ULTIMATE X-MEN

STORY
MARK **MILLAR**

PENCILS
ADAM **KUBERT**
ANDY **KUBERT**
WITH
TOM **RANEY**
TOM **DERENICK**

INKS
ART **THIBERT**
WITH
DANNY **MIKI**
SCOTT **HANNA**
JOE **KUBERT**
LARY **STUCKER**

COLORS
RICHARD **ISANOVE**
TRANSPARENCY
DIGITAL
WITH
BRIAN **HABERLIN**
DAVID **STEWART**

LETTERS
RICHARD **STARKINGS**
& COMICRAFT'S
WES 'N' SAIDA!

ASSISTANT EDITOR
PETE **FRANCO**

EDITOR
MARK **POWERS**

EDITOR IN CHIEF
JOE **QUESADA**

PRESIDENT
BILL **JEMAS**

ULTIMATE X-MEN VOL. 1. Contains material originally published in magazine form as ULTIMATE X-MEN #1-12 and GIANT-SIZE X-MEN #1. Second printing 2003. ISBN# 0-7851-1008-9. Published by MARVEL COMICS, a division of MARVEL ENTERTAINMENT GROUP, INC. OFFICE OF PUBLICATION: 10 East 40th Street, New York, NY 10016. Copyright © 1975, 2001 and 2002 Marvel Characters, Inc. All rights reserved. $29.99 per copy in the U.S. and $48.00 in Canada (GST #R127032852); Canadian Agreement #40668537. All characters featured in this issue and the distinctive names and likenesses thereof, and all related indicia are trademarks of Marvel Characters, Inc. No similarity between any of the names, characters, persons, and/or institutions in this magazine with those of any living or dead person or institution is intended, and any such similarity which may exist is purely coincidental. **Printed in Canada.** STAN LEE, Chairman Emeritus. For information regarding advertising in Marvel Comics or on Marvel.com, please contact Russell Brown, Executive Vice President, Consumer Products, Promotions and Media Sales at 212-576-8561 or rbrown@marvel.com

10 9 8 7 6 5 4 3 2

MARVEL

TABLE OF CONTENTS

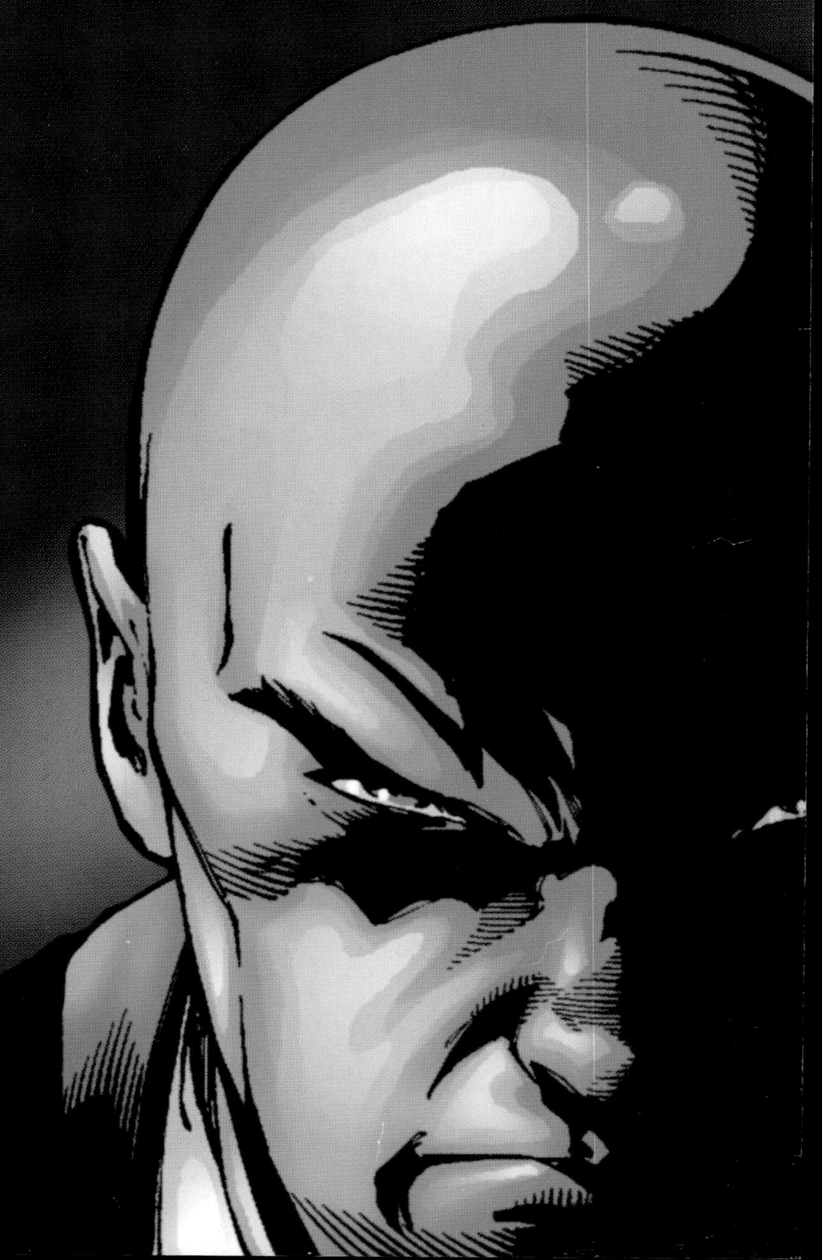

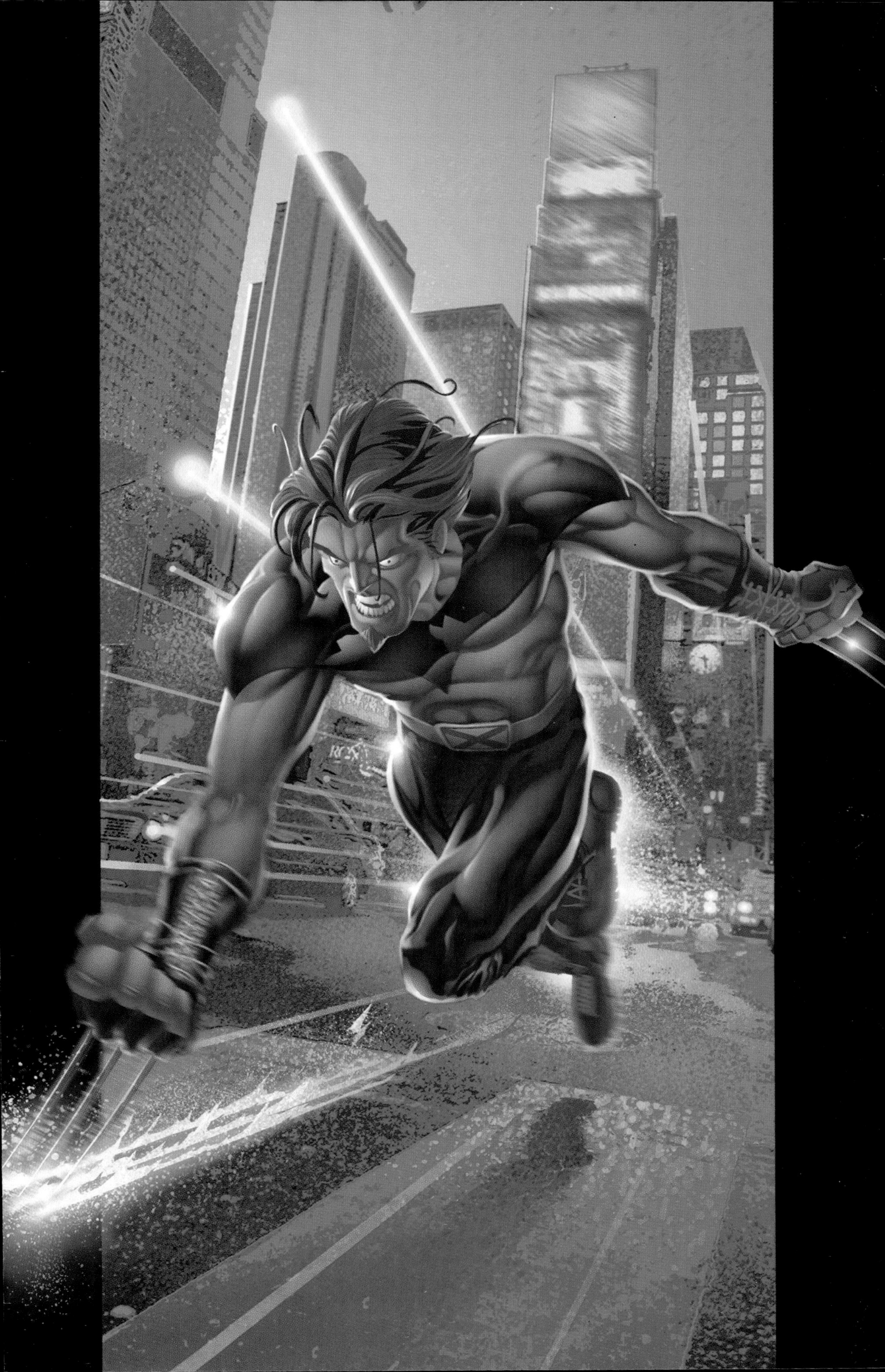

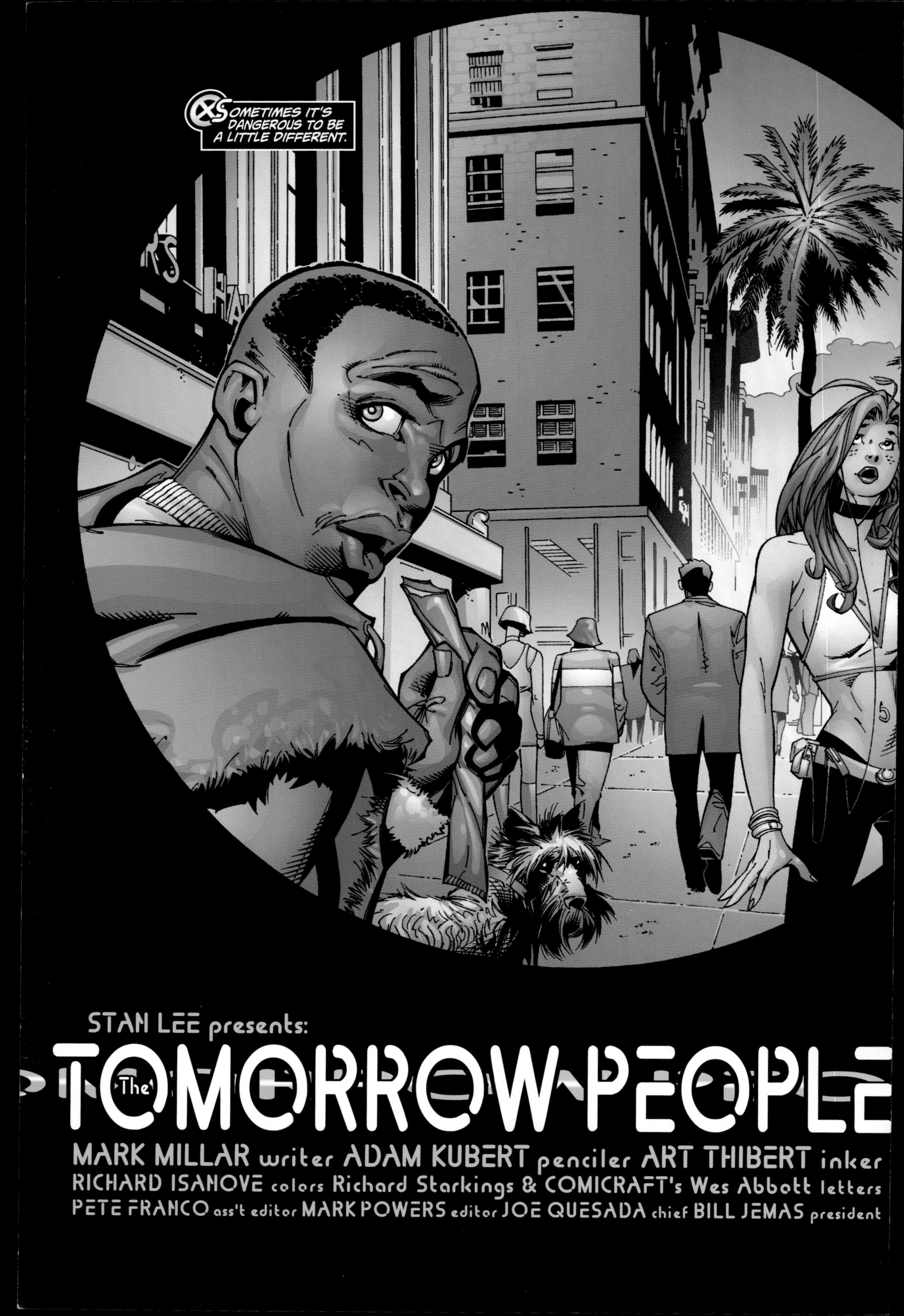

SOMETIMES IT'S DANGEROUS TO BE A LITTLE DIFFERENT.

STAN LEE presents:

The TOMORROW PEOPLE

MARK MILLAR writer ADAM KUBERT penciler ART THIBERT inker
RICHARD ISANOVE colors Richard Starkings & COMICRAFT's Wes Abbott letters
PETE FRANCO ass't editor MARK POWERS editor JOE QUESADA chief BILL JEMAS president

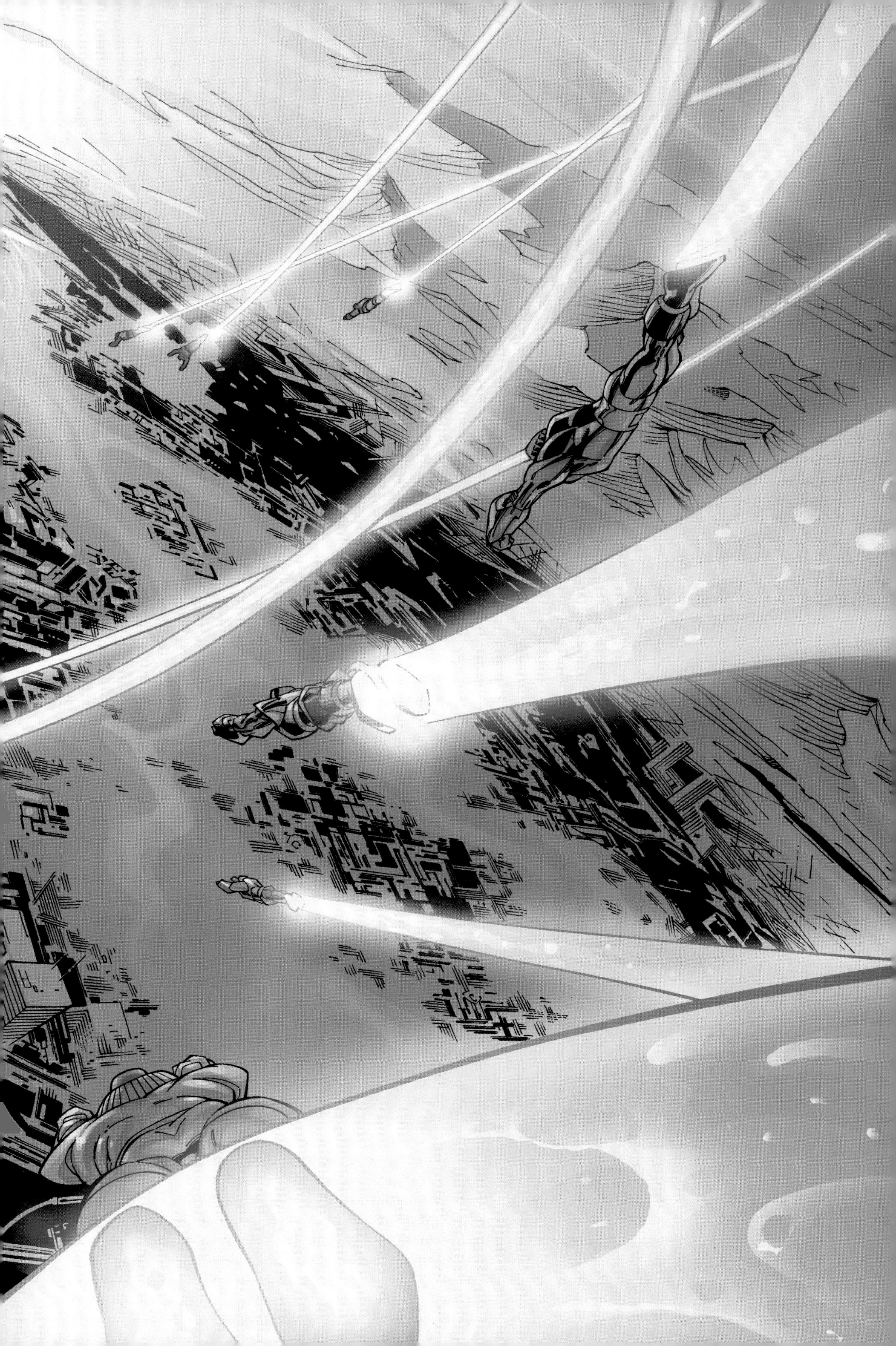

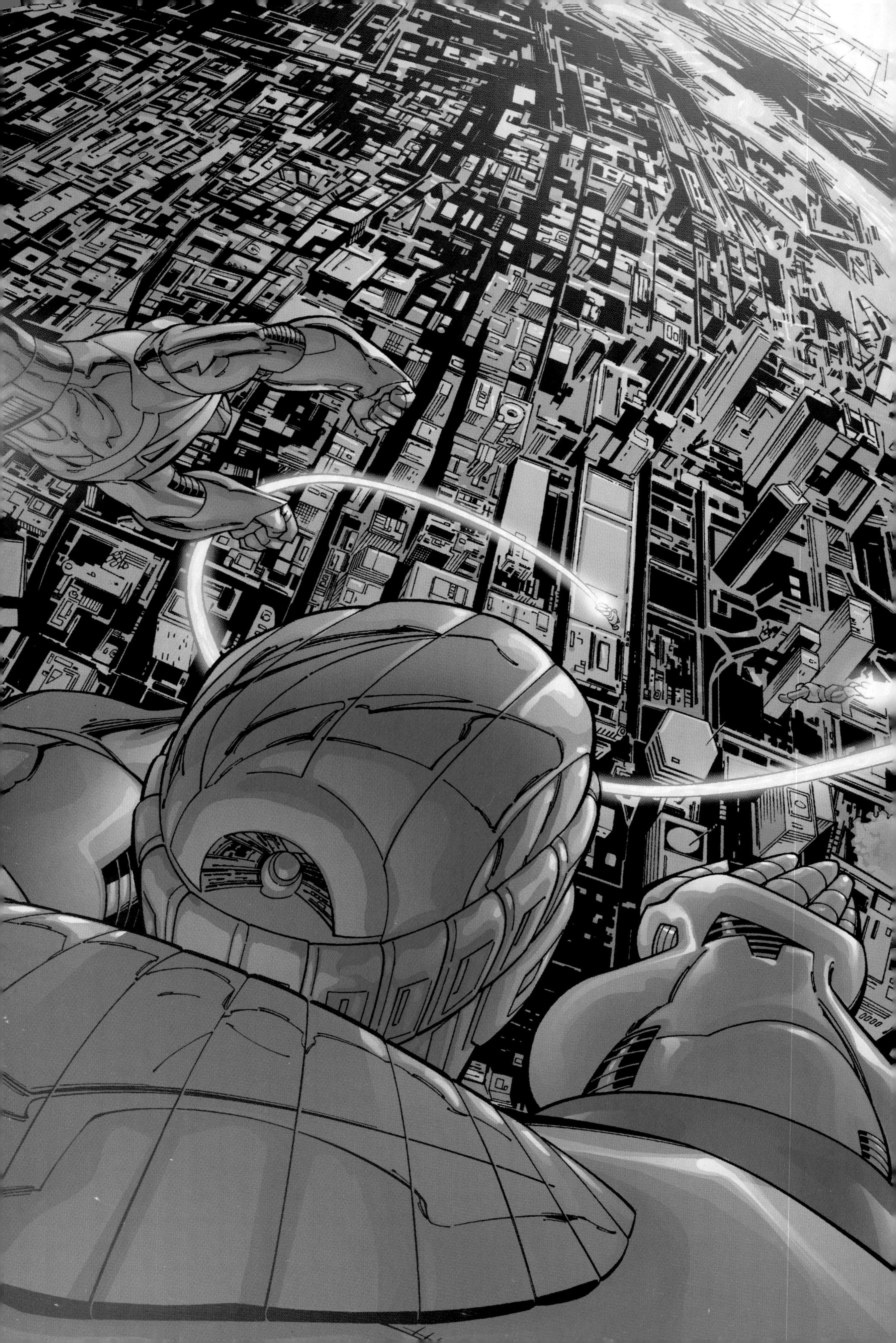

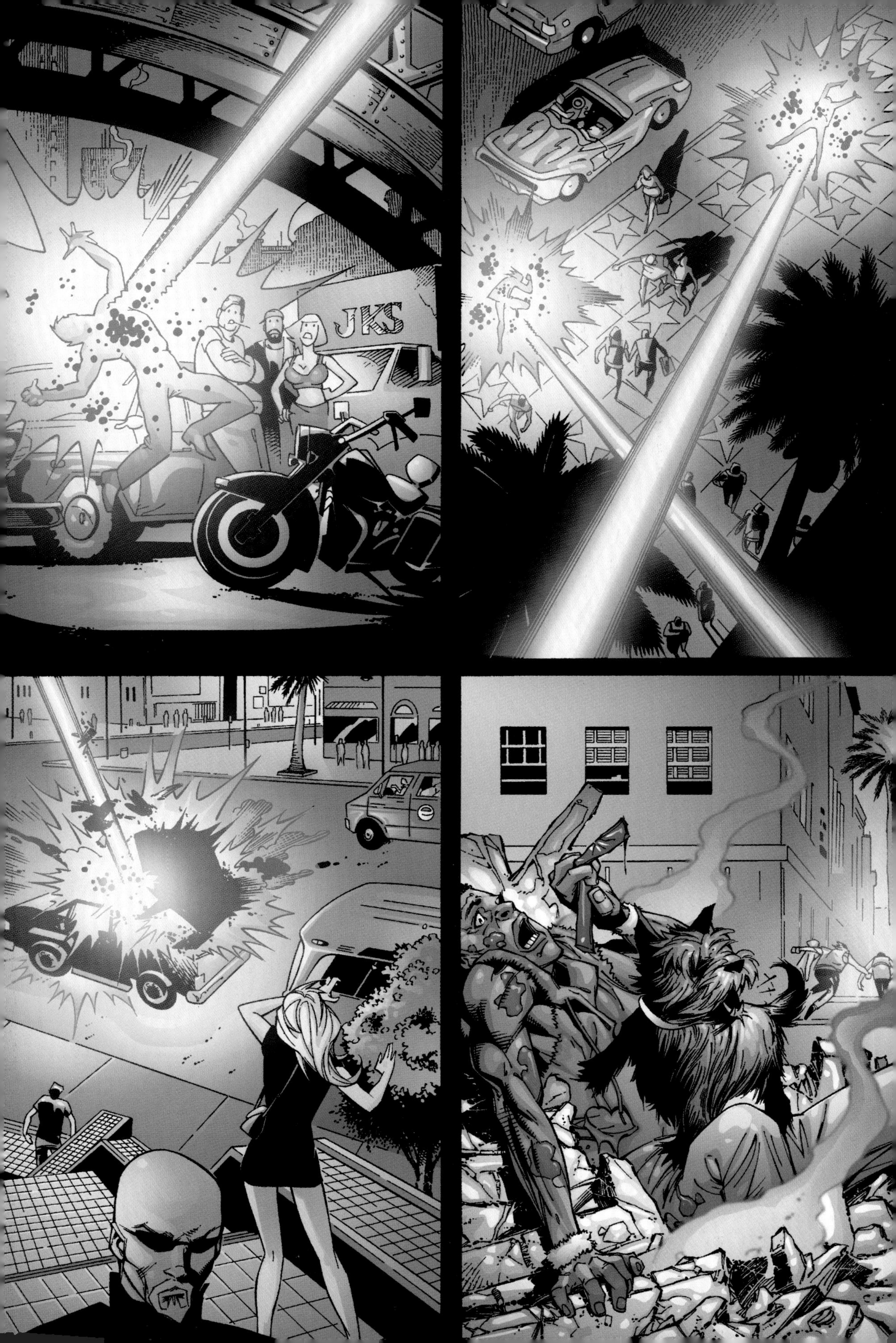
JKS

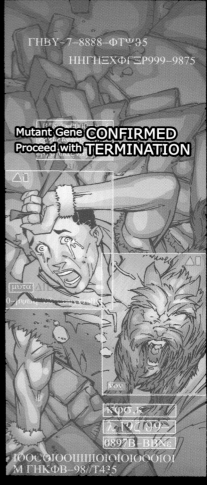

ΓΗΒΥ-7-8888-ΦΤΨ95
ΗΗΓΗΞΧΦΓΞΡ999-9875
Mutant Gene CONFIRMED
Proceed with TERMINATION
0897B-BBNε
Μ ΓΗΚΦΒ-98//T435
CRUNCH
TEM

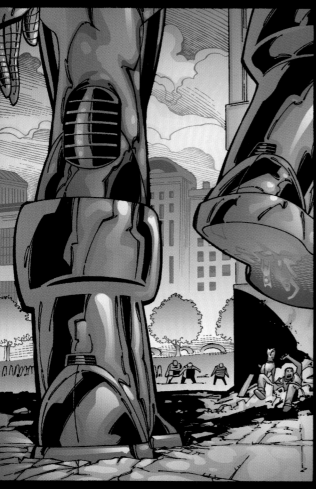

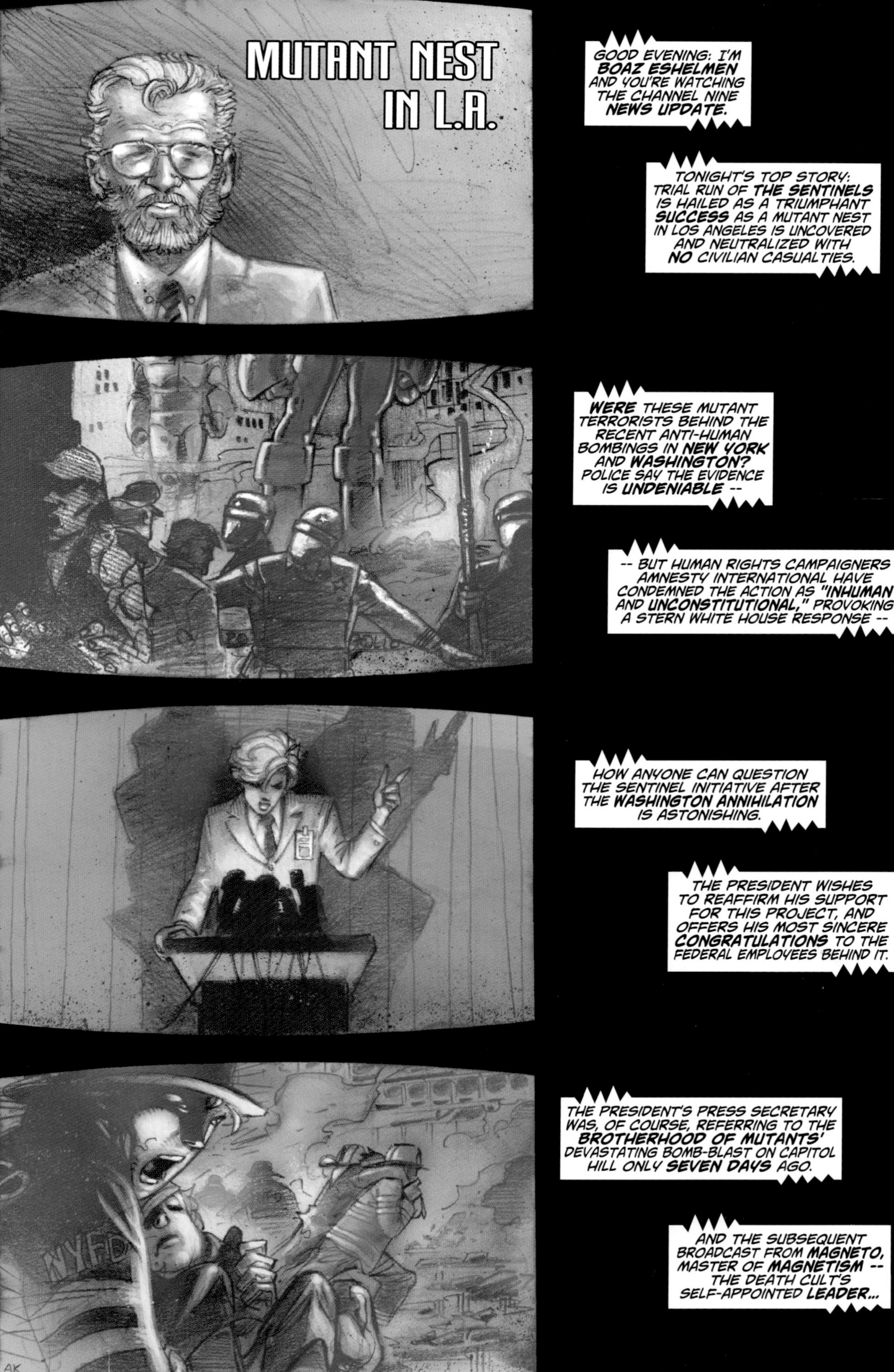
MUTANT NEST IN L.A.
GOOD EVENING: I'M BOAZ ESHELMEN AND YOU'RE WATCHING THE CHANNEL NINE NEWS UPDATE.
TONIGHT'S TOP STORY: TRIAL RUN OF THE SENTINELS IS HAILED AS A TRIUMPHANT SUCCESS AS A MUTANT NEST IN LOS ANGELES IS UNCOVERED AND NEUTRALIZED WITH NO CIVILIAN CASUALTIES.
WERE THESE MUTANT TERRORISTS BEHIND THE RECENT ANTI-HUMAN BOMBINGS IN NEW YORK AND WASHINGTON? POLICE SAY THE EVIDENCE IS UNDENIABLE --
-- BUT HUMAN RIGHTS CAMPAIGNERS AMNESTY INTERNATIONAL HAVE CONDEMNED THE ACTION AS "INHUMAN AND UNCONSTITUTIONAL," PROVOKING A STERN WHITE HOUSE RESPONSE --
HOW ANYONE CAN QUESTION THE SENTINEL INITIATIVE AFTER THE WASHINGTON ANNIHILATION IS ASTONISHING.
THE PRESIDENT WISHES TO REAFFIRM HIS SUPPORT FOR THIS PROJECT, AND OFFERS HIS MOST SINCERE CONGRATULATIONS TO THE FEDERAL EMPLOYEES BEHIND IT.
THE PRESIDENT'S PRESS SECRETARY WAS, OF COURSE, REFERRING TO THE BROTHERHOOD OF MUTANTS' DEVASTATING BOMB-BLAST ON CAPITOL HILL ONLY SEVEN DAYS AGO.
AND THE SUBSEQUENT BROADCAST FROM MAGNETO, MASTER OF MAGNETISM -- THE DEATH CULT'S SELF-APPOINTED LEADER...
NYFD
AK

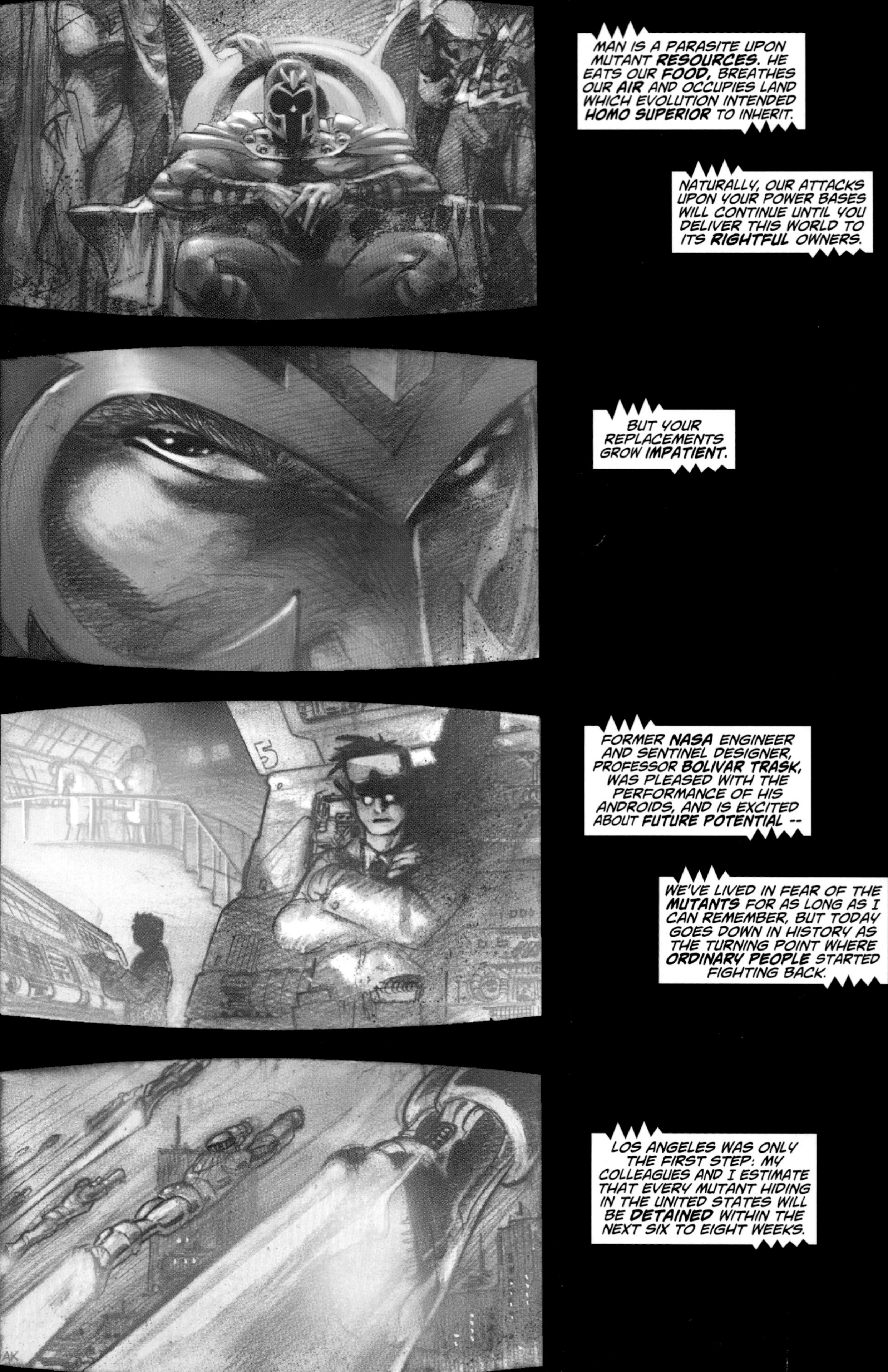
MAN IS A PARASITE UPON MUTANT **RESOURCES.** HE EATS OUR **FOOD,** BREATHES OUR **AIR** AND OCCUPIES LAND WHICH EVOLUTION INTENDED **HOMO SUPERIOR** TO INHERIT.
NATURALLY, OUR ATTACKS UPON YOUR POWER BASES WILL CONTINUE UNTIL YOU DELIVER THIS WORLD TO ITS **RIGHTFUL** OWNERS.
BUT YOUR REPLACEMENTS GROW **IMPATIENT.**
FORMER **NASA** ENGINEER AND SENTINEL DESIGNER, PROFESSOR **BOLIVAR TRASK,** WAS PLEASED WITH THE PERFORMANCE OF HIS ANDROIDS, AND IS EXCITED ABOUT **FUTURE POTENTIAL** --
WE'VE LIVED IN FEAR OF THE **MUTANTS** FOR AS LONG AS I CAN REMEMBER, BUT TODAY GOES DOWN IN HISTORY AS THE TURNING POINT WHERE **ORDINARY PEOPLE** STARTED FIGHTING BACK.
LOS ANGELES WAS ONLY THE FIRST STEP: MY COLLEAGUES AND I ESTIMATE THAT EVERY MUTANT HIDING IN THE UNITED STATES WILL BE **DETAINED** WITHIN THE NEXT SIX TO EIGHT WEEKS.

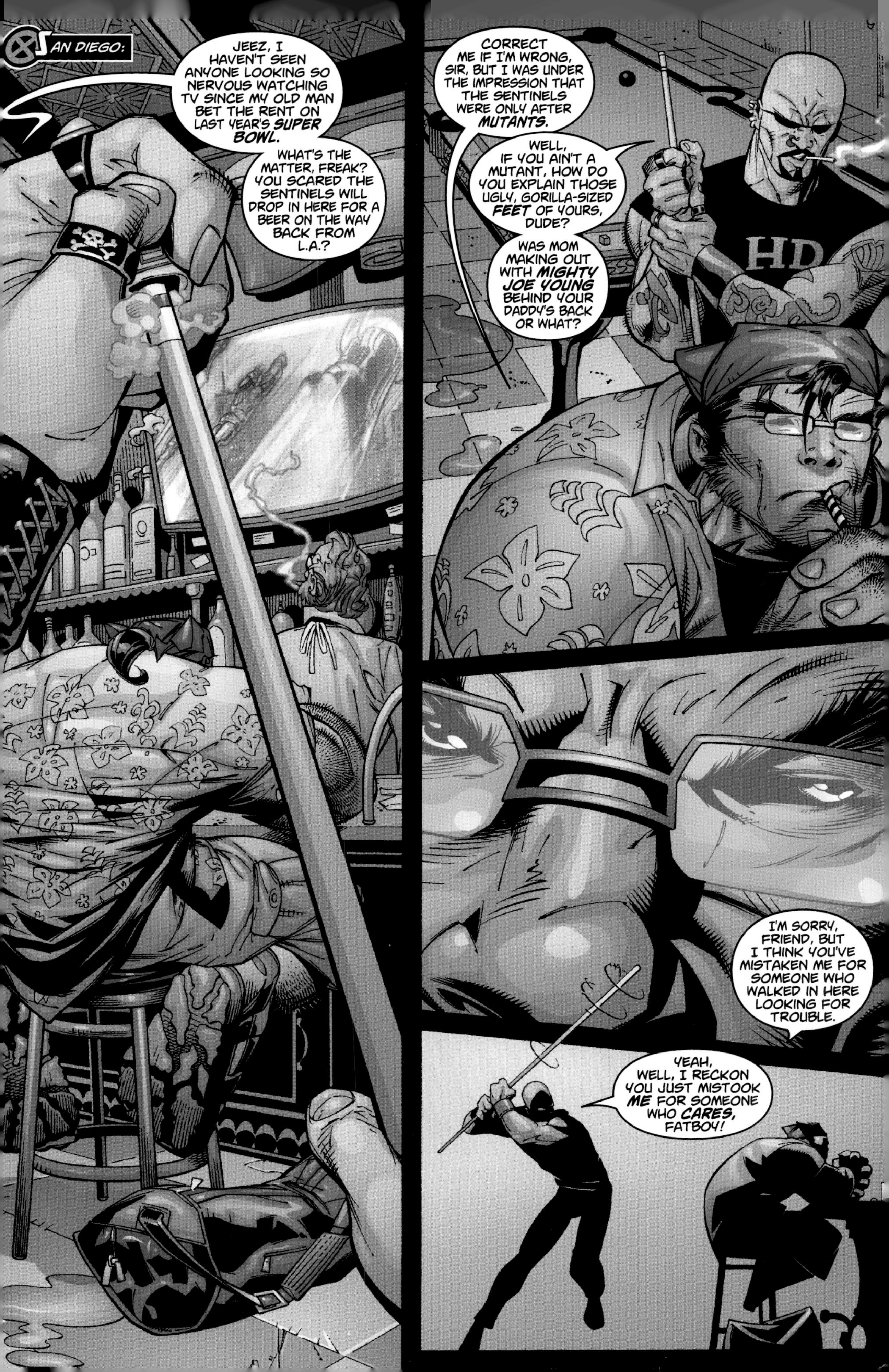
SAN DIEGO:
JEEZ, I HAVEN'T SEEN ANYONE LOOKING SO NERVOUS WATCHING TV SINCE MY OLD MAN BET THE RENT ON LAST YEAR'S SUPER BOWL.
WHAT'S THE MATTER, FREAK? YOU SCARED THE SENTINELS WILL DROP IN HERE FOR A BEER ON THE WAY BACK FROM L.A.?
CORRECT ME IF I'M WRONG, SIR, BUT I WAS UNDER THE IMPRESSION THAT THE SENTINELS WERE ONLY AFTER MUTANTS.
WELL, IF YOU AIN'T A MUTANT, HOW DO YOU EXPLAIN THOSE UGLY, GORILLA-SIZED FEET OF YOURS, DUDE?
WAS MOM MAKING OUT WITH MIGHTY JOE YOUNG BEHIND YOUR DADDY'S BACK OR WHAT?
HD
I'M SORRY, FRIEND, BUT I THINK YOU'VE MISTAKEN ME FOR SOMEONE WHO WALKED IN HERE LOOKING FOR TROUBLE.
YEAH, WELL, I RECKON YOU JUST MISTOOK ME FOR SOMEONE WHO CARES, FATBOY!

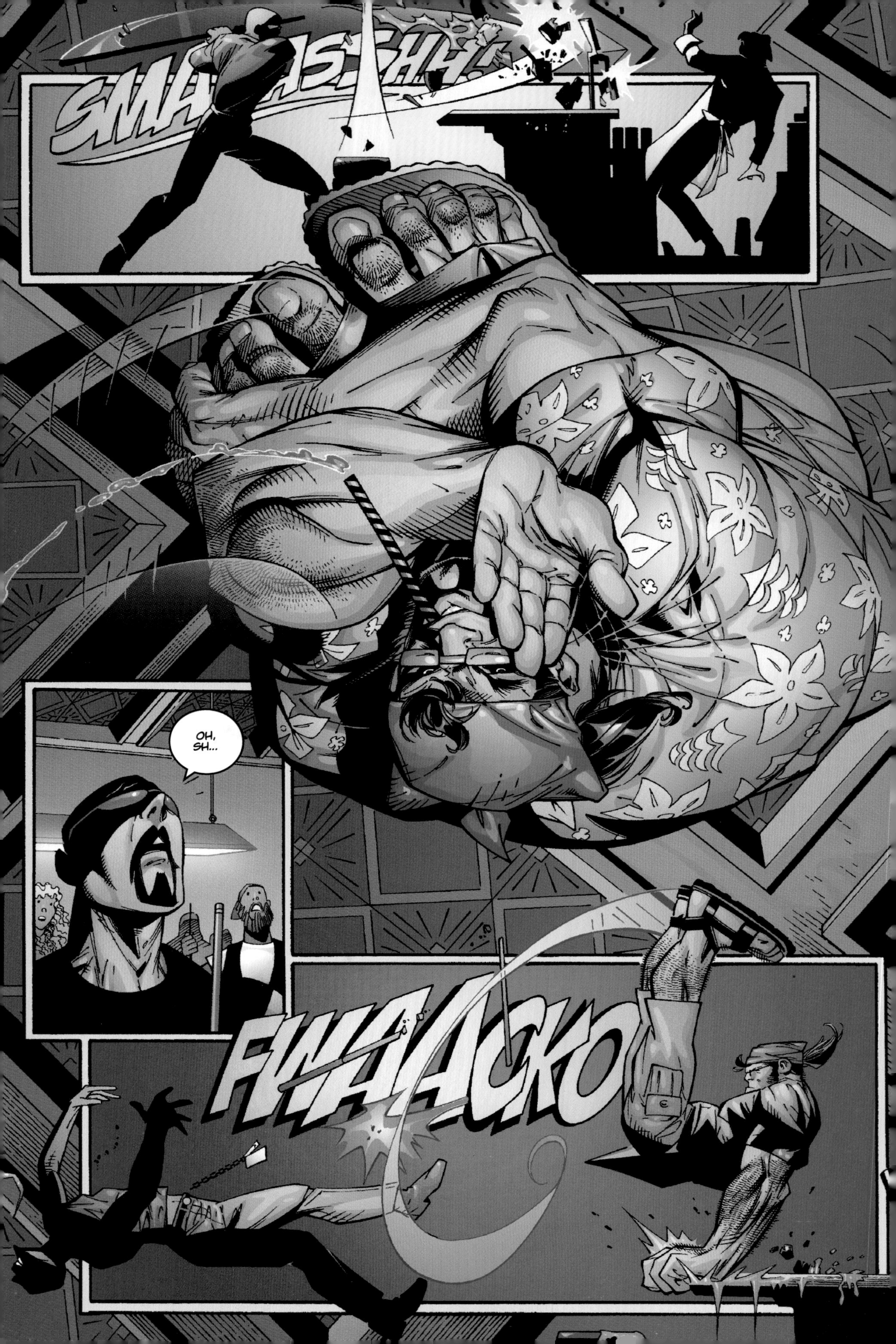
SMASSHH!
OH, SH...
FWHACKO

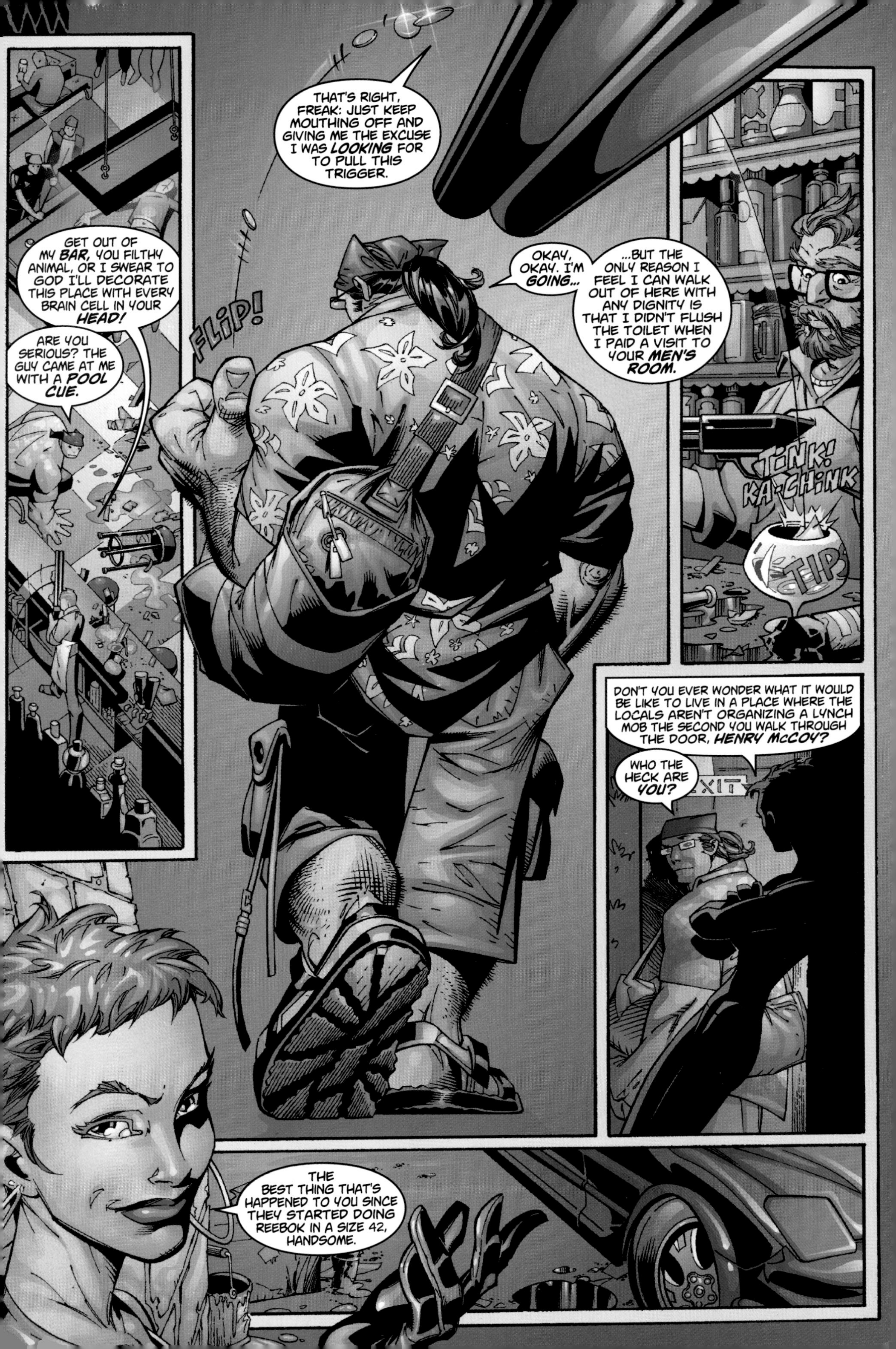
GET OUT OF MY BAR, YOU FILTHY ANIMAL, OR I SWEAR TO GOD I'LL DECORATE THIS PLACE WITH EVERY BRAIN CELL IN YOUR HEAD!
ARE YOU SERIOUS? THE GUY CAME AT ME WITH A POOL CUE.
THAT'S RIGHT, FREAK: JUST KEEP MOUTHING OFF AND GIVING ME THE EXCUSE I WAS LOOKING FOR TO PULL THIS TRIGGER.
FLIP!
OKAY, OKAY. I'M GOING...
...BUT THE ONLY REASON I FEEL I CAN WALK OUT OF HERE WITH ANY DIGNITY IS THAT I DIDN'T FLUSH THE TOILET WHEN I PAID A VISIT TO YOUR MEN'S ROOM.
TINK!
KA-CHINK
TIPS
DON'T YOU EVER WONDER WHAT IT WOULD BE LIKE TO LIVE IN A PLACE WHERE THE LOCALS AREN'T ORGANIZING A LYNCH MOB THE SECOND YOU WALK THROUGH THE DOOR, HENRY McCOY?
WHO THE HECK ARE YOU?
EXIT
THE BEST THING THAT'S HAPPENED TO YOU SINCE THEY STARTED DOING REEBOK IN A SIZE 42, HANDSOME.

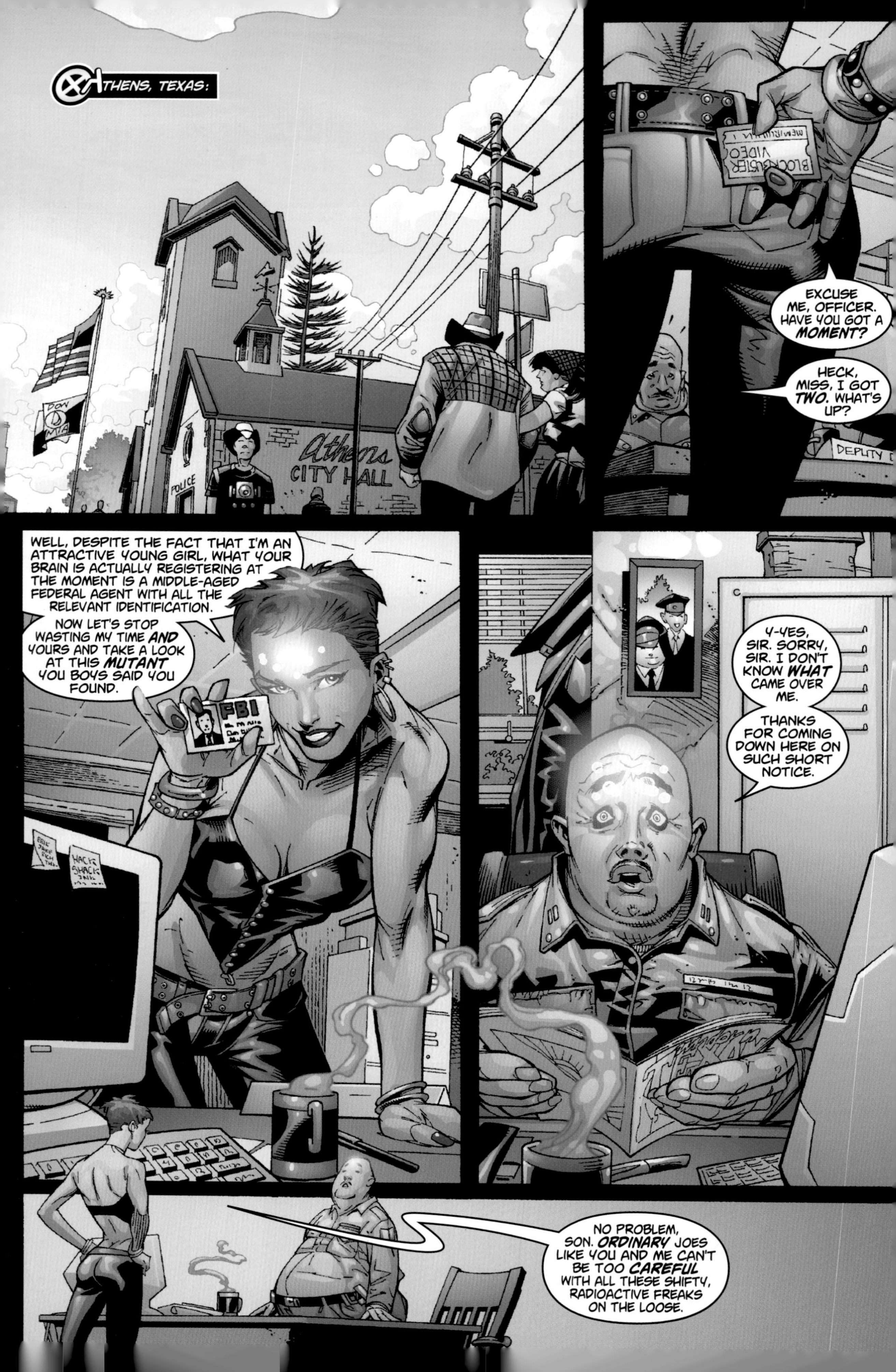
ATHENS, TEXAS:
POLICE
Athens CITY HALL
BLOCKBUSTER VIDEO
EXCUSE ME, OFFICER. HAVE YOU GOT A MOMENT?
HECK, MISS, I GOT TWO. WHAT'S UP?
WELL, DESPITE THE FACT THAT I'M AN ATTRACTIVE YOUNG GIRL, WHAT YOUR BRAIN IS ACTUALLY REGISTERING AT THE MOMENT IS A MIDDLE-AGED FEDERAL AGENT WITH ALL THE RELEVANT IDENTIFICATION.
NOW LET'S STOP WASTING MY TIME AND YOURS AND TAKE A LOOK AT THIS MUTANT YOU BOYS SAID YOU FOUND.
FBI
Y-YES, SIR. SORRY, SIR. I DON'T KNOW WHAT CAME OVER ME.
THANKS FOR COMING DOWN HERE ON SUCH SHORT NOTICE.
NO PROBLEM, SON. ORDINARY JOES LIKE YOU AND ME CAN'T BE TOO CAREFUL WITH ALL THESE SHIFTY, RADIOACTIVE FREAKS ON THE LOOSE.

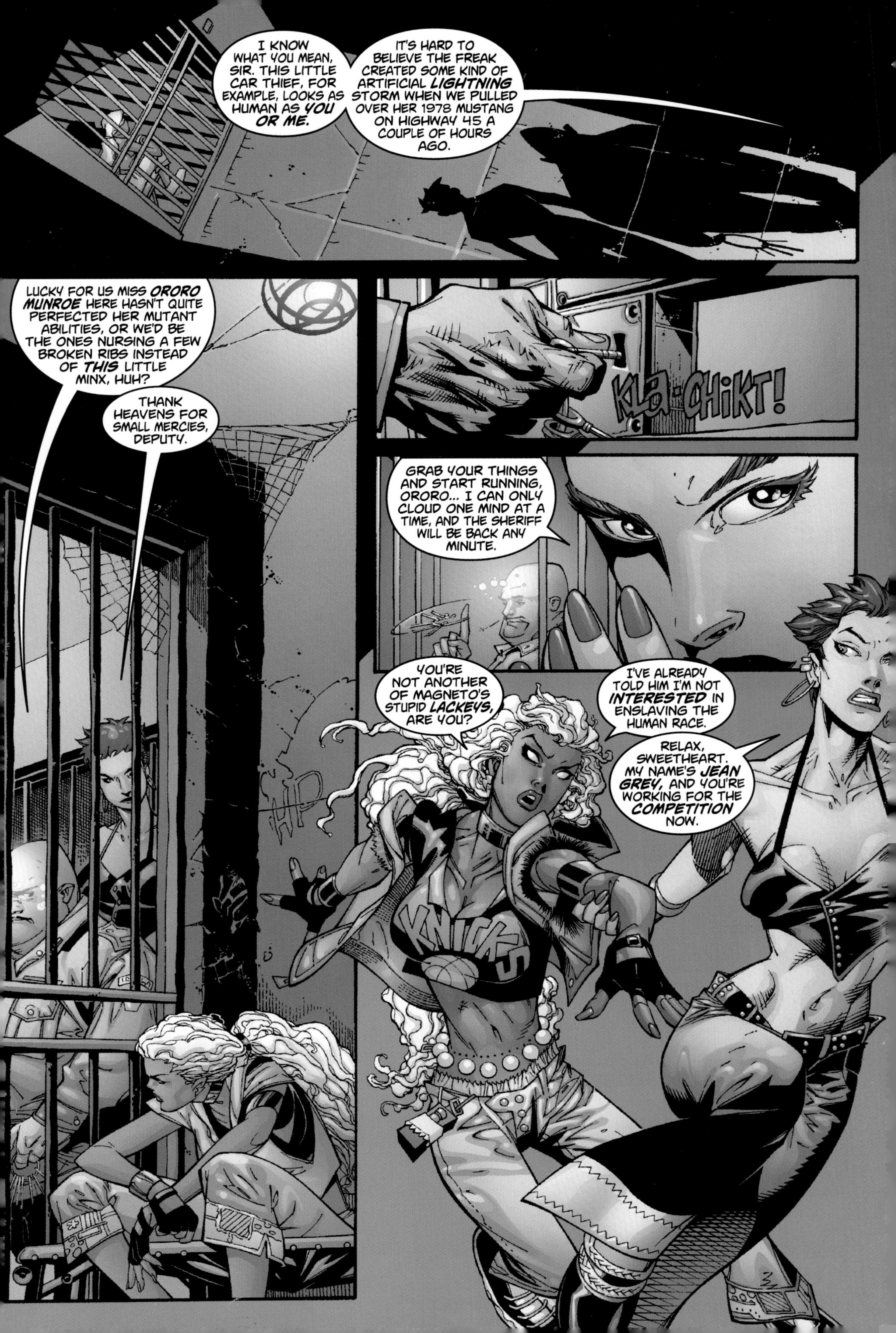

I KNOW WHAT YOU MEAN, SIR. THIS LITTLE CAR THIEF, FOR EXAMPLE, LOOKS AS HUMAN AS YOU OR ME.
IT'S HARD TO BELIEVE THE FREAK CREATED SOME KIND OF ARTIFICIAL LIGHTNING STORM WHEN WE PULLED OVER HER 1978 MUSTANG ON HIGHWAY 45 A COUPLE OF HOURS AGO.
LUCKY FOR US MISS ORORO MUNROE HERE HASN'T QUITE PERFECTED HER MUTANT ABILITIES, OR WE'D BE THE ONES NURSING A FEW BROKEN RIBS INSTEAD OF THIS LITTLE MINX, HUH?
THANK HEAVENS FOR SMALL MERCIES, DEPUTY.
KLA-CHIKT!
GRAB YOUR THINGS AND START RUNNING, ORORO... I CAN ONLY CLOUD ONE MIND AT A TIME, AND THE SHERIFF WILL BE BACK ANY MINUTE.
YOU'RE NOT ANOTHER OF MAGNETO'S STUPID LACKEYS, ARE YOU?
I'VE ALREADY TOLD HIM I'M NOT INTERESTED IN ENSLAVING THE HUMAN RACE.
RELAX, SWEETHEART. MY NAME'S JEAN GREY, AND YOU'RE WORKING FOR THE COMPETITION NOW.

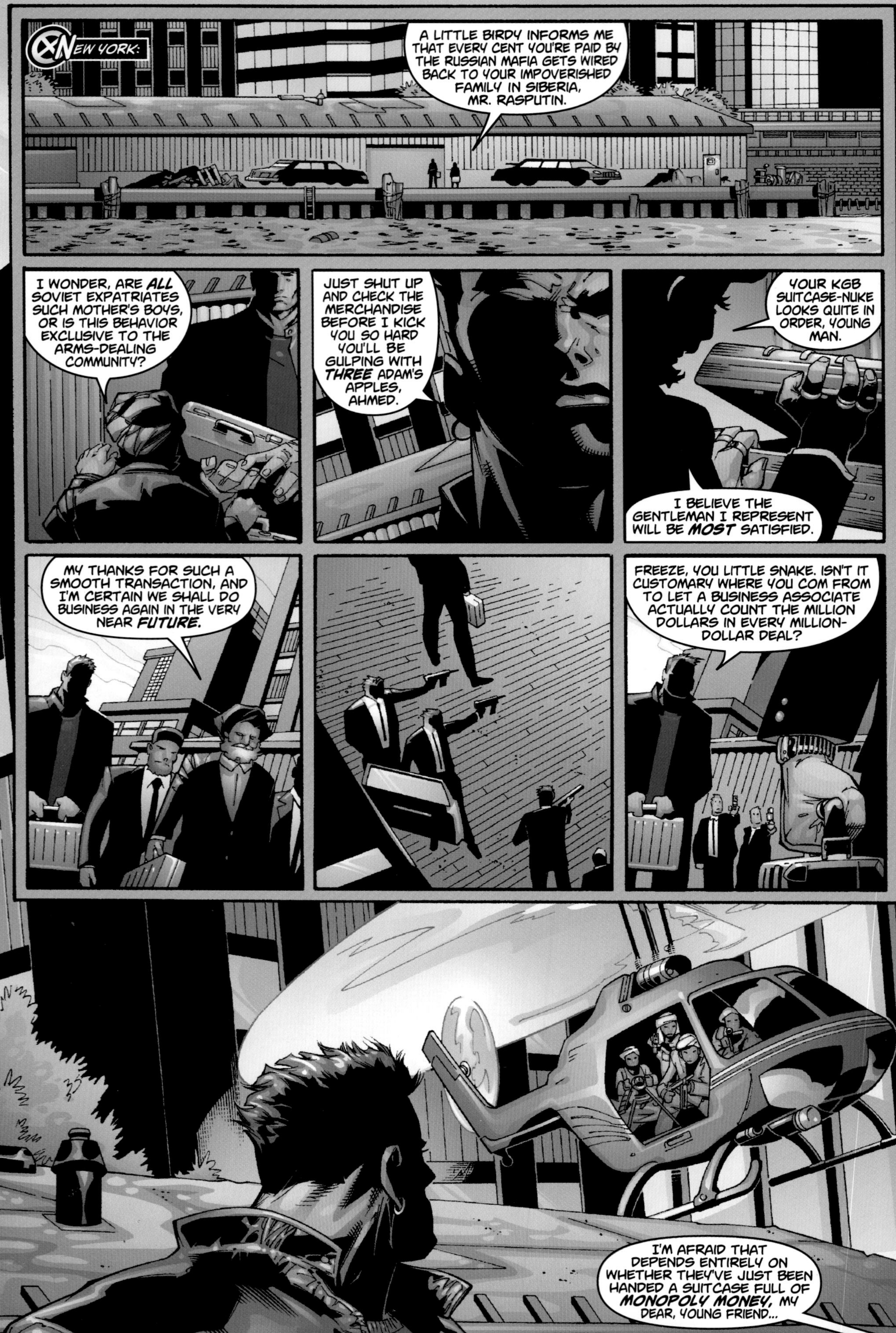
NEW YORK:
A LITTLE BIRDY INFORMS ME THAT EVERY CENT YOU'RE PAID BY THE RUSSIAN MAFIA GETS WIRED BACK TO YOUR IMPOVERISHED FAMILY IN SIBERIA, MR. RASPUTIN.
I WONDER, ARE ALL SOVIET EXPATRIATES SUCH MOTHER'S BOYS, OR IS THIS BEHAVIOR EXCLUSIVE TO THE ARMS-DEALING COMMUNITY?
JUST SHUT UP AND CHECK THE MERCHANDISE BEFORE I KICK YOU SO HARD YOU'LL BE GULPING WITH THREE ADAM'S APPLES, AHMED.
YOUR KGB SUITCASE-NUKE LOOKS QUITE IN ORDER, YOUNG MAN.
I BELIEVE THE GENTLEMAN I REPRESENT WILL BE MOST SATISFIED.
MY THANKS FOR SUCH A SMOOTH TRANSACTION, AND I'M CERTAIN WE SHALL DO BUSINESS AGAIN IN THE VERY NEAR FUTURE.
FREEZE, YOU LITTLE SNAKE. ISN'T IT CUSTOMARY WHERE YOU COM FROM TO LET A BUSINESS ASSOCIATE ACTUALLY COUNT THE MILLION DOLLARS IN EVERY MILLION-DOLLAR DEAL?
I'M AFRAID THAT DEPENDS ENTIRELY ON WHETHER THEY'VE JUST BEEN HANDED A SUITCASE FULL OF MONOPOLY MONEY, MY DEAR, YOUNG FRIEND...

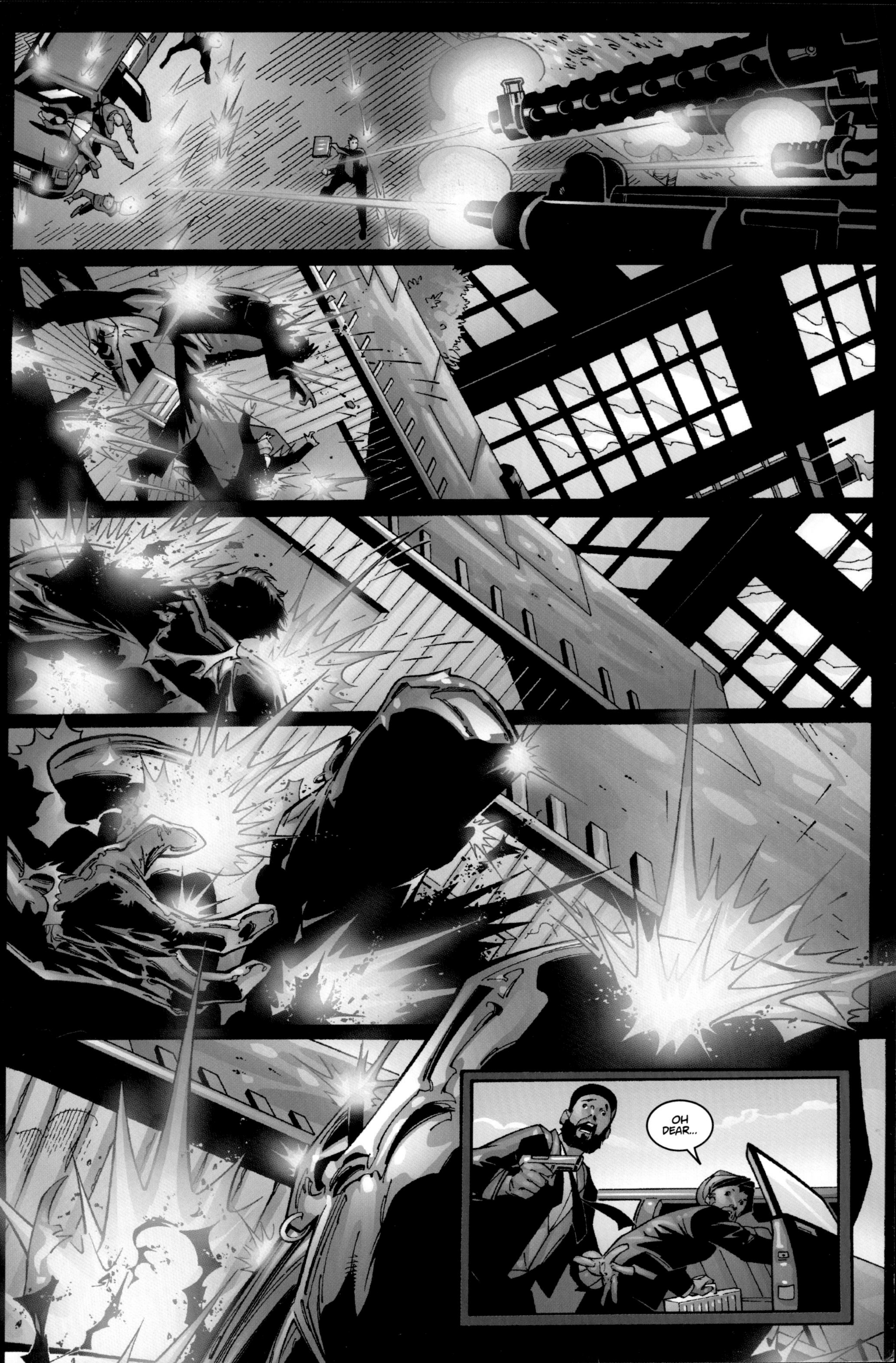
OH DEAR...

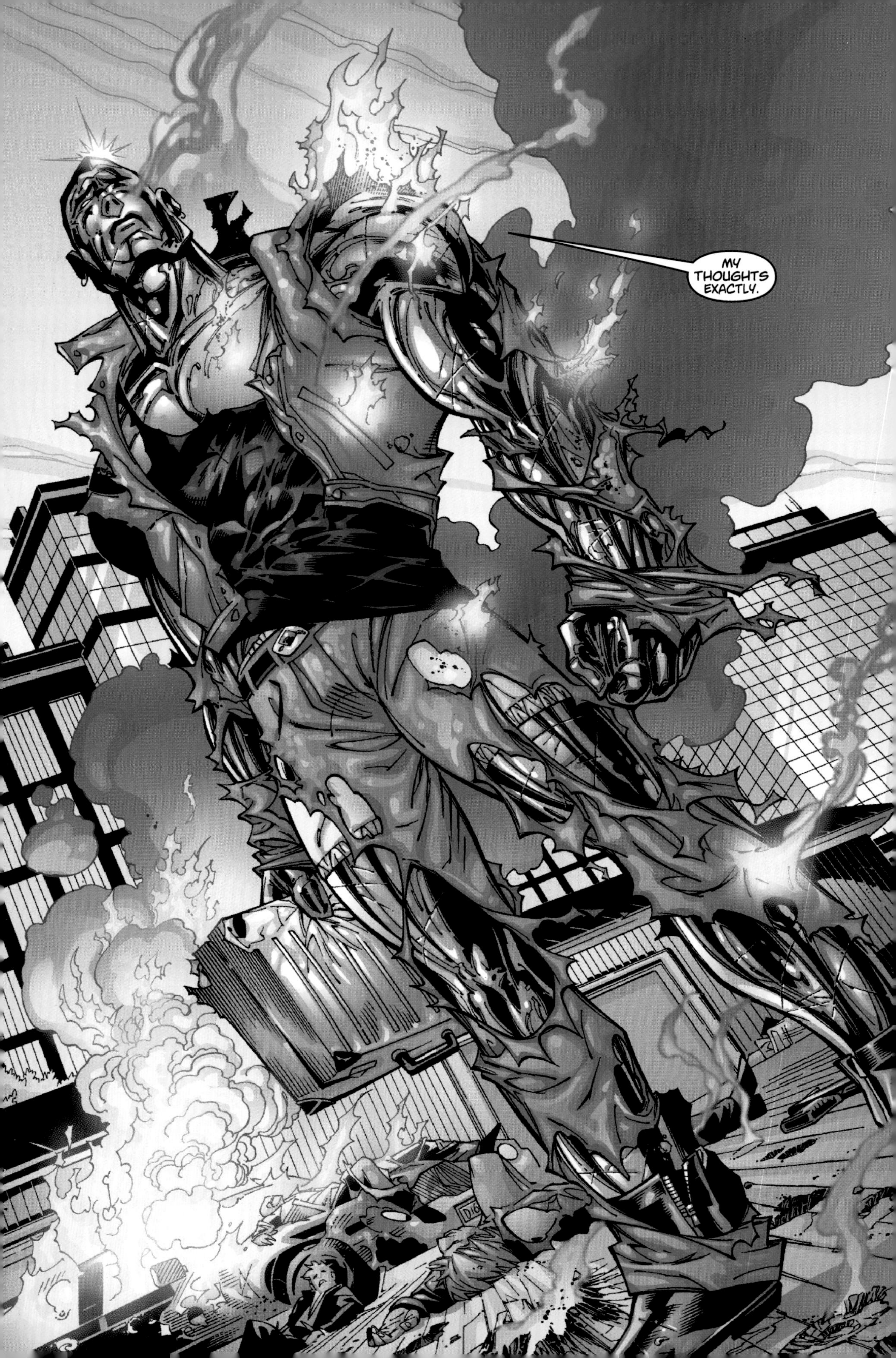
MY THOUGHTS EXACTLY.

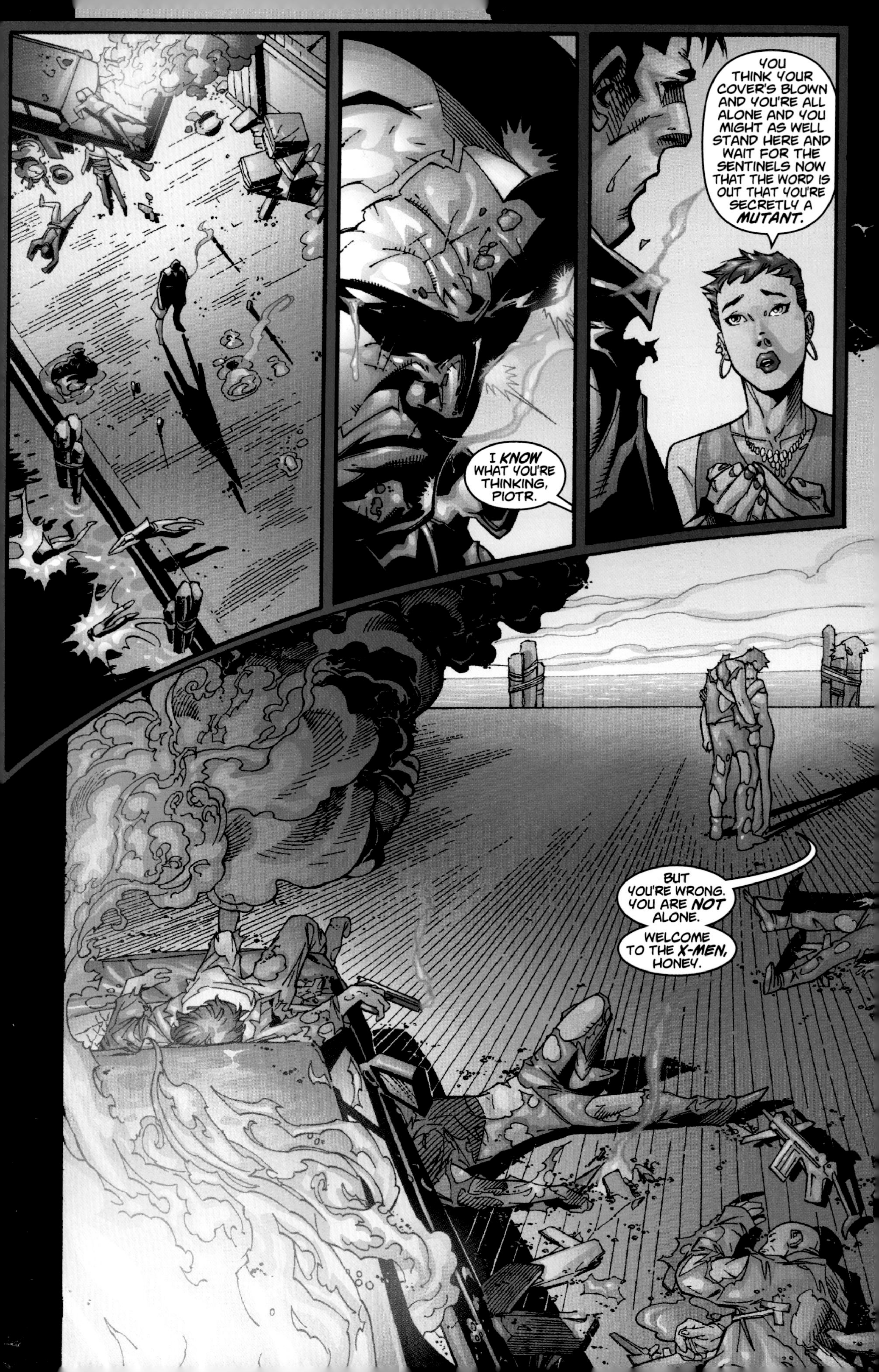
I KNOW WHAT YOU'RE THINKING, PIOTR.
YOU THINK YOUR COVER'S BLOWN AND YOU'RE ALL ALONE AND YOU MIGHT AS WELL STAND HERE AND WAIT FOR THE SENTINELS NOW THAT THE WORD IS OUT THAT YOU'RE SECRETLY A MUTANT.
BUT YOU'RE WRONG. YOU ARE NOT ALONE.
WELCOME TO THE X-MEN, HONEY.

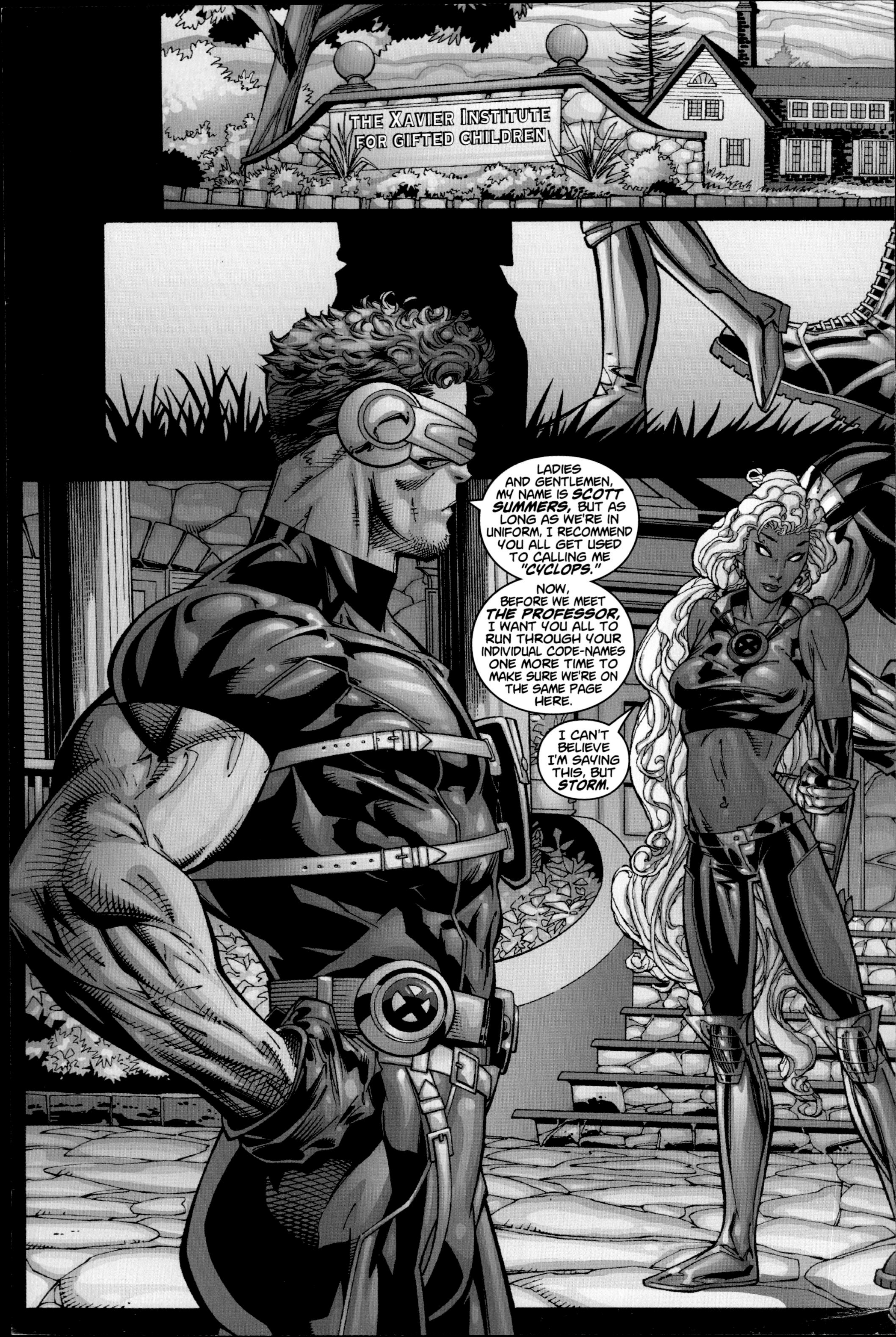
THE XAVIER INSTITUTE FOR GIFTED CHILDREN
LADIES AND GENTLEMEN, MY NAME IS SCOTT SUMMERS, BUT AS LONG AS WE'RE IN UNIFORM, I RECOMMEND YOU ALL GET USED TO CALLING ME "CYCLOPS."
NOW, BEFORE WE MEET THE PROFESSOR, I WANT YOU ALL TO RUN THROUGH YOUR INDIVIDUAL CODE-NAMES ONE MORE TIME TO MAKE SURE WE'RE ON THE SAME PAGE HERE.
I CAN'T BELIEVE I'M SAYING THIS, BUT STORM.

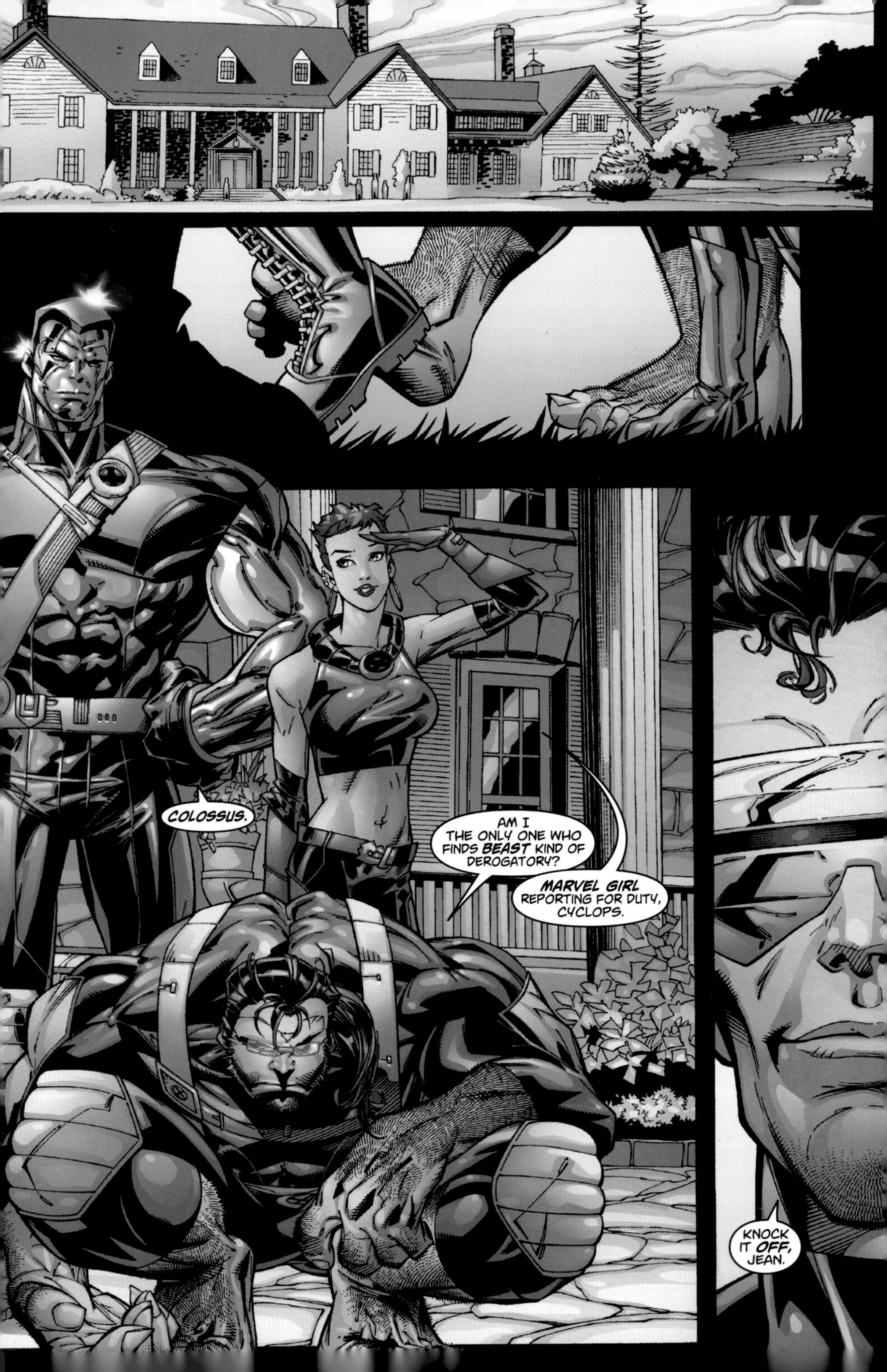
COLOSSUS.
AM I THE ONLY ONE WHO FINDS BEAST KIND OF DEROGATORY?
MARVEL GIRL REPORTING FOR DUTY, CYCLOPS.
KNOCK IT OFF, JEAN.

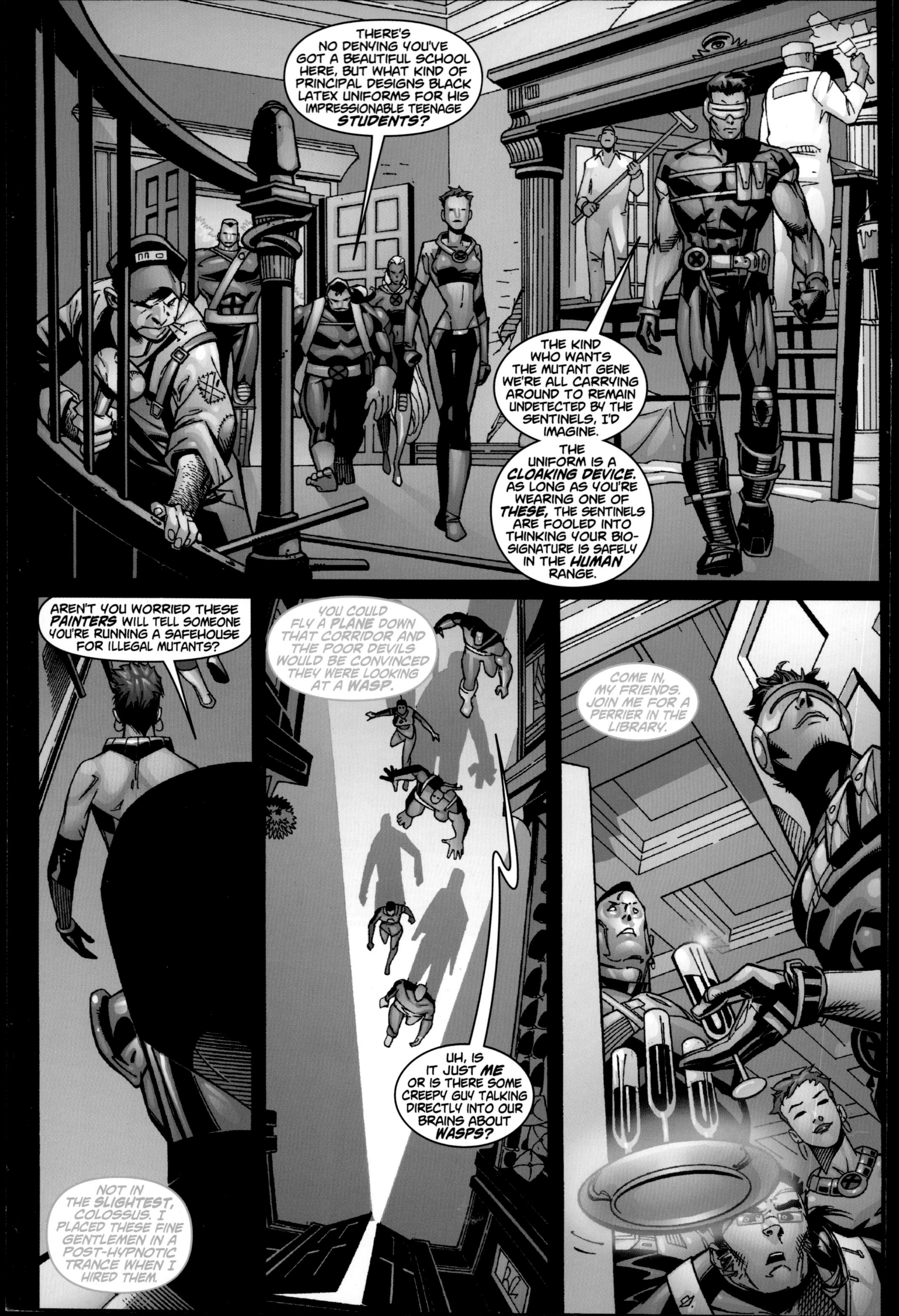
THERE'S NO DENYING YOU'VE GOT A BEAUTIFUL SCHOOL HERE, BUT WHAT KIND OF PRINCIPAL DESIGNS BLACK LATEX UNIFORMS FOR HIS IMPRESSIONABLE TEENAGE STUDENTS?
THE KIND WHO WANTS THE MUTANT GENE WE'RE ALL CARRYING AROUND TO REMAIN UNDETECTED BY THE SENTINELS, I'D IMAGINE.
THE UNIFORM IS A CLOAKING DEVICE. AS LONG AS YOU'RE WEARING ONE OF THESE, THE SENTINELS ARE FOOLED INTO THINKING YOUR BIO-SIGNATURE IS SAFELY IN THE HUMAN RANGE.
AREN'T YOU WORRIED THESE PAINTERS WILL TELL SOMEONE YOU'RE RUNNING A SAFEHOUSE FOR ILLEGAL MUTANTS?
NOT IN THE SLIGHTEST, COLOSSUS. I PLACED THESE FINE GENTLEMEN IN A POST-HYPNOTIC TRANCE WHEN I HIRED THEM.
YOU COULD FLY A PLANE DOWN THAT CORRIDOR AND THE POOR DEVILS WOULD BE CONVINCED THEY WERE LOOKING AT A WASP.
UH, IS IT JUST ME OR IS THERE SOME CREEPY GUY TALKING DIRECTLY INTO OUR BRAINS ABOUT WASPS?
COME IN, MY FRIENDS. JOIN ME FOR A PERRIER IN THE LIBRARY.

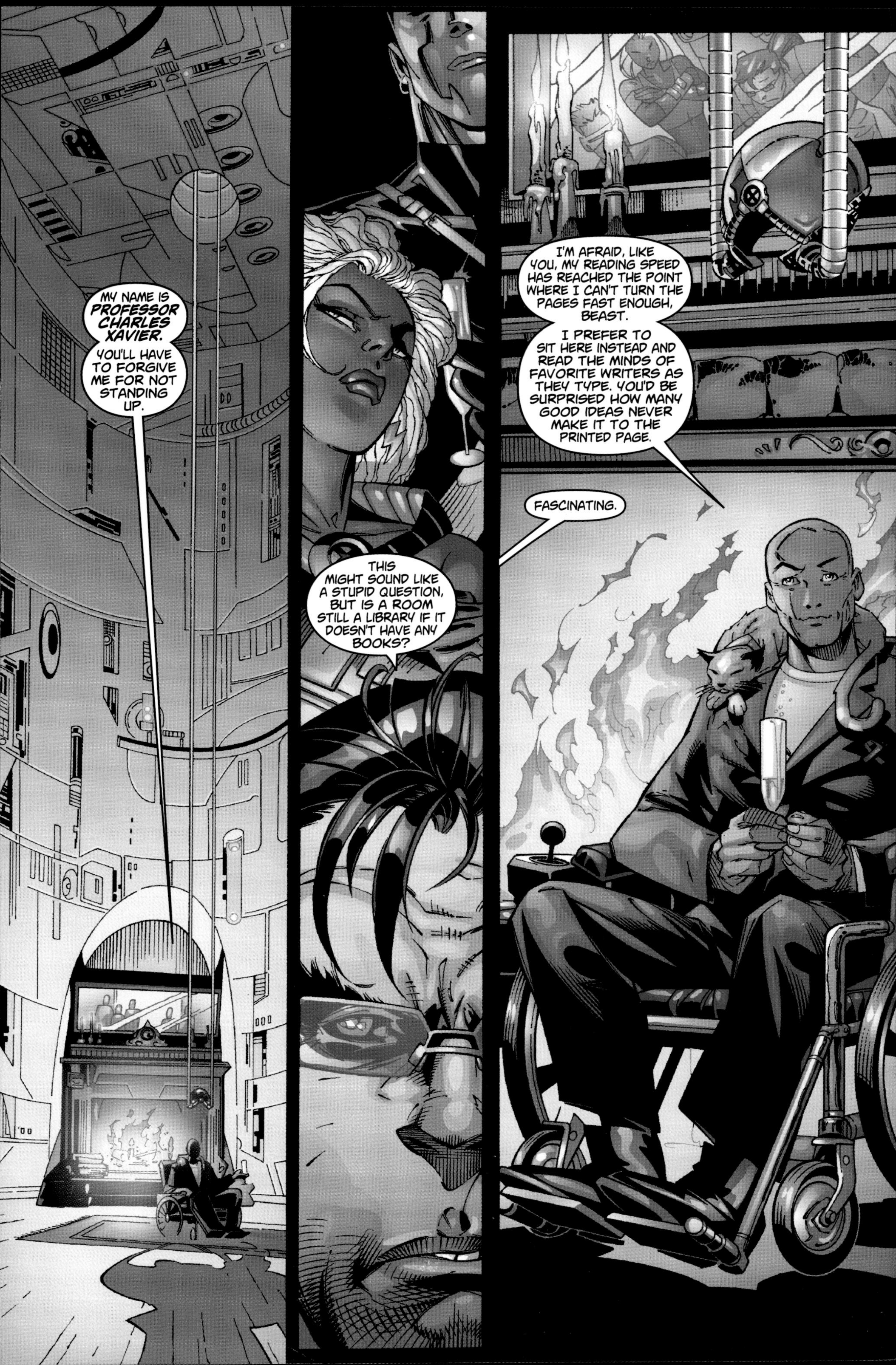
MY NAME IS PROFESSOR CHARLES XAVIER.
YOU'LL HAVE TO FORGIVE ME FOR NOT STANDING UP.
THIS MIGHT SOUND LIKE A STUPID QUESTION, BUT IS A ROOM STILL A LIBRARY IF IT DOESN'T HAVE ANY BOOKS?
I'M AFRAID, LIKE YOU, MY READING SPEED HAS REACHED THE POINT WHERE I CAN'T TURN THE PAGES FAST ENOUGH, BEAST.
I PREFER TO SIT HERE INSTEAD AND READ THE MINDS OF FAVORITE WRITERS AS THEY TYPE. YOU'D BE SURPRISED HOW MANY GOOD IDEAS NEVER MAKE IT TO THE PRINTED PAGE.
FASCINATING.

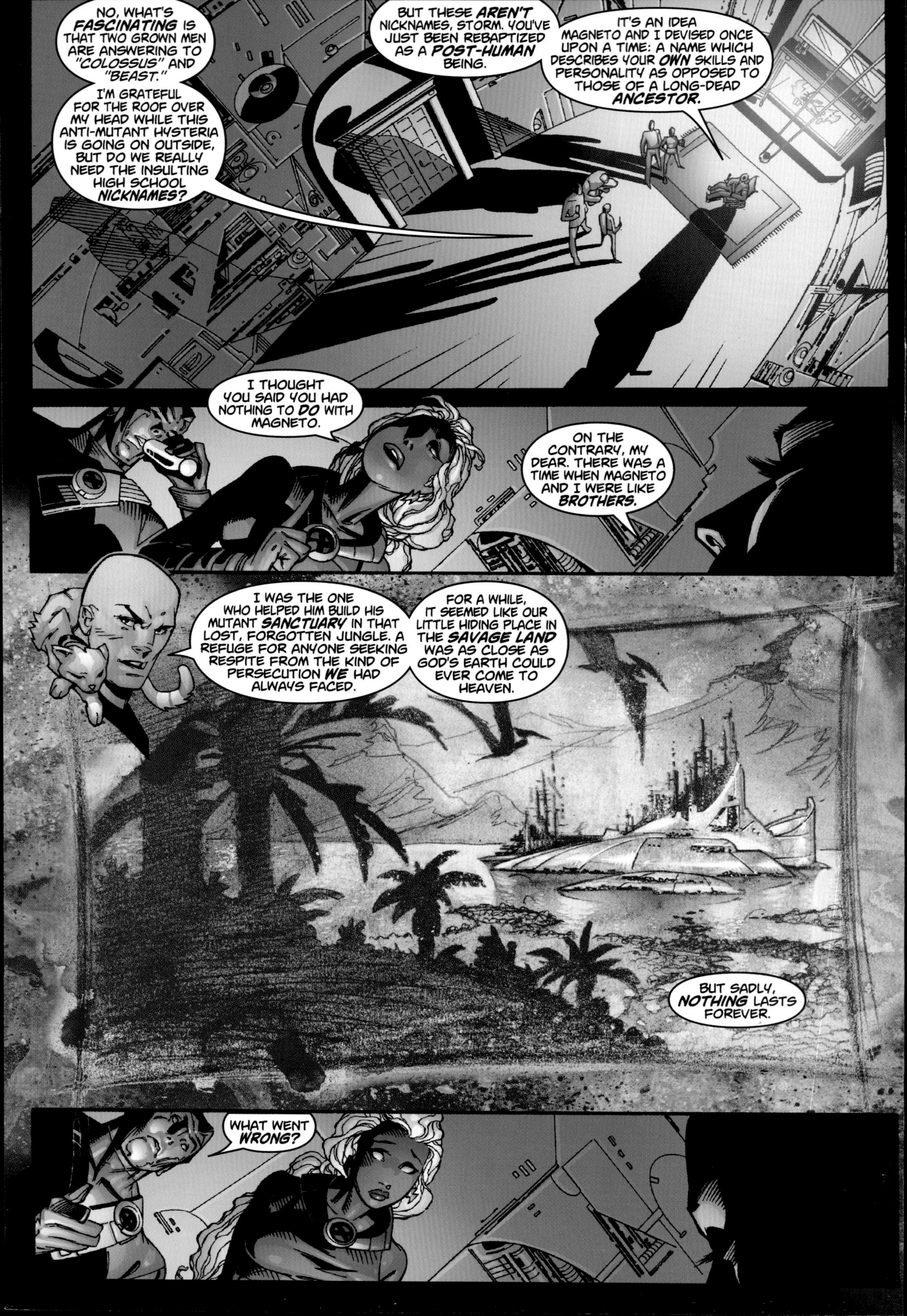
NO, WHAT'S FASCINATING IS THAT TWO GROWN MEN ARE ANSWERING TO "COLOSSUS" AND "BEAST."
I'M GRATEFUL FOR THE ROOF OVER MY HEAD WHILE THIS ANTI-MUTANT HYSTERIA IS GOING ON OUTSIDE, BUT DO WE REALLY NEED THE INSULTING HIGH SCHOOL NICKNAMES?
BUT THESE AREN'T NICKNAMES, STORM. YOU'VE JUST BEEN REBAPTIZED AS A POST-HUMAN BEING.
IT'S AN IDEA MAGNETO AND I DEVISED ONCE UPON A TIME: A NAME WHICH DESCRIBES YOUR OWN SKILLS AND PERSONALITY AS OPPOSED TO THOSE OF A LONG-DEAD ANCESTOR.
I THOUGHT YOU SAID YOU HAD NOTHING TO DO WITH MAGNETO.
ON THE CONTRARY, MY DEAR. THERE WAS A TIME WHEN MAGNETO AND I WERE LIKE BROTHERS.
I WAS THE ONE WHO HELPED HIM BUILD HIS MUTANT SANCTUARY IN THAT LOST, FORGOTTEN JUNGLE. A REFUGE FOR ANYONE SEEKING RESPITE FROM THE KIND OF PERSECUTION WE HAD ALWAYS FACED.
FOR A WHILE, IT SEEMED LIKE OUR LITTLE HIDING PLACE IN THE SAVAGE LAND WAS AS CLOSE AS GOD'S EARTH COULD EVER COME TO HEAVEN.
BUT SADLY, NOTHING LASTS FOREVER.
WHAT WENT WRONG?

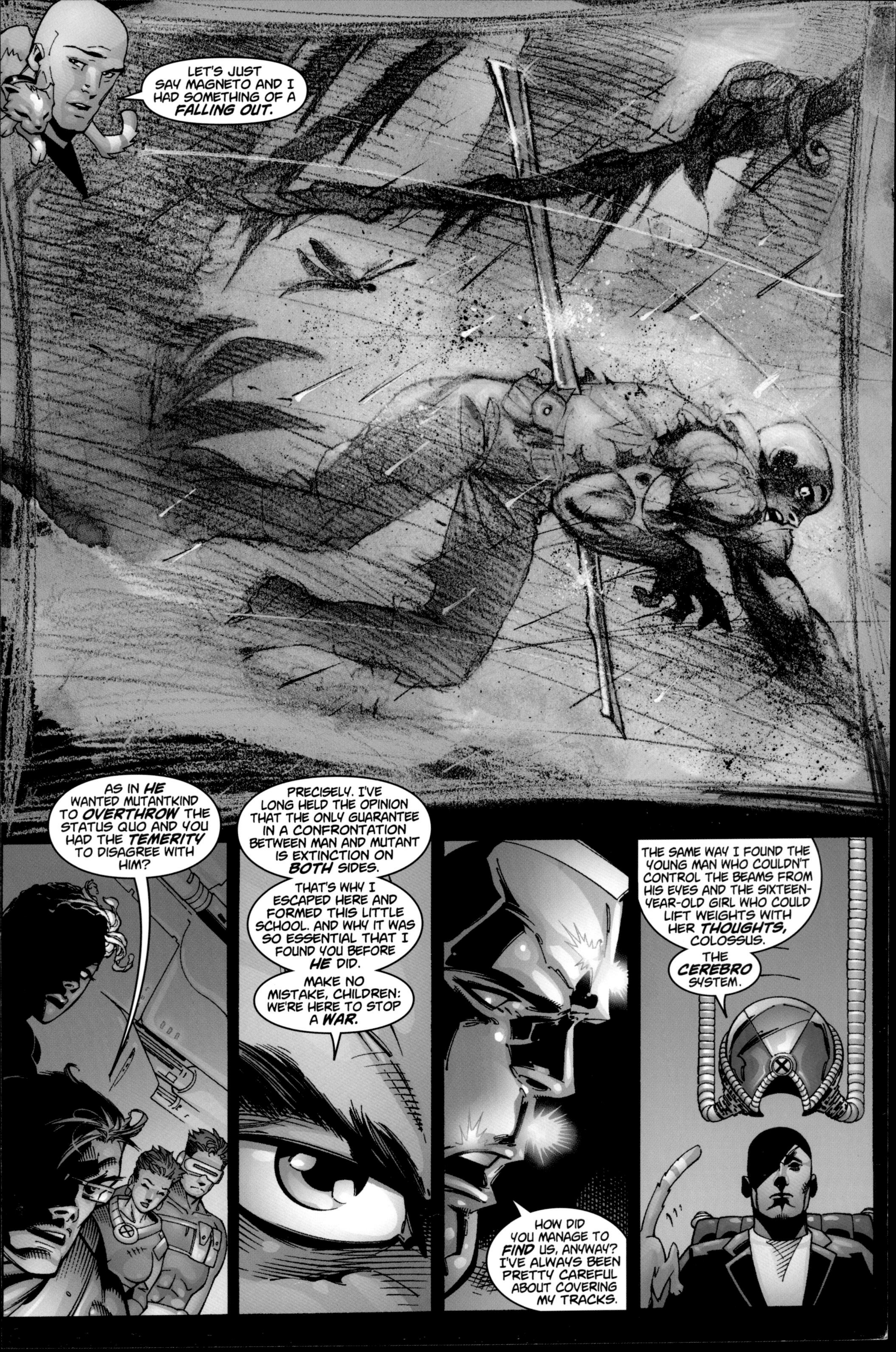
LET'S JUST SAY MAGNETO AND I HAD SOMETHING OF A FALLING OUT.
AS IN HE WANTED MUTANTKIND TO OVERTHROW THE STATUS QUO AND YOU HAD THE TEMERITY TO DISAGREE WITH HIM?
PRECISELY. I'VE LONG HELD THE OPINION THAT THE ONLY GUARANTEE IN A CONFRONTATION BETWEEN MAN AND MUTANT IS EXTINCTION ON BOTH SIDES.
THAT'S WHY I ESCAPED HERE AND FORMED THIS LITTLE SCHOOL. AND WHY IT WAS SO ESSENTIAL THAT I FOUND YOU BEFORE HE DID.
MAKE NO MISTAKE, CHILDREN: WE'RE HERE TO STOP A WAR.
HOW DID YOU MANAGE TO FIND US, ANYWAY? I'VE ALWAYS BEEN PRETTY CAREFUL ABOUT COVERING MY TRACKS.
THE SAME WAY I FOUND THE YOUNG MAN WHO COULDN'T CONTROL THE BEAMS FROM HIS EYES AND THE SIXTEEN-YEAR-OLD GIRL WHO COULD LIFT WEIGHTS WITH HER THOUGHTS, COLOSSUS.
THE CEREBRO SYSTEM.

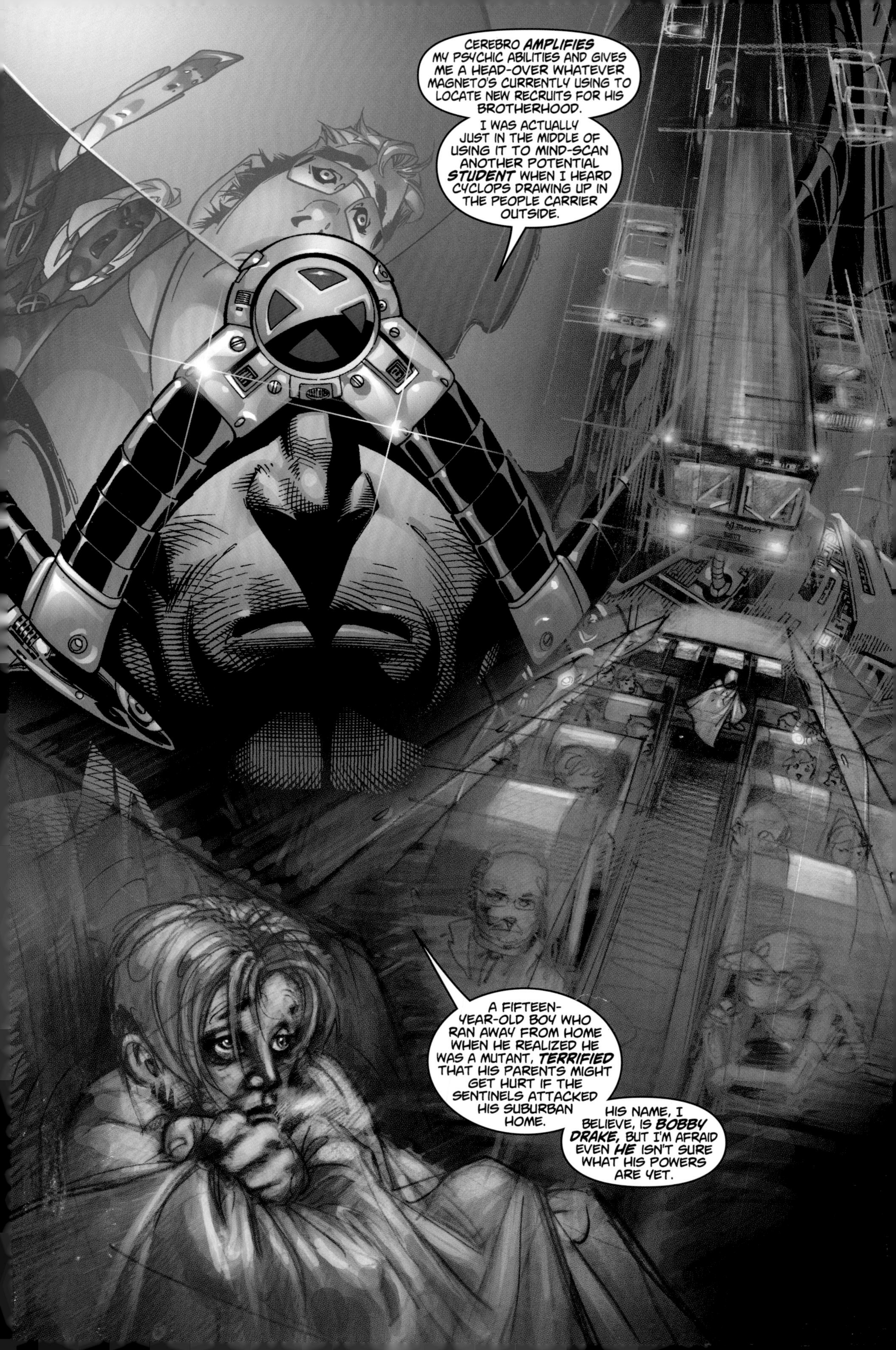
CEREBRO AMPLIFIES MY PSYCHIC ABILITIES AND GIVES ME A HEAD-OVER WHATEVER MAGNETO'S CURRENTLY USING TO LOCATE NEW RECRUITS FOR HIS BROTHERHOOD.
I WAS ACTUALLY JUST IN THE MIDDLE OF USING IT TO MIND-SCAN ANOTHER POTENTIAL STUDENT WHEN I HEARD CYCLOPS DRAWING UP IN THE PEOPLE CARRIER OUTSIDE.
A FIFTEEN-YEAR-OLD BOY WHO RAN AWAY FROM HOME WHEN HE REALIZED HE WAS A MUTANT, TERRIFIED THAT HIS PARENTS MIGHT GET HURT IF THE SENTINELS ATTACKED HIS SUBURBAN HOME.
HIS NAME, I BELIEVE, IS BOBBY DRAKE, BUT I'M AFRAID EVEN HE ISN'T SURE WHAT HIS POWERS ARE YET.

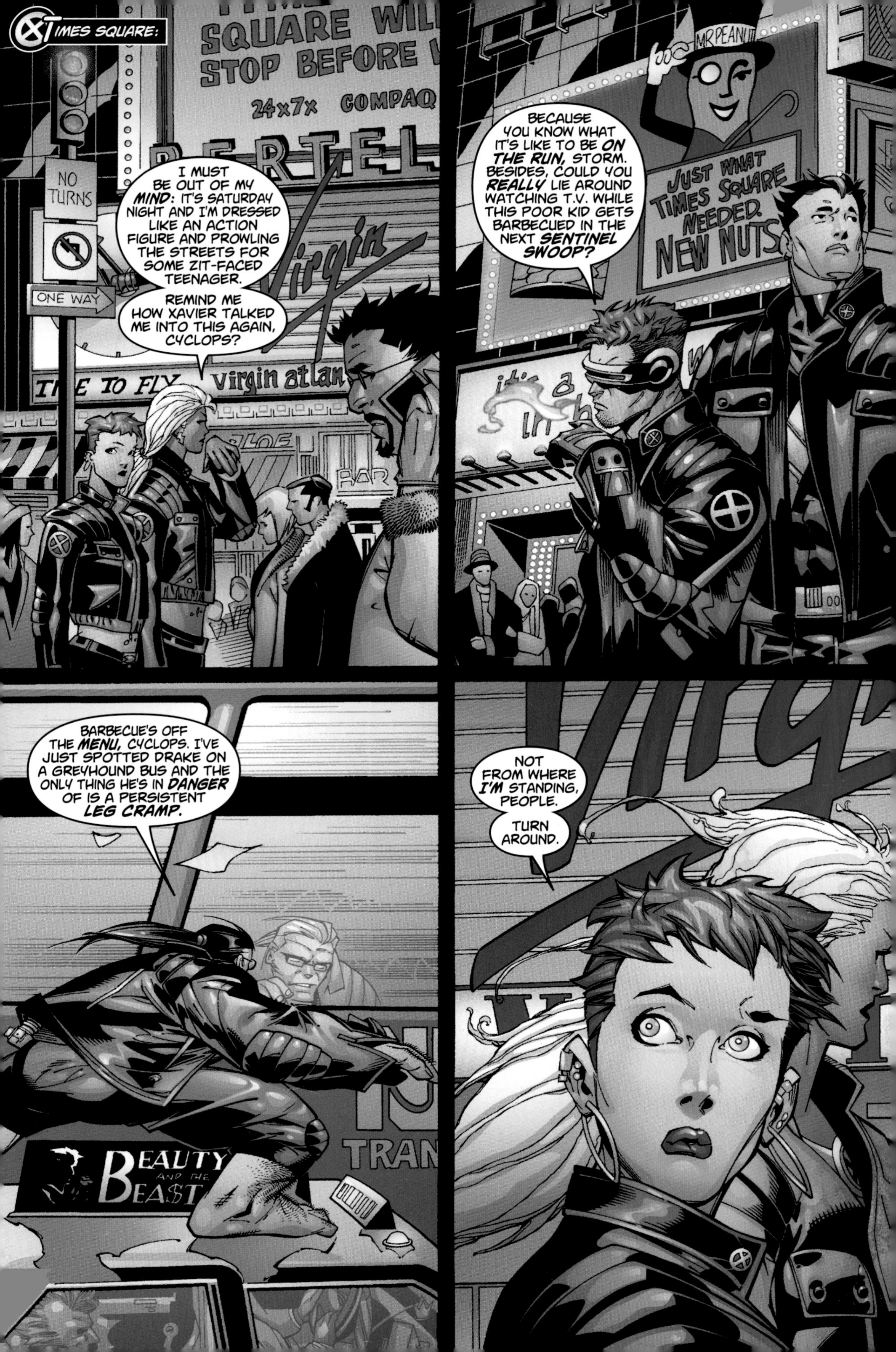
TIMES SQUARE:
SQUARE WILL STOP BEFORE
24x7x COMPAQ
NO TURNS
ONE WAY
I MUST BE OUT OF MY MIND: IT'S SATURDAY NIGHT AND I'M DRESSED LIKE AN ACTION FIGURE AND PROWLING THE STREETS FOR SOME ZIT-FACED TEENAGER.
REMIND ME HOW XAVIER TALKED ME INTO THIS AGAIN, CYCLOPS?
MR PEANUT
JUST WHAT TIMES SQUARE NEEDED. NEW NUTS
BECAUSE YOU KNOW WHAT IT'S LIKE TO BE ON THE RUN, STORM. BESIDES, COULD YOU REALLY LIE AROUND WATCHING T.V. WHILE THIS POOR KID GETS BARBECUED IN THE NEXT SENTINEL SWOOP?
BARBECUE'S OFF THE MENU, CYCLOPS. I'VE JUST SPOTTED DRAKE ON A GREYHOUND BUS AND THE ONLY THING HE'S IN DANGER OF IS A PERSISTENT LEG CRAMP.
BEAUTY AND THE BEAST
NOT FROM WHERE I'M STANDING, PEOPLE.
TURN AROUND.

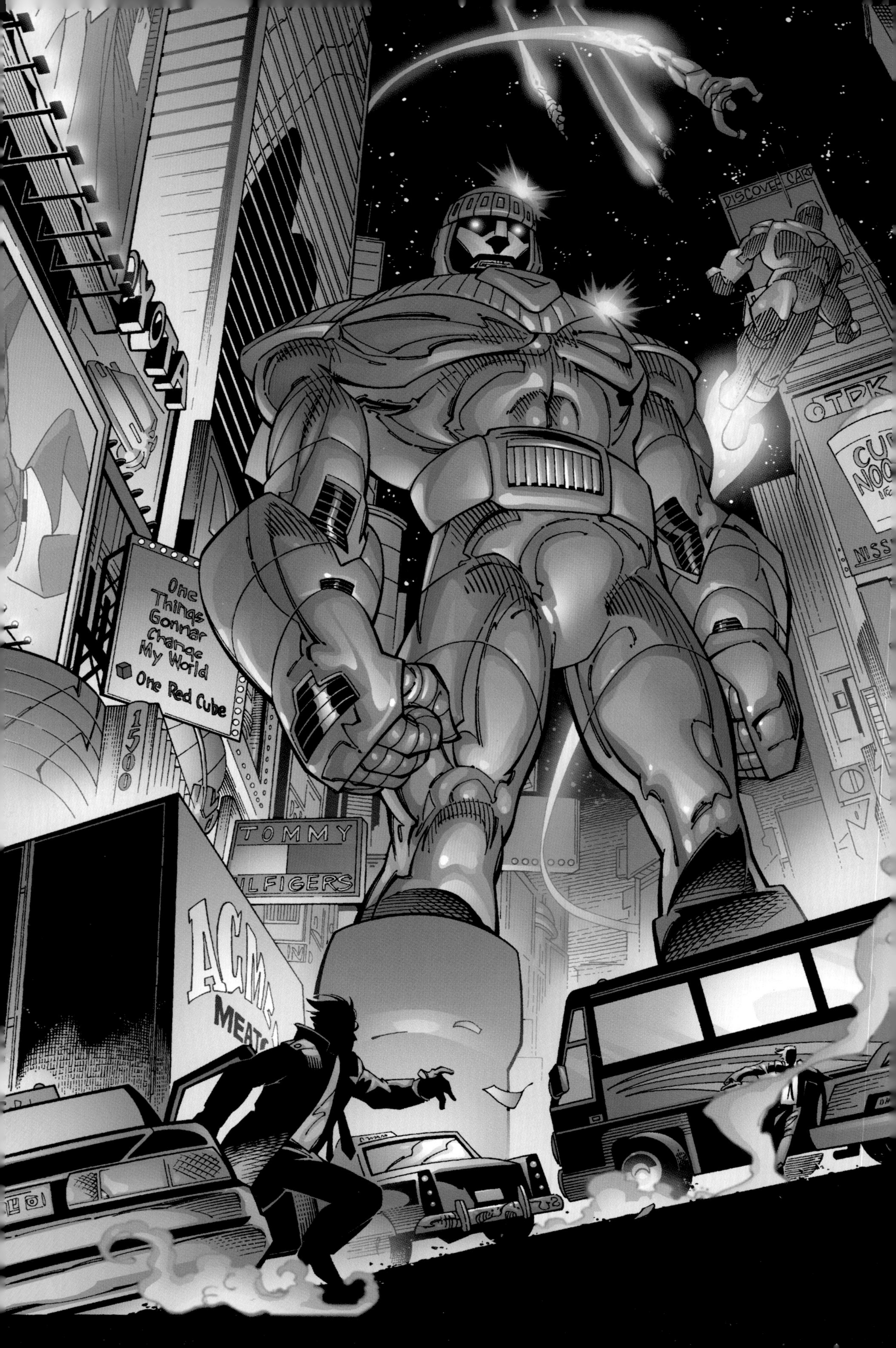
One Things Gonnar Change My World
One Red Cube
1500
TOMMY
ILFIGERS

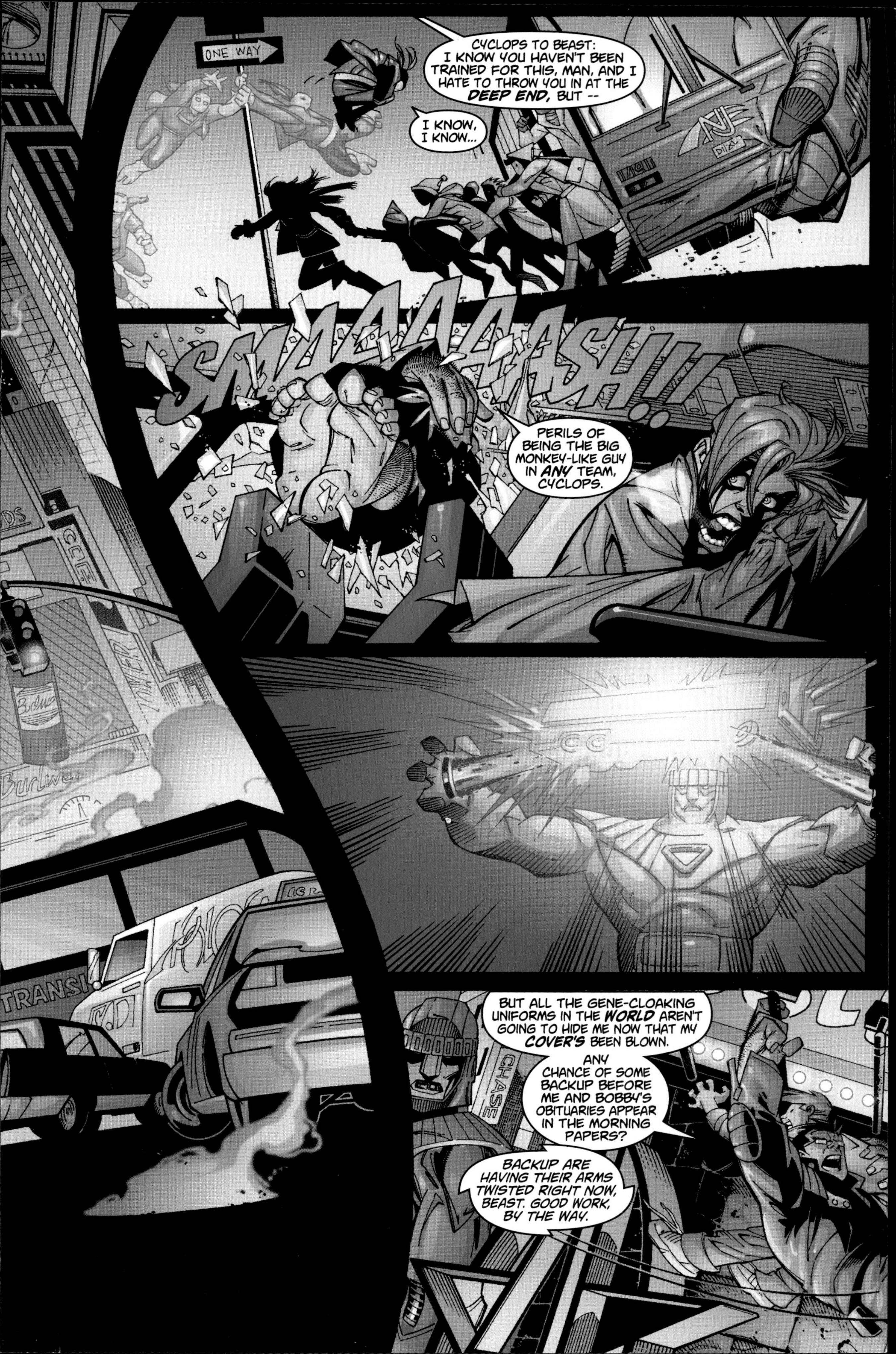
CYCLOPS TO BEAST: I KNOW YOU HAVEN'T BEEN TRAINED FOR THIS, MAN, AND I HATE TO THROW YOU IN AT THE DEEP END, BUT --
I KNOW, I KNOW...
ONE WAY
SMAAAAAASH!!
PERILS OF BEING THE BIG MONKEY-LIKE GUY IN ANY TEAM, CYCLOPS.
BUT ALL THE GENE-CLOAKING UNIFORMS IN THE WORLD AREN'T GOING TO HIDE ME NOW THAT MY COVER'S BEEN BLOWN.
ANY CHANCE OF SOME BACKUP BEFORE ME AND BOBBY'S OBITUARIES APPEAR IN THE MORNING PAPERS?
BACKUP ARE HAVING THEIR ARMS TWISTED RIGHT NOW, BEAST. GOOD WORK, BY THE WAY.
CHASE
TRANSI

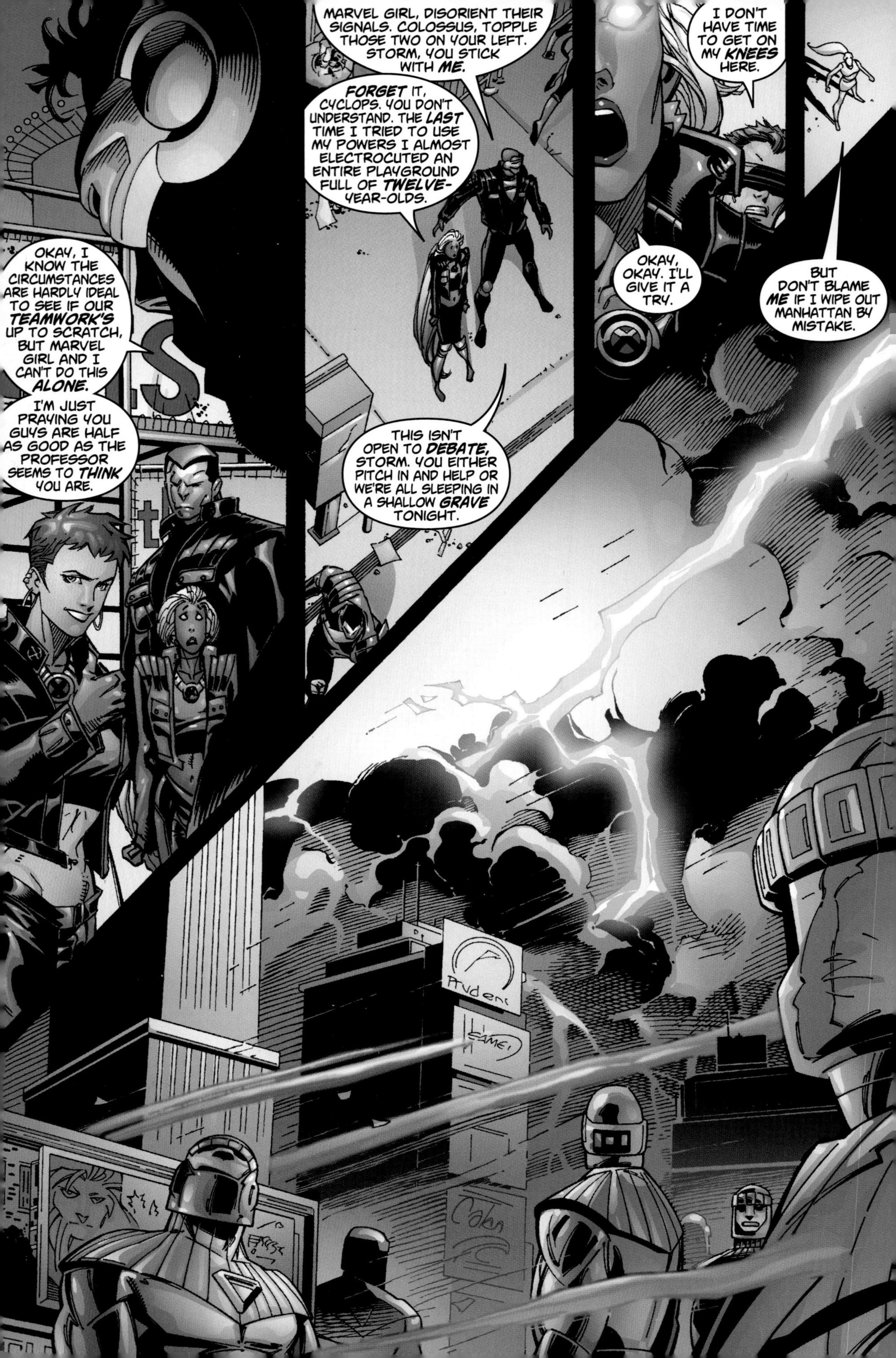

OKAY, I KNOW THE CIRCUMSTANCES ARE HARDLY IDEAL TO SEE IF OUR TEAMWORK'S UP TO SCRATCH, BUT MARVEL GIRL AND I CAN'T DO THIS ALONE.
I'M JUST PRAYING YOU GUYS ARE HALF AS GOOD AS THE PROFESSOR SEEMS TO THINK YOU ARE.
MARVEL GIRL, DISORIENT THEIR SIGNALS. COLOSSUS, TOPPLE THOSE TWO ON YOUR LEFT. STORM, YOU STICK WITH ME.
FORGET IT, CYCLOPS. YOU DON'T UNDERSTAND. THE LAST TIME I TRIED TO USE MY POWERS I ALMOST ELECTROCUTED AN ENTIRE PLAYGROUND FULL OF TWELVE-YEAR-OLDS.
THIS ISN'T OPEN TO DEBATE, STORM. YOU EITHER PITCH IN AND HELP OR WE'RE ALL SLEEPING IN A SHALLOW GRAVE TONIGHT.
I DON'T HAVE TIME TO GET ON MY KNEES HERE.
OKAY, OKAY. I'LL GIVE IT A TRY.
BUT DON'T BLAME ME IF I WIPE OUT MANHATTAN BY MISTAKE.

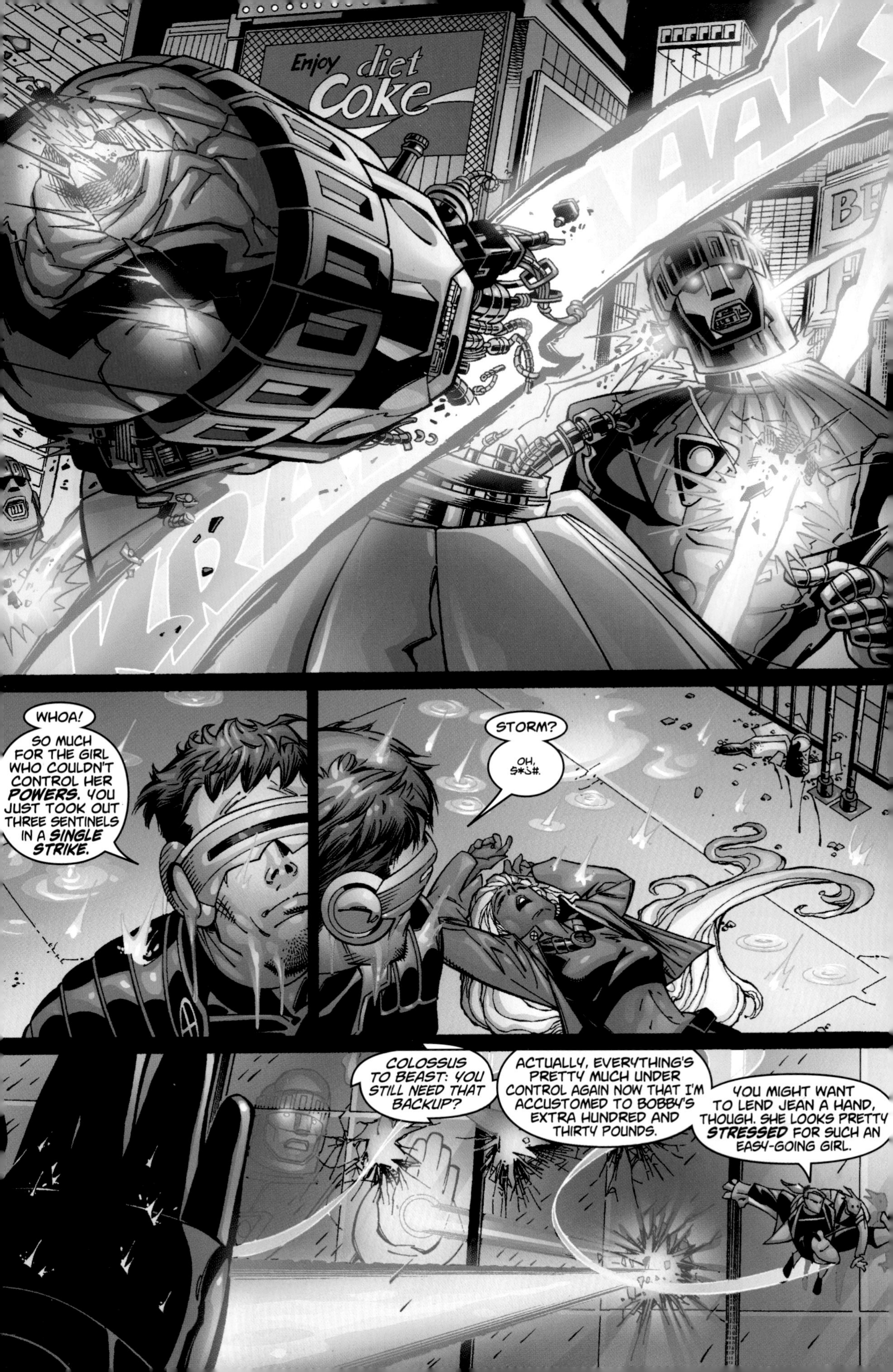
Enjoy diet Coke
KRAAAK
WHOA!
SO MUCH FOR THE GIRL WHO COULDN'T CONTROL HER POWERS. YOU JUST TOOK OUT THREE SENTINELS IN A SINGLE STRIKE.
STORM?
OH, S*J#.
COLOSSUS TO BEAST: YOU STILL NEED THAT BACKUP?
ACTUALLY, EVERYTHING'S PRETTY MUCH UNDER CONTROL AGAIN NOW THAT I'M ACCUSTOMED TO BOBBY'S EXTRA HUNDRED AND THIRTY POUNDS.
YOU MIGHT WANT TO LEND JEAN A HAND, THOUGH. SHE LOOKS PRETTY STRESSED FOR SUCH AN EASY-GOING GIRL.

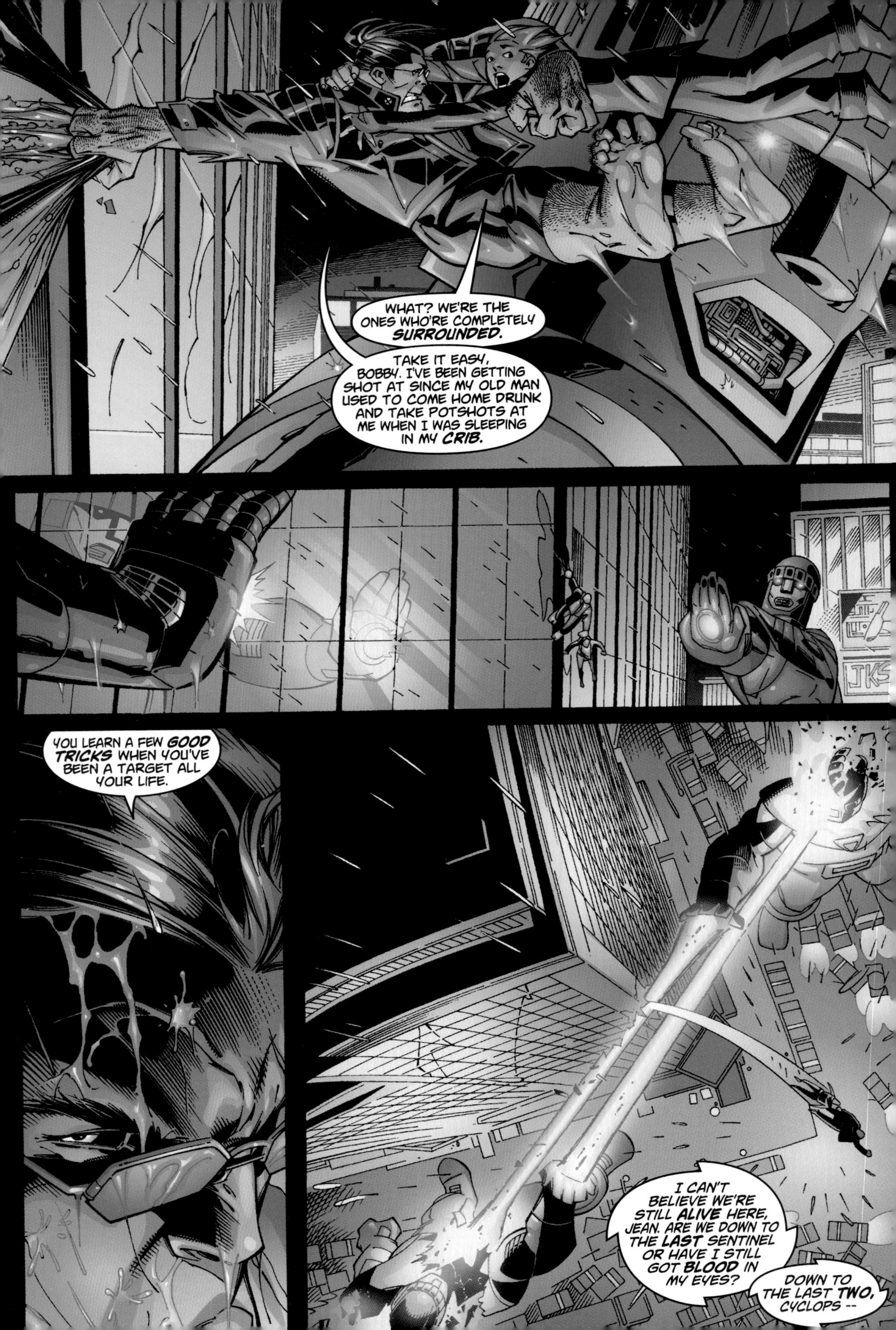
WHAT? WE'RE THE ONES WHO'RE COMPLETELY **SURROUNDED.**
TAKE IT EASY, BOBBY. I'VE BEEN GETTING SHOT AT SINCE MY OLD MAN USED TO COME HOME DRUNK AND TAKE POTSHOTS AT ME WHEN I WAS SLEEPING IN MY **CRIB.**
JKS
YOU LEARN A FEW **GOOD TRICKS** WHEN YOU'VE BEEN A TARGET ALL YOUR LIFE.
I CAN'T BELIEVE WE'RE STILL **ALIVE** HERE, JEAN. ARE WE DOWN TO THE **LAST** SENTINEL OR HAVE I STILL GOT **BLOOD** IN MY EYES?
DOWN TO THE LAST **TWO,** CYCLOPS --

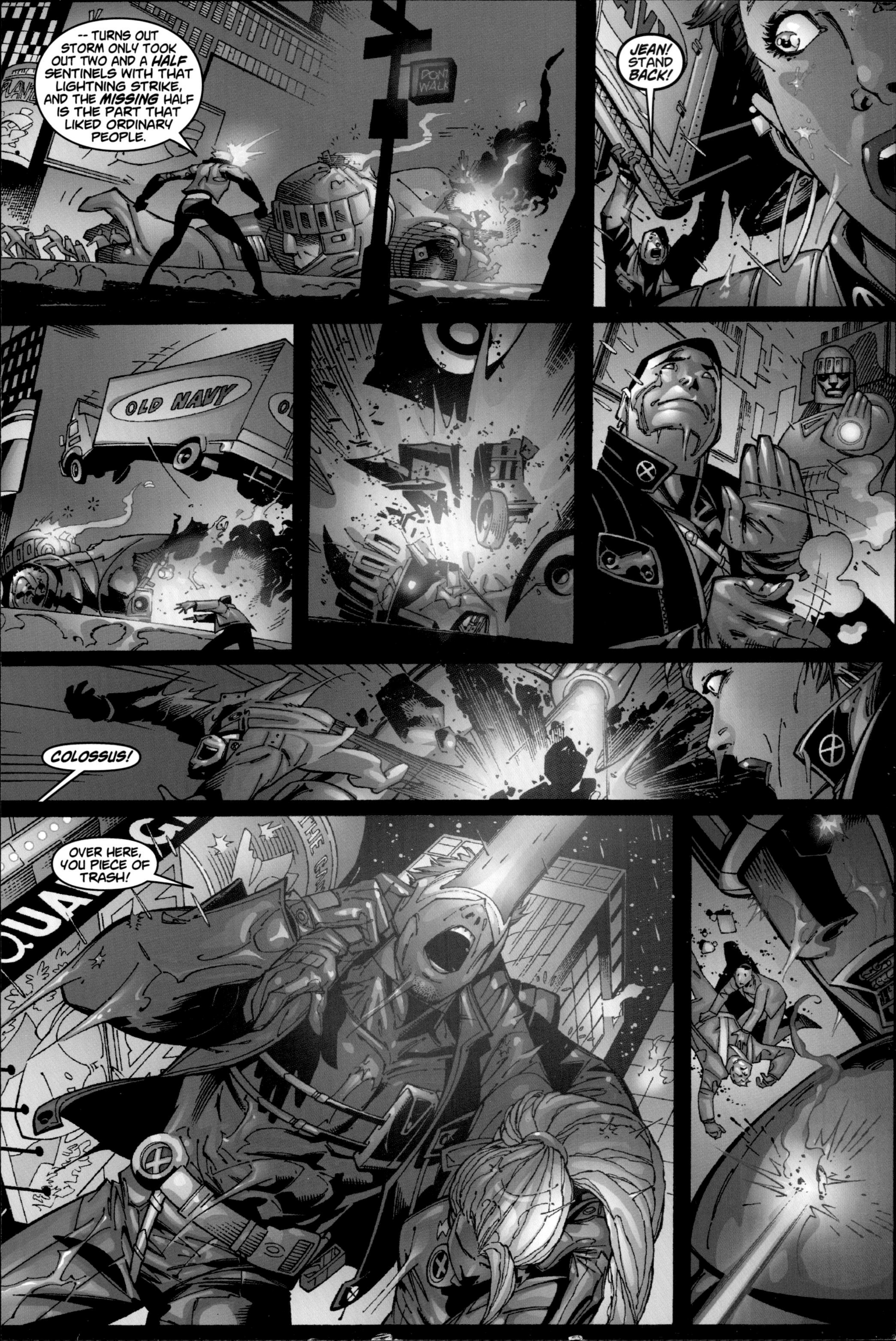
-- TURNS OUT STORM ONLY TOOK OUT TWO AND A HALF SENTINELS WITH THAT LIGHTNING STRIKE, AND THE MISSING HALF IS THE PART THAT LIKED ORDINARY PEOPLE.
DON'T WALK
JEAN! STAND BACK!
OLD NAVY
COLOSSUS!
OVER HERE, YOU PIECE OF TRASH!

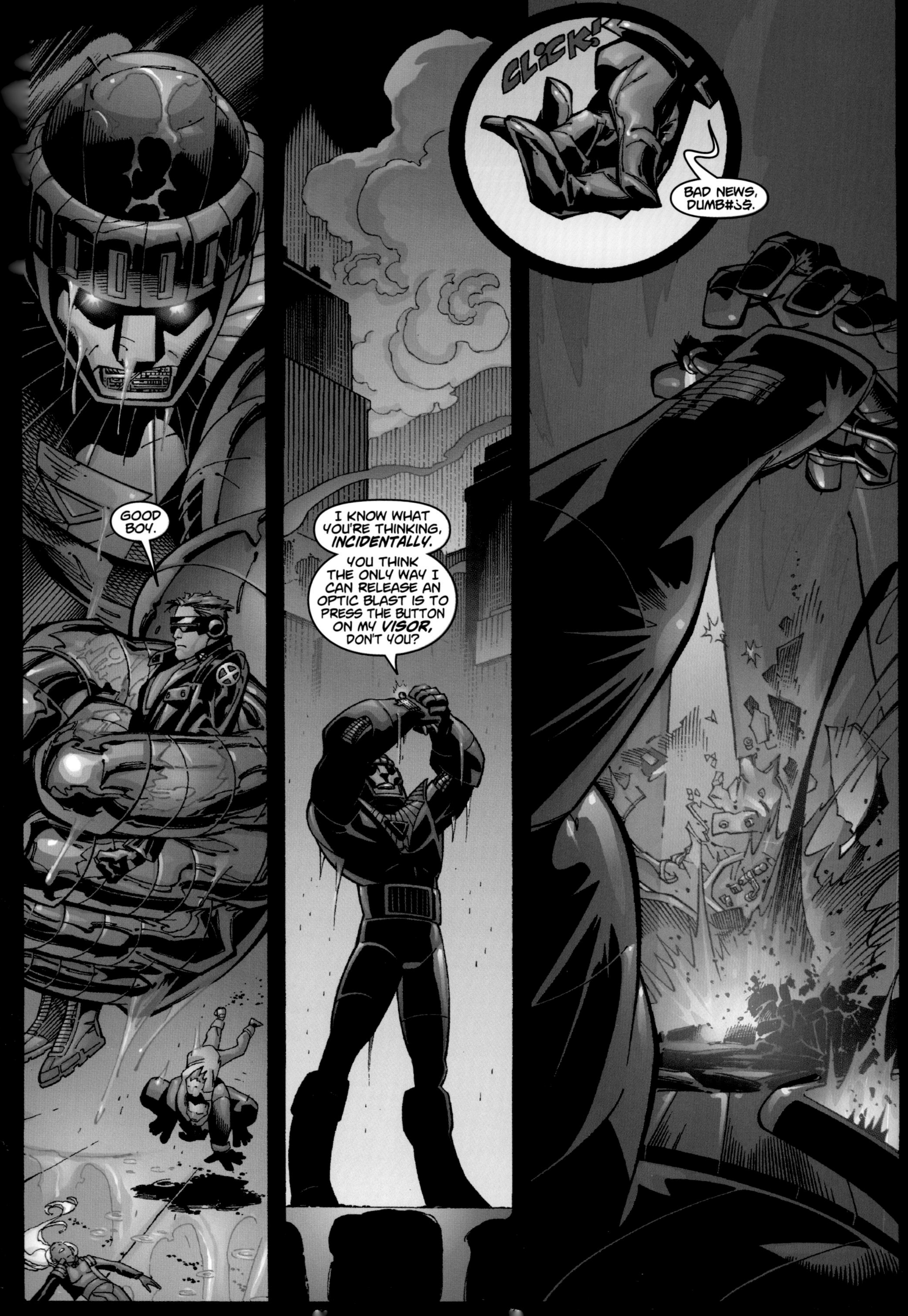

GOOD BOY.
I KNOW WHAT YOU'RE THINKING, INCIDENTALLY.
YOU THINK THE ONLY WAY I CAN RELEASE AN OPTIC BLAST IS TO PRESS THE BUTTON ON MY VISOR, DON'T YOU?
CLICK!
BAD NEWS, DUMB#$S.

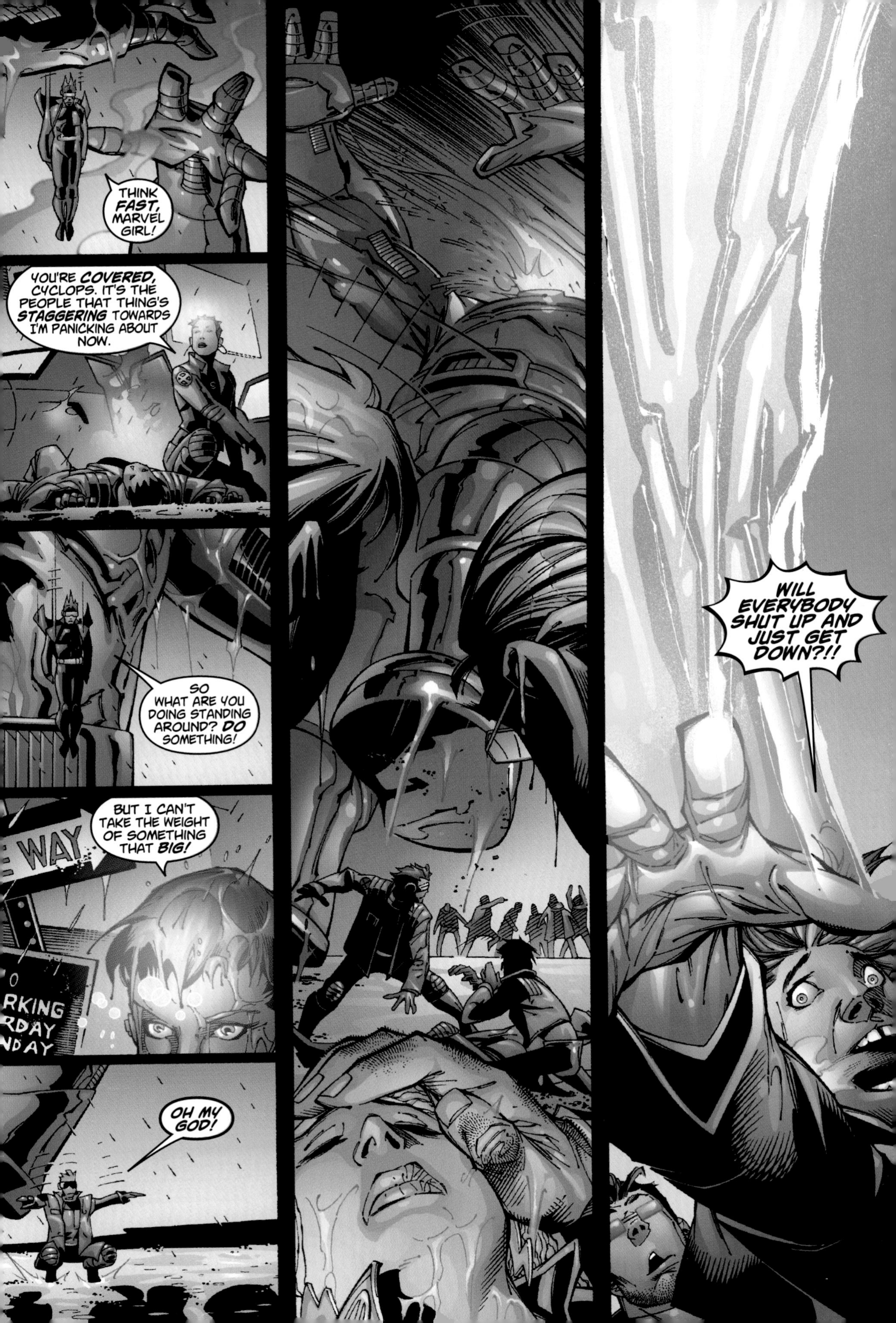
THINK FAST, MARVEL GIRL!
YOU'RE COVERED, CYCLOPS. IT'S THE PEOPLE THAT THING'S STAGGERING TOWARDS I'M PANICKING ABOUT NOW.
SO WHAT ARE YOU DOING STANDING AROUND? DO SOMETHING!
WAY
BUT I CAN'T TAKE THE WEIGHT OF SOMETHING THAT BIG!
RKING
RDAY
NDAY
OH MY GOD!
WILL EVERYBODY SHUT UP AND JUST GET DOWN?!!

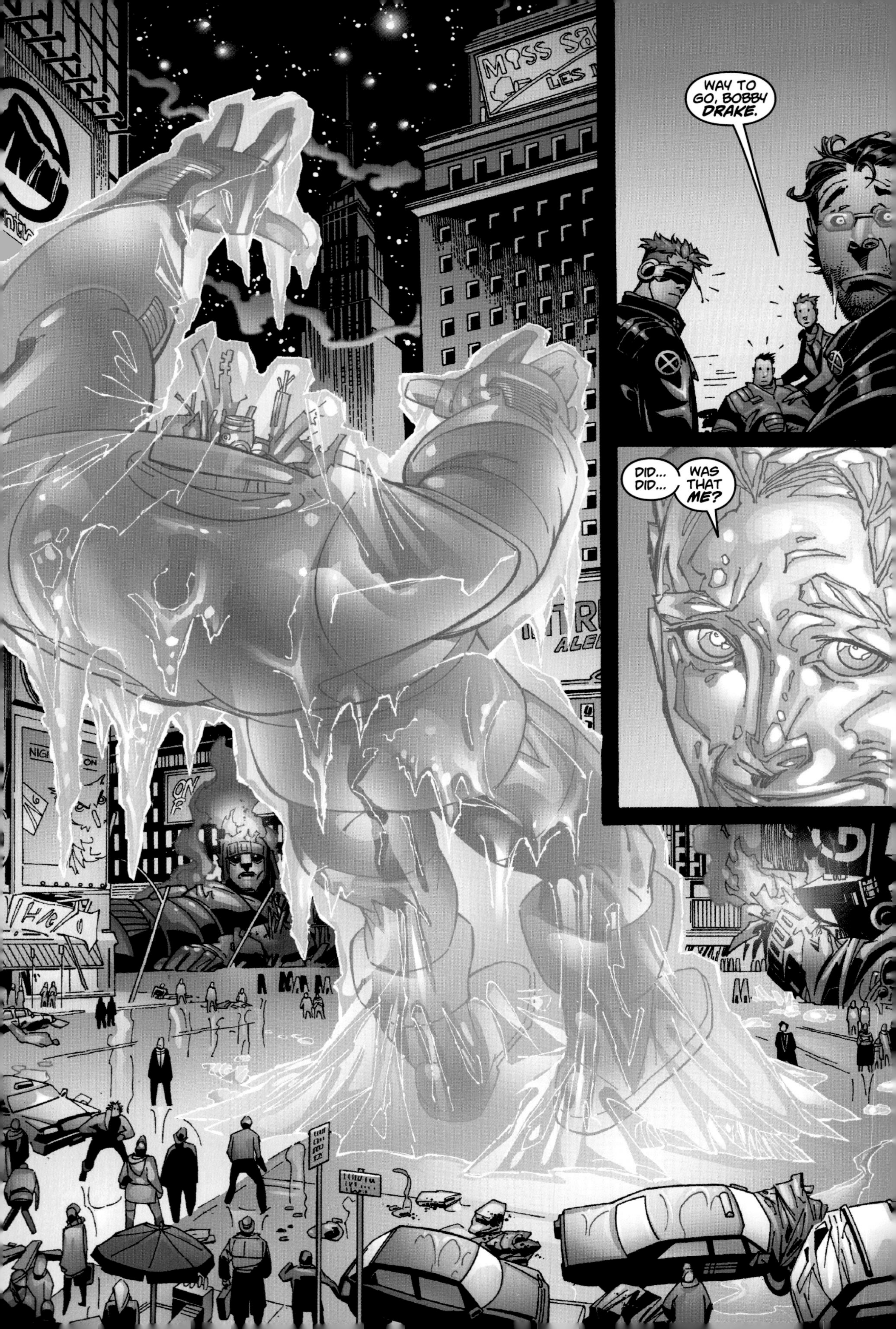
WAY TO GO, BOBBY DRAKE.
DID... DID...
WAS THAT ME?

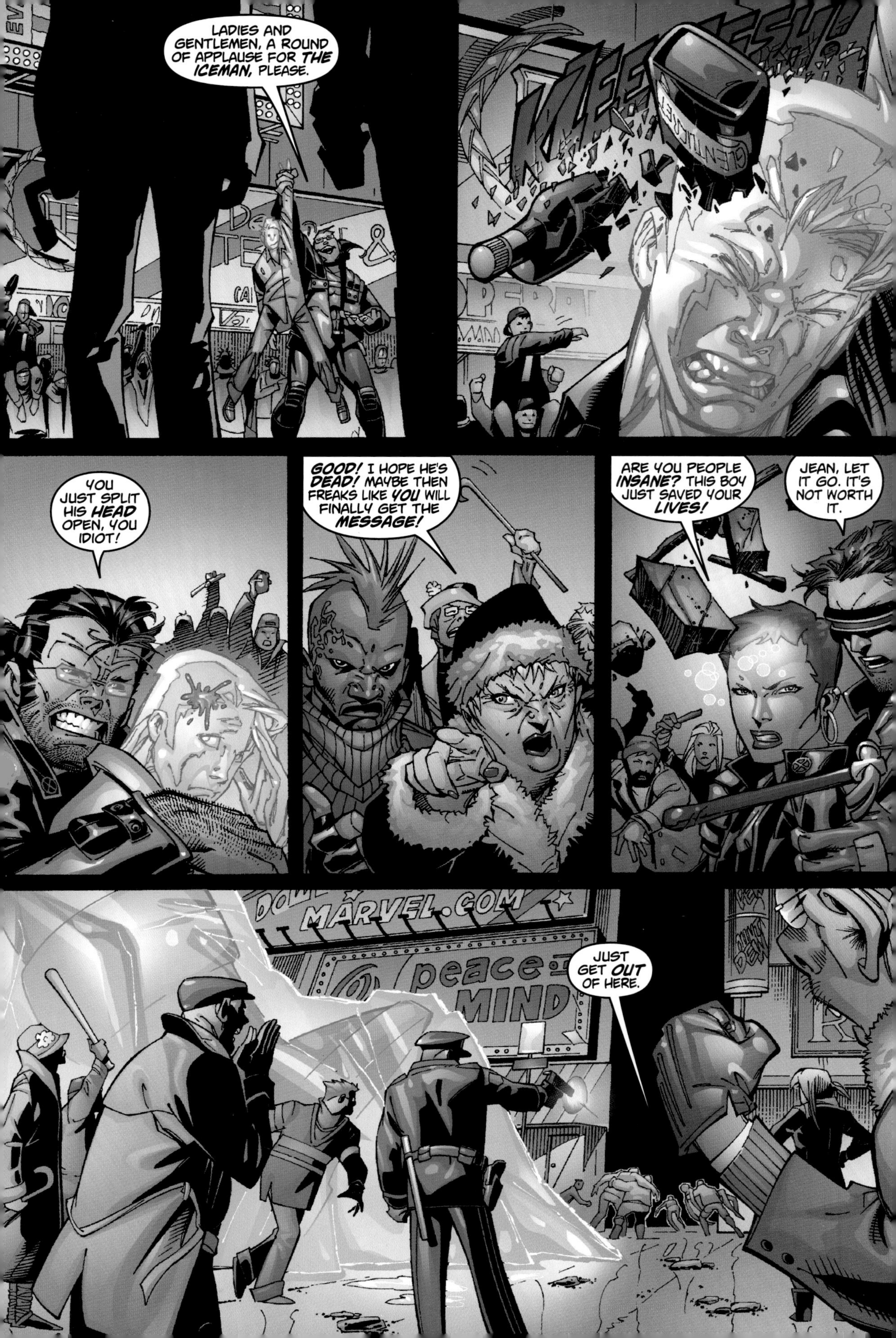
LADIES AND GENTLEMEN, A ROUND OF APPLAUSE FOR THE ICEMAN, PLEASE.
YOU JUST SPLIT HIS HEAD OPEN, YOU IDIOT!
GOOD! I HOPE HE'S DEAD! MAYBE THEN FREAKS LIKE YOU WILL FINALLY GET THE MESSAGE!
ARE YOU PEOPLE INSANE? THIS BOY JUST SAVED YOUR LIVES!
JEAN, LET IT GO. IT'S NOT WORTH IT.
MARVEL.COM
peace MIND
JUST GET OUT OF HERE.

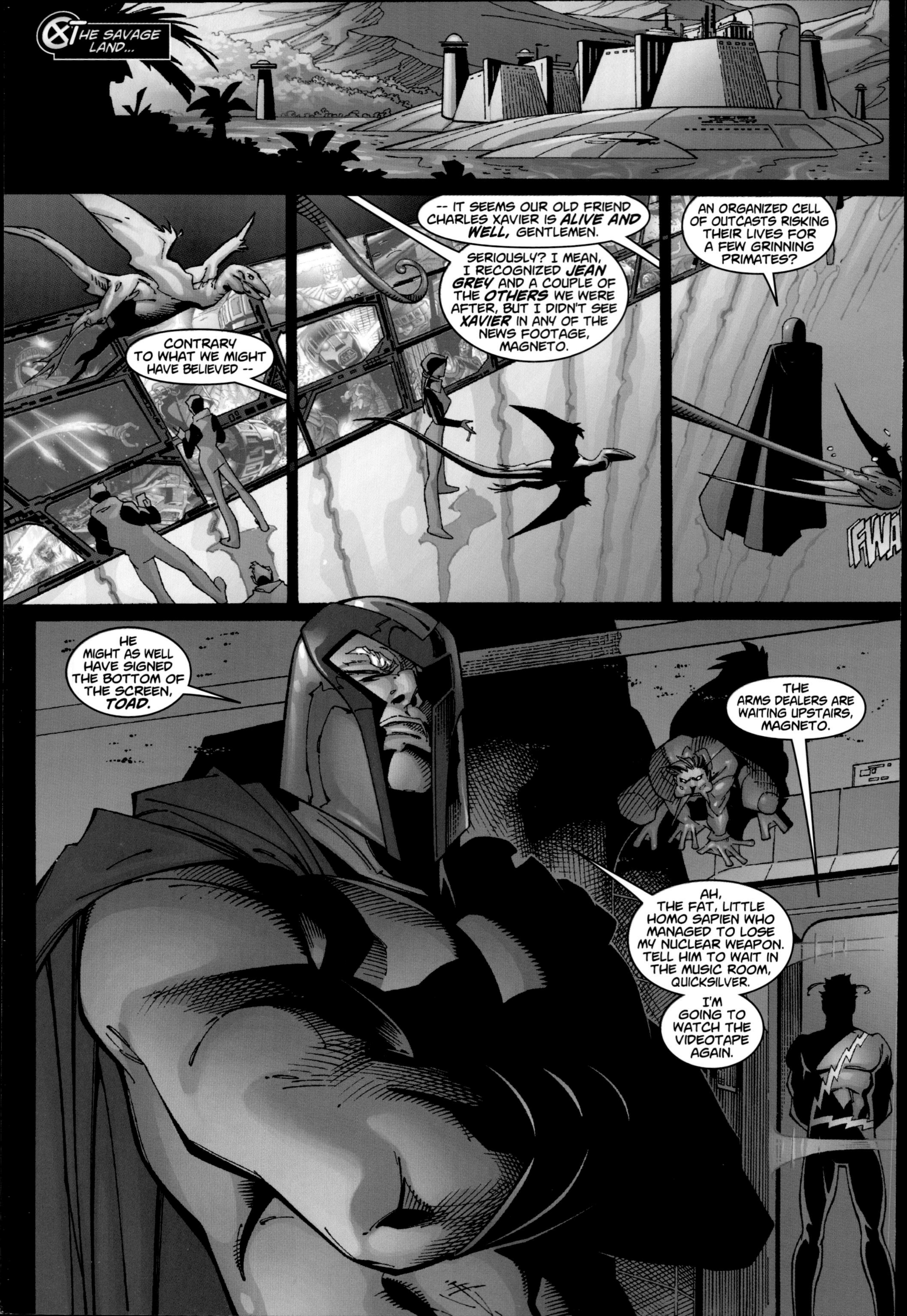
THE SAVAGE LAND...
CONTRARY TO WHAT WE MIGHT HAVE BELIEVED --
-- IT SEEMS OUR OLD FRIEND CHARLES XAVIER IS ALIVE AND WELL, GENTLEMEN.
SERIOUSLY? I MEAN, I RECOGNIZED JEAN GREY AND A COUPLE OF THE OTHERS WE WERE AFTER, BUT I DIDN'T SEE XAVIER IN ANY OF THE NEWS FOOTAGE, MAGNETO.
AN ORGANIZED CELL OF OUTCASTS RISKING THEIR LIVES FOR A FEW GRINNING PRIMATES?
HE MIGHT AS WELL HAVE SIGNED THE BOTTOM OF THE SCREEN, TOAD.
THE ARMS DEALERS ARE WAITING UPSTAIRS, MAGNETO.
AH, THE FAT, LITTLE HOMO SAPIEN WHO MANAGED TO LOSE MY NUCLEAR WEAPON. TELL HIM TO WAIT IN THE MUSIC ROOM, QUICKSILVER.
I'M GOING TO WATCH THE VIDEOTAPE AGAIN.

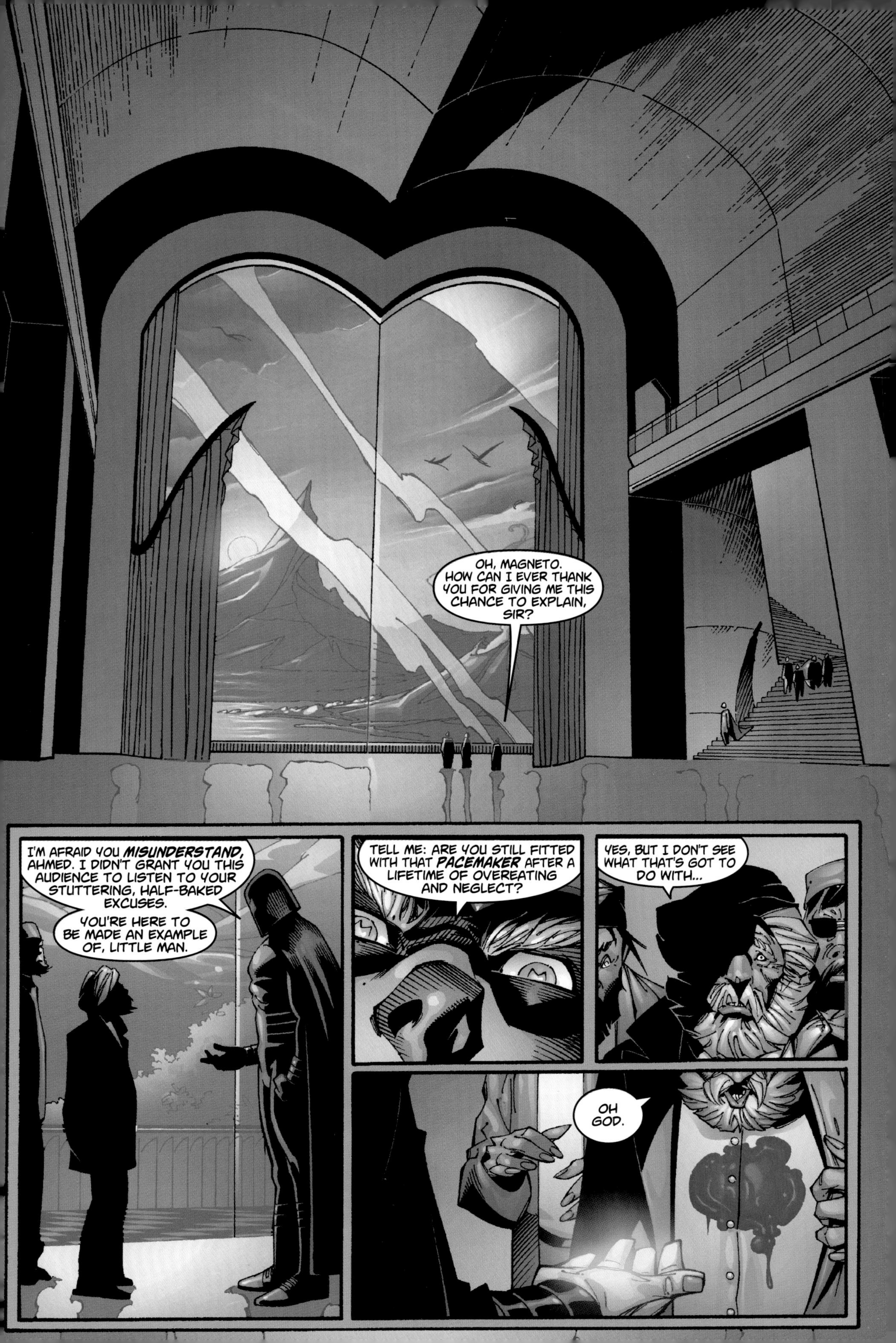
OH, MAGNETO. HOW CAN I EVER THANK YOU FOR GIVING ME THIS CHANCE TO EXPLAIN, SIR?
I'M AFRAID YOU MISUNDERSTAND, AHMED. I DIDN'T GRANT YOU THIS AUDIENCE TO LISTEN TO YOUR STUTTERING, HALF-BAKED EXCUSES.
YOU'RE HERE TO BE MADE AN EXAMPLE OF, LITTLE MAN.
TELL ME: ARE YOU STILL FITTED WITH THAT PACEMAKER AFTER A LIFETIME OF OVEREATING AND NEGLECT?
YES, BUT I DON'T SEE WHAT THAT'S GOT TO DO WITH...
OH GOD.

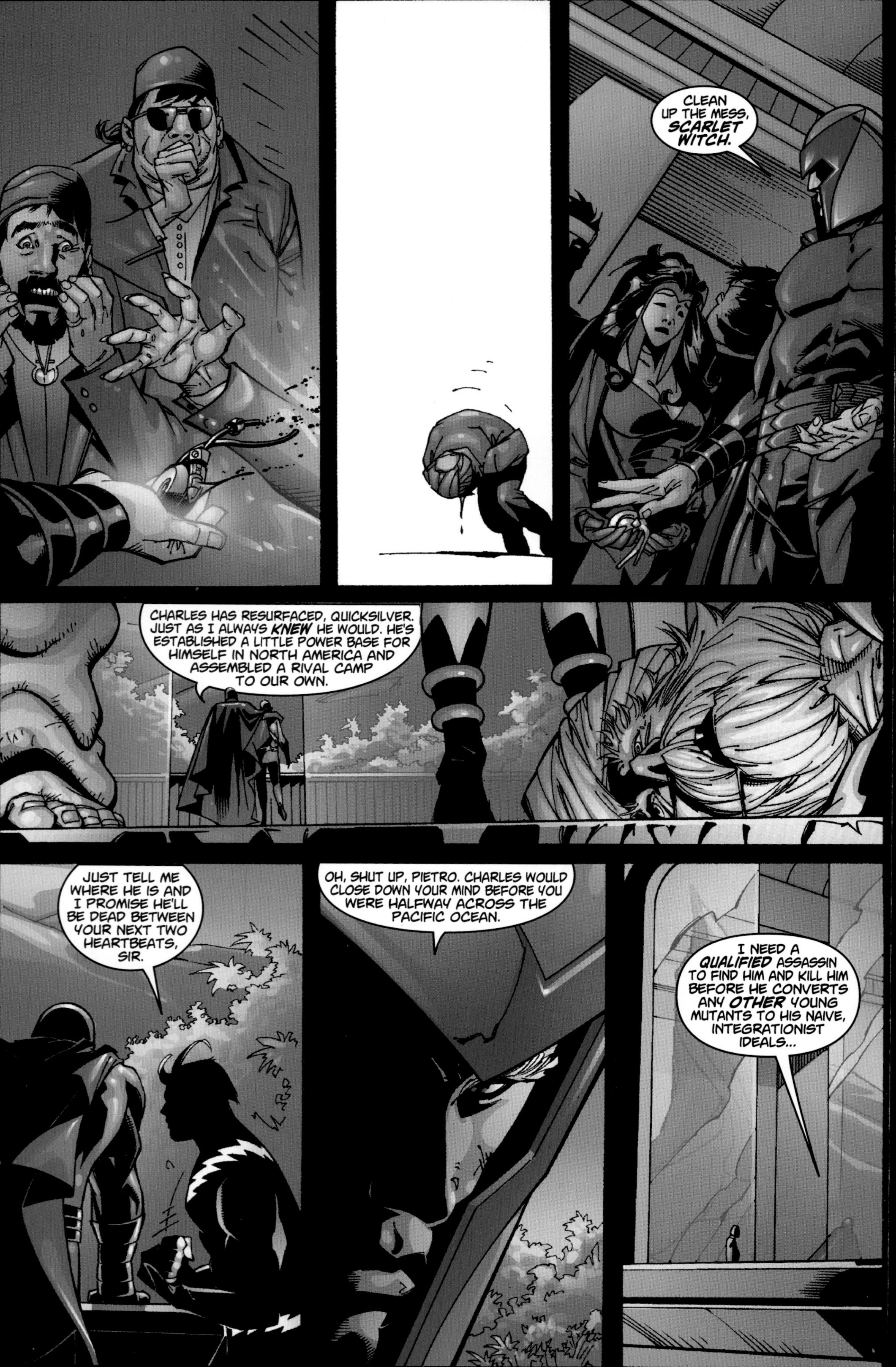
CLEAN UP THE MESS, SCARLET WITCH.
CHARLES HAS RESURFACED, QUICKSILVER. JUST AS I ALWAYS KNEW HE WOULD. HE'S ESTABLISHED A LITTLE POWER BASE FOR HIMSELF IN NORTH AMERICA AND ASSEMBLED A RIVAL CAMP TO OUR OWN.
JUST TELL ME WHERE HE IS AND I PROMISE HE'LL BE DEAD BETWEEN YOUR NEXT TWO HEARTBEATS, SIR.
OH, SHUT UP, PIETRO. CHARLES WOULD CLOSE DOWN YOUR MIND BEFORE YOU WERE HALFWAY ACROSS THE PACIFIC OCEAN.
I NEED A QUALIFIED ASSASSIN TO FIND HIM AND KILL HIM BEFORE HE CONVERTS ANY OTHER YOUNG MUTANTS TO HIS NAIVE, INTEGRATIONIST IDEALS...

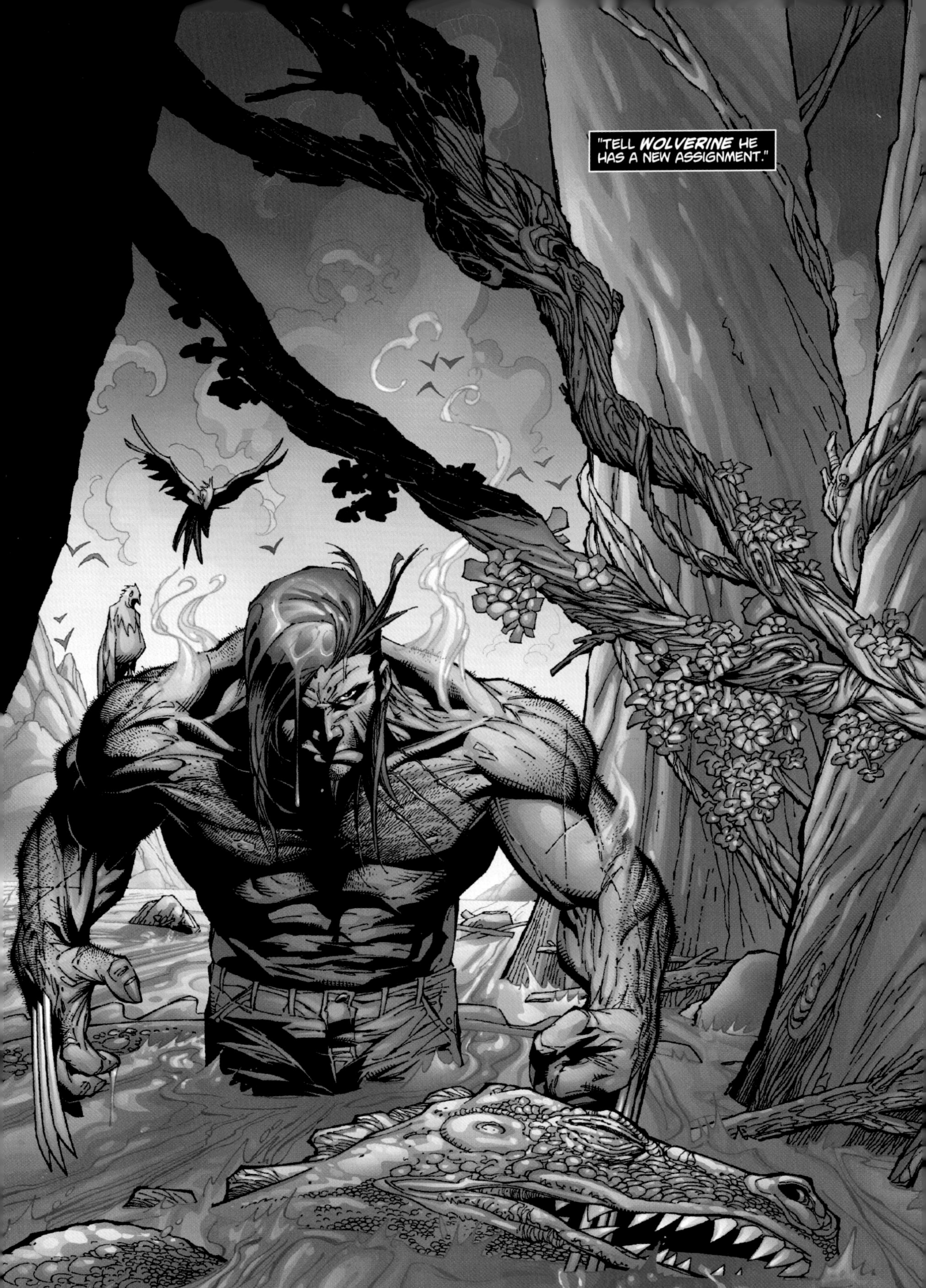
"TELL WOLVERINE HE HAS A NEW ASSIGNMENT."

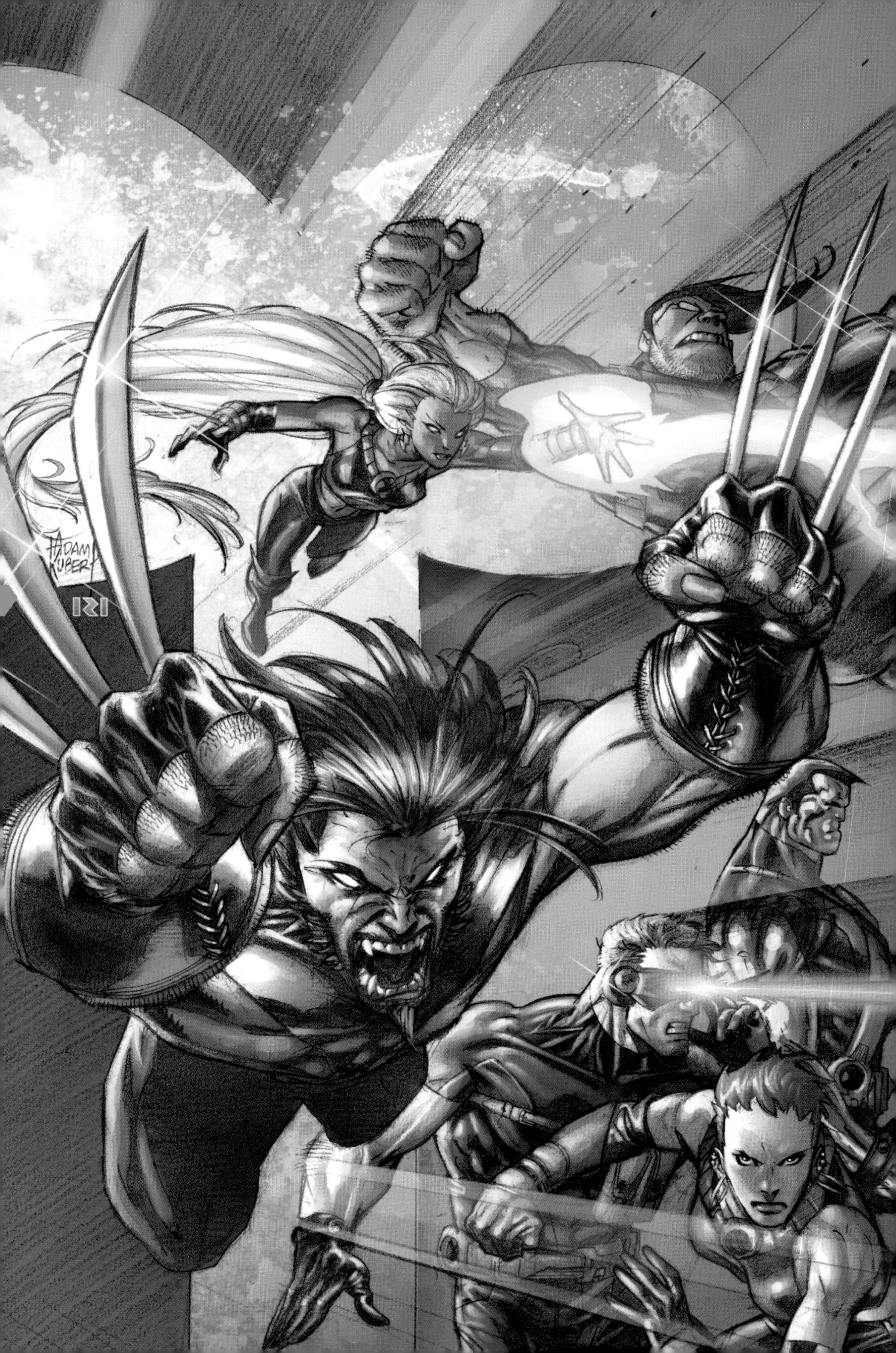

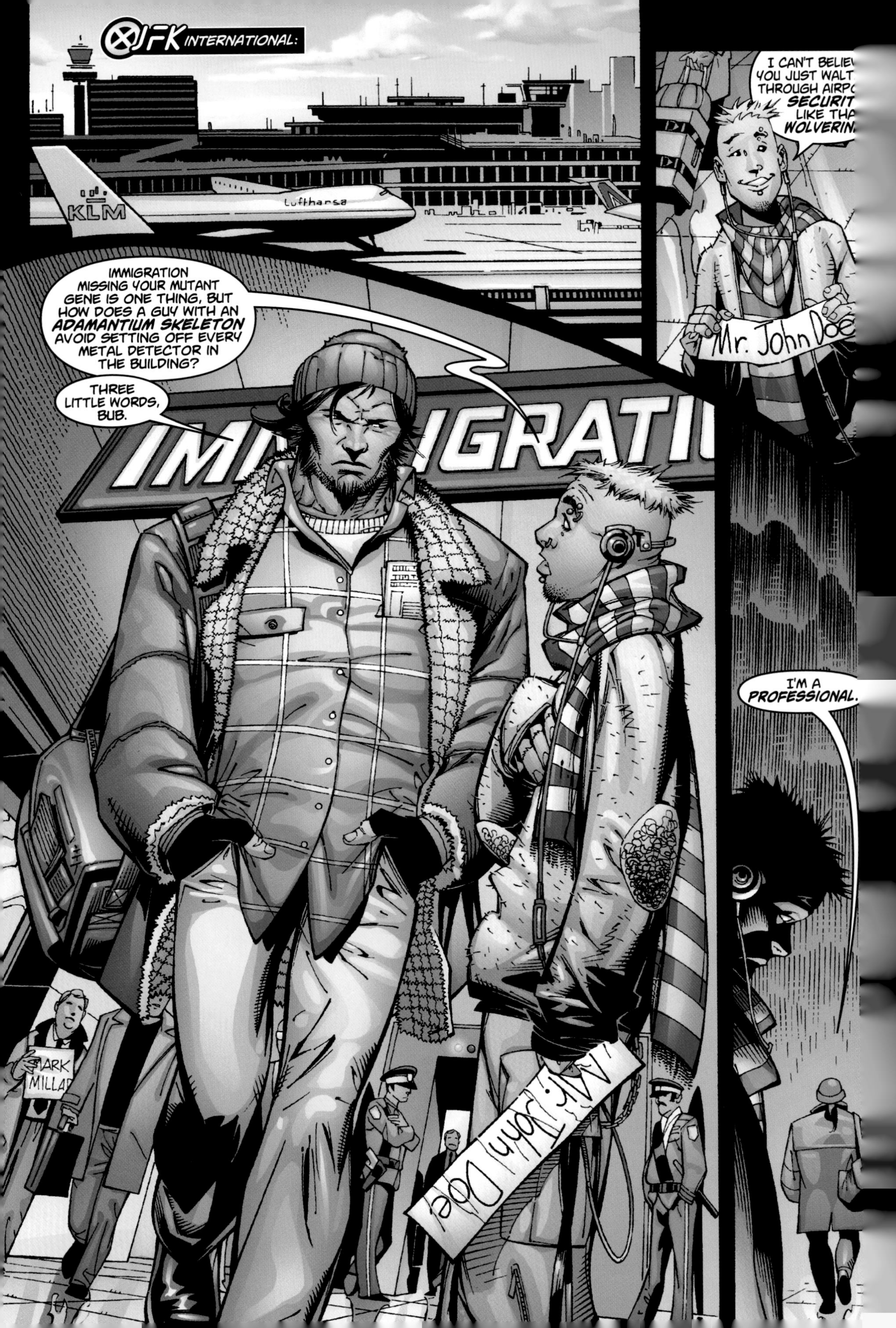
JFK INTERNATIONAL:
KLM
Lufthansa
I CAN'T BELIEV YOU JUST WALT THROUGH AIRPO SECURIT LIKE THA WOLVERIN
Mr. John Doe
IMMIGRATION MISSING YOUR MUTANT GENE IS ONE THING, BUT HOW DOES A GUY WITH AN ADAMANTIUM SKELETON AVOID SETTING OFF EVERY METAL DETECTOR IN THE BUILDING?
THREE LITTLE WORDS, BUB.
IMMIGRATI
I'M A PROFESSIONAL.
MARK MILLA
Mr. John Doe

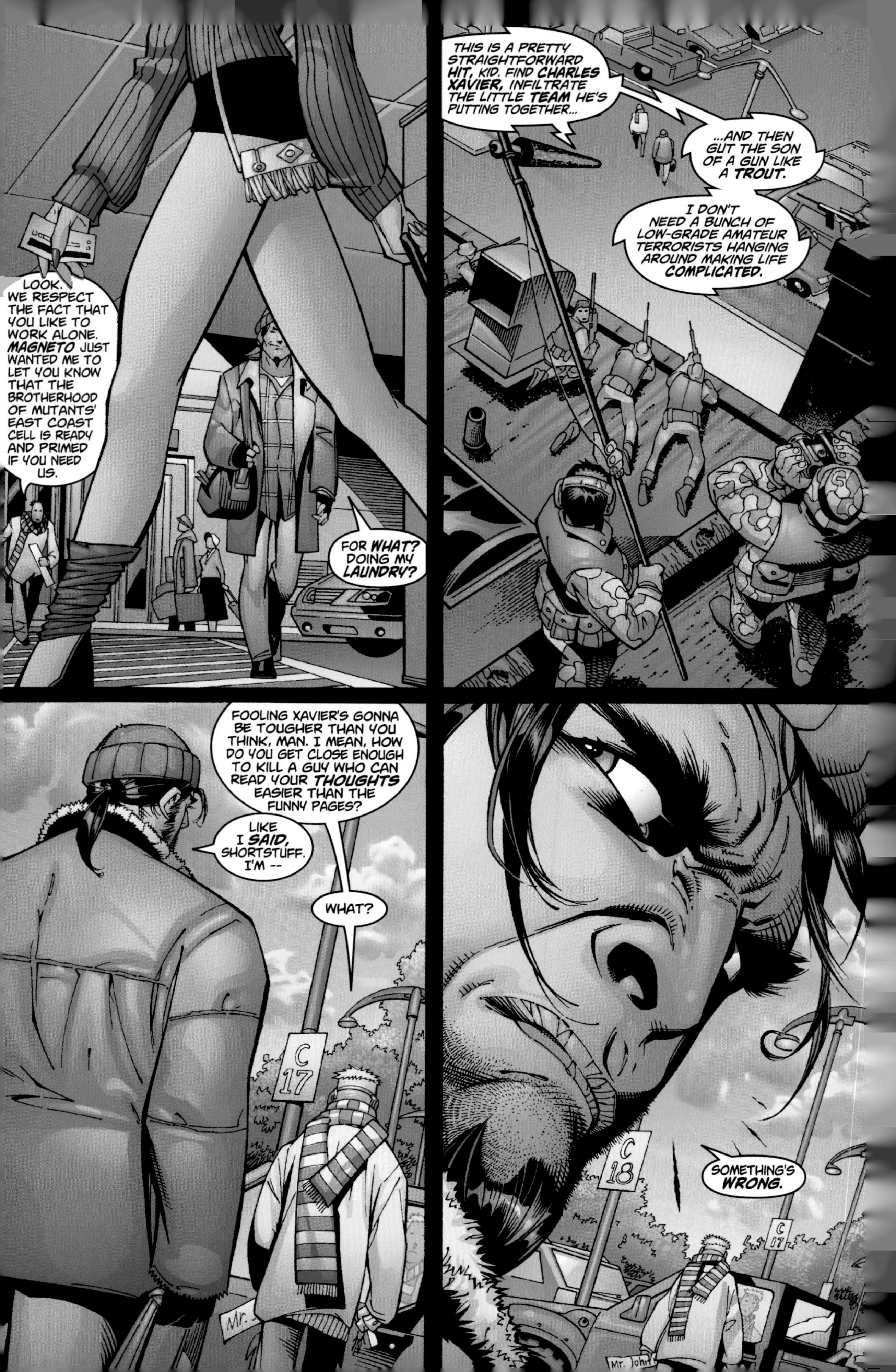
LOOK. WE RESPECT THE FACT THAT YOU LIKE TO WORK ALONE. MAGNETO JUST WANTED ME TO LET YOU KNOW THAT THE BROTHERHOOD OF MUTANTS' EAST COAST CELL IS READY AND PRIMED IF YOU NEED US.
FOR WHAT? DOING MY LAUNDRY?
THIS IS A PRETTY STRAIGHTFORWARD HIT, KID. FIND CHARLES XAVIER, INFILTRATE THE LITTLE TEAM HE'S PUTTING TOGETHER...
...AND THEN GUT THE SON OF A GUN LIKE A TROUT.
I DON'T NEED A BUNCH OF LOW-GRADE AMATEUR TERRORISTS HANGING AROUND MAKING LIFE COMPLICATED.
FOOLING XAVIER'S GONNA BE TOUGHER THAN YOU THINK, MAN. I MEAN, HOW DO YOU GET CLOSE ENOUGH TO KILL A GUY WHO CAN READ YOUR THOUGHTS EASIER THAN THE FUNNY PAGES?
LIKE I SAID, SHORTSTUFF. I'M --
WHAT?
SOMETHING'S WRONG.
C 17
C 18
C 07

HOLD YOUR *FIRE*, BOYS.

WE *GOT* HIM.

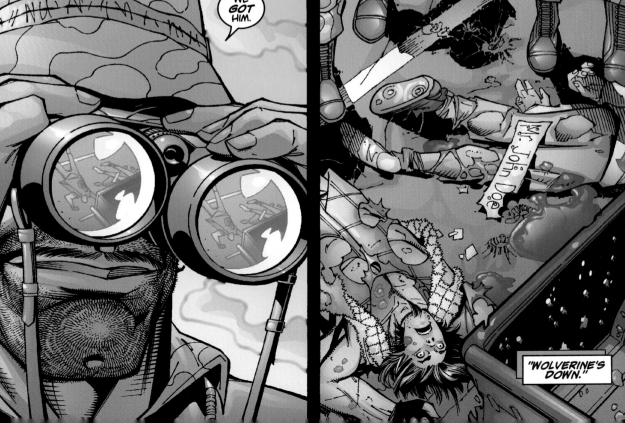

"WOLVERINE'S DOWN."

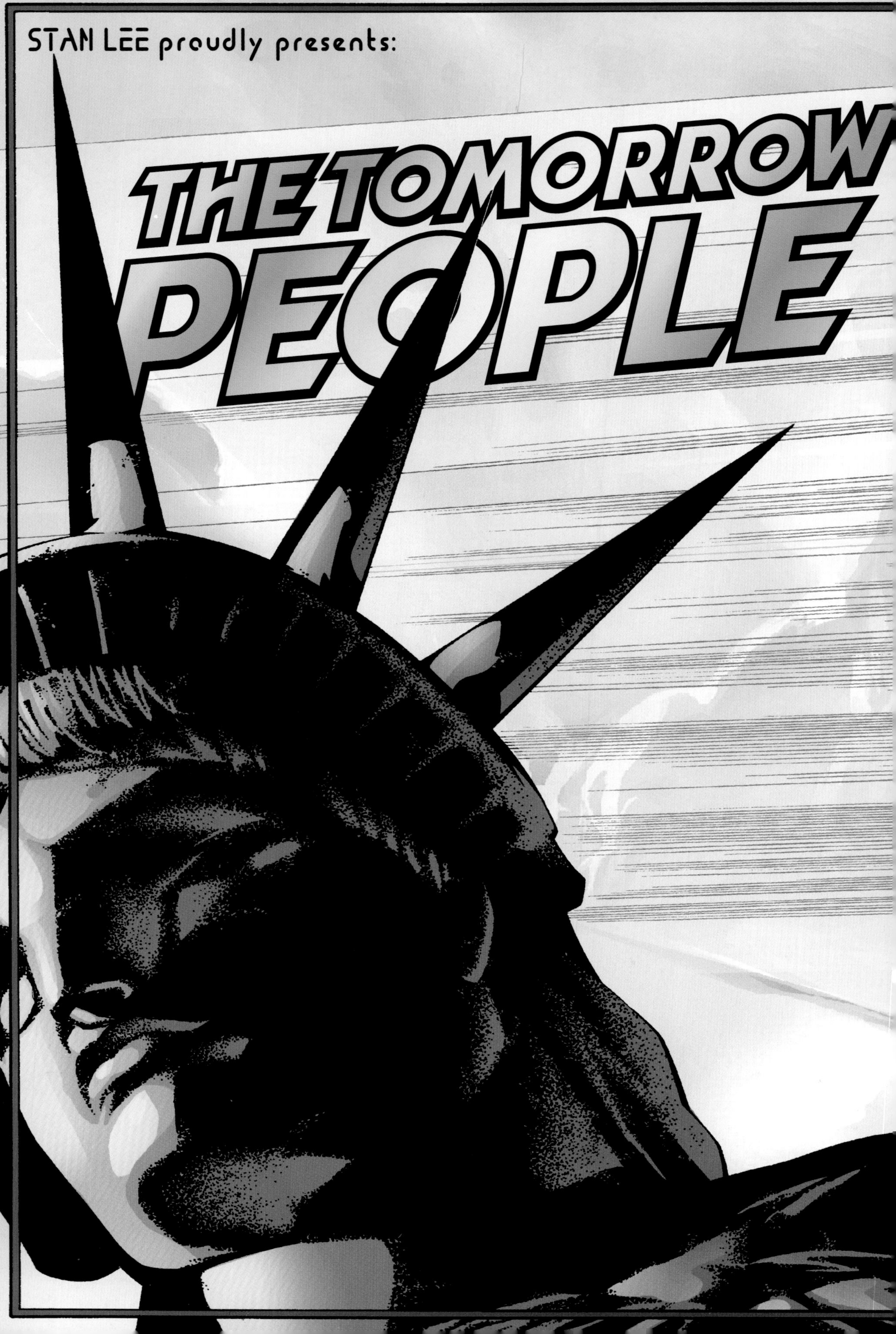
STAN LEE proudly presents:
THE TOMORROW PEOPLE

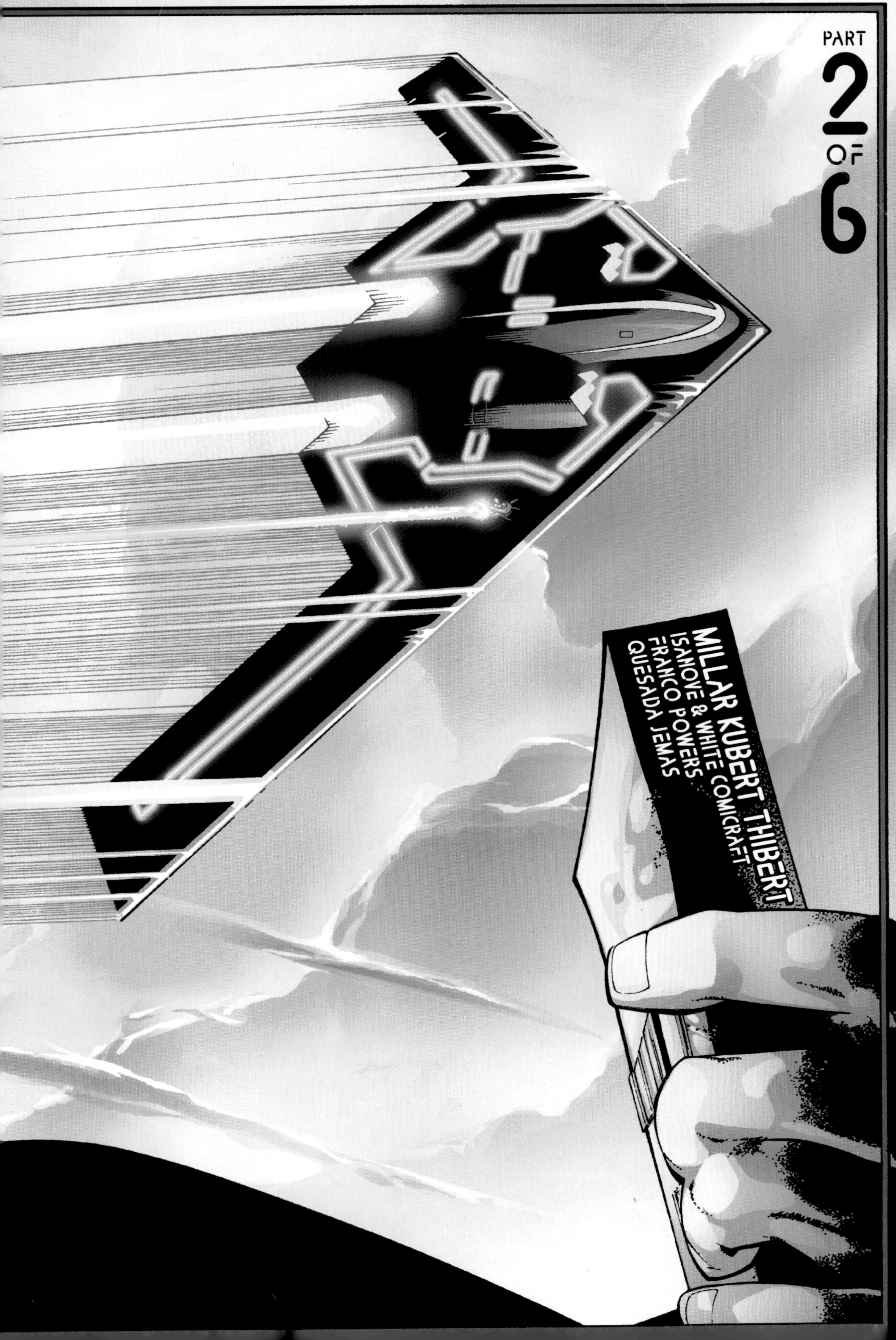
PART 2 OF 6
MILLAR KUBERT THIBERT
ISANOVE & WHITE COMICRAFT
FRANCO POWERS
QUESADA JEMAS

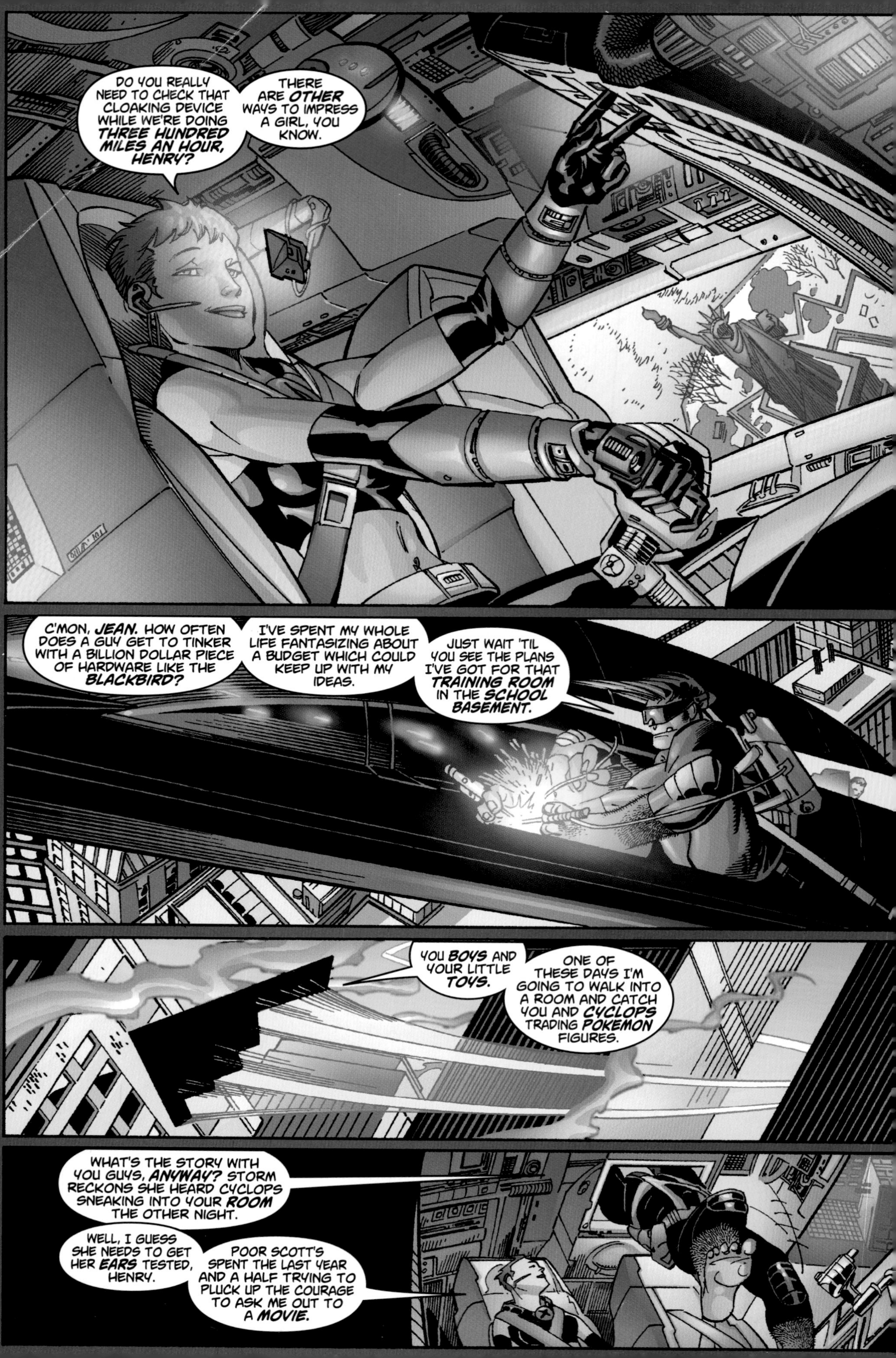

DO YOU REALLY NEED TO CHECK THAT CLOAKING DEVICE WHILE WE'RE DOING THREE HUNDRED MILES AN HOUR, HENRY?
THERE ARE OTHER WAYS TO IMPRESS A GIRL, YOU KNOW.
C'MON, JEAN. HOW OFTEN DOES A GUY GET TO TINKER WITH A BILLION DOLLAR PIECE OF HARDWARE LIKE THE BLACKBIRD?
I'VE SPENT MY WHOLE LIFE FANTASIZING ABOUT A BUDGET WHICH COULD KEEP UP WITH MY IDEAS.
JUST WAIT 'TIL YOU SEE THE PLANS I'VE GOT FOR THAT TRAINING ROOM IN THE SCHOOL BASEMENT.
YOU BOYS AND YOUR LITTLE TOYS.
ONE OF THESE DAYS I'M GOING TO WALK INTO A ROOM AND CATCH YOU AND CYCLOPS TRADING POKEMON FIGURES.
WHAT'S THE STORY WITH YOU GUYS, ANYWAY? STORM RECKONS SHE HEARD CYCLOPS SNEAKING INTO YOUR ROOM THE OTHER NIGHT.
WELL, I GUESS SHE NEEDS TO GET HER EARS TESTED, HENRY.
POOR SCOTT'S SPENT THE LAST YEAR AND A HALF TRYING TO PLUCK UP THE COURAGE TO ASK ME OUT TO A MOVIE.

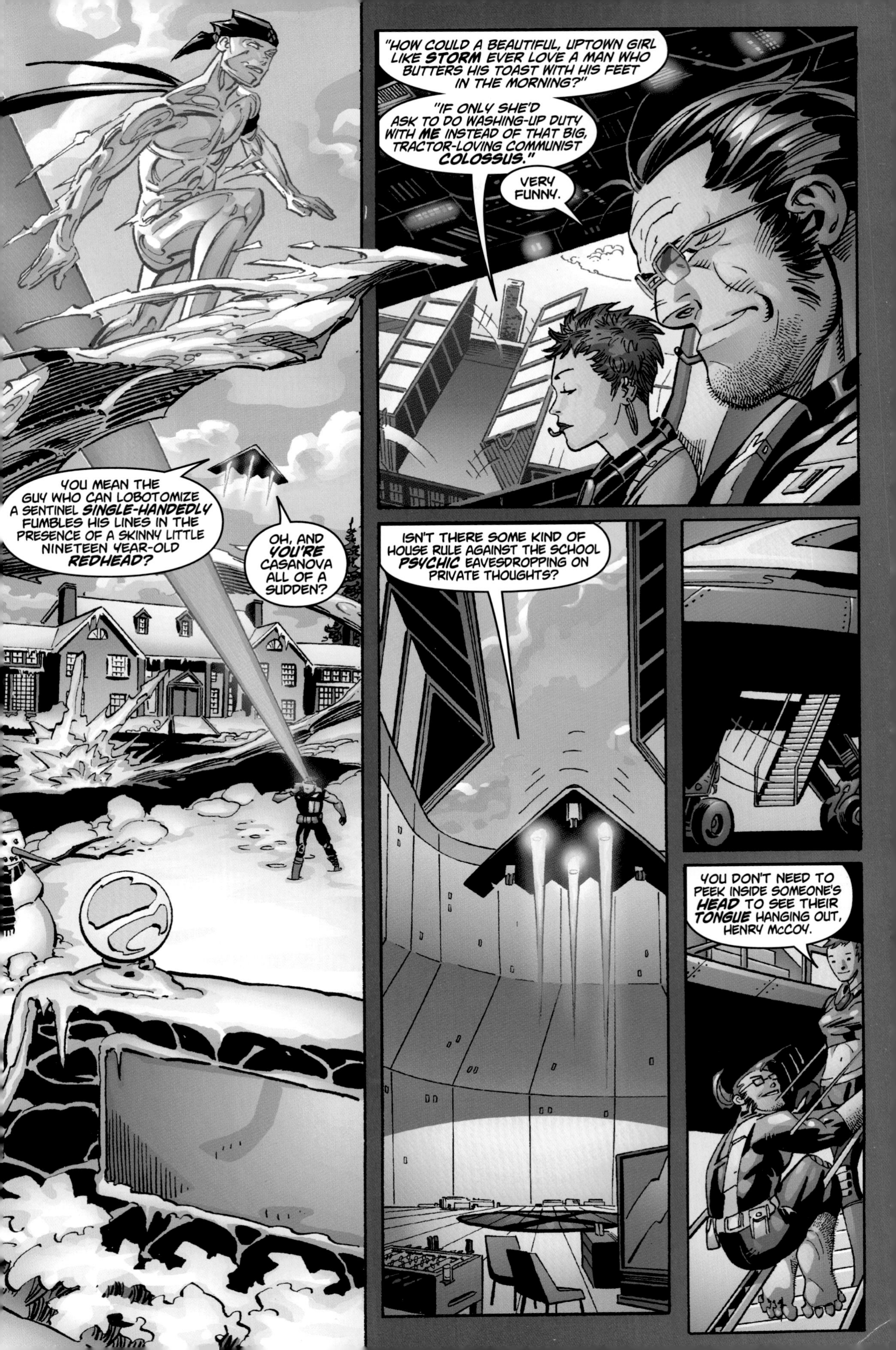
YOU MEAN THE GUY WHO CAN LOBOTOMIZE A SENTINEL SINGLE-HANDEDLY FUMBLES HIS LINES IN THE PRESENCE OF A SKINNY LITTLE NINETEEN YEAR-OLD REDHEAD?
OH, AND YOU'RE CASANOVA ALL OF A SUDDEN?
"HOW COULD A BEAUTIFUL, UPTOWN GIRL LIKE STORM EVER LOVE A MAN WHO BUTTERS HIS TOAST WITH HIS FEET IN THE MORNING?"
"IF ONLY SHE'D ASK TO DO WASHING-UP DUTY WITH ME INSTEAD OF THAT BIG, TRACTOR-LOVING COMMUNIST COLOSSUS."
VERY FUNNY.
ISN'T THERE SOME KIND OF HOUSE RULE AGAINST THE SCHOOL PSYCHIC EAVESDROPPING ON PRIVATE THOUGHTS?
YOU DON'T NEED TO PEEK INSIDE SOMEONE'S HEAD TO SEE THEIR TONGUE HANGING OUT, HENRY McCOY.

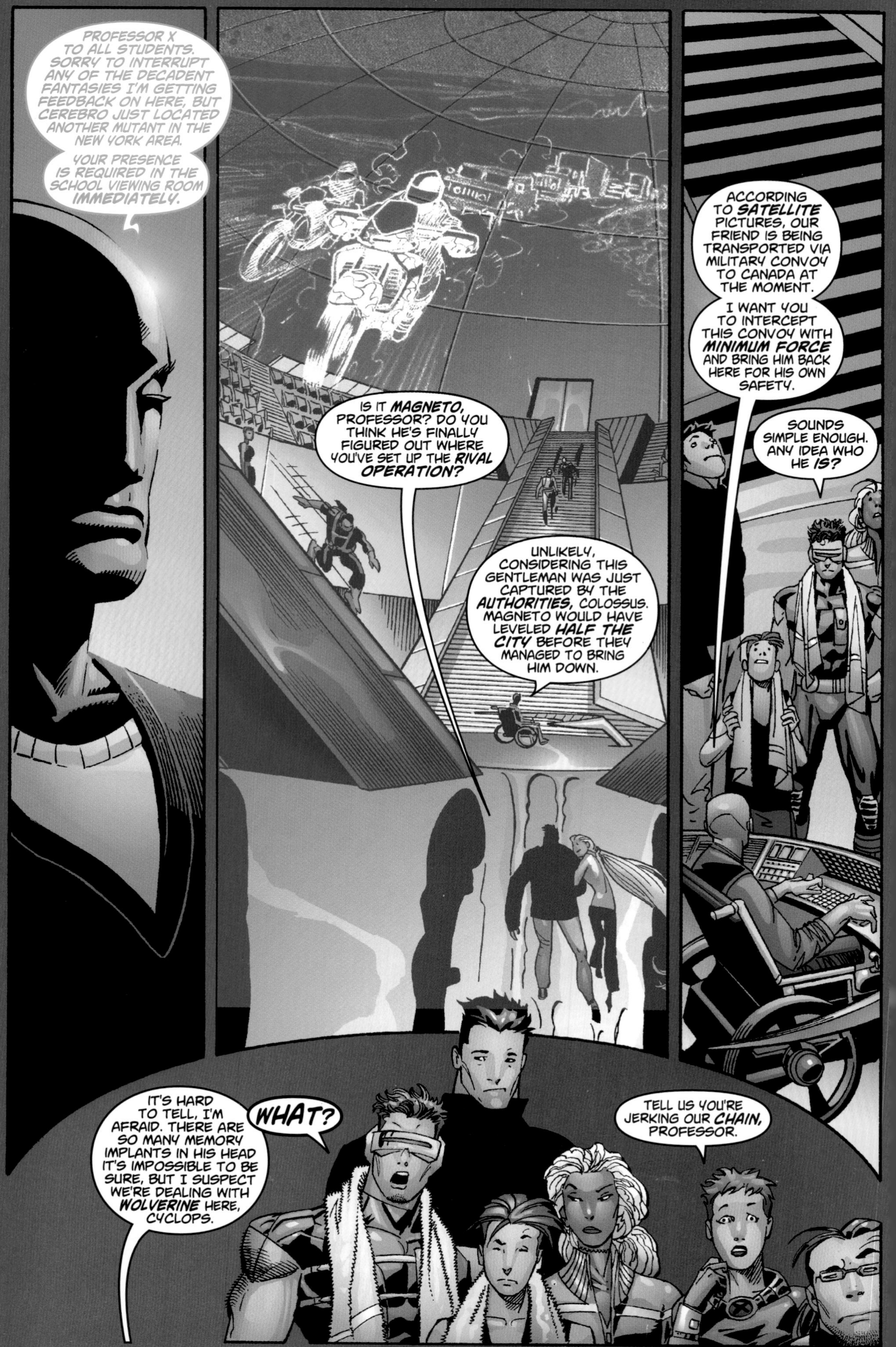
PROFESSOR X TO ALL STUDENTS. SORRY TO INTERRUPT ANY OF THE DECADENT FANTASIES I'M GETTING FEEDBACK ON HERE, BUT CEREBRO JUST LOCATED ANOTHER MUTANT IN THE NEW YORK AREA.
YOUR PRESENCE IS REQUIRED IN THE SCHOOL VIEWING ROOM IMMEDIATELY.
IS IT MAGNETO, PROFESSOR? DO YOU THINK HE'S FINALLY FIGURED OUT WHERE YOU'VE SET UP THE RIVAL OPERATION?
UNLIKELY, CONSIDERING THIS GENTLEMAN WAS JUST CAPTURED BY THE AUTHORITIES, COLOSSUS. MAGNETO WOULD HAVE LEVELED HALF THE CITY BEFORE THEY MANAGED TO BRING HIM DOWN.
ACCORDING TO SATELLITE PICTURES, OUR FRIEND IS BEING TRANSPORTED VIA MILITARY CONVOY TO CANADA AT THE MOMENT.
I WANT YOU TO INTERCEPT THIS CONVOY WITH MINIMUM FORCE AND BRING HIM BACK HERE FOR HIS OWN SAFETY.
SOUNDS SIMPLE ENOUGH. ANY IDEA WHO HE IS?
IT'S HARD TO TELL, I'M AFRAID. THERE ARE SO MANY MEMORY IMPLANTS IN HIS HEAD IT'S IMPOSSIBLE TO BE SURE, BUT I SUSPECT WE'RE DEALING WITH WOLVERINE HERE, CYCLOPS.
WHAT?
TELL US YOU'RE JERKING OUR CHAIN, PROFESSOR.

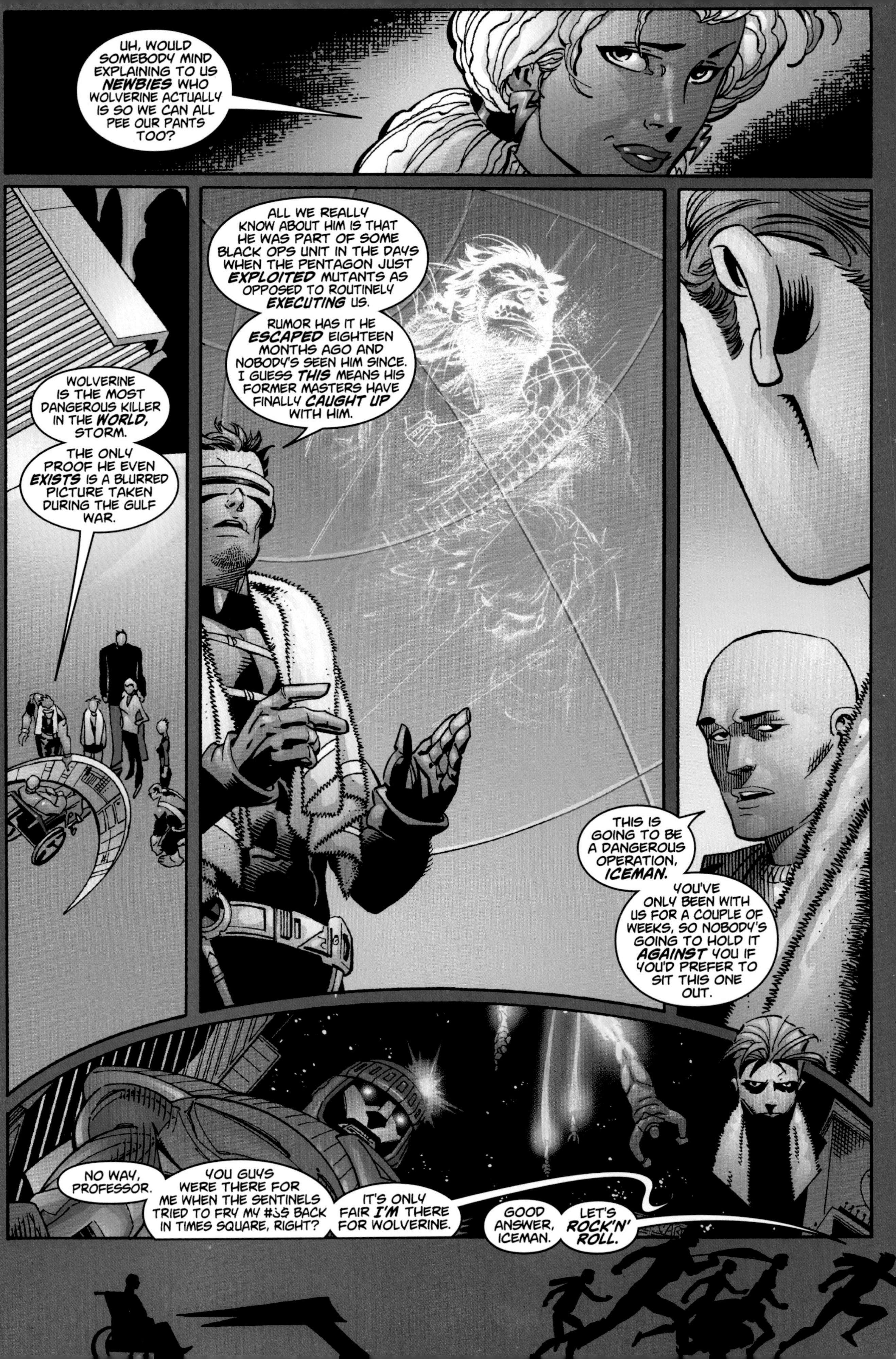
UH, WOULD SOMEBODY MIND EXPLAINING TO US NEWBIES WHO WOLVERINE ACTUALLY IS SO WE CAN ALL PEE OUR PANTS TOO?
WOLVERINE IS THE MOST DANGEROUS KILLER IN THE WORLD, STORM.
THE ONLY PROOF HE EVEN EXISTS IS A BLURRED PICTURE TAKEN DURING THE GULF WAR.
ALL WE REALLY KNOW ABOUT HIM IS THAT HE WAS PART OF SOME BLACK OPS UNIT IN THE DAYS WHEN THE PENTAGON JUST EXPLOITED MUTANTS AS OPPOSED TO ROUTINELY EXECUTING US.
RUMOR HAS IT HE ESCAPED EIGHTEEN MONTHS AGO AND NOBODY'S SEEN HIM SINCE. I GUESS THIS MEANS HIS FORMER MASTERS HAVE FINALLY CAUGHT UP WITH HIM.
THIS IS GOING TO BE A DANGEROUS OPERATION, ICEMAN.
YOU'VE ONLY BEEN WITH US FOR A COUPLE OF WEEKS, SO NOBODY'S GOING TO HOLD IT AGAINST YOU IF YOU'D PREFER TO SIT THIS ONE OUT.
NO WAY, PROFESSOR.
YOU GUYS WERE THERE FOR ME WHEN THE SENTINELS TRIED TO FRY MY #¿$ BACK IN TIMES SQUARE, RIGHT?
IT'S ONLY FAIR I'M THERE FOR WOLVERINE.
GOOD ANSWER, ICEMAN.
LET'S ROCK'N' ROLL.

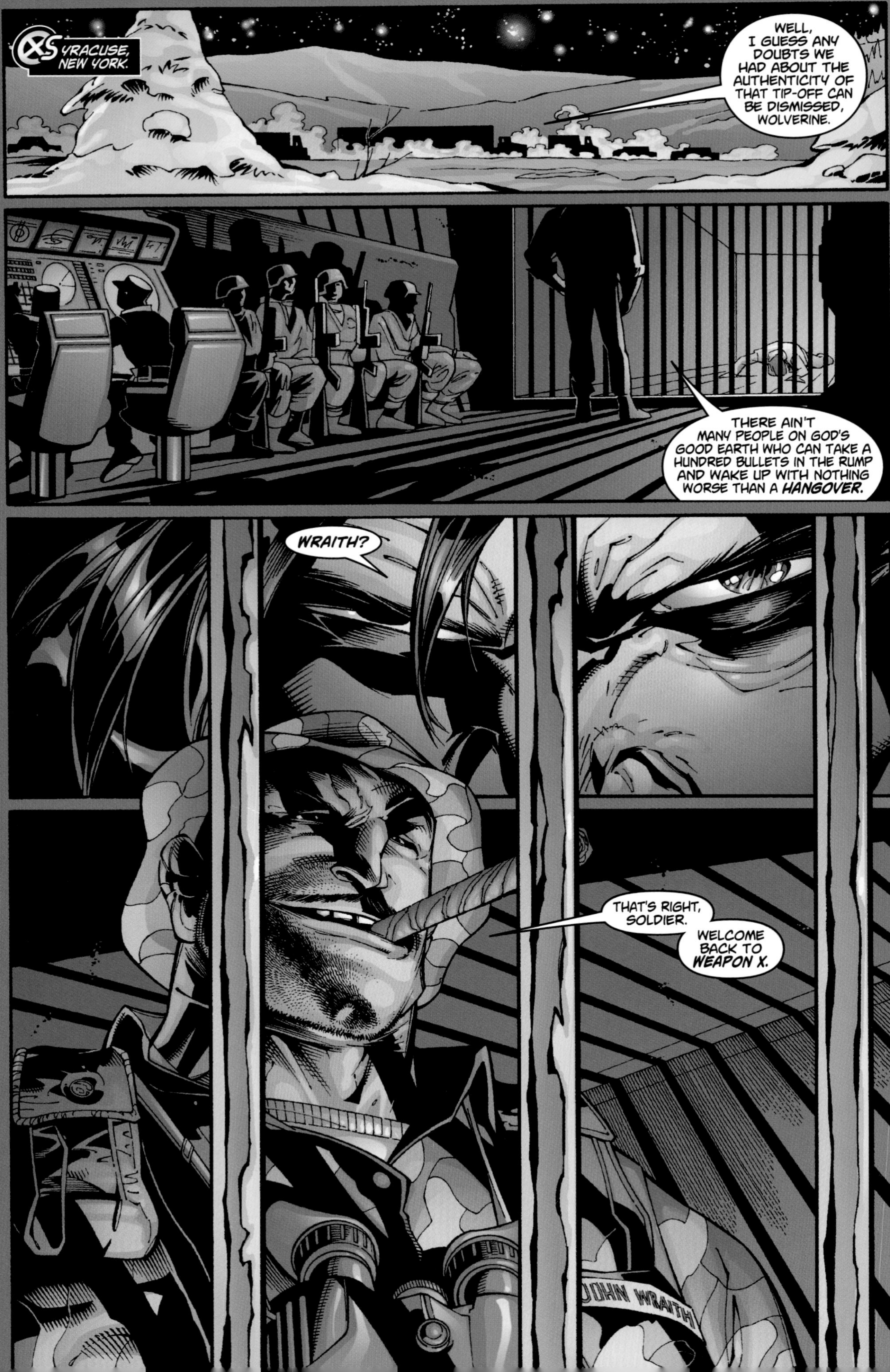
SYRACUSE, NEW YORK.
WELL, I GUESS ANY DOUBTS WE HAD ABOUT THE AUTHENTICITY OF THAT TIP-OFF CAN BE DISMISSED, WOLVERINE.
THERE AIN'T MANY PEOPLE ON GOD'S GOOD EARTH WHO CAN TAKE A HUNDRED BULLETS IN THE RUMP AND WAKE UP WITH NOTHING WORSE THAN A HANGOVER.
WRAITH?
THAT'S RIGHT, SOLDIER.
WELCOME BACK TO WEAPON X.
JOHN WRAITH

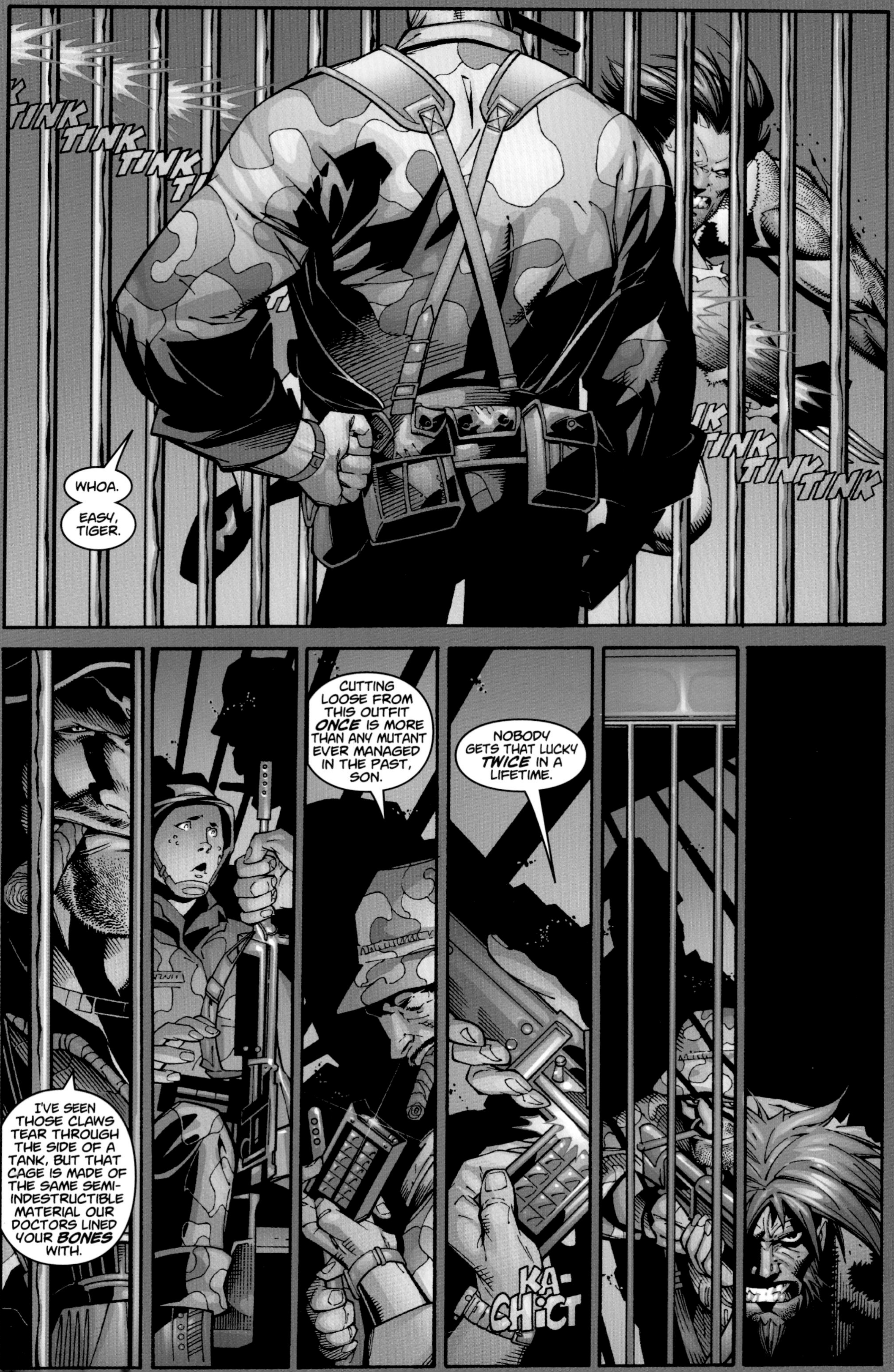
TINK TINK TINK
WHOA.
EASY, TIGER.
TINK TINK TINK
I'VE SEEN THOSE CLAWS TEAR THROUGH THE SIDE OF A TANK, BUT THAT CAGE IS MADE OF THE SAME SEMI-INDESTRUCTIBLE MATERIAL OUR DOCTORS LINED YOUR BONES WITH.
CUTTING LOOSE FROM THIS OUTFIT ONCE IS MORE THAN ANY MUTANT EVER MANAGED IN THE PAST, SON.
NOBODY GETS THAT LUCKY TWICE IN A LIFETIME.
KA-CHICT

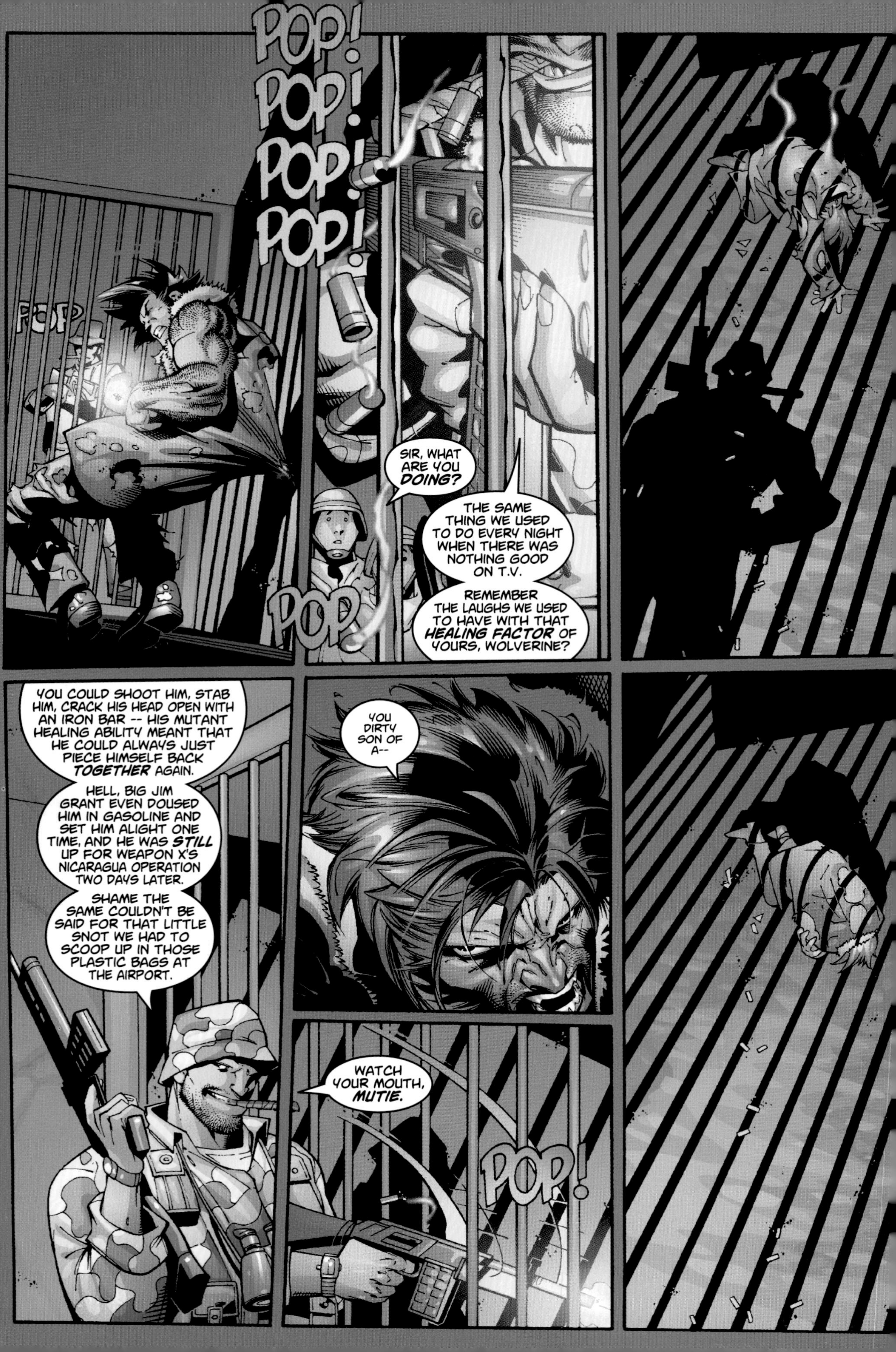
POP! POP! POP! POP!
POP
SIR, WHAT ARE YOU DOING?
THE SAME THING WE USED TO DO EVERY NIGHT WHEN THERE WAS NOTHING GOOD ON T.V.
REMEMBER THE LAUGHS WE USED TO HAVE WITH THAT HEALING FACTOR OF YOURS, WOLVERINE?
POP
YOU COULD SHOOT HIM, STAB HIM, CRACK HIS HEAD OPEN WITH AN IRON BAR -- HIS MUTANT HEALING ABILITY MEANT THAT HE COULD ALWAYS JUST PIECE HIMSELF BACK TOGETHER AGAIN.
HELL, BIG JIM GRANT EVEN DOUSED HIM IN GASOLINE AND SET HIM ALIGHT ONE TIME, AND HE WAS STILL UP FOR WEAPON X'S NICARAGUA OPERATION TWO DAYS LATER.
SHAME THE SAME COULDN'T BE SAID FOR THAT LITTLE SNOT WE HAD TO SCOOP UP IN THOSE PLASTIC BAGS AT THE AIRPORT.
YOU DIRTY SON OF A--
WATCH YOUR MOUTH, MUTIE.
POP!

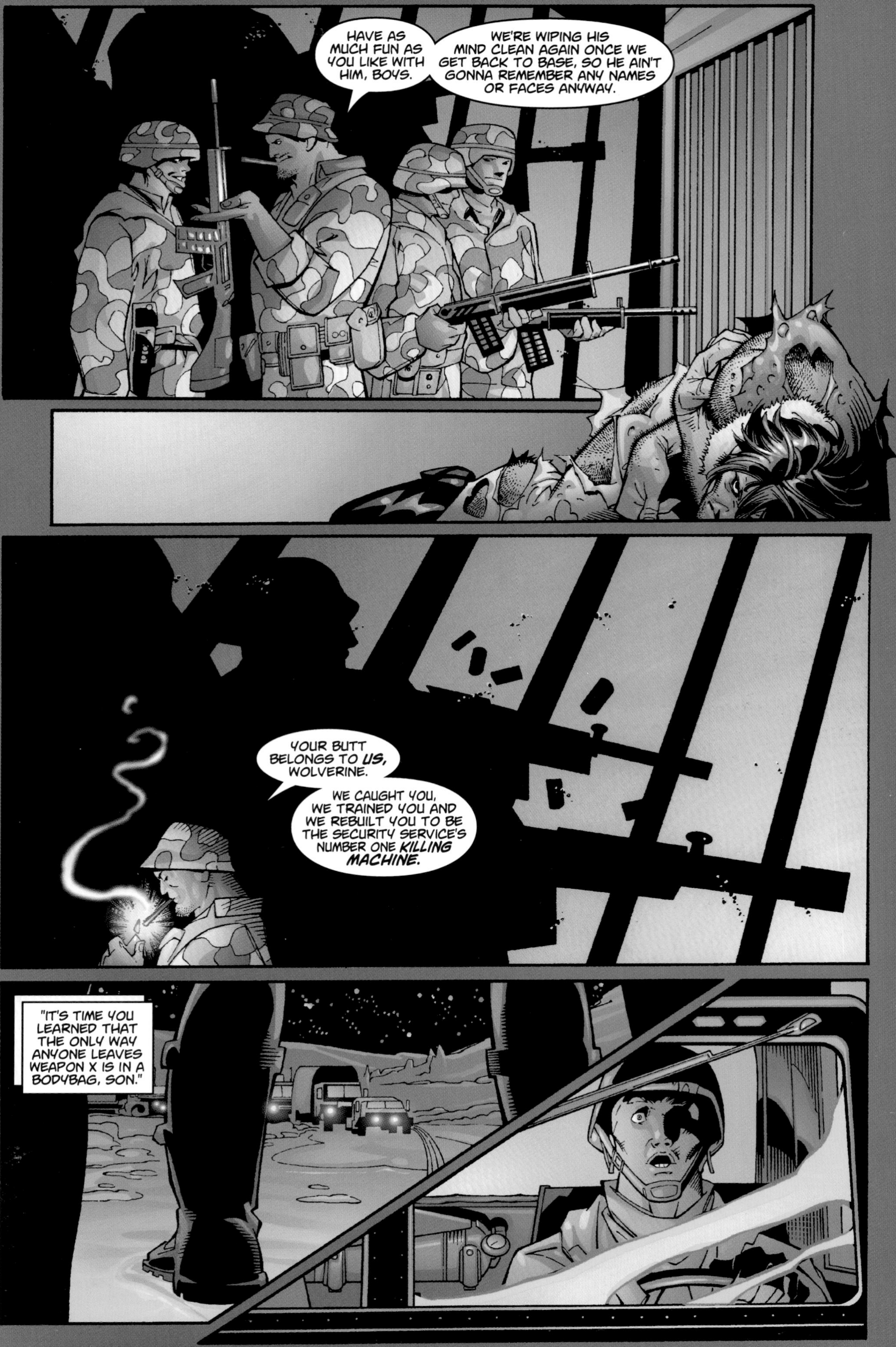
HAVE AS MUCH FUN AS YOU LIKE WITH HIM, BOYS.
WE'RE WIPING HIS MIND CLEAN AGAIN ONCE WE GET BACK TO BASE, SO HE AIN'T GONNA REMEMBER ANY NAMES OR FACES ANYWAY.
YOUR BUTT BELONGS TO US, WOLVERINE.
WE CAUGHT YOU, WE TRAINED YOU AND WE REBUILT YOU TO BE THE SECURITY SERVICE'S NUMBER ONE KILLING MACHINE.
"IT'S TIME YOU LEARNED THAT THE ONLY WAY ANYONE LEAVES WEAPON X IS IN A BODYBAG, SON."

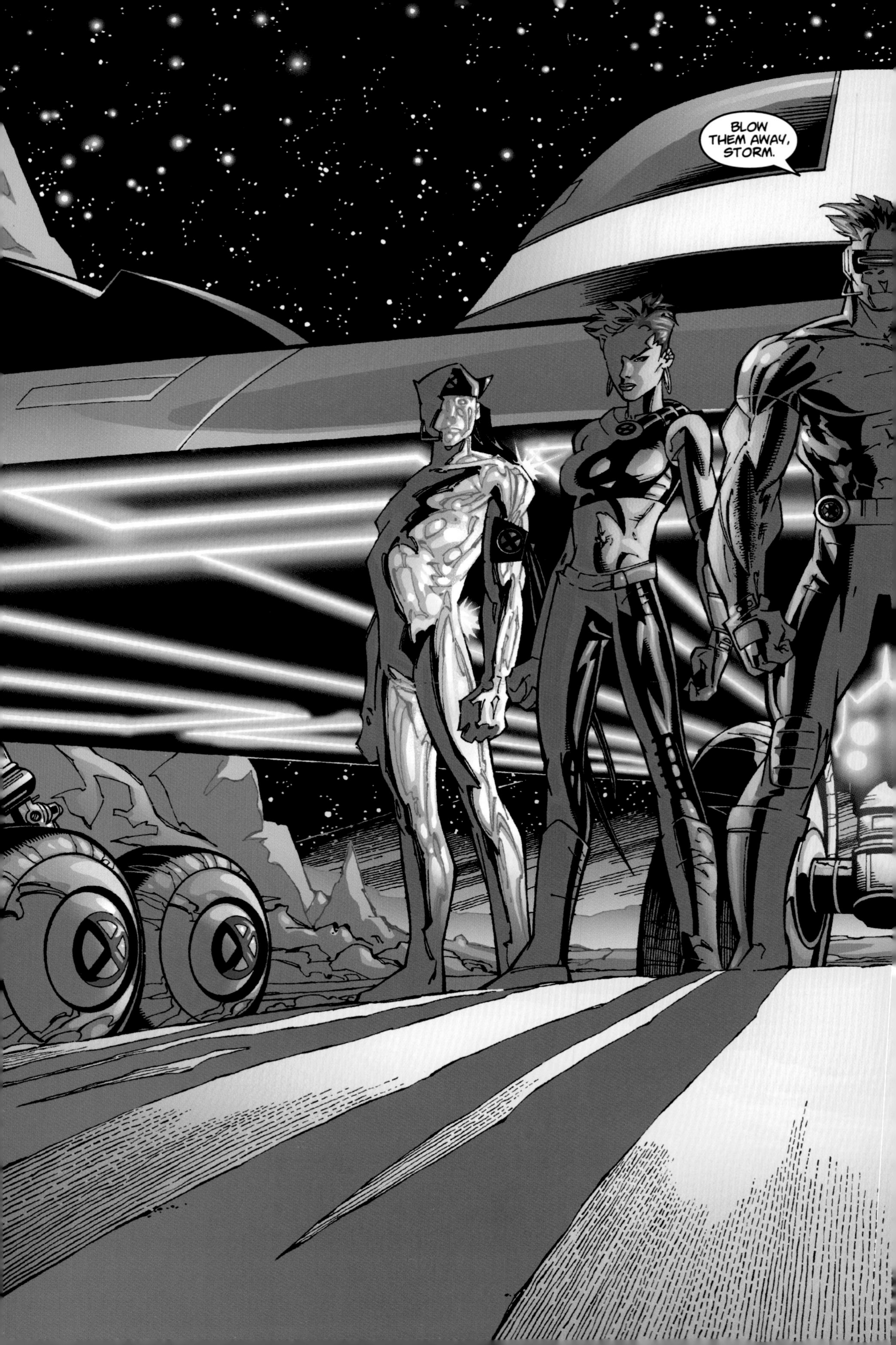
BLOW THEM AWAY, STORM.

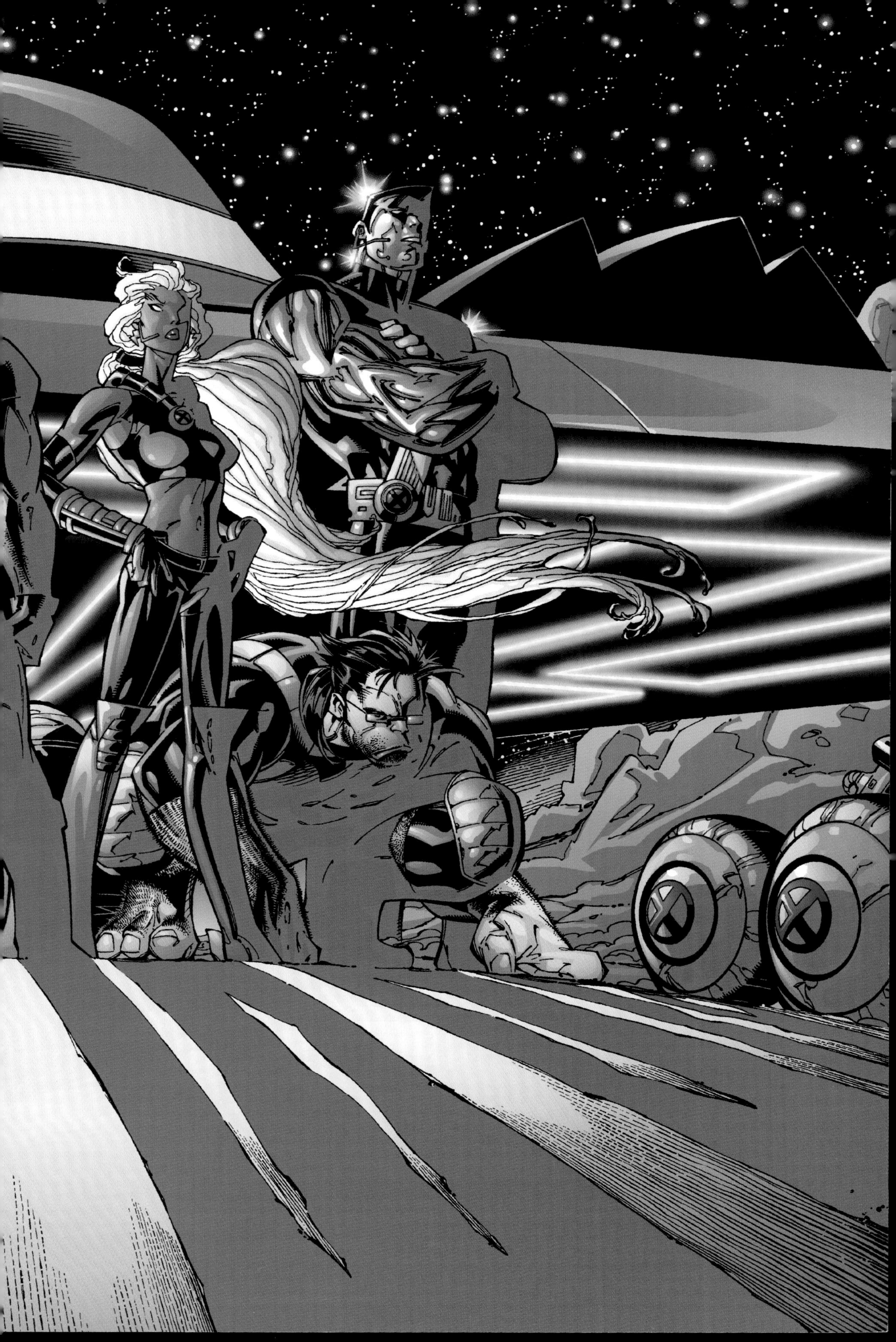

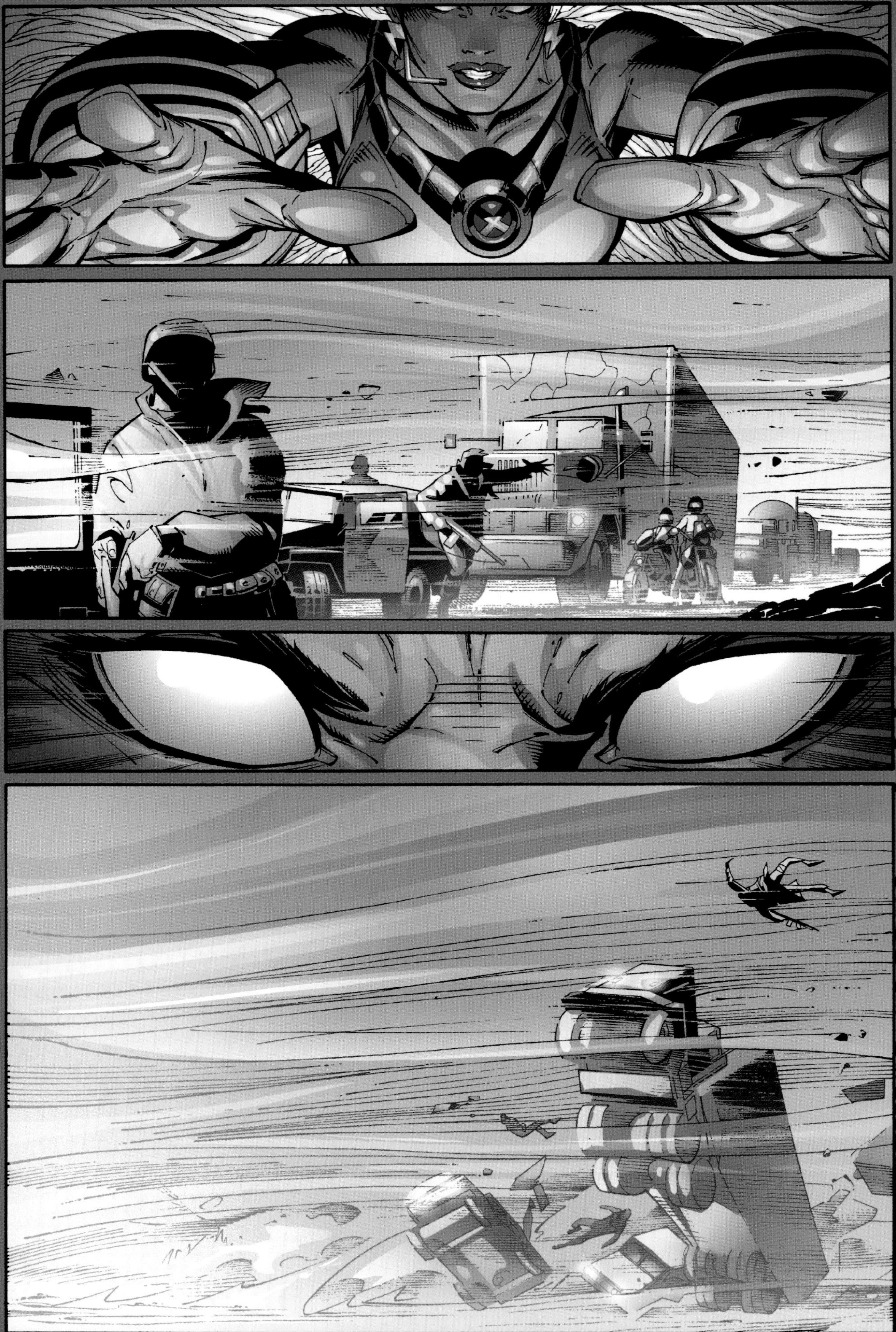

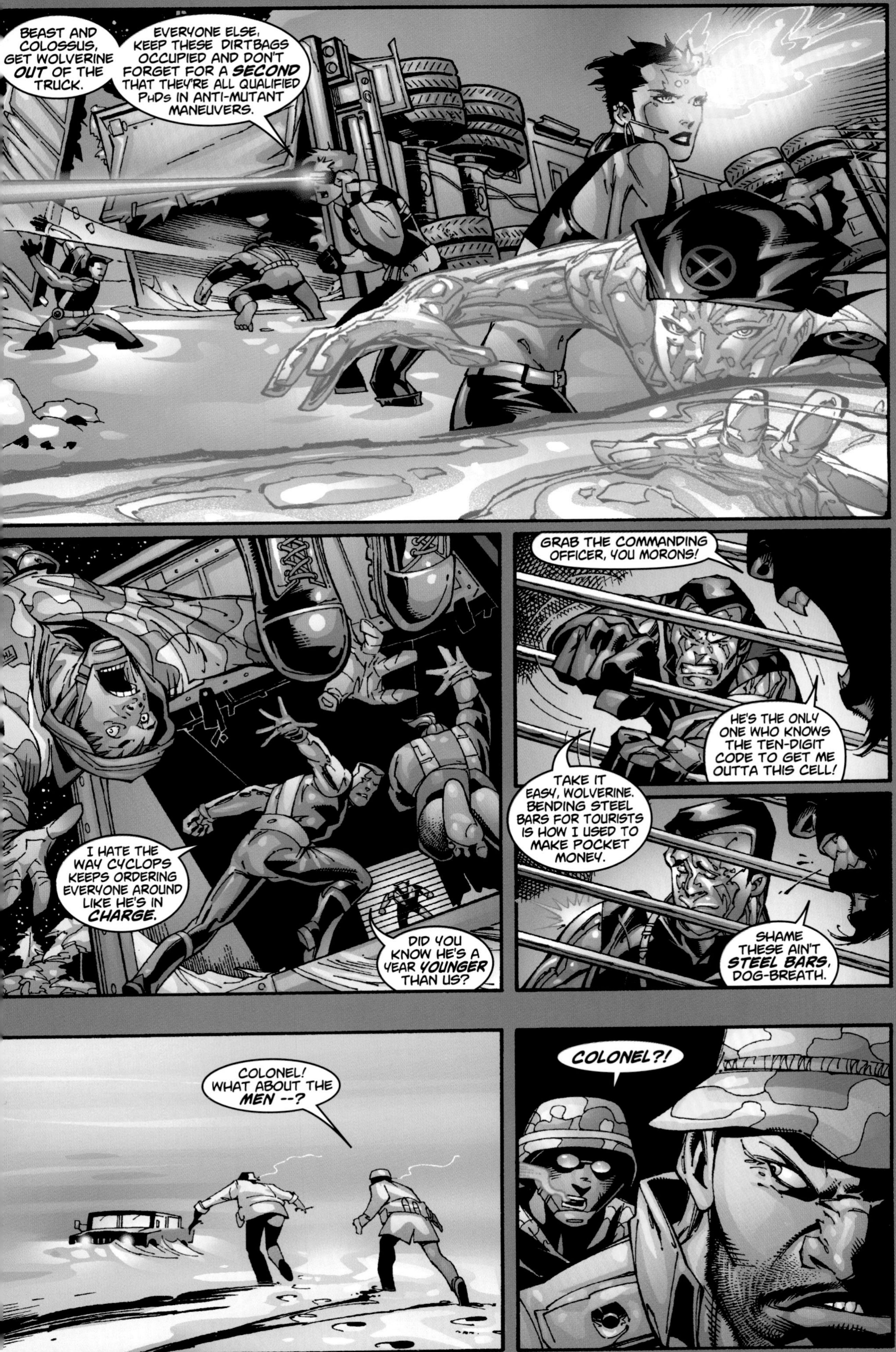

BEAST AND COLOSSUS, GET WOLVERINE OUT OF THE TRUCK.
EVERYONE ELSE, KEEP THESE DIRTBAGS OCCUPIED AND DON'T FORGET FOR A SECOND THAT THEY'RE ALL QUALIFIED PhDs IN ANTI-MUTANT MANEUVERS.
I HATE THE WAY CYCLOPS KEEPS ORDERING EVERYONE AROUND LIKE HE'S IN CHARGE.
DID YOU KNOW HE'S A YEAR YOUNGER THAN US?
GRAB THE COMMANDING OFFICER, YOU MORONS!
HE'S THE ONLY ONE WHO KNOWS THE TEN-DIGIT CODE TO GET ME OUTTA THIS CELL!
TAKE IT EASY, WOLVERINE. BENDING STEEL BARS FOR TOURISTS IS HOW I USED TO MAKE POCKET MONEY.
SHAME THESE AIN'T STEEL BARS, DOG-BREATH.
COLONEL! WHAT ABOUT THE MEN --?
COLONEL?!

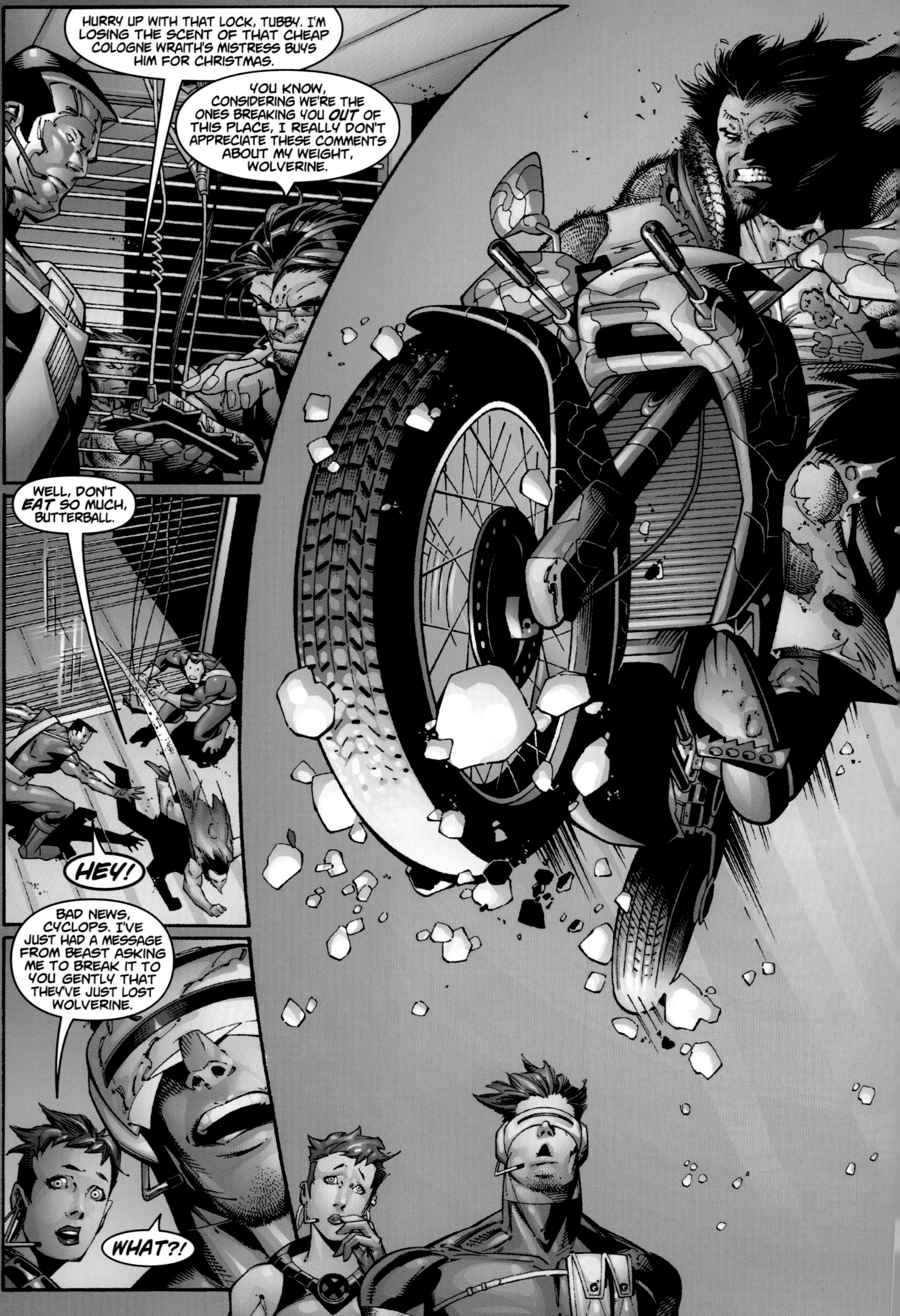
HURRY UP WITH THAT LOCK, TUBBY. I'M LOSING THE SCENT OF THAT CHEAP COLOGNE WRAITH'S MISTRESS BUYS HIM FOR CHRISTMAS.
YOU KNOW, CONSIDERING WE'RE THE ONES BREAKING YOU OUT OF THIS PLACE, I REALLY DON'T APPRECIATE THESE COMMENTS ABOUT MY WEIGHT, WOLVERINE.
WELL, DON'T EAT SO MUCH, BUTTERBALL.
HEY!
BAD NEWS, CYCLOPS. I'VE JUST HAD A MESSAGE FROM BEAST ASKING ME TO BREAK IT TO YOU GENTLY THAT THEY'VE JUST LOST WOLVERINE.
WHAT?!

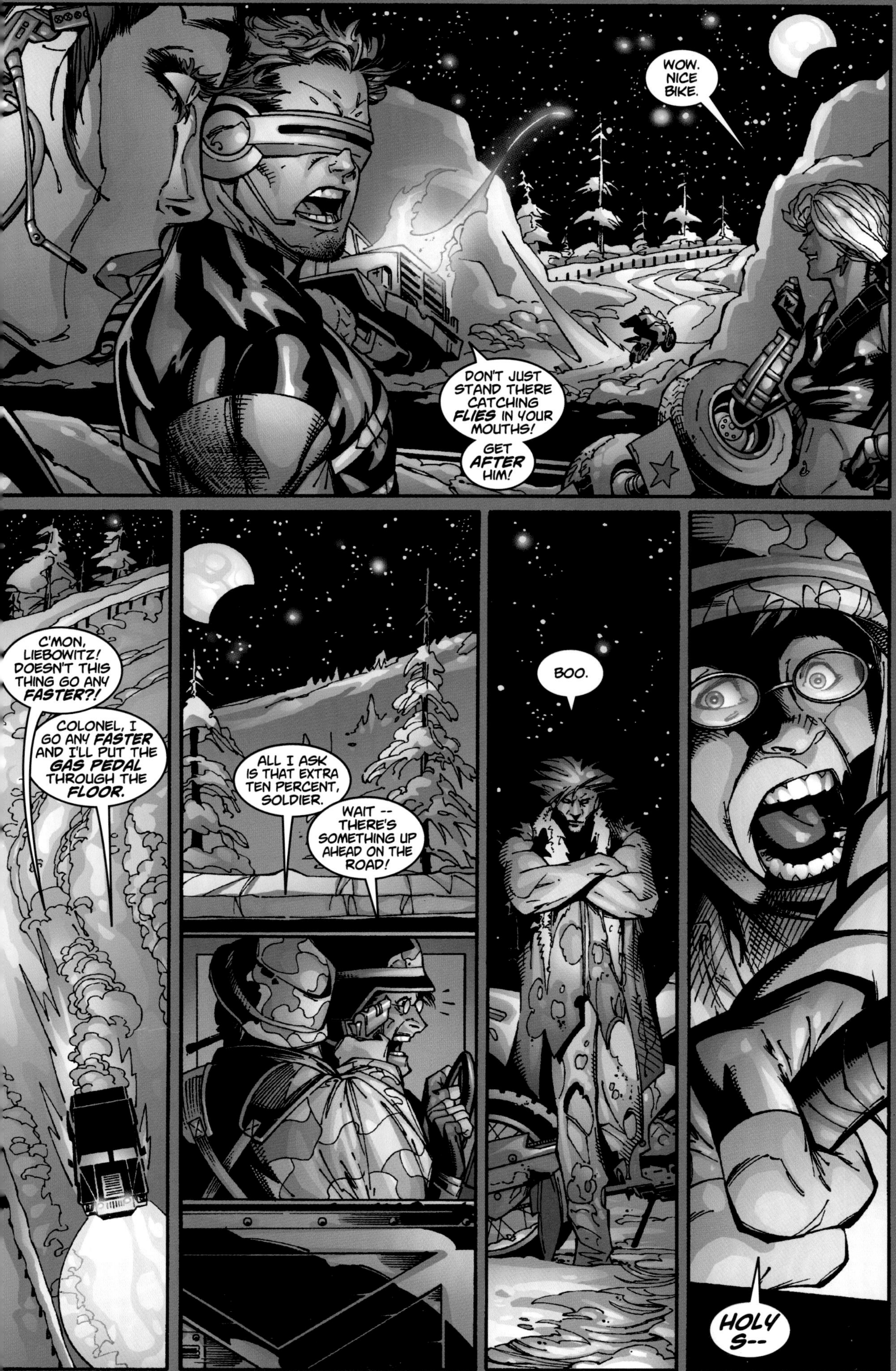
WOW. NICE BIKE.
DON'T JUST STAND THERE CATCHING FLIES IN YOUR MOUTHS!
GET AFTER HIM!
C'MON, LIEBOWITZ! DOESN'T THIS THING GO ANY FASTER?!
COLONEL, I GO ANY FASTER AND I'LL PUT THE GAS PEDAL THROUGH THE FLOOR.
ALL I ASK IS THAT EXTRA TEN PERCENT, SOLDIER.
WAIT -- THERE'S SOMETHING UP AHEAD ON THE ROAD!
BOO.
HOLY S--

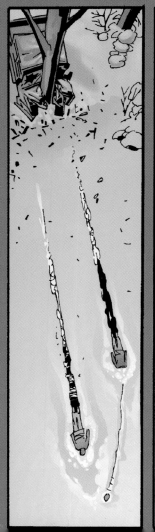

LIEBOWITZ?! HOLY MOTHER OF GOD --! YOU JUST BROKE HIS FREAKIN' NECK!

LUCKY LIEBOWITZ.

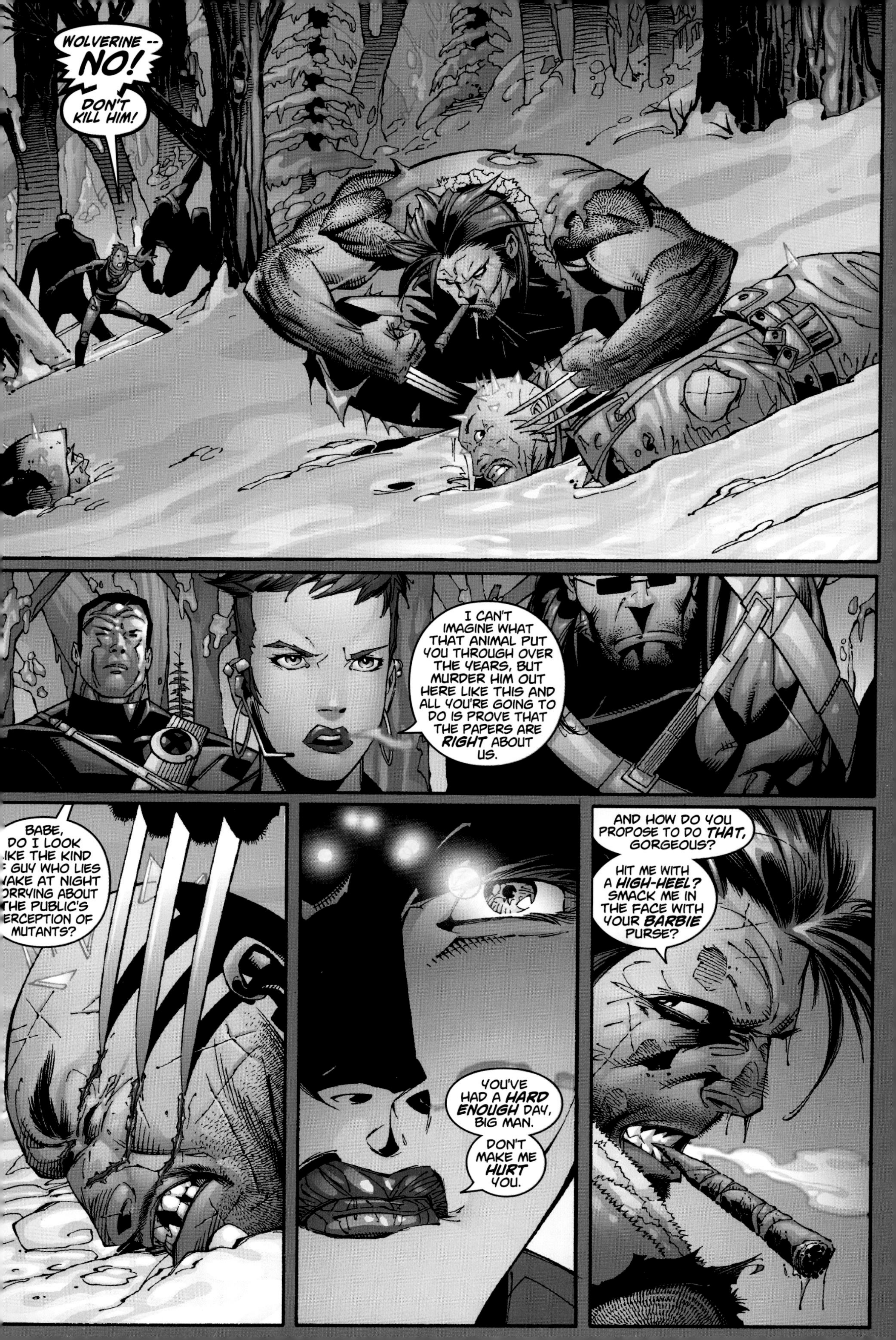

WOLVERINE -- NO!
DON'T KILL HIM!
I CAN'T IMAGINE WHAT THAT ANIMAL PUT YOU THROUGH OVER THE YEARS, BUT MURDER HIM OUT HERE LIKE THIS AND ALL YOU'RE GOING TO DO IS PROVE THAT THE PAPERS ARE RIGHT ABOUT US.
BABE, DO I LOOK LIKE THE KIND OF GUY WHO LIES AWAKE AT NIGHT WORRYING ABOUT THE PUBLIC'S PERCEPTION OF MUTANTS?
YOU'VE HAD A HARD ENOUGH DAY, BIG MAN.
DON'T MAKE ME HURT YOU.
AND HOW DO YOU PROPOSE TO DO THAT, GORGEOUS?
HIT ME WITH A HIGH-HEEL? SMACK ME IN THE FACE WITH YOUR BARBIE PURSE?

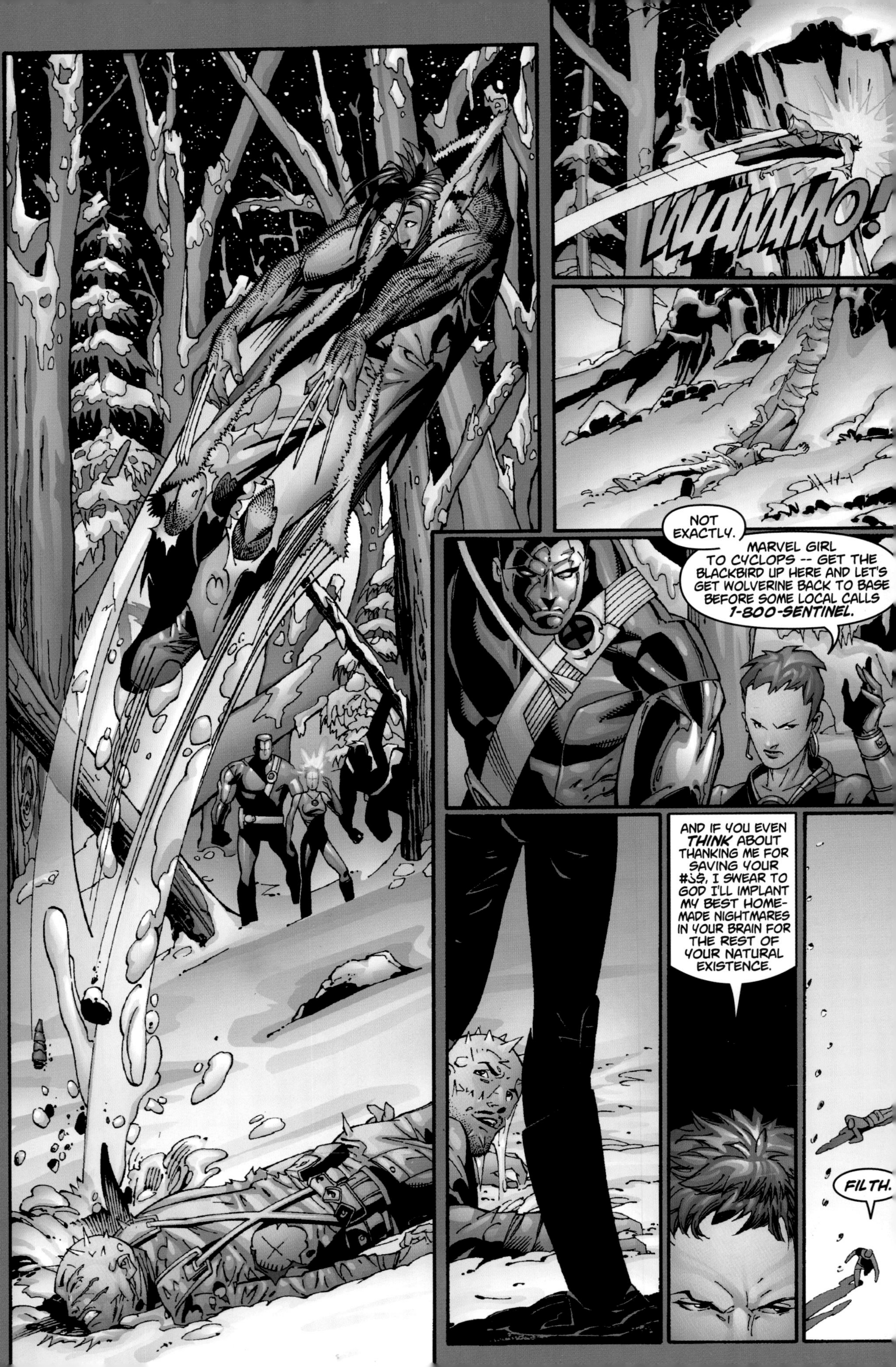
VVVANNNO!
NOT EXACTLY.
MARVEL GIRL TO CYCLOPS -- GET THE BLACKBIRD UP HERE AND LET'S GET WOLVERINE BACK TO BASE BEFORE SOME LOCAL CALLS 1-800-SENTINEL.
AND IF YOU EVEN THINK ABOUT THANKING ME FOR SAVING YOUR #$S, I SWEAR TO GOD I'LL IMPLANT MY BEST HOME-MADE NIGHTMARES IN YOUR BRAIN FOR THE REST OF YOUR NATURAL EXISTENCE.
FILTH.

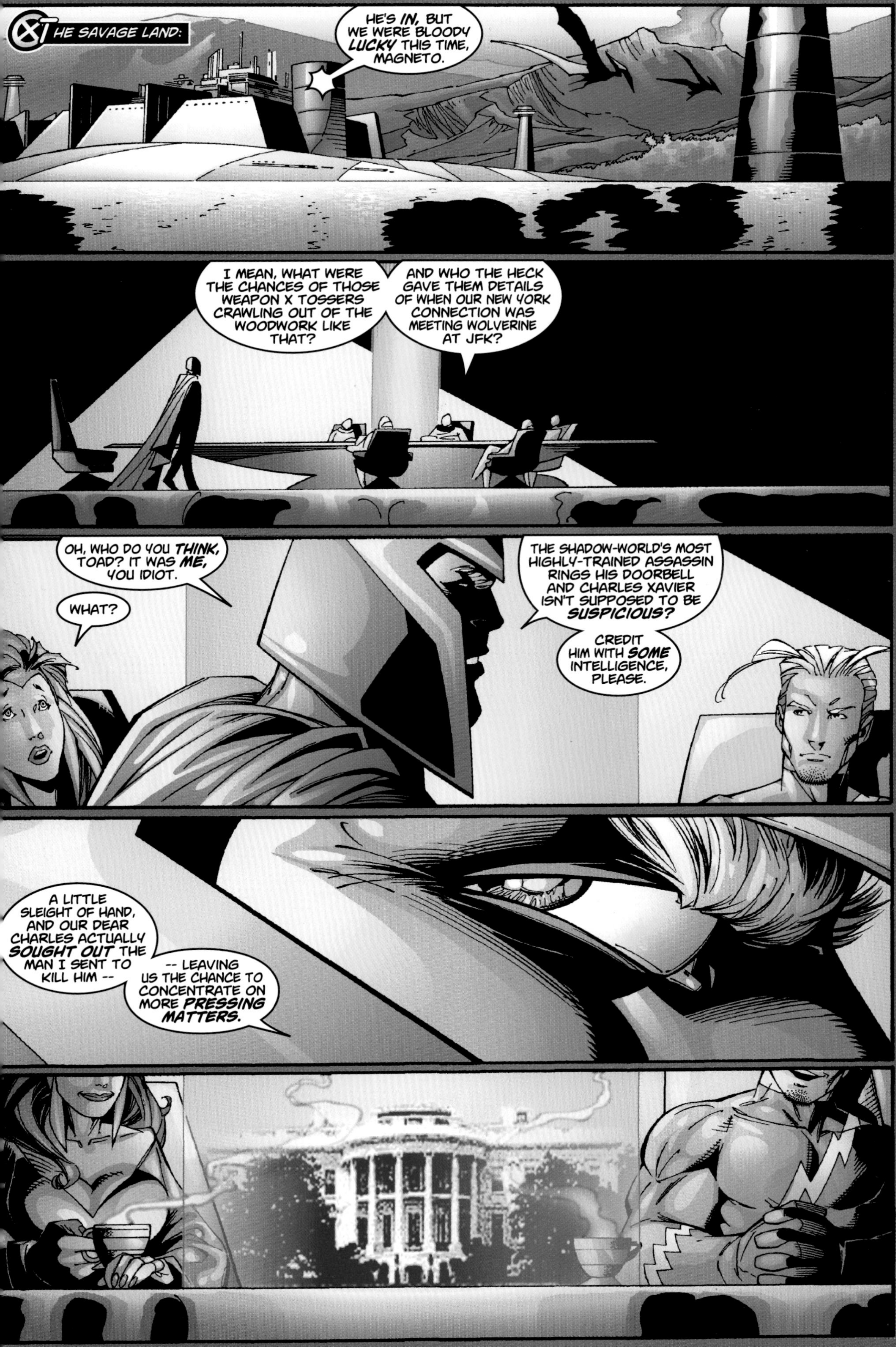
THE SAVAGE LAND:
HE'S IN, BUT WE WERE BLOODY LUCKY THIS TIME, MAGNETO.
I MEAN, WHAT WERE THE CHANCES OF THOSE WEAPON X TOSSERS CRAWLING OUT OF THE WOODWORK LIKE THAT?
AND WHO THE HECK GAVE THEM DETAILS OF WHEN OUR NEW YORK CONNECTION WAS MEETING WOLVERINE AT JFK?
OH, WHO DO YOU THINK, TOAD? IT WAS ME, YOU IDIOT.
WHAT?
THE SHADOW-WORLD'S MOST HIGHLY-TRAINED ASSASSIN RINGS HIS DOORBELL AND CHARLES XAVIER ISN'T SUPPOSED TO BE SUSPICIOUS?
CREDIT HIM WITH SOME INTELLIGENCE, PLEASE.
A LITTLE SLEIGHT OF HAND, AND OUR DEAR CHARLES ACTUALLY SOUGHT OUT THE MAN I SENT TO KILL HIM --
-- LEAVING US THE CHANCE TO CONCENTRATE ON MORE PRESSING MATTERS.

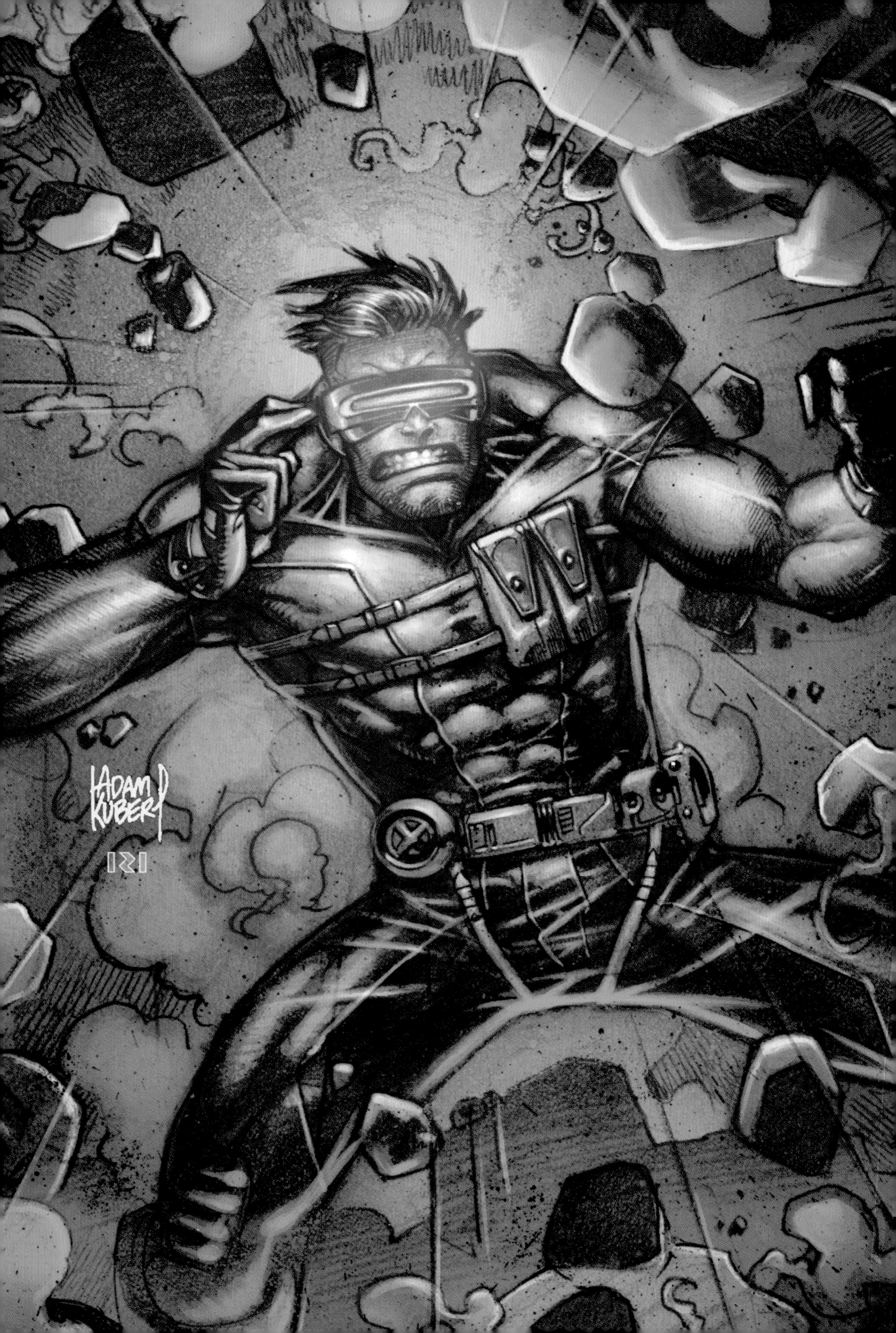
ADAM KUBERT

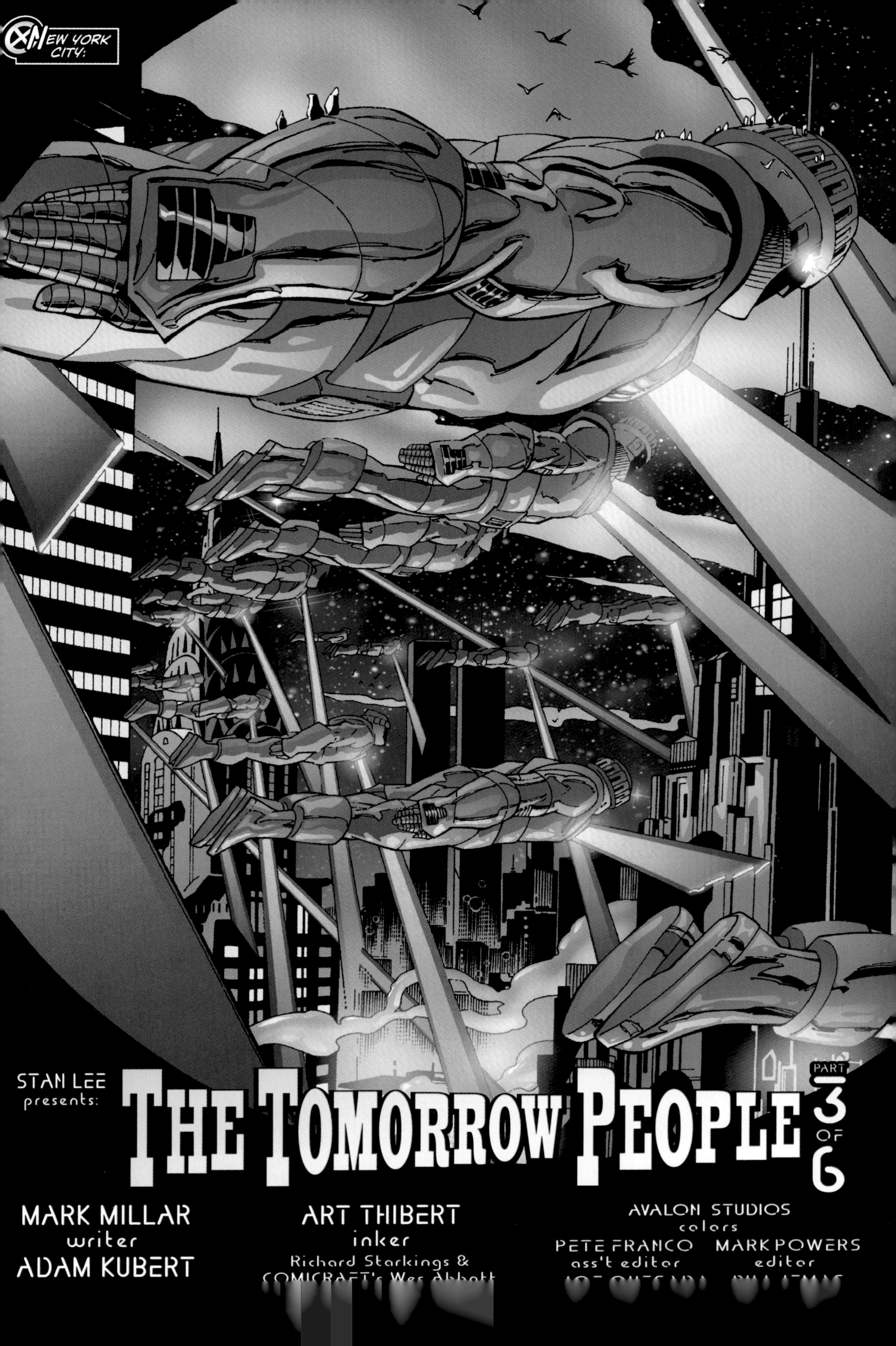

NEW YORK CITY:
STAN LEE presents:
THE TOMORROW PEOPLE
PART 3 OF 6
MARK MILLAR writer
ADAM KUBERT
ART THIBERT inker
Richard Starkings & COMICRAFT's Wes Abbott
AVALON STUDIOS colors
PETE FRANCO ass't editor
MARK POWERS editor

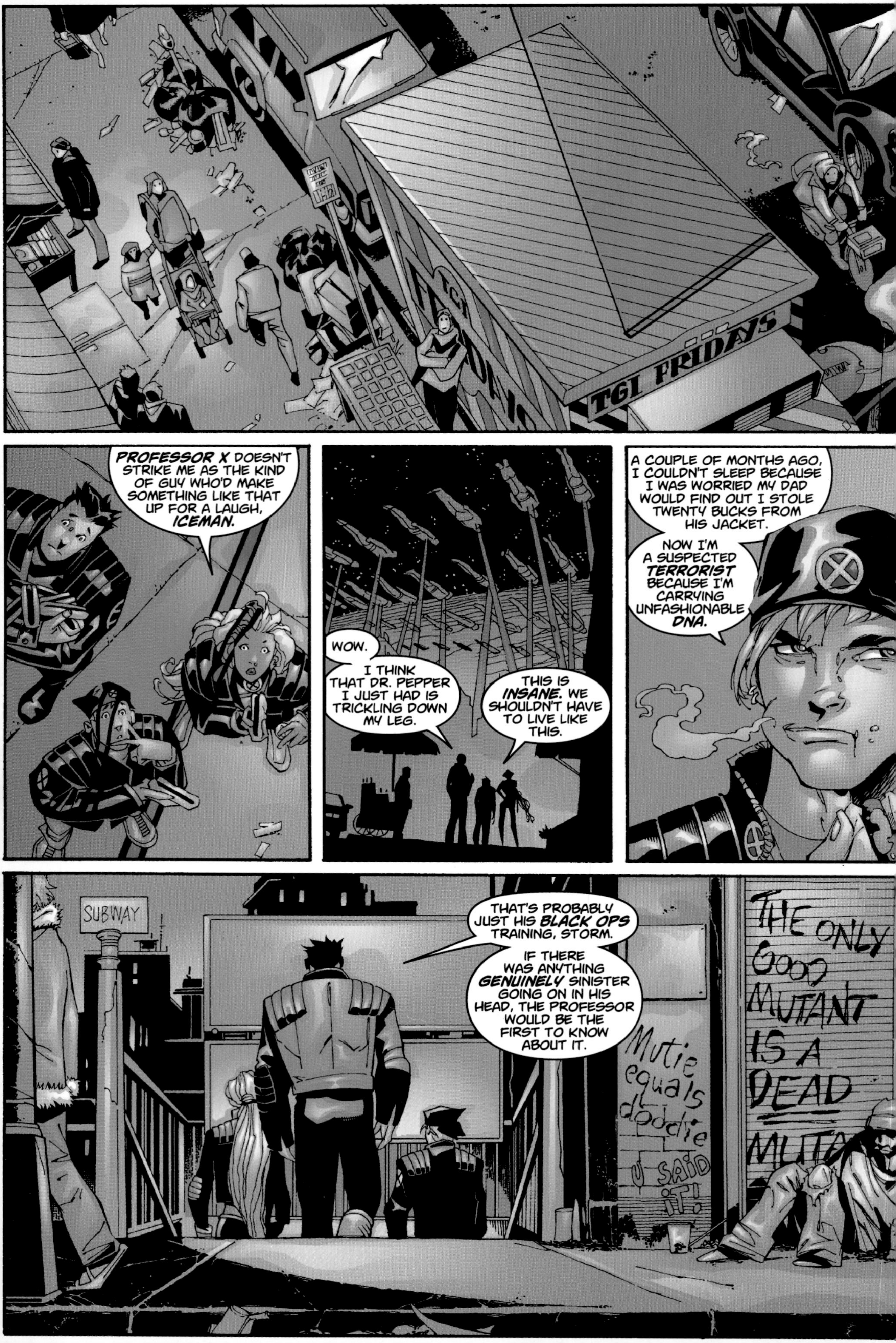
TGI FRIDAYS
PROFESSOR X DOESN'T STRIKE ME AS THE KIND OF GUY WHO'D MAKE SOMETHING LIKE THAT UP FOR A LAUGH, ICEMAN.
WOW.
I THINK THAT DR. PEPPER I JUST HAD IS TRICKLING DOWN MY LEG.
THIS IS INSANE. WE SHOULDN'T HAVE TO LIVE LIKE THIS.
A COUPLE OF MONTHS AGO, I COULDN'T SLEEP BECAUSE I WAS WORRIED MY DAD WOULD FIND OUT I STOLE TWENTY BUCKS FROM HIS JACKET.
NOW I'M A SUSPECTED TERRORIST BECAUSE I'M CARRYING UNFASHIONABLE DNA.
SUBWAY
THAT'S PROBABLY JUST HIS BLACK OPS TRAINING, STORM.
IF THERE WAS ANYTHING GENUINELY SINISTER GOING ON IN HIS HEAD, THE PROFESSOR WOULD BE THE FIRST TO KNOW ABOUT IT.
Mutie equals doodie
U SAID IT!
THE ONLY GOOD MUTANT IS A DEAD MUTA

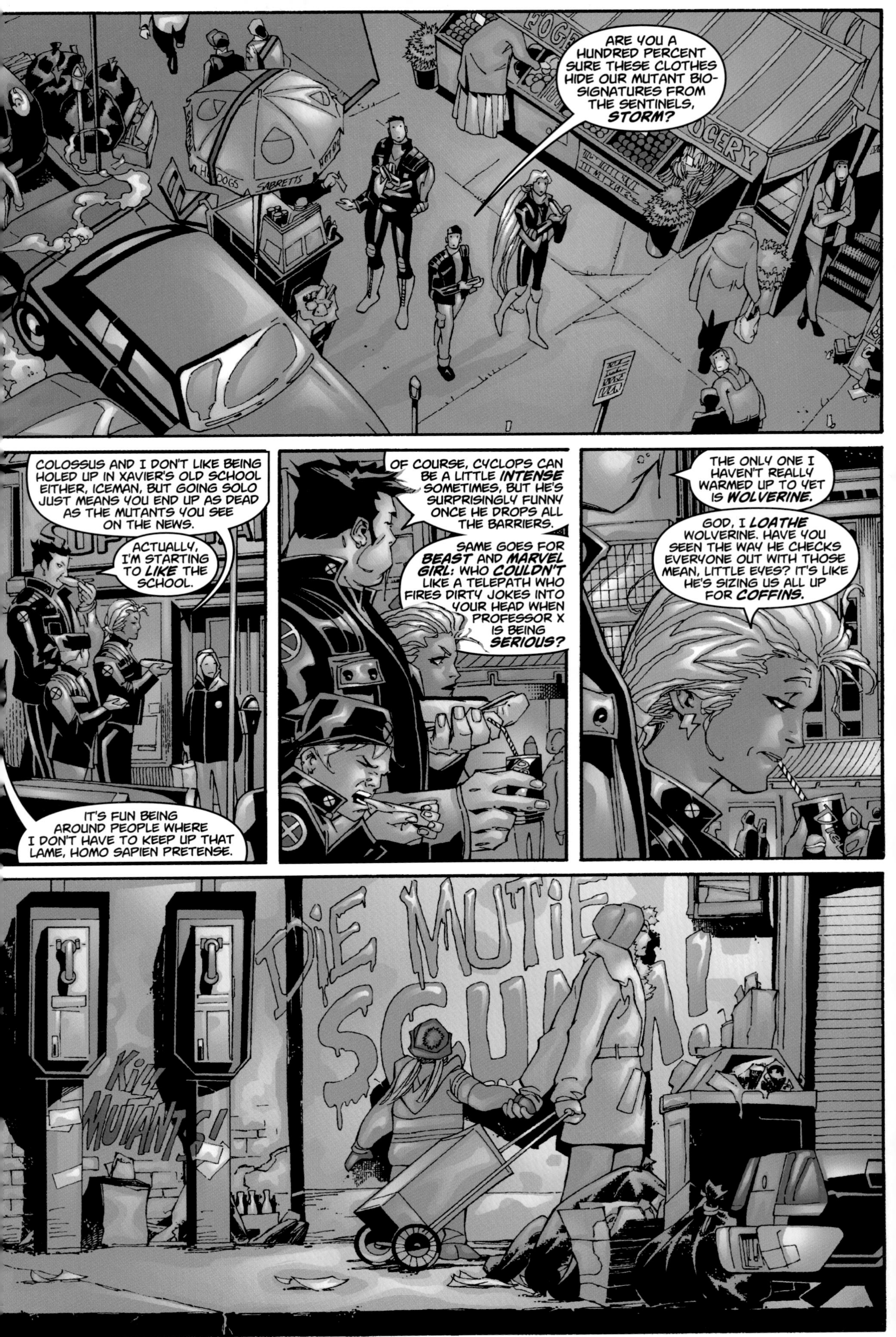

ARE YOU A HUNDRED PERCENT SURE THESE CLOTHES HIDE OUR MUTANT BIO-SIGNATURES FROM THE SENTINELS, **STORM?**
SABRETTS
COLOSSUS AND I DON'T LIKE BEING HOLED UP IN XAVIER'S OLD SCHOOL EITHER, ICEMAN, BUT GOING SOLO JUST MEANS YOU END UP AS DEAD AS THE MUTANTS YOU SEE ON THE NEWS.
ACTUALLY, I'M STARTING TO ***LIKE*** THE SCHOOL.
IT'S FUN BEING AROUND PEOPLE WHERE I DON'T HAVE TO KEEP UP THAT LAME, HOMO SAPIEN PRETENSE.
OF COURSE, CYCLOPS CAN BE A LITTLE ***INTENSE*** SOMETIMES, BUT HE'S SURPRISINGLY FUNNY ONCE HE DROPS ALL THE BARRIERS.
SAME GOES FOR ***BEAST*** AND ***MARVEL GIRL***: WHO ***COULDN'T*** LIKE A TELEPATH WHO FIRES DIRTY JOKES INTO YOUR HEAD WHEN PROFESSOR X IS BEING ***SERIOUS?***
THE ONLY ONE I HAVEN'T REALLY WARMED UP TO YET IS ***WOLVERINE.***
GOD, I ***LOATHE*** WOLVERINE. HAVE YOU SEEN THE WAY HE CHECKS EVERYONE OUT WITH THOSE MEAN, LITTLE EYES? IT'S LIKE HE'S SIZING US ALL UP FOR ***COFFINS.***
DIE MUTIE
KILL MUTANTS!

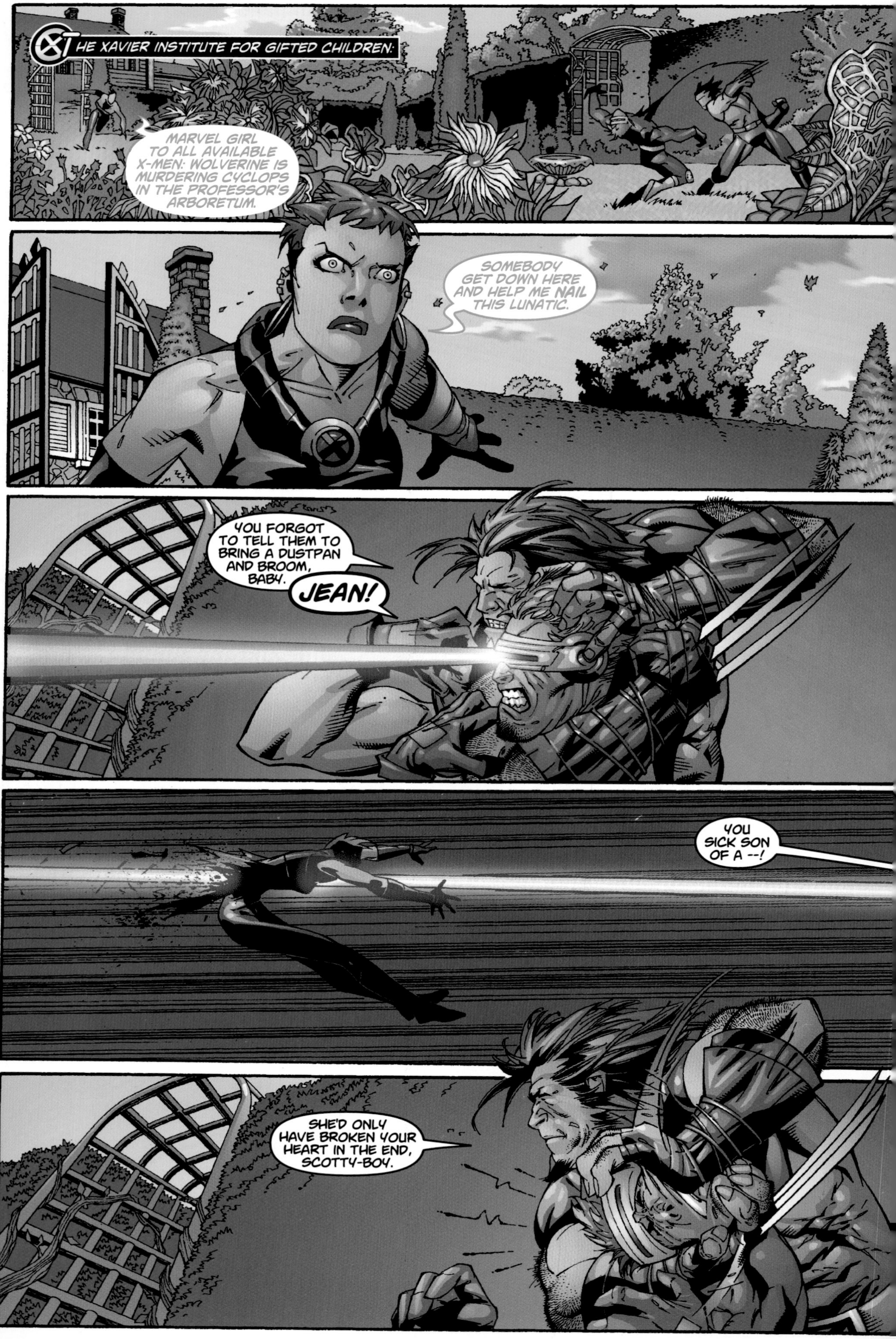
THE XAVIER INSTITUTE FOR GIFTED CHILDREN:
MARVEL GIRL TO ALL AVAILABLE X-MEN: WOLVERINE IS MURDERING CYCLOPS IN THE PROFESSOR'S ARBORETUM.
SOMEBODY GET DOWN HERE AND HELP ME NAIL THIS LUNATIC.
YOU FORGOT TO TELL THEM TO BRING A DUSTPAN AND BROOM, BABY.
JEAN!
YOU SICK SON OF A --!
SHE'D ONLY HAVE BROKEN YOUR HEART IN THE END, SCOTTY-BOY.

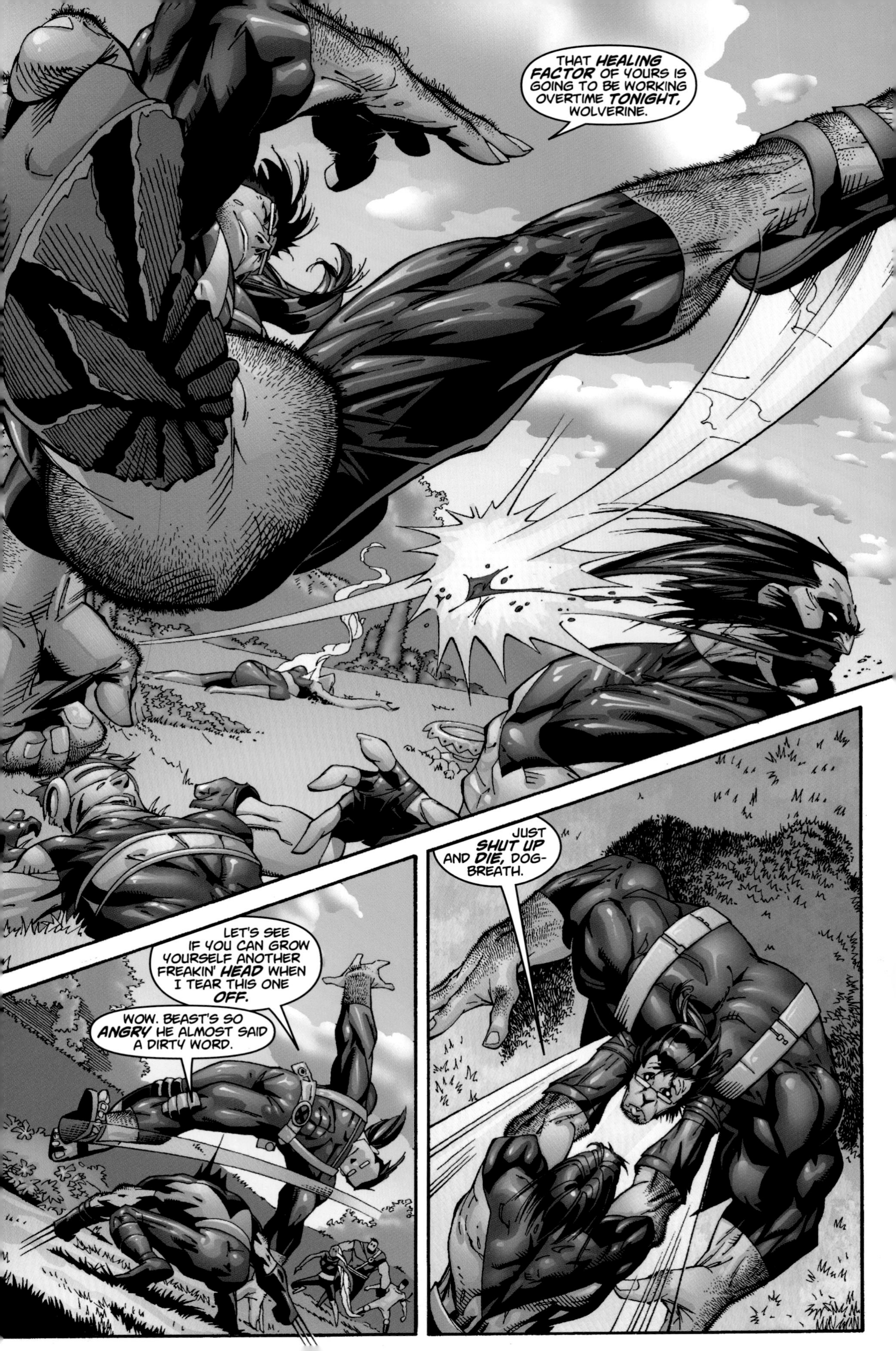
THAT HEALING FACTOR OF YOURS IS GOING TO BE WORKING OVERTIME TONIGHT, WOLVERINE.
LET'S SEE IF YOU CAN GROW YOURSELF ANOTHER FREAKIN' HEAD WHEN I TEAR THIS ONE OFF.
WOW. BEAST'S SO ANGRY HE ALMOST SAID A DIRTY WORD.
JUST SHUT UP AND DIE, DOG-BREATH.

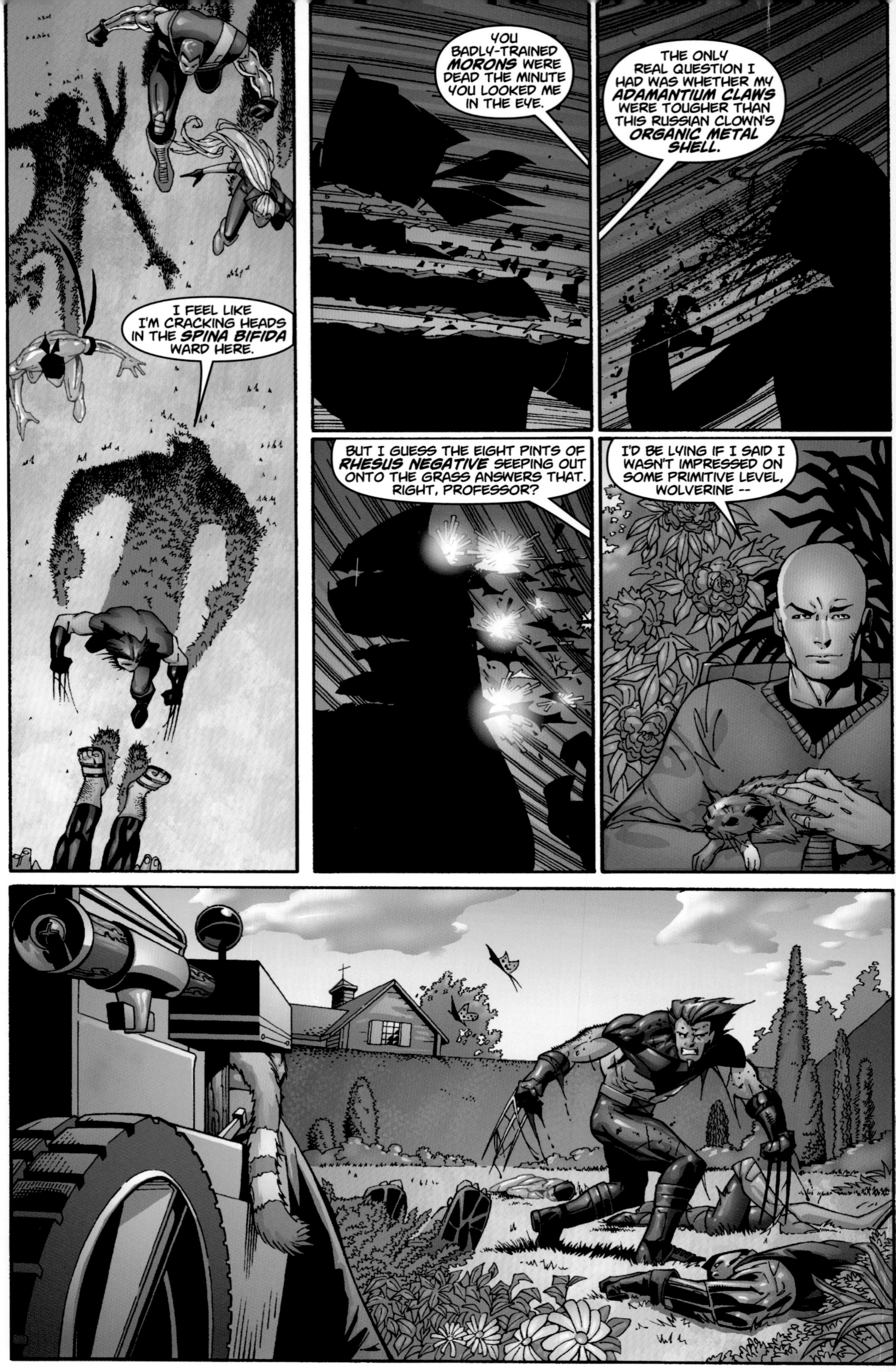
I FEEL LIKE I'M CRACKING HEADS IN THE SPINA BIFIDA WARD HERE.
YOU BADLY-TRAINED MORONS WERE DEAD THE MINUTE YOU LOOKED ME IN THE EYE.
THE ONLY REAL QUESTION I HAD WAS WHETHER MY ADAMANTIUM CLAWS WERE TOUGHER THAN THIS RUSSIAN CLOWN'S ORGANIC METAL SHELL.
BUT I GUESS THE EIGHT PINTS OF RHESUS NEGATIVE SEEPING OUT ONTO THE GRASS ANSWERS THAT. RIGHT, PROFESSOR?
I'D BE LYING IF I SAID I WASN'T IMPRESSED ON SOME PRIMITIVE LEVEL, WOLVERINE --

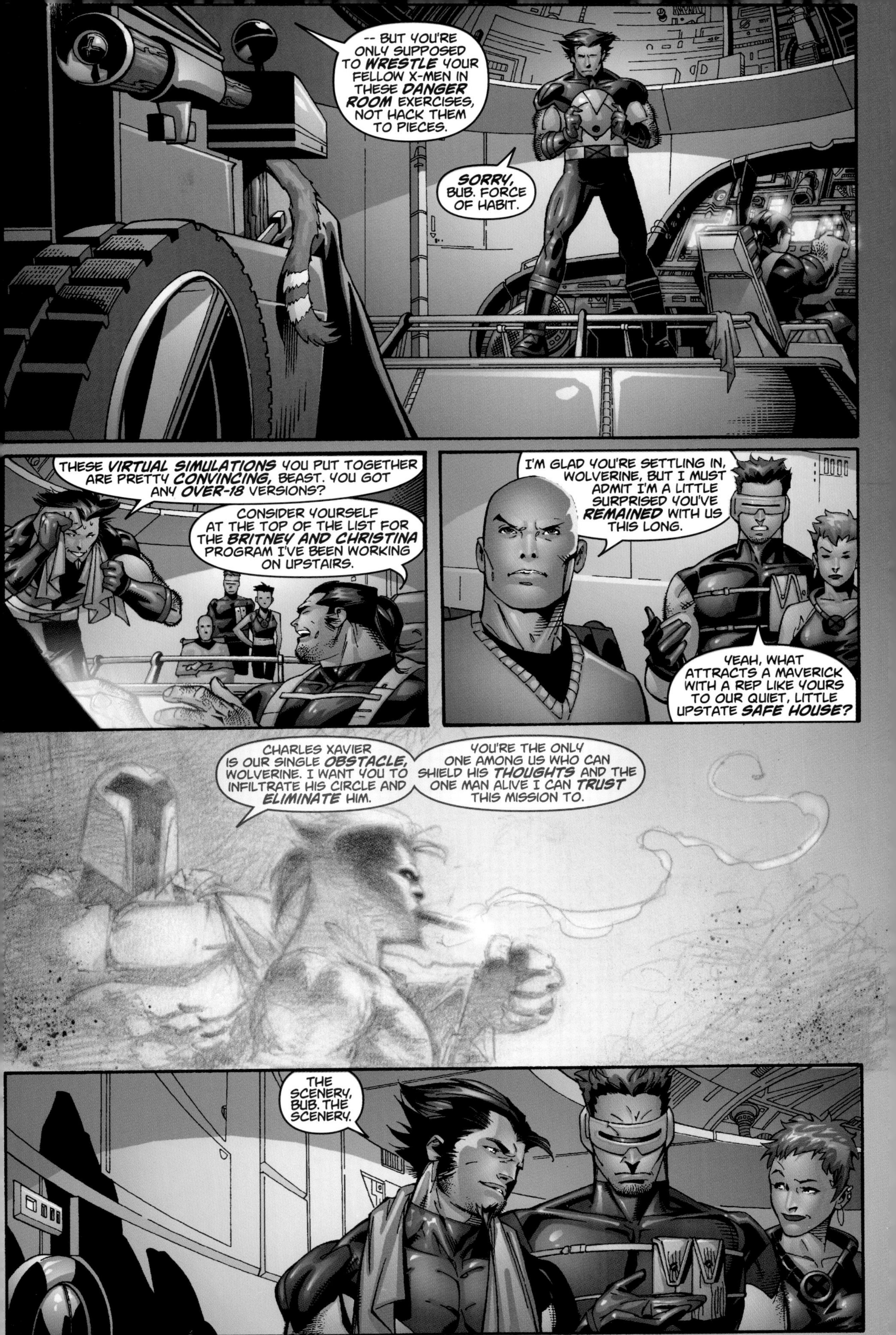
-- BUT YOU'RE ONLY SUPPOSED TO WRESTLE YOUR FELLOW X-MEN IN THESE DANGER ROOM EXERCISES, NOT HACK THEM TO PIECES.
SORRY, BUB. FORCE OF HABIT.
THESE VIRTUAL SIMULATIONS YOU PUT TOGETHER ARE PRETTY CONVINCING, BEAST. YOU GOT ANY OVER-18 VERSIONS?
CONSIDER YOURSELF AT THE TOP OF THE LIST FOR THE BRITNEY AND CHRISTINA PROGRAM I'VE BEEN WORKING ON UPSTAIRS.
I'M GLAD YOU'RE SETTLING IN, WOLVERINE, BUT I MUST ADMIT I'M A LITTLE SURPRISED YOU'VE REMAINED WITH US THIS LONG.
YEAH, WHAT ATTRACTS A MAVERICK WITH A REP LIKE YOURS TO OUR QUIET, LITTLE UPSTATE SAFE HOUSE?
CHARLES XAVIER IS OUR SINGLE OBSTACLE, WOLVERINE. I WANT YOU TO INFILTRATE HIS CIRCLE AND ELIMINATE HIM.
YOU'RE THE ONLY ONE AMONG US WHO CAN SHIELD HIS THOUGHTS AND THE ONE MAN ALIVE I CAN TRUST THIS MISSION TO.
THE SCENERY, BUB. THE SCENERY.

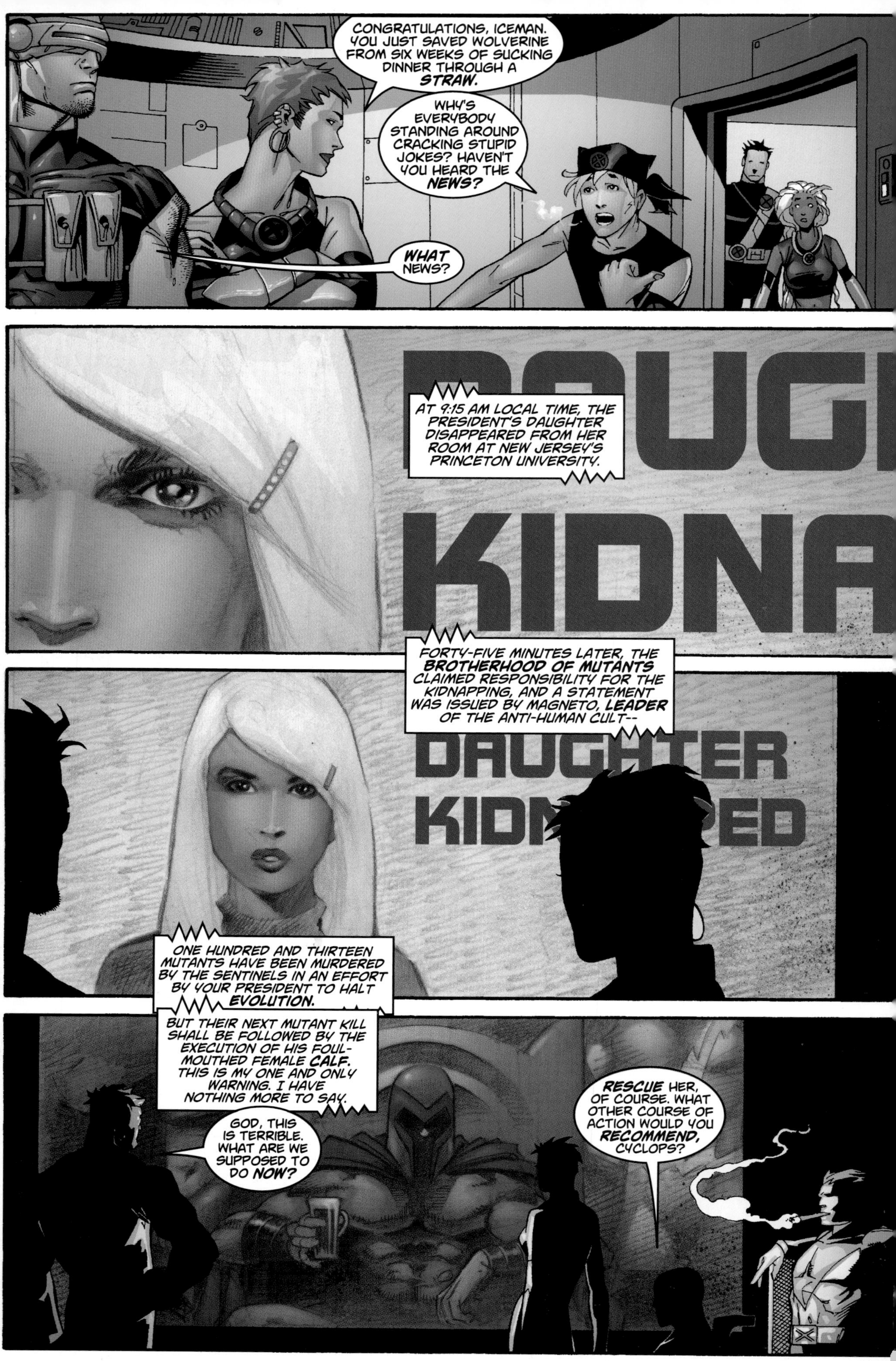
CONGRATULATIONS, ICEMAN. YOU JUST SAVED WOLVERINE FROM SIX WEEKS OF SUCKING DINNER THROUGH A STRAW.
WHY'S EVERYBODY STANDING AROUND CRACKING STUPID JOKES? HAVEN'T YOU HEARD THE NEWS?
WHAT NEWS?
AT 9:15 AM LOCAL TIME, THE PRESIDENT'S DAUGHTER DISAPPEARED FROM HER ROOM AT NEW JERSEY'S PRINCETON UNIVERSITY.
FORTY-FIVE MINUTES LATER, THE BROTHERHOOD OF MUTANTS CLAIMED RESPONSIBILITY FOR THE KIDNAPPING, AND A STATEMENT WAS ISSUED BY MAGNETO, LEADER OF THE ANTI-HUMAN CULT--
ONE HUNDRED AND THIRTEEN MUTANTS HAVE BEEN MURDERED BY THE SENTINELS IN AN EFFORT BY YOUR PRESIDENT TO HALT EVOLUTION.
BUT THEIR NEXT MUTANT KILL SHALL BE FOLLOWED BY THE EXECUTION OF HIS FOUL-MOUTHED FEMALE CALF. THIS IS MY ONE AND ONLY WARNING. I HAVE NOTHING MORE TO SAY.
GOD, THIS IS TERRIBLE. WHAT ARE WE SUPPOSED TO DO NOW?
RESCUE HER, OF COURSE. WHAT OTHER COURSE OF ACTION WOULD YOU RECOMMEND, CYCLOPS?

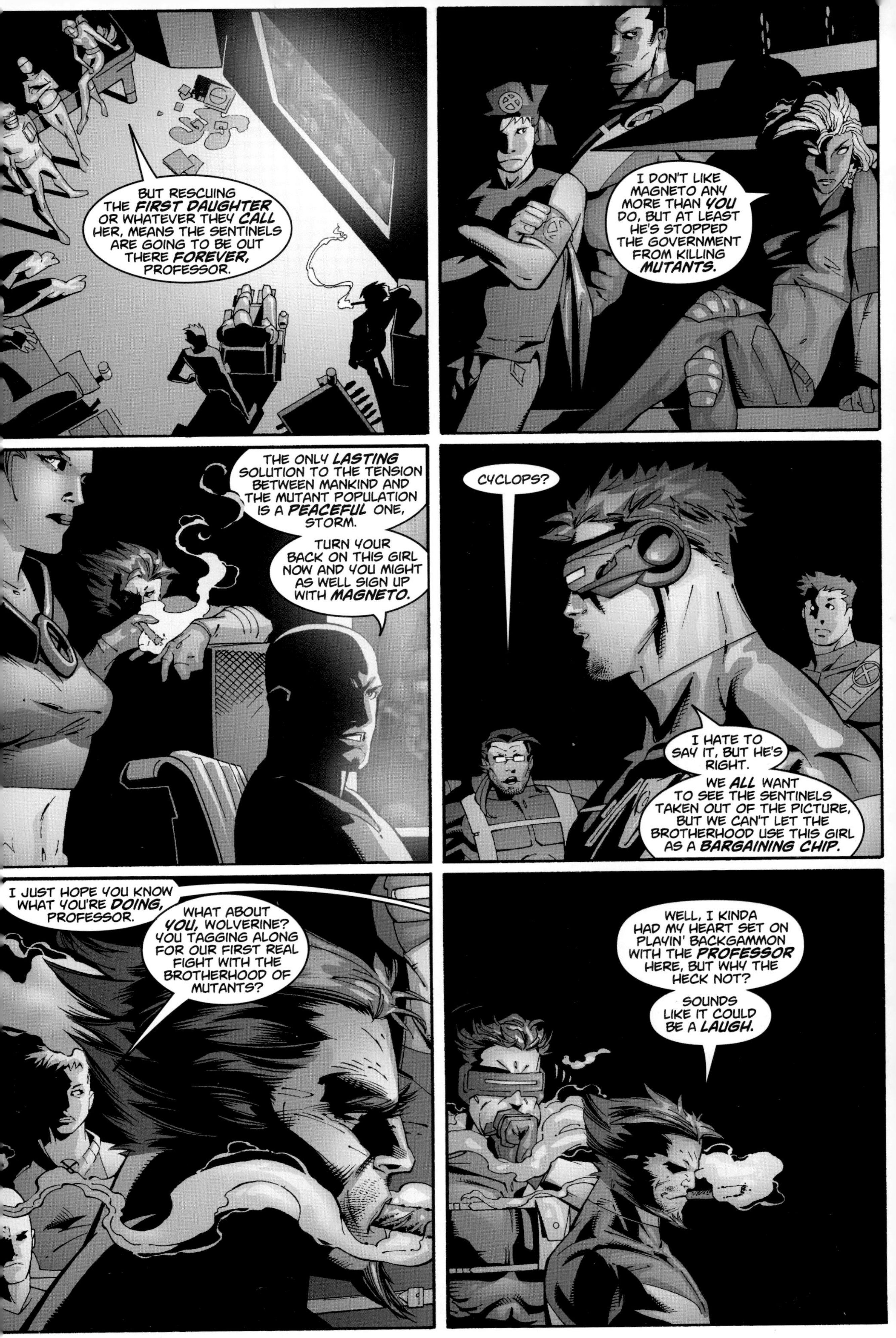
BUT RESCUING THE FIRST DAUGHTER OR WHATEVER THEY CALL HER, MEANS THE SENTINELS ARE GOING TO BE OUT THERE FOREVER, PROFESSOR.
I DON'T LIKE MAGNETO ANY MORE THAN YOU DO, BUT AT LEAST HE'S STOPPED THE GOVERNMENT FROM KILLING MUTANTS.
THE ONLY LASTING SOLUTION TO THE TENSION BETWEEN MANKIND AND THE MUTANT POPULATION IS A PEACEFUL ONE, STORM.
TURN YOUR BACK ON THIS GIRL NOW AND YOU MIGHT AS WELL SIGN UP WITH MAGNETO.
CYCLOPS?
I HATE TO SAY IT, BUT HE'S RIGHT.
WE ALL WANT TO SEE THE SENTINELS TAKEN OUT OF THE PICTURE, BUT WE CAN'T LET THE BROTHERHOOD USE THIS GIRL AS A BARGAINING CHIP.
I JUST HOPE YOU KNOW WHAT YOU'RE DOING, PROFESSOR.
WHAT ABOUT YOU, WOLVERINE? YOU TAGGING ALONG FOR OUR FIRST REAL FIGHT WITH THE BROTHERHOOD OF MUTANTS?
WELL, I KINDA HAD MY HEART SET ON PLAYIN' BACKGAMMON WITH THE PROFESSOR HERE, BUT WHY THE HECK NOT?
SOUNDS LIKE IT COULD BE A LAUGH.

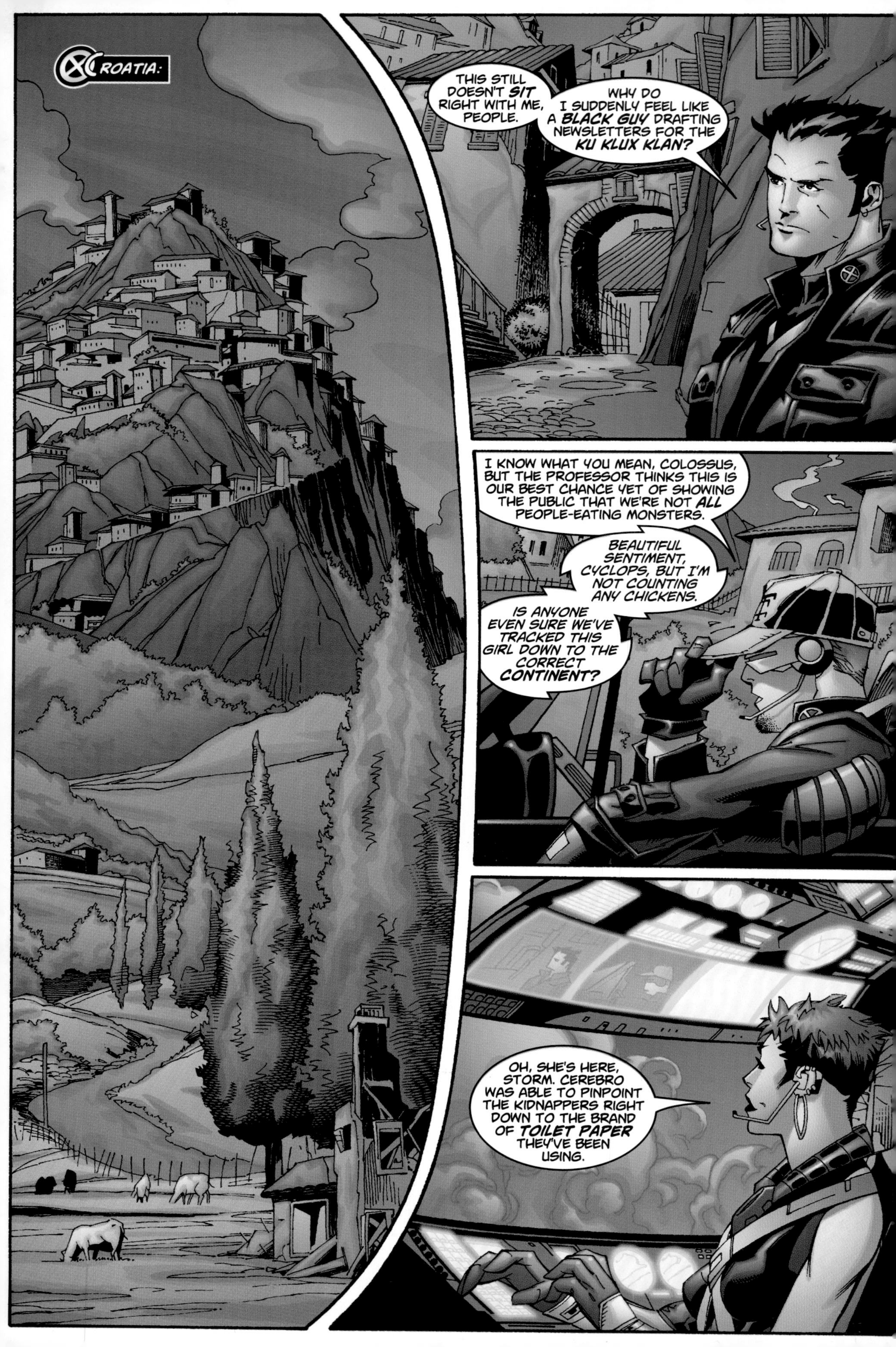
CROATIA:
THIS STILL DOESN'T SIT RIGHT WITH ME, PEOPLE.
WHY DO I SUDDENLY FEEL LIKE A BLACK GUY DRAFTING NEWSLETTERS FOR THE KU KLUX KLAN?
I KNOW WHAT YOU MEAN, COLOSSUS, BUT THE PROFESSOR THINKS THIS IS OUR BEST CHANCE YET OF SHOWING THE PUBLIC THAT WE'RE NOT ALL PEOPLE-EATING MONSTERS.
BEAUTIFUL SENTIMENT, CYCLOPS, BUT I'M NOT COUNTING ANY CHICKENS.
IS ANYONE EVEN SURE WE'VE TRACKED THIS GIRL DOWN TO THE CORRECT CONTINENT?
OH, SHE'S HERE, STORM. CEREBRO WAS ABLE TO PINPOINT THE KIDNAPPERS RIGHT DOWN TO THE BRAND OF TOILET PAPER THEY'VE BEEN USING.

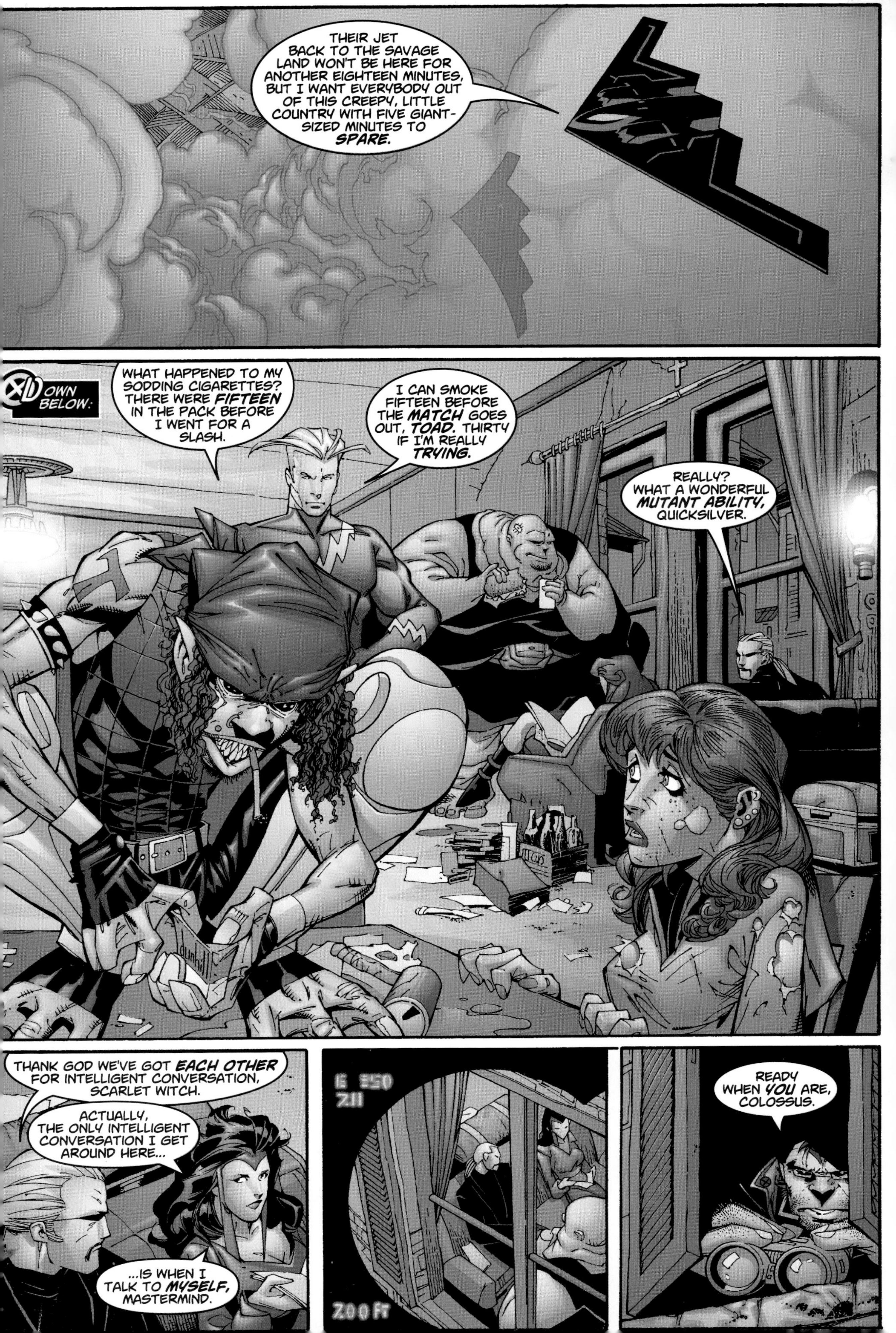

THEIR JET BACK TO THE SAVAGE LAND WON'T BE HERE FOR ANOTHER EIGHTEEN MINUTES, BUT I WANT EVERYBODY OUT OF THIS CREEPY, LITTLE COUNTRY WITH FIVE GIANT-SIZED MINUTES TO SPARE.
DOWN BELOW:
WHAT HAPPENED TO MY SODDING CIGARETTES? THERE WERE FIFTEEN IN THE PACK BEFORE I WENT FOR A SLASH.
I CAN SMOKE FIFTEEN BEFORE THE MATCH GOES OUT, TOAD. THIRTY IF I'M REALLY TRYING.
REALLY? WHAT A WONDERFUL MUTANT ABILITY, QUICKSILVER.
THANK GOD WE'VE GOT EACH OTHER FOR INTELLIGENT CONVERSATION, SCARLET WITCH.
ACTUALLY, THE ONLY INTELLIGENT CONVERSATION I GET AROUND HERE...
...IS WHEN I TALK TO MYSELF, MASTERMIND.
READY WHEN YOU ARE, COLOSSUS.

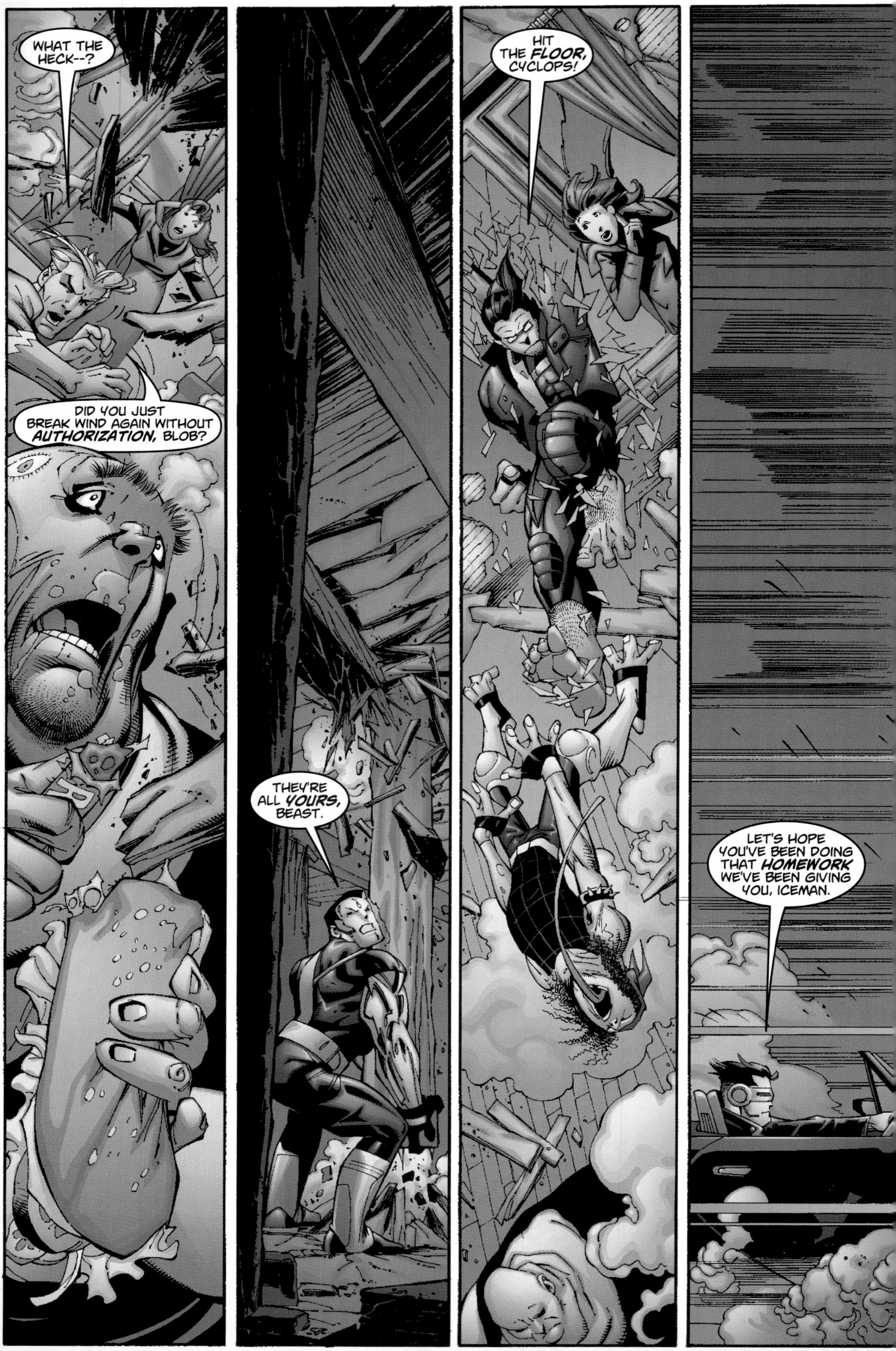

WHAT THE HECK--?
DID YOU JUST BREAK WIND AGAIN WITHOUT AUTHORIZATION, BLOB?
THEY'RE ALL YOURS, BEAST.
HIT THE FLOOR, CYCLOPS!
LET'S HOPE YOU'VE BEEN DOING THAT HOMEWORK WE'VE BEEN GIVING YOU, ICEMAN.

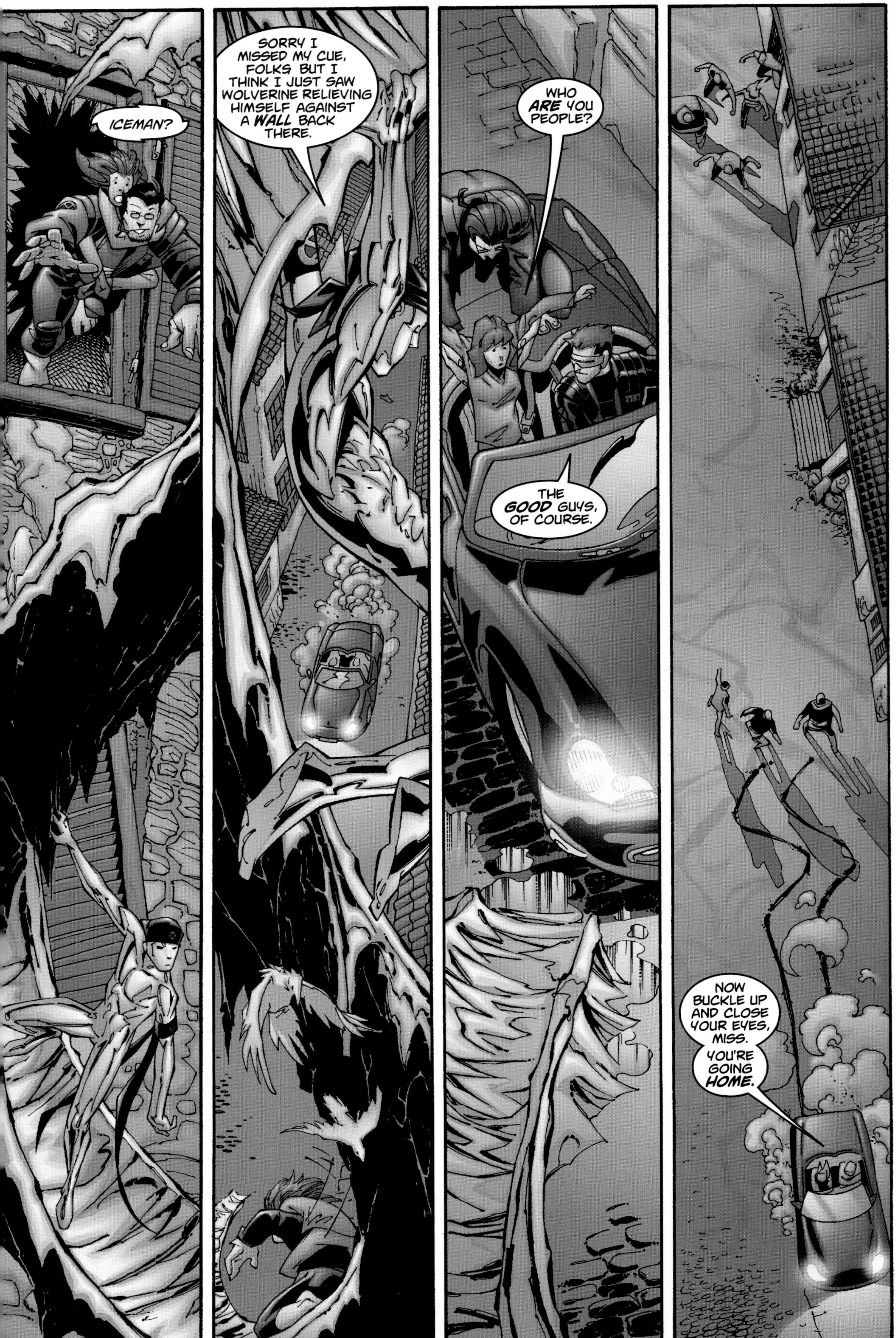
ICEMAN?
SORRY I MISSED MY CUE, FOLKS, BUT I THINK I JUST SAW WOLVERINE RELIEVING HIMSELF AGAINST A WALL BACK THERE.
WHO ARE YOU PEOPLE?
THE GOOD GUYS, OF COURSE.
NOW BUCKLE UP AND CLOSE YOUR EYES, MISS.
YOU'RE GOING HOME.

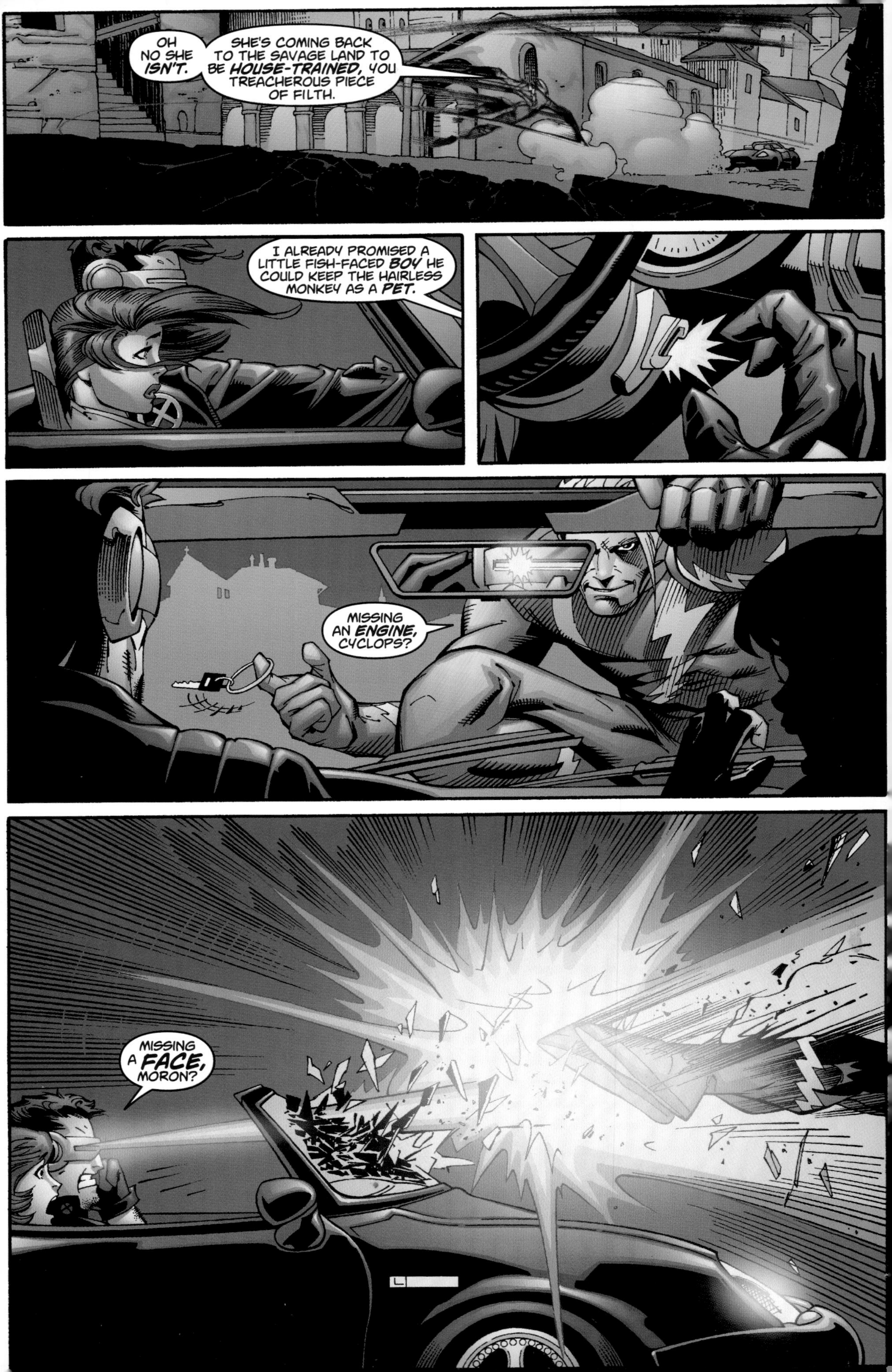
OH NO SHE ISN'T.
SHE'S COMING BACK TO THE SAVAGE LAND TO BE HOUSE-TRAINED, YOU TREACHEROUS PIECE OF FILTH.
I ALREADY PROMISED A LITTLE FISH-FACED BOY HE COULD KEEP THE HAIRLESS MONKEY AS A PET.
MISSING AN ENGINE, CYCLOPS?
MISSING A FACE, MORON?

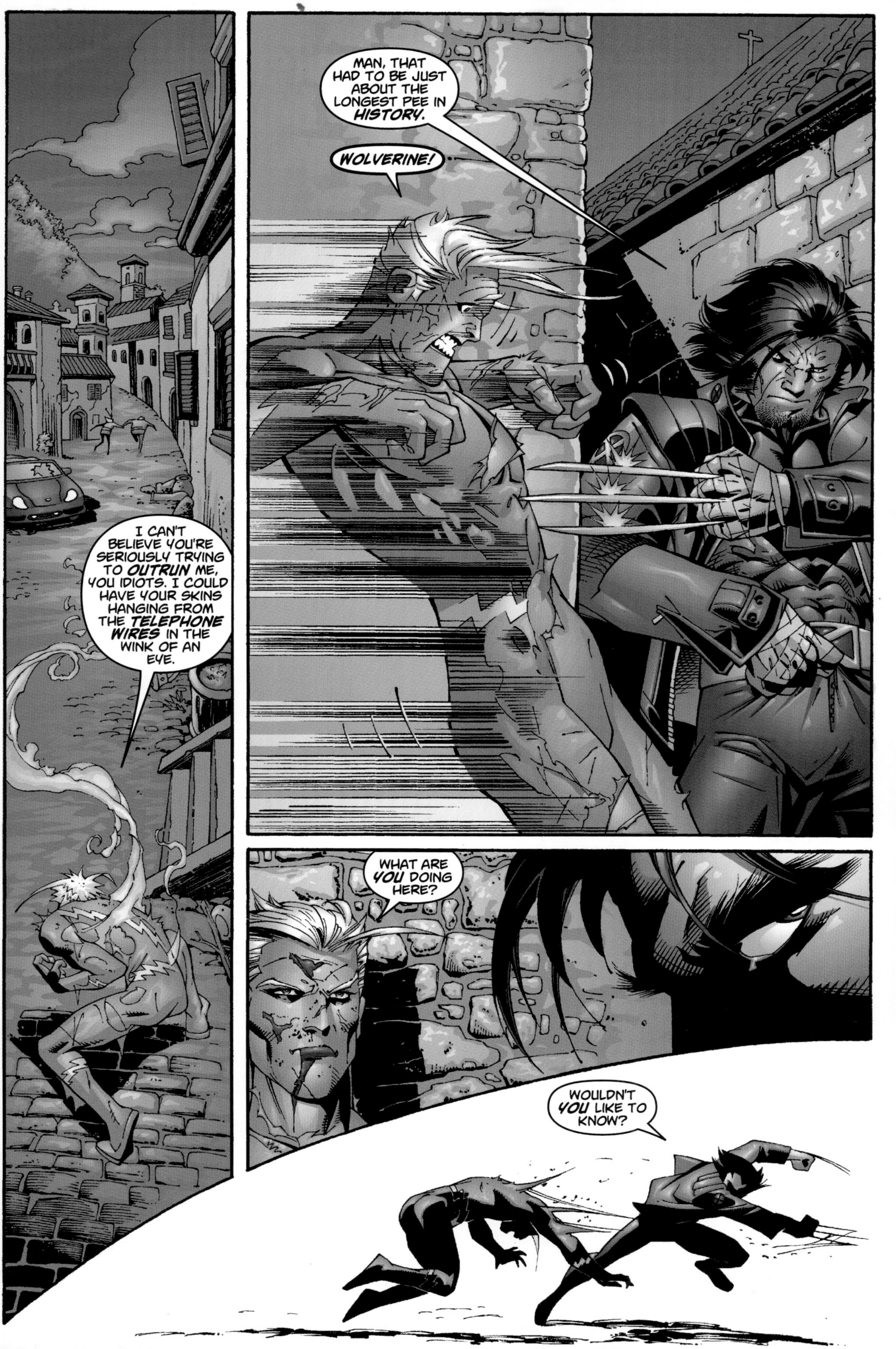

I CAN'T BELIEVE YOU'RE SERIOUSLY TRYING TO OUTRUN ME, YOU IDIOTS. I COULD HAVE YOUR SKINS HANGING FROM THE TELEPHONE WIRES IN THE WINK OF AN EYE.
MAN, THAT HAD TO BE JUST ABOUT THE LONGEST PEE IN HISTORY.
WOLVERINE!
WHAT ARE YOU DOING HERE?
WOULDN'T YOU LIKE TO KNOW?

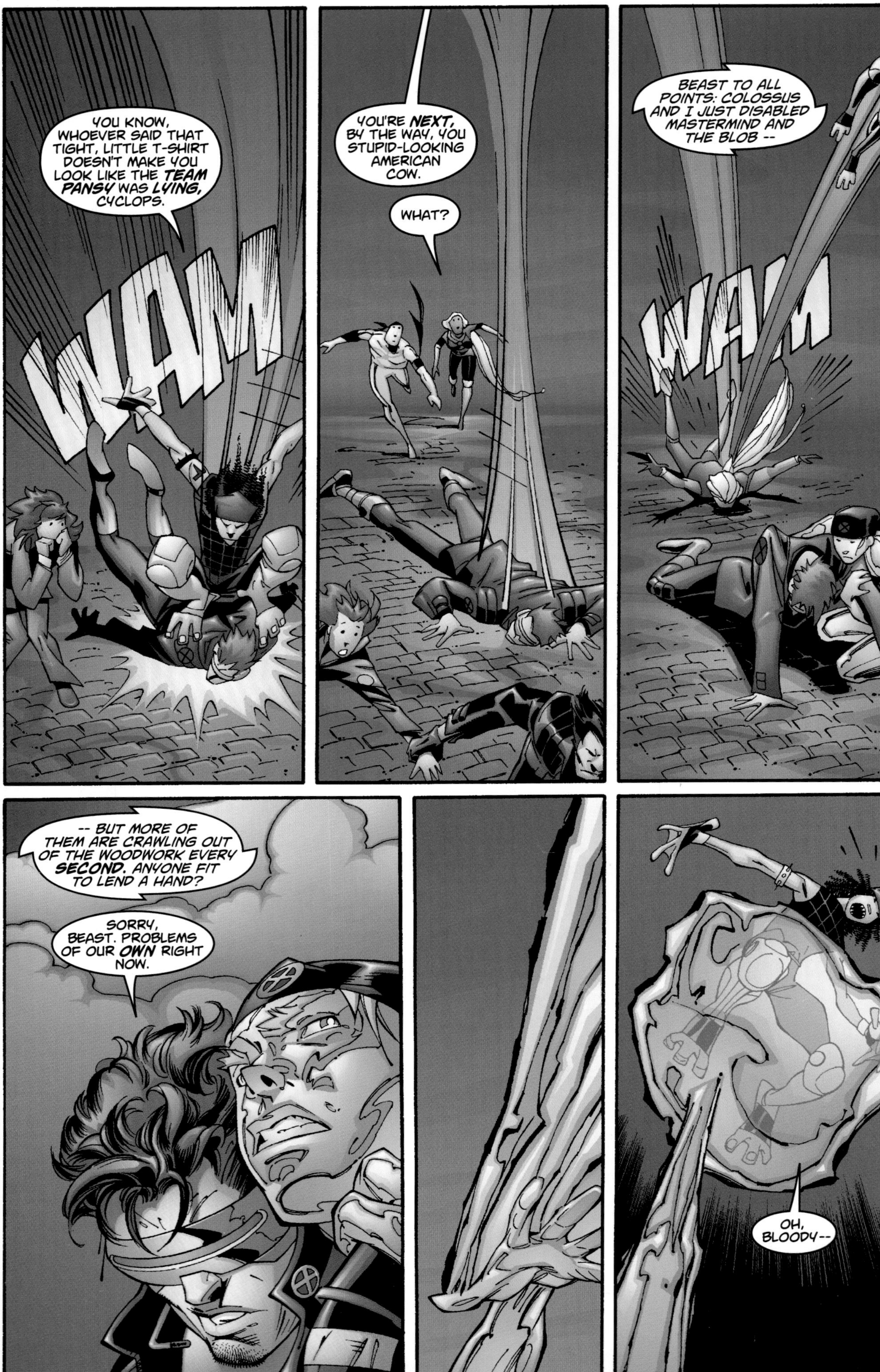
YOU KNOW, WHOEVER SAID THAT TIGHT, LITTLE T-SHIRT DOESN'T MAKE YOU LOOK LIKE THE TEAM PANSY WAS LYING, CYCLOPS.
WAM
YOU'RE NEXT, BY THE WAY, YOU STUPID-LOOKING AMERICAN COW.
WHAT?
BEAST TO ALL POINTS: COLOSSUS AND I JUST DISABLED MASTERMIND AND THE BLOB --
WAM
-- BUT MORE OF THEM ARE CRAWLING OUT OF THE WOODWORK EVERY SECOND. ANYONE FIT TO LEND A HAND?
SORRY, BEAST. PROBLEMS OF OUR OWN RIGHT NOW.
OH, BLOODY--

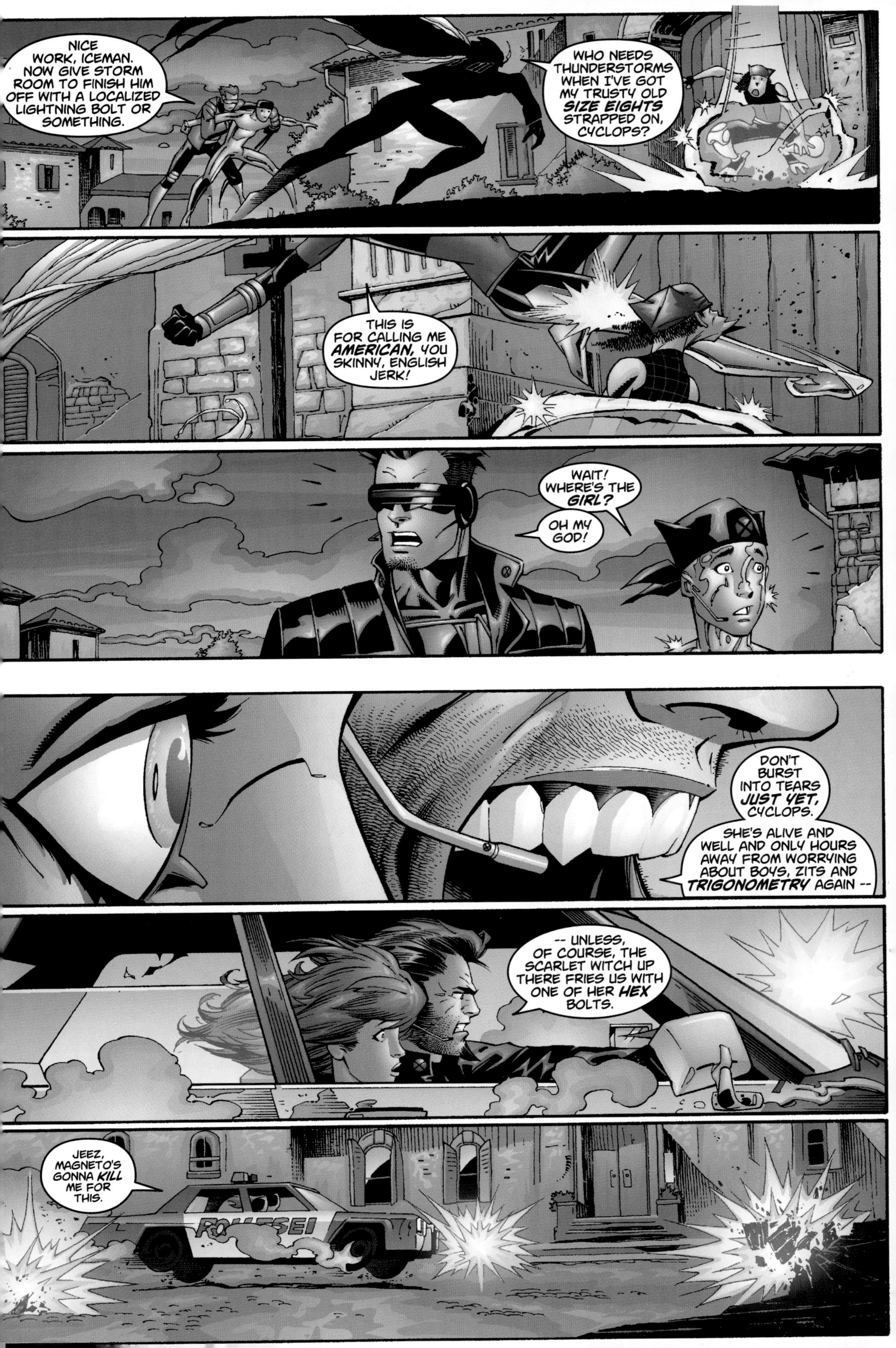
NICE WORK, ICEMAN. NOW GIVE STORM ROOM TO FINISH HIM OFF WITH A LOCALIZED LIGHTNING BOLT OR SOMETHING.
WHO NEEDS THUNDERSTORMS WHEN I'VE GOT MY TRUSTY OLD SIZE EIGHTS STRAPPED ON, CYCLOPS?
THIS IS FOR CALLING ME AMERICAN, YOU SKINNY, ENGLISH JERK!
WAIT! WHERE'S THE GIRL?
OH MY GOD!
DON'T BURST INTO TEARS JUST YET, CYCLOPS.
SHE'S ALIVE AND WELL AND ONLY HOURS AWAY FROM WORRYING ABOUT BOYS, ZITS AND TRIGONOMETRY AGAIN --
-- UNLESS, OF COURSE, THE SCARLET WITCH UP THERE FRIES US WITH ONE OF HER HEX BOLTS.
JEEZ, MAGNETO'S GONNA KILL ME FOR THIS.
POLIZEI

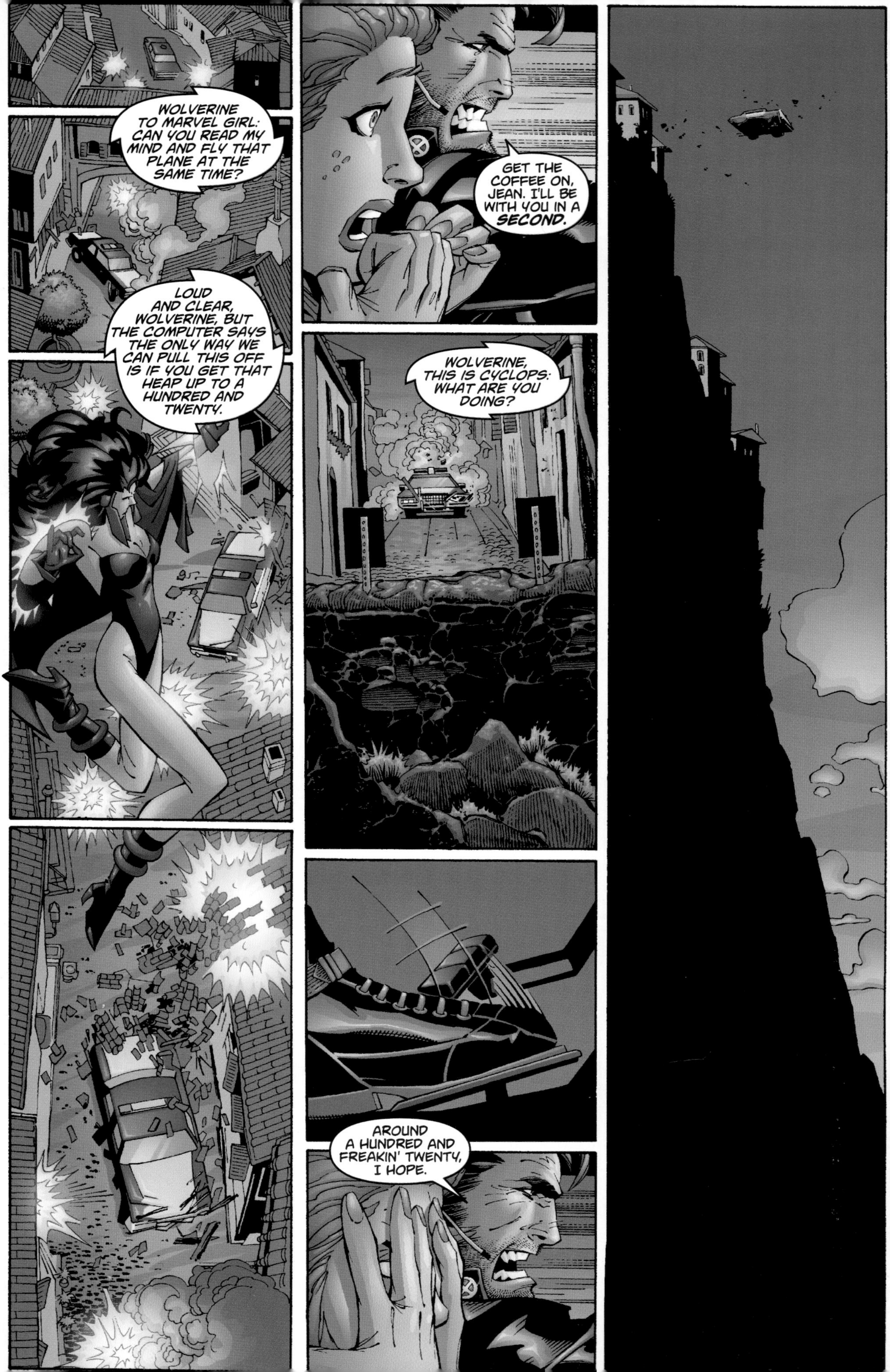
WOLVERINE TO MARVEL GIRL: CAN YOU READ MY MIND AND FLY THAT PLANE AT THE SAME TIME?
LOUD AND CLEAR, WOLVERINE, BUT THE COMPUTER SAYS THE ONLY WAY WE CAN PULL THIS OFF IS IF YOU GET THAT HEAP UP TO A HUNDRED AND TWENTY.
GET THE COFFEE ON, JEAN. I'LL BE WITH YOU IN A SECOND.
WOLVERINE, THIS IS CYCLOPS: WHAT ARE YOU DOING?
AROUND A HUNDRED AND FREAKIN' TWENTY, I HOPE.

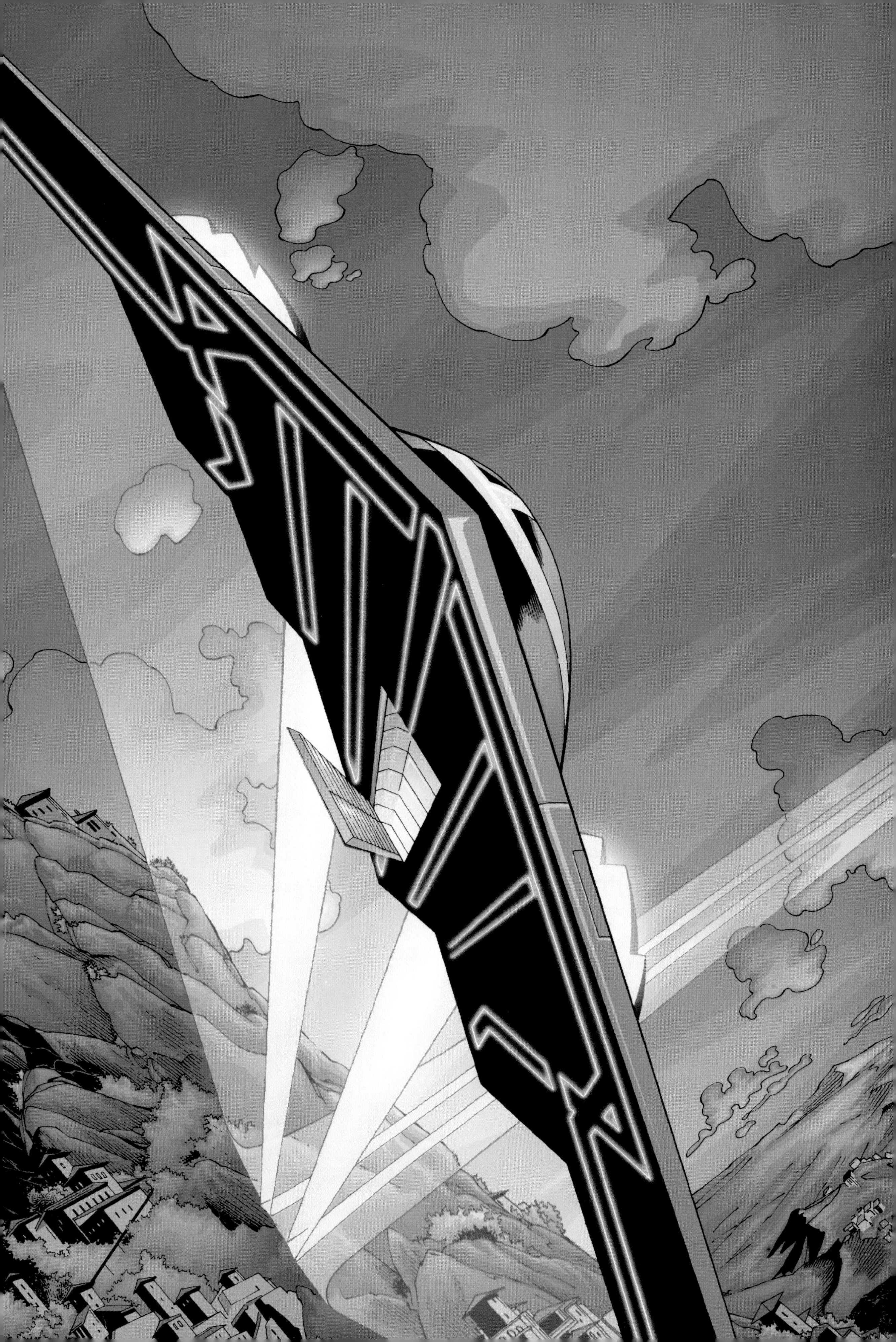

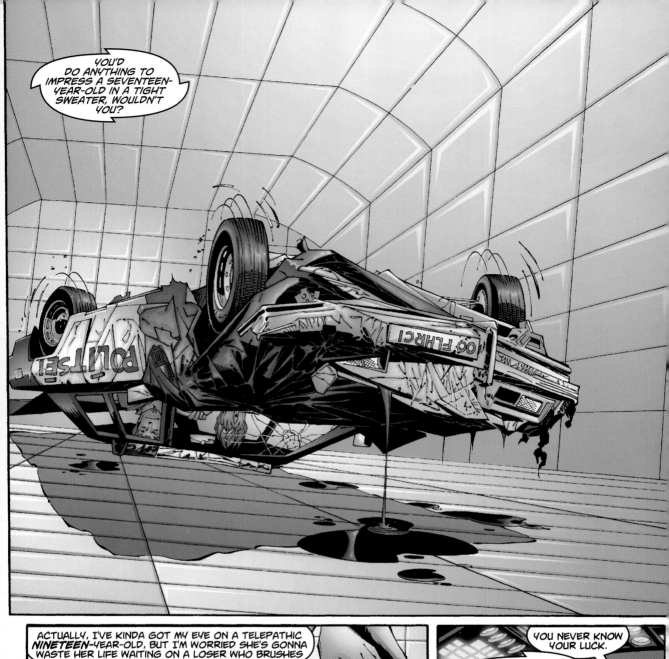

YOU'D DO ANYTHING TO IMPRESS A SEVENTEEN-YEAR-OLD IN A TIGHT SWEATER, WOULDN'T YOU?

ACTUALLY, I'VE KINDA GOT MY EYE ON A TELEPATHIC *NINETEEN*-YEAR-OLD, BUT I'M WORRIED SHE'S GONNA WASTE HER LIFE WAITING ON A LOSER WHO BRUSHES HIS *TEETH* SIX TIMES A DAY.

DON'T GIVE UP HOPE, WOLVERINE.

YOU NEVER KNOW YOUR LUCK.

CYCLOPS TO MARVEL GIRL: GIVE YOURSELF A PAT ON THE BACK AND RENDEZVOUS FIVE MILES WEST AS PLANNED, JEAN.

OH, AND *WOLVERINE* --?

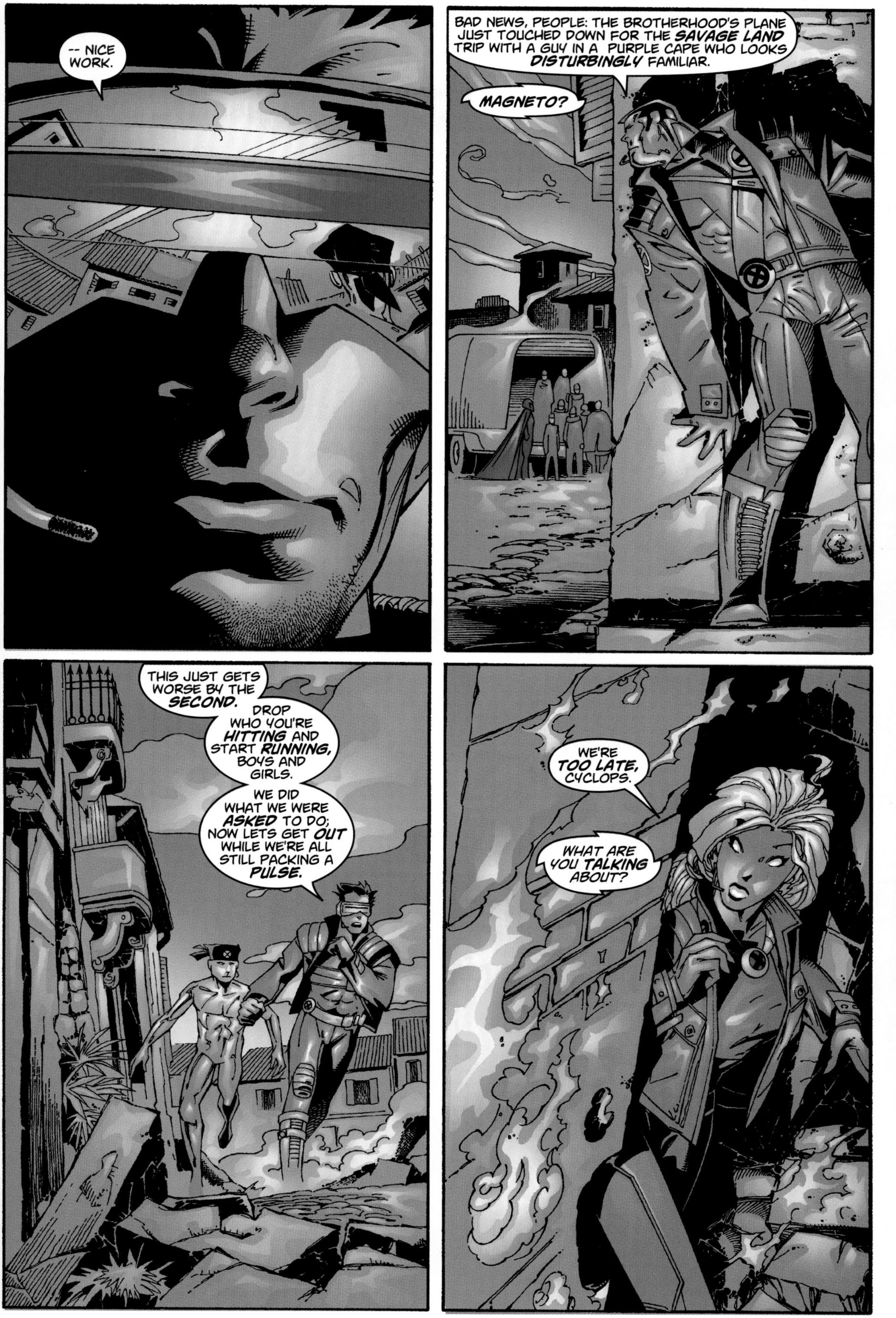
-- NICE WORK.
BAD NEWS, PEOPLE: THE BROTHERHOOD'S PLANE JUST TOUCHED DOWN FOR THE SAVAGE LAND TRIP WITH A GUY IN A PURPLE CAPE WHO LOOKS DISTURBINGLY FAMILIAR.
MAGNETO?
THIS JUST GETS WORSE BY THE SECOND.
DROP WHO YOU'RE HITTING AND START RUNNING, BOYS AND GIRLS.
WE DID WHAT WE WERE ASKED TO DO; NOW LETS GET OUT WHILE WE'RE ALL STILL PACKING A PULSE.
WE'RE TOO LATE, CYCLOPS.
WHAT ARE YOU TALKING ABOUT?

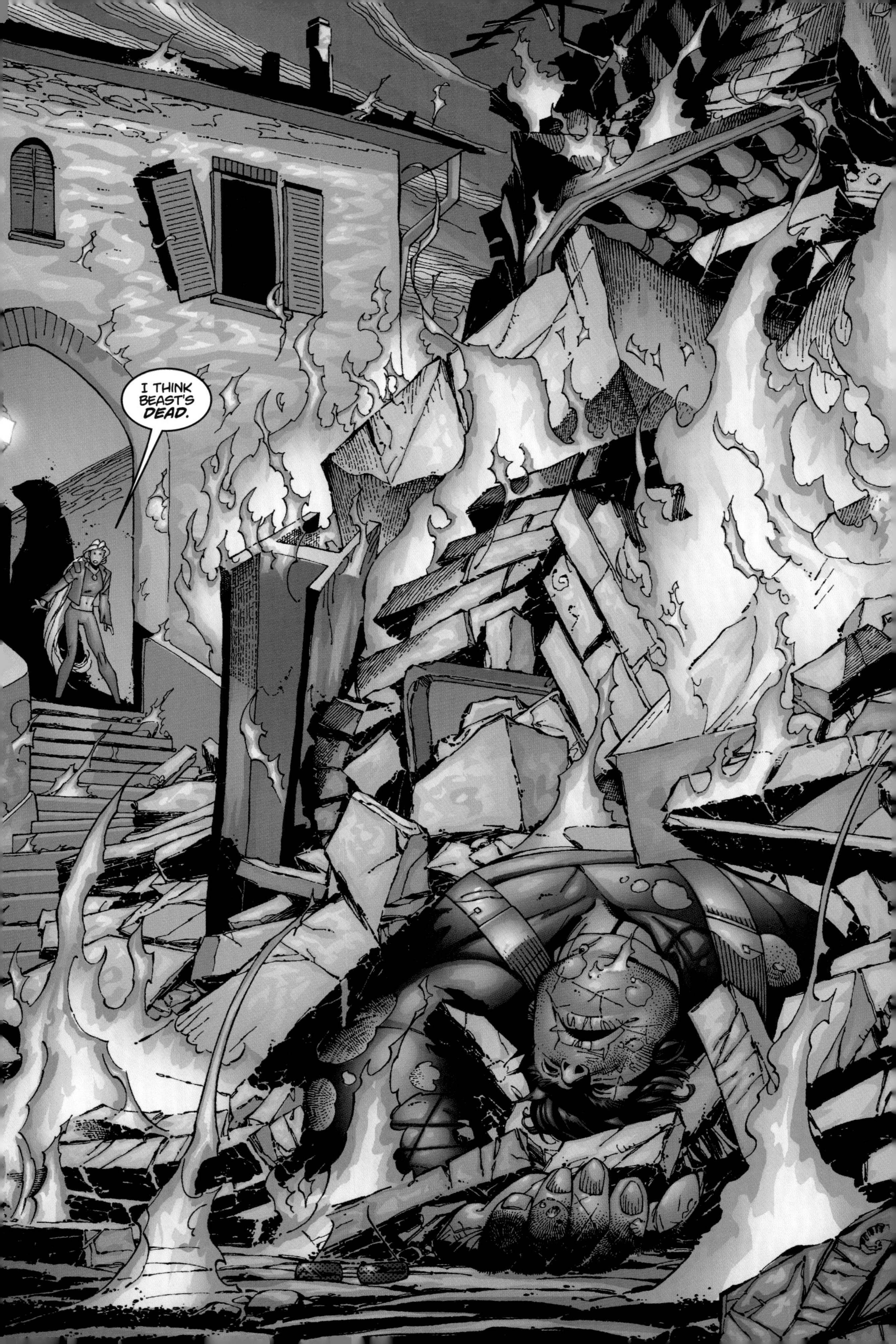
I THINK BEAST'S DEAD.

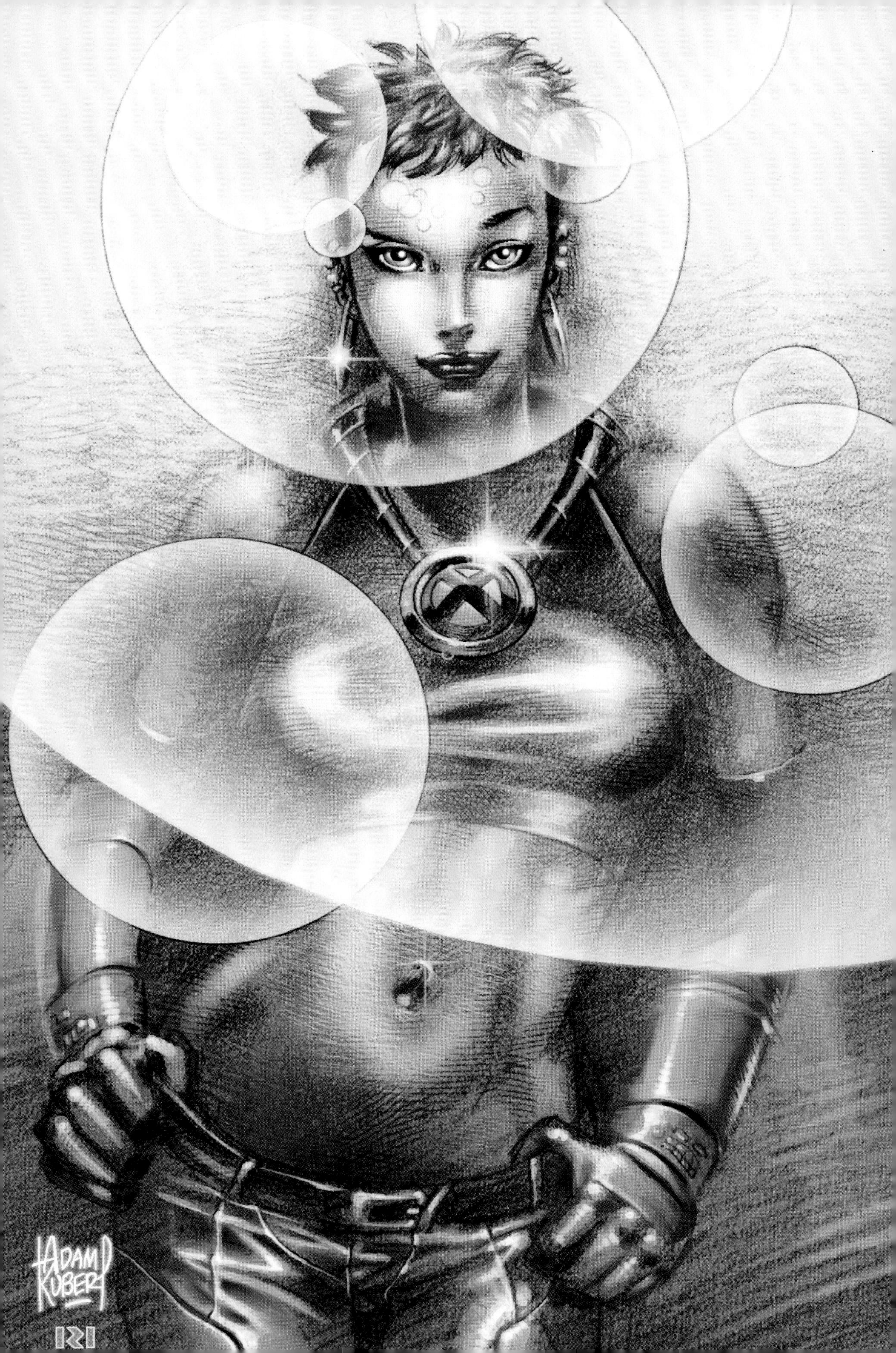
ADAM KUBERT

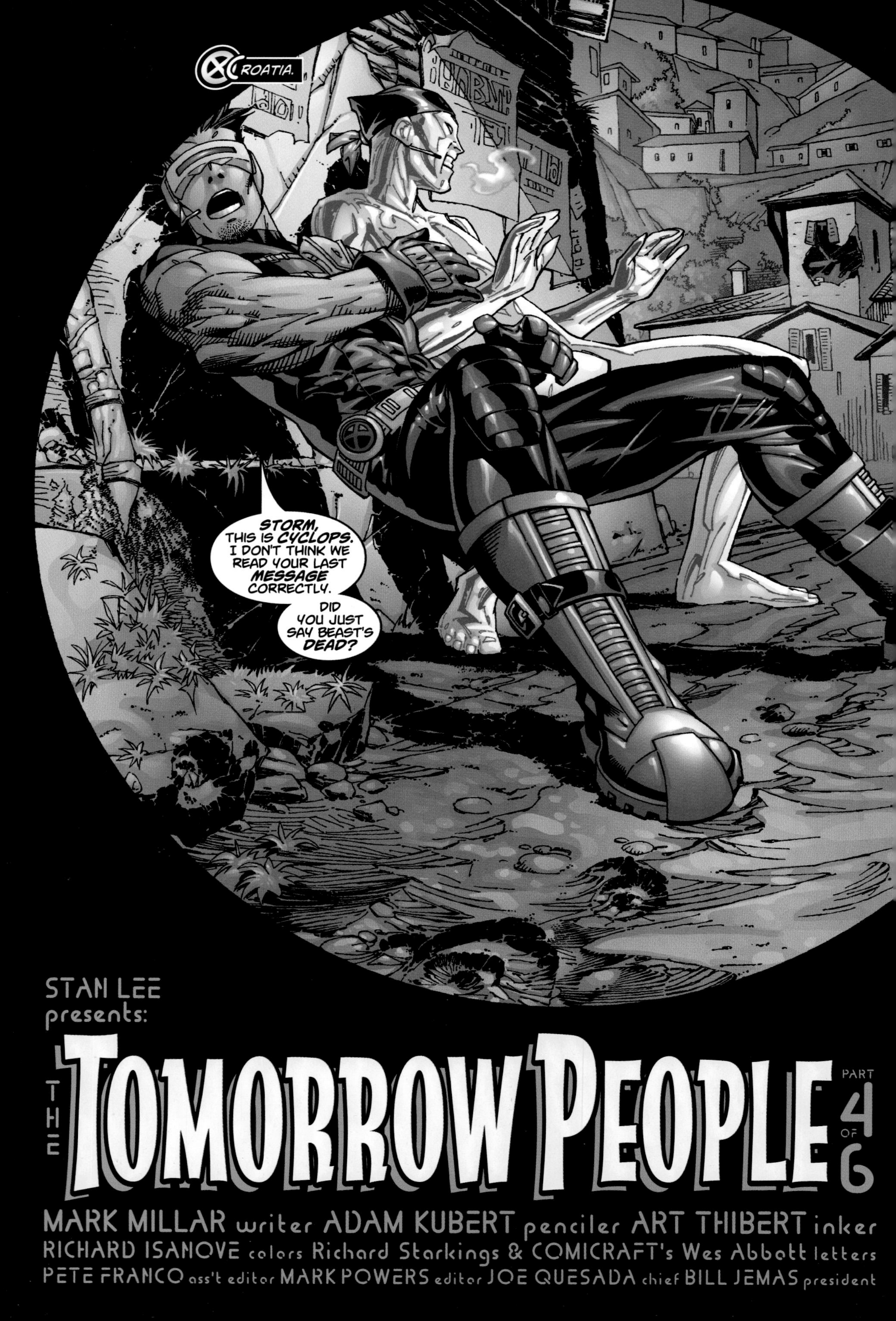
CROATIA.
STORM, THIS IS CYCLOPS. I DON'T THINK WE READ YOUR LAST MESSAGE CORRECTLY.
DID YOU JUST SAY BEAST'S DEAD?

STAN LEE presents:

THE TOMORROW PEOPLE PART 4 OF 6

MARK MILLAR writer ADAM KUBERT penciler ART THIBERT inker
RICHARD ISANOVE colors Richard Starkings & COMICRAFT's Wes Abbott letters
PETE FRANCO ass't editor MARK POWERS editor JOE QUESADA chief BILL JEMAS president

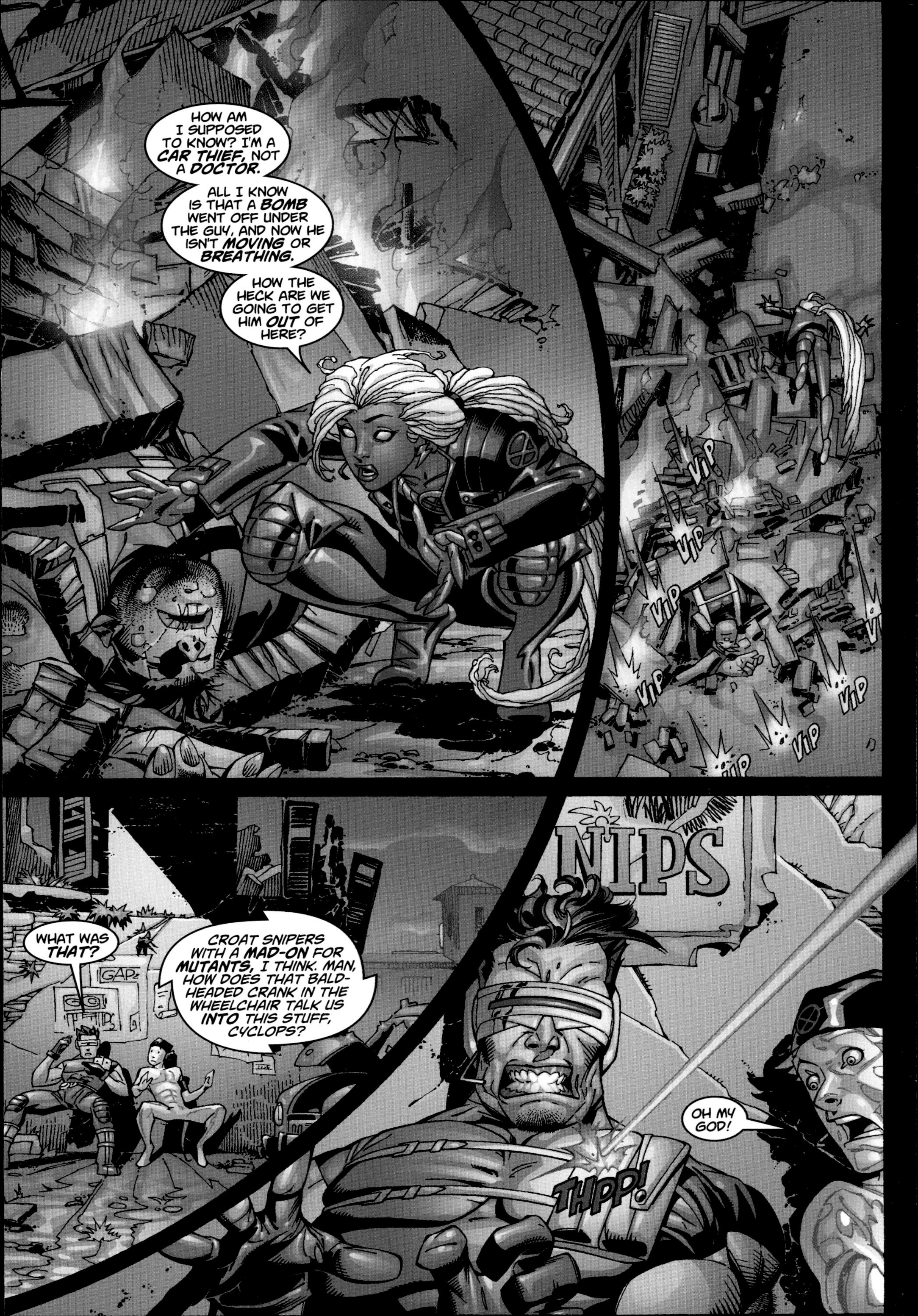
HOW AM I SUPPOSED TO KNOW? I'M A CAR THIEF, NOT A DOCTOR.
ALL I KNOW IS THAT A BOMB WENT OFF UNDER THE GUY, AND NOW HE ISN'T MOVING OR BREATHING.
HOW THE HECK ARE WE GOING TO GET HIM OUT OF HERE?
VIP
VIP
VIP
VIP
VIP
VIP
VIP
NIPS
WHAT WAS THAT?
CROAT SNIPERS WITH A MAD-ON FOR MUTANTS, I THINK. MAN, HOW DOES THAT BALD-HEADED CRANK IN THE WHEELCHAIR TALK US INTO THIS STUFF, CYCLOPS?
GAP
OH MY GOD!
THPP!

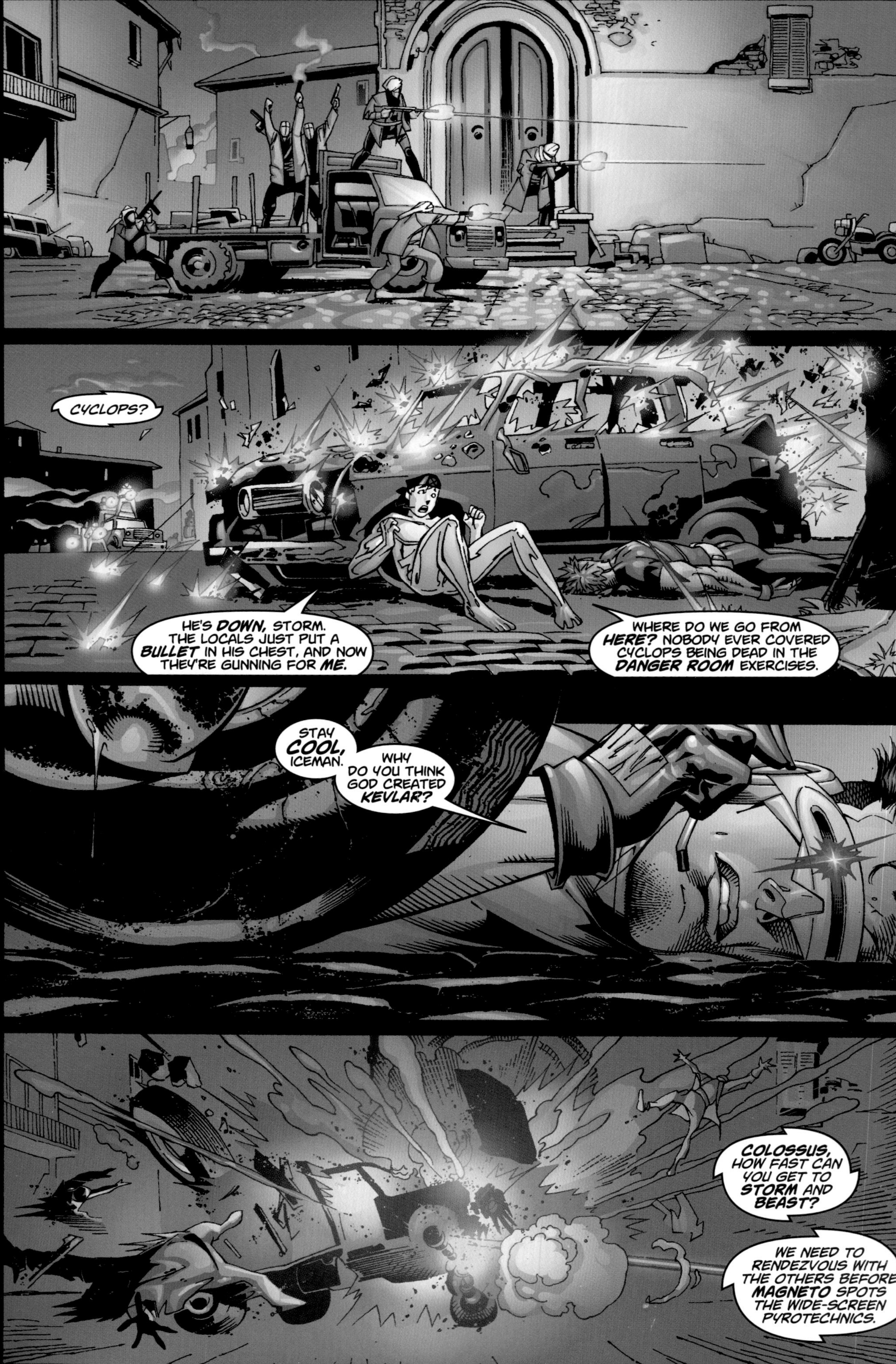
CYCLOPS?
HE'S DOWN, STORM. THE LOCALS JUST PUT A BULLET IN HIS CHEST, AND NOW THEY'RE GUNNING FOR ME.
WHERE DO WE GO FROM HERE? NOBODY EVER COVERED CYCLOPS BEING DEAD IN THE DANGER ROOM EXERCISES.
STAY COOL, ICEMAN.
WHY DO YOU THINK GOD CREATED KEVLAR?
COLOSSUS, HOW FAST CAN YOU GET TO STORM AND BEAST?
WE NEED TO RENDEZVOUS WITH THE OTHERS BEFORE MAGNETO SPOTS THE WIDE-SCREEN PYROTECHNICS.

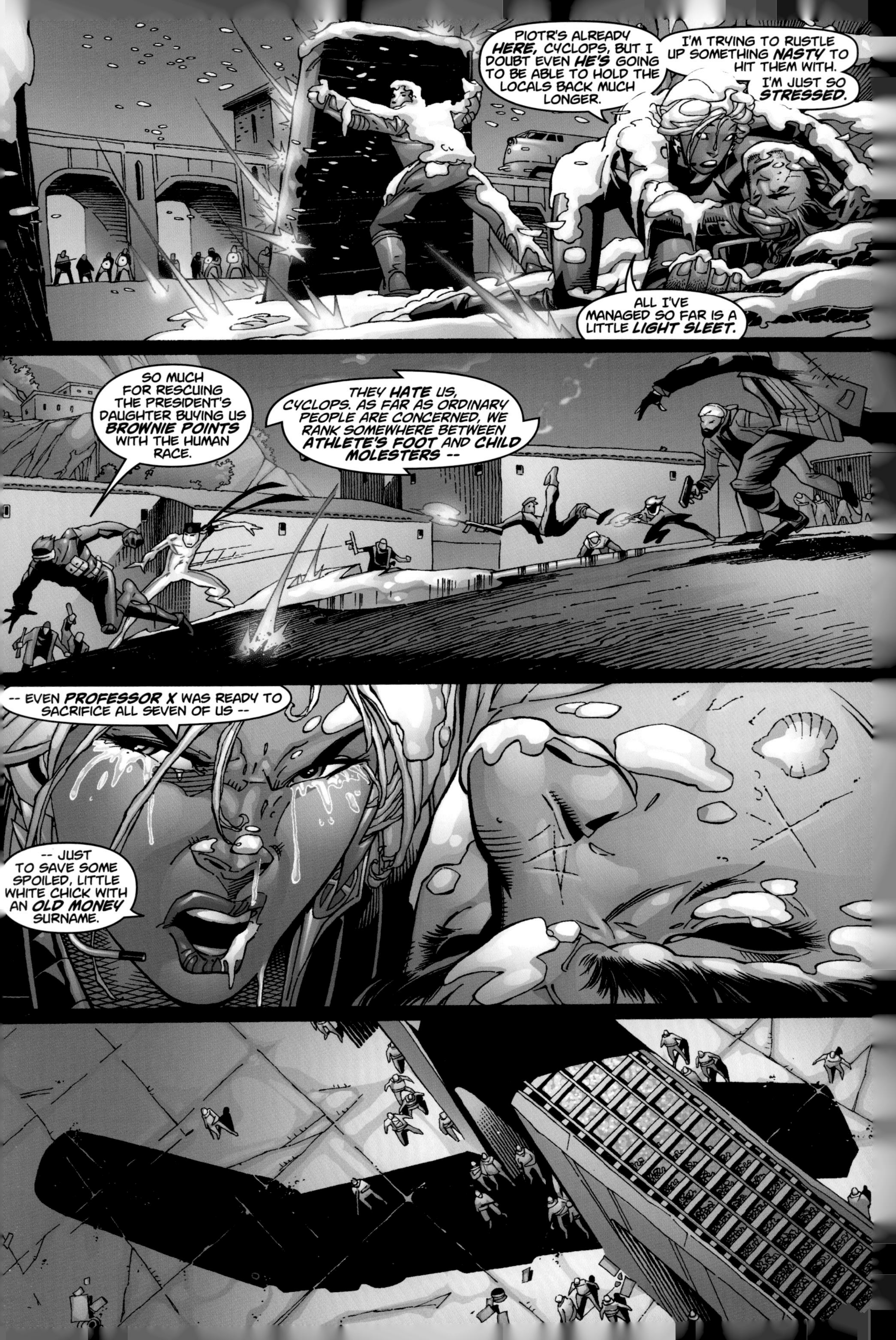
PIOTR'S ALREADY HERE, CYCLOPS, BUT I DOUBT EVEN HE'S GOING TO BE ABLE TO HOLD THE LOCALS BACK MUCH LONGER.
I'M TRYING TO RUSTLE UP SOMETHING NASTY TO HIT THEM WITH.
I'M JUST SO STRESSED.
ALL I'VE MANAGED SO FAR IS A LITTLE LIGHT SLEET.
SO MUCH FOR RESCUING THE PRESIDENT'S DAUGHTER BUYING US BROWNIE POINTS WITH THE HUMAN RACE.
THEY HATE US, CYCLOPS. AS FAR AS ORDINARY PEOPLE ARE CONCERNED, WE RANK SOMEWHERE BETWEEN ATHLETE'S FOOT AND CHILD MOLESTERS --
-- EVEN PROFESSOR X WAS READY TO SACRIFICE ALL SEVEN OF US --
-- JUST TO SAVE SOME SPOILED, LITTLE WHITE CHICK WITH AN OLD MONEY SURNAME.

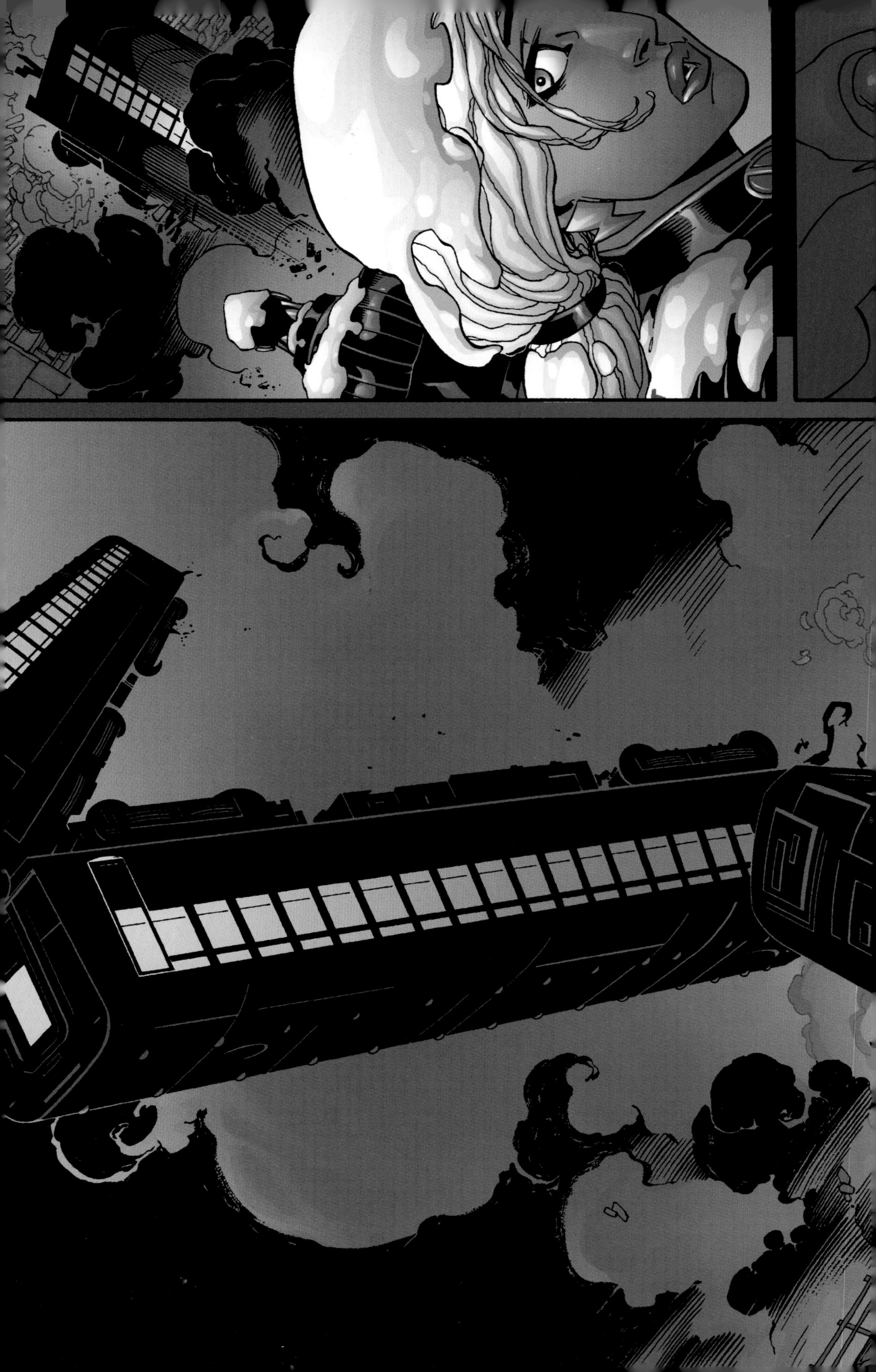

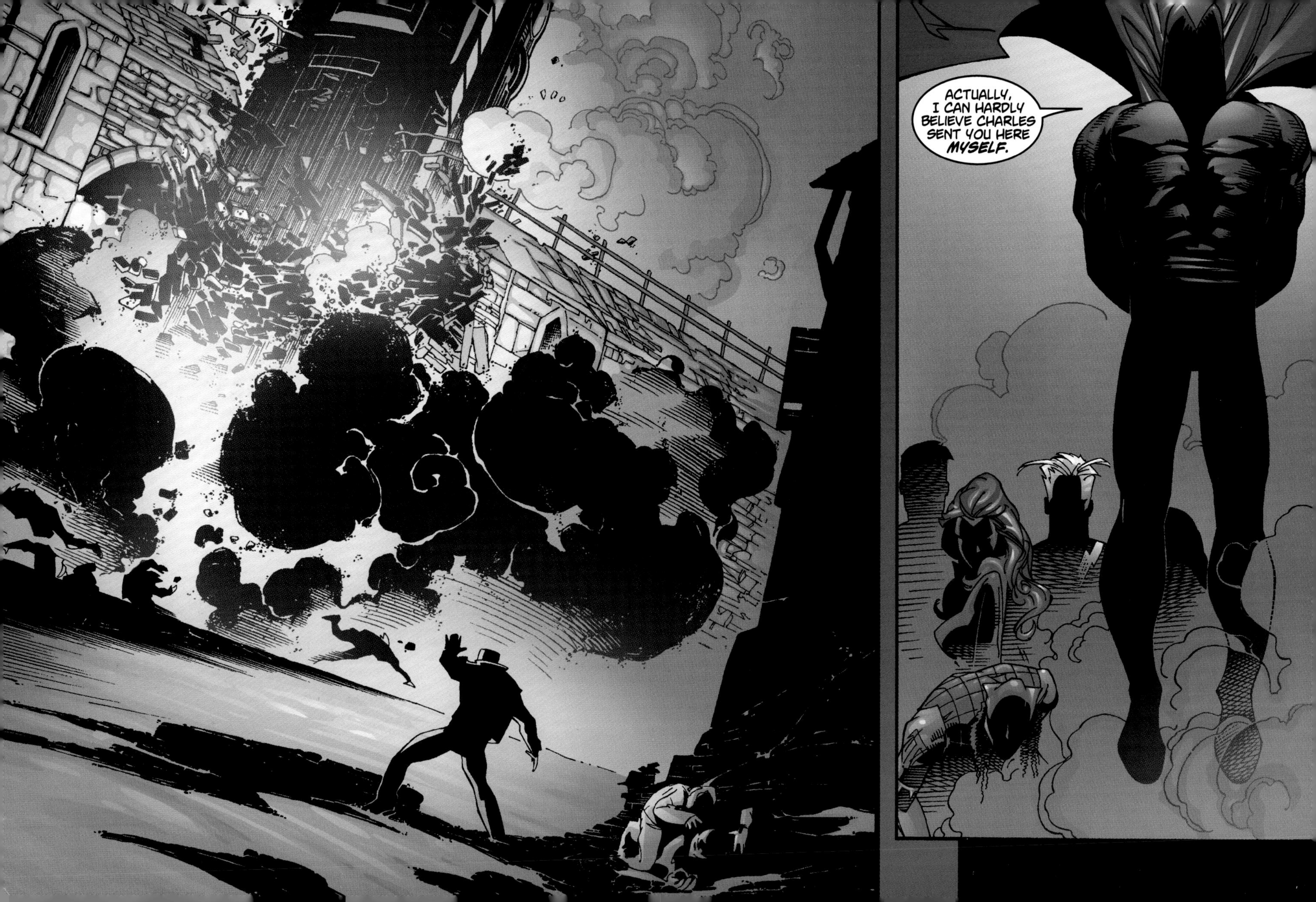
ACTUALLY, I CAN HARDLY BELIEVE CHARLES SENT YOU HERE MYSELF.

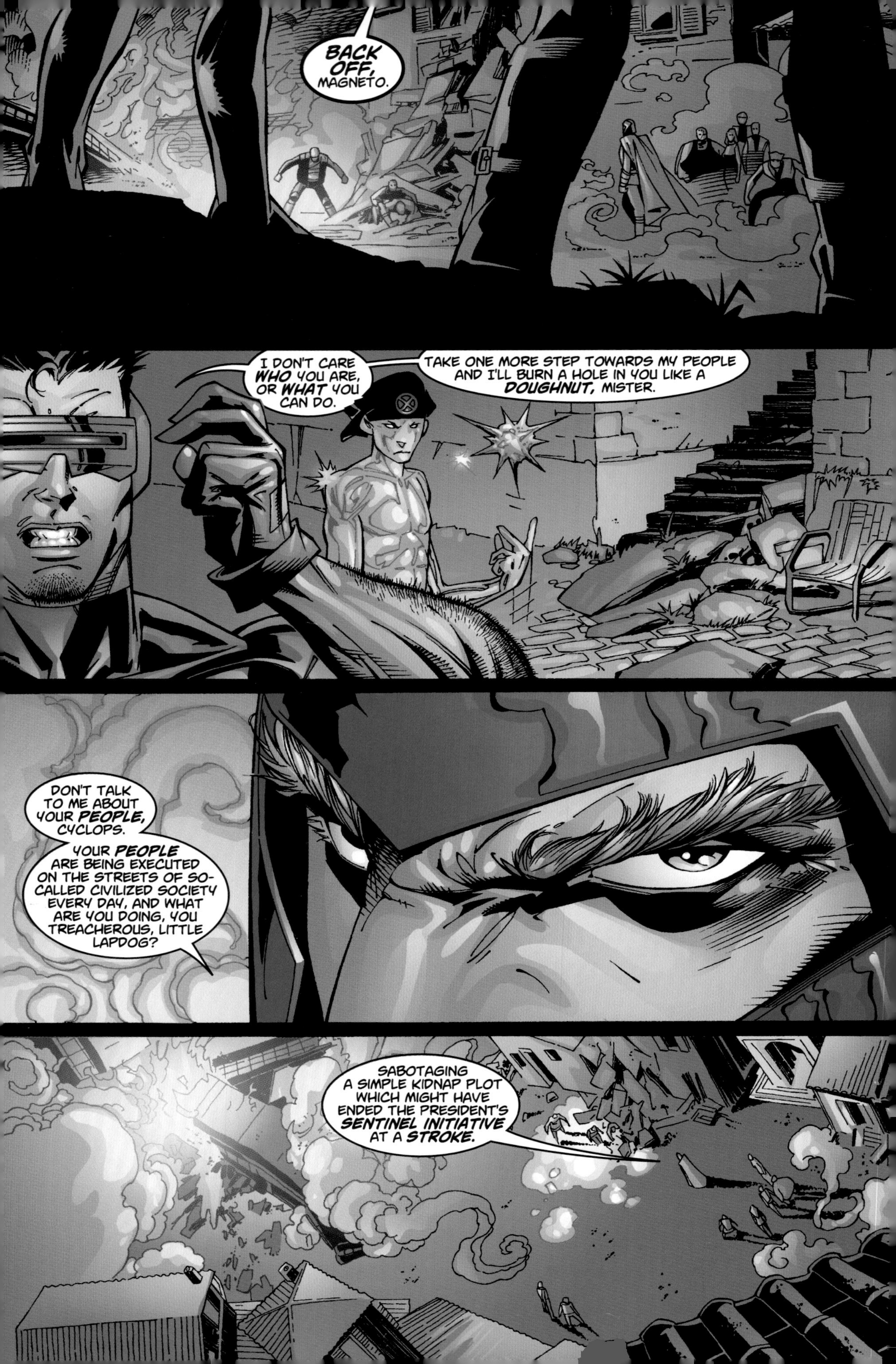
BACK OFF, MAGNETO.
I DON'T CARE WHO YOU ARE, OR WHAT YOU CAN DO.
TAKE ONE MORE STEP TOWARDS MY PEOPLE AND I'LL BURN A HOLE IN YOU LIKE A DOUGHNUT, MISTER.
DON'T TALK TO ME ABOUT YOUR PEOPLE, CYCLOPS.
YOUR PEOPLE ARE BEING EXECUTED ON THE STREETS OF SO-CALLED CIVILIZED SOCIETY EVERY DAY, AND WHAT ARE YOU DOING, YOU TREACHEROUS, LITTLE LAPDOG?
SABOTAGING A SIMPLE KIDNAP PLOT WHICH MIGHT HAVE ENDED THE PRESIDENT'S SENTINEL INITIATIVE AT A STROKE.

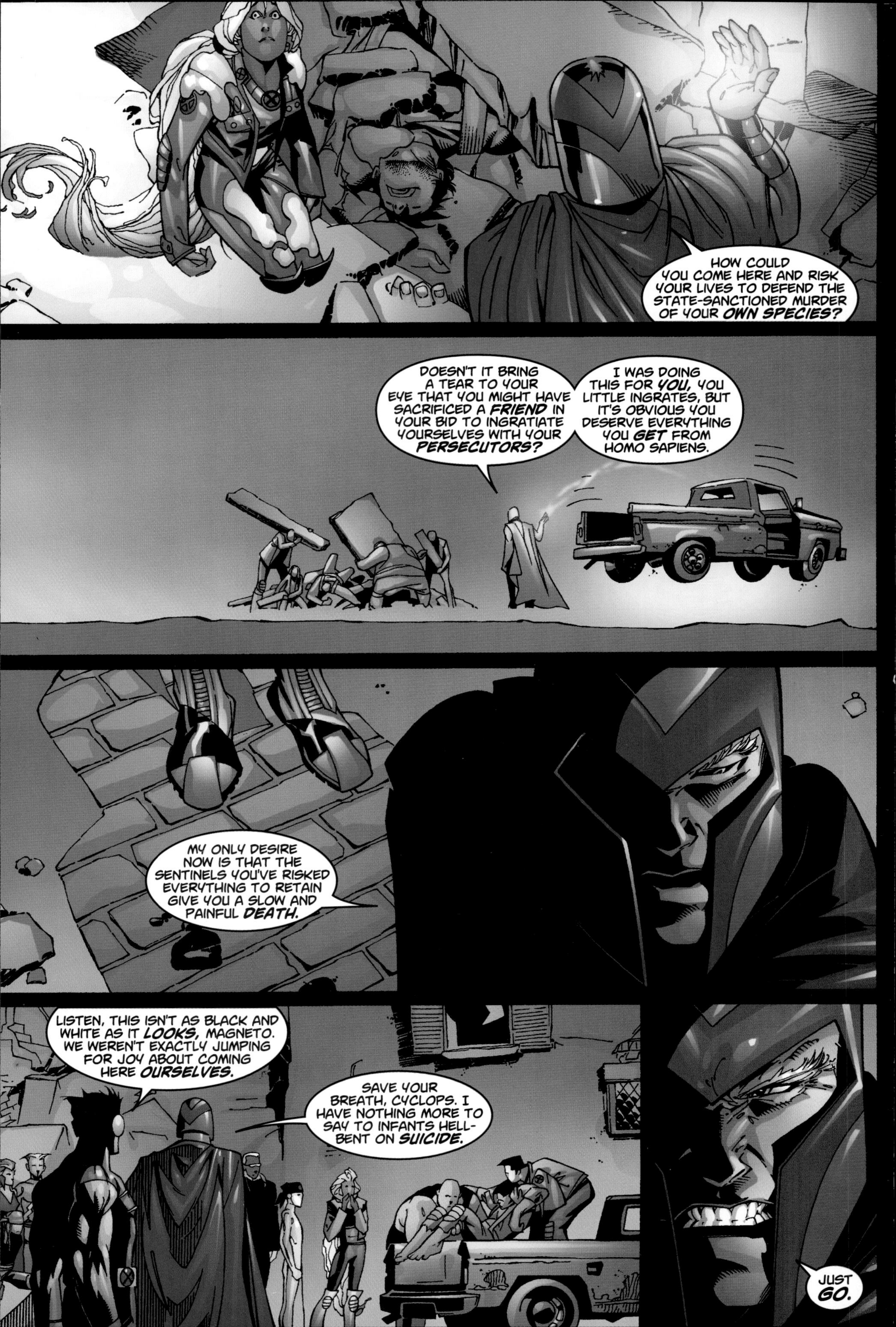
HOW COULD YOU COME HERE AND RISK YOUR LIVES TO DEFEND THE STATE-SANCTIONED MURDER OF YOUR OWN SPECIES?
DOESN'T IT BRING A TEAR TO YOUR EYE THAT YOU MIGHT HAVE SACRIFICED A FRIEND IN YOUR BID TO INGRATIATE YOURSELVES WITH YOUR PERSECUTORS?
I WAS DOING THIS FOR YOU, YOU LITTLE INGRATES, BUT IT'S OBVIOUS YOU DESERVE EVERYTHING YOU GET FROM HOMO SAPIENS.
MY ONLY DESIRE NOW IS THAT THE SENTINELS YOU'VE RISKED EVERYTHING TO RETAIN GIVE YOU A SLOW AND PAINFUL DEATH.
LISTEN, THIS ISN'T AS BLACK AND WHITE AS IT LOOKS, MAGNETO. WE WEREN'T EXACTLY JUMPING FOR JOY ABOUT COMING HERE OURSELVES.
SAVE YOUR BREATH, CYCLOPS. I HAVE NOTHING MORE TO SAY TO INFANTS HELL-BENT ON SUICIDE.
JUST GO.

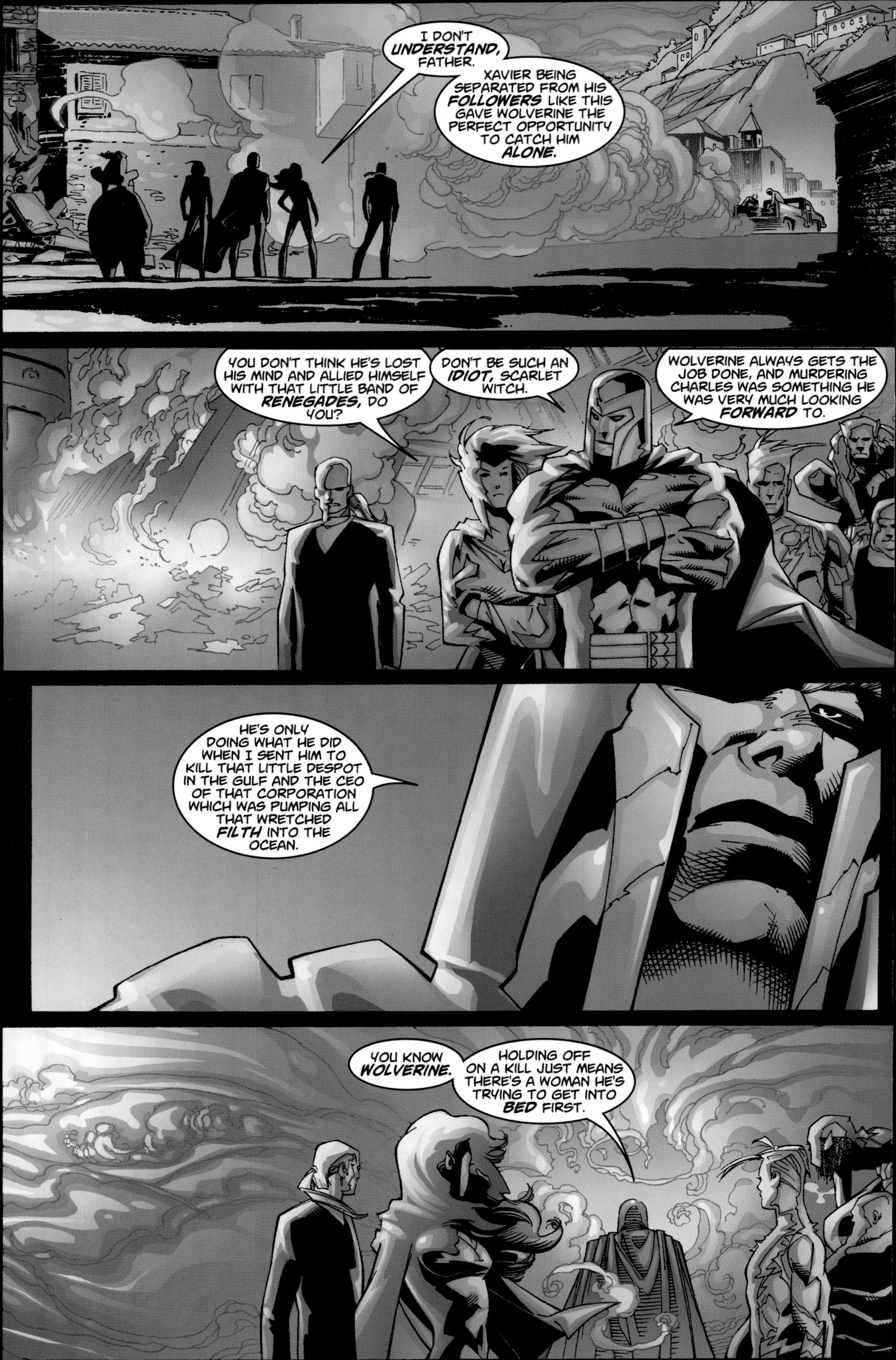
I DON'T UNDERSTAND, FATHER.
XAVIER BEING SEPARATED FROM HIS FOLLOWERS LIKE THIS GAVE WOLVERINE THE PERFECT OPPORTUNITY TO CATCH HIM ALONE.
YOU DON'T THINK HE'S LOST HIS MIND AND ALLIED HIMSELF WITH THAT LITTLE BAND OF RENEGADES, DO YOU?
DON'T BE SUCH AN IDIOT, SCARLET WITCH.
WOLVERINE ALWAYS GETS THE JOB DONE, AND MURDERING CHARLES WAS SOMETHING HE WAS VERY MUCH LOOKING FORWARD TO.
HE'S ONLY DOING WHAT HE DID WHEN I SENT HIM TO KILL THAT LITTLE DESPOT IN THE GULF AND THE CEO OF THAT CORPORATION WHICH WAS PUMPING ALL THAT WRETCHED FILTH INTO THE OCEAN.
YOU KNOW WOLVERINE.
HOLDING OFF ON A KILL JUST MEANS THERE'S A WOMAN HE'S TRYING TO GET INTO BED FIRST.

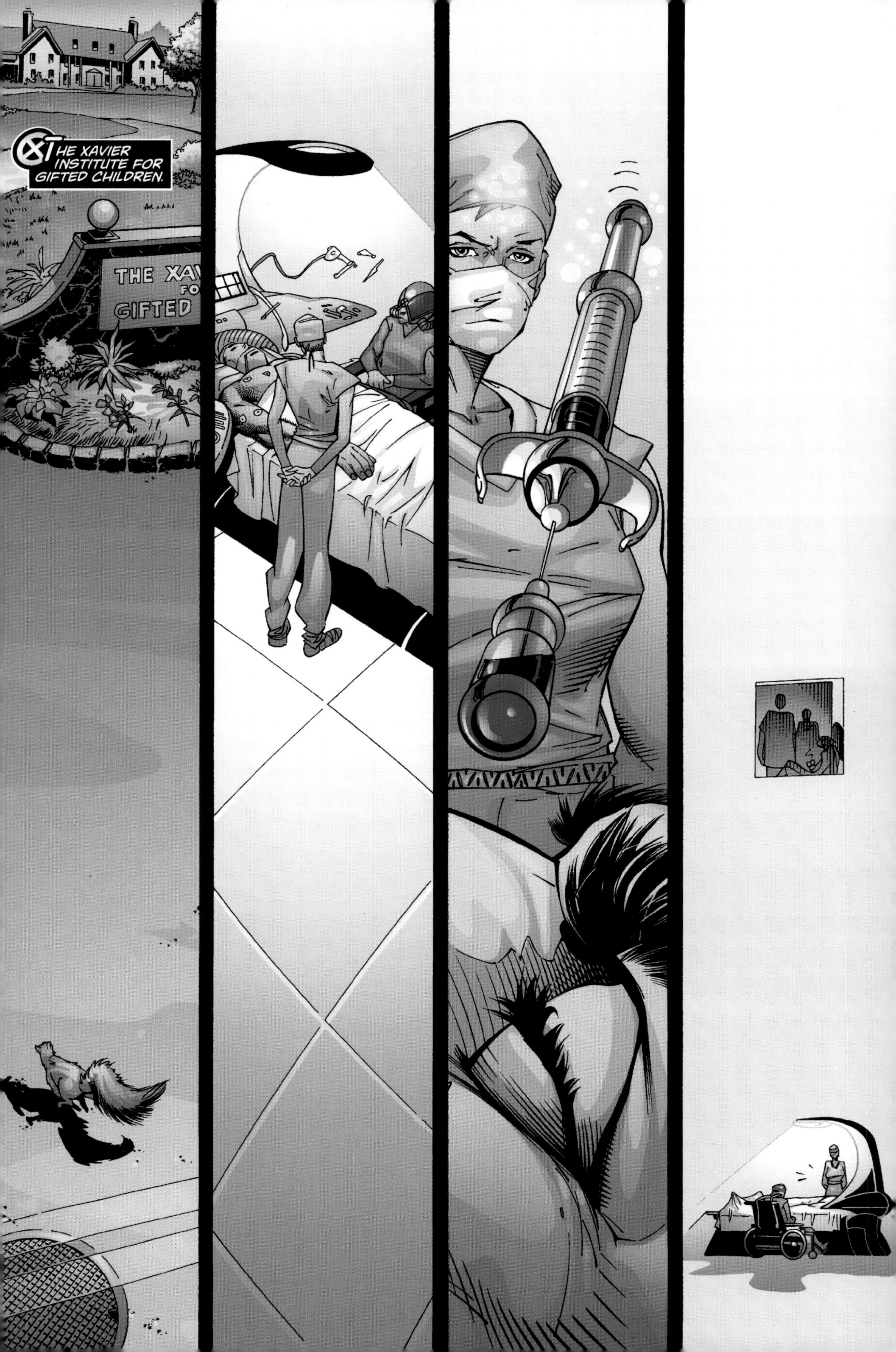
THE XAVIER INSTITUTE FOR GIFTED CHILDREN.
THE XAV
FO
GIFTED

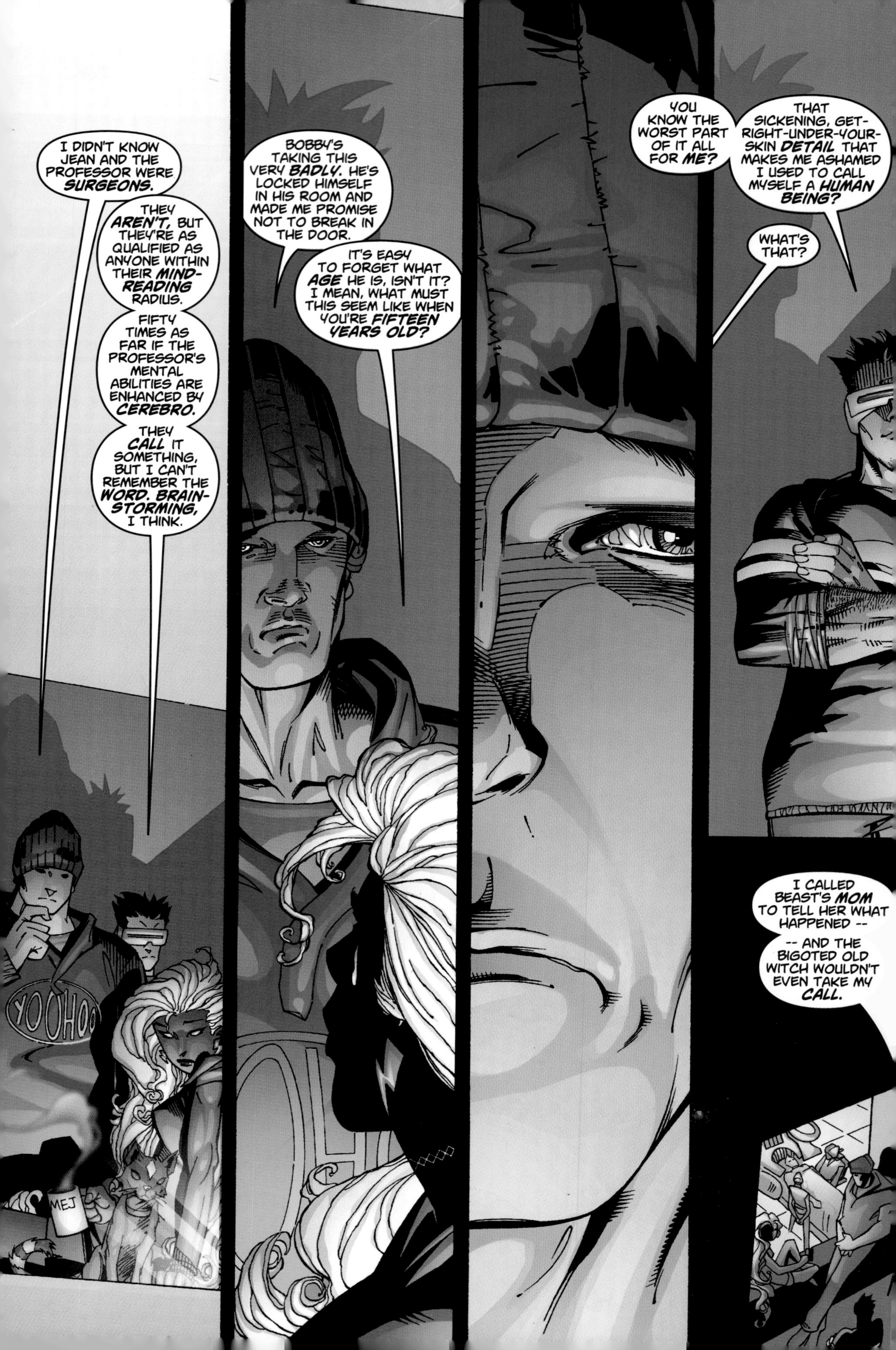
I DIDN'T KNOW JEAN AND THE PROFESSOR WERE SURGEONS.
THEY AREN'T, BUT THEY'RE AS QUALIFIED AS ANYONE WITHIN THEIR MIND-READING RADIUS.
FIFTY TIMES AS FAR IF THE PROFESSOR'S MENTAL ABILITIES ARE ENHANCED BY CEREBRO.
THEY CALL IT SOMETHING, BUT I CAN'T REMEMBER THE WORD. BRAIN-STORMING, I THINK.
YOOHOO
MEJ
BOBBY'S TAKING THIS VERY BADLY. HE'S LOCKED HIMSELF IN HIS ROOM AND MADE ME PROMISE NOT TO BREAK IN THE DOOR.
IT'S EASY TO FORGET WHAT AGE HE IS, ISN'T IT? I MEAN, WHAT MUST THIS SEEM LIKE WHEN YOU'RE FIFTEEN YEARS OLD?
YOU KNOW THE WORST PART OF IT ALL FOR ME?
WHAT'S THAT?
THAT SICKENING, GET-RIGHT-UNDER-YOUR-SKIN DETAIL THAT MAKES ME ASHAMED I USED TO CALL MYSELF A HUMAN BEING?
I CALLED BEAST'S MOM TO TELL HER WHAT HAPPENED --
-- AND THE BIGOTED OLD WITCH WOULDN'T EVEN TAKE MY CALL.

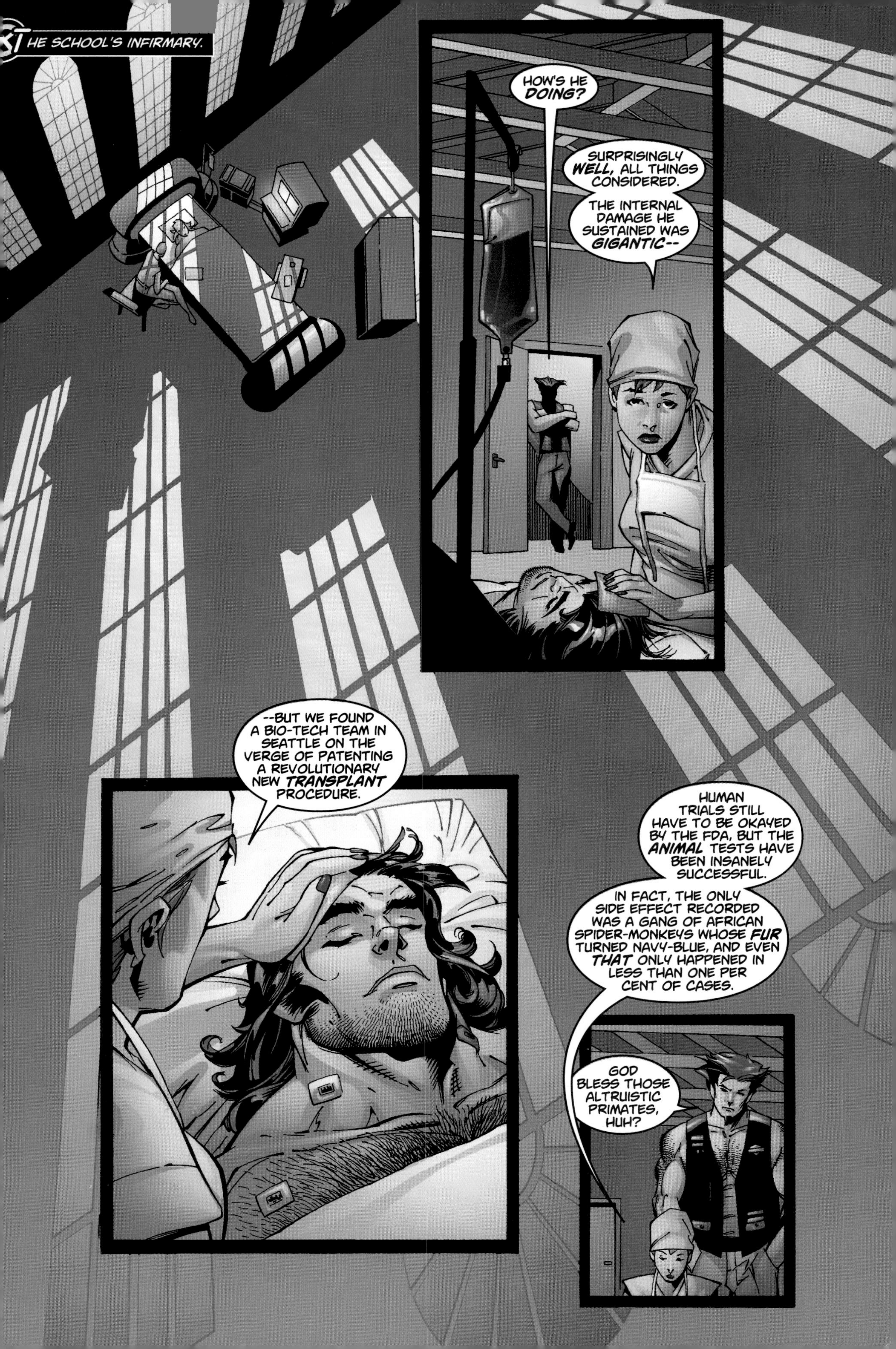
THE SCHOOL'S INFIRMARY.
HOW'S HE DOING?
SURPRISINGLY WELL, ALL THINGS CONSIDERED.
THE INTERNAL DAMAGE HE SUSTAINED WAS GIGANTIC--
--BUT WE FOUND A BIO-TECH TEAM IN SEATTLE ON THE VERGE OF PATENTING A REVOLUTIONARY NEW TRANSPLANT PROCEDURE.
HUMAN TRIALS STILL HAVE TO BE OKAYED BY THE FDA, BUT THE ANIMAL TESTS HAVE BEEN INSANELY SUCCESSFUL.
IN FACT, THE ONLY SIDE EFFECT RECORDED WAS A GANG OF AFRICAN SPIDER-MONKEYS WHOSE FUR TURNED NAVY-BLUE, AND EVEN THAT ONLY HAPPENED IN LESS THAN ONE PER CENT OF CASES.
GOD BLESS THOSE ALTRUISTIC PRIMATES, HUH?

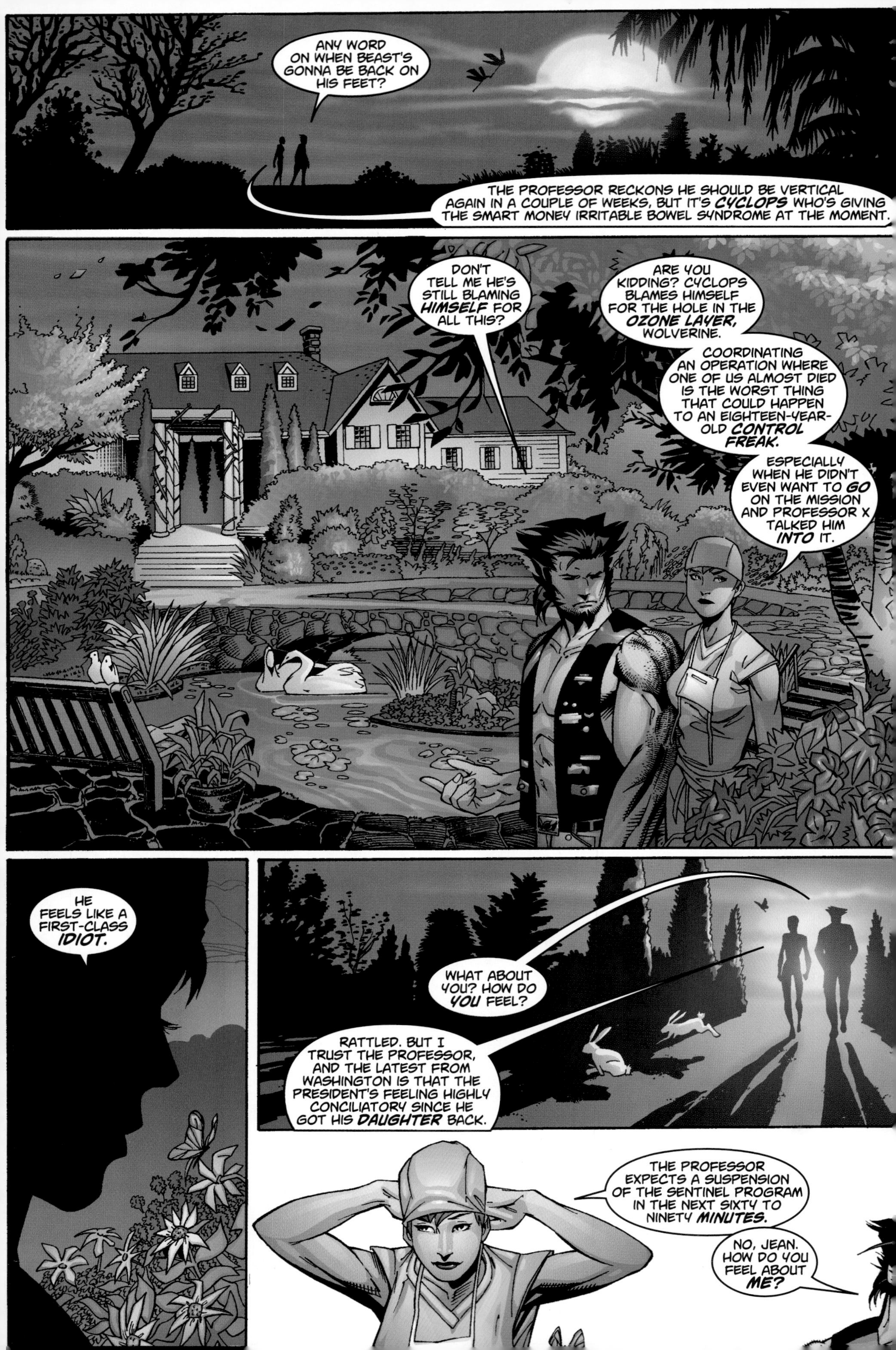
ANY WORD ON WHEN BEAST'S GONNA BE BACK ON HIS FEET?
THE PROFESSOR RECKONS HE SHOULD BE VERTICAL AGAIN IN A COUPLE OF WEEKS, BUT IT'S CYCLOPS WHO'S GIVING THE SMART MONEY IRRITABLE BOWEL SYNDROME AT THE MOMENT.
DON'T TELL ME HE'S STILL BLAMING HIMSELF FOR ALL THIS?
ARE YOU KIDDING? CYCLOPS BLAMES HIMSELF FOR THE HOLE IN THE OZONE LAYER, WOLVERINE.
COORDINATING AN OPERATION WHERE ONE OF US ALMOST DIED IS THE WORST THING THAT COULD HAPPEN TO AN EIGHTEEN-YEAR-OLD CONTROL FREAK.
ESPECIALLY WHEN HE DIDN'T EVEN WANT TO GO ON THE MISSION AND PROFESSOR X TALKED HIM INTO IT.
HE FEELS LIKE A FIRST-CLASS IDIOT.
WHAT ABOUT YOU? HOW DO YOU FEEL?
RATTLED. BUT I TRUST THE PROFESSOR, AND THE LATEST FROM WASHINGTON IS THAT THE PRESIDENT'S FEELING HIGHLY CONCILIATORY SINCE HE GOT HIS DAUGHTER BACK.
THE PROFESSOR EXPECTS A SUSPENSION OF THE SENTINEL PROGRAM IN THE NEXT SIXTY TO NINETY MINUTES.
NO, JEAN. HOW DO YOU FEEL ABOUT ME?

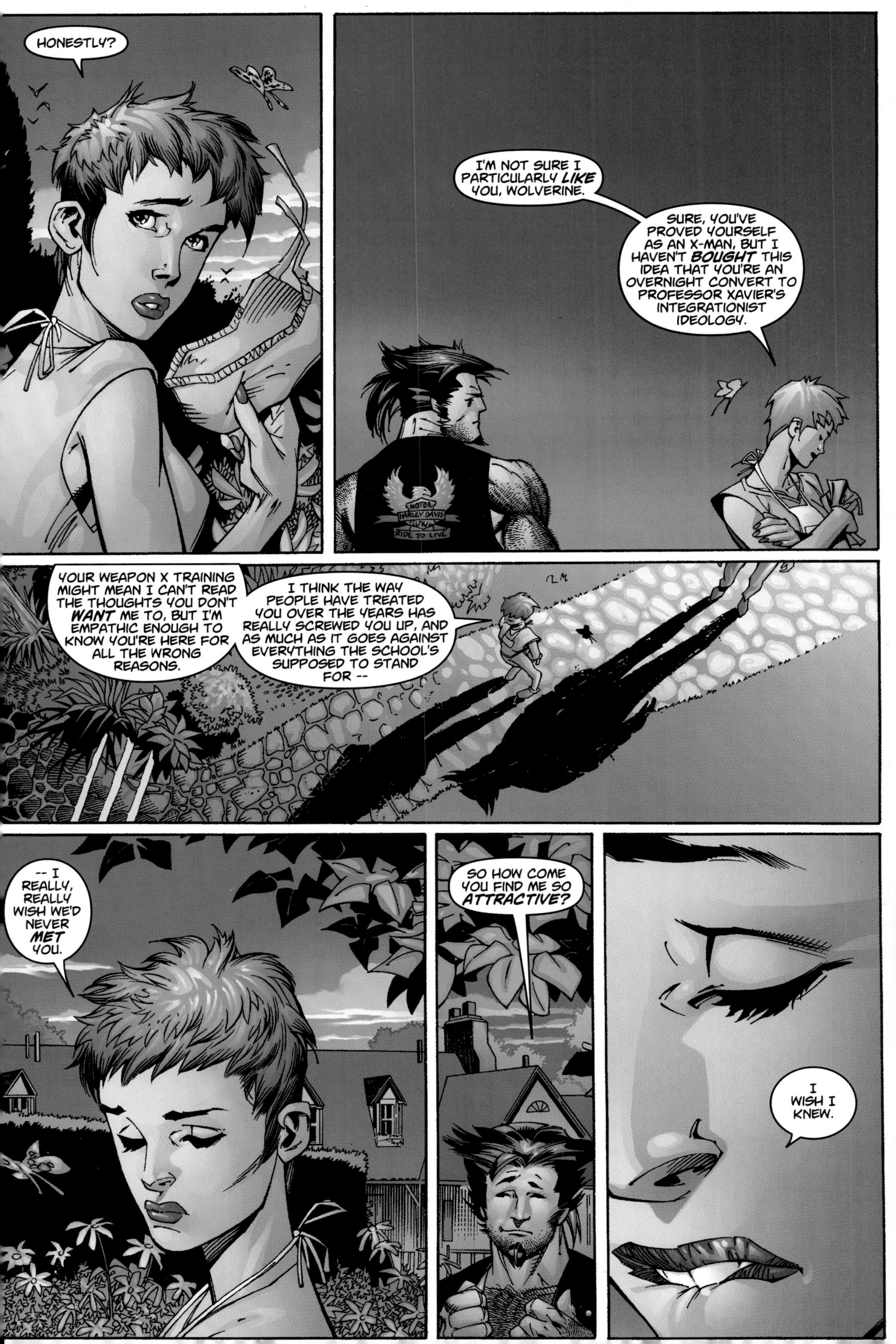
HONESTLY?
I'M NOT SURE I PARTICULARLY LIKE YOU, WOLVERINE.
SURE, YOU'VE PROVED YOURSELF AS AN X-MAN, BUT I HAVEN'T BOUGHT THIS IDEA THAT YOU'RE AN OVERNIGHT CONVERT TO PROFESSOR XAVIER'S INTEGRATIONIST IDEOLOGY.
MOTOR HARLEY DAVIS RIDE TO LIVE
YOUR WEAPON X TRAINING MIGHT MEAN I CAN'T READ THE THOUGHTS YOU DON'T WANT ME TO, BUT I'M EMPATHIC ENOUGH TO KNOW YOU'RE HERE FOR ALL THE WRONG REASONS.
I THINK THE WAY PEOPLE HAVE TREATED YOU OVER THE YEARS HAS REALLY SCREWED YOU UP, AND AS MUCH AS IT GOES AGAINST EVERYTHING THE SCHOOL'S SUPPOSED TO STAND FOR --
-- I REALLY, REALLY WISH WE'D NEVER MET YOU.
SO HOW COME YOU FIND ME SO ATTRACTIVE?
I WISH I KNEW.

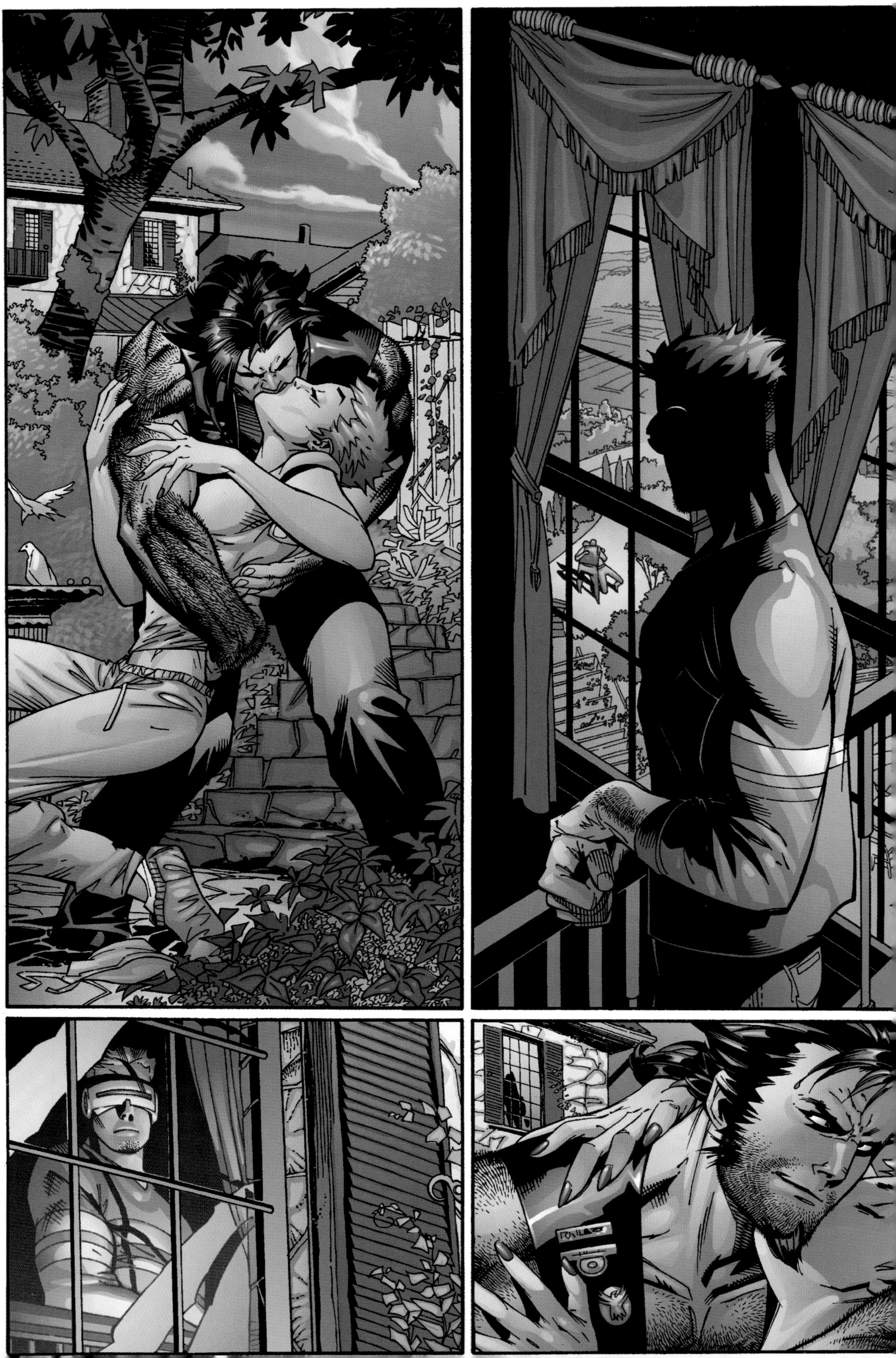

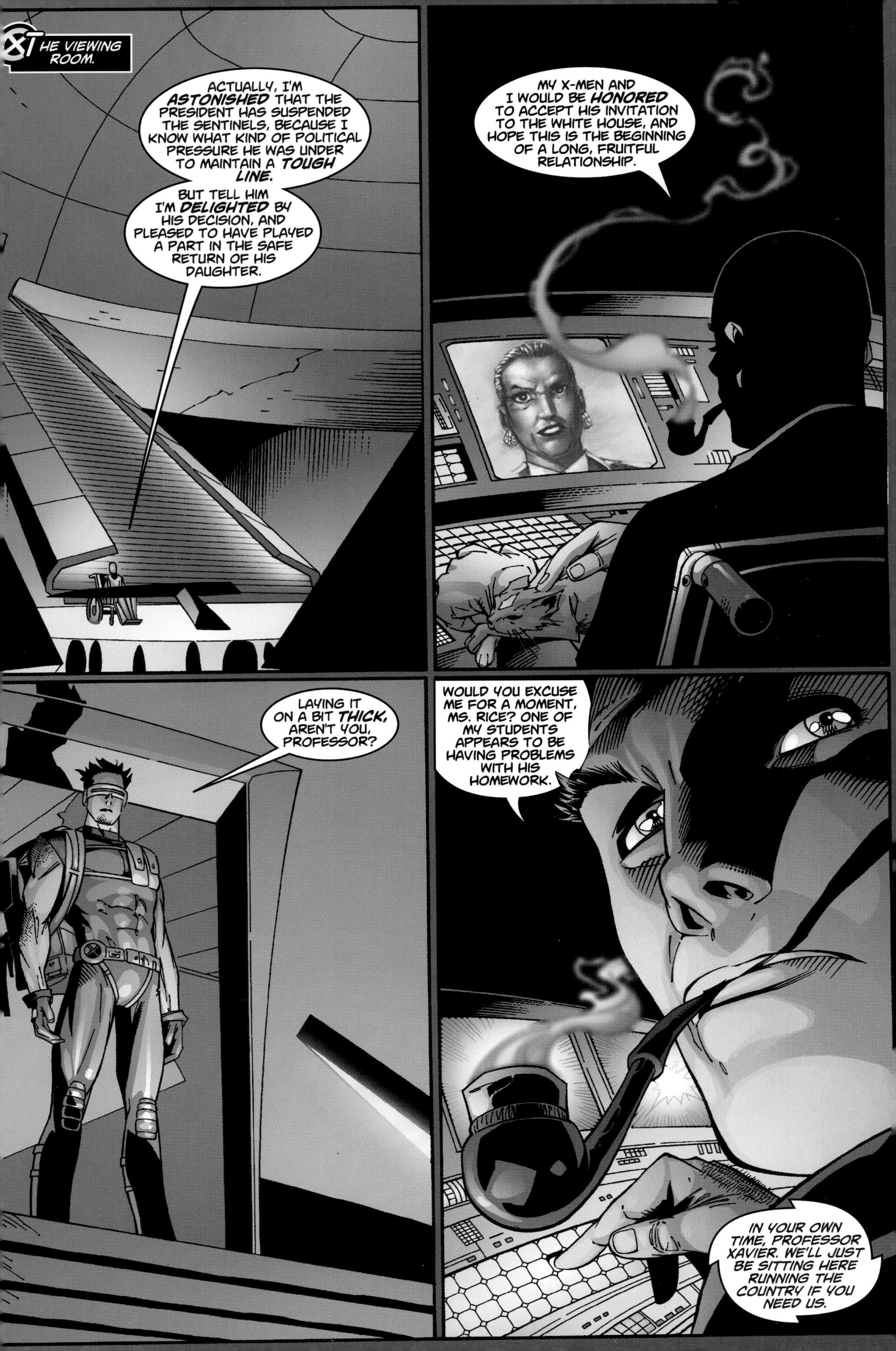
THE VIEWING ROOM.
ACTUALLY, I'M ASTONISHED THAT THE PRESIDENT HAS SUSPENDED THE SENTINELS, BECAUSE I KNOW WHAT KIND OF POLITICAL PRESSURE HE WAS UNDER TO MAINTAIN A TOUGH LINE.
BUT TELL HIM I'M DELIGHTED BY HIS DECISION, AND PLEASED TO HAVE PLAYED A PART IN THE SAFE RETURN OF HIS DAUGHTER.
MY X-MEN AND I WOULD BE HONORED TO ACCEPT HIS INVITATION TO THE WHITE HOUSE, AND HOPE THIS IS THE BEGINNING OF A LONG, FRUITFUL RELATIONSHIP.
LAYING IT ON A BIT THICK, AREN'T YOU, PROFESSOR?
WOULD YOU EXCUSE ME FOR A MOMENT, MS. RICE? ONE OF MY STUDENTS APPEARS TO BE HAVING PROBLEMS WITH HIS HOMEWORK.
IN YOUR OWN TIME, PROFESSOR XAVIER. WE'LL JUST BE SITTING HERE RUNNING THE COUNTRY IF YOU NEED US.

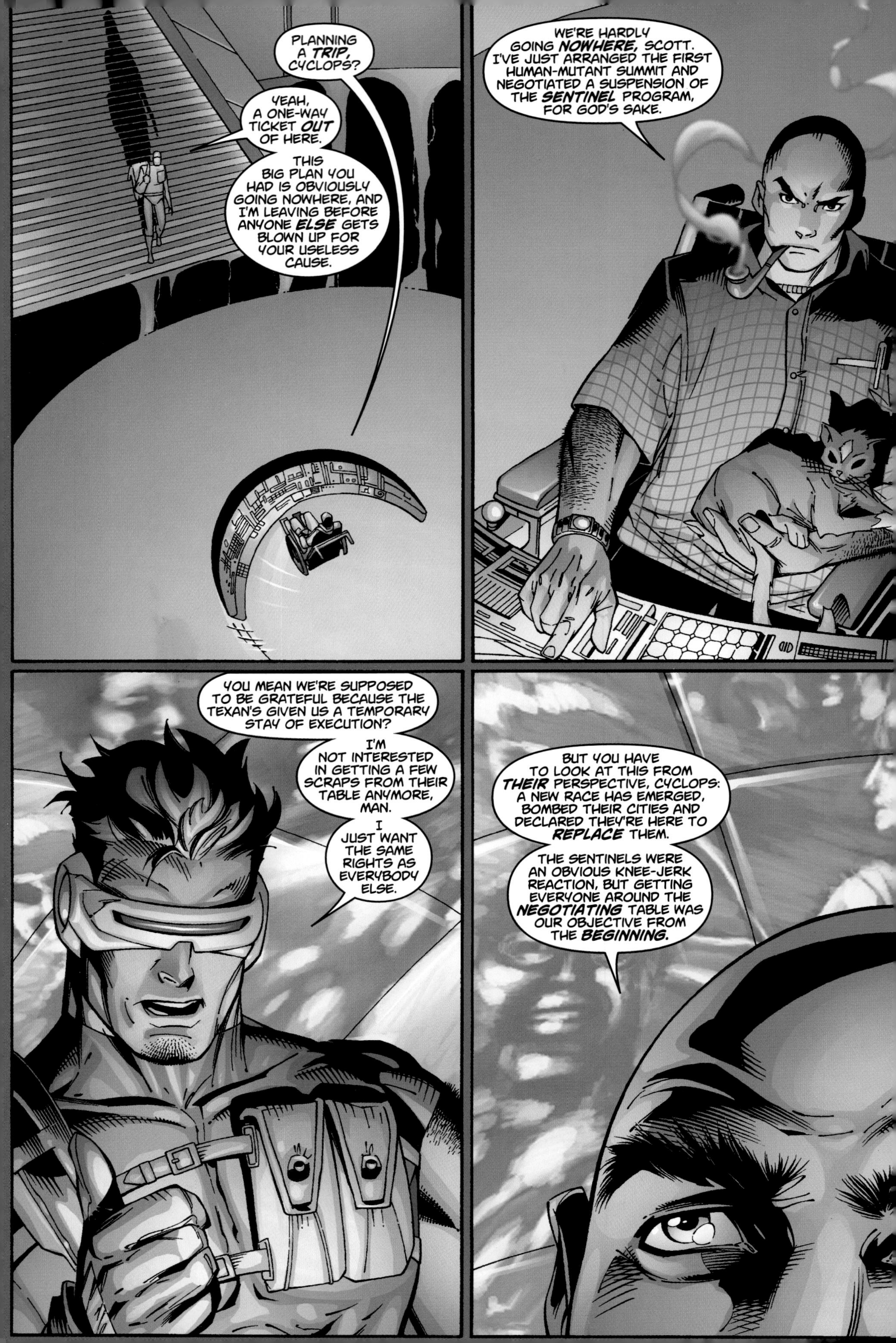
PLANNING A TRIP, CYCLOPS?
YEAH, A ONE-WAY TICKET OUT OF HERE.
THIS BIG PLAN YOU HAD IS OBVIOUSLY GOING NOWHERE, AND I'M LEAVING BEFORE ANYONE ELSE GETS BLOWN UP FOR YOUR USELESS CAUSE.
WE'RE HARDLY GOING NOWHERE, SCOTT. I'VE JUST ARRANGED THE FIRST HUMAN-MUTANT SUMMIT AND NEGOTIATED A SUSPENSION OF THE SENTINEL PROGRAM, FOR GOD'S SAKE.
YOU MEAN WE'RE SUPPOSED TO BE GRATEFUL BECAUSE THE TEXAN'S GIVEN US A TEMPORARY STAY OF EXECUTION?
I'M NOT INTERESTED IN GETTING A FEW SCRAPS FROM THEIR TABLE ANYMORE, MAN.
I JUST WANT THE SAME RIGHTS AS EVERYBODY ELSE.
BUT YOU HAVE TO LOOK AT THIS FROM THEIR PERSPECTIVE, CYCLOPS: A NEW RACE HAS EMERGED, BOMBED THEIR CITIES AND DECLARED THEY'RE HERE TO REPLACE THEM.
THE SENTINELS WERE AN OBVIOUS KNEE-JERK REACTION, BUT GETTING EVERYONE AROUND THE NEGOTIATING TABLE WAS OUR OBJECTIVE FROM THE BEGINNING.

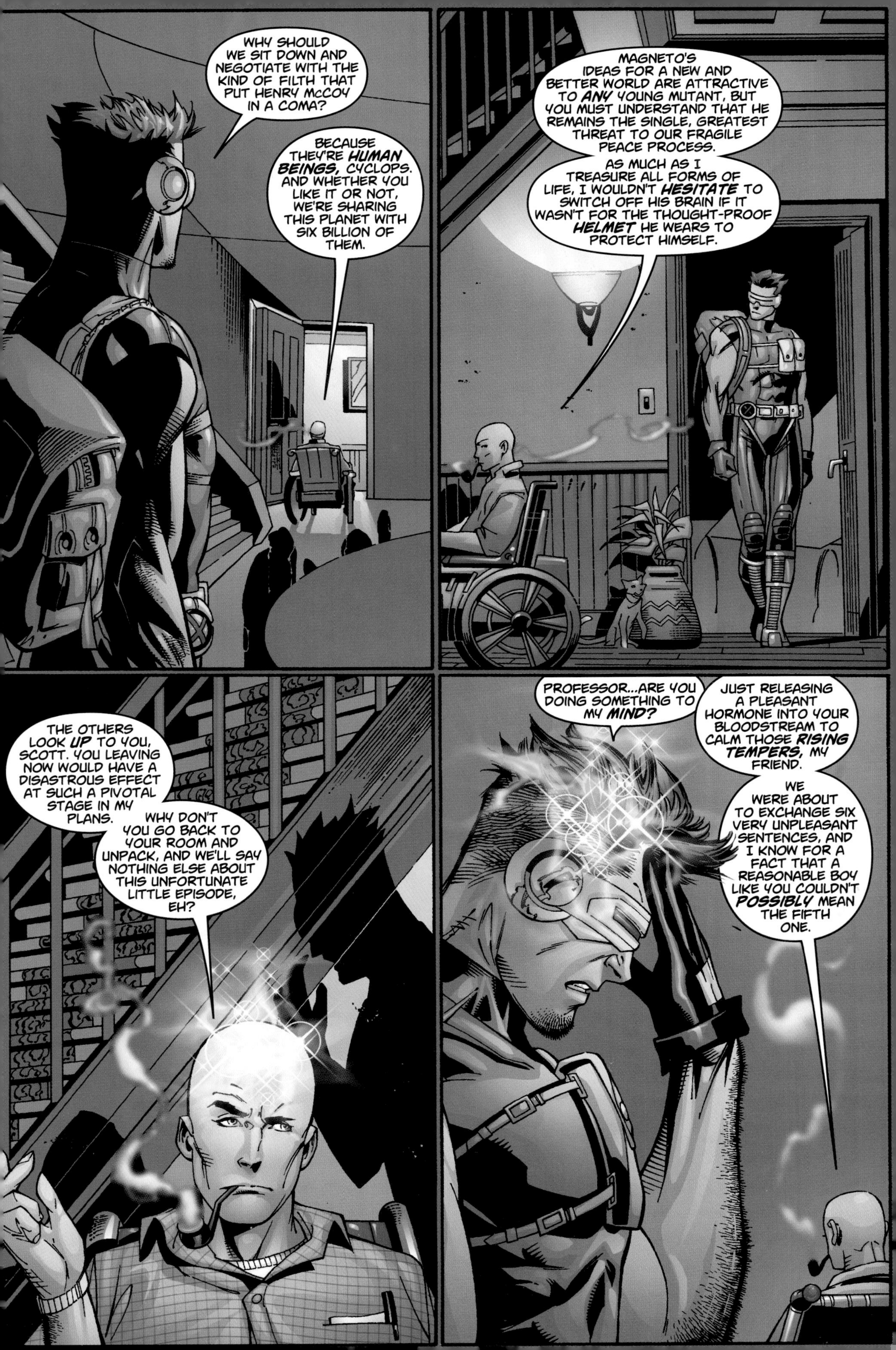
WHY SHOULD WE SIT DOWN AND NEGOTIATE WITH THE KIND OF FILTH THAT PUT HENRY McCOY IN A COMA?
BECAUSE THEY'RE HUMAN BEINGS, CYCLOPS. AND WHETHER YOU LIKE IT OR NOT, WE'RE SHARING THIS PLANET WITH SIX BILLION OF THEM.
MAGNETO'S IDEAS FOR A NEW AND BETTER WORLD ARE ATTRACTIVE TO ANY YOUNG MUTANT, BUT YOU MUST UNDERSTAND THAT HE REMAINS THE SINGLE, GREATEST THREAT TO OUR FRAGILE PEACE PROCESS.
AS MUCH AS I TREASURE ALL FORMS OF LIFE, I WOULDN'T HESITATE TO SWITCH OFF HIS BRAIN IF IT WASN'T FOR THE THOUGHT-PROOF HELMET HE WEARS TO PROTECT HIMSELF.
THE OTHERS LOOK UP TO YOU, SCOTT. YOU LEAVING NOW WOULD HAVE A DISASTROUS EFFECT AT SUCH A PIVOTAL STAGE IN MY PLANS.
WHY DON'T YOU GO BACK TO YOUR ROOM AND UNPACK, AND WE'LL SAY NOTHING ELSE ABOUT THIS UNFORTUNATE LITTLE EPISODE, EH?
PROFESSOR...ARE YOU DOING SOMETHING TO MY MIND?
JUST RELEASING A PLEASANT HORMONE INTO YOUR BLOODSTREAM TO CALM THOSE RISING TEMPERS, MY FRIEND.
WE WERE ABOUT TO EXCHANGE SIX VERY UNPLEASANT SENTENCES, AND I KNOW FOR A FACT THAT A REASONABLE BOY LIKE YOU COULDN'T POSSIBLY MEAN THE FIFTH ONE.

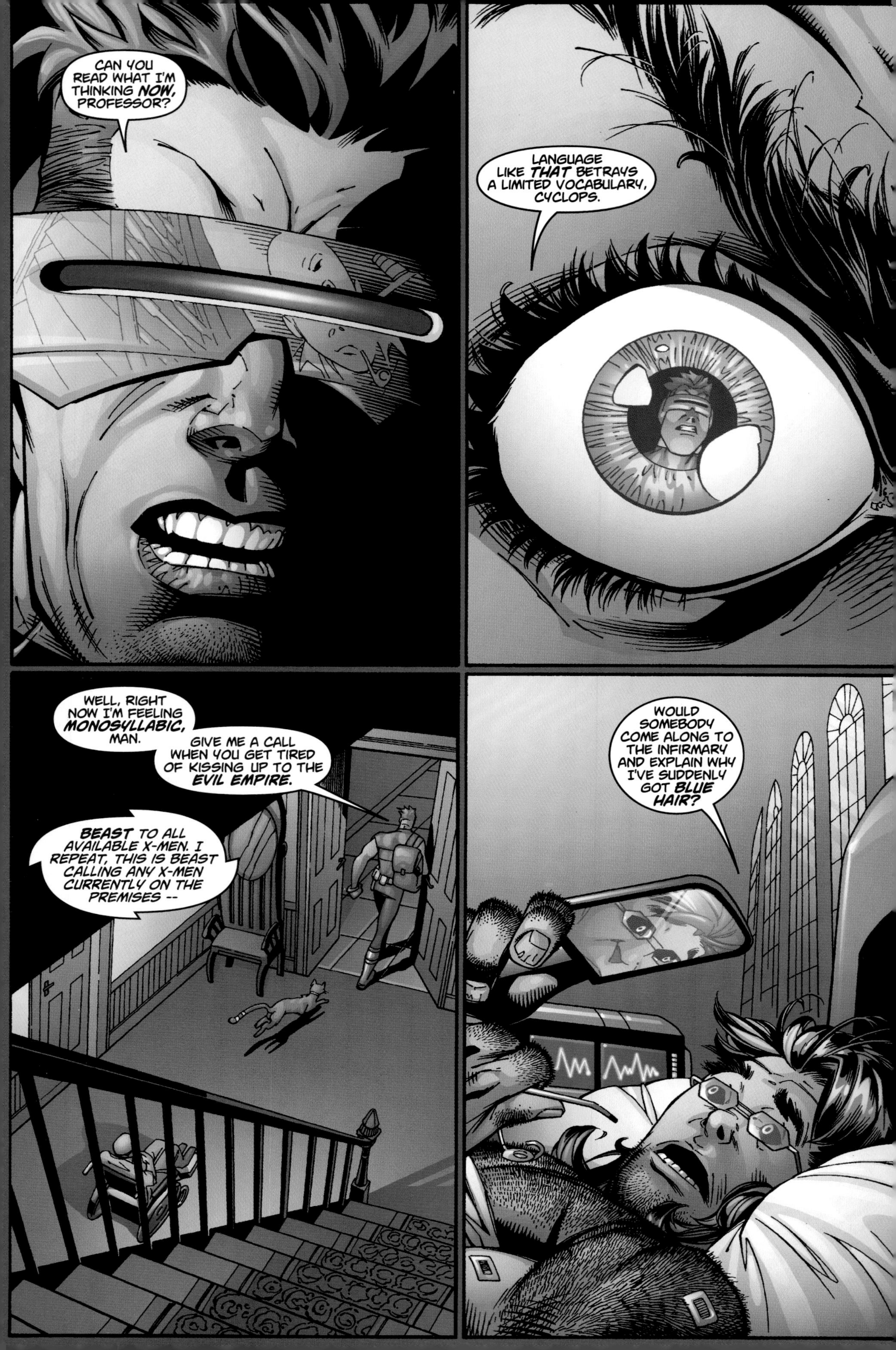
CAN YOU READ WHAT I'M THINKING NOW, PROFESSOR?
LANGUAGE LIKE THAT BETRAYS A LIMITED VOCABULARY, CYCLOPS.
WELL, RIGHT NOW I'M FEELING MONOSYLLABIC, MAN.
GIVE ME A CALL WHEN YOU GET TIRED OF KISSING UP TO THE EVIL EMPIRE.
BEAST TO ALL AVAILABLE X-MEN. I REPEAT, THIS IS BEAST CALLING ANY X-MEN CURRENTLY ON THE PREMISES --
WOULD SOMEBODY COME ALONG TO THE INFIRMARY AND EXPLAIN WHY I'VE SUDDENLY GOT BLUE HAIR?

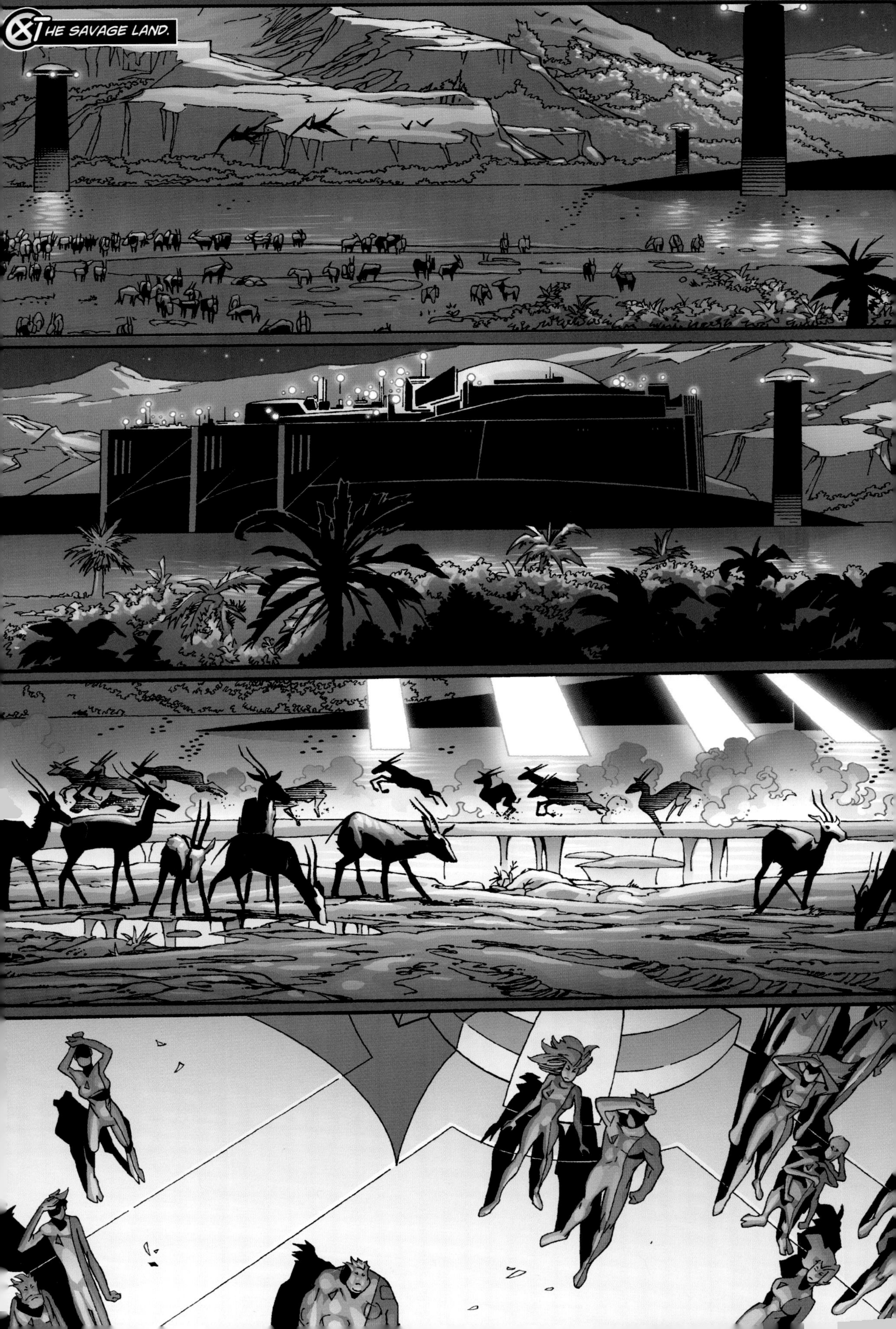
THE SAVAGE LAND.

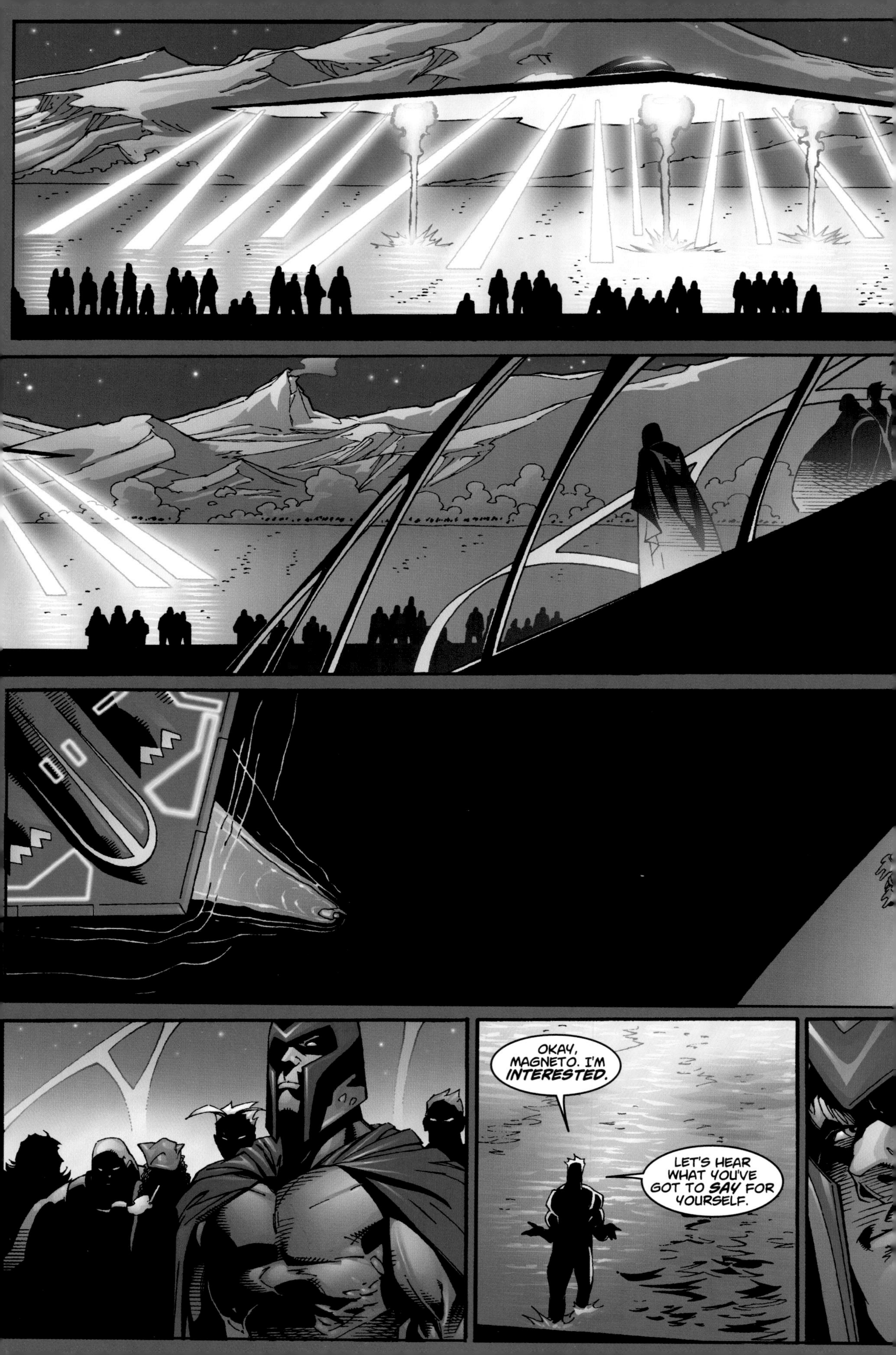
OKAY, MAGNETO. I'M INTERESTED.
LET'S HEAR WHAT YOU'VE GOT TO SAY FOR YOURSELF.

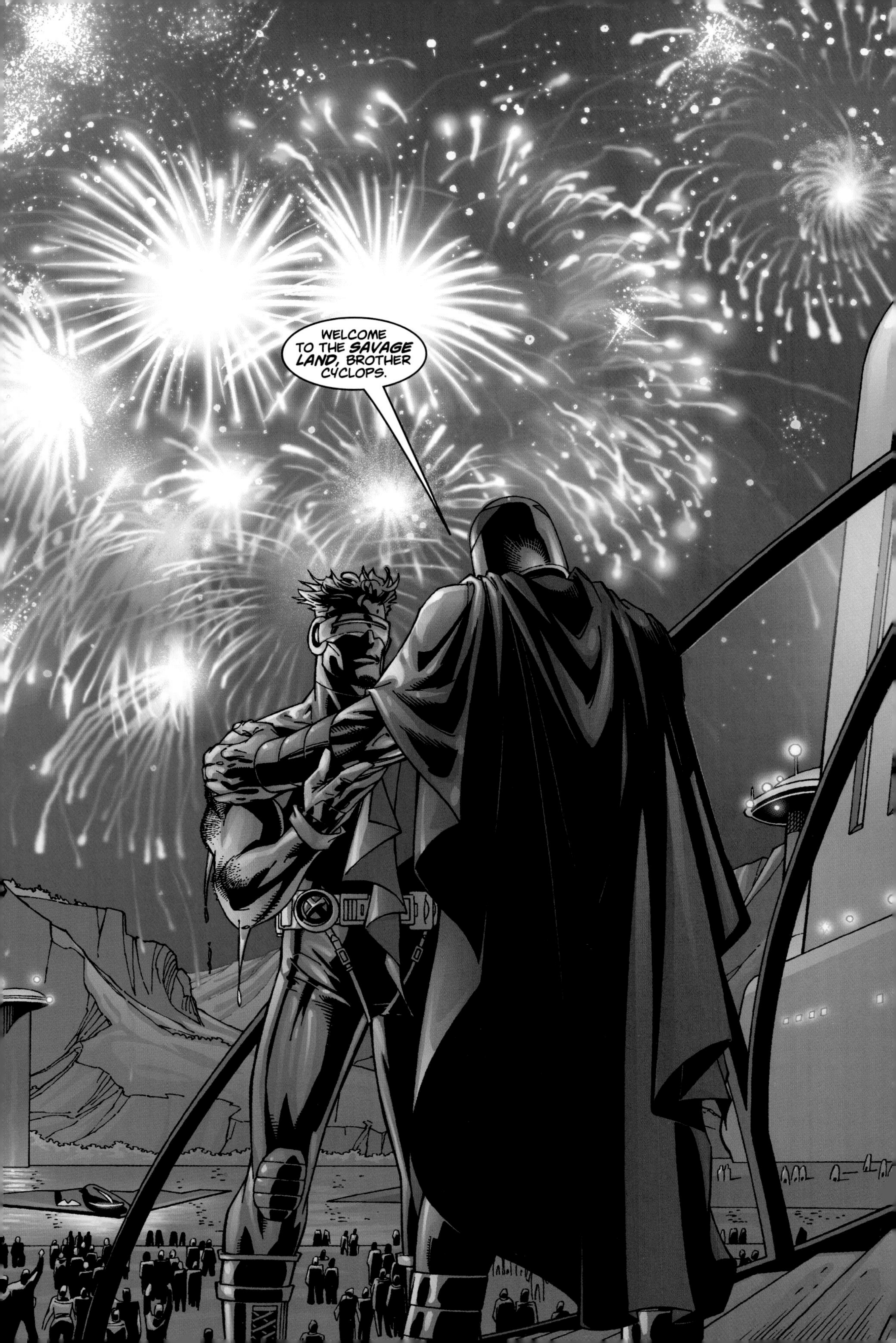
WELCOME TO THE SAVAGE LAND, BROTHER CYCLOPS.

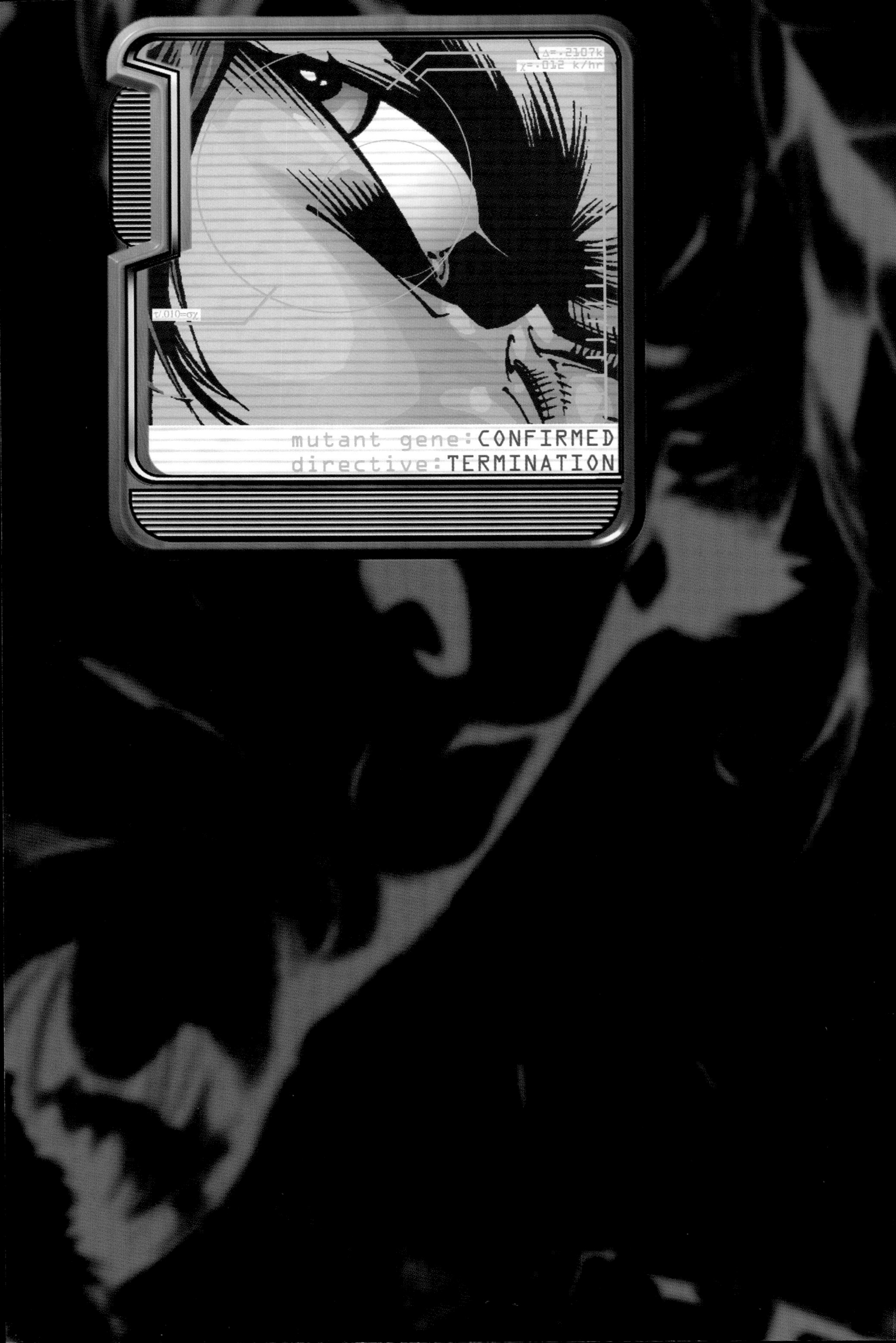
mutant gene:CONFIRMED
directive:TERMINATION

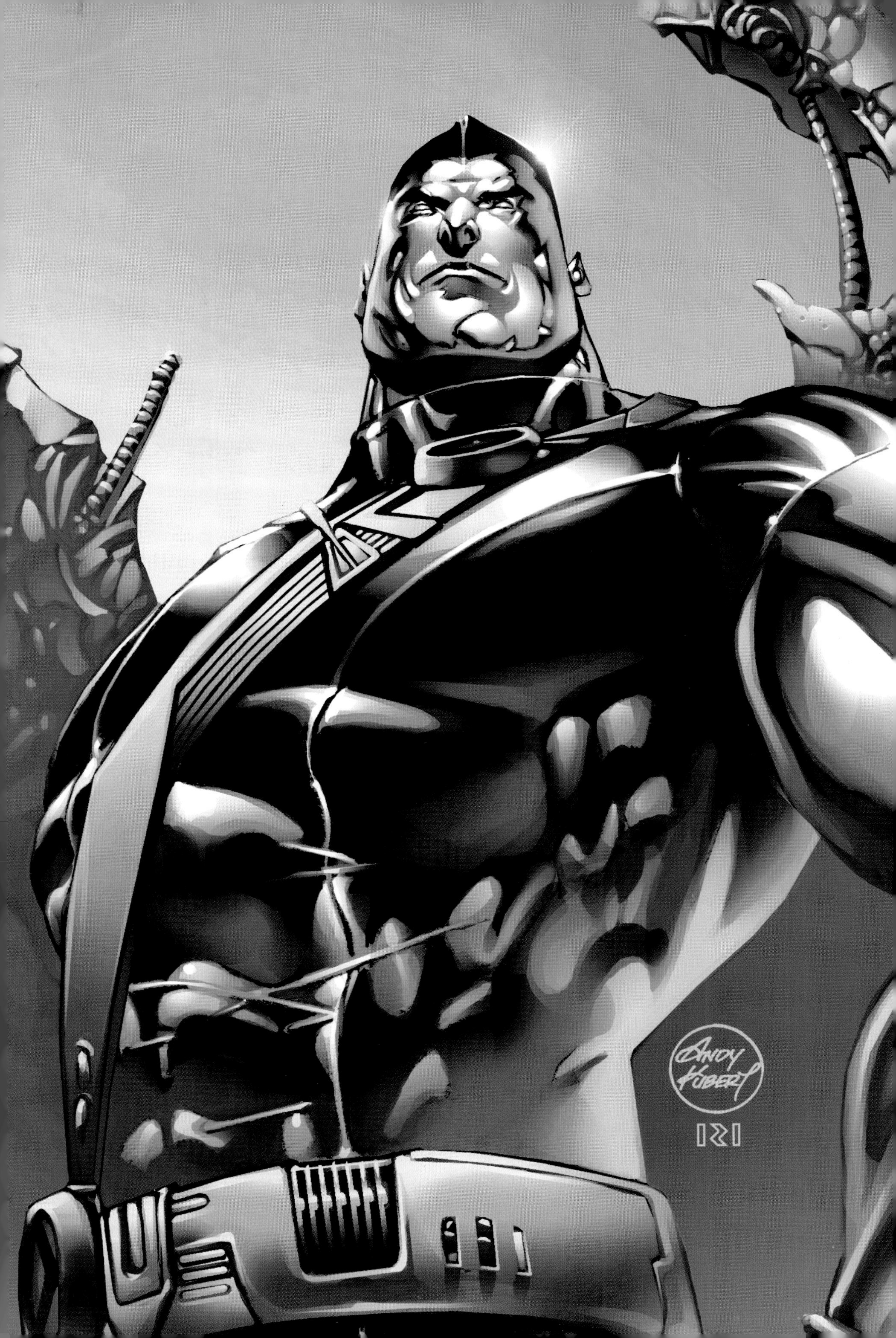
ANDY KUBERT

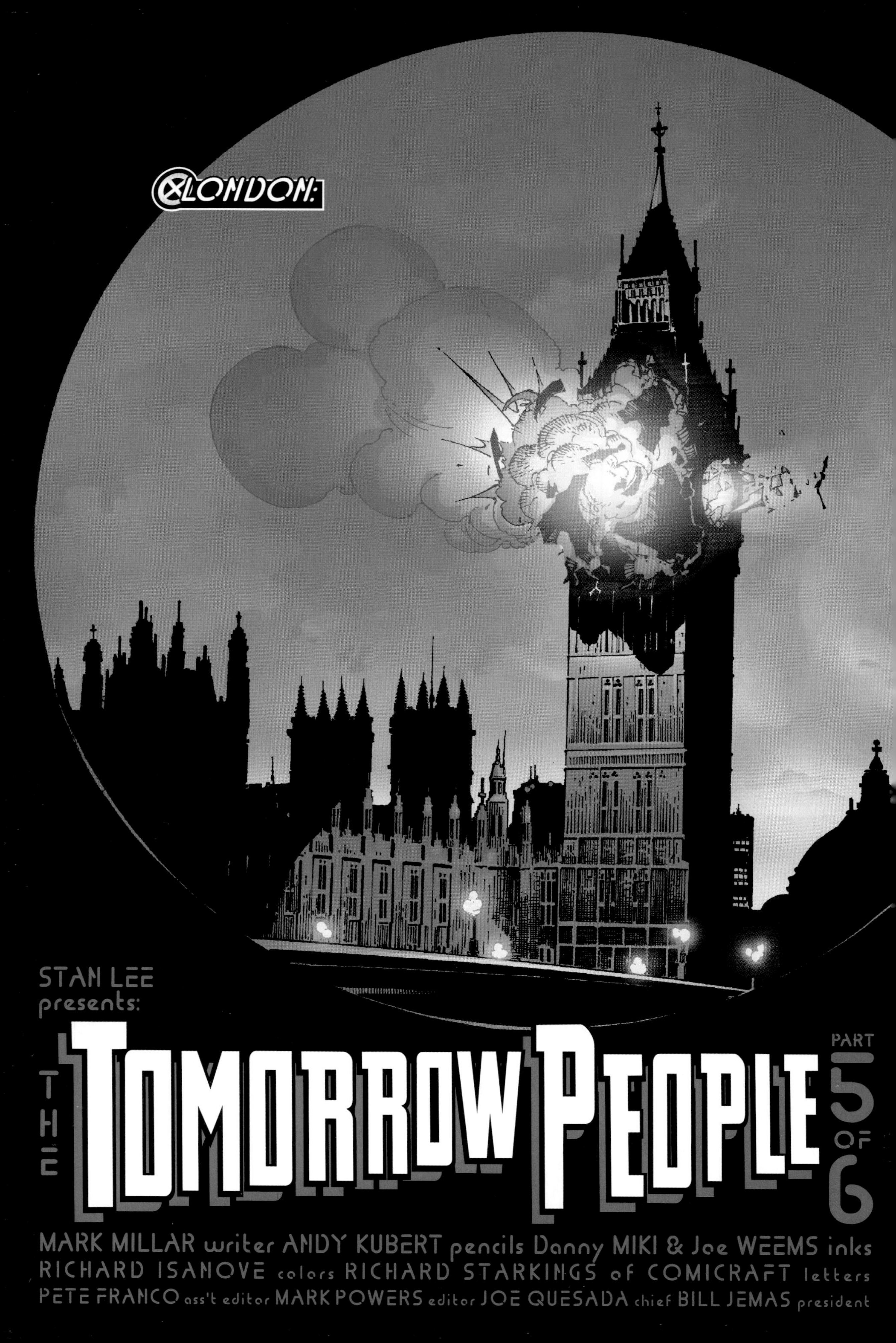
X LONDON:
STAN LEE presents:
THE TOMORROW PEOPLE
PART 5 OF 6
MARK MILLAR writer ANDY KUBERT pencils Danny MIKI & Joe WEEMS inks
RICHARD ISANOVE colors RICHARD STARKINGS of COMICRAFT letters
PETE FRANCO ass't editor MARK POWERS editor JOE QUESADA chief BILL JEMAS president

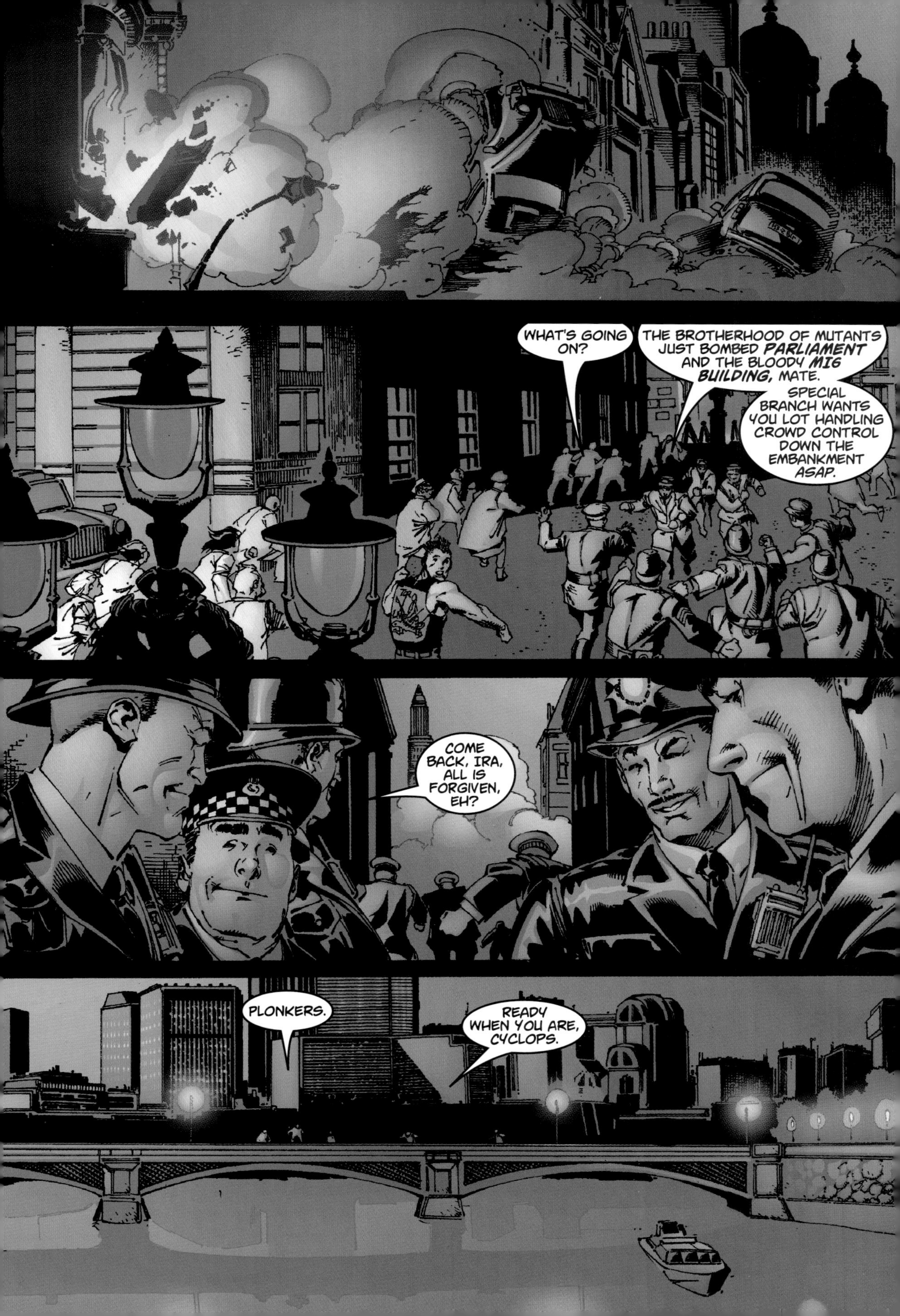
WHAT'S GOING ON?
THE BROTHERHOOD OF MUTANTS JUST BOMBED *PARLIAMENT* AND THE BLOODY *MI6 BUILDING,* MATE.
SPECIAL BRANCH WANTS YOU LOT HANDLING CROWD CONTROL DOWN THE EMBANKMENT *ASAP.*
COME BACK, IRA, ALL IS FORGIVEN, EH?
PLONKERS.
READY WHEN YOU ARE, CYCLOPS.

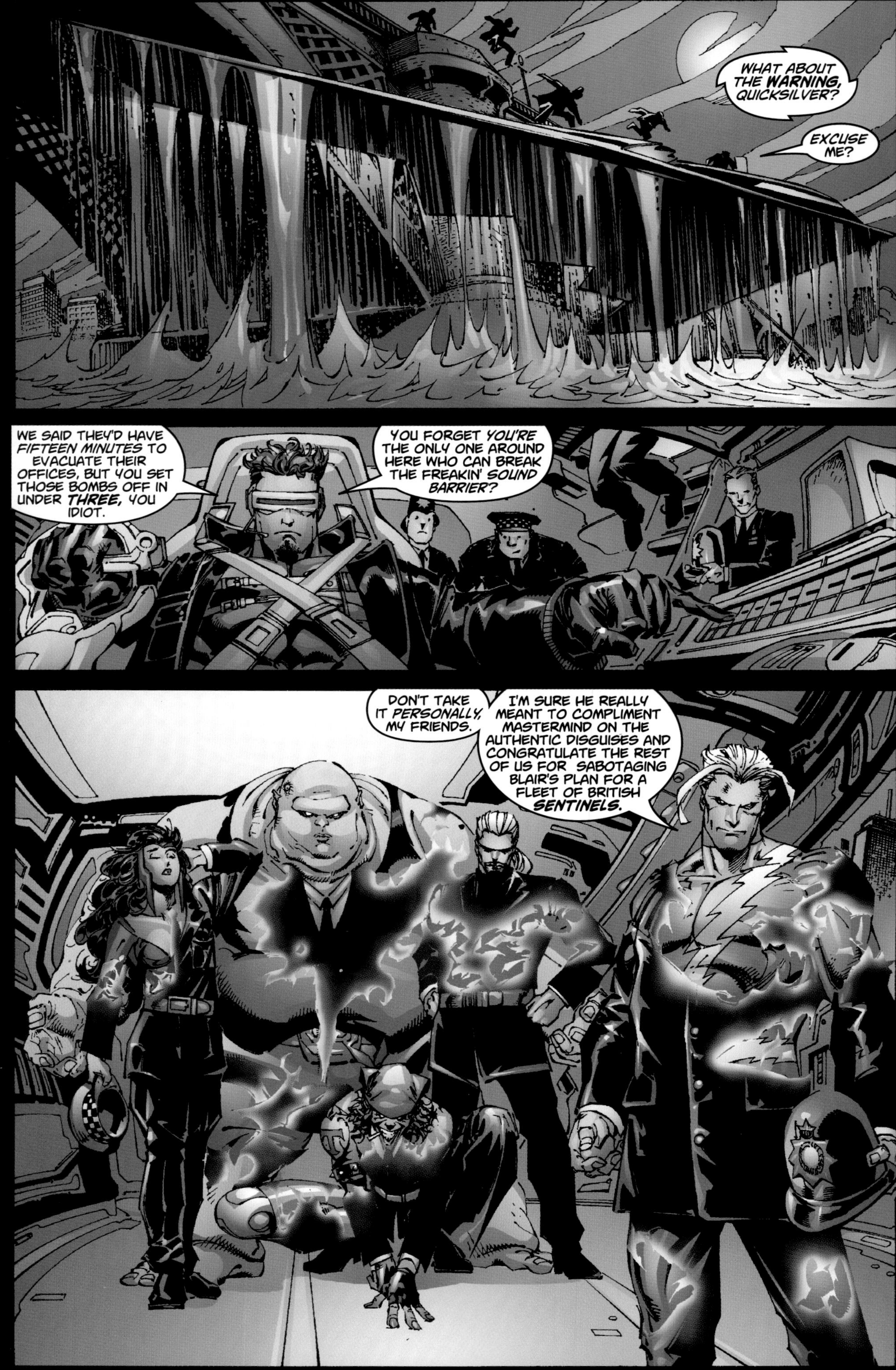
WHAT ABOUT THE **WARNING,** QUICKSILVER?
EXCUSE ME?
WE SAID THEY'D HAVE *FIFTEEN MINUTES* TO EVACUATE THEIR OFFICES, BUT YOU SET THOSE BOMBS OFF IN UNDER **THREE,** YOU IDIOT.
YOU FORGET *YOU'RE* THE ONLY ONE AROUND HERE WHO CAN BREAK THE FREAKIN' *SOUND* BARRIER?
DON'T TAKE IT *PERSONALLY,* MY FRIENDS.
I'M SURE HE REALLY MEANT TO COMPLIMENT MASTERMIND ON THE AUTHENTIC DISGUISES AND CONGRATULATE THE REST OF US FOR SABOTAGING BLAIR'S PLAN FOR A FLEET OF BRITISH ***SENTINELS.***

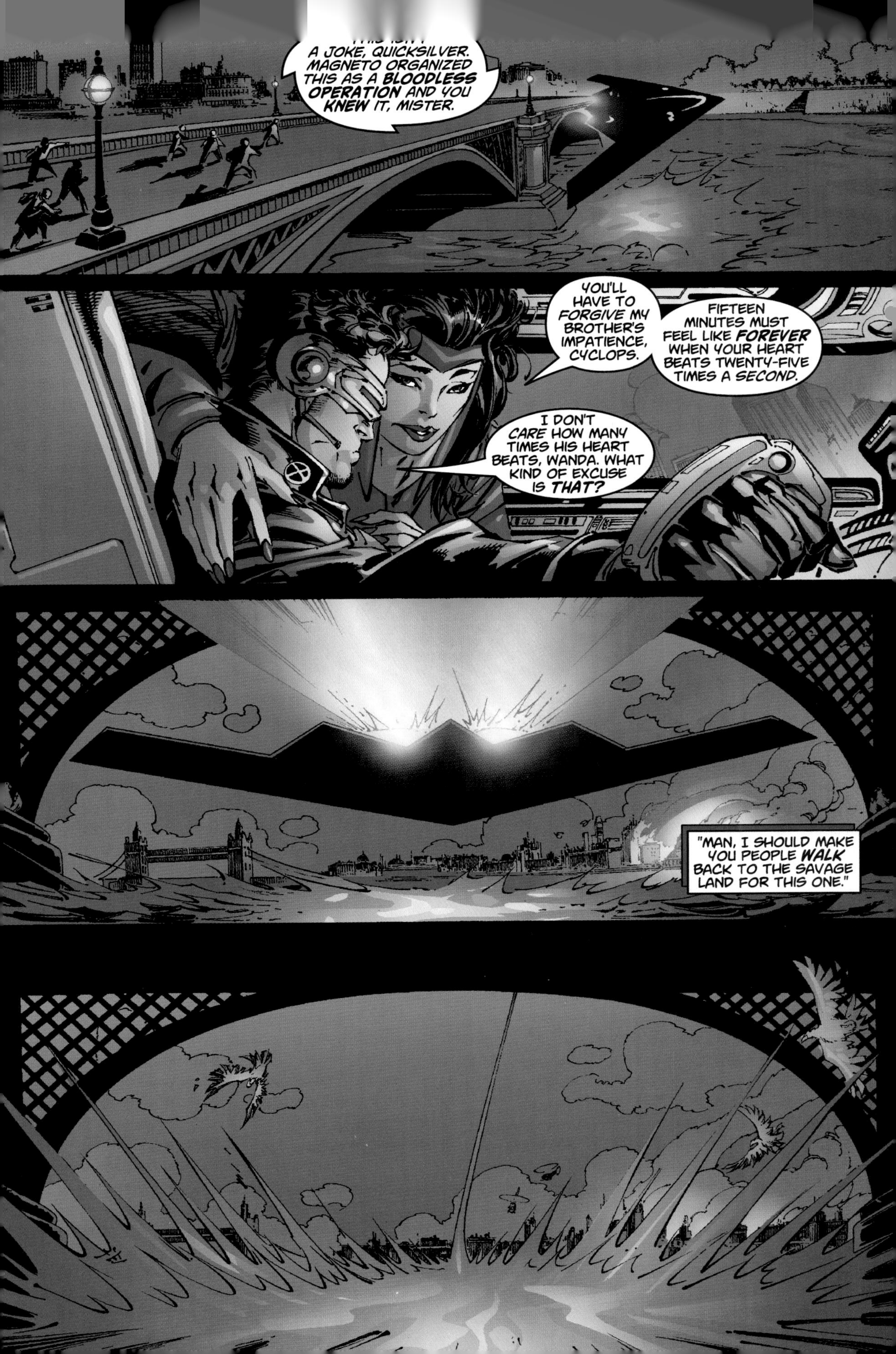
A JOKE, QUICKSILVER. MAGNETO ORGANIZED THIS AS A **BLOODLESS OPERATION** AND YOU **KNEW** IT, MISTER.
YOU'LL HAVE TO *FORGIVE* MY BROTHER'S IMPATIENCE, CYCLOPS.
FIFTEEN MINUTES MUST FEEL LIKE **FOREVER** WHEN YOUR HEART BEATS TWENTY-FIVE TIMES A *SECOND*.
I DON'T *CARE* HOW MANY TIMES HIS HEART BEATS, WANDA. WHAT KIND OF EXCUSE IS **THAT?**
"MAN, I SHOULD MAKE YOU PEOPLE **WALK** BACK TO THE SAVAGE LAND FOR THIS ONE."

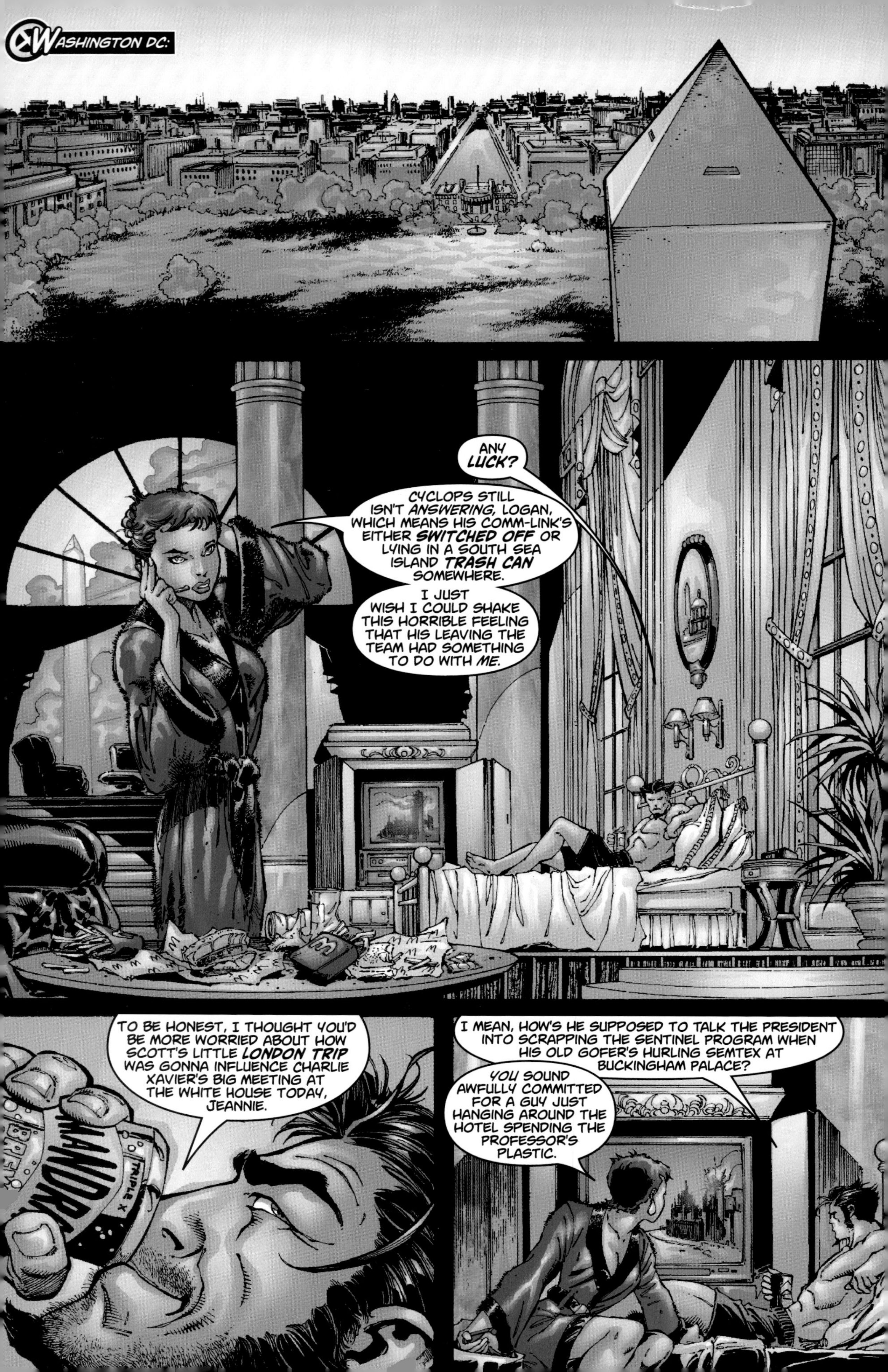
WASHINGTON DC:
ANY LUCK?
CYCLOPS STILL ISN'T ANSWERING, LOGAN, WHICH MEANS HIS COMM-LINK'S EITHER SWITCHED OFF OR LYING IN A SOUTH SEA ISLAND TRASH CAN SOMEWHERE.
I JUST WISH I COULD SHAKE THIS HORRIBLE FEELING THAT HIS LEAVING THE TEAM HAD SOMETHING TO DO WITH ME.
TO BE HONEST, I THOUGHT YOU'D BE MORE WORRIED ABOUT HOW SCOTT'S LITTLE LONDON TRIP WAS GONNA INFLUENCE CHARLIE XAVIER'S BIG MEETING AT THE WHITE HOUSE TODAY, JEANNIE.
I MEAN, HOW'S HE SUPPOSED TO TALK THE PRESIDENT INTO SCRAPPING THE SENTINEL PROGRAM WHEN HIS OLD GOFER'S HURLING SEMTEX AT BUCKINGHAM PALACE?
YOU SOUND AWFULLY COMMITTED FOR A GUY JUST HANGING AROUND THE HOTEL SPENDING THE PROFESSOR'S PLASTIC.
TRIPLE X

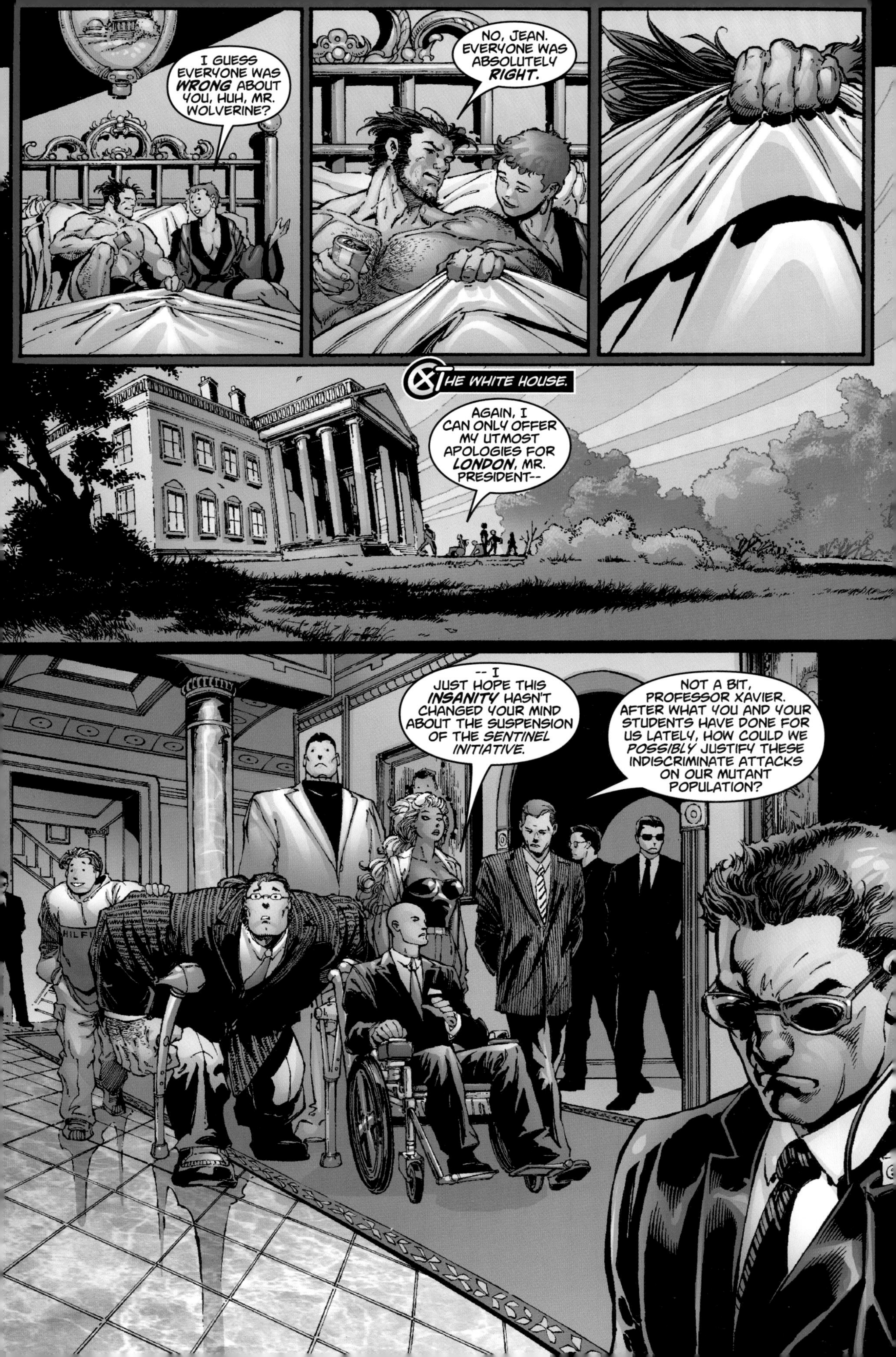
I GUESS EVERYONE WAS WRONG ABOUT YOU, HUH, MR. WOLVERINE?
NO, JEAN. EVERYONE WAS ABSOLUTELY RIGHT.
THE WHITE HOUSE.
AGAIN, I CAN ONLY OFFER MY UTMOST APOLOGIES FOR LONDON, MR. PRESIDENT--
-- I JUST HOPE THIS INSANITY HASN'T CHANGED YOUR MIND ABOUT THE SUSPENSION OF THE SENTINEL INITIATIVE.
NOT A BIT, PROFESSOR XAVIER. AFTER WHAT YOU AND YOUR STUDENTS HAVE DONE FOR US LATELY, HOW COULD WE POSSIBLY JUSTIFY THESE INDISCRIMINATE ATTACKS ON OUR MUTANT POPULATION?

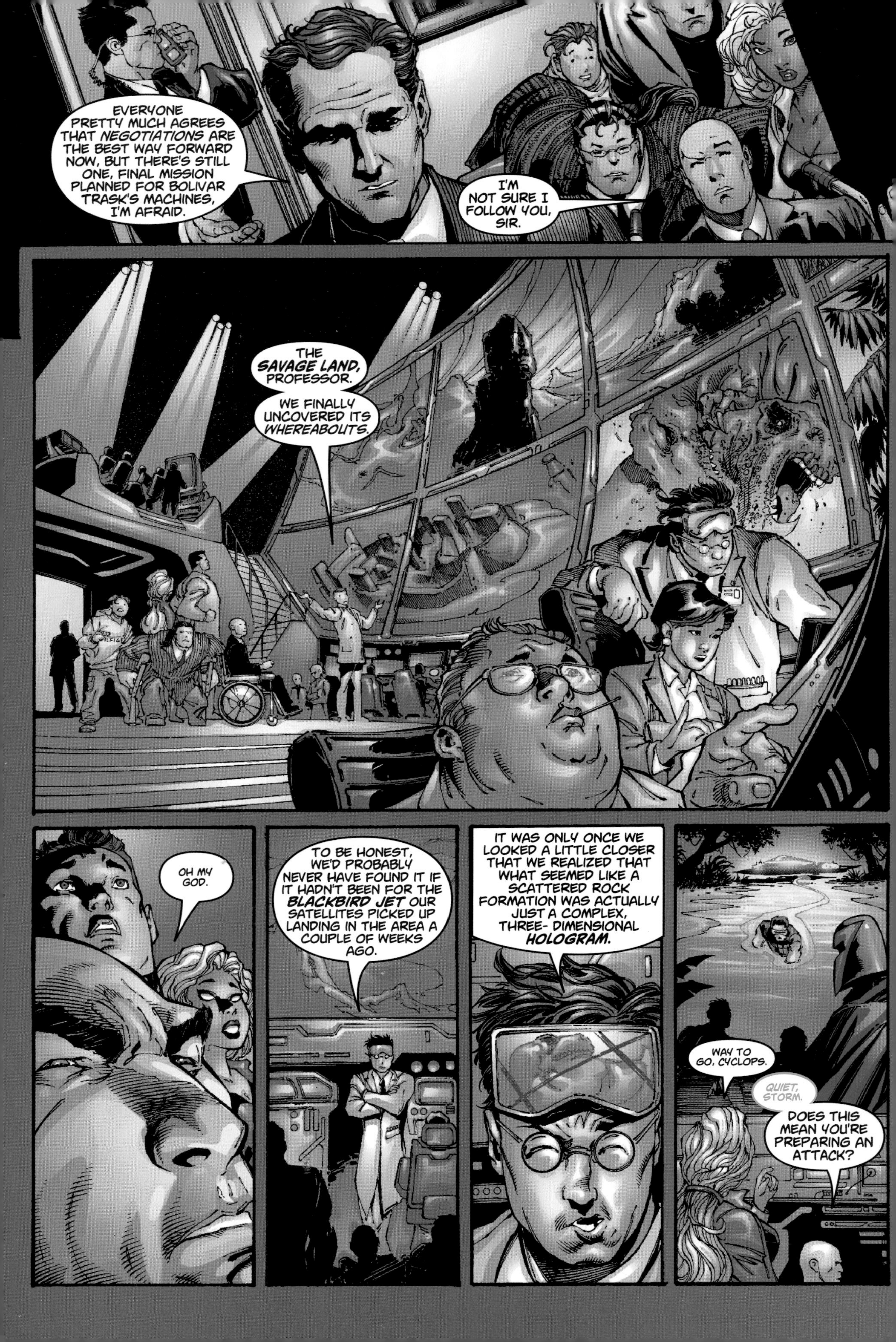
EVERYONE PRETTY MUCH AGREES THAT NEGOTIATIONS ARE THE BEST WAY FORWARD NOW, BUT THERE'S STILL ONE, FINAL MISSION PLANNED FOR BOLIVAR TRASK'S MACHINES, I'M AFRAID.
I'M NOT SURE I FOLLOW YOU, SIR.
THE SAVAGE LAND, PROFESSOR.
WE FINALLY UNCOVERED ITS WHEREABOUTS.
OH MY GOD.
TO BE HONEST, WE'D PROBABLY NEVER HAVE FOUND IT IF IT HADN'T BEEN FOR THE BLACKBIRD JET OUR SATELLITES PICKED UP LANDING IN THE AREA A COUPLE OF WEEKS AGO.
IT WAS ONLY ONCE WE LOOKED A LITTLE CLOSER THAT WE REALIZED THAT WHAT SEEMED LIKE A SCATTERED ROCK FORMATION WAS ACTUALLY JUST A COMPLEX, THREE- DIMENSIONAL HOLOGRAM.
WAY TO GO, CYCLOPS.
QUIET, STORM.
DOES THIS MEAN YOU'RE PREPARING AN ATTACK?

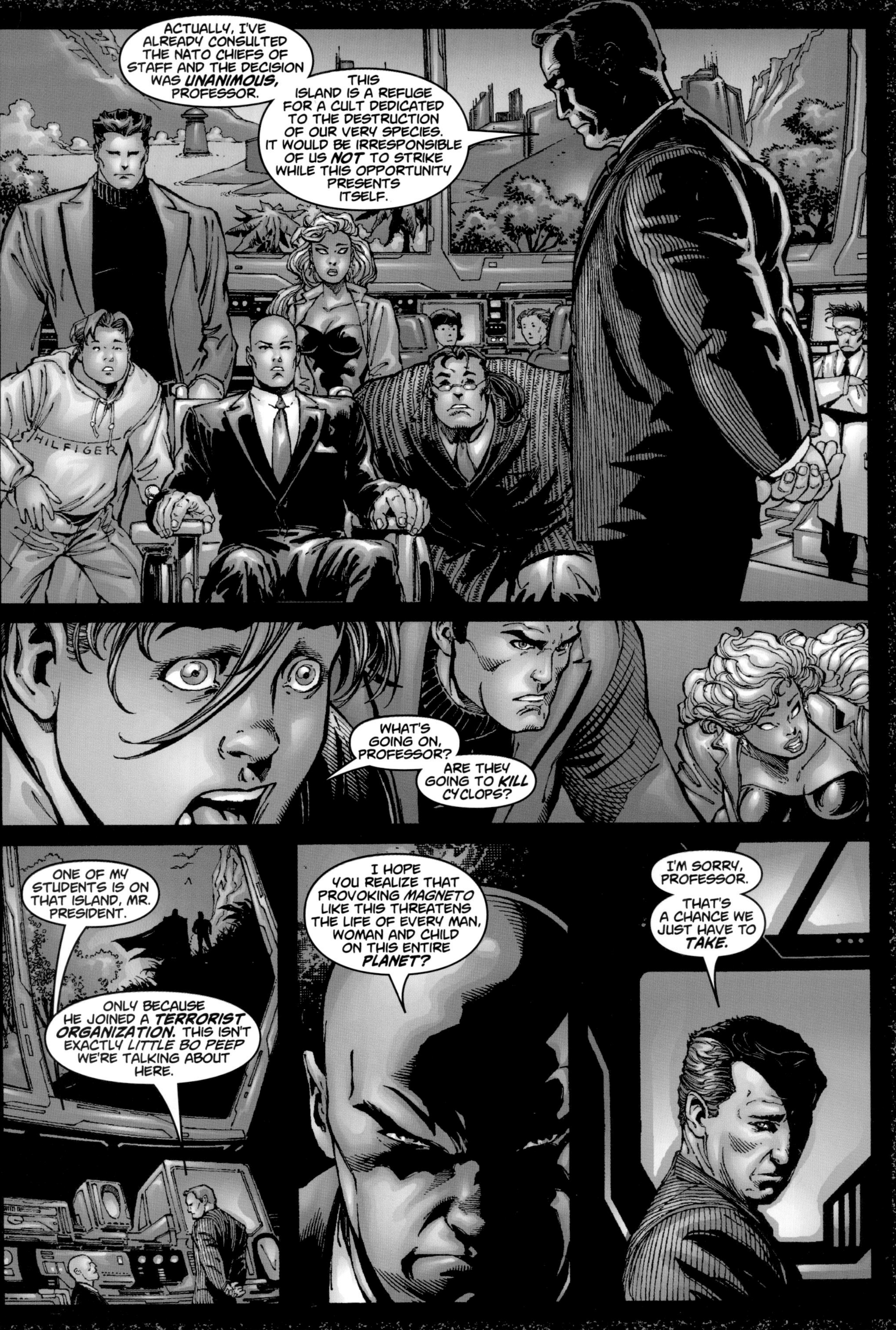
ACTUALLY, I'VE ALREADY CONSULTED THE NATO CHIEFS OF STAFF AND THE DECISION WAS UNANIMOUS, PROFESSOR.
THIS ISLAND IS A REFUGE FOR A CULT DEDICATED TO THE DESTRUCTION OF OUR VERY SPECIES. IT WOULD BE IRRESPONSIBLE OF US NOT TO STRIKE WHILE THIS OPPORTUNITY PRESENTS ITSELF.
HILFIGER
WHAT'S GOING ON, PROFESSOR?
ARE THEY GOING TO KILL CYCLOPS?
ONE OF MY STUDENTS IS ON THAT ISLAND, MR. PRESIDENT.
ONLY BECAUSE HE JOINED A TERRORIST ORGANIZATION. THIS ISN'T EXACTLY LITTLE BO PEEP WE'RE TALKING ABOUT HERE.
I HOPE YOU REALIZE THAT PROVOKING MAGNETO LIKE THIS THREATENS THE LIFE OF EVERY MAN, WOMAN AND CHILD ON THIS ENTIRE PLANET?
I'M SORRY, PROFESSOR.
THAT'S A CHANCE WE JUST HAVE TO TAKE.

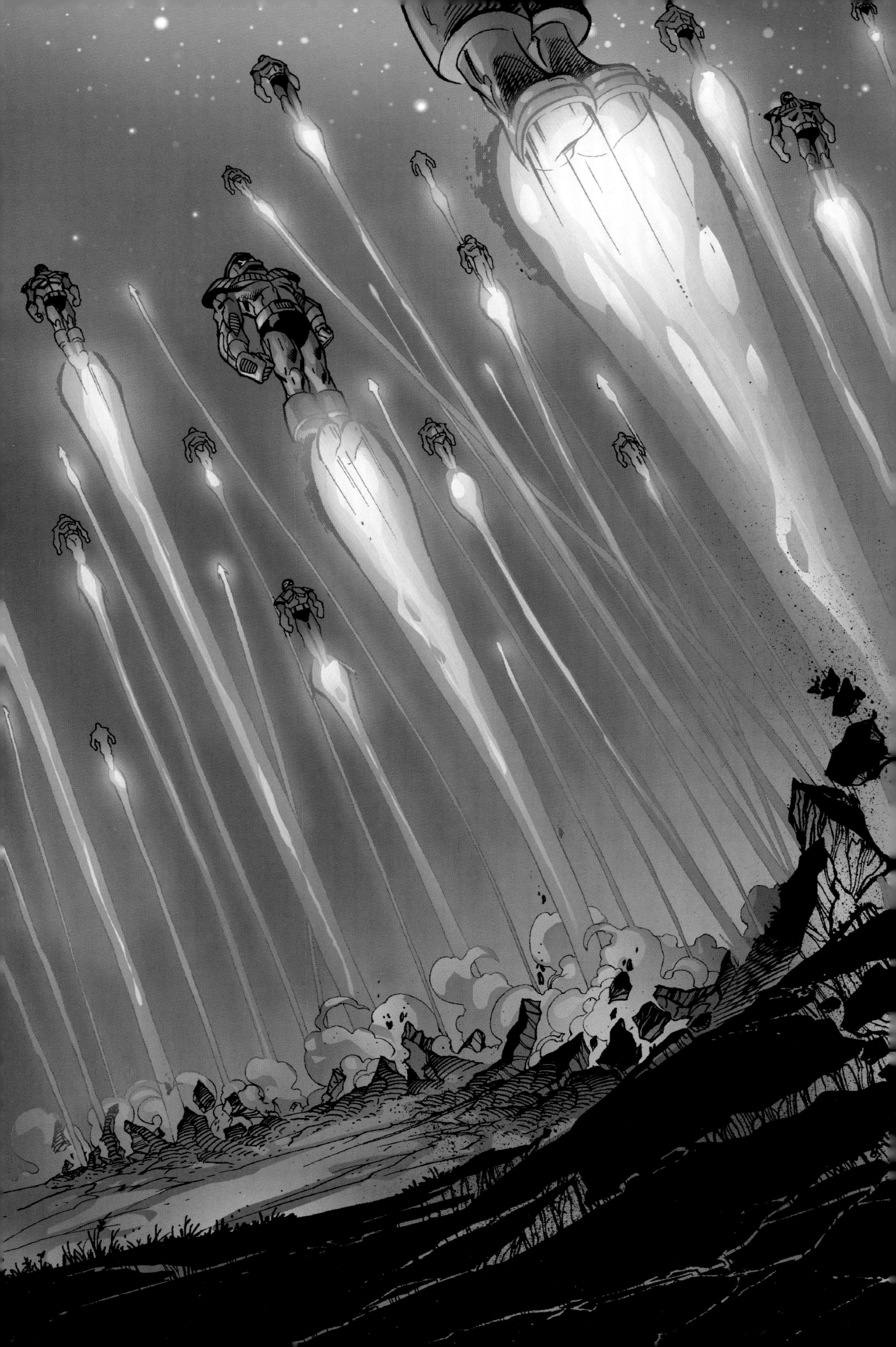

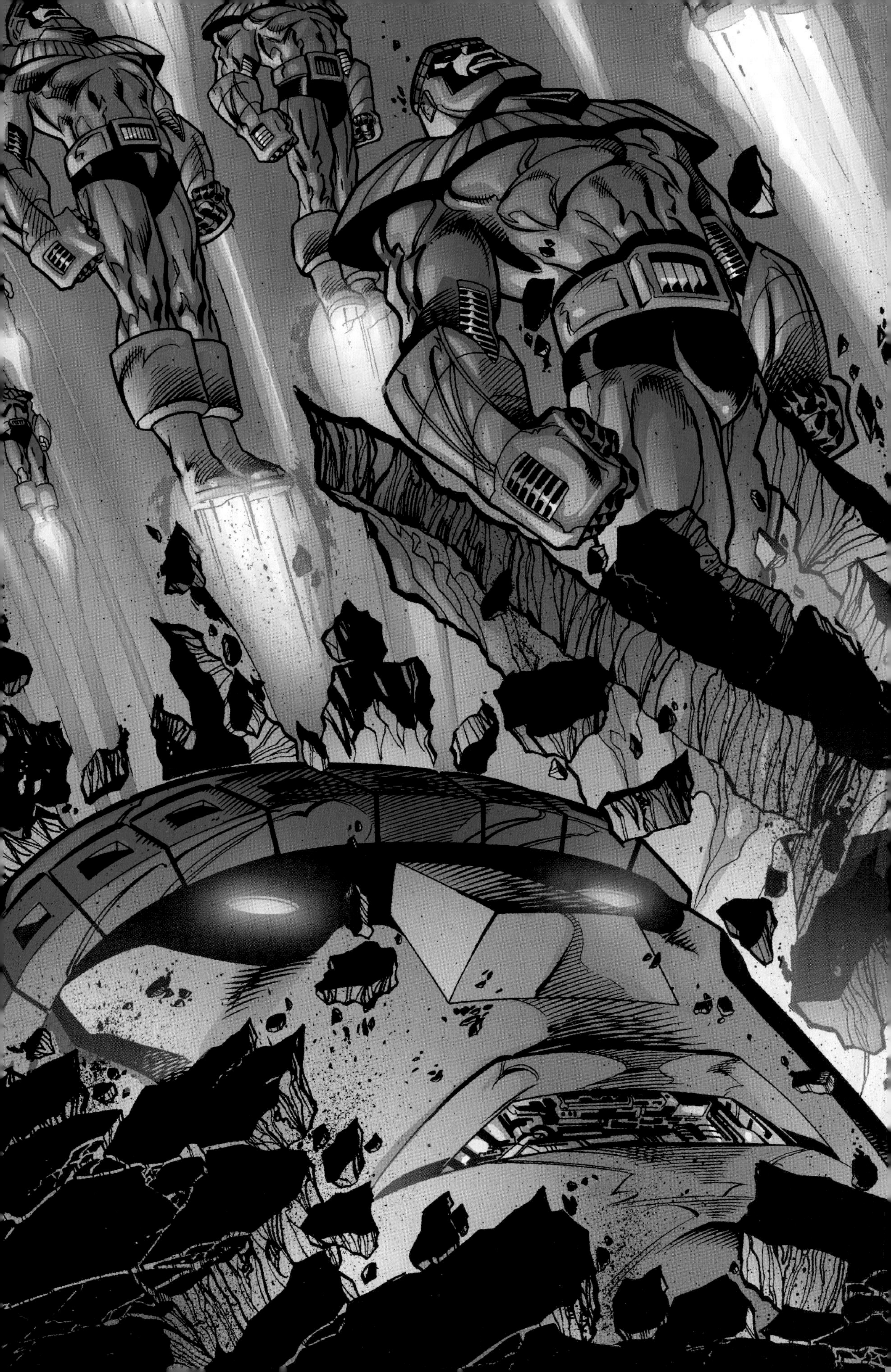

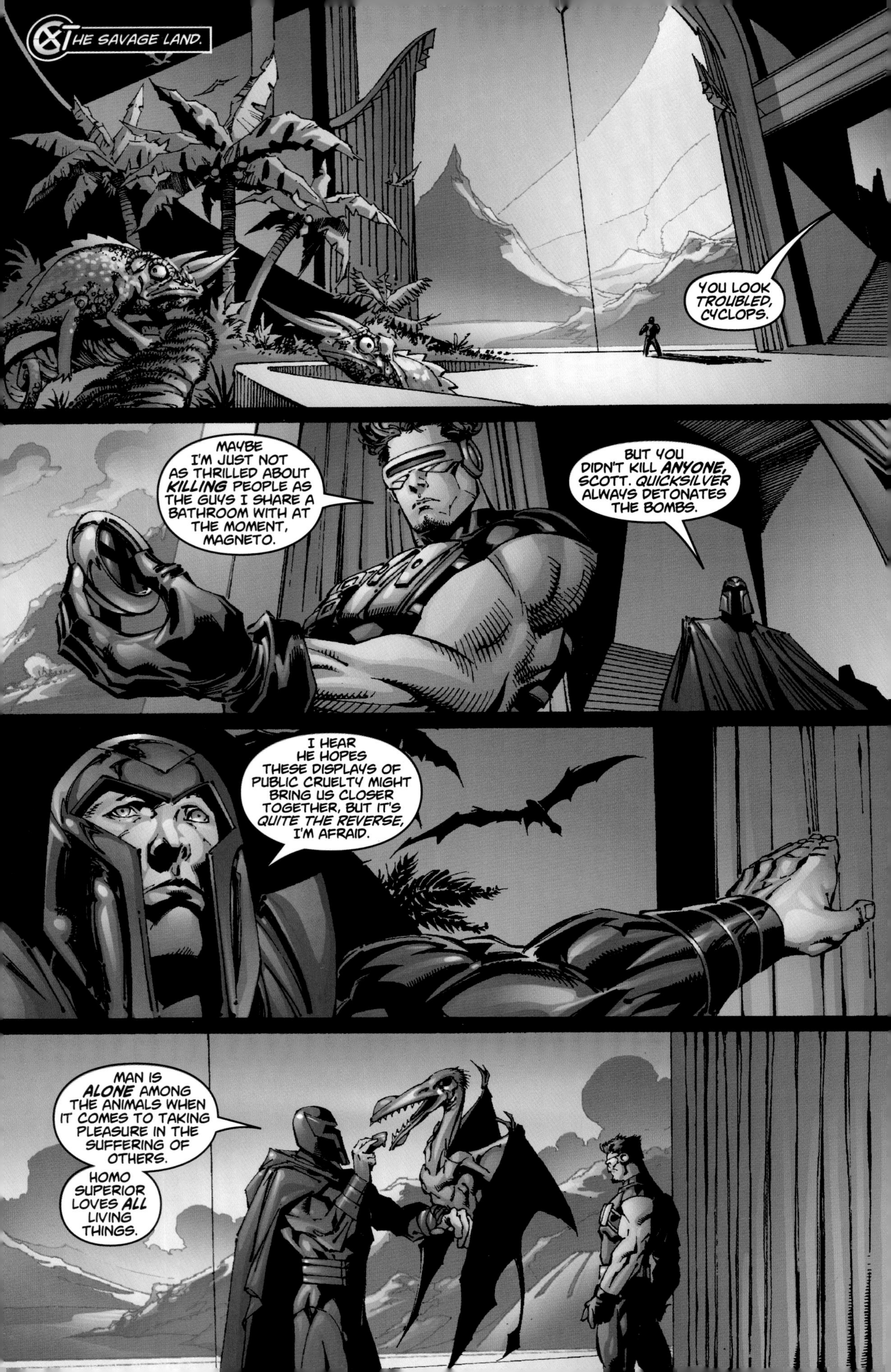
THE SAVAGE LAND.
YOU LOOK TROUBLED, CYCLOPS.
MAYBE I'M JUST NOT AS THRILLED ABOUT KILLING PEOPLE AS THE GUYS I SHARE A BATHROOM WITH AT THE MOMENT, MAGNETO.
BUT YOU DIDN'T KILL ANYONE, SCOTT. QUICKSILVER ALWAYS DETONATES THE BOMBS.
I HEAR HE HOPES THESE DISPLAYS OF PUBLIC CRUELTY MIGHT BRING US CLOSER TOGETHER, BUT IT'S QUITE THE REVERSE, I'M AFRAID.
MAN IS ALONE AMONG THE ANIMALS WHEN IT COMES TO TAKING PLEASURE IN THE SUFFERING OF OTHERS.
HOMO SUPERIOR LOVES ALL LIVING THINGS.

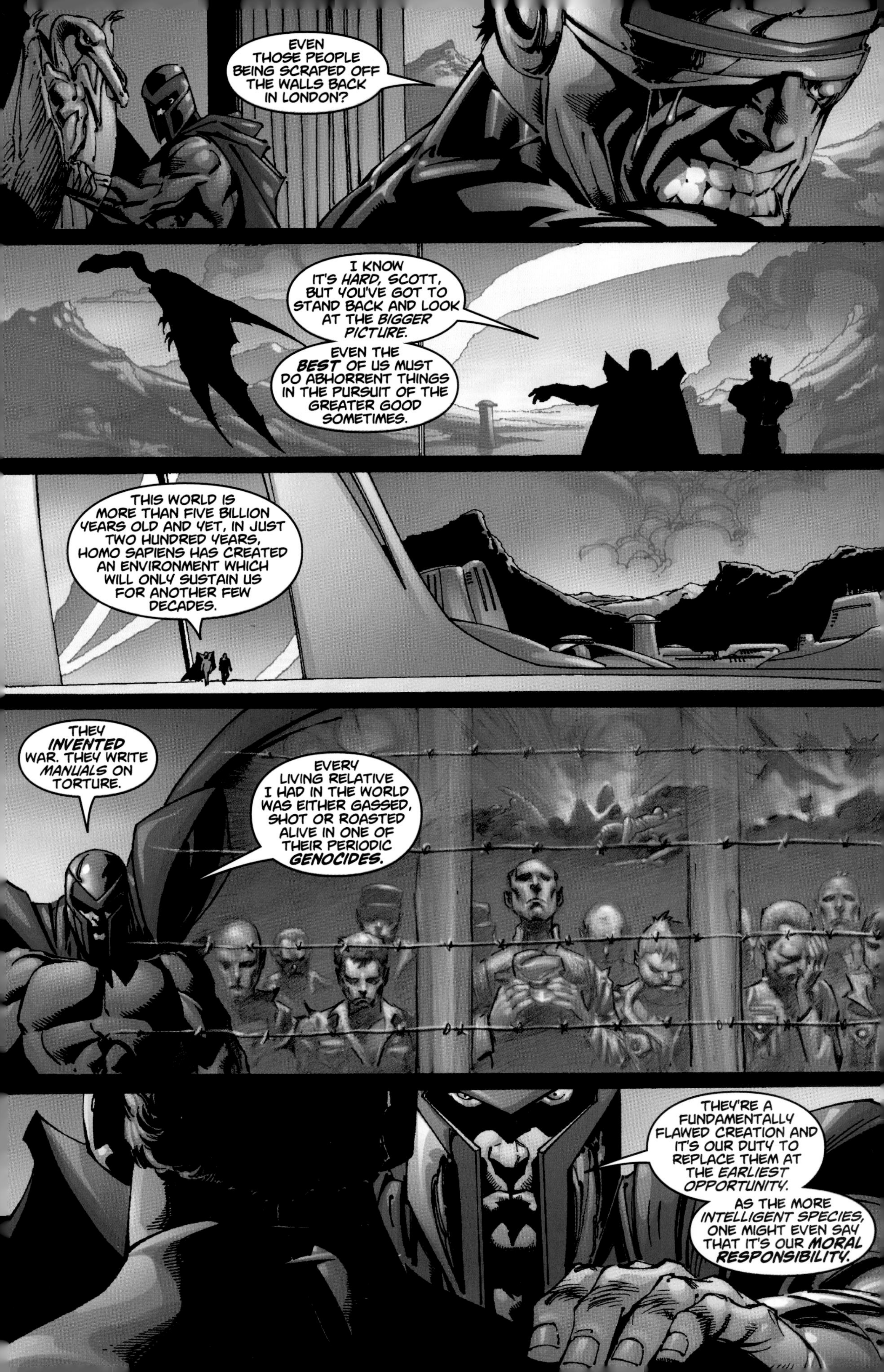
EVEN THOSE PEOPLE BEING SCRAPED OFF THE WALLS BACK IN LONDON?
I KNOW IT'S HARD, SCOTT, BUT YOU'VE GOT TO STAND BACK AND LOOK AT THE BIGGER PICTURE.
EVEN THE BEST OF US MUST DO ABHORRENT THINGS IN THE PURSUIT OF THE GREATER GOOD SOMETIMES.
THIS WORLD IS MORE THAN FIVE BILLION YEARS OLD AND YET, IN JUST TWO HUNDRED YEARS, HOMO SAPIENS HAS CREATED AN ENVIRONMENT WHICH WILL ONLY SUSTAIN US FOR ANOTHER FEW DECADES.
THEY INVENTED WAR. THEY WRITE MANUALS ON TORTURE.
EVERY LIVING RELATIVE I HAD IN THE WORLD WAS EITHER GASSED, SHOT OR ROASTED ALIVE IN ONE OF THEIR PERIODIC GENOCIDES.
THEY'RE A FUNDAMENTALLY FLAWED CREATION AND IT'S OUR DUTY TO REPLACE THEM AT THE EARLIEST OPPORTUNITY.
AS THE MORE INTELLIGENT SPECIES, ONE MIGHT EVEN SAY THAT IT'S OUR MORAL RESPONSIBILITY.

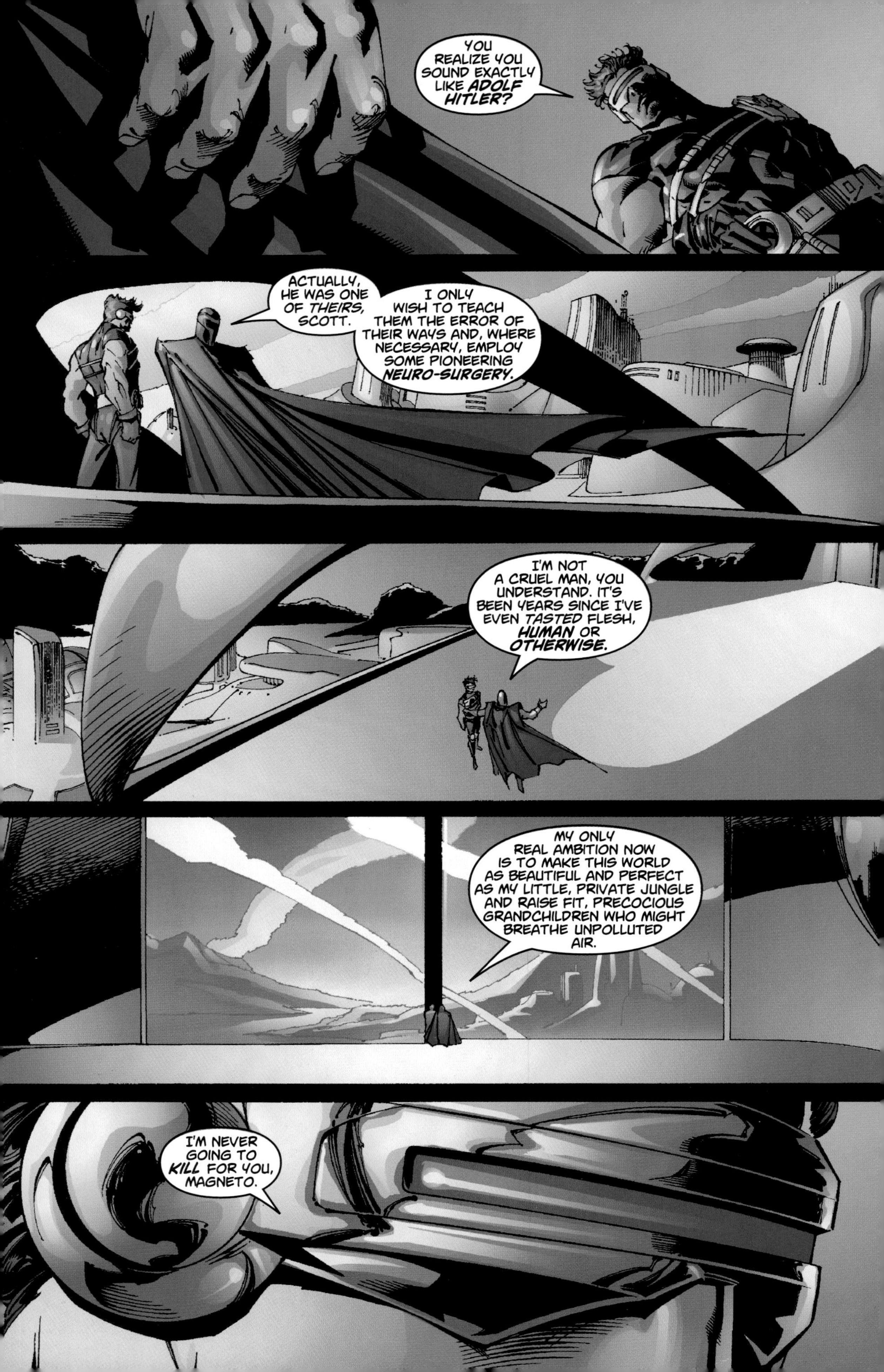
YOU REALIZE YOU SOUND EXACTLY LIKE ADOLF HITLER?
ACTUALLY, HE WAS ONE OF THEIRS, SCOTT.
I ONLY WISH TO TEACH THEM THE ERROR OF THEIR WAYS AND, WHERE NECESSARY, EMPLOY SOME PIONEERING NEURO-SURGERY.
I'M NOT A CRUEL MAN, YOU UNDERSTAND. IT'S BEEN YEARS SINCE I'VE EVEN TASTED FLESH, HUMAN OR OTHERWISE.
MY ONLY REAL AMBITION NOW IS TO MAKE THIS WORLD AS BEAUTIFUL AND PERFECT AS MY LITTLE, PRIVATE JUNGLE AND RAISE FIT, PRECOCIOUS GRANDCHILDREN WHO MIGHT BREATHE UNPOLLUTED AIR.
I'M NEVER GOING TO KILL FOR YOU, MAGNETO.

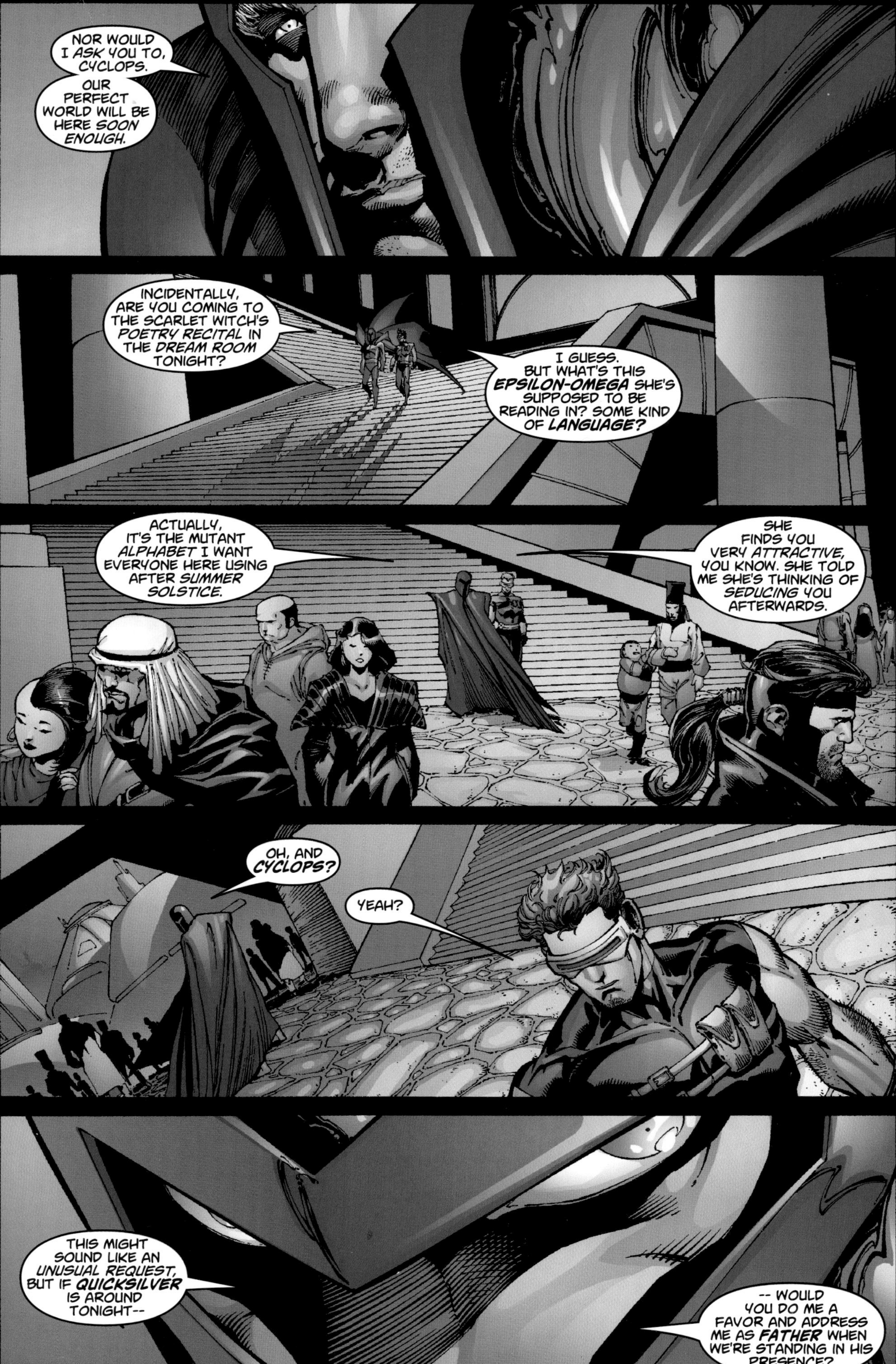
NOR WOULD I ASK YOU TO, CYCLOPS.
OUR PERFECT WORLD WILL BE HERE SOON ENOUGH.
INCIDENTALLY, ARE YOU COMING TO THE SCARLET WITCH'S POETRY RECITAL IN THE DREAM ROOM TONIGHT?
I GUESS. BUT WHAT'S THIS EPSILON-OMEGA SHE'S SUPPOSED TO BE READING IN? SOME KIND OF LANGUAGE?
ACTUALLY, IT'S THE MUTANT ALPHABET I WANT EVERYONE HERE USING AFTER SUMMER SOLSTICE.
SHE FINDS YOU VERY ATTRACTIVE, YOU KNOW. SHE TOLD ME SHE'S THINKING OF SEDUCING YOU AFTERWARDS.
OH, AND CYCLOPS?
YEAH?
THIS MIGHT SOUND LIKE AN UNUSUAL REQUEST, BUT IF QUICKSILVER IS AROUND TONIGHT--
-- WOULD YOU DO ME A FAVOR AND ADDRESS ME AS FATHER WHEN WE'RE STANDING IN HIS PRESENCE?

WHY DOES HE TAKE SUCH PLEASURE IN *HURTING* ME, WANDA?

HAVE I REALLY BEEN SUCH A BAD SON THAT I DESERVE TO CRY MYSELF TO SLEEP LIKE THIS EVERY NIGHT?

MAGNETO COULDN'T ASK FOR A MORE PERFECT SON, PIETRO.

BLOB SAYS HE JUST RESENTS US BECAUSE WE'RE CONSTANT, LIVING REMINDERS OF HIS ONE MOMENT OF WEAKNESS WITH A *HOMO SAPIEN* FEMALE ALL THOSE YEARS AGO.

BUT I WISH HE'D STOP CRITICIZING ME IN FRONT OF PEOPLE. HE EVEN SAID MY MUTANT POWER WAS *EFFEMINATE* THIS MORNING.

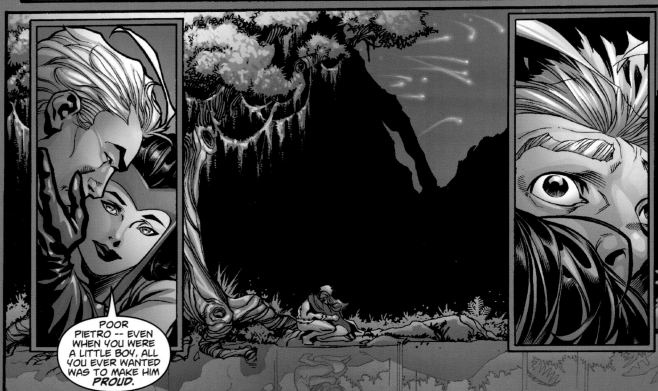

POOR PIETRO -- EVEN WHEN YOU WERE A LITTLE BOY, ALL YOU EVER WANTED WAS TO MAKE HIM *PROUD.*

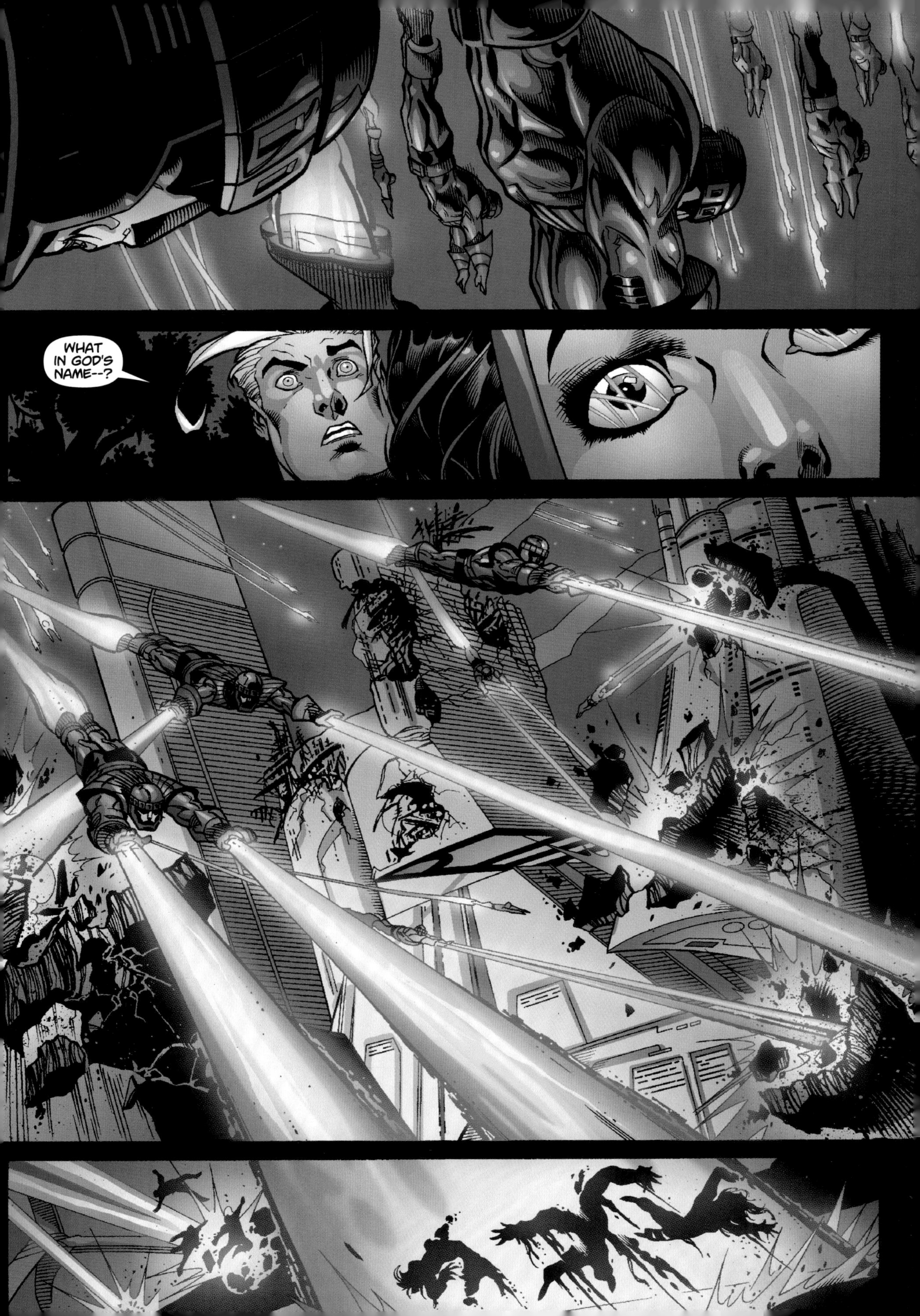
WHAT IN GOD'S NAME--?

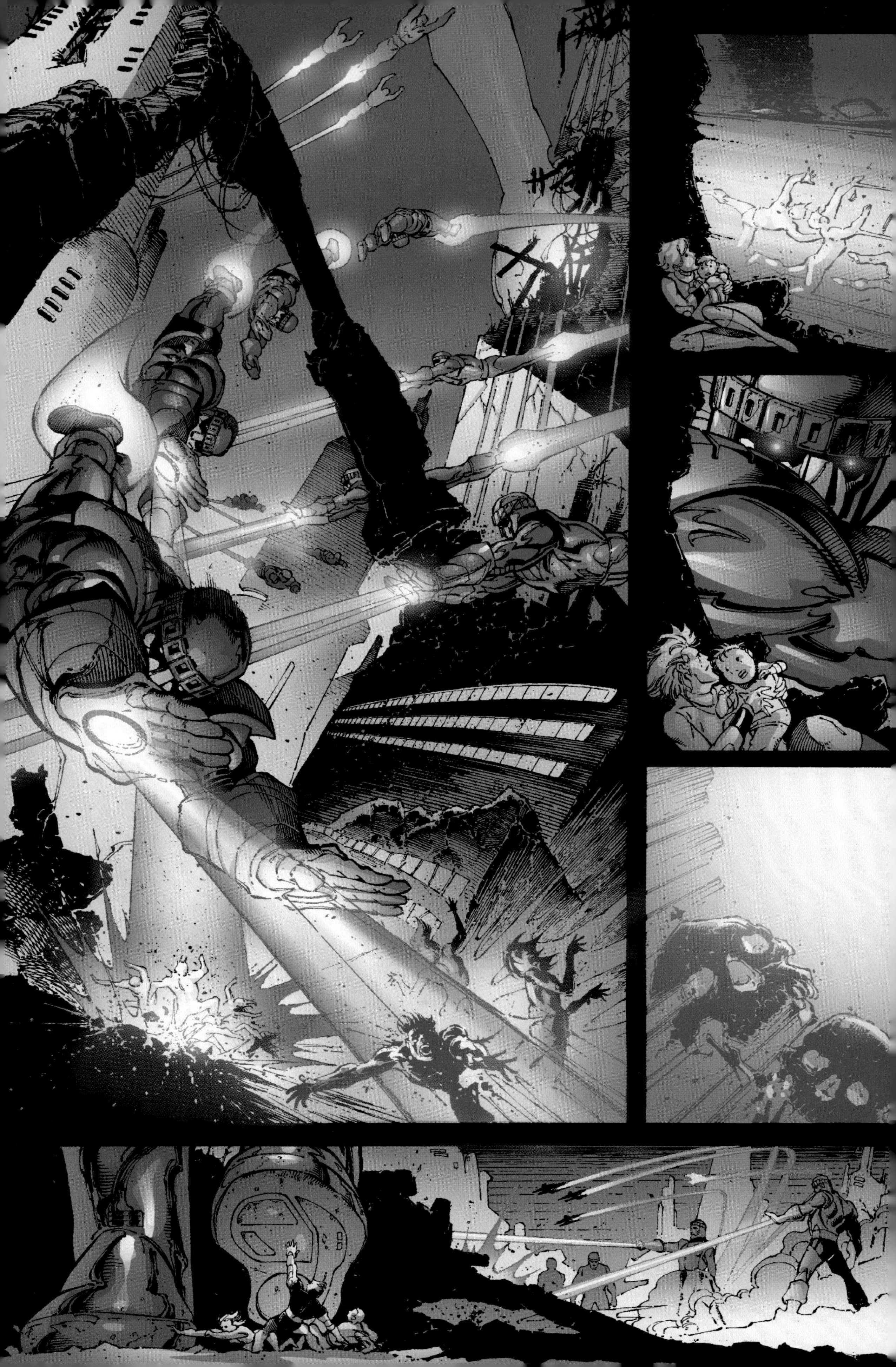

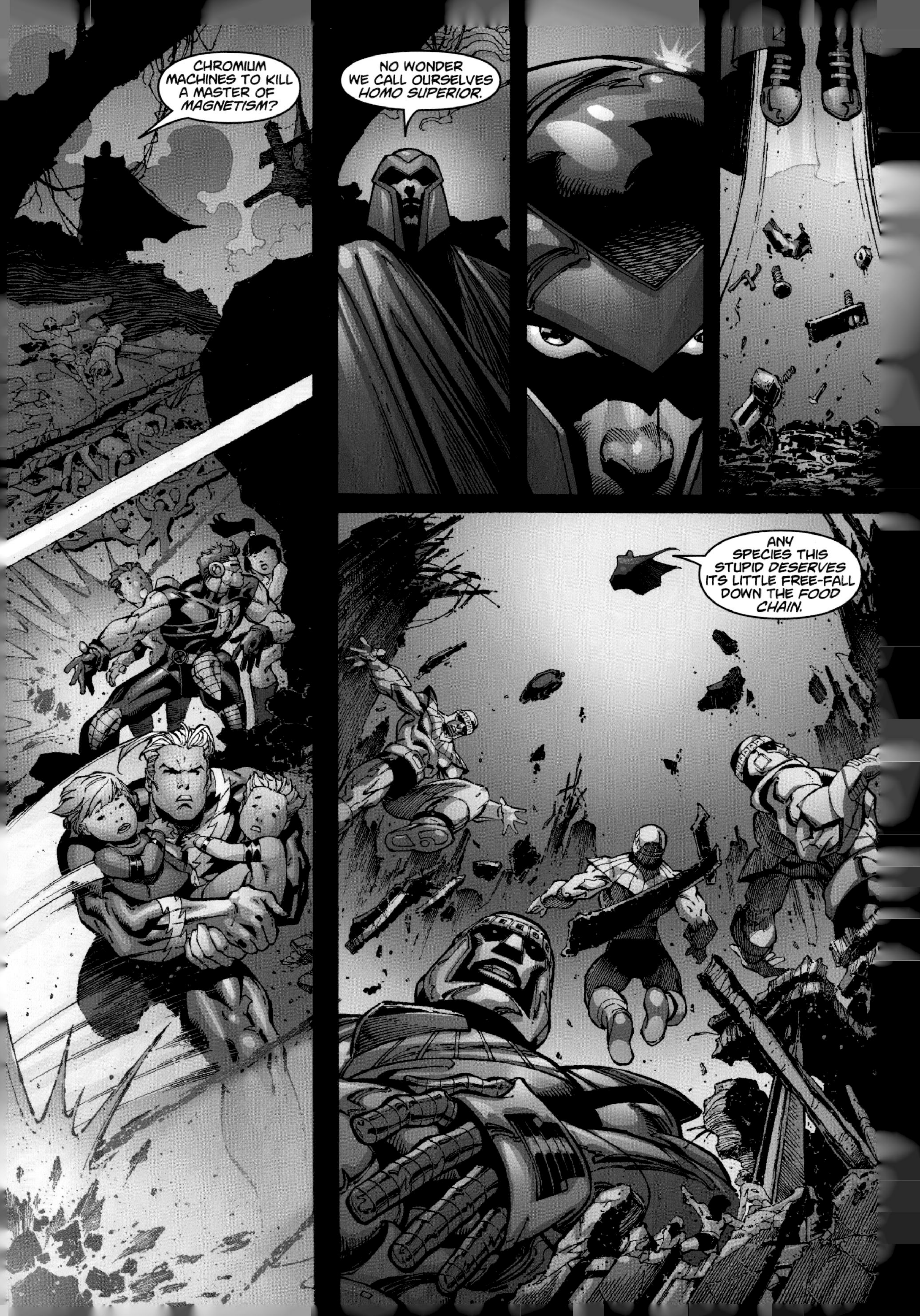
CHROMIUM MACHINES TO KILL A MASTER OF MAGNETISM?
NO WONDER WE CALL OURSELVES HOMO SUPERIOR.
ANY SPECIES THIS STUPID DESERVES ITS LITTLE FREE-FALL DOWN THE FOOD CHAIN.

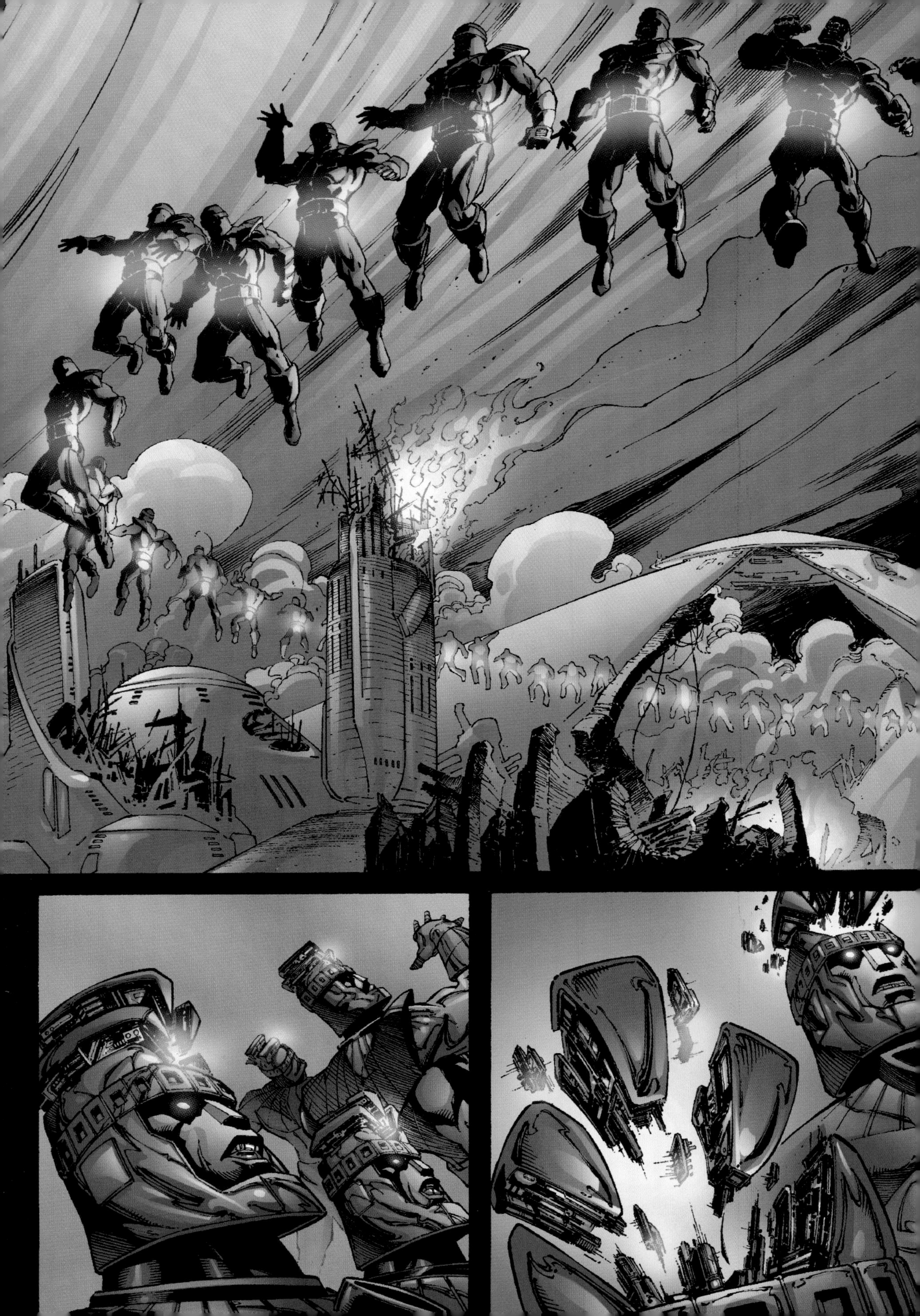

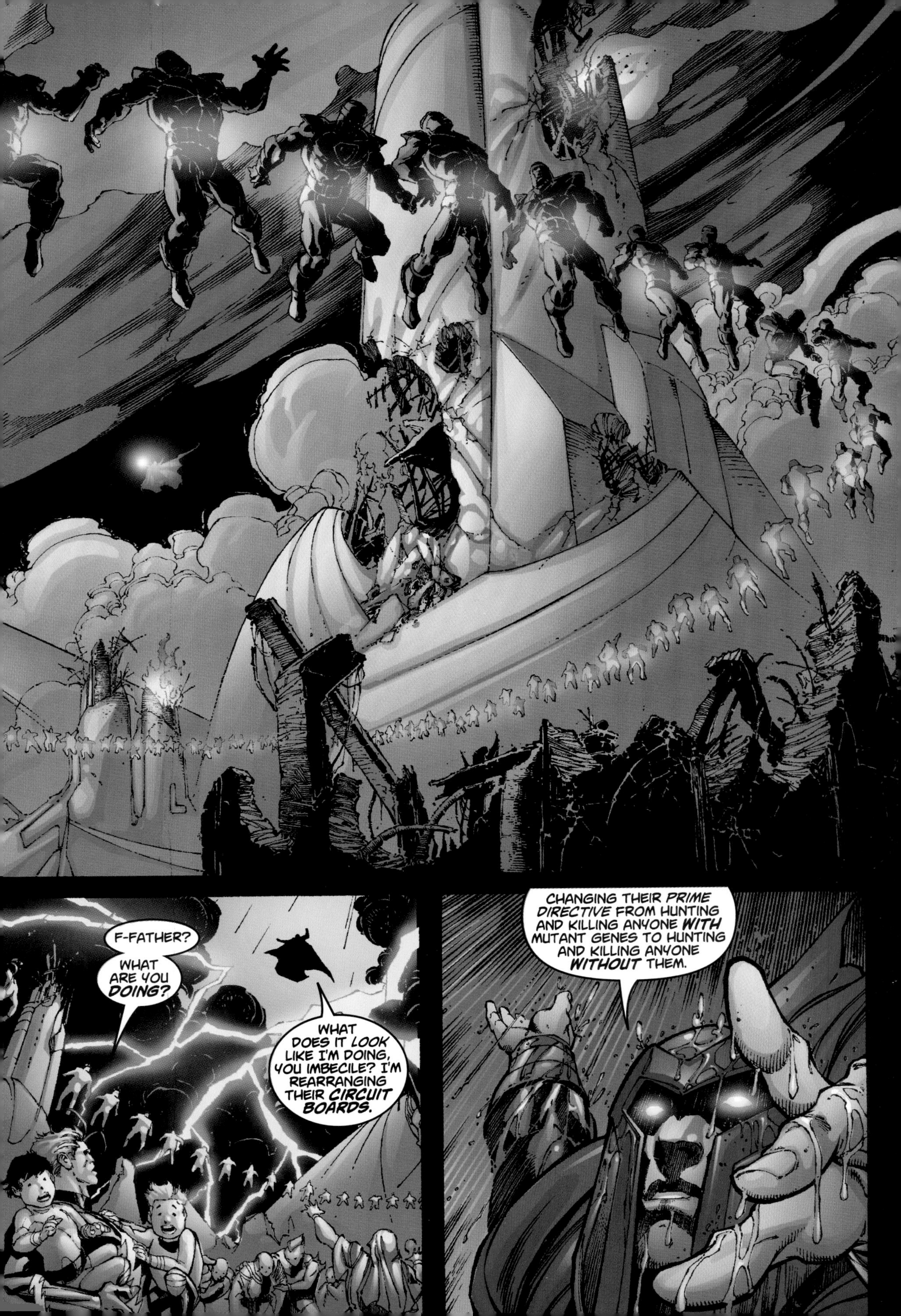
F-FATHER?
WHAT ARE YOU DOING?
WHAT DOES IT LOOK LIKE I'M DOING, YOU IMBECILE? I'M REARRANGING THEIR CIRCUIT BOARDS.
CHANGING THEIR PRIME DIRECTIVE FROM HUNTING AND KILLING ANYONE WITH MUTANT GENES TO HUNTING AND KILLING ANYONE WITHOUT THEM.

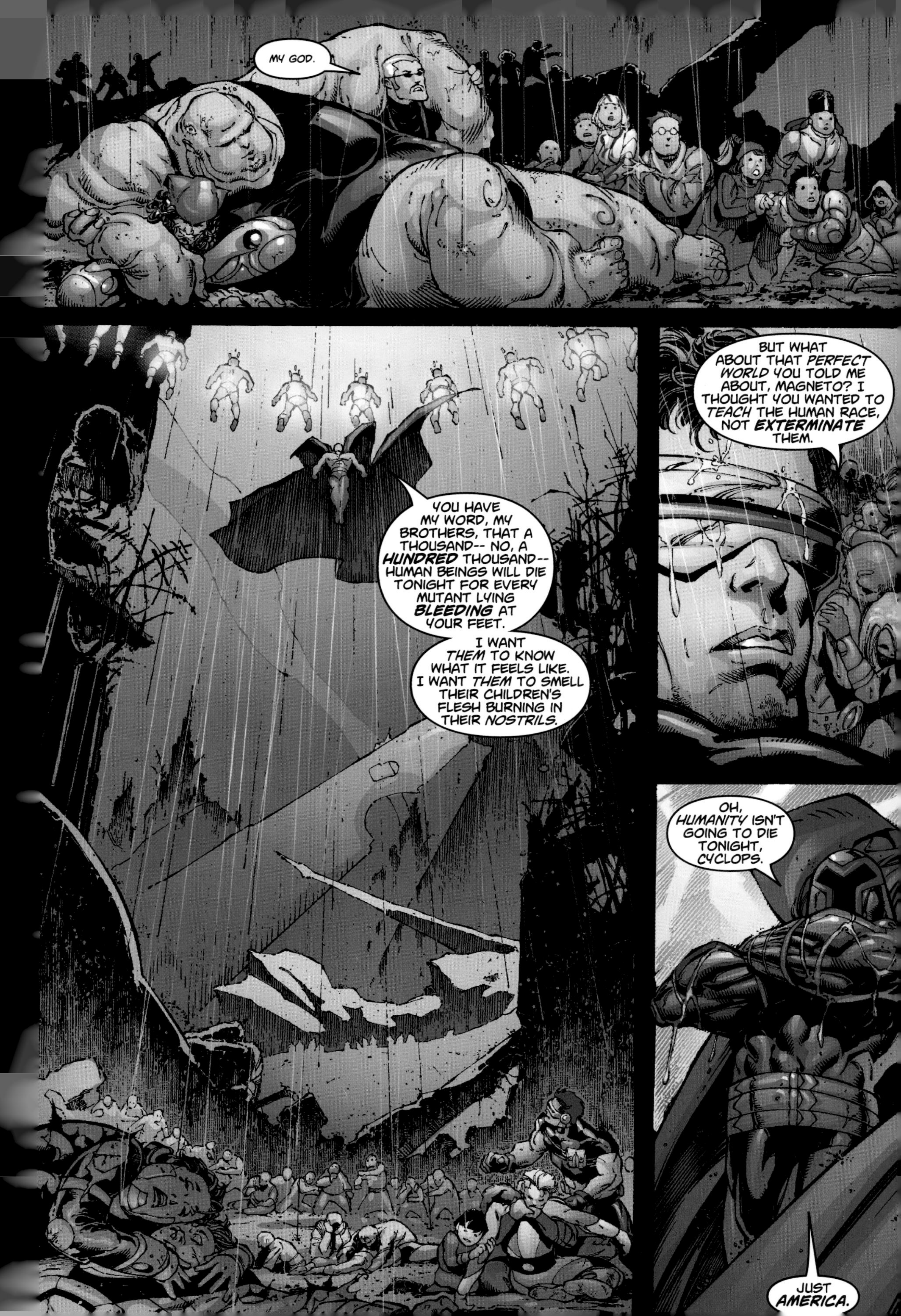
MY GOD.
YOU HAVE MY WORD, MY BROTHERS, THAT A THOUSAND-- NO, A HUNDRED THOUSAND-- HUMAN BEINGS WILL DIE TONIGHT FOR EVERY MUTANT LYING BLEEDING AT YOUR FEET.
I WANT THEM TO KNOW WHAT IT FEELS LIKE. I WANT THEM TO SMELL THEIR CHILDREN'S FLESH BURNING IN THEIR NOSTRILS.
BUT WHAT ABOUT THAT PERFECT WORLD YOU TOLD ME ABOUT, MAGNETO? I THOUGHT YOU WANTED TO TEACH THE HUMAN RACE, NOT EXTERMINATE THEM.
OH, HUMANITY ISN'T GOING TO DIE TONIGHT, CYCLOPS.
JUST AMERICA.

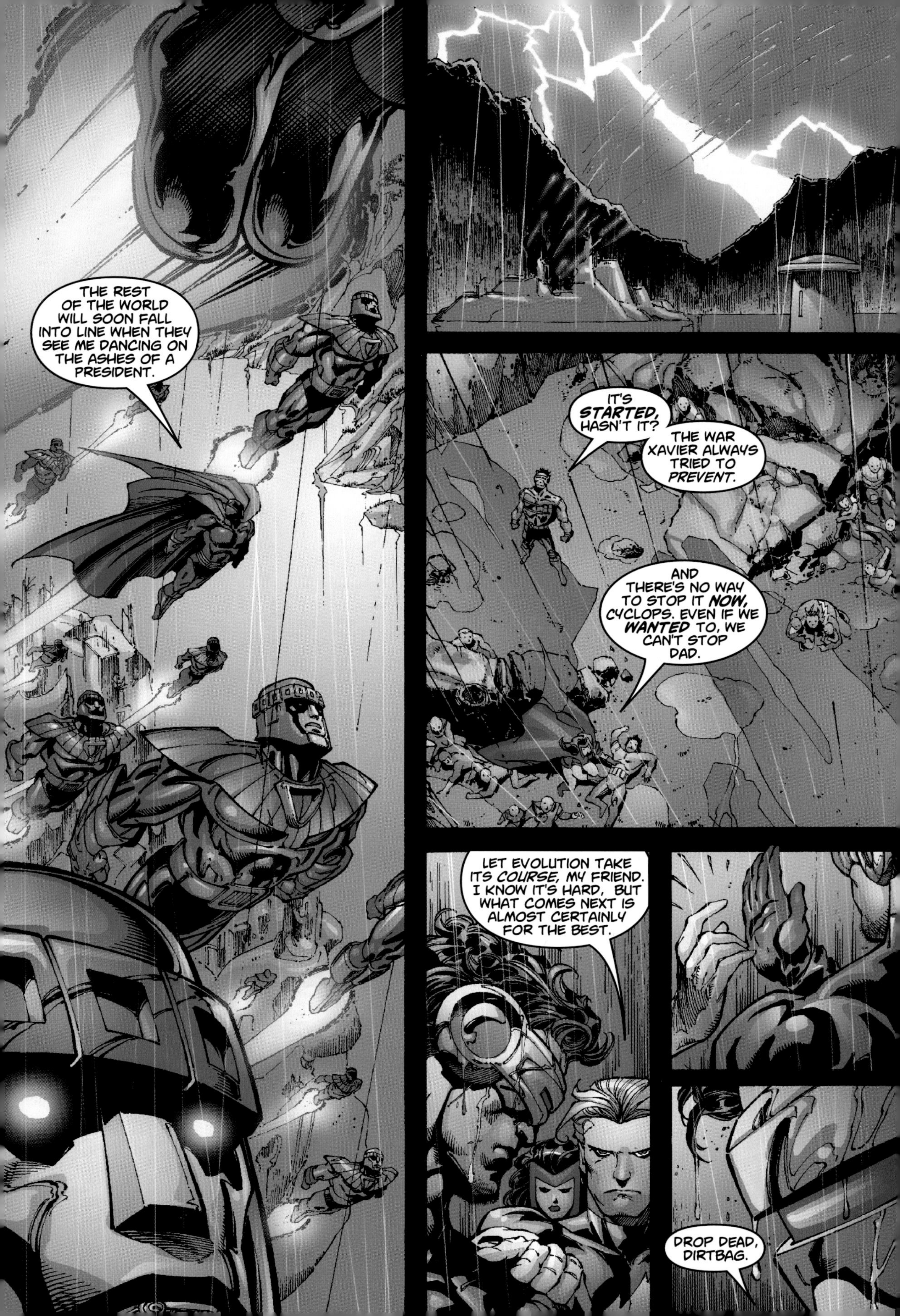
THE REST OF THE WORLD WILL SOON FALL INTO LINE WHEN THEY SEE ME DANCING ON THE ASHES OF A PRESIDENT.
IT'S STARTED, HASN'T IT?
THE WAR XAVIER ALWAYS TRIED TO PREVENT.
AND THERE'S NO WAY TO STOP IT NOW, CYCLOPS. EVEN IF WE WANTED TO, WE CAN'T STOP DAD.
LET EVOLUTION TAKE ITS COURSE, MY FRIEND. I KNOW IT'S HARD, BUT WHAT COMES NEXT IS ALMOST CERTAINLY FOR THE BEST.
DROP DEAD, DIRTBAG.

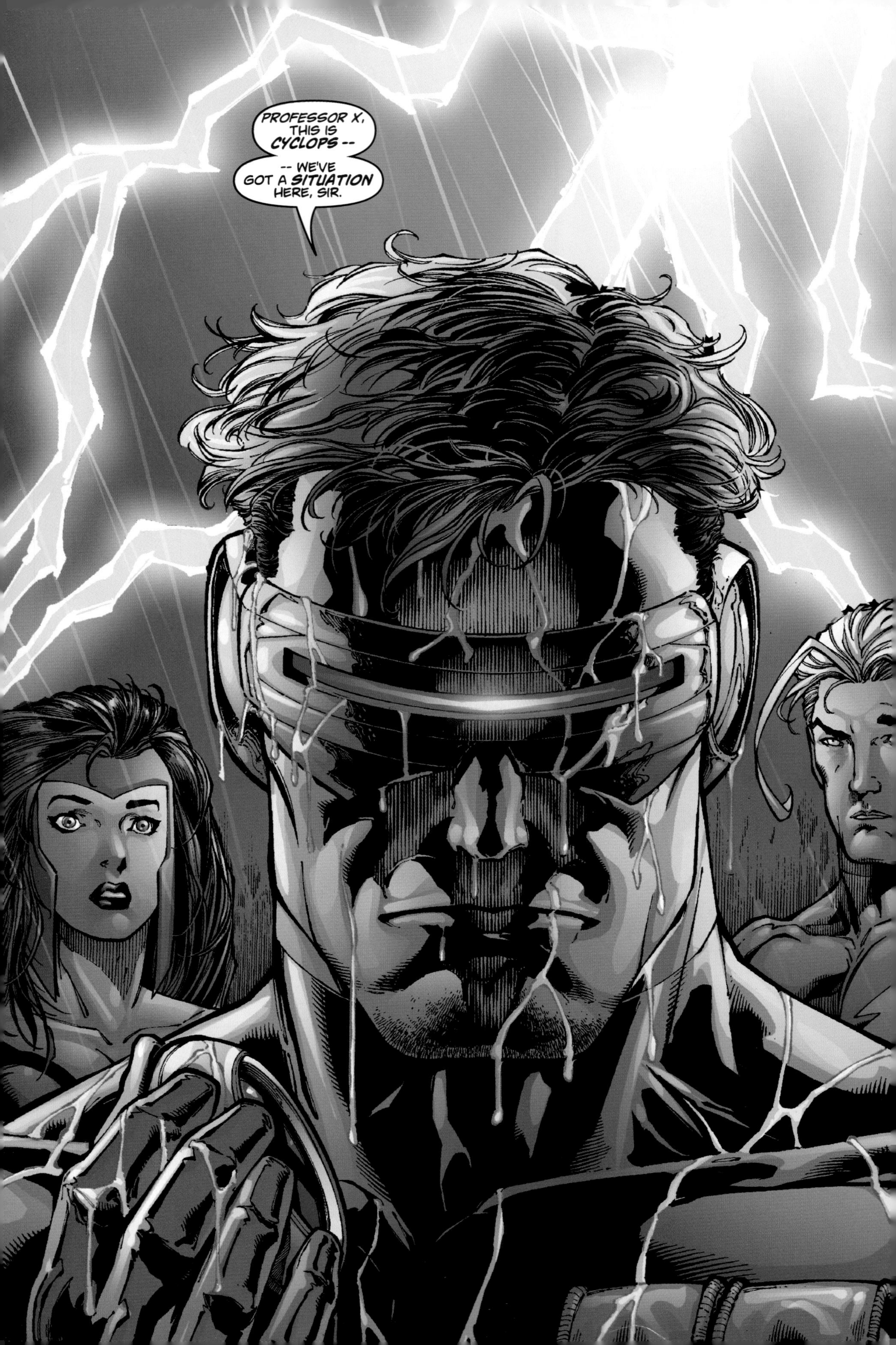
PROFESSOR X, THIS IS CYCLOPS --
-- WE'VE GOT A SITUATION HERE, SIR.

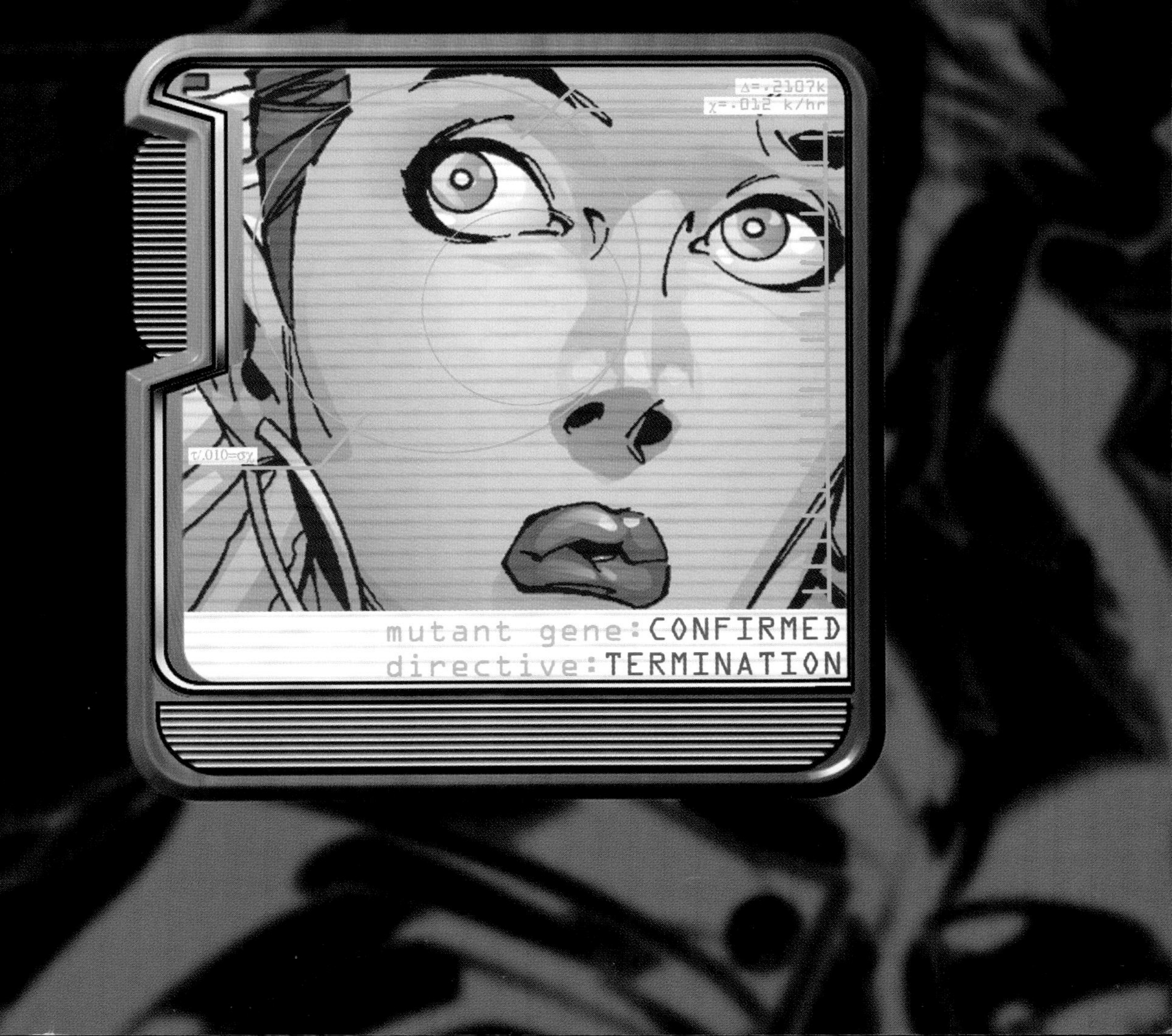
Δ=.2107k
χ=.012 k/hr
τ/.010=σχ
mutant gene:CONFIRMED
directive:TERMINATION

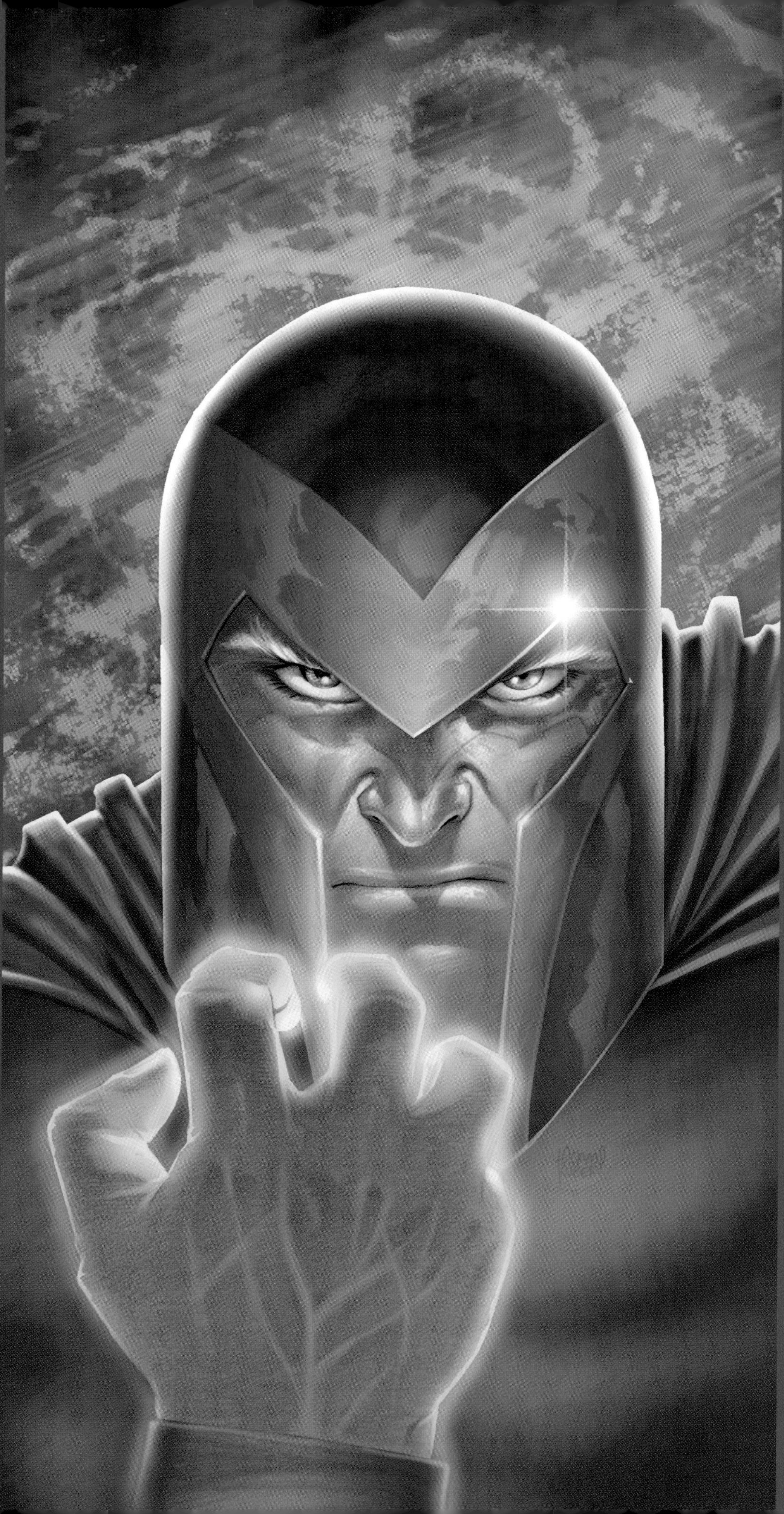

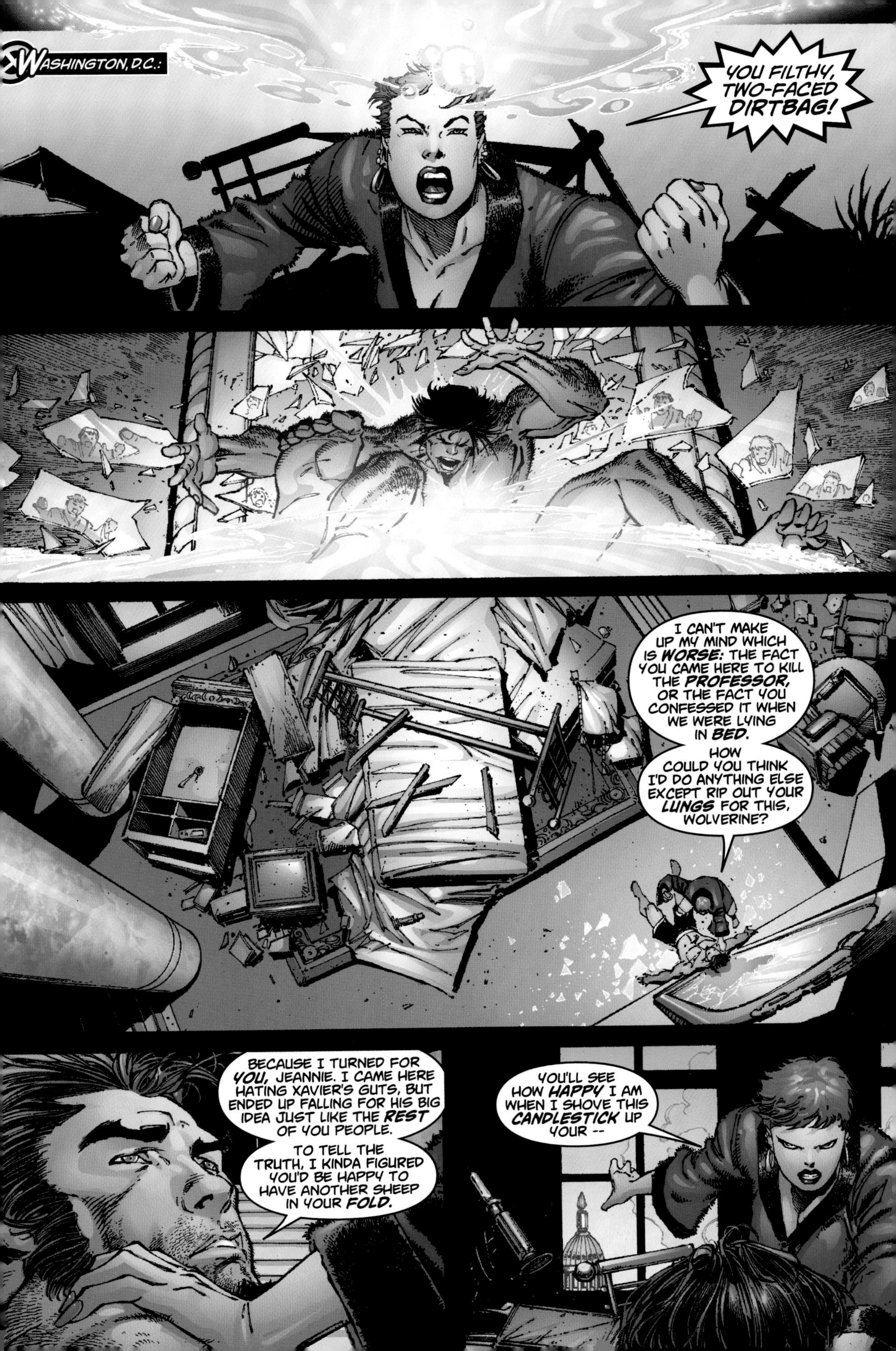
WASHINGTON, D.C.:
YOU FILTHY, TWO-FACED DIRTBAG!
I CAN'T MAKE UP MY MIND WHICH IS WORSE: THE FACT YOU CAME HERE TO KILL THE PROFESSOR, OR THE FACT YOU CONFESSED IT WHEN WE WERE LYING IN BED.
HOW COULD YOU THINK I'D DO ANYTHING ELSE EXCEPT RIP OUT YOUR LUNGS FOR THIS, WOLVERINE?
BECAUSE I TURNED FOR YOU, JEANNIE. I CAME HERE HATING XAVIER'S GUTS, BUT ENDED UP FALLING FOR HIS BIG IDEA JUST LIKE THE REST OF YOU PEOPLE.
TO TELL THE TRUTH, I KINDA FIGURED YOU'D BE HAPPY TO HAVE ANOTHER SHEEP IN YOUR FOLD.
YOU'LL SEE HOW HAPPY I AM WHEN I SHOVE THIS CANDLESTICK UP YOUR --

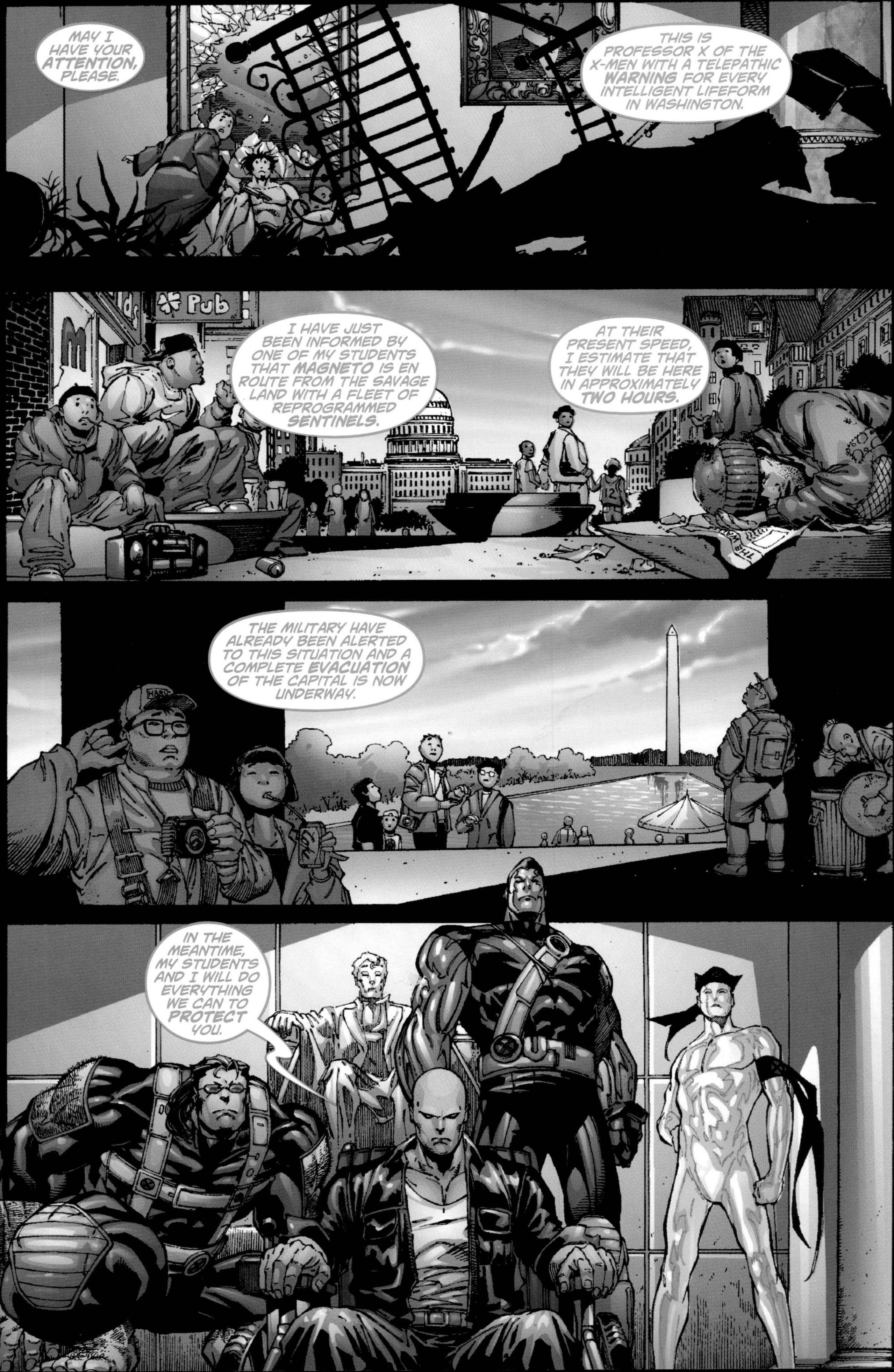

MAY I HAVE YOUR ATTENTION, PLEASE.
THIS IS PROFESSOR X OF THE X-MEN WITH A TELEPATHIC WARNING FOR EVERY INTELLIGENT LIFEFORM IN WASHINGTON.
Pub
I HAVE JUST BEEN INFORMED BY ONE OF MY STUDENTS THAT MAGNETO IS EN ROUTE FROM THE SAVAGE LAND WITH A FLEET OF REPROGRAMMED SENTINELS.
AT THEIR PRESENT SPEED, I ESTIMATE THAT THEY WILL BE HERE IN APPROXIMATELY TWO HOURS.
THE MILITARY HAVE ALREADY BEEN ALERTED TO THIS SITUATION AND A COMPLETE EVACUATION OF THE CAPITAL IS NOW UNDERWAY.
IN THE MEANTIME, MY STUDENTS AND I WILL DO EVERYTHING WE CAN TO PROTECT YOU.

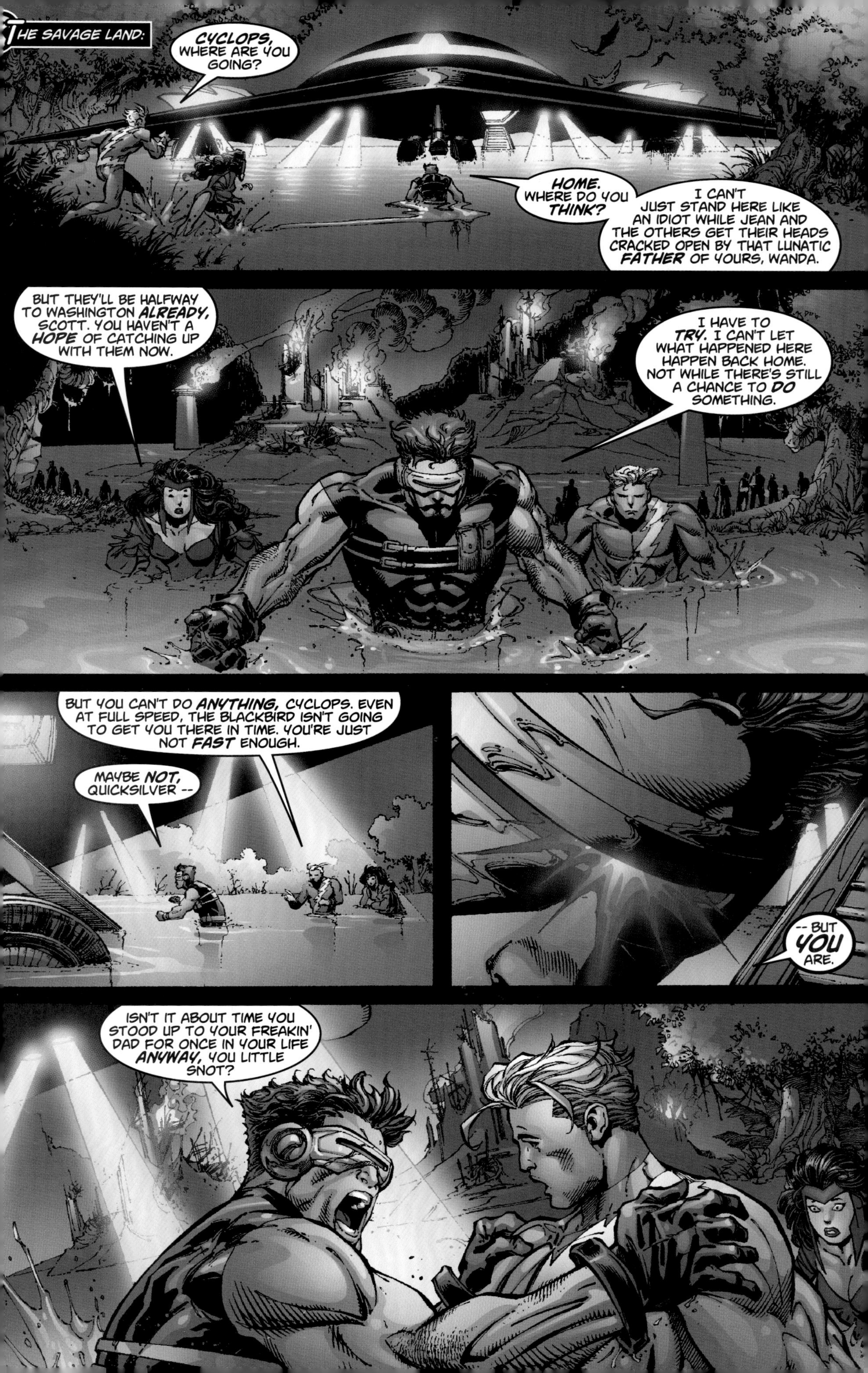
THE SAVAGE LAND:
CYCLOPS, WHERE ARE YOU GOING?
HOME. WHERE DO YOU THINK?
I CAN'T JUST STAND HERE LIKE AN IDIOT WHILE JEAN AND THE OTHERS GET THEIR HEADS CRACKED OPEN BY THAT LUNATIC FATHER OF YOURS, WANDA.
BUT THEY'LL BE HALFWAY TO WASHINGTON ALREADY, SCOTT. YOU HAVEN'T A HOPE OF CATCHING UP WITH THEM NOW.
I HAVE TO TRY. I CAN'T LET WHAT HAPPENED HERE HAPPEN BACK HOME. NOT WHILE THERE'S STILL A CHANCE TO DO SOMETHING.
BUT YOU CAN'T DO ANYTHING, CYCLOPS. EVEN AT FULL SPEED, THE BLACKBIRD ISN'T GOING TO GET YOU THERE IN TIME. YOU'RE JUST NOT FAST ENOUGH.
MAYBE NOT, QUICKSILVER --
-- BUT YOU ARE.
ISN'T IT ABOUT TIME YOU STOOD UP TO YOUR FREAKIN' DAD FOR ONCE IN YOUR LIFE ANYWAY, YOU LITTLE SNOT?

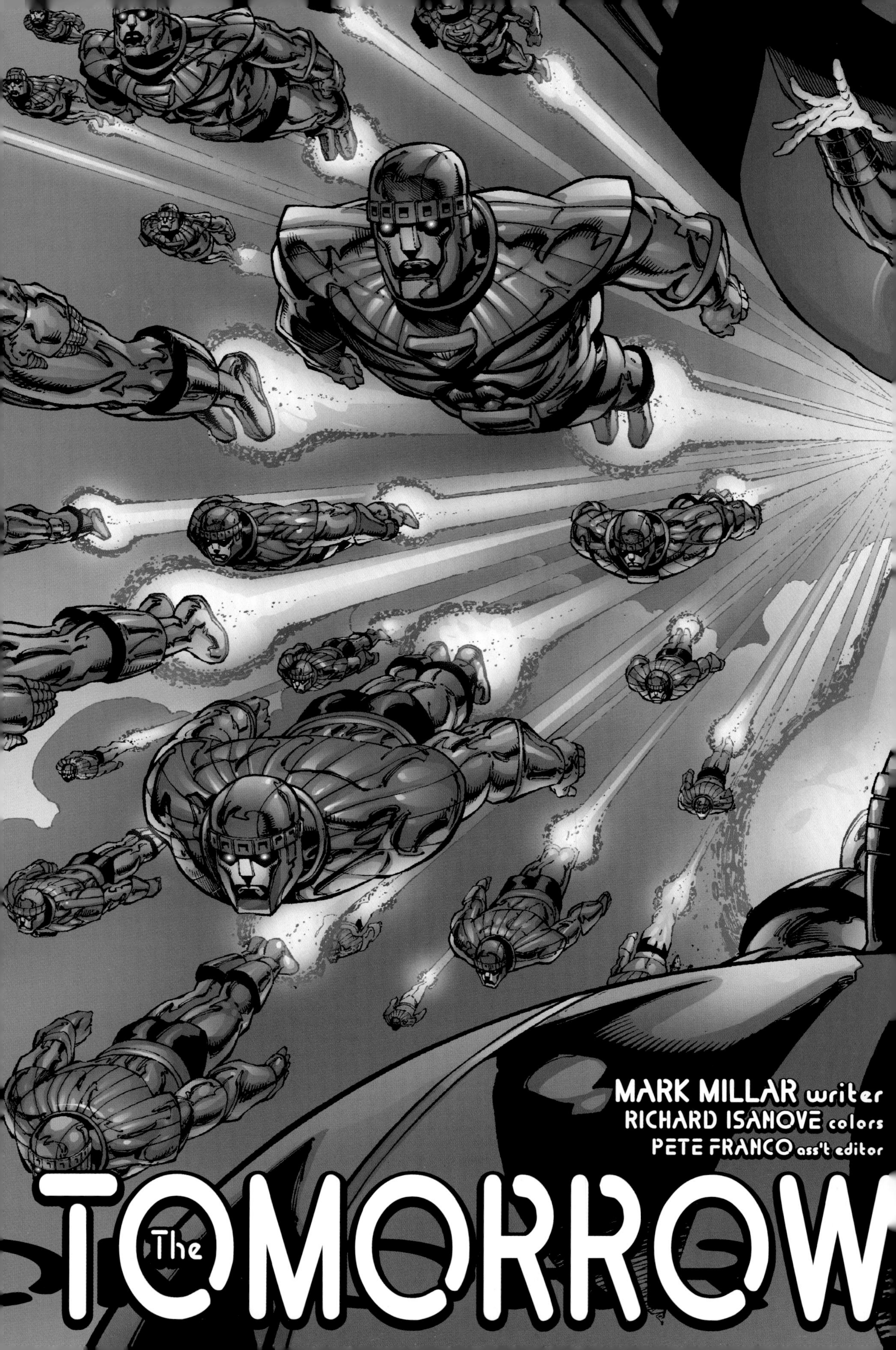
MARK MILLAR writer
RICHARD ISANOVE colors
PETE FRANCO ass't editor
The TOMORROW

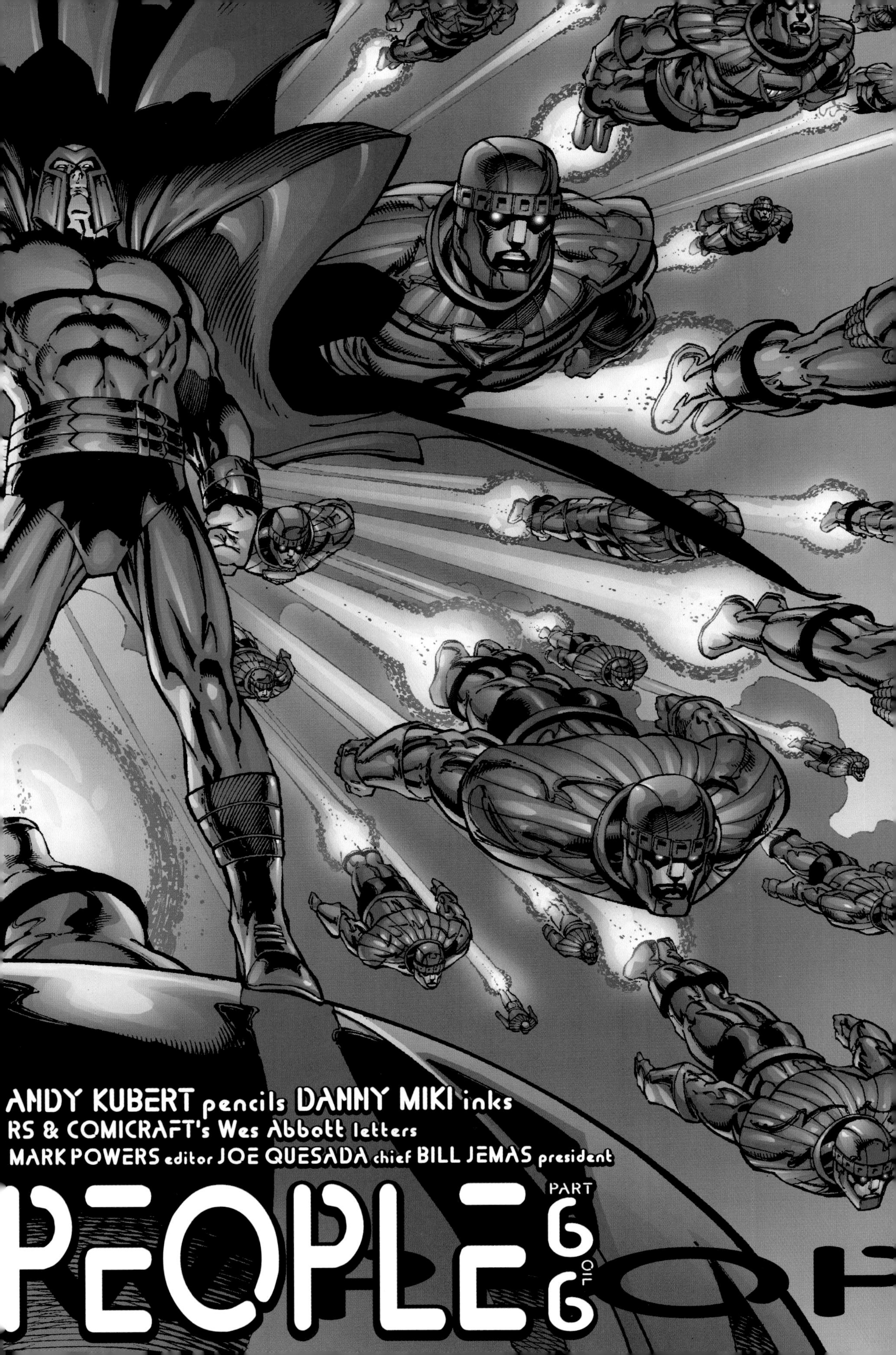
ANDY KUBERT pencils DANNY MIKI inks
RS & COMICRAFT's Wes Abbott letters
MARK POWERS editor JOE QUESADA chief BILL JEMAS president
PEOPLE
PART 6 OF 6

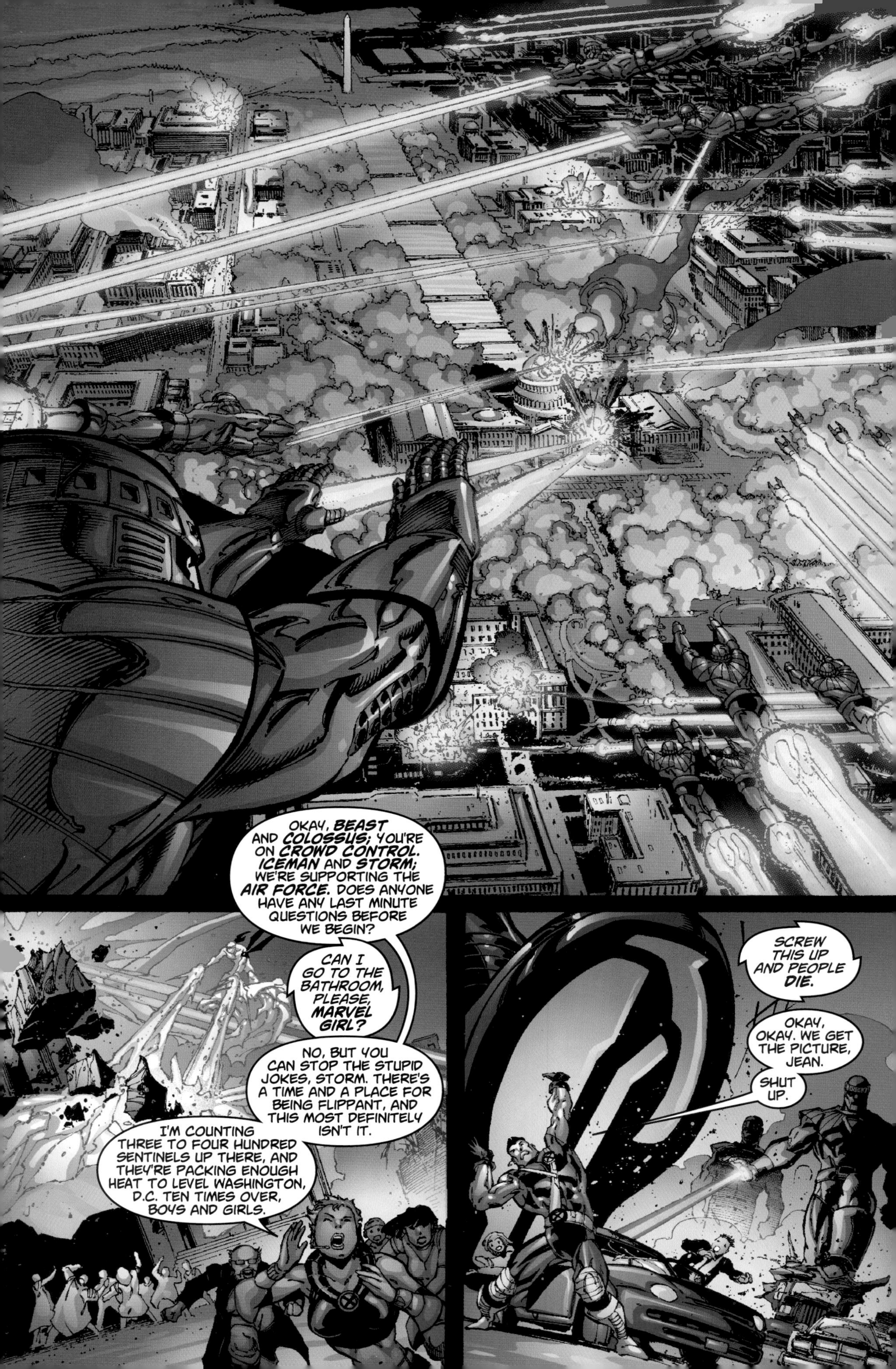
OKAY, BEAST AND COLOSSUS; YOU'RE ON CROWD CONTROL. ICEMAN AND STORM; WE'RE SUPPORTING THE AIR FORCE. DOES ANYONE HAVE ANY LAST MINUTE QUESTIONS BEFORE WE BEGIN?
CAN I GO TO THE BATHROOM, PLEASE, MARVEL GIRL?
NO, BUT YOU CAN STOP THE STUPID JOKES, STORM. THERE'S A TIME AND A PLACE FOR BEING FLIPPANT, AND THIS MOST DEFINITELY ISN'T IT.
I'M COUNTING THREE TO FOUR HUNDRED SENTINELS UP THERE, AND THEY'RE PACKING ENOUGH HEAT TO LEVEL WASHINGTON, D.C. TEN TIMES OVER, BOYS AND GIRLS.
SCREW THIS UP AND PEOPLE DIE.
OKAY, OKAY. WE GET THE PICTURE, JEAN.
SHUT UP.

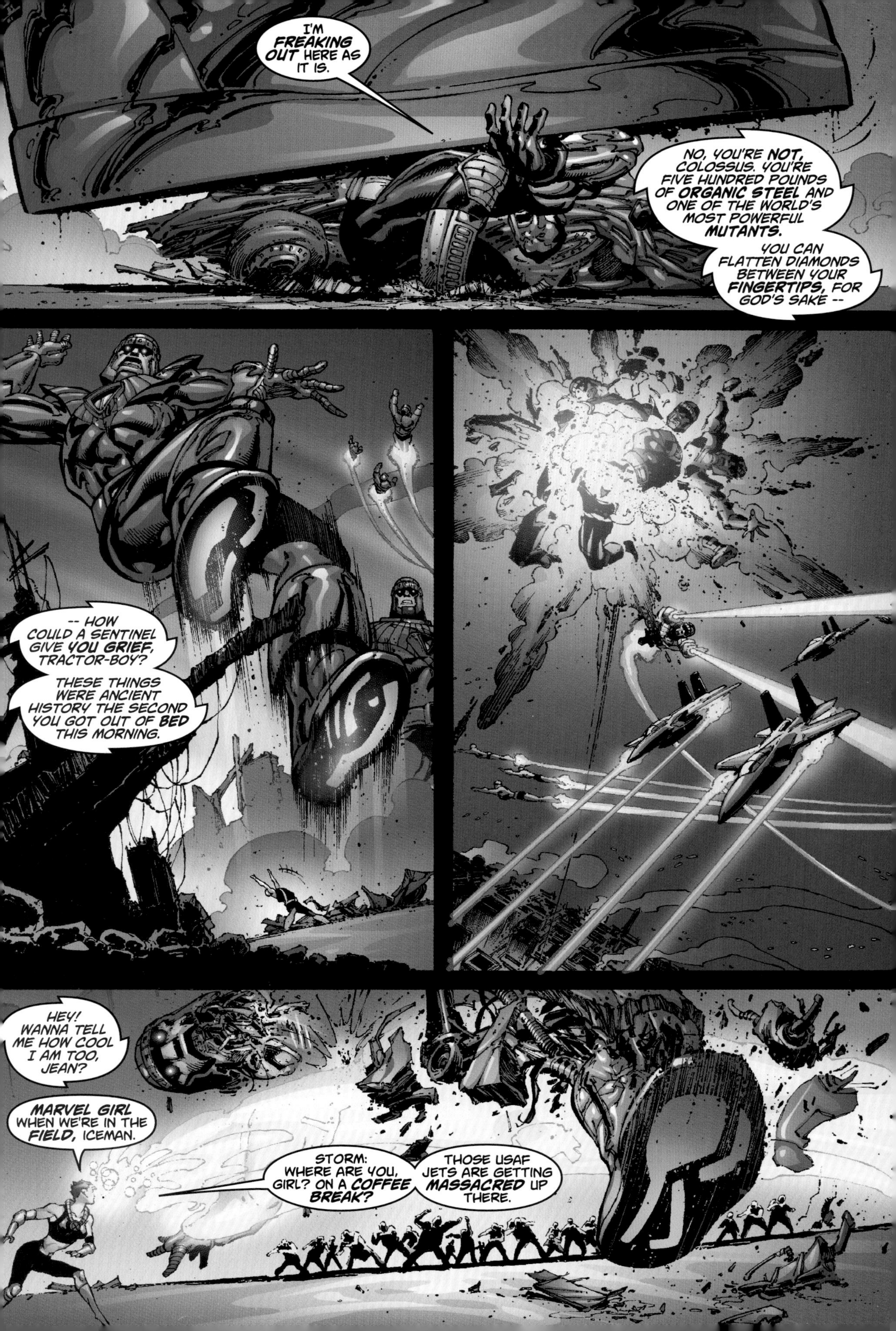
I'M FREAKING OUT HERE AS IT IS.
NO, YOU'RE NOT, COLOSSUS. YOU'RE FIVE HUNDRED POUNDS OF ORGANIC STEEL AND ONE OF THE WORLD'S MOST POWERFUL MUTANTS.
YOU CAN FLATTEN DIAMONDS BETWEEN YOUR FINGERTIPS, FOR GOD'S SAKE --
-- HOW COULD A SENTINEL GIVE YOU GRIEF, TRACTOR-BOY?
THESE THINGS WERE ANCIENT HISTORY THE SECOND YOU GOT OUT OF BED THIS MORNING.
HEY! WANNA TELL ME HOW COOL I AM TOO, JEAN?
MARVEL GIRL WHEN WE'RE IN THE FIELD, ICEMAN.
STORM: WHERE ARE YOU, GIRL? ON A COFFEE BREAK?
THOSE USAF JETS ARE GETTING MASSACRED UP THERE.

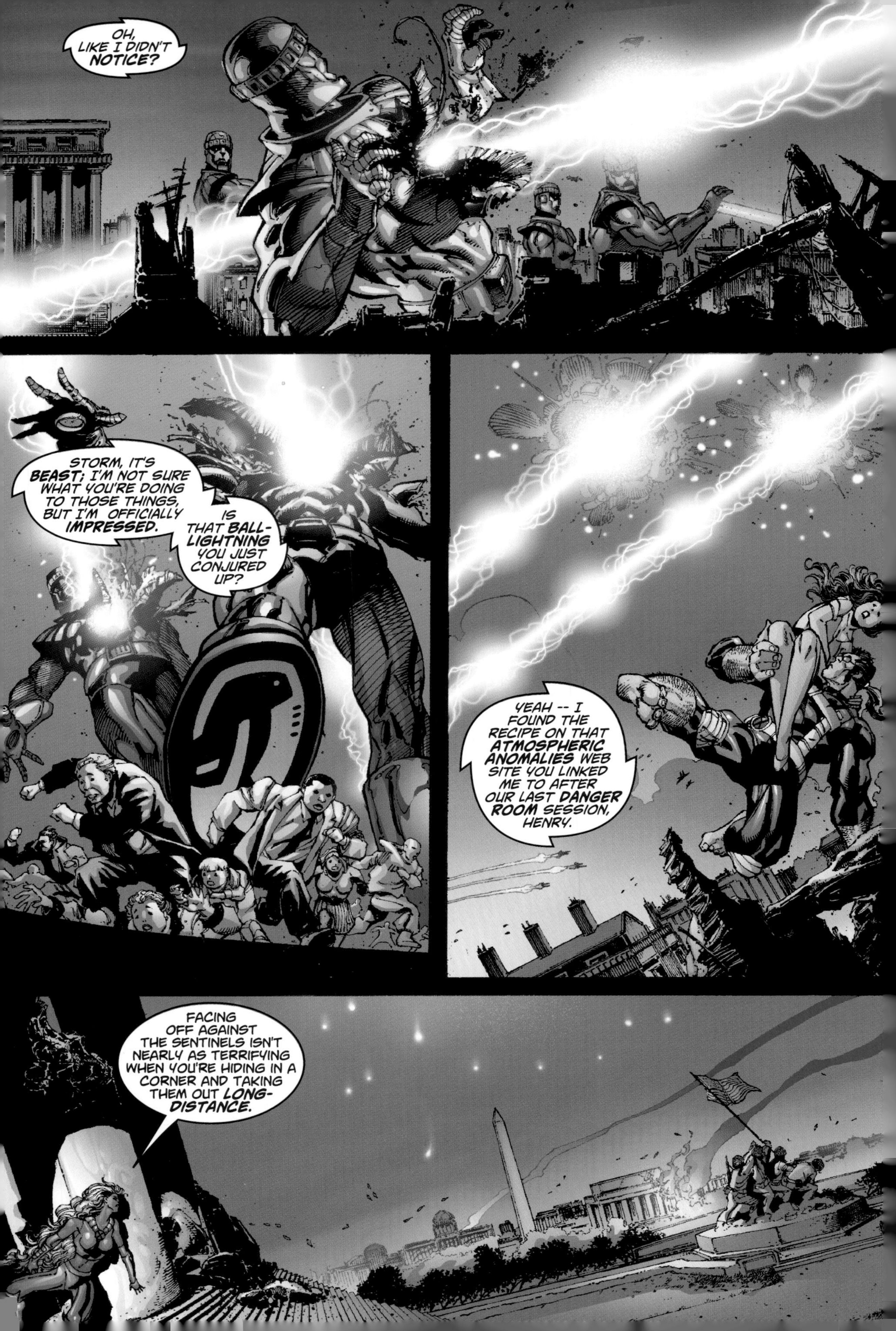
OH, LIKE I DIDN'T NOTICE?
STORM, IT'S BEAST; I'M NOT SURE WHAT YOU'RE DOING TO THOSE THINGS, BUT I'M OFFICIALLY IMPRESSED.
IS THAT BALL-LIGHTNING YOU JUST CONJURED UP?
YEAH -- I FOUND THE RECIPE ON THAT ATMOSPHERIC ANOMALIES WEB SITE YOU LINKED ME TO AFTER OUR LAST DANGER ROOM SESSION, HENRY.
FACING OFF AGAINST THE SENTINELS ISN'T NEARLY AS TERRIFYING WHEN YOU'RE HIDING IN A CORNER AND TAKING THEM OUT LONG-DISTANCE.

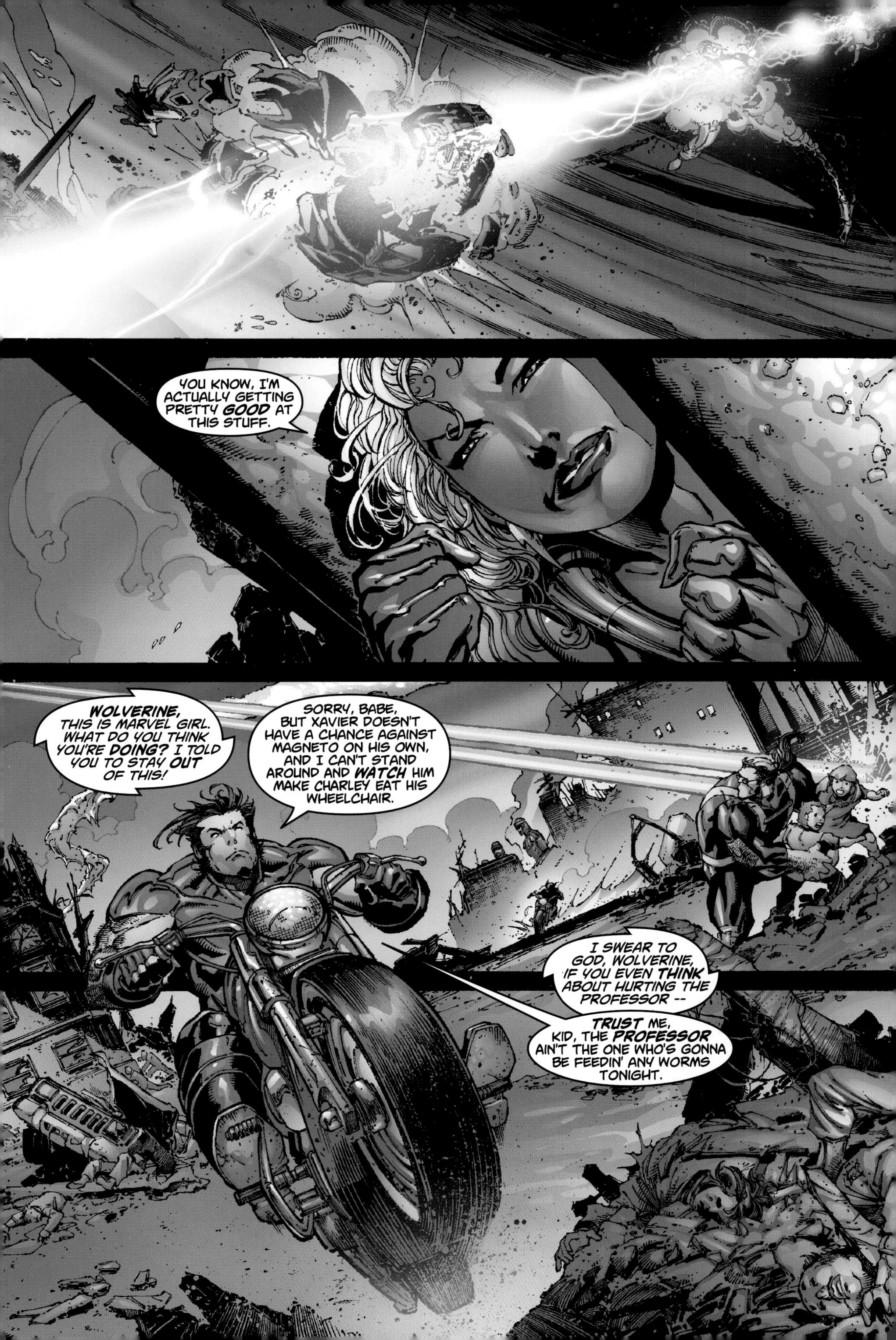

YOU KNOW, I'M ACTUALLY GETTING PRETTY GOOD AT THIS STUFF.
WOLVERINE, THIS IS MARVEL GIRL. WHAT DO YOU THINK YOU'RE DOING? I TOLD YOU TO STAY OUT OF THIS!
SORRY, BABE, BUT XAVIER DOESN'T HAVE A CHANCE AGAINST MAGNETO ON HIS OWN, AND I CAN'T STAND AROUND AND WATCH HIM MAKE CHARLEY EAT HIS WHEELCHAIR.
I SWEAR TO GOD, WOLVERINE, IF YOU EVEN THINK ABOUT HURTING THE PROFESSOR --
TRUST ME, KID, THE PROFESSOR AIN'T THE ONE WHO'S GONNA BE FEEDIN' ANY WORMS TONIGHT.

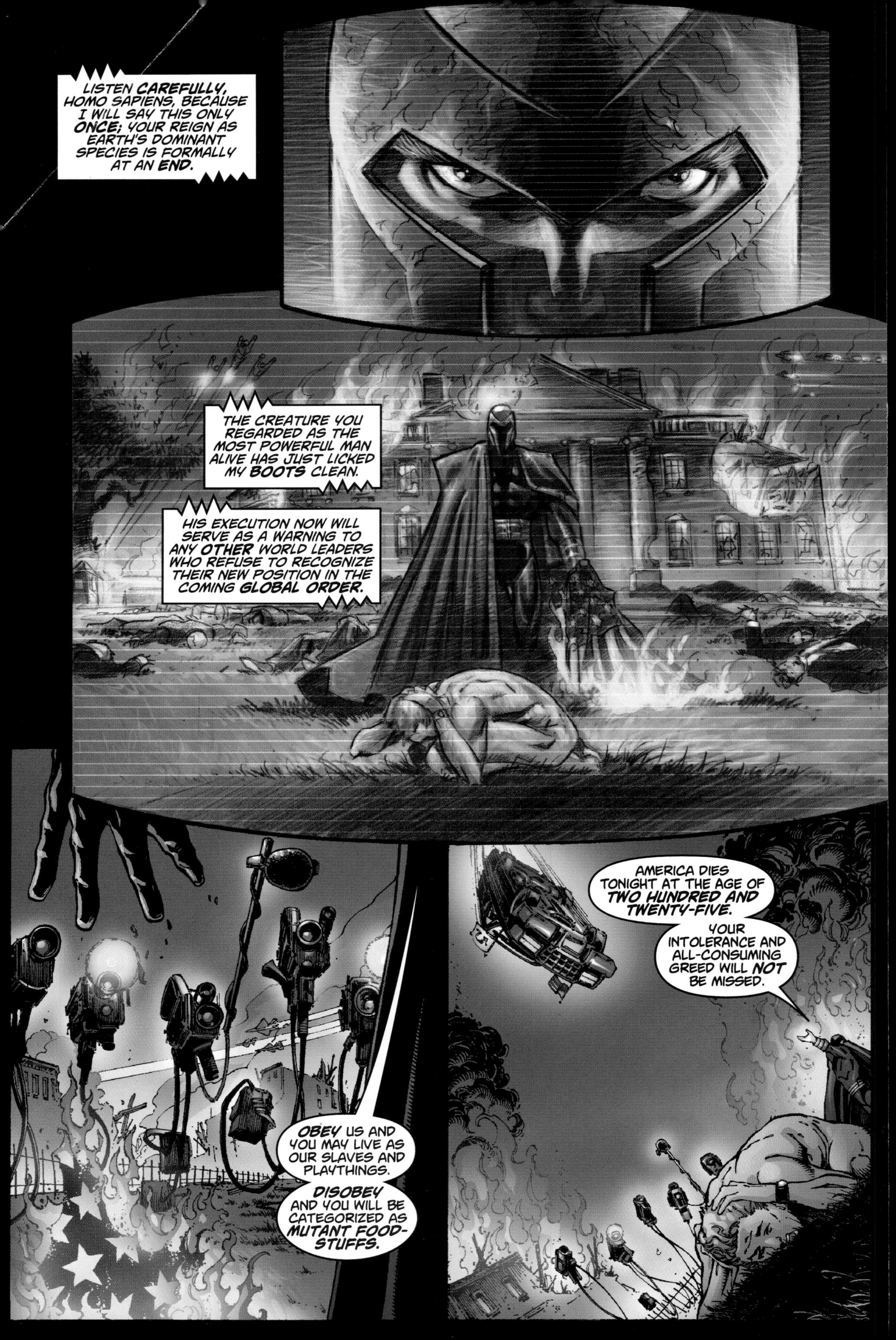
LISTEN CAREFULLY, HOMO SAPIENS, BECAUSE I WILL SAY THIS ONLY ONCE; YOUR REIGN AS EARTH'S DOMINANT SPECIES IS FORMALLY AT AN END.
THE CREATURE YOU REGARDED AS THE MOST POWERFUL MAN ALIVE HAS JUST LICKED MY BOOTS CLEAN.
HIS EXECUTION NOW WILL SERVE AS A WARNING TO ANY OTHER WORLD LEADERS WHO REFUSE TO RECOGNIZE THEIR NEW POSITION IN THE COMING GLOBAL ORDER.
OBEY US AND YOU MAY LIVE AS OUR SLAVES AND PLAYTHINGS.
DISOBEY AND YOU WILL BE CATEGORIZED AS MUTANT FOOD-STUFFS.
AMERICA DIES TONIGHT AT THE AGE OF TWO HUNDRED AND TWENTY-FIVE.
YOUR INTOLERANCE AND ALL-CONSUMING GREED WILL NOT BE MISSED.

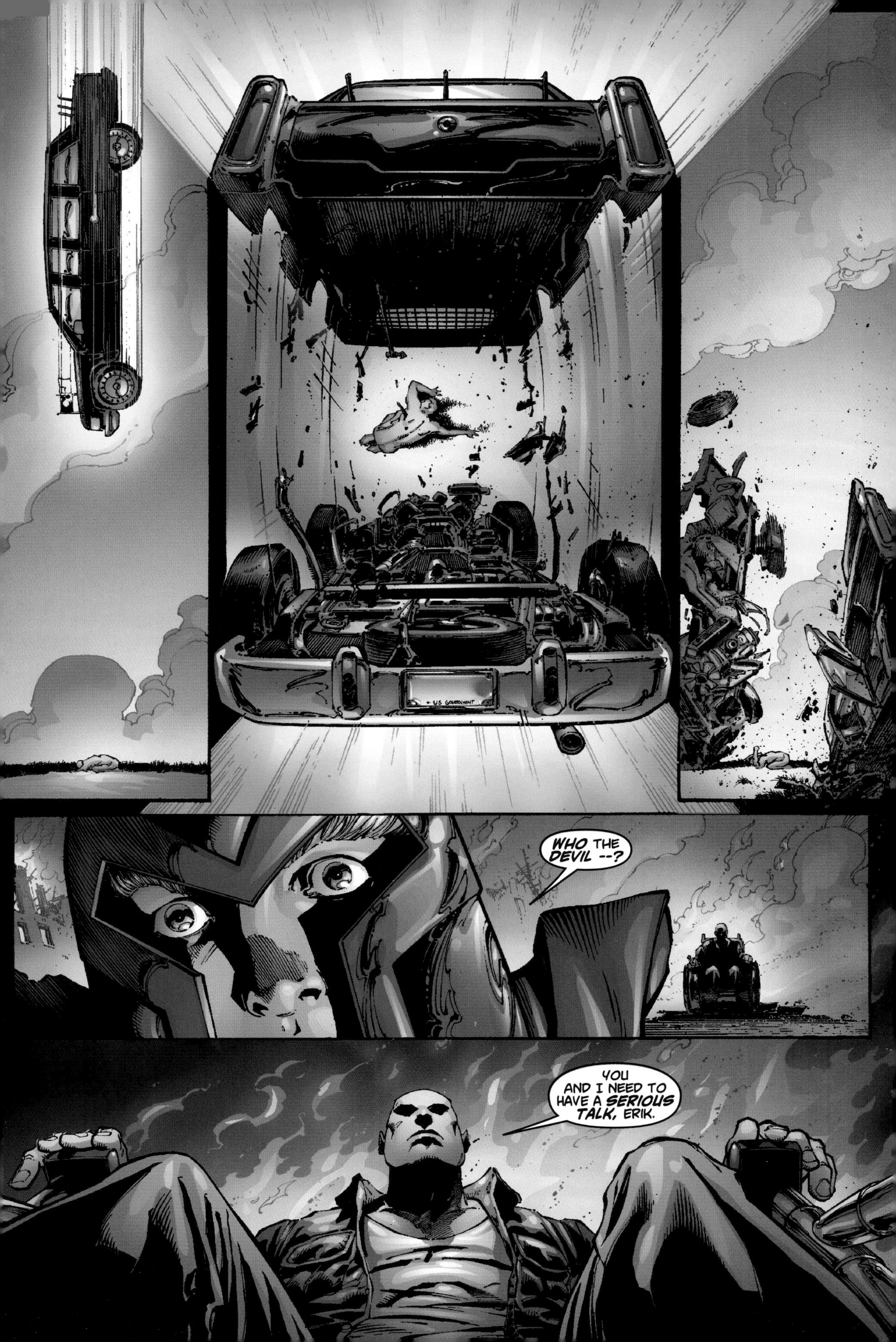
US GOVERNMENT
WHO THE DEVIL --?
YOU AND I NEED TO HAVE A SERIOUS TALK, ERIK.

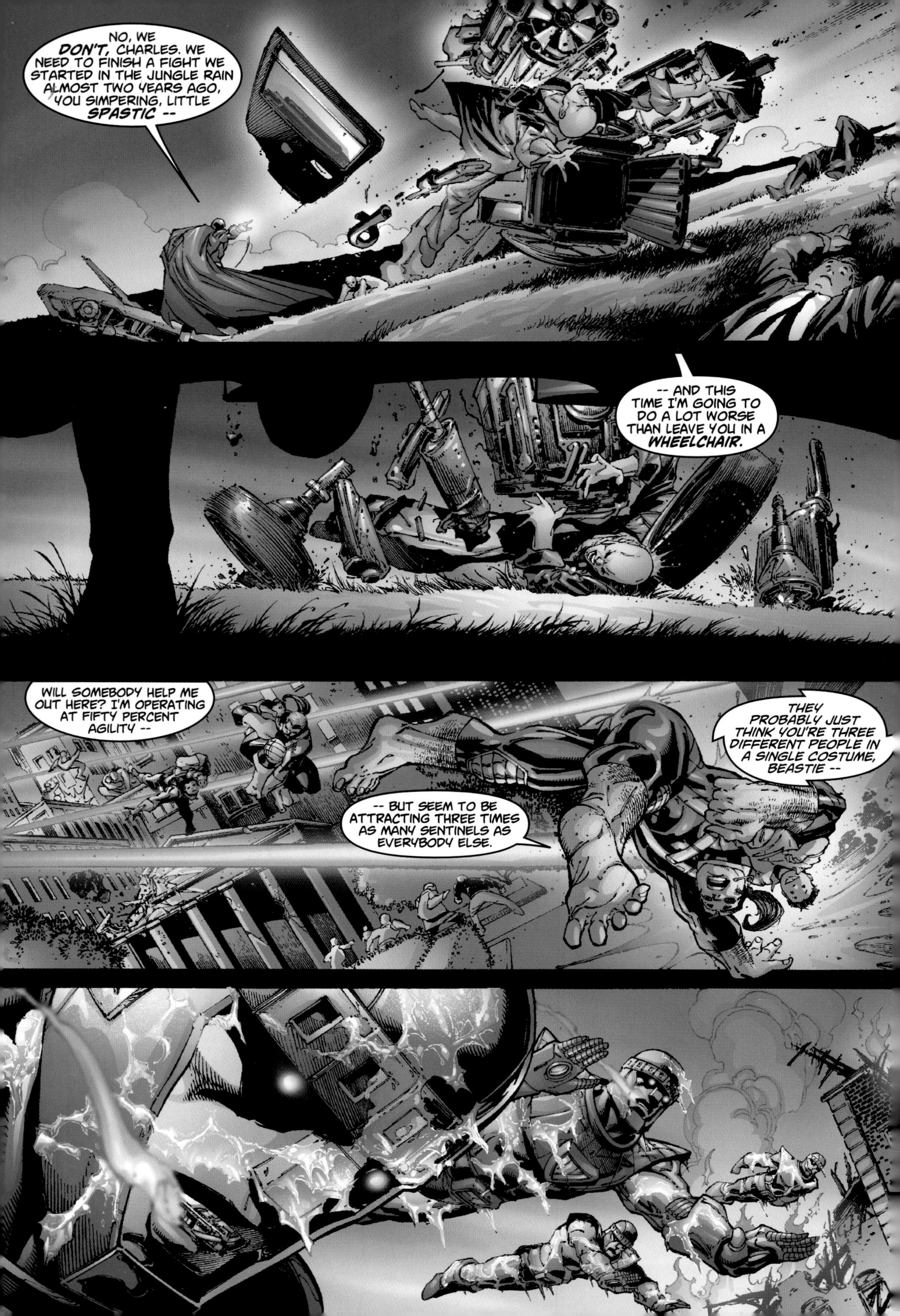
NO, WE DON'T, CHARLES. WE NEED TO FINISH A FIGHT WE STARTED IN THE JUNGLE RAIN ALMOST TWO YEARS AGO, YOU SIMPERING, LITTLE SPASTIC --
-- AND THIS TIME I'M GOING TO DO A LOT WORSE THAN LEAVE YOU IN A WHEELCHAIR.
WILL SOMEBODY HELP ME OUT HERE? I'M OPERATING AT FIFTY PERCENT AGILITY --
-- BUT SEEM TO BE ATTRACTING THREE TIMES AS MANY SENTINELS AS EVERYBODY ELSE.
THEY PROBABLY JUST THINK YOU'RE THREE DIFFERENT PEOPLE IN A SINGLE COSTUME, BEASTIE --

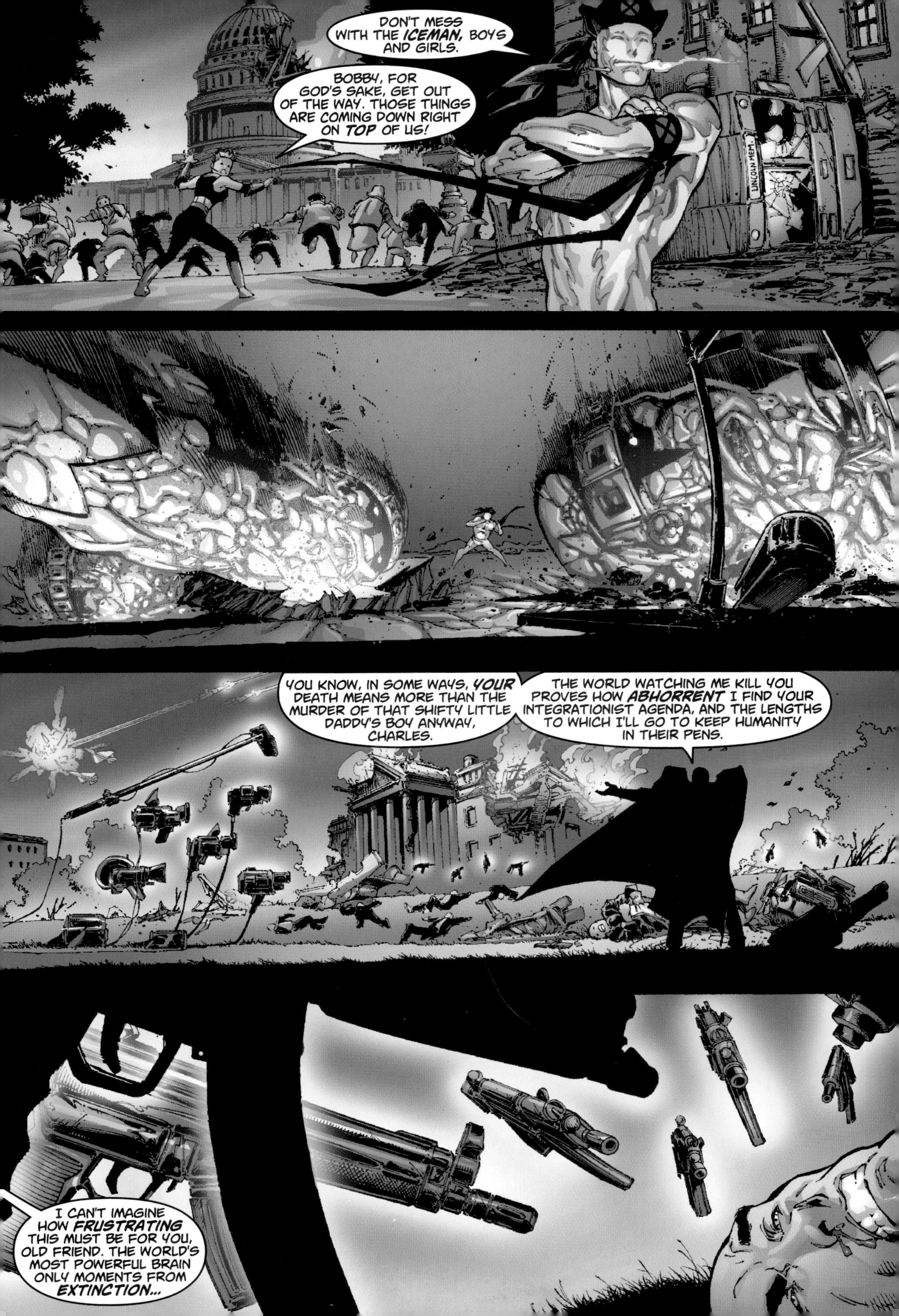
DON'T MESS WITH THE ICEMAN, BOYS AND GIRLS.
BOBBY, FOR GOD'S SAKE, GET OUT OF THE WAY. THOSE THINGS ARE COMING DOWN RIGHT ON TOP OF US!
LINCOLN MEM.
YOU KNOW, IN SOME WAYS, YOUR DEATH MEANS MORE THAN THE MURDER OF THAT SHIFTY LITTLE DADDY'S BOY ANYWAY, CHARLES.
THE WORLD WATCHING ME KILL YOU PROVES HOW ABHORRENT I FIND YOUR INTEGRATIONIST AGENDA, AND THE LENGTHS TO WHICH I'LL GO TO KEEP HUMANITY IN THEIR PENS.
I CAN'T IMAGINE HOW FRUSTRATING THIS MUST BE FOR YOU, OLD FRIEND. THE WORLD'S MOST POWERFUL BRAIN ONLY MOMENTS FROM EXTINCTION...

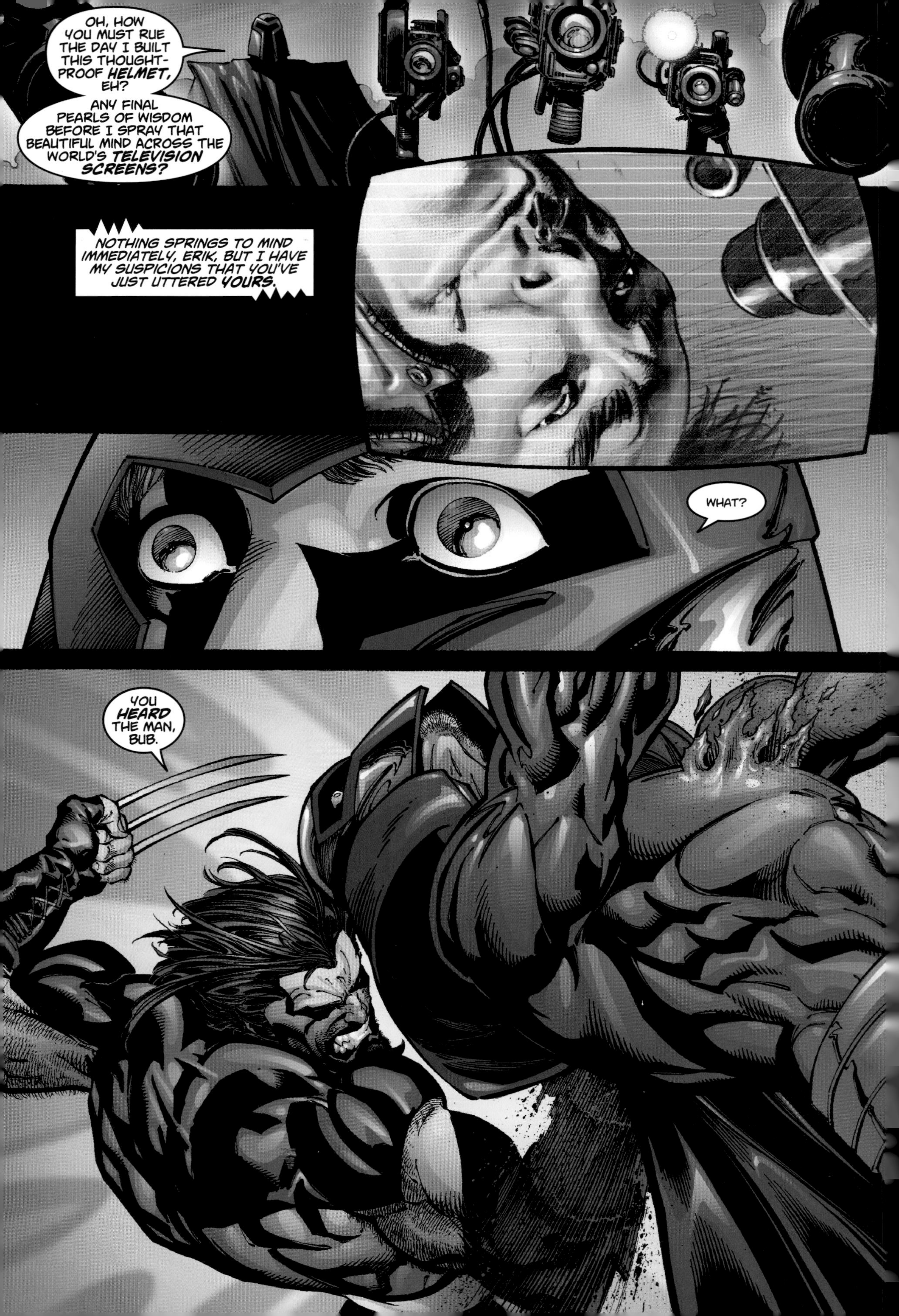
OH, HOW YOU MUST RUE THE DAY I BUILT THIS THOUGHT-PROOF HELMET, EH?
ANY FINAL PEARLS OF WISDOM BEFORE I SPRAY THAT BEAUTIFUL MIND ACROSS THE WORLD'S TELEVISION SCREENS?
NOTHING SPRINGS TO MIND IMMEDIATELY, ERIK, BUT I HAVE MY SUSPICIONS THAT YOU'VE JUST UTTERED YOURS.
WHAT?
YOU HEARD THE MAN, BUB.

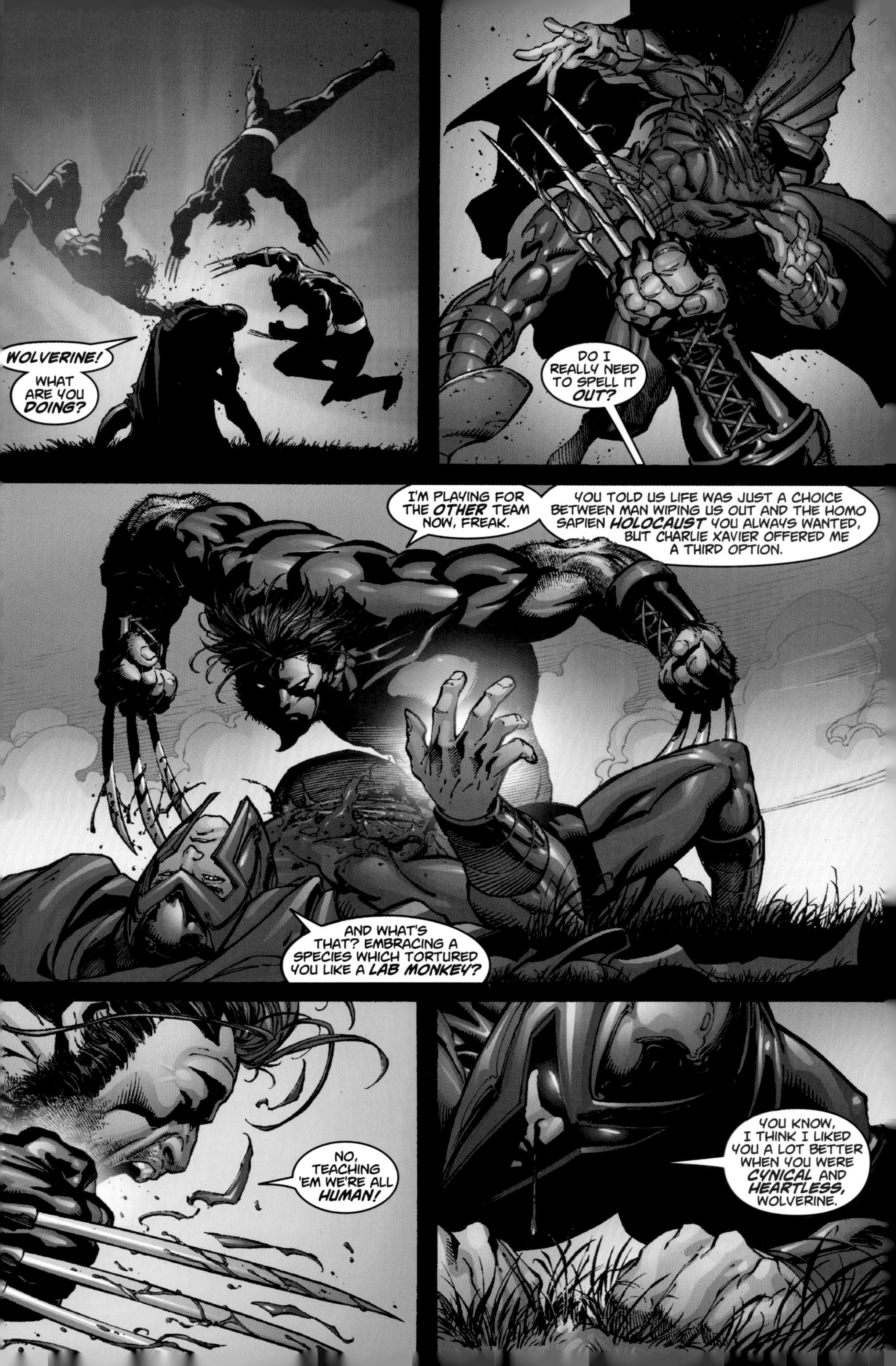
WOLVERINE! WHAT ARE YOU DOING?
DO I REALLY NEED TO SPELL IT OUT?
I'M PLAYING FOR THE OTHER TEAM NOW, FREAK.
YOU TOLD US LIFE WAS JUST A CHOICE BETWEEN MAN WIPING US OUT AND THE HOMO SAPIEN HOLOCAUST YOU ALWAYS WANTED, BUT CHARLIE XAVIER OFFERED ME A THIRD OPTION.
AND WHAT'S THAT? EMBRACING A SPECIES WHICH TORTURED YOU LIKE A LAB MONKEY?
NO, TEACHING 'EM WE'RE ALL HUMAN!
YOU KNOW, I THINK I LIKED YOU A LOT BETTER WHEN YOU WERE CYNICAL AND HEARTLESS, WOLVERINE.

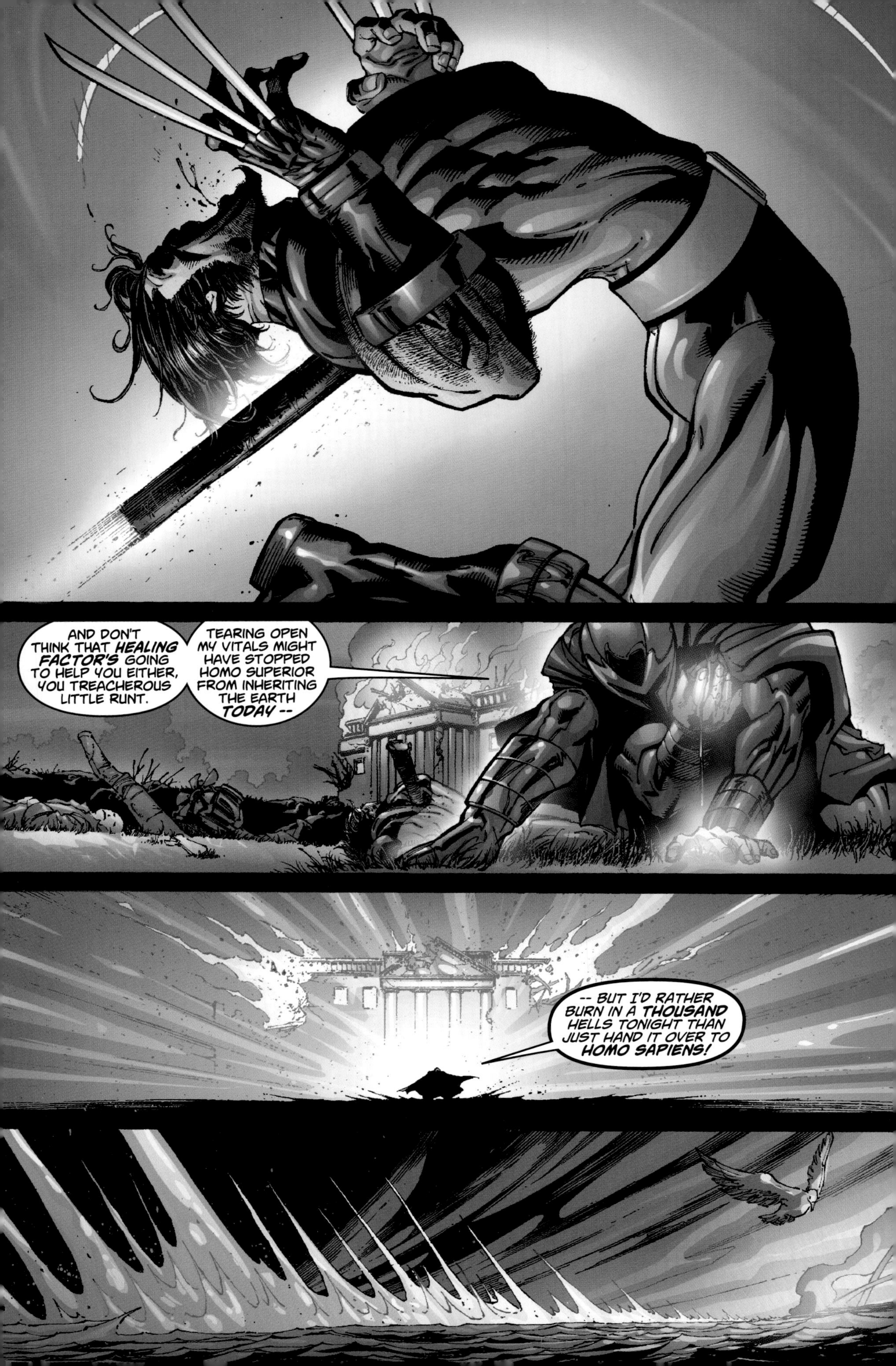
AND DON'T THINK THAT HEALING FACTOR'S GOING TO HELP YOU EITHER, YOU TREACHEROUS LITTLE RUNT.
TEARING OPEN MY VITALS MIGHT HAVE STOPPED HOMO SUPERIOR FROM INHERITING THE EARTH TODAY --
-- BUT I'D RATHER BURN IN A THOUSAND HELLS TONIGHT THAN JUST HAND IT OVER TO HOMO SAPIENS!

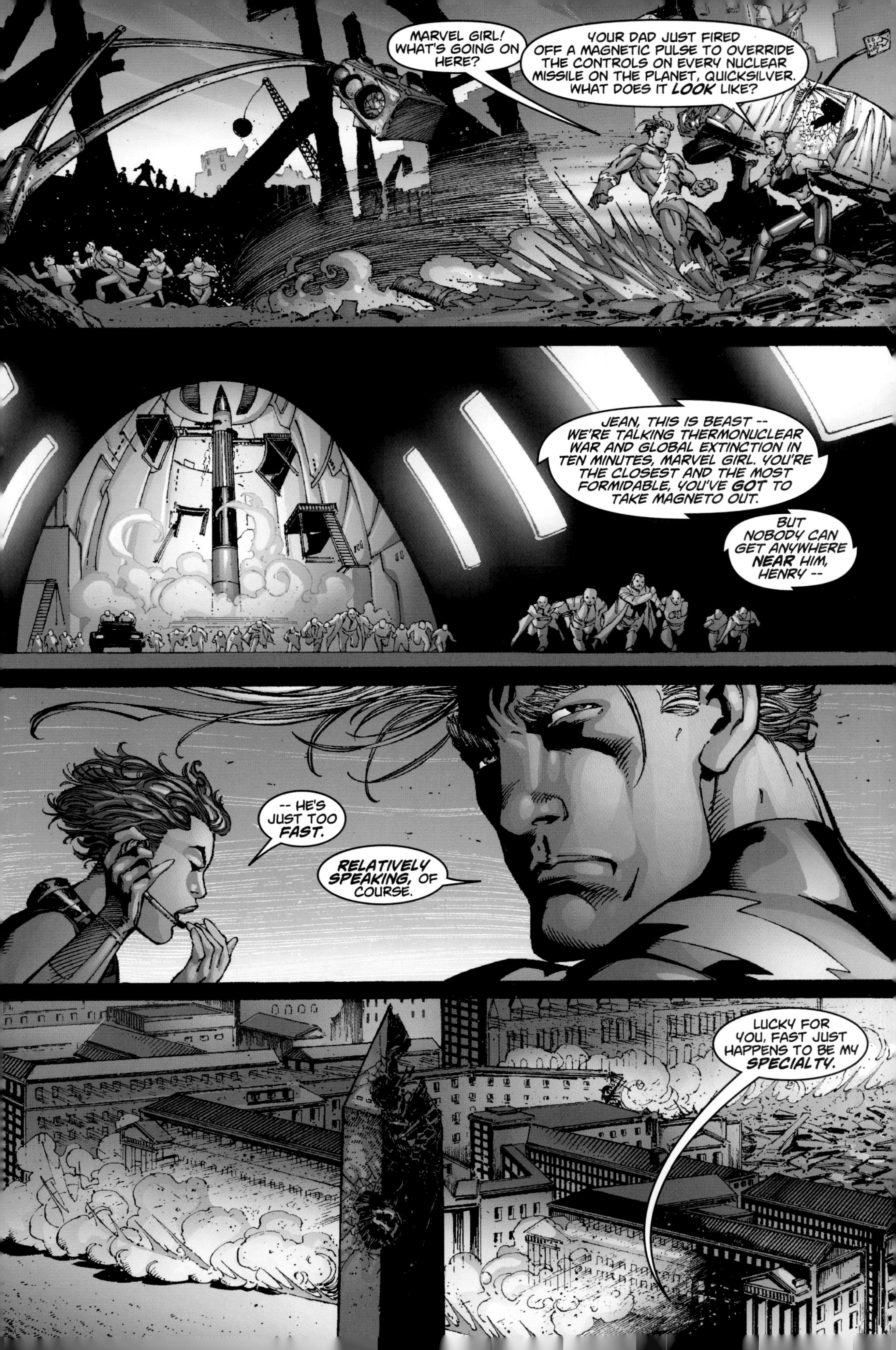
MARVEL GIRL! WHAT'S GOING ON HERE?
YOUR DAD JUST FIRED OFF A MAGNETIC PULSE TO OVERRIDE THE CONTROLS ON EVERY NUCLEAR MISSILE ON THE PLANET, QUICKSILVER. WHAT DOES IT *LOOK* LIKE?
JEAN, THIS IS BEAST -- WE'RE TALKING THERMONUCLEAR WAR AND GLOBAL EXTINCTION IN TEN MINUTES, MARVEL GIRL. YOU'RE THE CLOSEST AND THE MOST FORMIDABLE, YOU'VE *GOT* TO TAKE MAGNETO OUT.
BUT NOBODY CAN GET ANYWHERE *NEAR* HIM, HENRY --
-- HE'S JUST TOO *FAST*.
RELATIVELY SPEAKING, OF COURSE.
LUCKY FOR YOU, FAST JUST HAPPENS TO BE MY *SPECIALTY*.

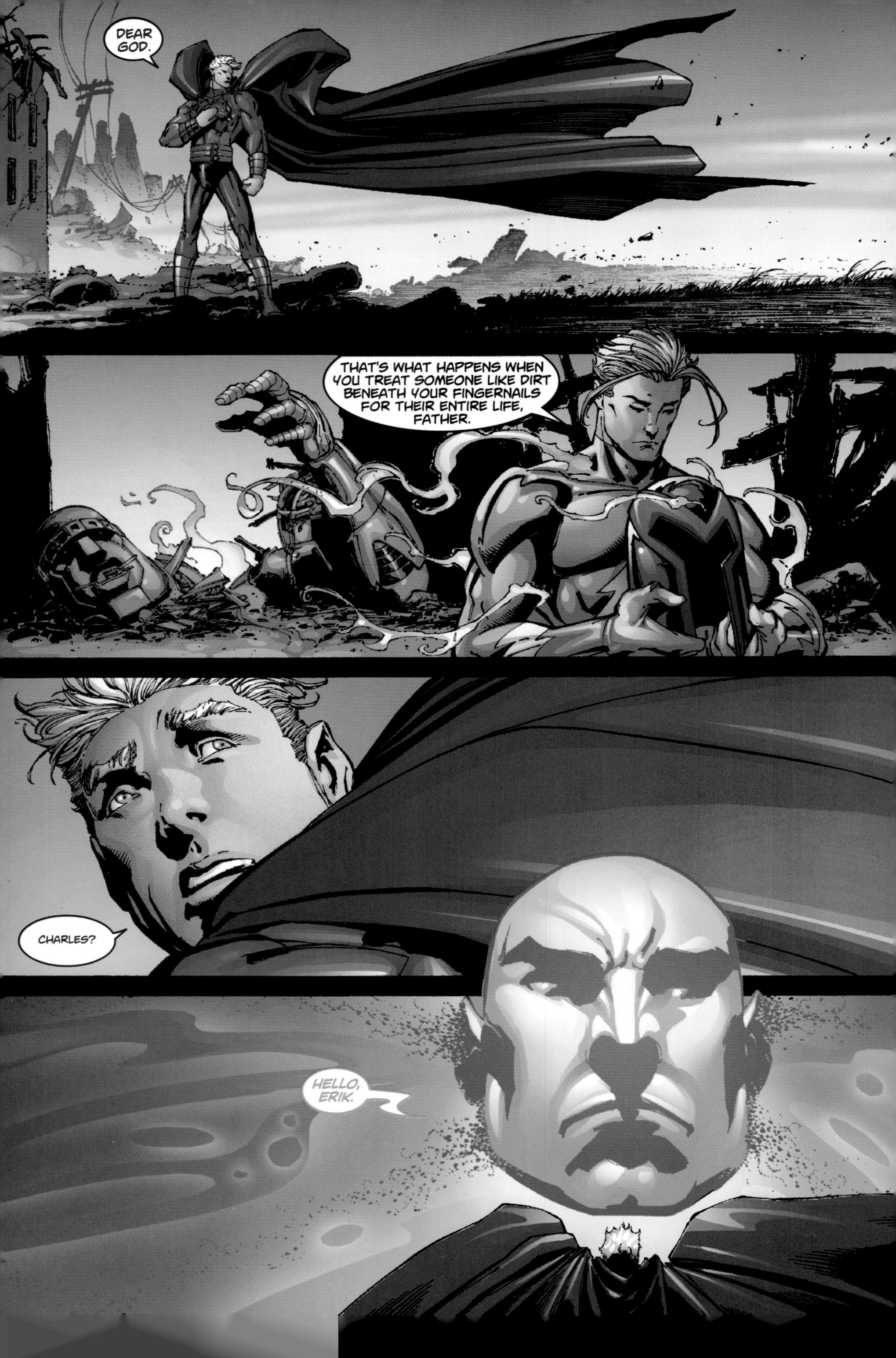
DEAR GOD.
THAT'S WHAT HAPPENS WHEN YOU TREAT SOMEONE LIKE DIRT BENEATH YOUR FINGERNAILS FOR THEIR ENTIRE LIFE, FATHER.
CHARLES?
HELLO, ERIK.

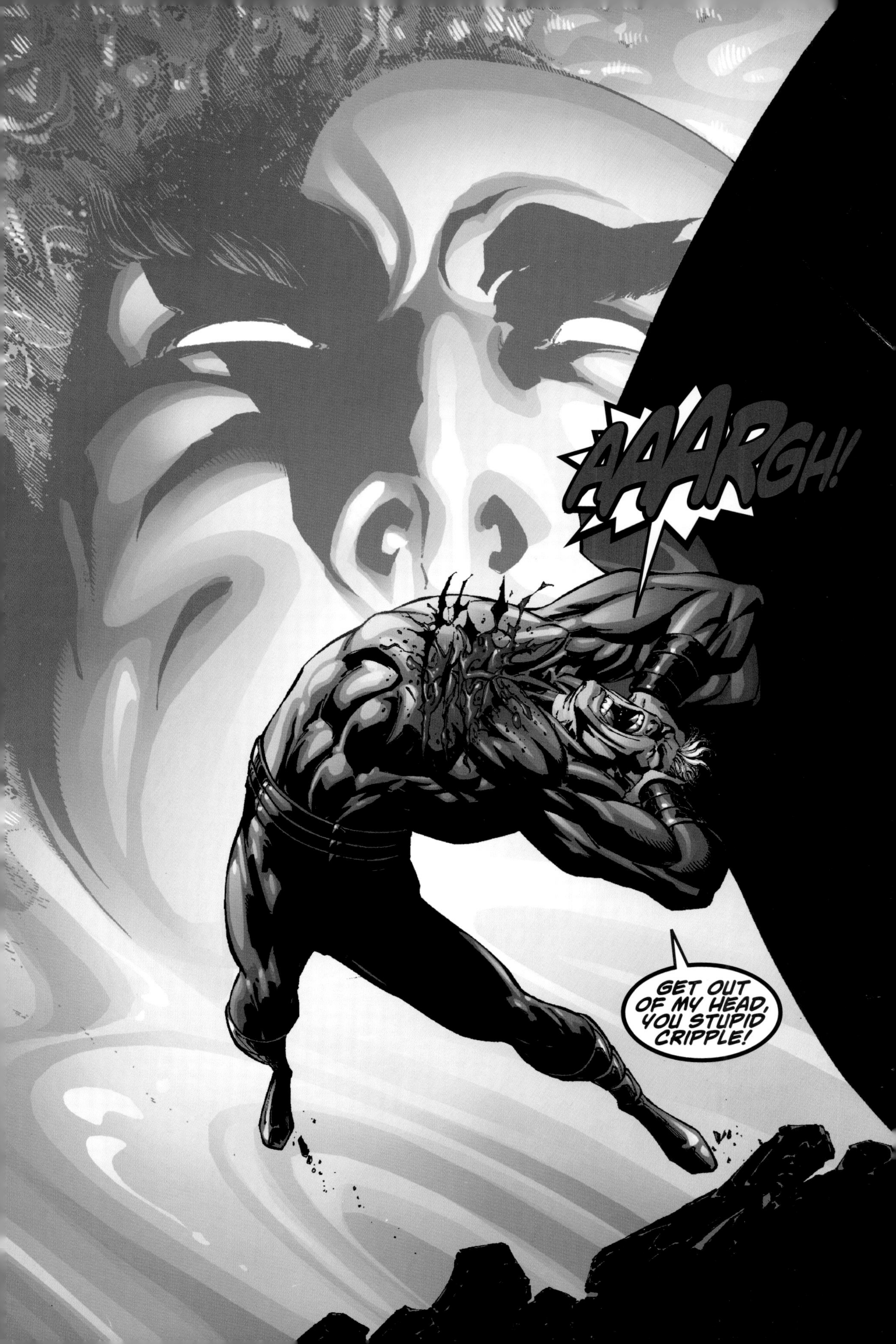
AAARGH!
GET OUT OF MY HEAD, YOU STUPID CRIPPLE!

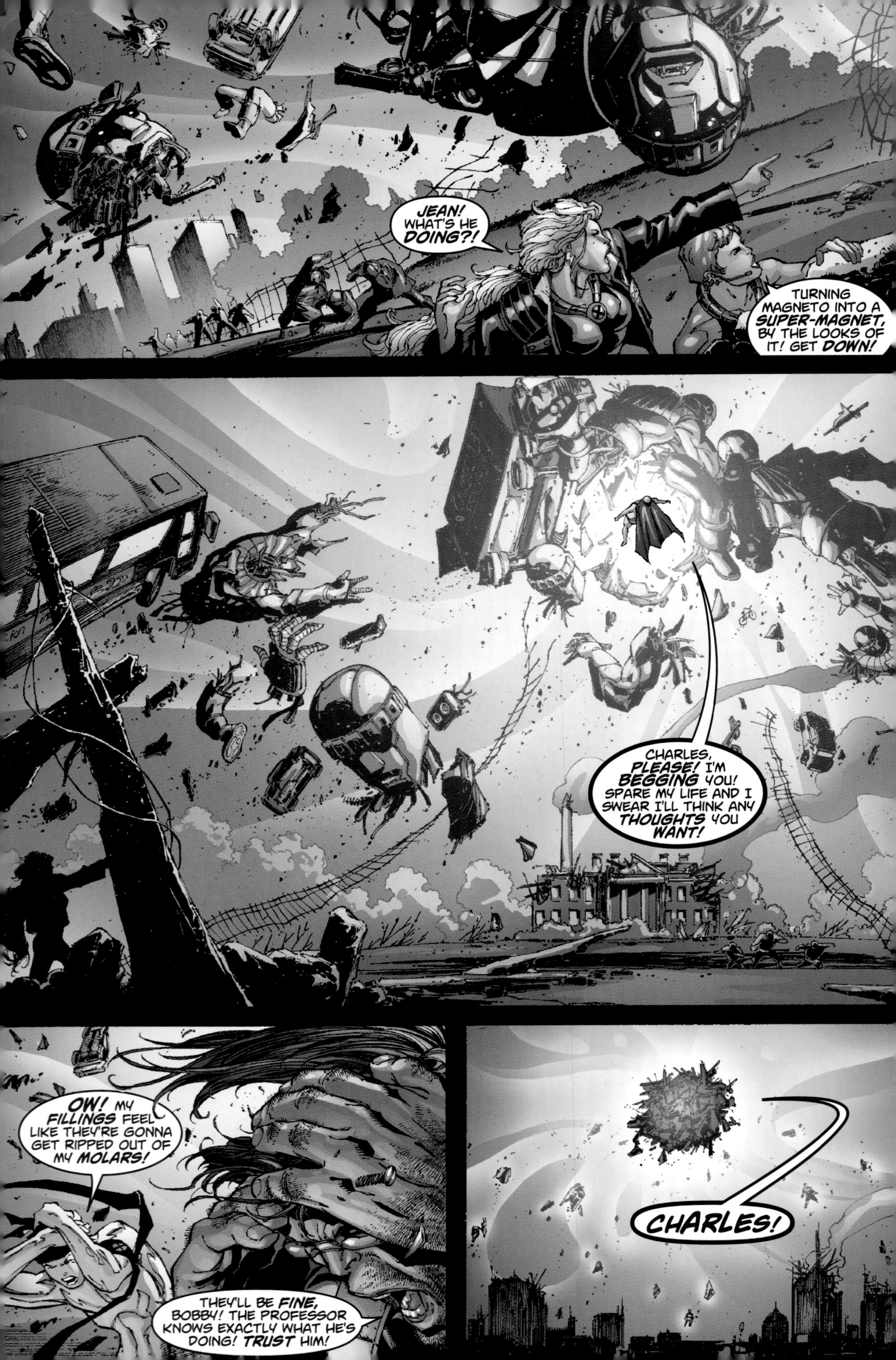
JEAN! WHAT'S HE DOING?!
TURNING MAGNETO INTO A SUPER-MAGNET, BY THE LOOKS OF IT! GET DOWN!
CHARLES, PLEASE! I'M BEGGING YOU! SPARE MY LIFE AND I SWEAR I'LL THINK ANY THOUGHTS YOU WANT!
OW! MY FILLINGS FEEL LIKE THEY'RE GONNA GET RIPPED OUT OF MY MOLARS!
THEY'LL BE FINE, BOBBY! THE PROFESSOR KNOWS EXACTLY WHAT HE'S DOING! TRUST HIM!
CHARLES!

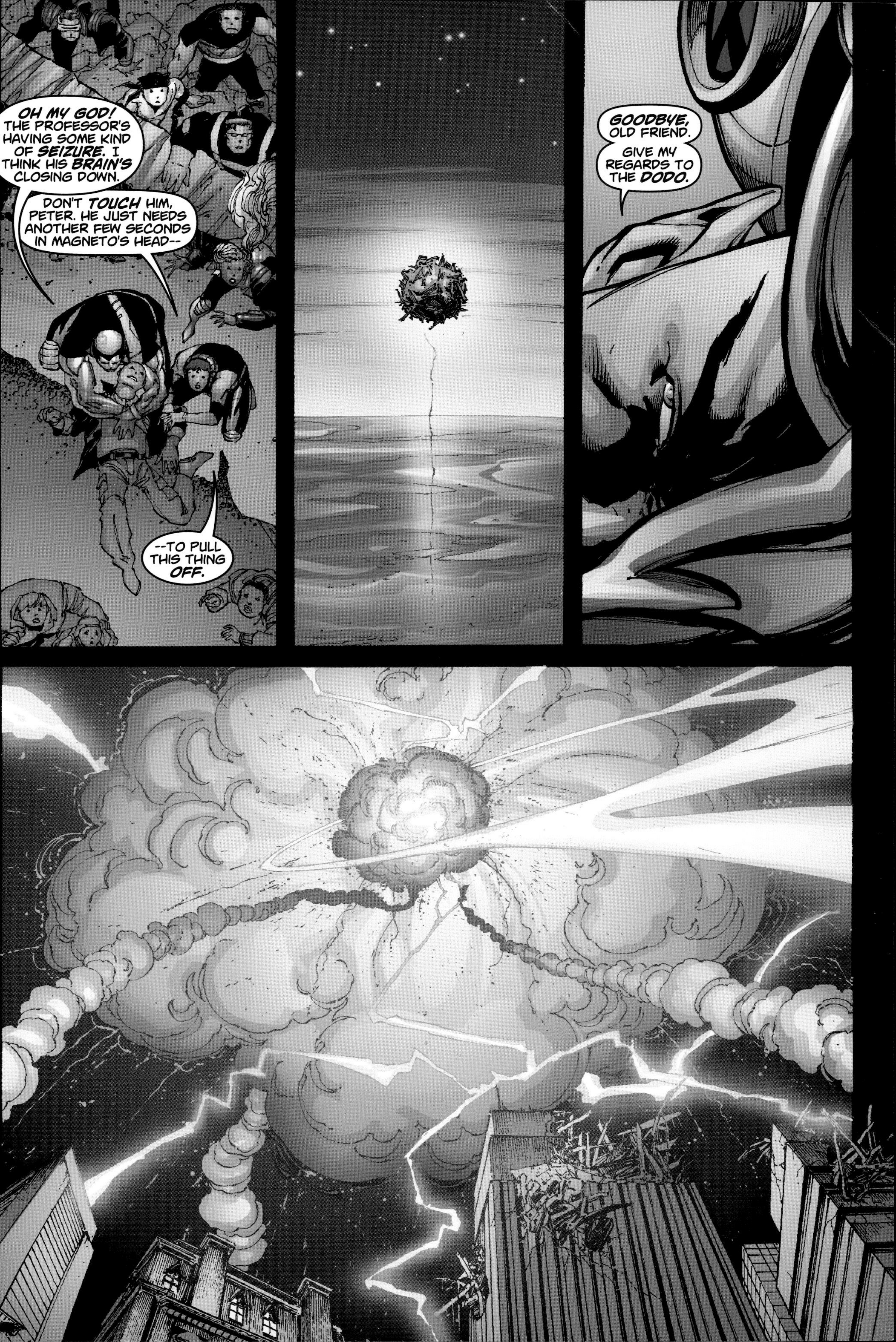

OH MY GOD! THE PROFESSOR'S HAVING SOME KIND OF SEIZURE. I THINK HIS BRAIN'S CLOSING DOWN.
DON'T TOUCH HIM, PETER. HE JUST NEEDS ANOTHER FEW SECONDS IN MAGNETO'S HEAD--
--TO PULL THIS THING OFF.
GOODBYE, OLD FRIEND.
GIVE MY REGARDS TO THE DODO.

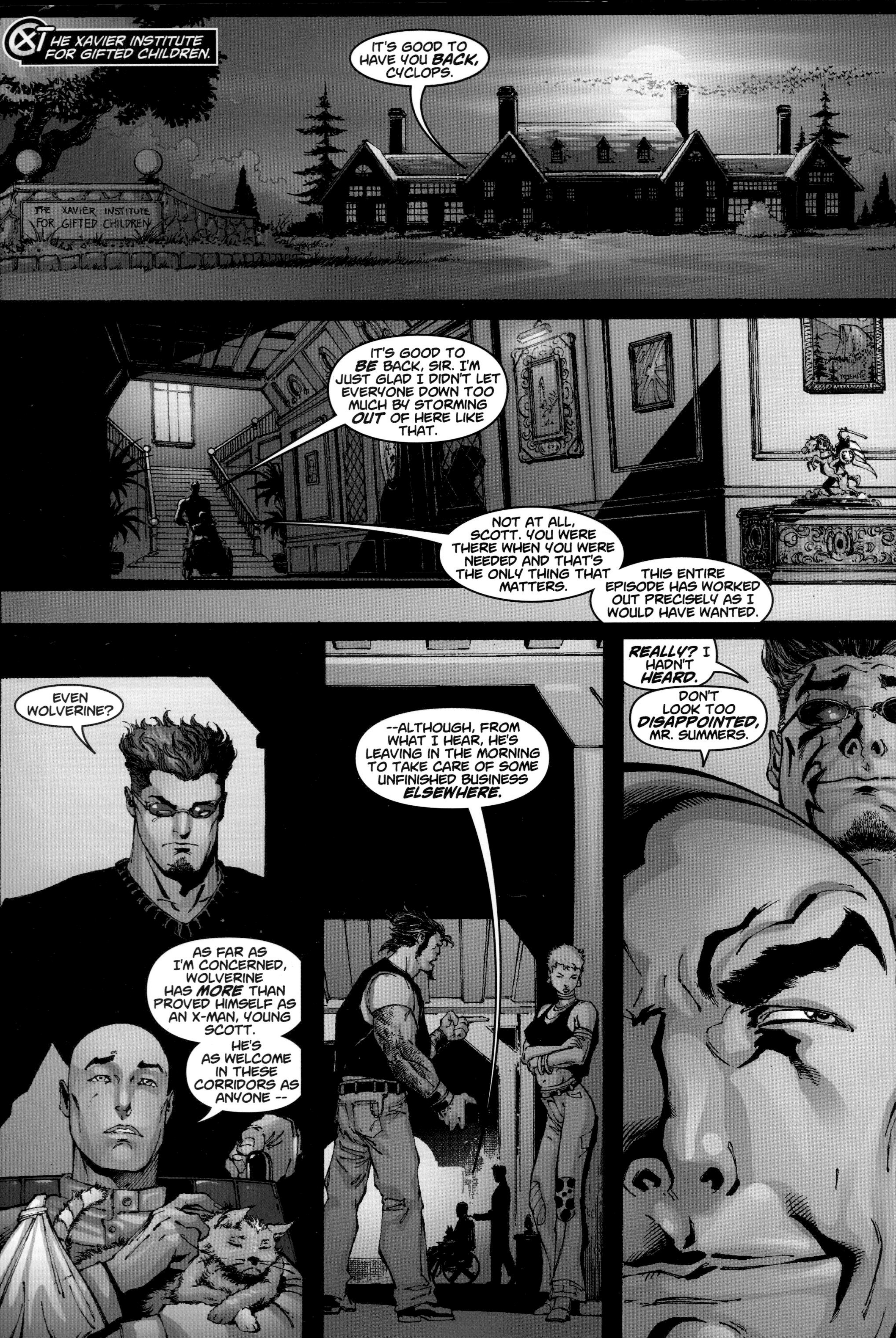
THE XAVIER INSTITUTE FOR GIFTED CHILDREN.
IT'S GOOD TO HAVE YOU BACK, CYCLOPS.
THE XAVIER INSTITUTE FOR GIFTED CHILDREN
IT'S GOOD TO BE BACK, SIR. I'M JUST GLAD I DIDN'T LET EVERYONE DOWN TOO MUCH BY STORMING OUT OF HERE LIKE THAT.
NOT AT ALL, SCOTT. YOU WERE THERE WHEN YOU WERE NEEDED AND THAT'S THE ONLY THING THAT MATTERS.
THIS ENTIRE EPISODE HAS WORKED OUT PRECISELY AS I WOULD HAVE WANTED.
EVEN WOLVERINE?
AS FAR AS I'M CONCERNED, WOLVERINE HAS MORE THAN PROVED HIMSELF AS AN X-MAN, YOUNG SCOTT.
HE'S AS WELCOME IN THESE CORRIDORS AS ANYONE --
--ALTHOUGH, FROM WHAT I HEAR, HE'S LEAVING IN THE MORNING TO TAKE CARE OF SOME UNFINISHED BUSINESS ELSEWHERE.
REALLY? I HADN'T HEARD.
DON'T LOOK TOO DISAPPOINTED, MR. SUMMERS.

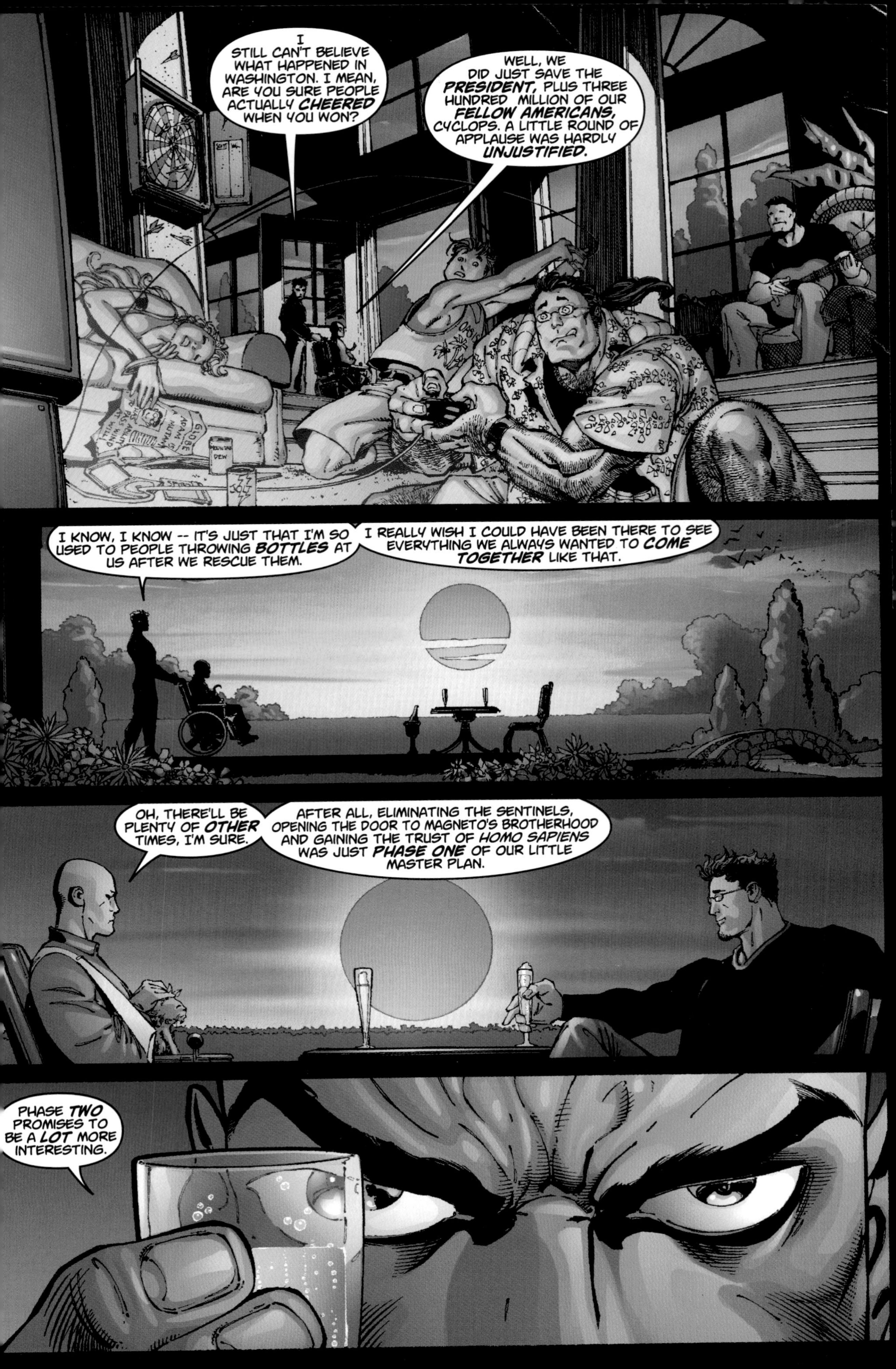
I STILL CAN'T BELIEVE WHAT HAPPENED IN WASHINGTON. I MEAN, ARE YOU SURE PEOPLE ACTUALLY CHEERED WHEN YOU WON?
WELL, WE DID JUST SAVE THE PRESIDENT, PLUS THREE HUNDRED MILLION OF OUR FELLOW AMERICANS, CYCLOPS. A LITTLE ROUND OF APPLAUSE WAS HARDLY UNJUSTIFIED.
I KNOW, I KNOW -- IT'S JUST THAT I'M SO USED TO PEOPLE THROWING BOTTLES AT US AFTER WE RESCUE THEM.
I REALLY WISH I COULD HAVE BEEN THERE TO SEE EVERYTHING WE ALWAYS WANTED TO COME TOGETHER LIKE THAT.
OH, THERE'LL BE PLENTY OF OTHER TIMES, I'M SURE.
AFTER ALL, ELIMINATING THE SENTINELS, OPENING THE DOOR TO MAGNETO'S BROTHERHOOD AND GAINING THE TRUST OF HOMO SAPIENS WAS JUST PHASE ONE OF OUR LITTLE MASTER PLAN.
PHASE TWO PROMISES TO BE A LOT MORE INTERESTING.

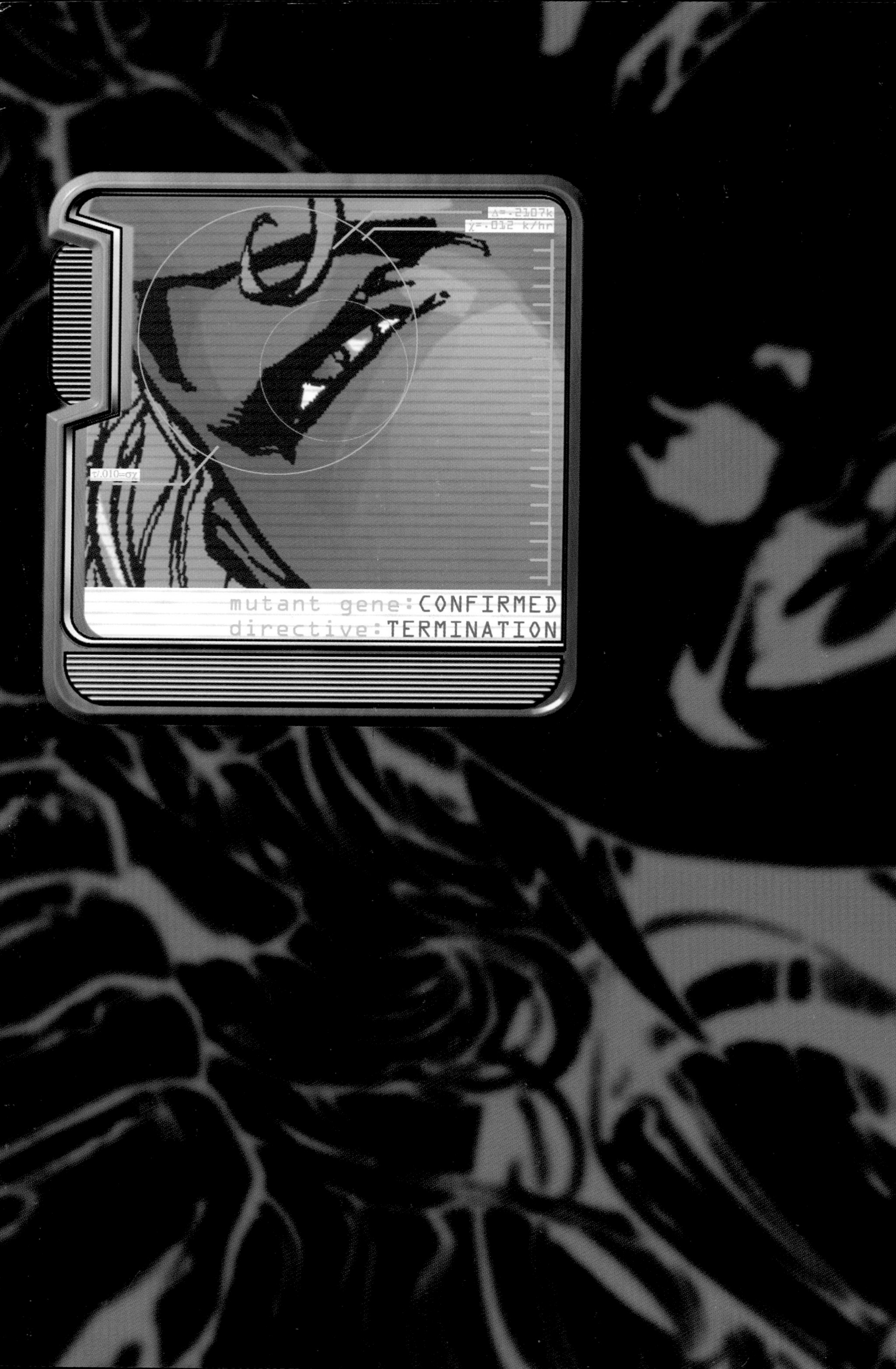
mutant gene:CONFIRMED
directive:TERMINATION

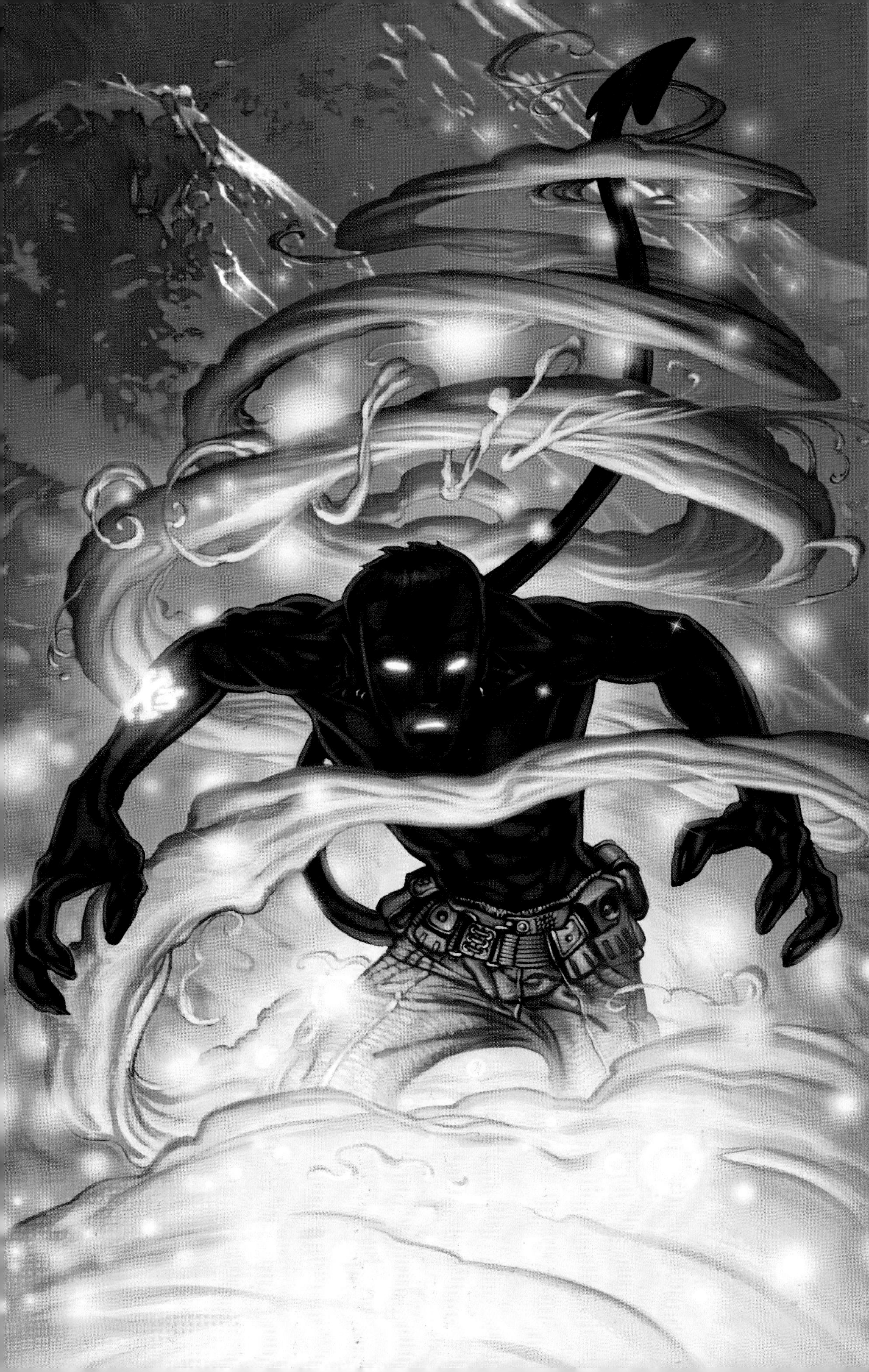

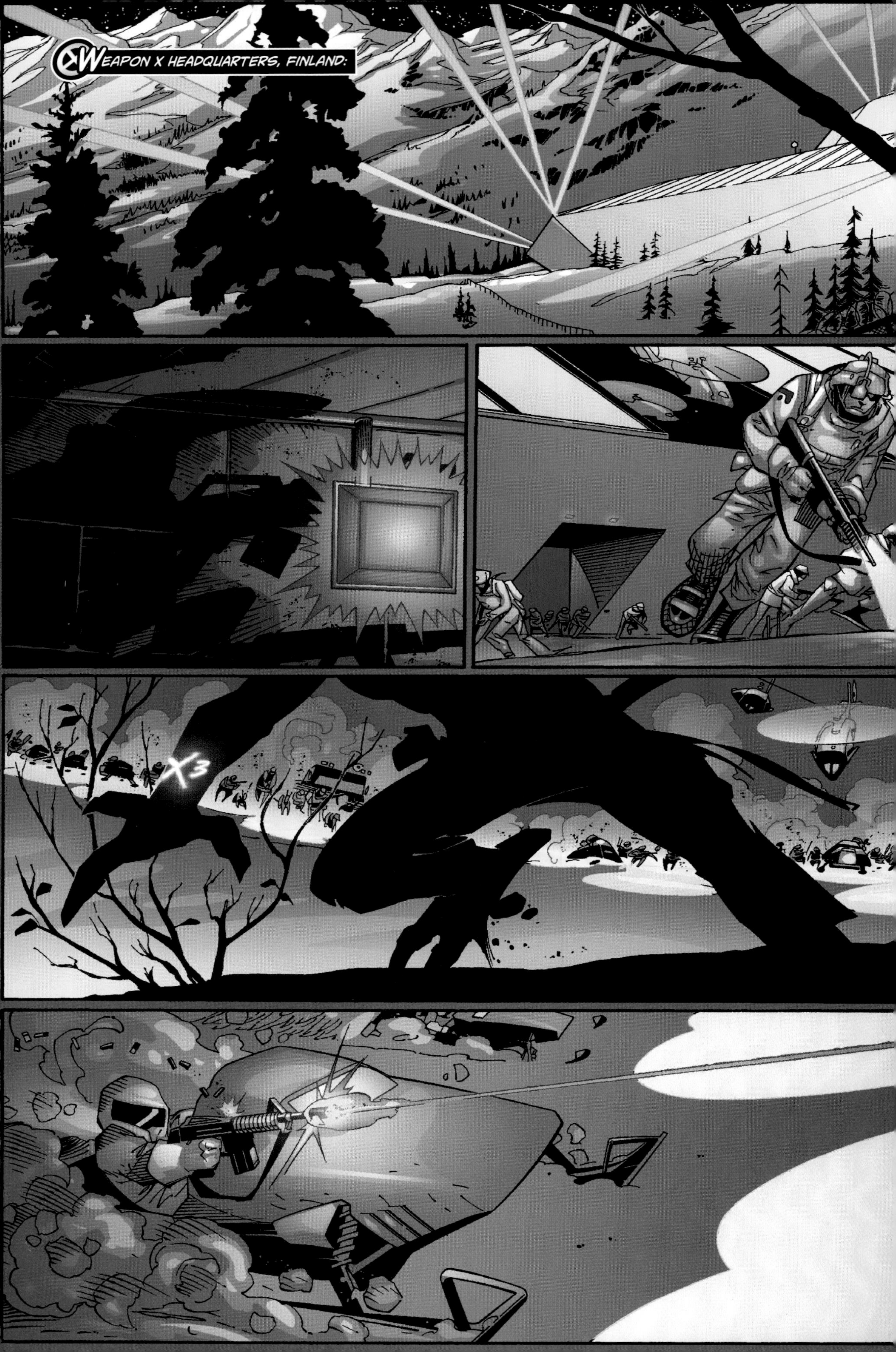
WEAPON X HEADQUARTERS, FINLAND:
X3

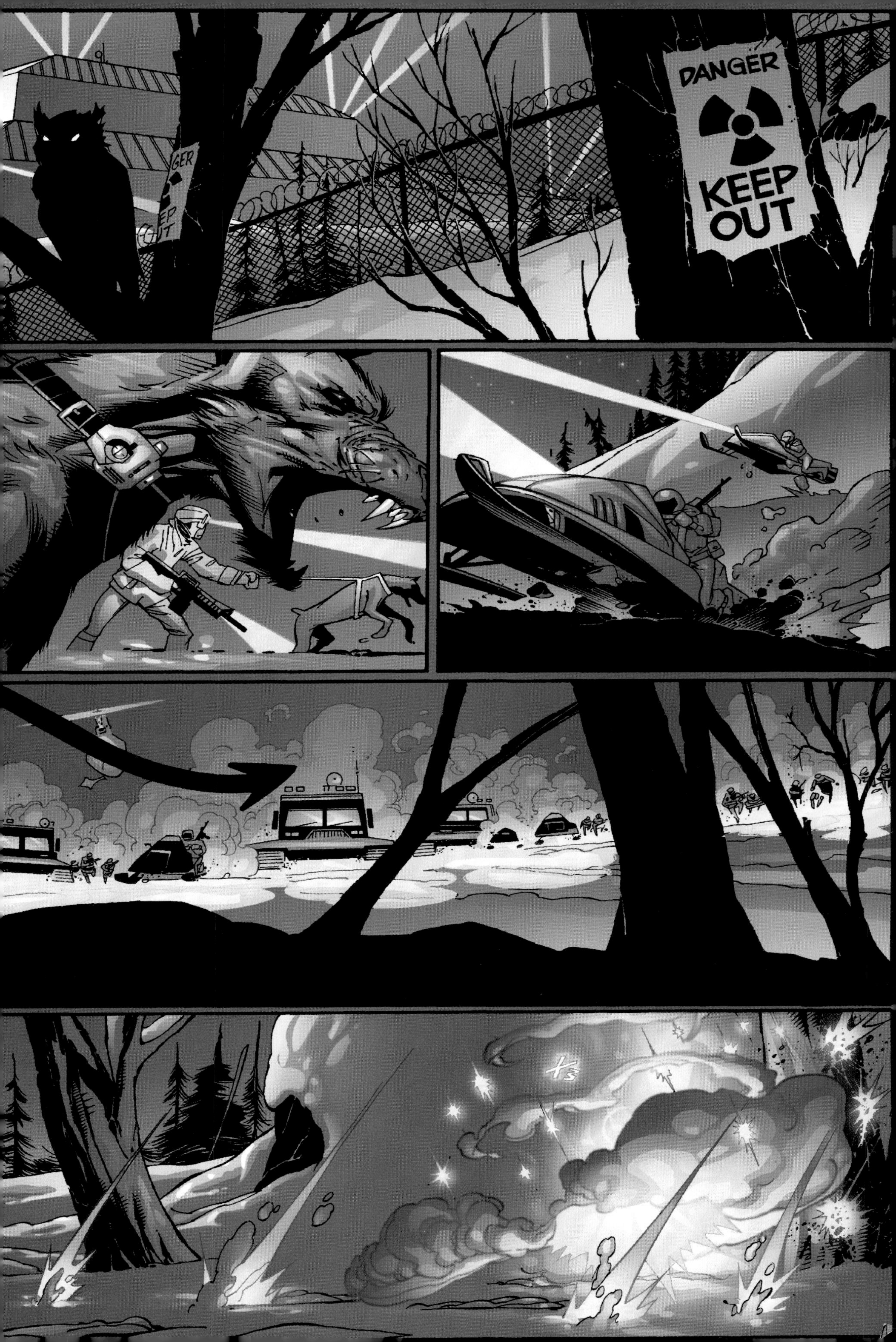
DANGER
KEEP OUT

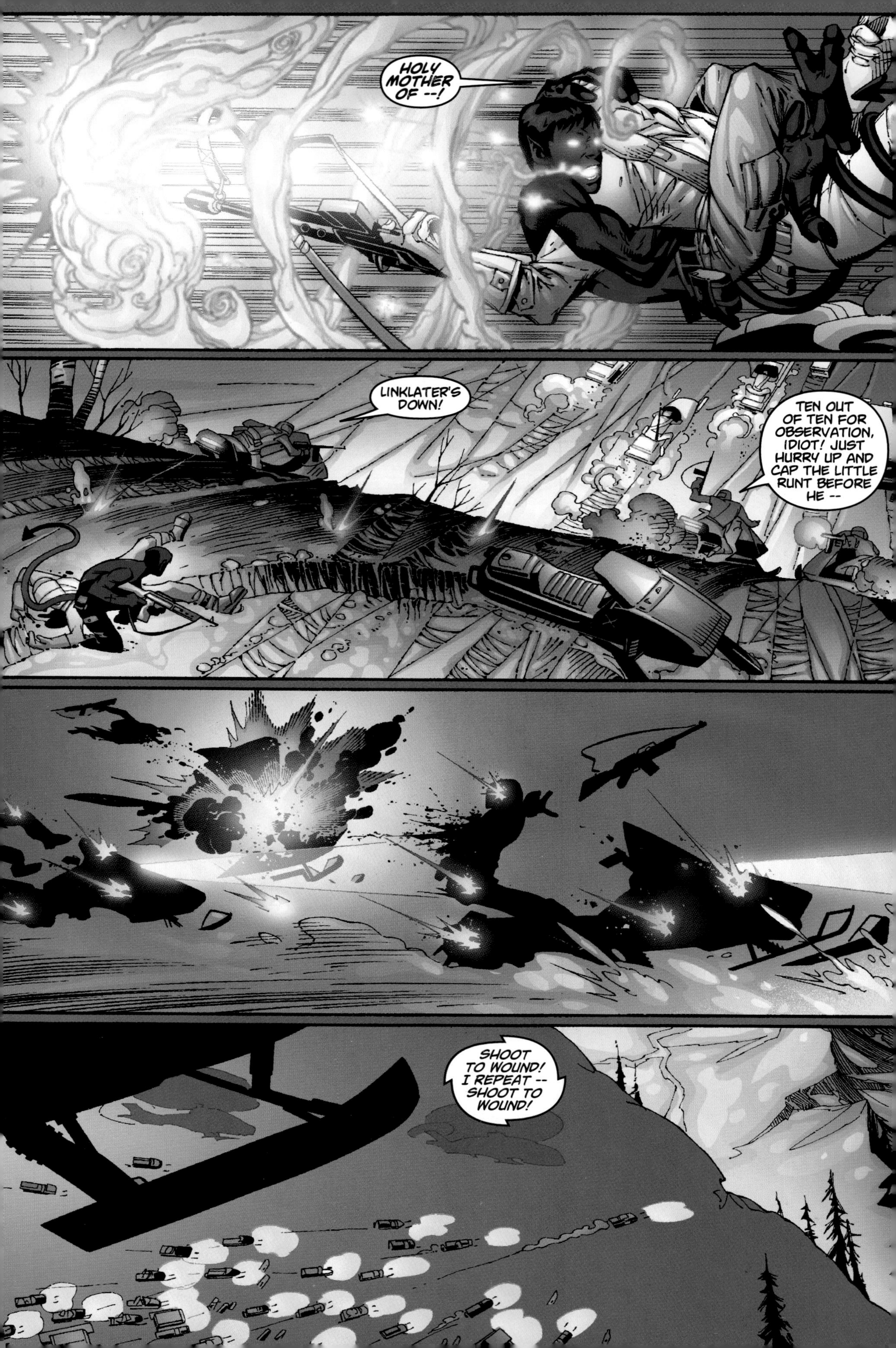
HOLY MOTHER OF --!
LINKLATER'S DOWN!
TEN OUT OF TEN FOR OBSERVATION, IDIOT! JUST HURRY UP AND CAP THE LITTLE RUNT BEFORE HE --
SHOOT TO WOUND! I REPEAT -- SHOOT TO WOUND!

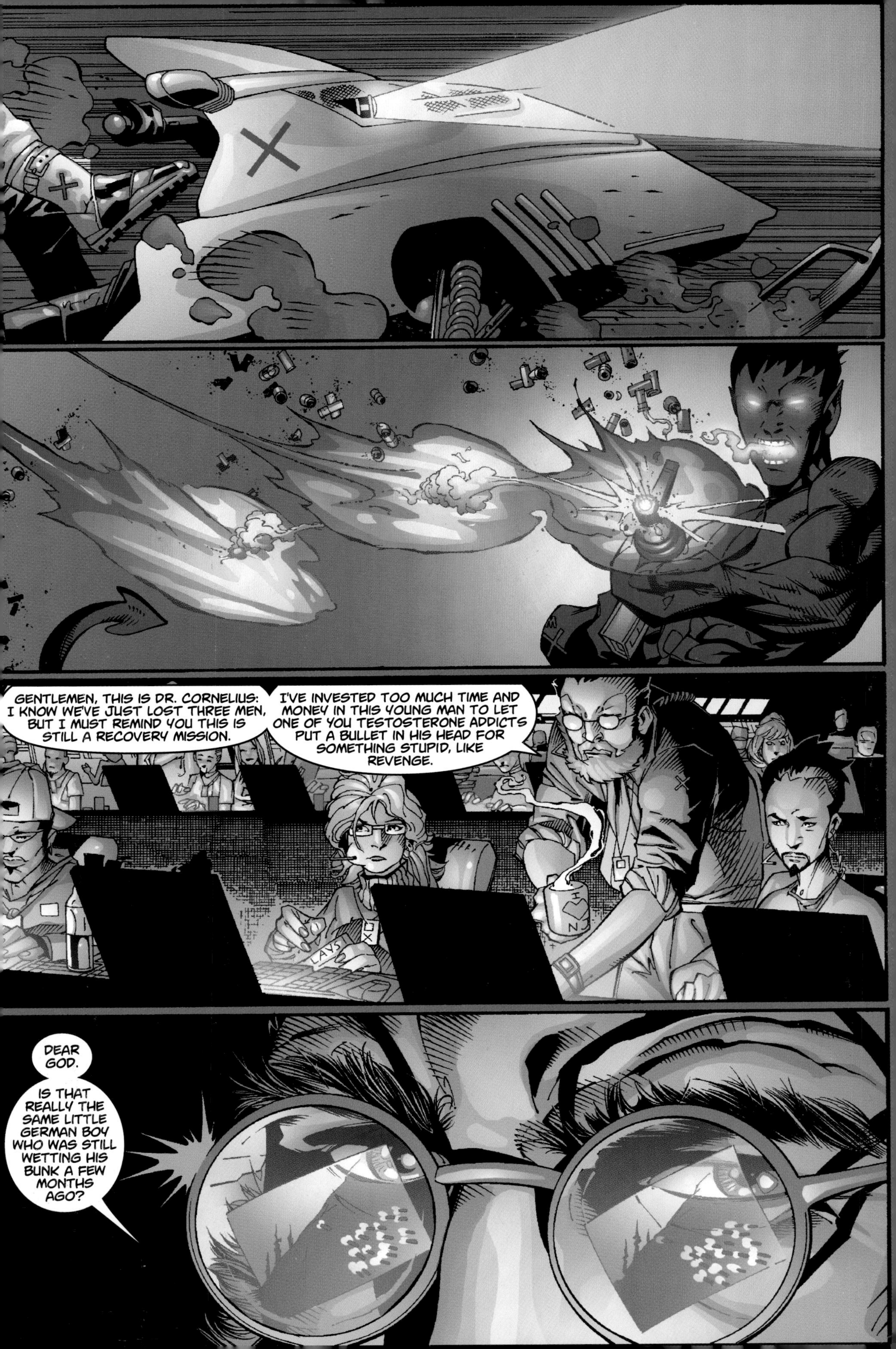
GENTLEMEN, THIS IS DR. CORNELIUS: I KNOW WE'VE JUST LOST THREE MEN, BUT I MUST REMIND YOU THIS IS STILL A RECOVERY MISSION.
I'VE INVESTED TOO MUCH TIME AND MONEY IN THIS YOUNG MAN TO LET ONE OF YOU TESTOSTERONE ADDICTS PUT A BULLET IN HIS HEAD FOR SOMETHING STUPID, LIKE REVENGE.
LAYS
DEAR GOD.
IS THAT REALLY THE SAME LITTLE GERMAN BOY WHO WAS STILL WETTING HIS BUNK A FEW MONTHS AGO?

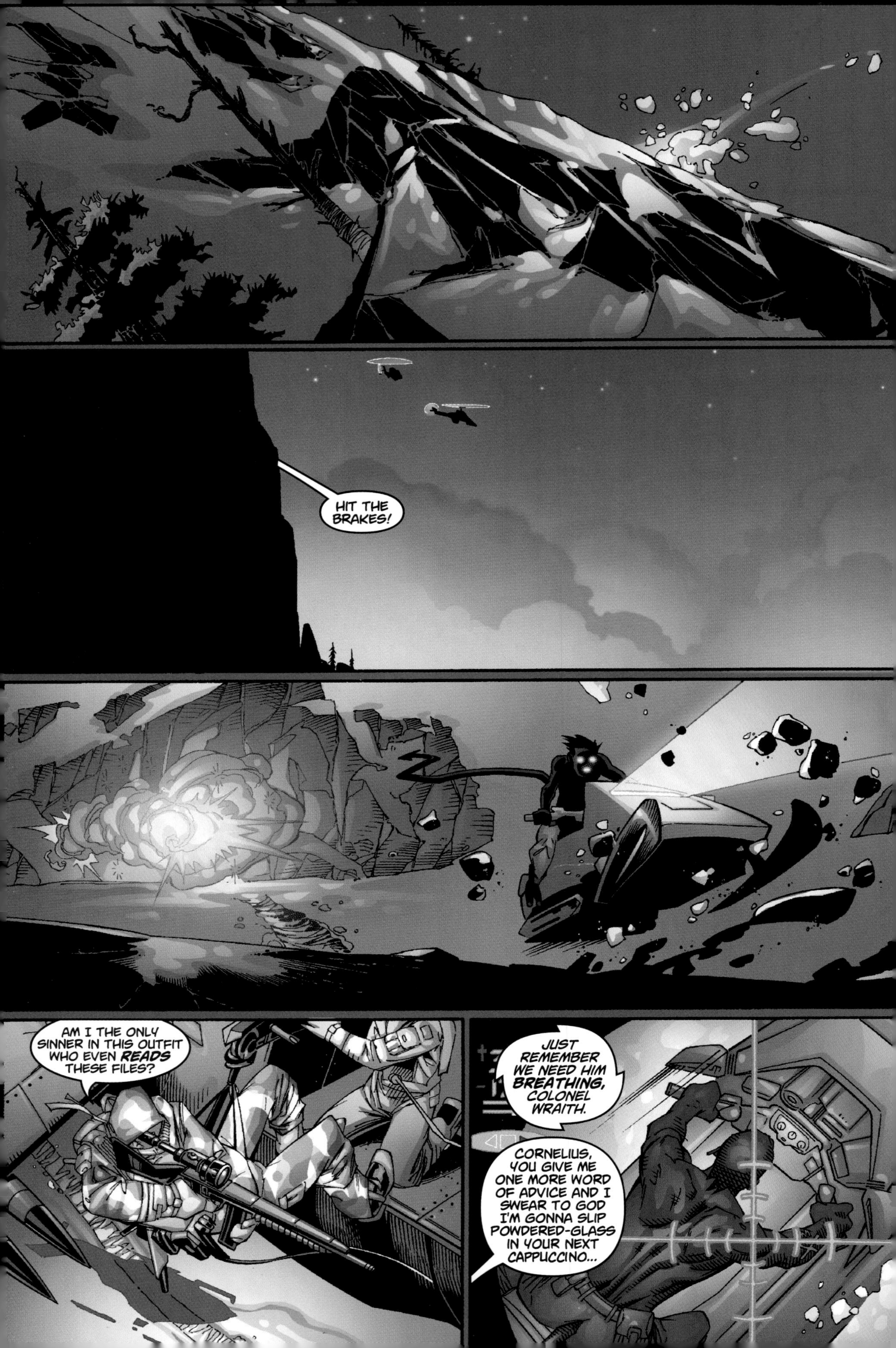
HIT THE BRAKES!
AM I THE ONLY SINNER IN THIS OUTFIT WHO EVEN **READS** THESE FILES?
JUST REMEMBER WE NEED HIM **BREATHING,** COLONEL WRAITH.
CORNELIUS, YOU GIVE ME ONE MORE WORD OF ADVICE AND I SWEAR TO GOD I'M GONNA SLIP POWDERED-GLASS IN YOUR NEXT CAPPUCCINO...

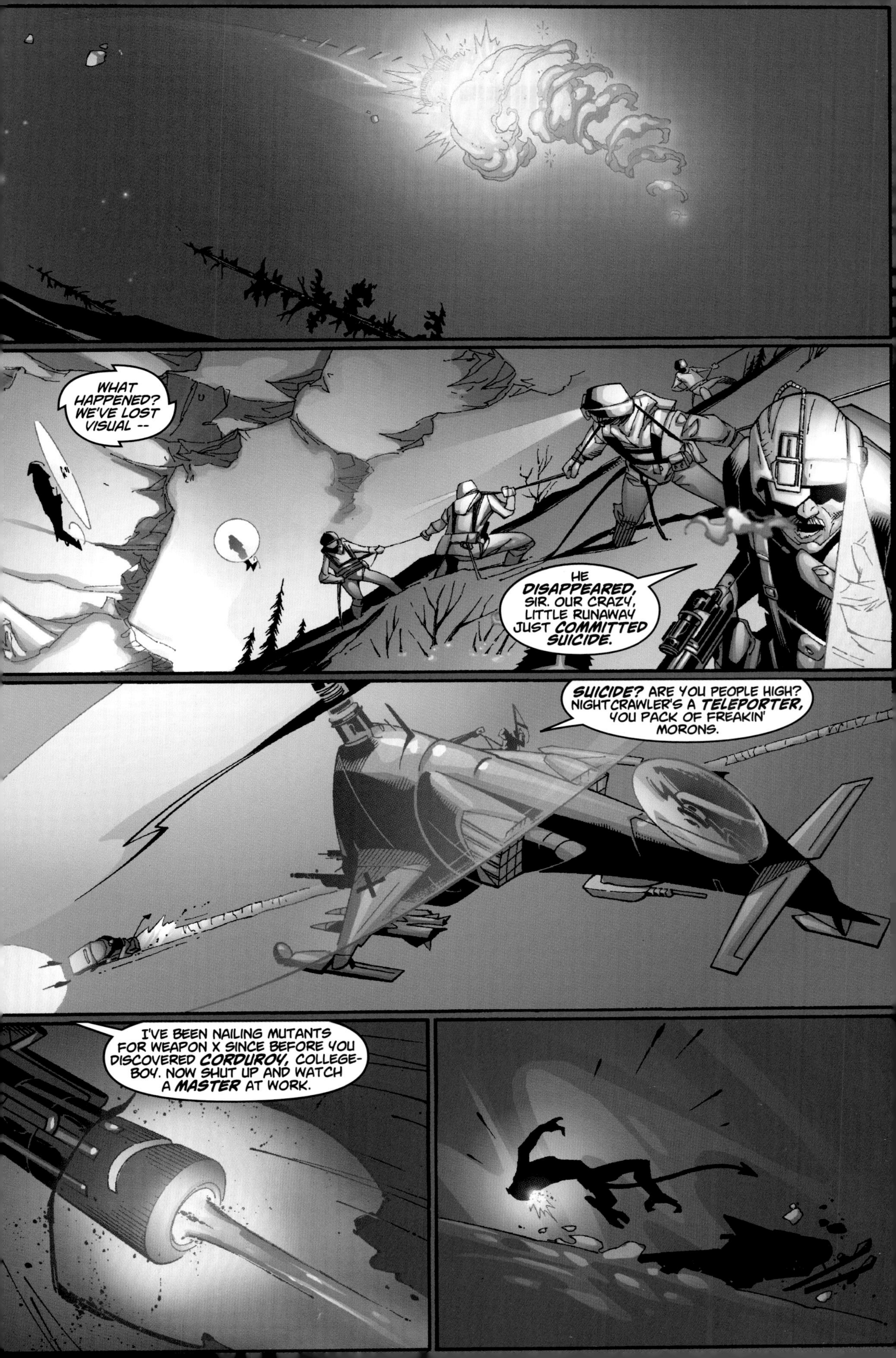
WHAT HAPPENED? WE'VE LOST VISUAL --
HE DISAPPEARED, SIR. OUR CRAZY, LITTLE RUNAWAY JUST COMMITTED SUICIDE.
SUICIDE? ARE YOU PEOPLE HIGH? NIGHTCRAWLER'S A TELEPORTER, YOU PACK OF FREAKIN' MORONS.
I'VE BEEN NAILING MUTANTS FOR WEAPON X SINCE BEFORE YOU DISCOVERED CORDUROY, COLLEGE-BOY. NOW SHUT UP AND WATCH A MASTER AT WORK.

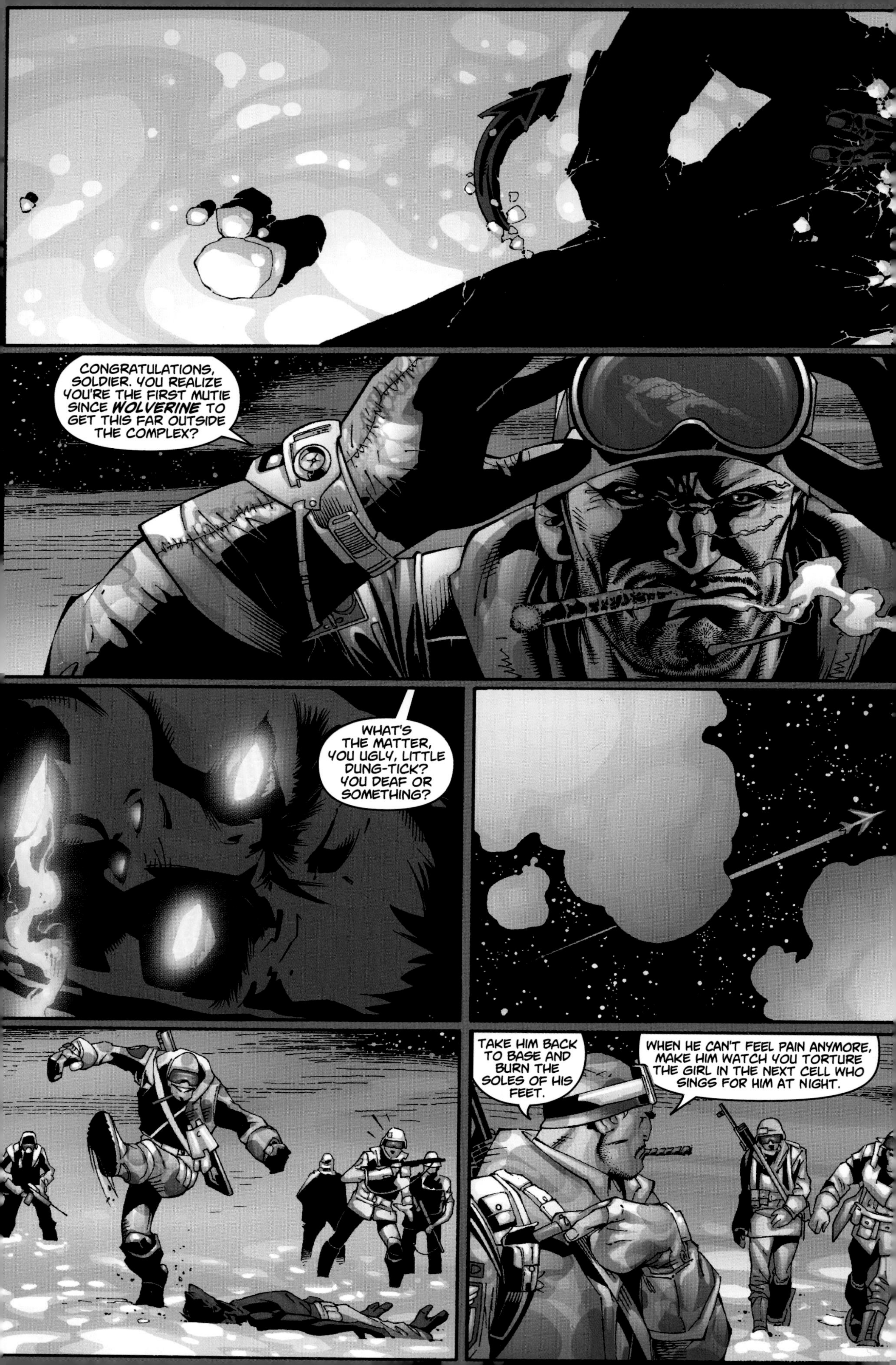
CONGRATULATIONS, SOLDIER. YOU REALIZE YOU'RE THE FIRST MUTIE SINCE WOLVERINE TO GET THIS FAR OUTSIDE THE COMPLEX?
WHAT'S THE MATTER, YOU UGLY, LITTLE DUNG-TICK? YOU DEAF OR SOMETHING?
TAKE HIM BACK TO BASE AND BURN THE SOLES OF HIS FEET.
WHEN HE CAN'T FEEL PAIN ANYMORE, MAKE HIM WATCH YOU TORTURE THE GIRL IN THE NEXT CELL WHO SINGS FOR HIM AT NIGHT.

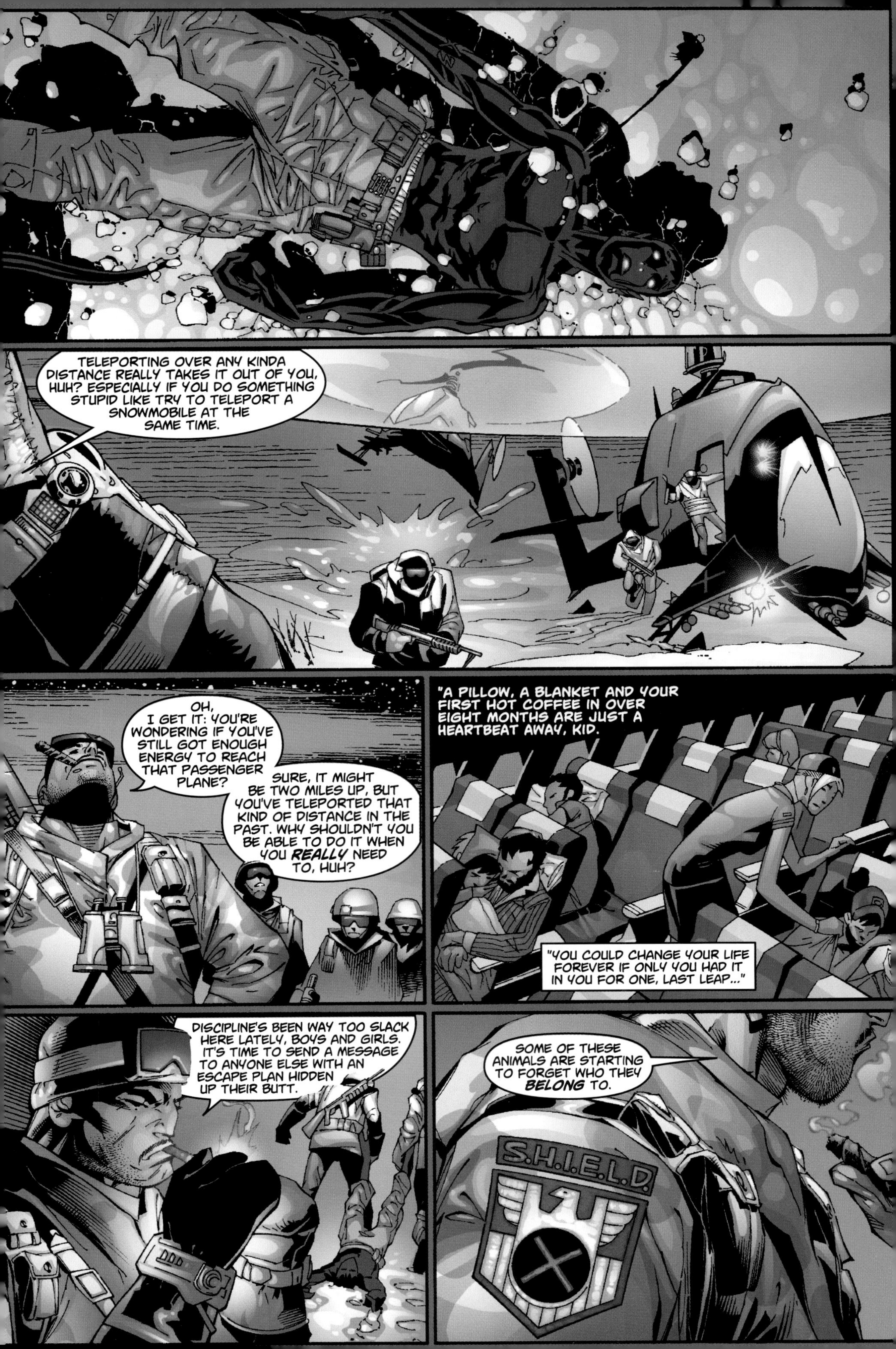
TELEPORTING OVER ANY KINDA DISTANCE REALLY TAKES IT OUT OF YOU, HUH? ESPECIALLY IF YOU DO SOMETHING STUPID LIKE TRY TO TELEPORT A SNOWMOBILE AT THE SAME TIME.
OH, I GET IT: YOU'RE WONDERING IF YOU'VE STILL GOT ENOUGH ENERGY TO REACH THAT PASSENGER PLANE?
SURE, IT MIGHT BE TWO MILES UP, BUT YOU'VE TELEPORTED THAT KIND OF DISTANCE IN THE PAST. WHY SHOULDN'T YOU BE ABLE TO DO IT WHEN YOU *REALLY* NEED TO, HUH?
"A PILLOW, A BLANKET AND YOUR FIRST HOT COFFEE IN OVER EIGHT MONTHS ARE JUST A HEARTBEAT AWAY, KID.
"YOU COULD CHANGE YOUR LIFE FOREVER IF ONLY YOU HAD IT IN YOU FOR ONE, LAST LEAP..."
DISCIPLINE'S BEEN WAY TOO SLACK HERE LATELY, BOYS AND GIRLS. IT'S TIME TO SEND A MESSAGE TO ANYONE ELSE WITH AN ESCAPE PLAN HIDDEN UP THEIR BUTT.
SOME OF THESE ANIMALS ARE STARTING TO FORGET WHO THEY *BELONG* TO.
S.H.I.E.L.D.

MARK MILLAR
writer

ADAM KUBERT
pencils

ART THIBERT
inks

RICHARD ISANOVE
colors

RICHARD STARKINGS
& COMICRAFT'S
WES ABBOTT
letters

PETE FRANCO
assistant editor

MARK POWERS
editor

JOE QUESADA
editor in chief

BILL JEMAS
president

RETURN TO WEAPON X

A STAN LEE PRESENTATION

PART ONE OF SIX

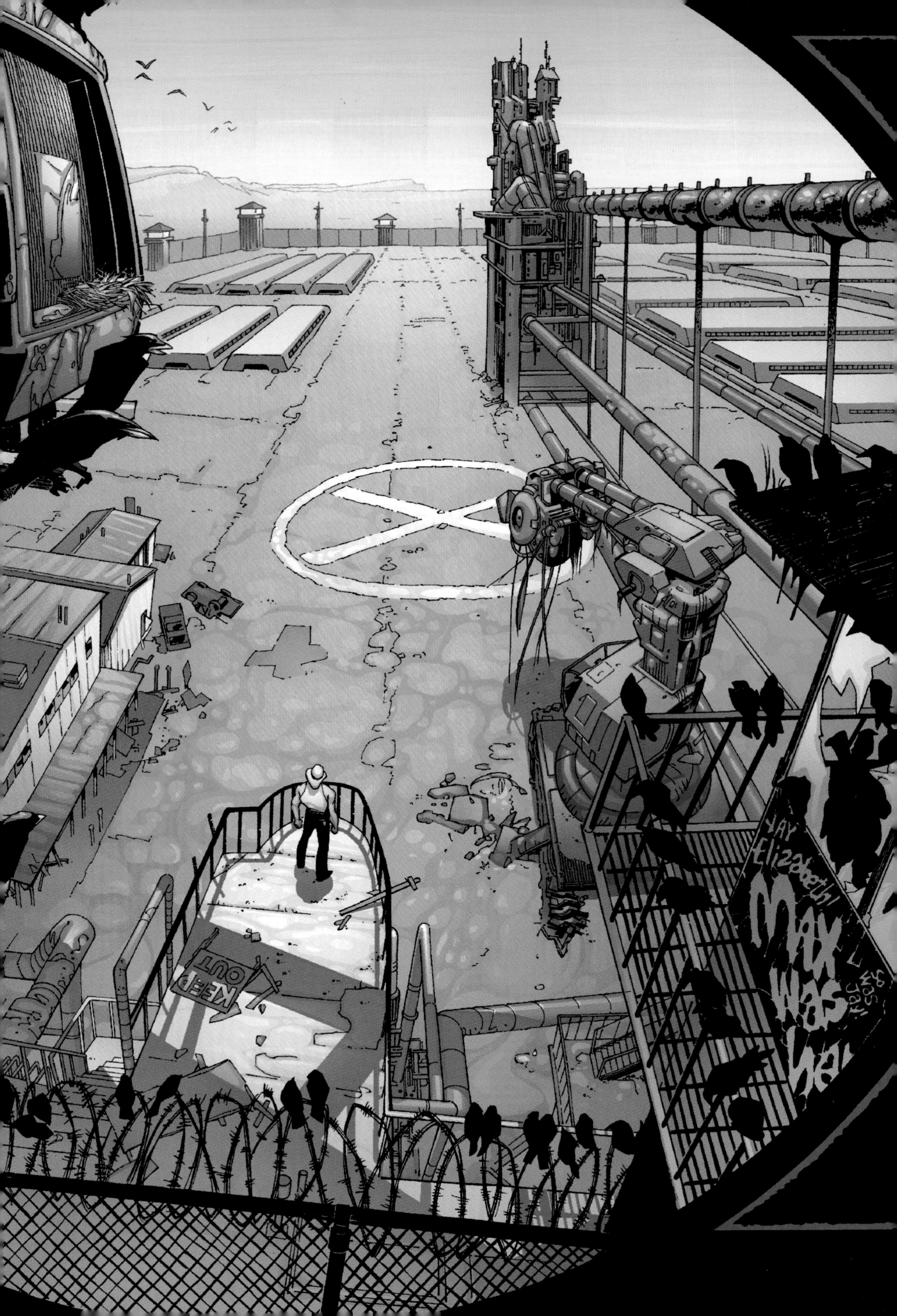
KEEP OUT
YAY Elizabeth!
Max was
so was Jay!

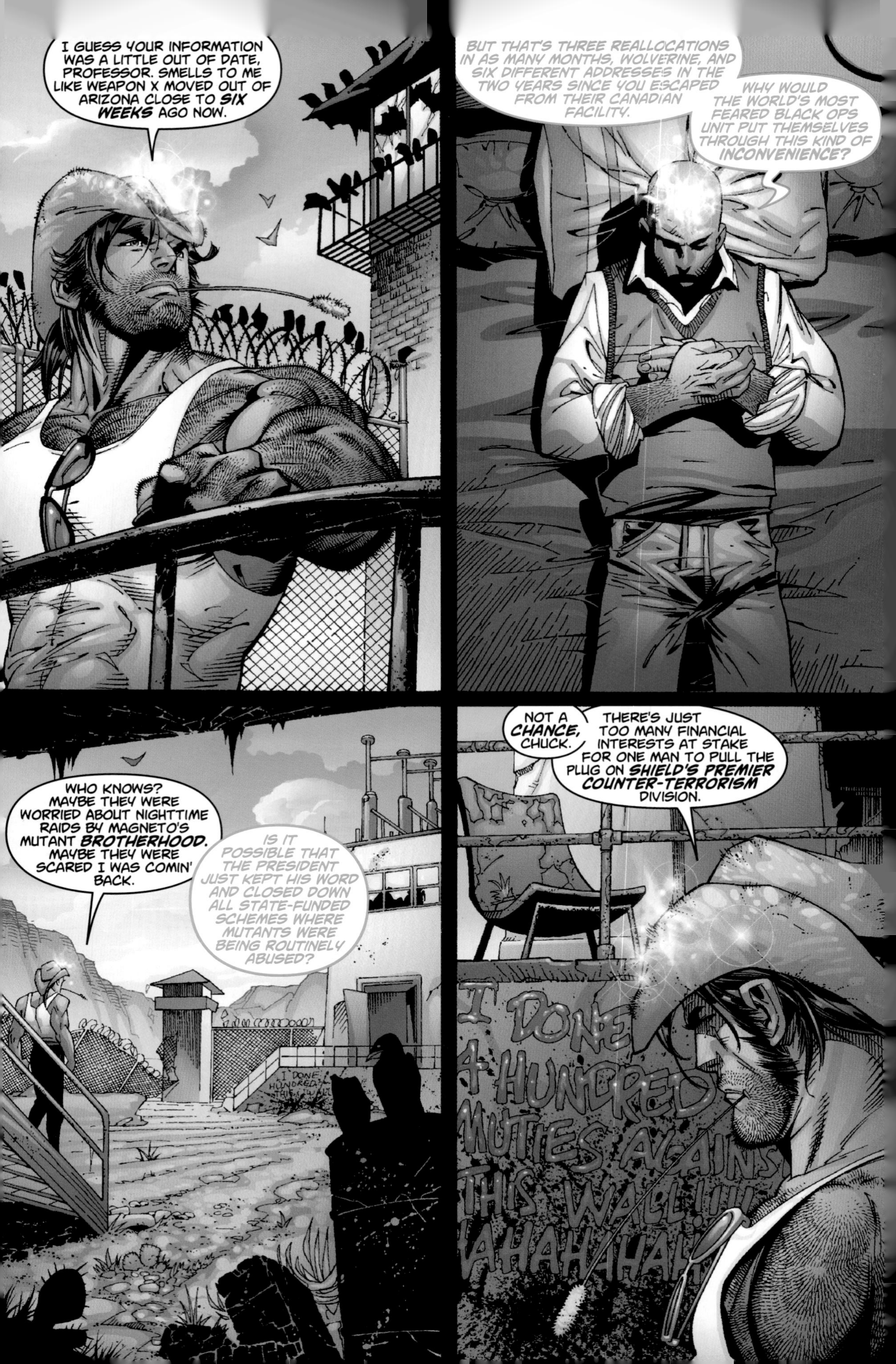
I GUESS YOUR INFORMATION WAS A LITTLE OUT OF DATE, PROFESSOR. SMELLS TO ME LIKE WEAPON X MOVED OUT OF ARIZONA CLOSE TO SIX WEEKS AGO NOW.
BUT THAT'S THREE REALLOCATIONS IN AS MANY MONTHS, WOLVERINE, AND SIX DIFFERENT ADDRESSES IN THE TWO YEARS SINCE YOU ESCAPED FROM THEIR CANADIAN FACILITY.
WHY WOULD THE WORLD'S MOST FEARED BLACK OPS UNIT PUT THEMSELVES THROUGH THIS KIND OF INCONVENIENCE?
WHO KNOWS? MAYBE THEY WERE WORRIED ABOUT NIGHTTIME RAIDS BY MAGNETO'S MUTANT BROTHERHOOD. MAYBE THEY WERE SCARED I WAS COMIN' BACK.
IS IT POSSIBLE THAT THE PRESIDENT JUST KEPT HIS WORD AND CLOSED DOWN ALL STATE-FUNDED SCHEMES WHERE MUTANTS WERE BEING ROUTINELY ABUSED?
NOT A CHANCE, CHUCK.
THERE'S JUST TOO MANY FINANCIAL INTERESTS AT STAKE FOR ONE MAN TO PULL THE PLUG ON SHIELD'S PREMIER COUNTER-TERRORISM DIVISION.
I DONE 4 HUNDRED MUTIES AGAINS THIS WALL!!! HAHAHAHA!

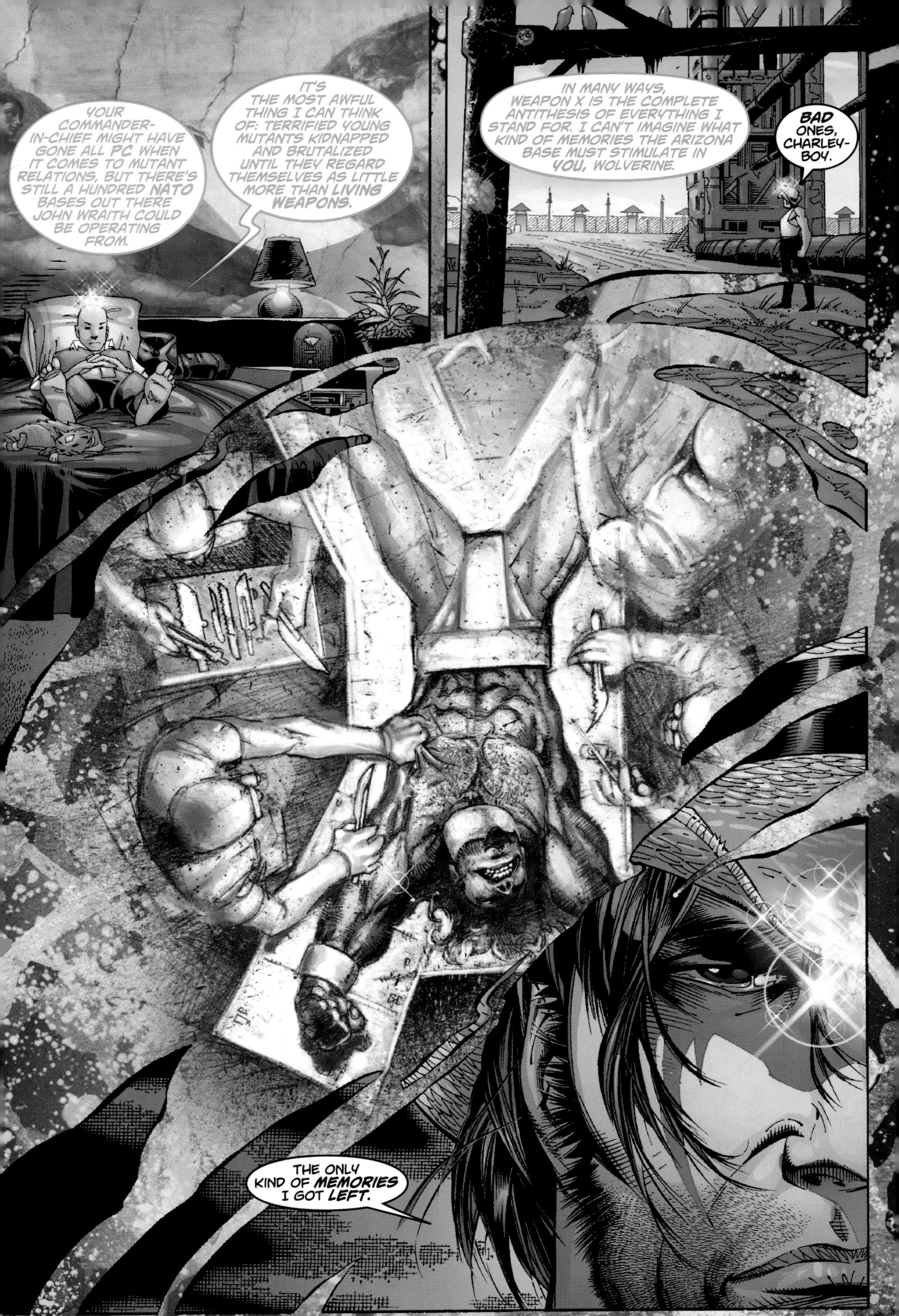
YOUR COMMANDER-IN-CHIEF MIGHT HAVE GONE ALL PC WHEN IT COMES TO MUTANT RELATIONS, BUT THERE'S STILL A HUNDRED NATO BASES OUT THERE JOHN WRAITH COULD BE OPERATING FROM.
IT'S THE MOST AWFUL THING I CAN THINK OF: TERRIFIED YOUNG MUTANTS KIDNAPPED AND BRUTALIZED UNTIL THEY REGARD THEMSELVES AS LITTLE MORE THAN LIVING WEAPONS.
IN MANY WAYS, WEAPON X IS THE COMPLETE ANTITHESIS OF EVERYTHING I STAND FOR. I CAN'T IMAGINE WHAT KIND OF MEMORIES THE ARIZONA BASE MUST STIMULATE IN YOU, WOLVERINE.
BAD ONES, CHARLEY-BOY.
THE ONLY KIND OF MEMORIES I GOT LEFT.

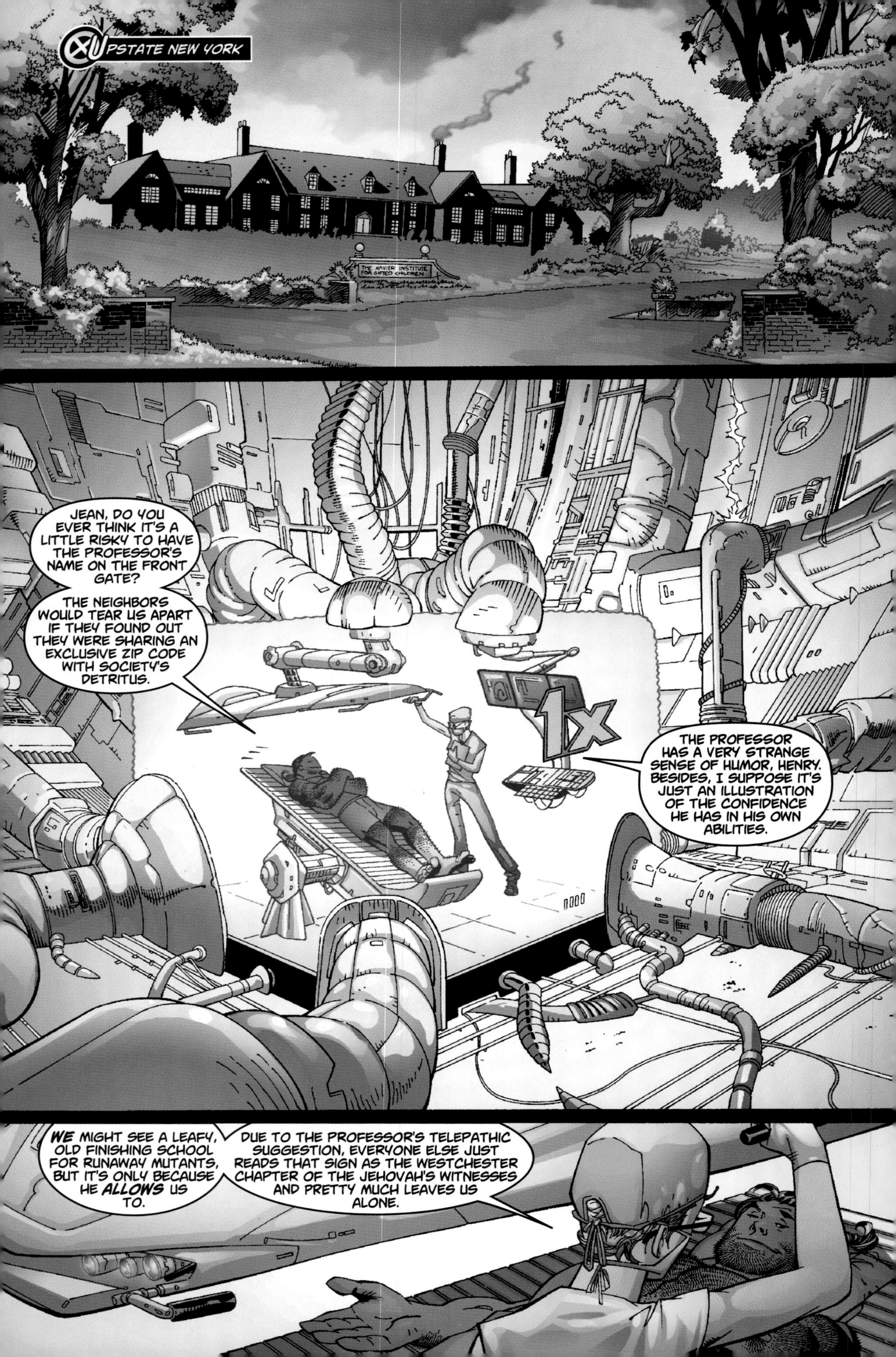
UPSTATE NEW YORK
THE XAVIER INSTITUTE FOR GIFTED CHILDREN
JEAN, DO YOU EVER THINK IT'S A LITTLE RISKY TO HAVE THE PROFESSOR'S NAME ON THE FRONT GATE?
THE NEIGHBORS WOULD TEAR US APART IF THEY FOUND OUT THEY WERE SHARING AN EXCLUSIVE ZIP CODE WITH SOCIETY'S DETRITUS.
THE PROFESSOR HAS A VERY STRANGE SENSE OF HUMOR, HENRY. BESIDES, I SUPPOSE IT'S JUST AN ILLUSTRATION OF THE CONFIDENCE HE HAS IN HIS OWN ABILITIES.
1X
WE MIGHT SEE A LEAFY, OLD FINISHING SCHOOL FOR RUNAWAY MUTANTS, BUT IT'S ONLY BECAUSE HE ALLOWS US TO.
DUE TO THE PROFESSOR'S TELEPATHIC SUGGESTION, EVERYONE ELSE JUST READS THAT SIGN AS THE WESTCHESTER CHAPTER OF THE JEHOVAH'S WITNESSES AND PRETTY MUCH LEAVES US ALONE.

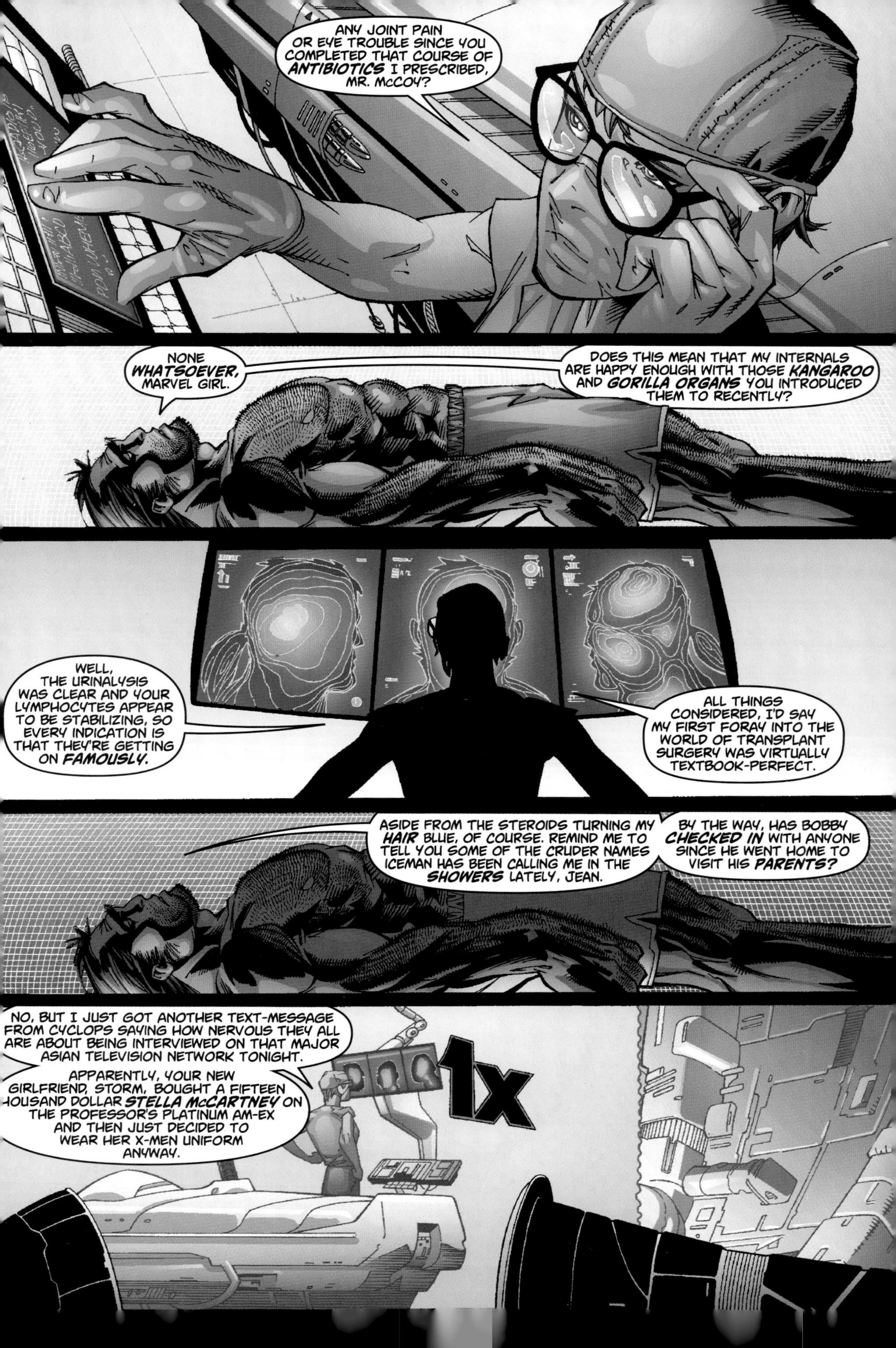
ANY JOINT PAIN OR EYE TROUBLE SINCE YOU COMPLETED THAT COURSE OF ANTIBIOTICS I PRESCRIBED, MR. McCOY?
NONE WHATSOEVER, MARVEL GIRL.
DOES THIS MEAN THAT MY INTERNALS ARE HAPPY ENOUGH WITH THOSE KANGAROO AND GORILLA ORGANS YOU INTRODUCED THEM TO RECENTLY?
WELL, THE URINALYSIS WAS CLEAR AND YOUR LYMPHOCYTES APPEAR TO BE STABILIZING, SO EVERY INDICATION IS THAT THEY'RE GETTING ON FAMOUSLY.
ALL THINGS CONSIDERED, I'D SAY MY FIRST FORAY INTO THE WORLD OF TRANSPLANT SURGERY WAS VIRTUALLY TEXTBOOK-PERFECT.
ASIDE FROM THE STEROIDS TURNING MY HAIR BLUE, OF COURSE. REMIND ME TO TELL YOU SOME OF THE CRUDER NAMES ICEMAN HAS BEEN CALLING ME IN THE SHOWERS LATELY, JEAN.
BY THE WAY, HAS BOBBY CHECKED IN WITH ANYONE SINCE HE WENT HOME TO VISIT HIS PARENTS?
NO, BUT I JUST GOT ANOTHER TEXT-MESSAGE FROM CYCLOPS SAYING HOW NERVOUS THEY ALL ARE ABOUT BEING INTERVIEWED ON THAT MAJOR ASIAN TELEVISION NETWORK TONIGHT.
APPARENTLY, YOUR NEW GIRLFRIEND, STORM, BOUGHT A FIFTEEN THOUSAND DOLLAR STELLA McCARTNEY ON THE PROFESSOR'S PLATINUM AM-EX AND THEN JUST DECIDED TO WEAR HER X-MEN UNIFORM ANYWAY.
1X

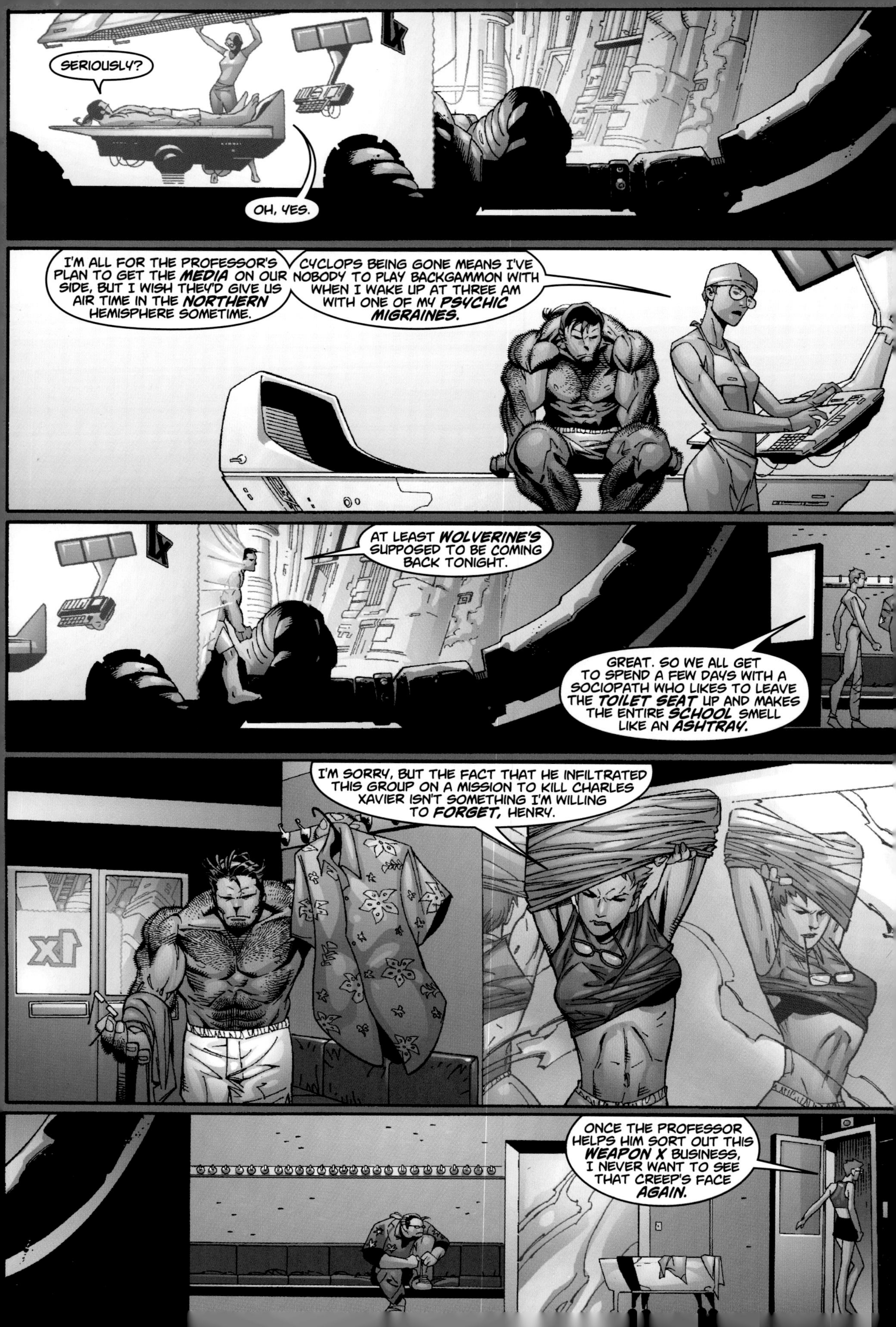

SERIOUSLY?
OH, YES.
I'M ALL FOR THE PROFESSOR'S PLAN TO GET THE MEDIA ON OUR SIDE, BUT I WISH THEY'D GIVE US AIR TIME IN THE NORTHERN HEMISPHERE SOMETIME.
CYCLOPS BEING GONE MEANS I'VE NOBODY TO PLAY BACKGAMMON WITH WHEN I WAKE UP AT THREE AM WITH ONE OF MY PSYCHIC MIGRAINES.
AT LEAST WOLVERINE'S SUPPOSED TO BE COMING BACK TONIGHT.
GREAT. SO WE ALL GET TO SPEND A FEW DAYS WITH A SOCIOPATH WHO LIKES TO LEAVE THE TOILET SEAT UP AND MAKES THE ENTIRE SCHOOL SMELL LIKE AN ASHTRAY.
I'M SORRY, BUT THE FACT THAT HE INFILTRATED THIS GROUP ON A MISSION TO KILL CHARLES XAVIER ISN'T SOMETHING I'M WILLING TO FORGET, HENRY.
ONCE THE PROFESSOR HELPS HIM SORT OUT THIS WEAPON X BUSINESS, I NEVER WANT TO SEE THAT CREEP'S FACE AGAIN.

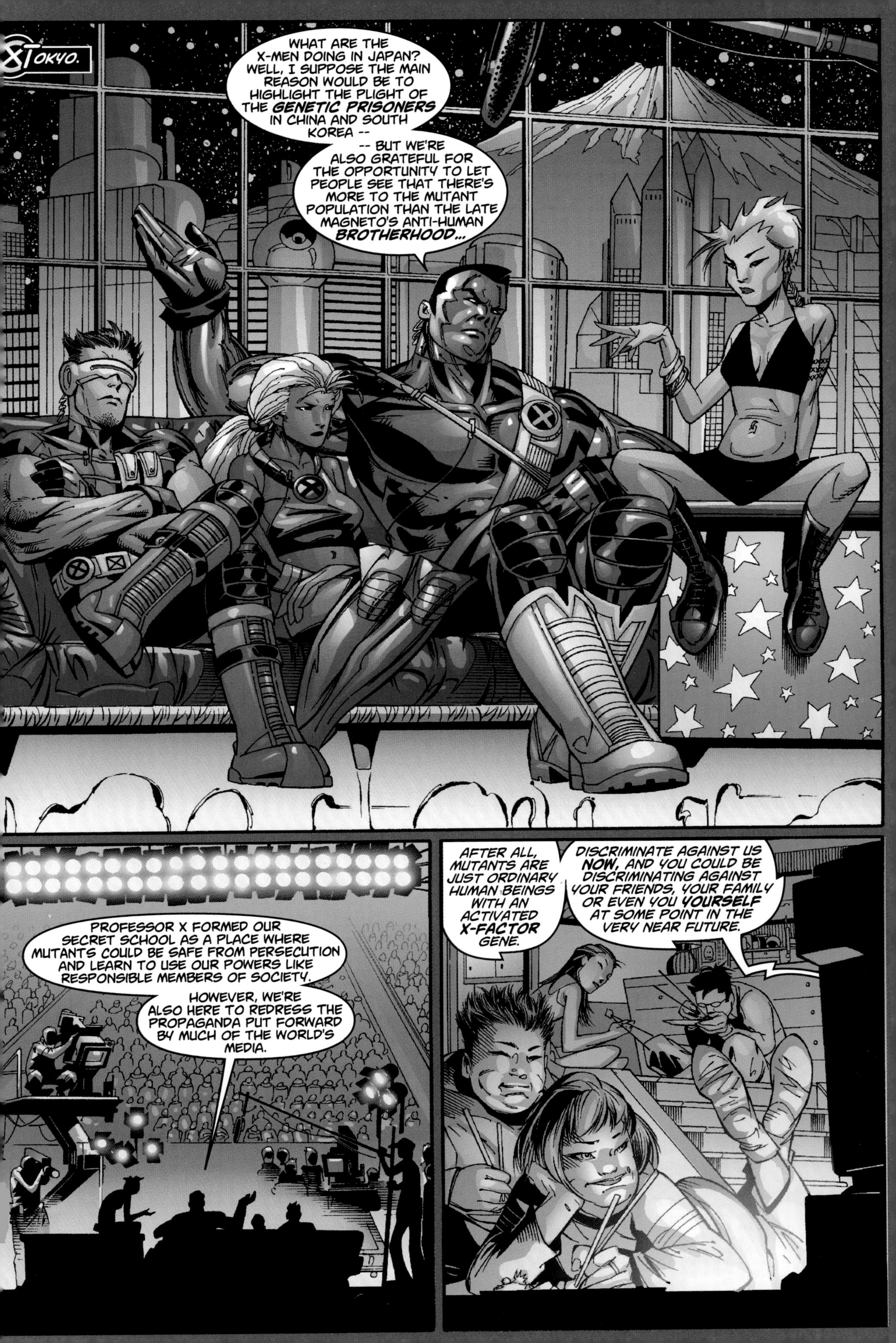
TOKYO.
WHAT ARE THE X-MEN DOING IN JAPAN? WELL, I SUPPOSE THE MAIN REASON WOULD BE TO HIGHLIGHT THE PLIGHT OF THE GENETIC PRISONERS IN CHINA AND SOUTH KOREA --
-- BUT WE'RE ALSO GRATEFUL FOR THE OPPORTUNITY TO LET PEOPLE SEE THAT THERE'S MORE TO THE MUTANT POPULATION THAN THE LATE MAGNETO'S ANTI-HUMAN BROTHERHOOD...
PROFESSOR X FORMED OUR SECRET SCHOOL AS A PLACE WHERE MUTANTS COULD BE SAFE FROM PERSECUTION AND LEARN TO USE OUR POWERS LIKE RESPONSIBLE MEMBERS OF SOCIETY.
HOWEVER, WE'RE ALSO HERE TO REDRESS THE PROPAGANDA PUT FORWARD BY MUCH OF THE WORLD'S MEDIA.
AFTER ALL, MUTANTS ARE JUST ORDINARY HUMAN BEINGS WITH AN ACTIVATED X-FACTOR GENE.
DISCRIMINATE AGAINST US NOW, AND YOU COULD BE DISCRIMINATING AGAINST YOUR FRIENDS, YOUR FAMILY OR EVEN YOU YOURSELF AT SOME POINT IN THE VERY NEAR FUTURE.

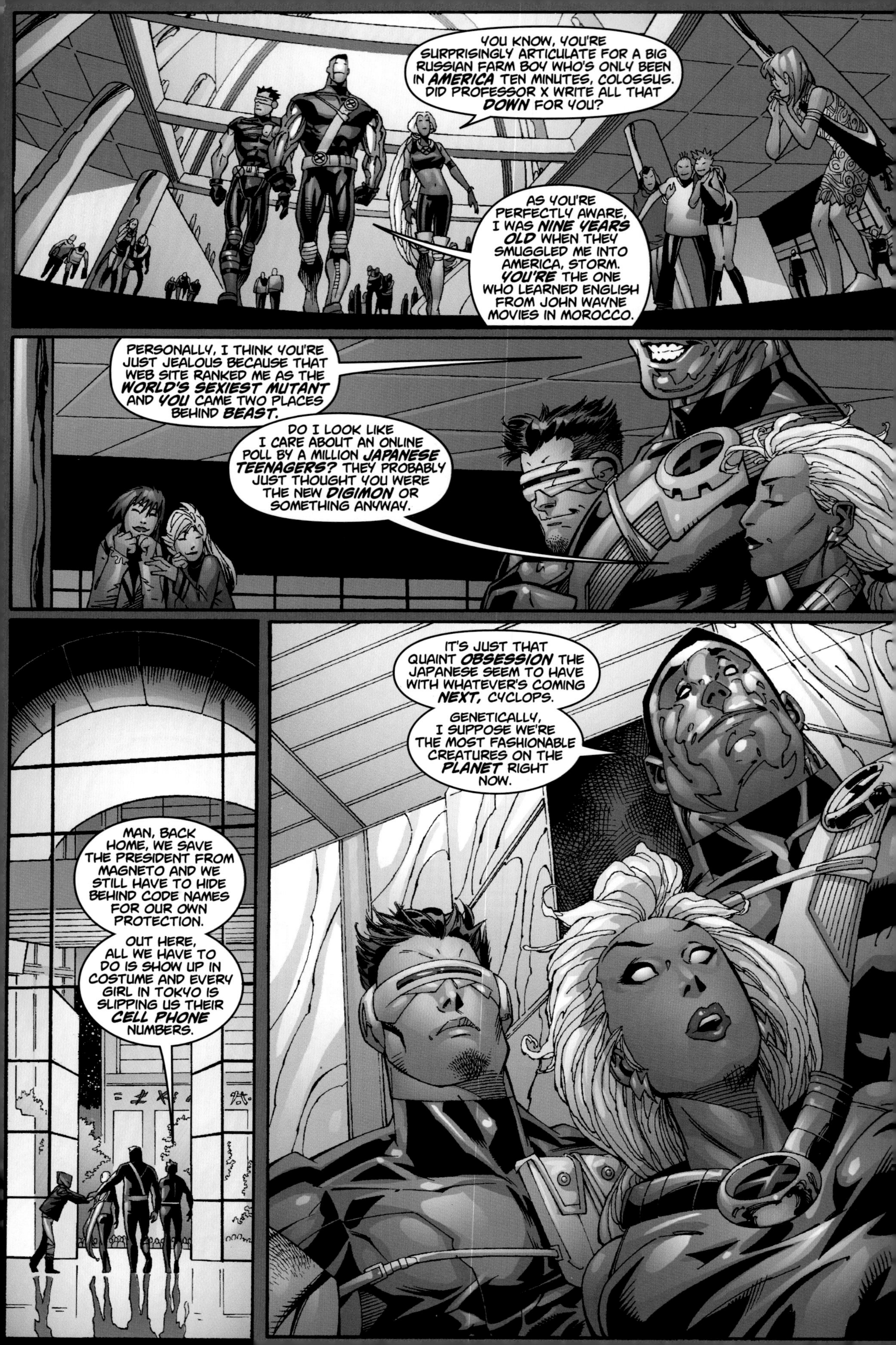
YOU KNOW, YOU'RE SURPRISINGLY ARTICULATE FOR A BIG RUSSIAN FARM BOY WHO'S ONLY BEEN IN AMERICA TEN MINUTES, COLOSSUS. DID PROFESSOR X WRITE ALL THAT DOWN FOR YOU?
AS YOU'RE PERFECTLY AWARE, I WAS NINE YEARS OLD WHEN THEY SMUGGLED ME INTO AMERICA, STORM. YOU'RE THE ONE WHO LEARNED ENGLISH FROM JOHN WAYNE MOVIES IN MOROCCO.
PERSONALLY, I THINK YOU'RE JUST JEALOUS BECAUSE THAT WEB SITE RANKED ME AS THE WORLD'S SEXIEST MUTANT AND YOU CAME TWO PLACES BEHIND BEAST.
DO I LOOK LIKE I CARE ABOUT AN ONLINE POLL BY A MILLION JAPANESE TEENAGERS? THEY PROBABLY JUST THOUGHT YOU WERE THE NEW DIGIMON OR SOMETHING ANYWAY.
MAN, BACK HOME, WE SAVE THE PRESIDENT FROM MAGNETO AND WE STILL HAVE TO HIDE BEHIND CODE NAMES FOR OUR OWN PROTECTION.
OUT HERE, ALL WE HAVE TO DO IS SHOW UP IN COSTUME AND EVERY GIRL IN TOKYO IS SLIPPING US THEIR CELL PHONE NUMBERS.
IT'S JUST THAT QUAINT OBSESSION THE JAPANESE SEEM TO HAVE WITH WHATEVER'S COMING NEXT, CYCLOPS.
GENETICALLY, I SUPPOSE WE'RE THE MOST FASHIONABLE CREATURES ON THE PLANET RIGHT NOW.

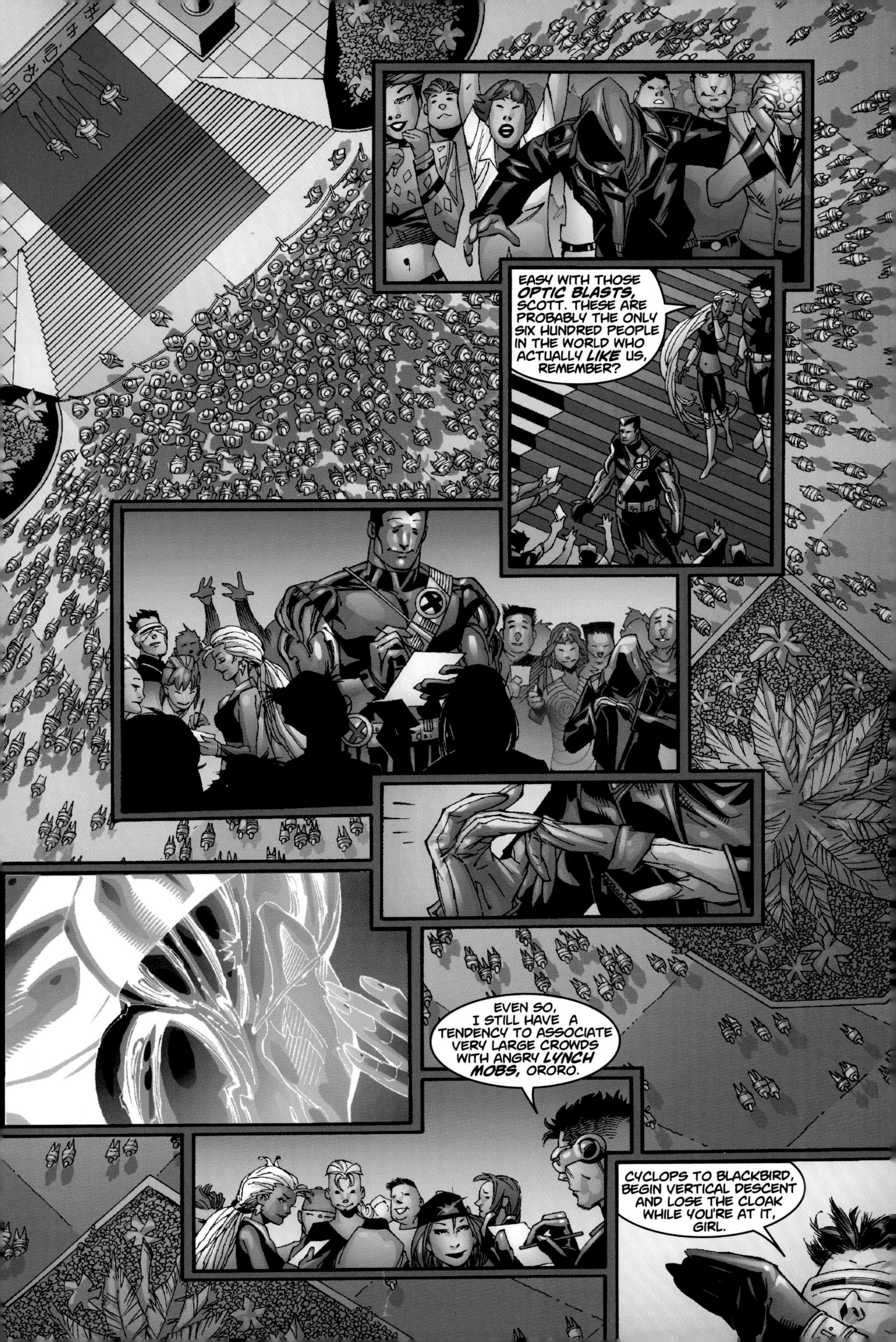
EASY WITH THOSE OPTIC BLASTS, SCOTT. THESE ARE PROBABLY THE ONLY SIX HUNDRED PEOPLE IN THE WORLD WHO ACTUALLY LIKE US, REMEMBER?
EVEN SO, I STILL HAVE A TENDENCY TO ASSOCIATE VERY LARGE CROWDS WITH ANGRY LYNCH MOBS, ORORO.
CYCLOPS TO BLACKBIRD, BEGIN VERTICAL DESCENT AND LOSE THE CLOAK WHILE YOU'RE AT IT, GIRL.

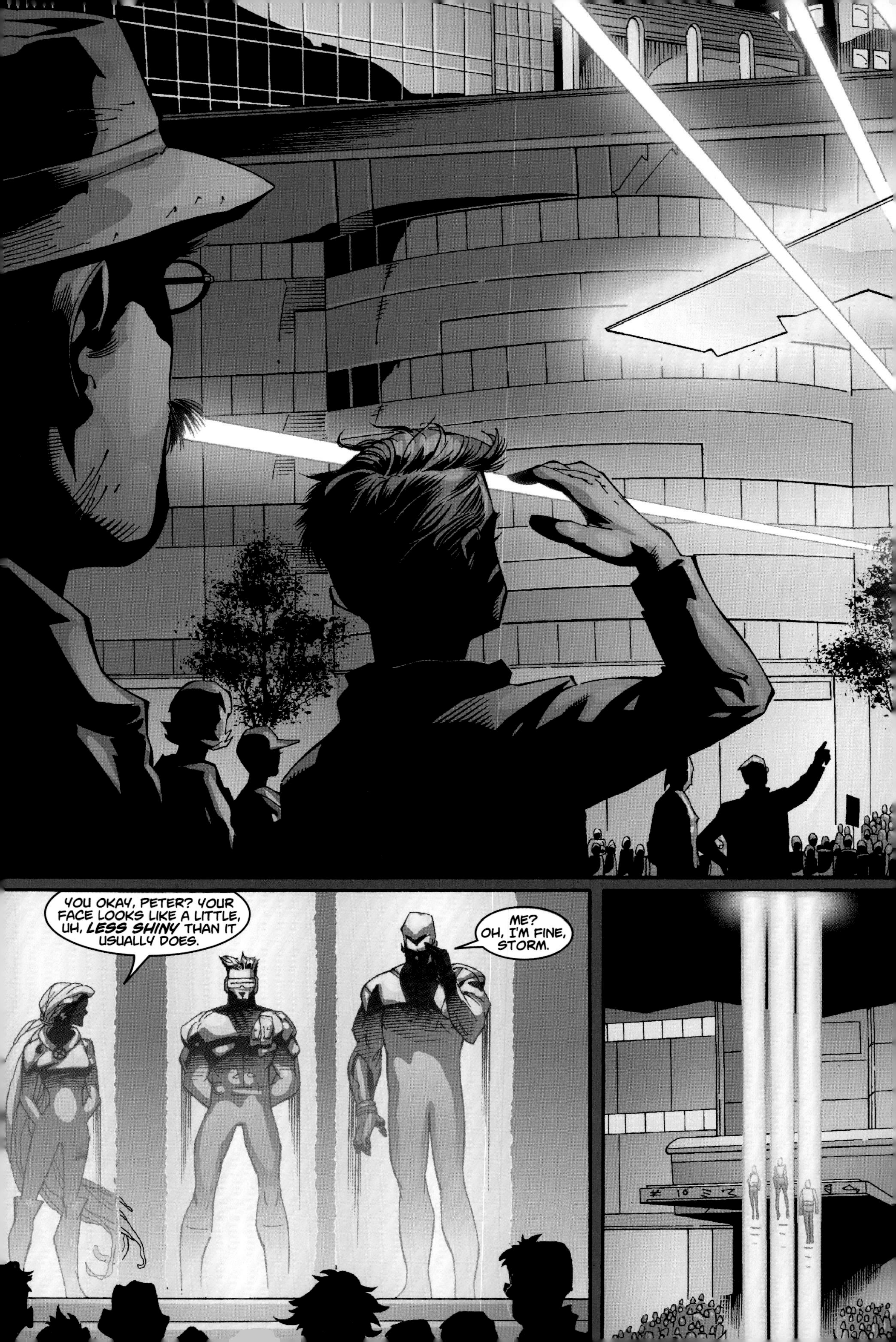
YOU OKAY, PETER? YOUR FACE LOOKS LIKE A LITTLE, UH, LESS SHINY THAN IT USUALLY DOES.
ME? OH, I'M FINE, STORM.

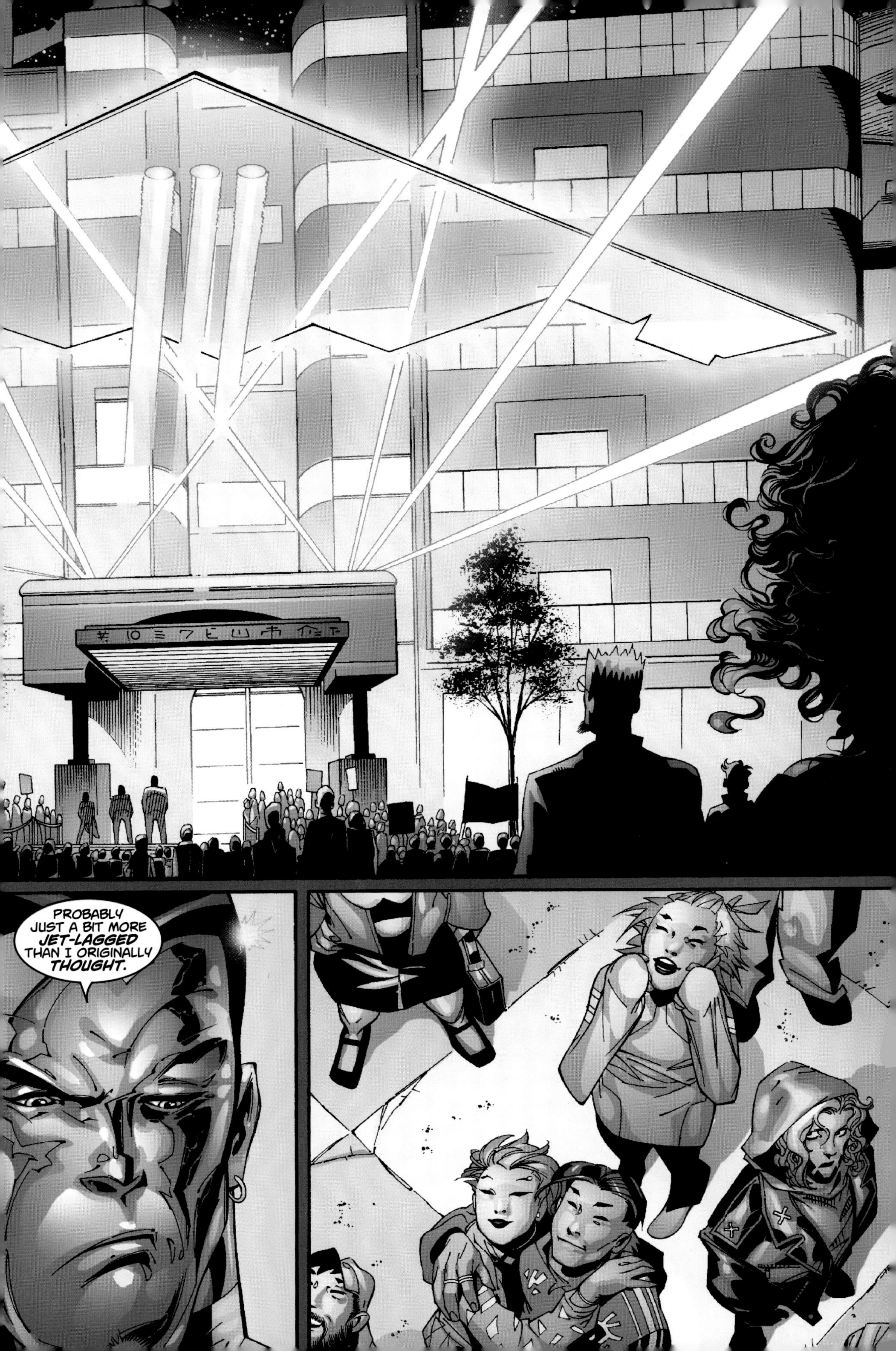
PROBABLY JUST A BIT MORE *JET-LAGGED* THAN I ORIGINALLY *THOUGHT.*

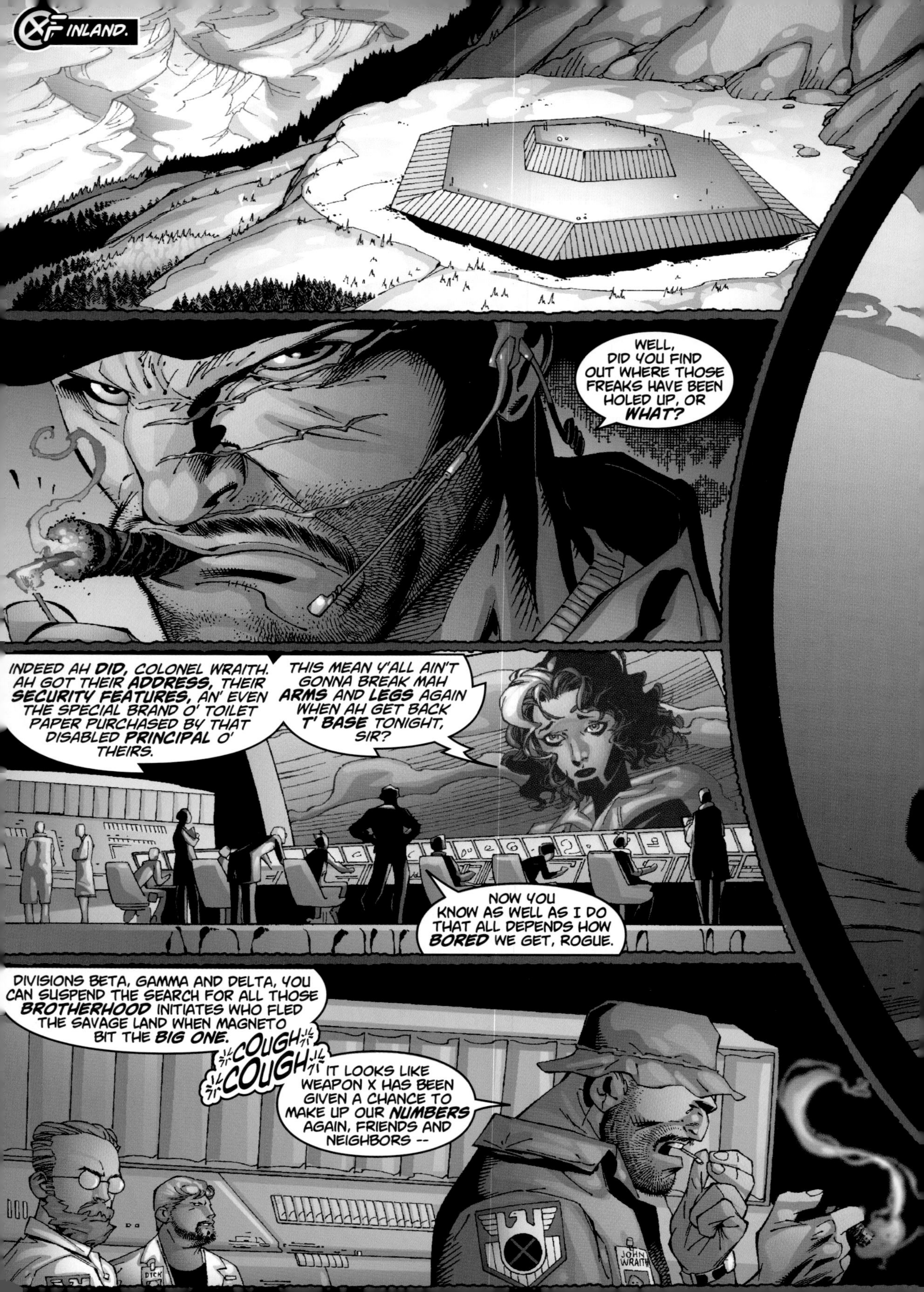
FINLAND.
WELL, DID YOU FIND OUT WHERE THOSE FREAKS HAVE BEEN HOLED UP, OR WHAT?
INDEED AH DID, COLONEL WRAITH. AH GOT THEIR ADDRESS, THEIR SECURITY FEATURES, AN' EVEN THE SPECIAL BRAND O' TOILET PAPER PURCHASED BY THAT DISABLED PRINCIPAL O' THEIRS.
THIS MEAN Y'ALL AIN'T GONNA BREAK MAH ARMS AND LEGS AGAIN WHEN AH GET BACK T' BASE TONIGHT, SIR?
NOW YOU KNOW AS WELL AS I DO THAT ALL DEPENDS HOW BORED WE GET, ROGUE.
DIVISIONS BETA, GAMMA AND DELTA, YOU CAN SUSPEND THE SEARCH FOR ALL THOSE BROTHERHOOD INITIATES WHO FLED THE SAVAGE LAND WHEN MAGNETO BIT THE BIG ONE.
COUGH COUGH
IT LOOKS LIKE WEAPON X HAS BEEN GIVEN A CHANCE TO MAKE UP OUR NUMBERS AGAIN, FRIENDS AND NEIGHBORS --
JOHN WRAITH
DICK

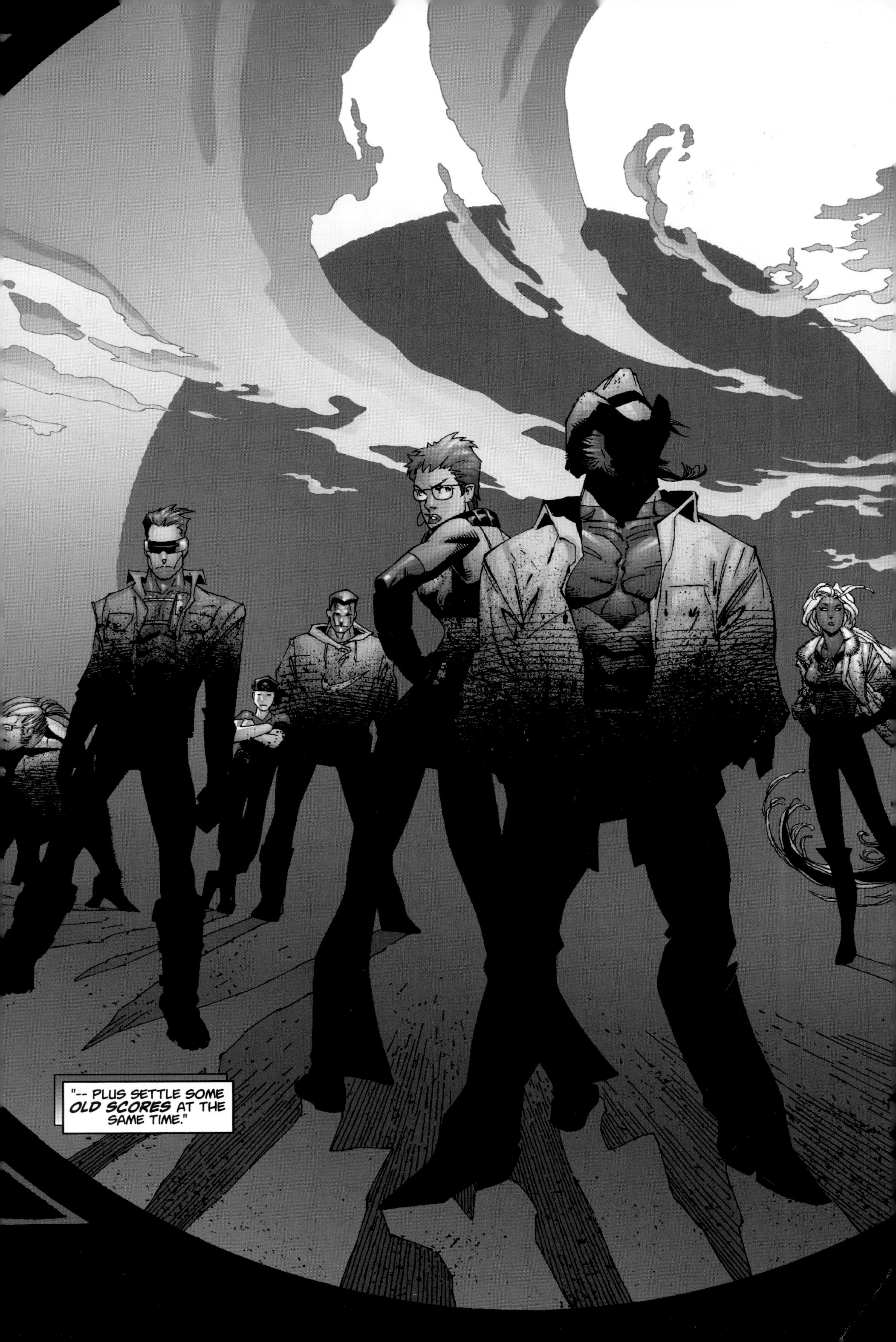
"-- PLUS SETTLE SOME OLD SCORES AT THE SAME TIME."

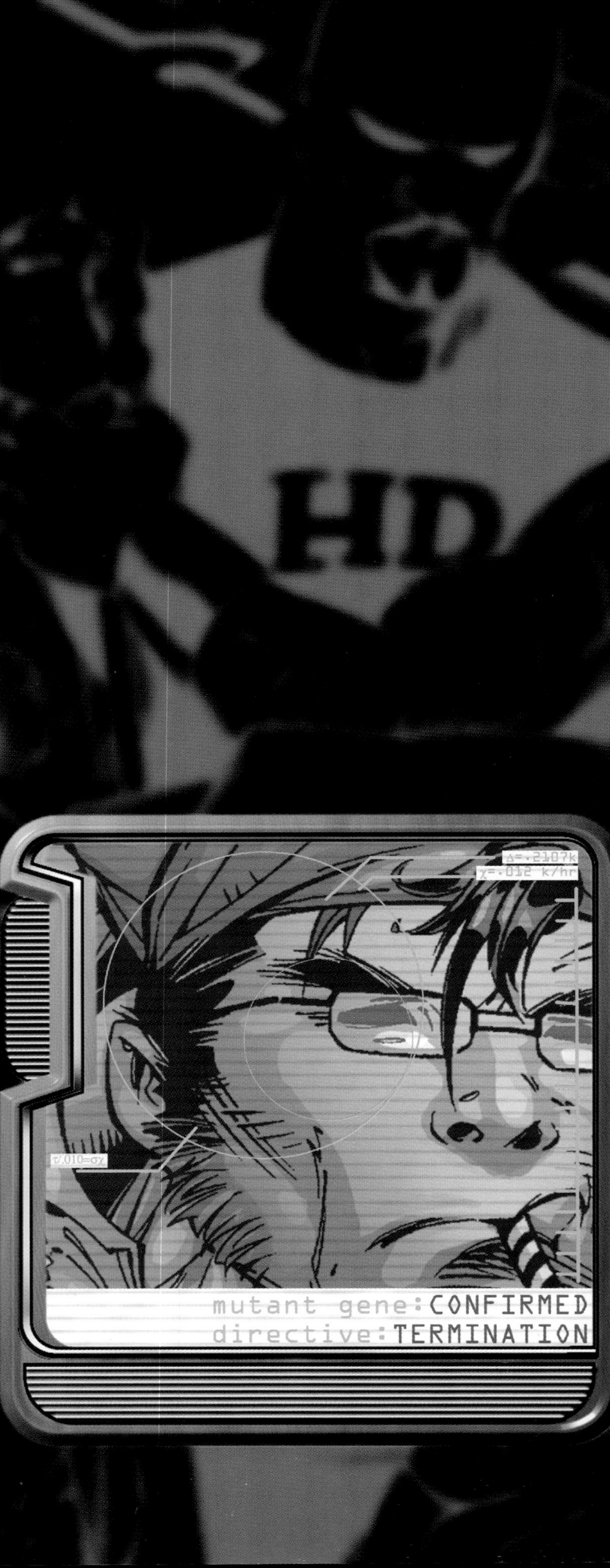
HD
Δ=.2107k
χ=.012 k/hr
mutant gene:CONFIRMED
directive:TERMINATION

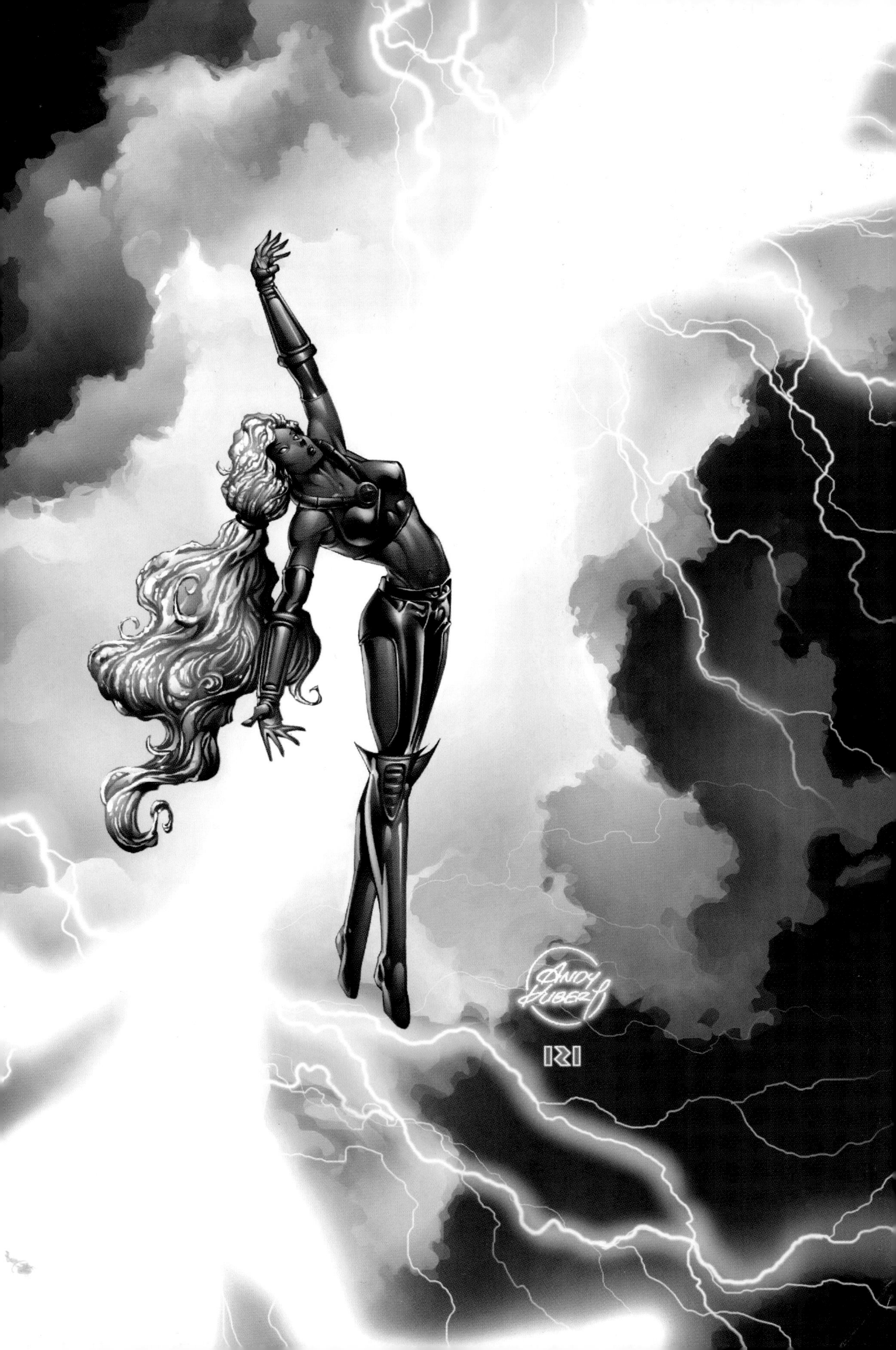

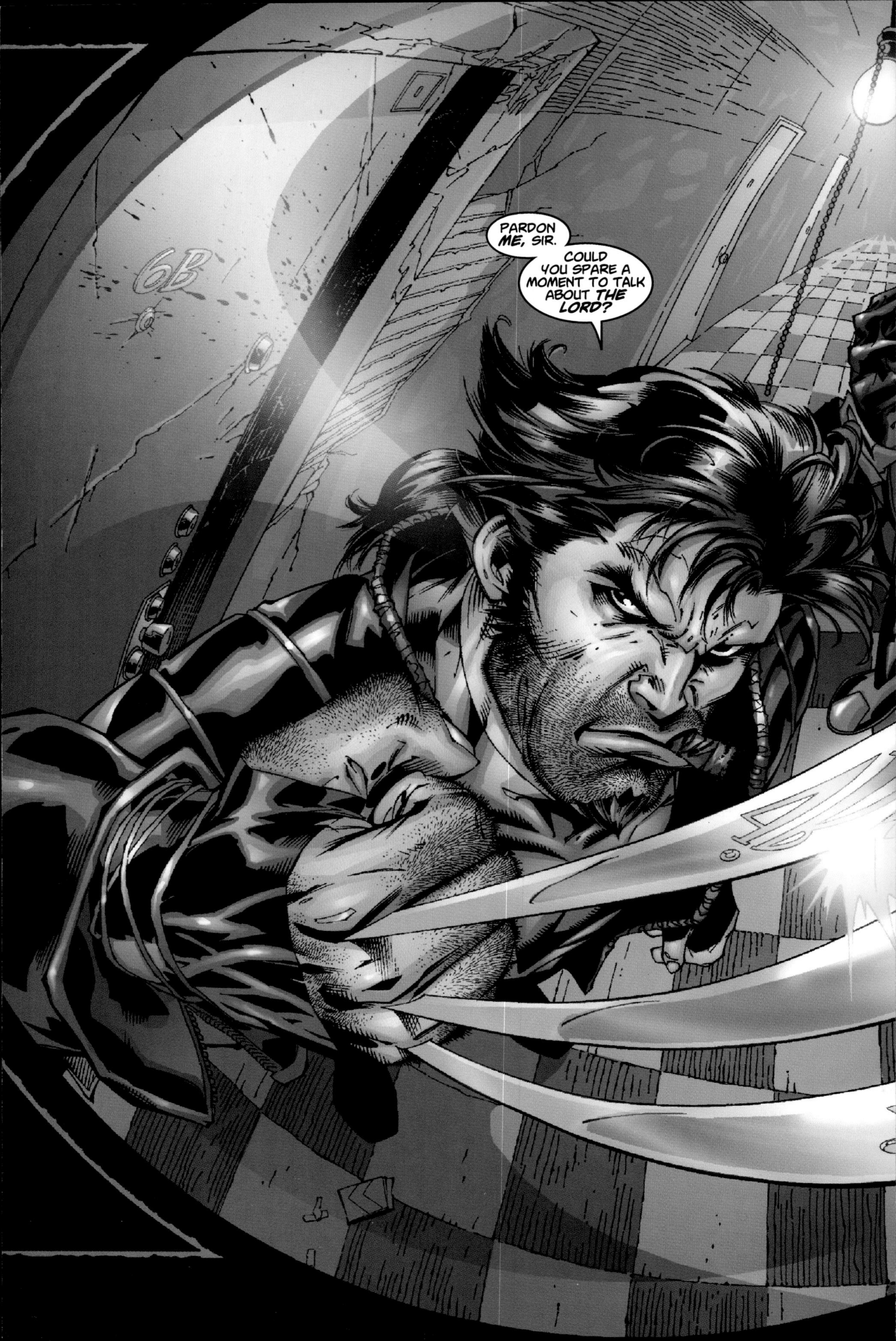
PARDON ME, SIR.
COULD YOU SPARE A MOMENT TO TALK ABOUT THE LORD?

RETURN TO WEAPON X

PART TWO OF SIX

MARK MILLAR
writer

ADAM KUBERT
pencils

ART THIBERT
inks

JUNG CHOI
colors

**RICHARD STARKINGS
& COMICRAFT'S
WES ABBOTT**
letters

PETE FRANCO
assistant editor

MARK POWERS
editor

JOE QUESADA
editor in chief

BILL JEMAS
president

A STAN LEE PRESENTATION

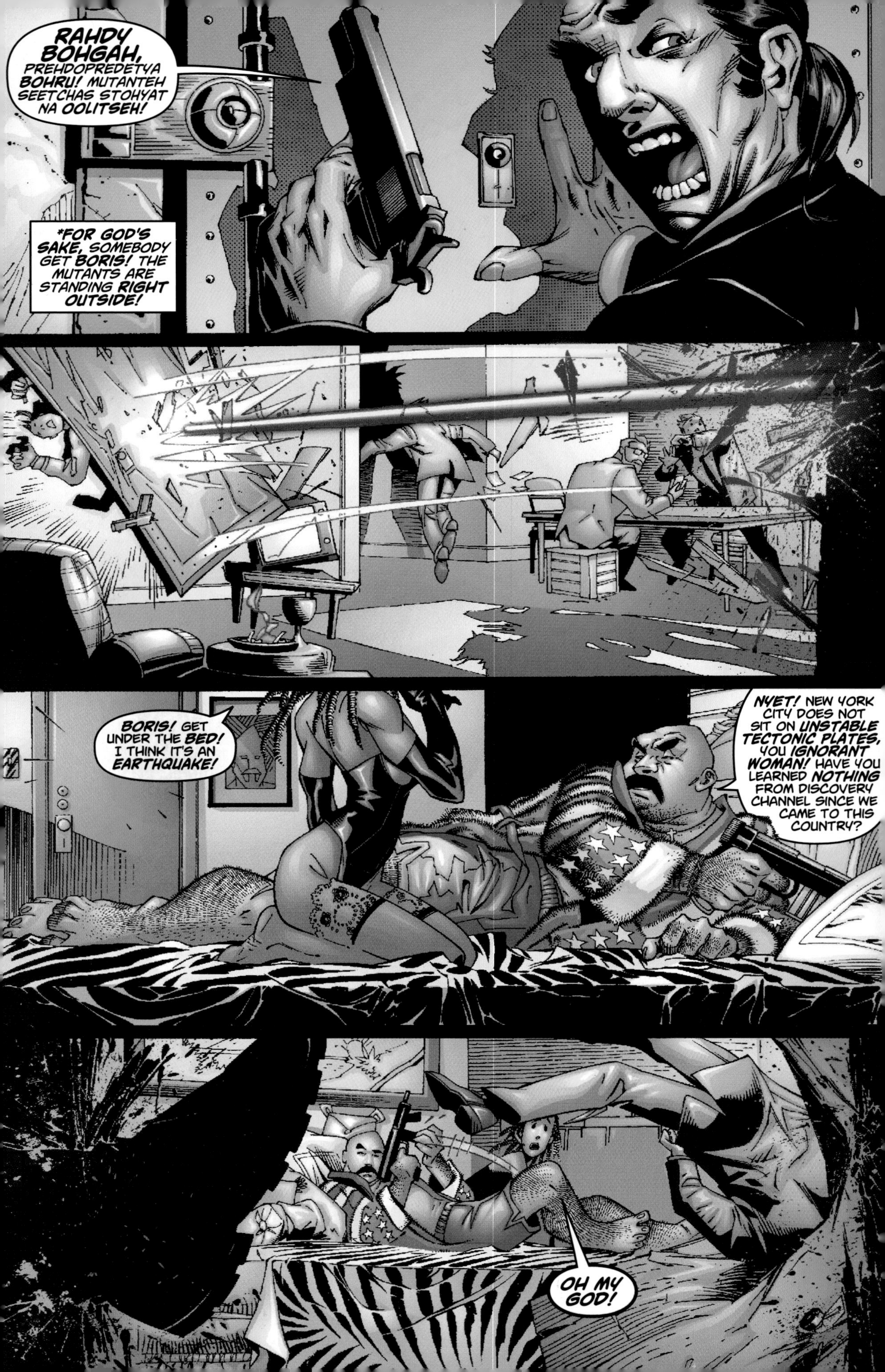
RAHDY BOHGAH, PREHDOPREDETYA BOHRU! MUTANTEH SEETCHAS STOHYAT NA OOLITSEH!
*FOR GOD'S SAKE, SOMEBODY GET BORIS! THE MUTANTS ARE STANDING RIGHT OUTSIDE!
BORIS! GET UNDER THE BED! I THINK IT'S AN EARTHQUAKE!
NYET! NEW YORK CITY DOES NOT SIT ON UNSTABLE TECTONIC PLATES, YOU IGNORANT WOMAN! HAVE YOU LEARNED NOTHING FROM DISCOVERY CHANNEL SINCE WE CAME TO THIS COUNTRY?
OH MY GOD!

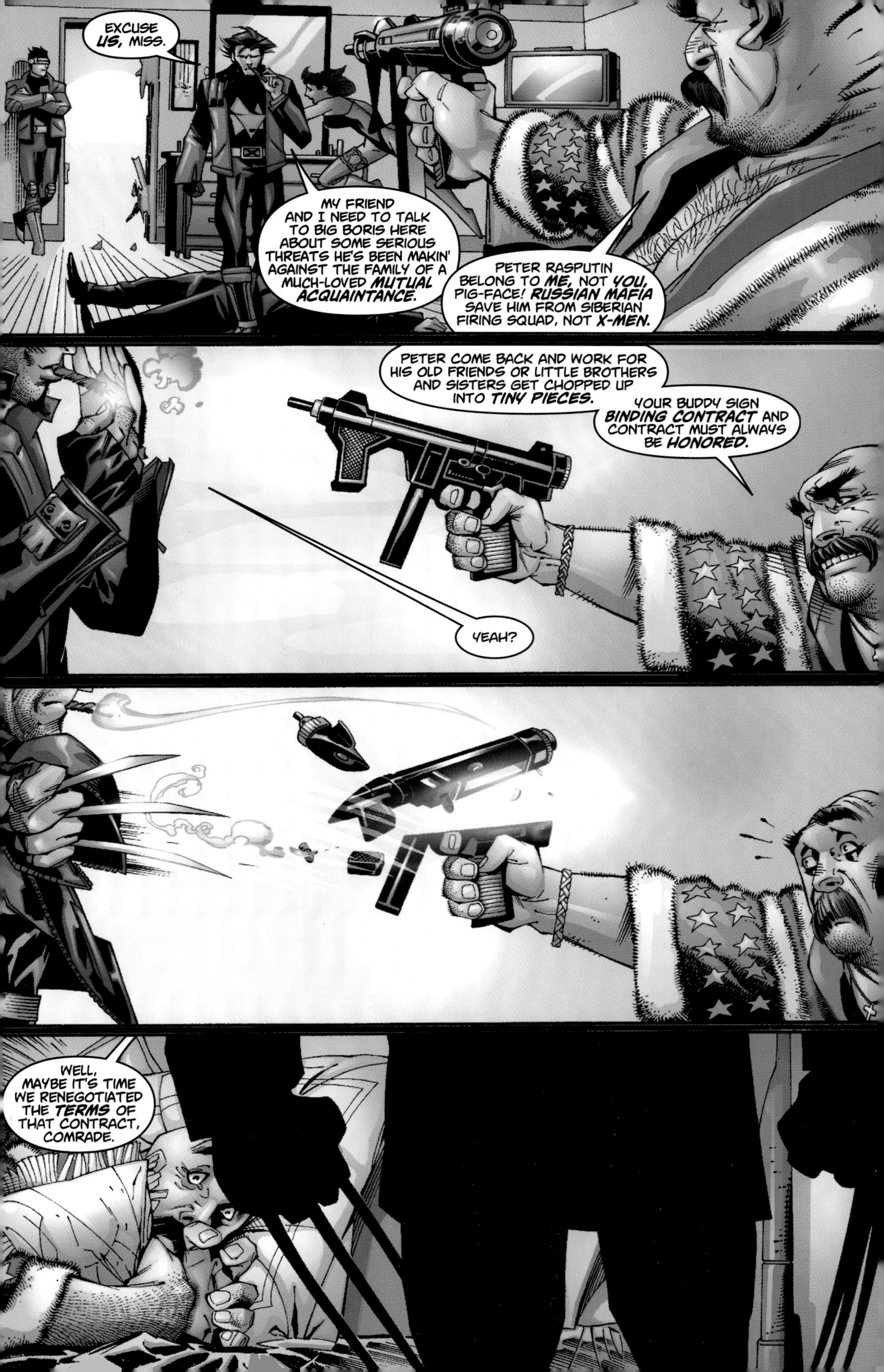
EXCUSE *US,* MISS.
MY FRIEND AND I NEED TO TALK TO BIG BORIS HERE ABOUT SOME SERIOUS THREATS HE'S BEEN MAKIN' AGAINST THE FAMILY OF A MUCH-LOVED ***MUTUAL ACQUAINTANCE***.
PETER RASPUTIN BELONG TO ***ME,*** NOT ***YOU,*** PIG-FACE! ***RUSSIAN MAFIA*** SAVE HIM FROM SIBERIAN FIRING SQUAD, NOT ***X-MEN***.
PETER COME BACK AND WORK FOR HIS OLD FRIENDS OR LITTLE BROTHERS AND SISTERS GET CHOPPED UP INTO ***TINY PIECES***.
YOUR BUDDY SIGN ***BINDING CONTRACT*** AND CONTRACT MUST ALWAYS BE ***HONORED***.
YEAH?
WELL, MAYBE IT'S TIME WE RENEGOTIATED THE ***TERMS*** OF THAT CONTRACT, COMRADE.

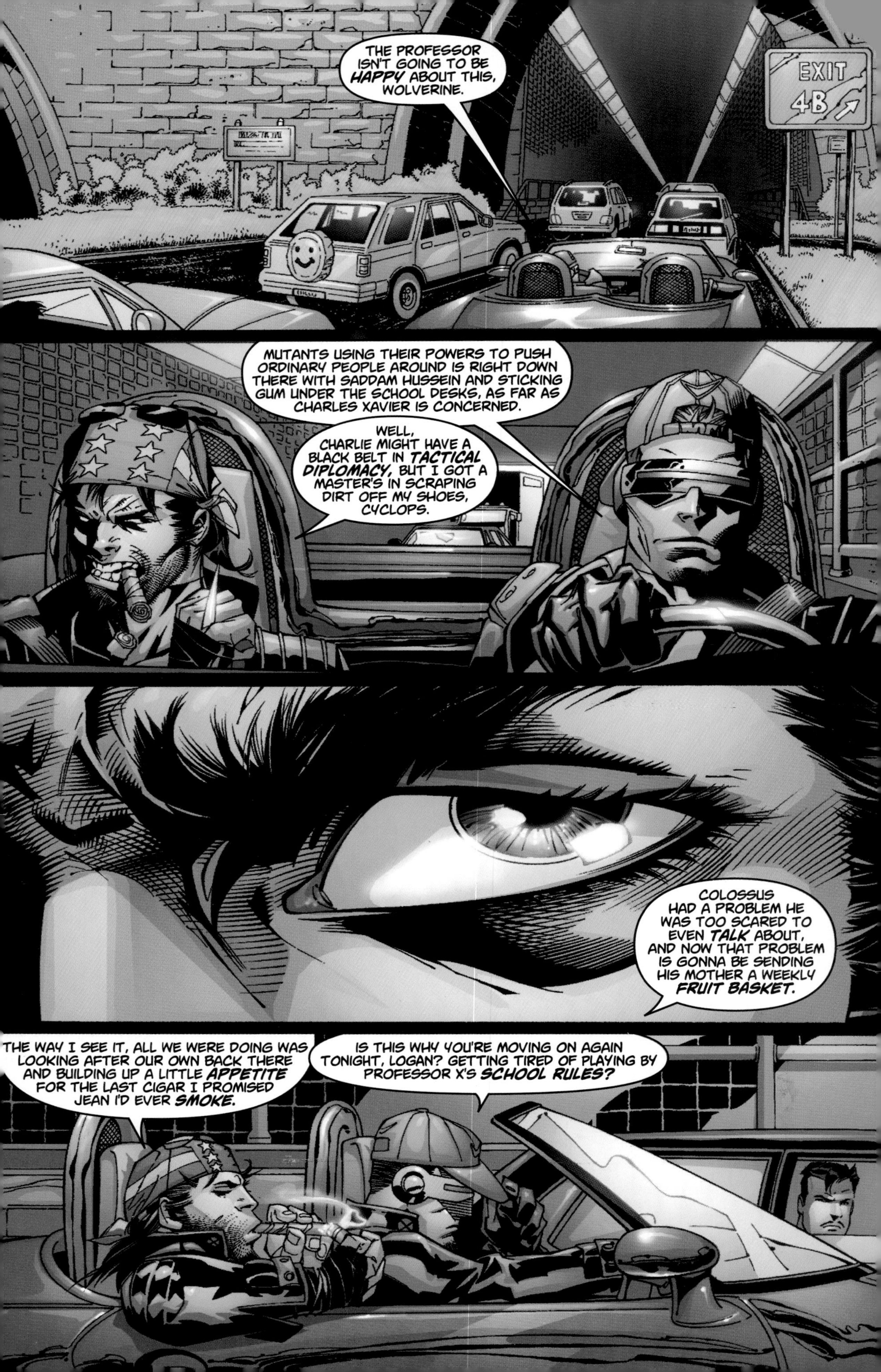
THE PROFESSOR ISN'T GOING TO BE HAPPY ABOUT THIS, WOLVERINE.
EXIT 4B
MUTANTS USING THEIR POWERS TO PUSH ORDINARY PEOPLE AROUND IS RIGHT DOWN THERE WITH SADDAM HUSSEIN AND STICKING GUM UNDER THE SCHOOL DESKS, AS FAR AS CHARLES XAVIER IS CONCERNED.
WELL, CHARLIE MIGHT HAVE A BLACK BELT IN TACTICAL DIPLOMACY, BUT I GOT A MASTER'S IN SCRAPING DIRT OFF MY SHOES, CYCLOPS.
COLOSSUS HAD A PROBLEM HE WAS TOO SCARED TO EVEN TALK ABOUT, AND NOW THAT PROBLEM IS GONNA BE SENDING HIS MOTHER A WEEKLY FRUIT BASKET.
THE WAY I SEE IT, ALL WE WERE DOING WAS LOOKING AFTER OUR OWN BACK THERE AND BUILDING UP A LITTLE APPETITE FOR THE LAST CIGAR I PROMISED JEAN I'D EVER SMOKE.
IS THIS WHY YOU'RE MOVING ON AGAIN TONIGHT, LOGAN? GETTING TIRED OF PLAYING BY PROFESSOR X'S SCHOOL RULES?

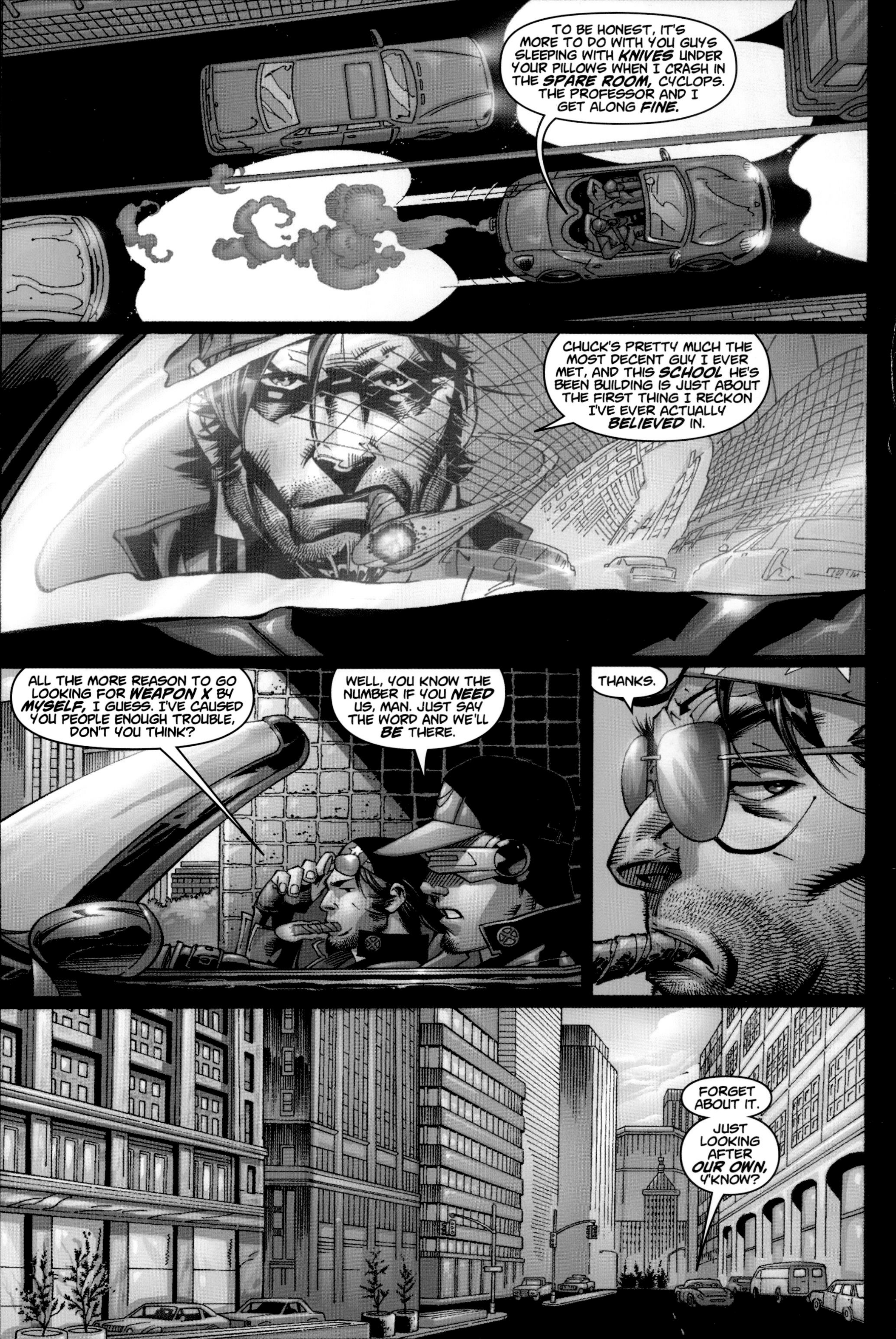
TO BE HONEST, IT'S MORE TO DO WITH YOU GUYS SLEEPING WITH KNIVES UNDER YOUR PILLOWS WHEN I CRASH IN THE SPARE ROOM, CYCLOPS. THE PROFESSOR AND I GET ALONG FINE.
CHUCK'S PRETTY MUCH THE MOST DECENT GUY I EVER MET, AND THIS SCHOOL HE'S BEEN BUILDING IS JUST ABOUT THE FIRST THING I RECKON I'VE EVER ACTUALLY BELIEVED IN.
ALL THE MORE REASON TO GO LOOKING FOR WEAPON X BY MYSELF, I GUESS. I'VE CAUSED YOU PEOPLE ENOUGH TROUBLE, DON'T YOU THINK?
WELL, YOU KNOW THE NUMBER IF YOU NEED US, MAN. JUST SAY THE WORD AND WE'LL BE THERE.
THANKS.
FORGET ABOUT IT.
JUST LOOKING AFTER OUR OWN, Y'KNOW?

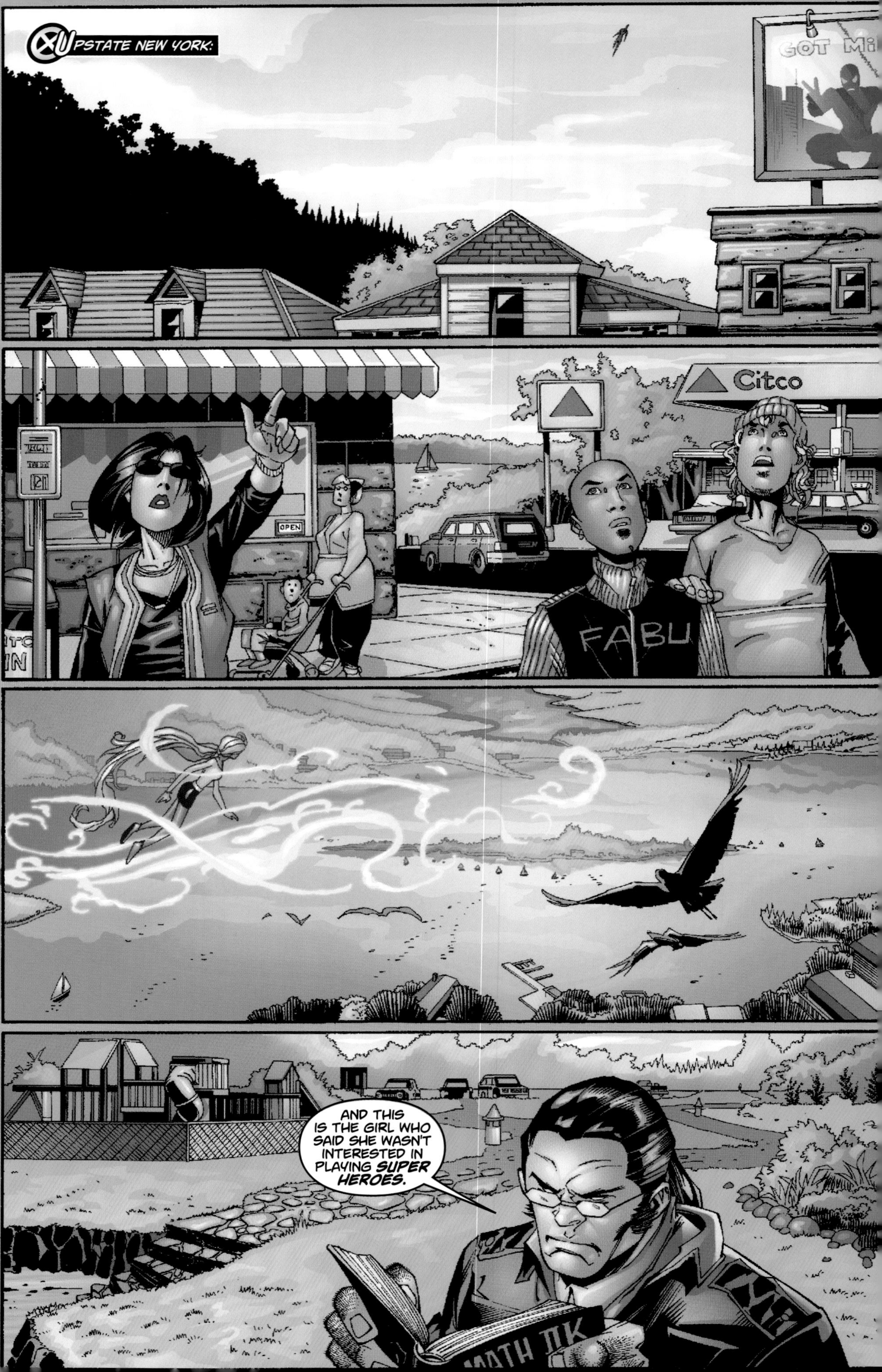
UPSTATE NEW YORK:
GOT MI
Citco
OPEN
FABU
AND THIS IS THE GIRL WHO SAID SHE WASN'T INTERESTED IN PLAYING SUPER HEROES.
MATH IIK

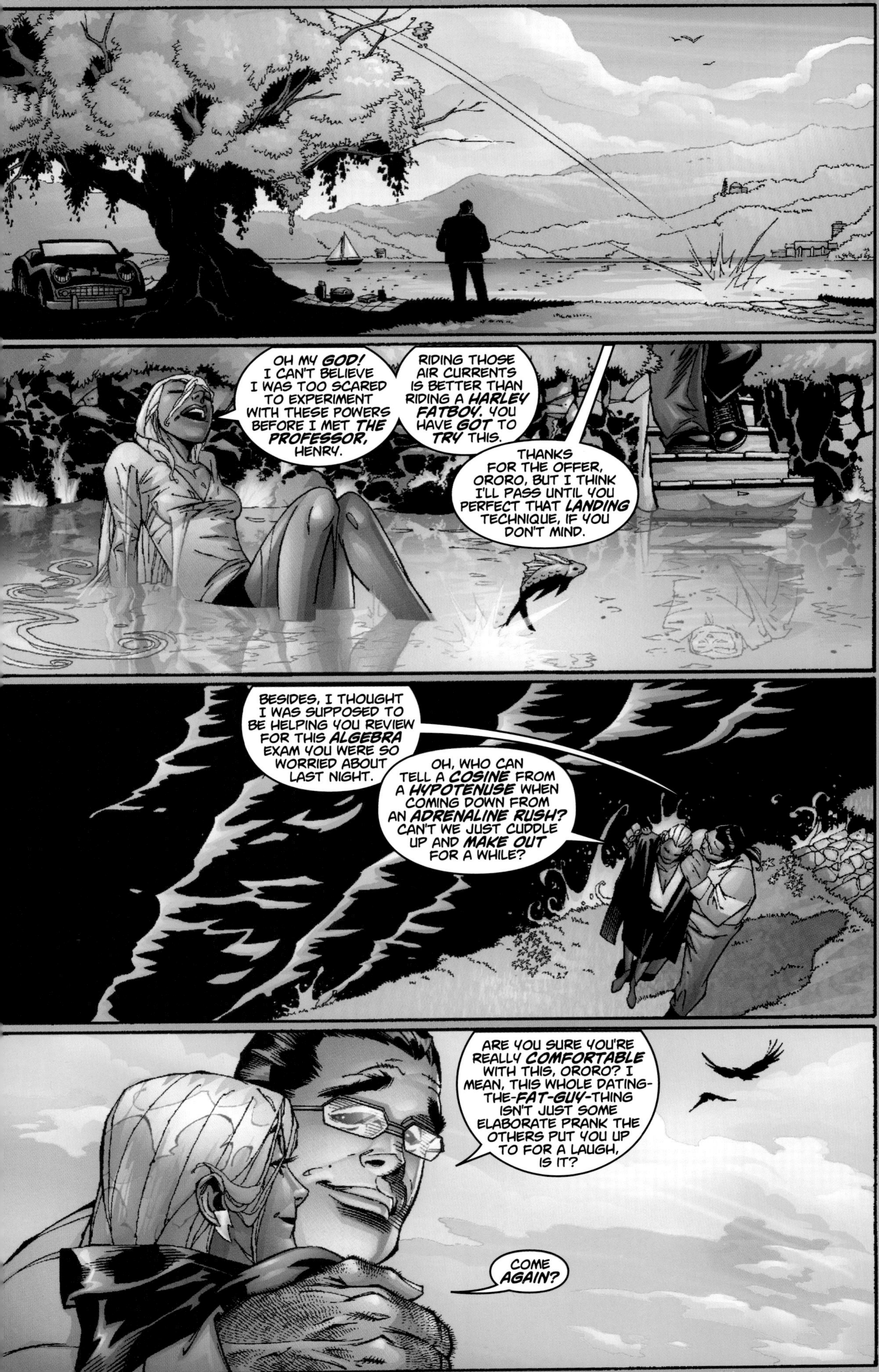
OH MY GOD! I CAN'T BELIEVE I WAS TOO SCARED TO EXPERIMENT WITH THESE POWERS BEFORE I MET THE PROFESSOR, HENRY.
RIDING THOSE AIR CURRENTS IS BETTER THAN RIDING A HARLEY FATBOY. YOU HAVE GOT TO TRY THIS.
THANKS FOR THE OFFER, ORORO, BUT I THINK I'LL PASS UNTIL YOU PERFECT THAT LANDING TECHNIQUE, IF YOU DON'T MIND.
BESIDES, I THOUGHT I WAS SUPPOSED TO BE HELPING YOU REVIEW FOR THIS ALGEBRA EXAM YOU WERE SO WORRIED ABOUT LAST NIGHT.
OH, WHO CAN TELL A COSINE FROM A HYPOTENUSE WHEN COMING DOWN FROM AN ADRENALINE RUSH? CAN'T WE JUST CUDDLE UP AND MAKE OUT FOR A WHILE?
ARE YOU SURE YOU'RE REALLY COMFORTABLE WITH THIS, ORORO? I MEAN, THIS WHOLE DATING-THE-FAT-GUY-THING ISN'T JUST SOME ELABORATE PRANK THE OTHERS PUT YOU UP TO FOR A LAUGH, IS IT?
COME AGAIN?

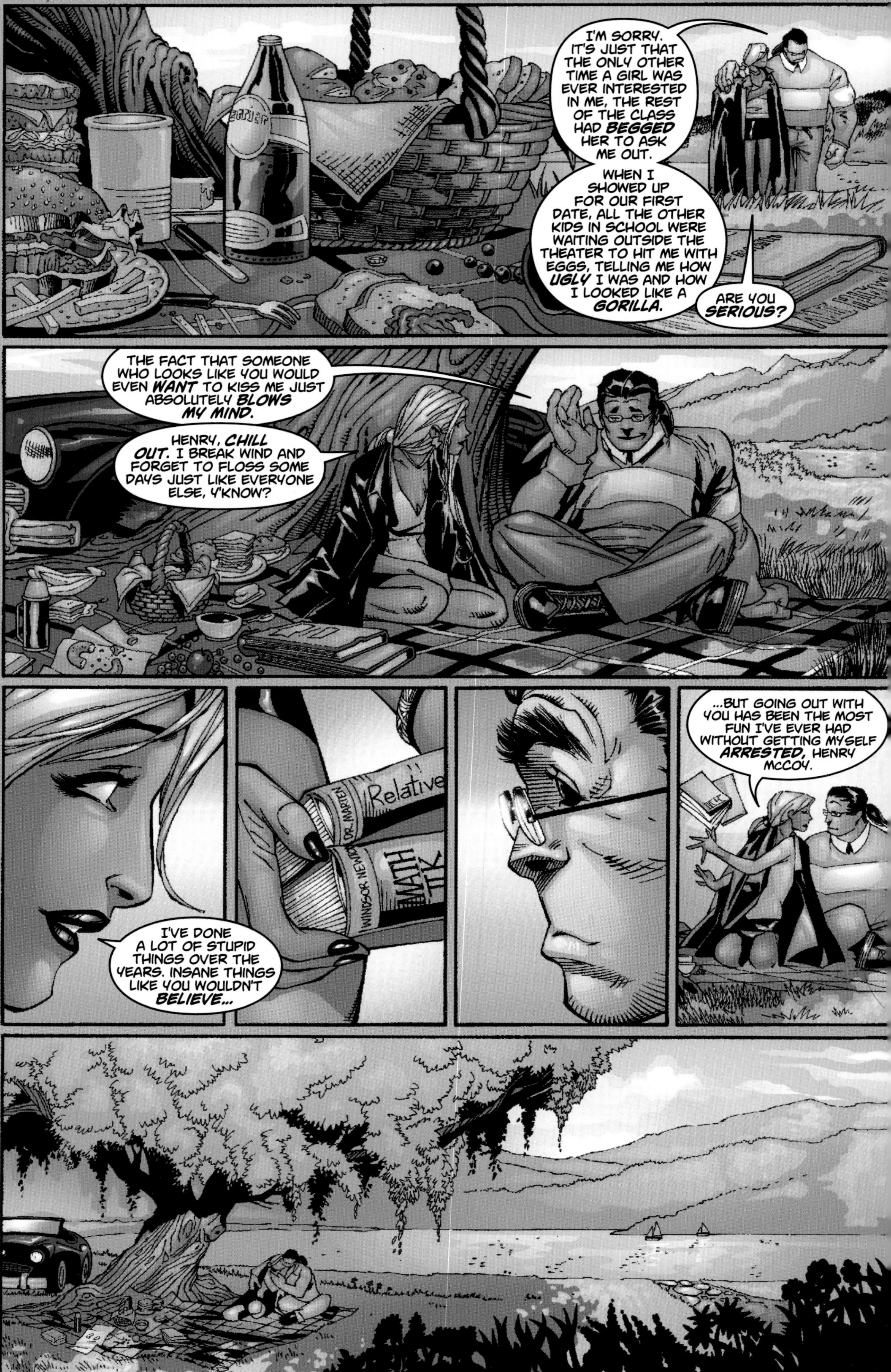
I'M SORRY. IT'S JUST THAT THE ONLY OTHER TIME A GIRL WAS EVER INTERESTED IN ME, THE REST OF THE CLASS HAD BEGGED HER TO ASK ME OUT.
WHEN I SHOWED UP FOR OUR FIRST DATE, ALL THE OTHER KIDS IN SCHOOL WERE WAITING OUTSIDE THE THEATER TO HIT ME WITH EGGS, TELLING ME HOW UGLY I WAS AND HOW I LOOKED LIKE A GORILLA.
ARE YOU SERIOUS?
THE FACT THAT SOMEONE WHO LOOKS LIKE YOU WOULD EVEN WANT TO KISS ME JUST ABSOLUTELY BLOWS MY MIND.
HENRY, CHILL OUT. I BREAK WIND AND FORGET TO FLOSS SOME DAYS JUST LIKE EVERYONE ELSE, Y'KNOW?
I'VE DONE A LOT OF STUPID THINGS OVER THE YEARS. INSANE THINGS LIKE YOU WOULDN'T BELIEVE...
Relative
DR. MARTEN
WINDSOR NEWTON
MATH
...BUT GOING OUT WITH YOU HAS BEEN THE MOST FUN I'VE EVER HAD WITHOUT GETTING MYSELF ARRESTED, HENRY McCOY.

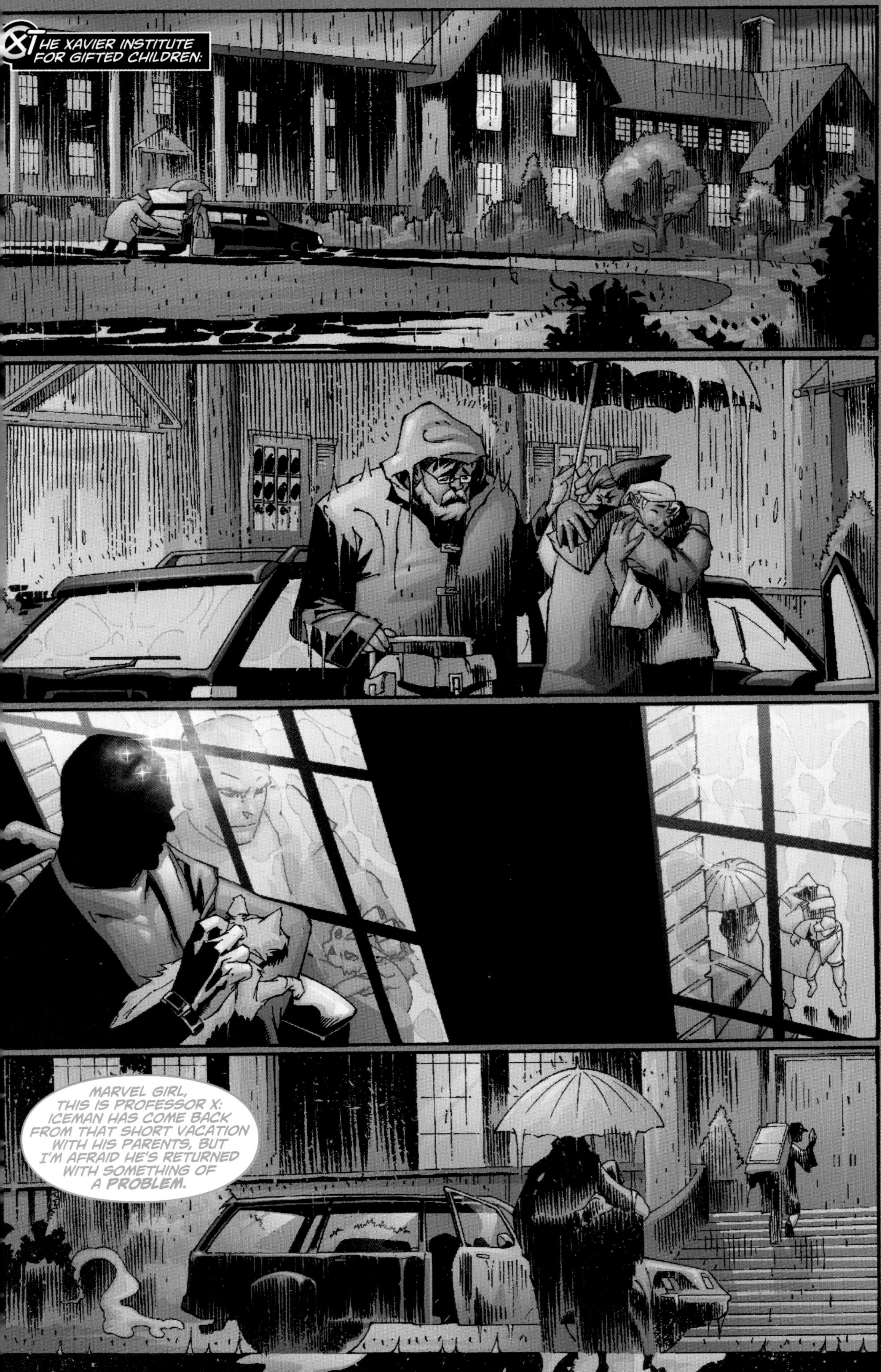
THE XAVIER INSTITUTE FOR GIFTED CHILDREN:
MARVEL GIRL, THIS IS PROFESSOR X: ICEMAN HAS COME BACK FROM THAT SHORT VACATION WITH HIS PARENTS, BUT I'M AFRAID HE'S RETURNED WITH SOMETHING OF A PROBLEM.

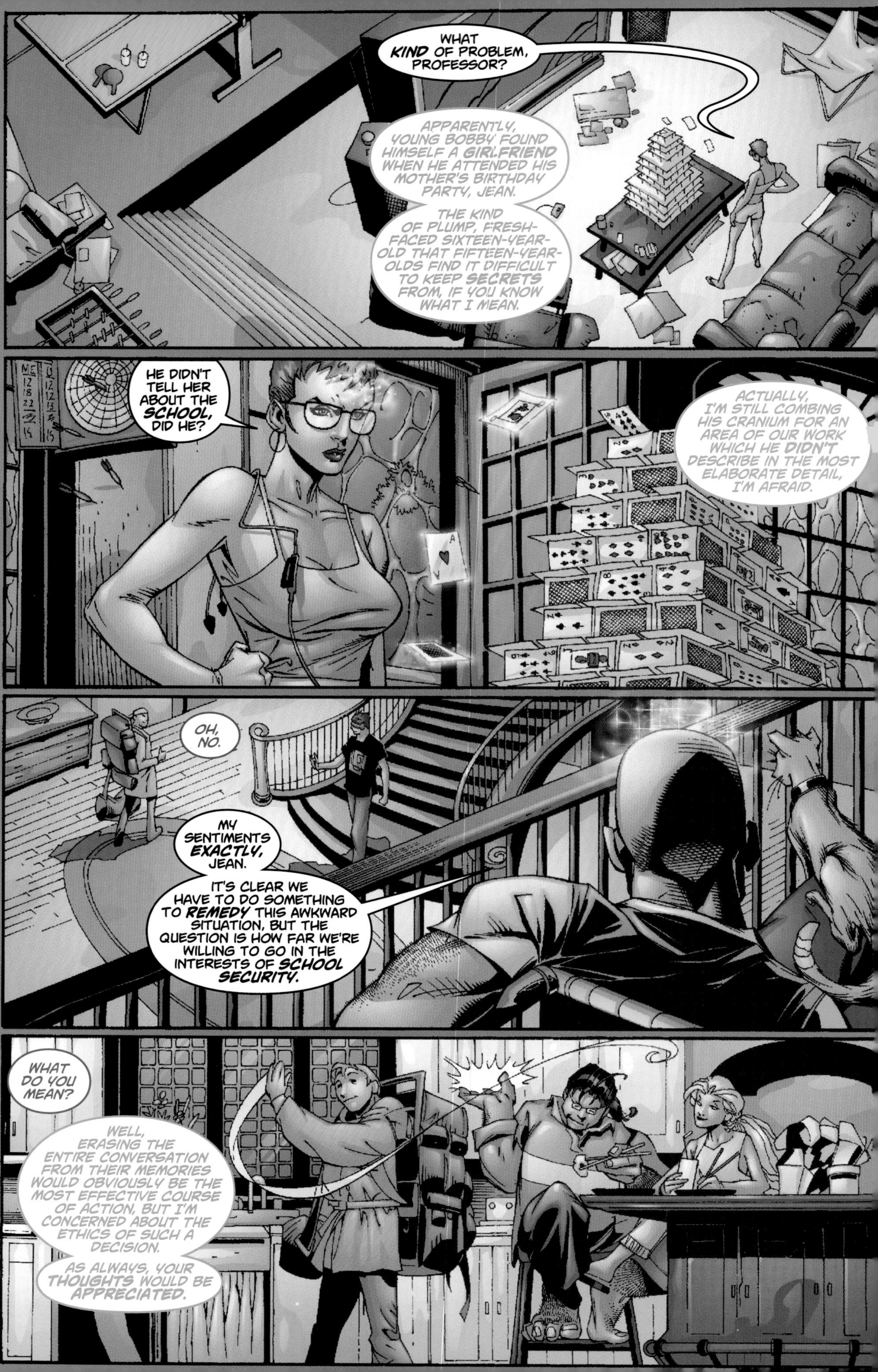
WHAT KIND OF PROBLEM, PROFESSOR?
APPARENTLY, YOUNG BOBBY FOUND HIMSELF A GIRLFRIEND WHEN HE ATTENDED HIS MOTHER'S BIRTHDAY PARTY, JEAN.
THE KIND OF PLUMP, FRESH-FACED SIXTEEN-YEAR-OLD THAT FIFTEEN-YEAR-OLDS FIND IT DIFFICULT TO KEEP SECRETS FROM, IF YOU KNOW WHAT I MEAN.
HE DIDN'T TELL HER ABOUT THE SCHOOL, DID HE?
ACTUALLY, I'M STILL COMBING HIS CRANIUM FOR AN AREA OF OUR WORK WHICH HE DIDN'T DESCRIBE IN THE MOST ELABORATE DETAIL, I'M AFRAID.
OH, NO.
MY SENTIMENTS EXACTLY, JEAN.
IT'S CLEAR WE HAVE TO DO SOMETHING TO REMEDY THIS AWKWARD SITUATION, BUT THE QUESTION IS HOW FAR WE'RE WILLING TO GO IN THE INTERESTS OF SCHOOL SECURITY.
WHAT DO YOU MEAN?
WELL, ERASING THE ENTIRE CONVERSATION FROM THEIR MEMORIES WOULD OBVIOUSLY BE THE MOST EFFECTIVE COURSE OF ACTION, BUT I'M CONCERNED ABOUT THE ETHICS OF SUCH A DECISION.
AS ALWAYS, YOUR THOUGHTS WOULD BE APPRECIATED.

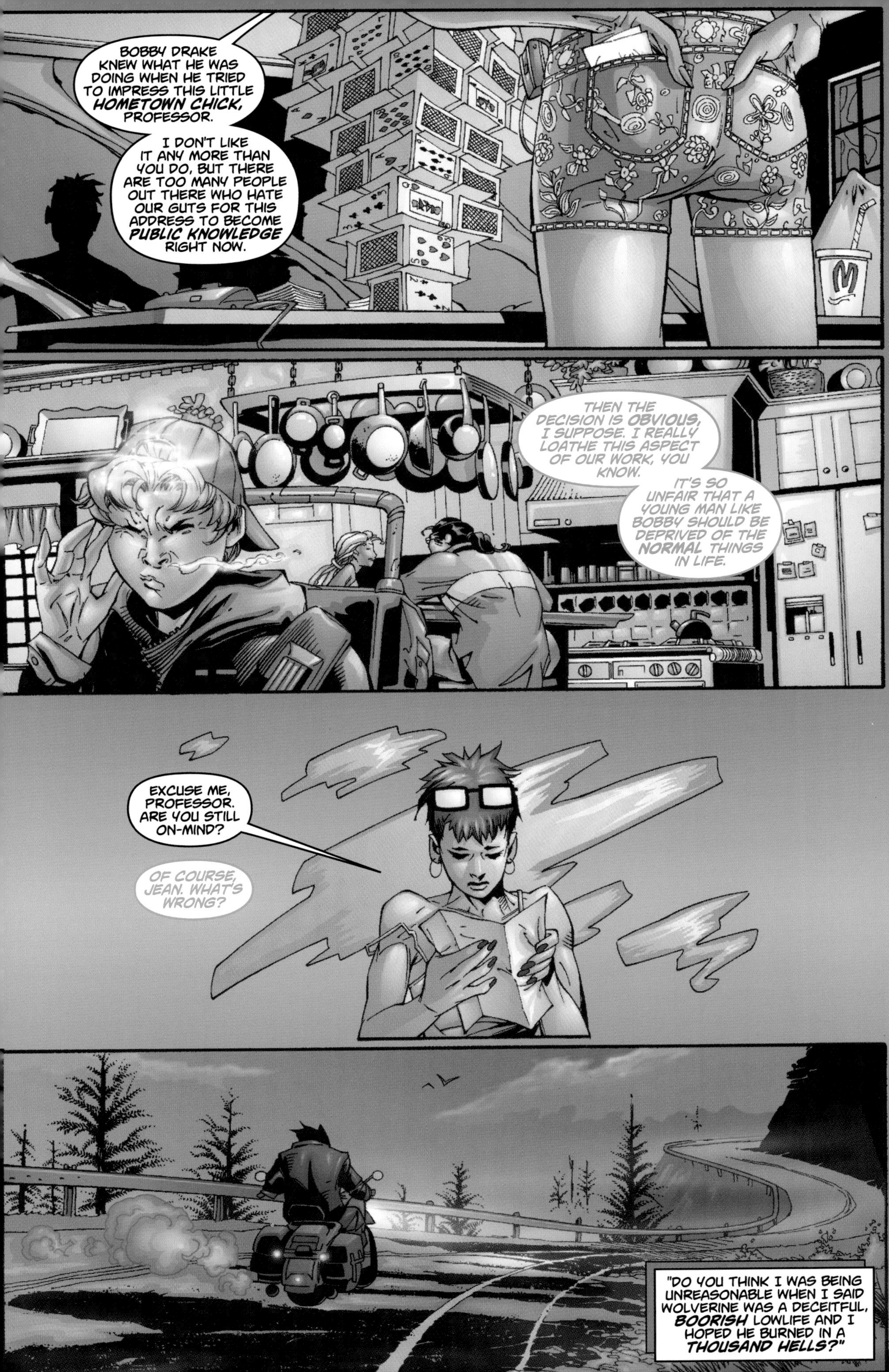
BOBBY DRAKE KNEW WHAT HE WAS DOING WHEN HE TRIED TO IMPRESS THIS LITTLE HOMETOWN CHICK, PROFESSOR.
I DON'T LIKE IT ANY MORE THAN YOU DO, BUT THERE ARE TOO MANY PEOPLE OUT THERE WHO HATE OUR GUTS FOR THIS ADDRESS TO BECOME PUBLIC KNOWLEDGE RIGHT NOW.
THEN THE DECISION IS OBVIOUS, I SUPPOSE. I REALLY LOATHE THIS ASPECT OF OUR WORK, YOU KNOW.
IT'S SO UNFAIR THAT A YOUNG MAN LIKE BOBBY SHOULD BE DEPRIVED OF THE NORMAL THINGS IN LIFE.
EXCUSE ME, PROFESSOR. ARE YOU STILL ON-MIND?
OF COURSE, JEAN. WHAT'S WRONG?
"DO YOU THINK I WAS BEING UNREASONABLE WHEN I SAID WOLVERINE WAS A DECEITFUL, BOORISH LOWLIFE AND I HOPED HE BURNED IN A THOUSAND HELLS?"

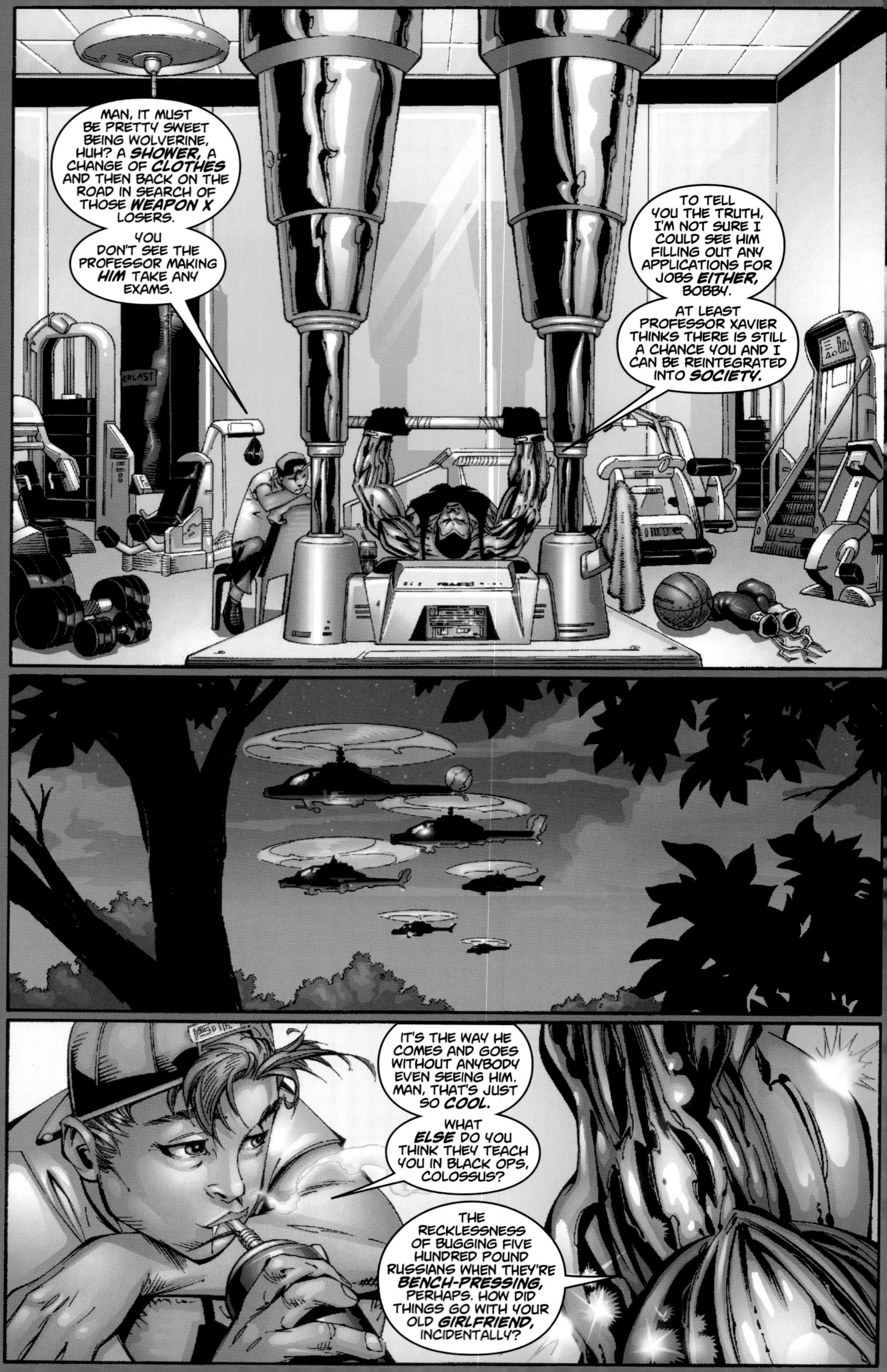
MAN, IT MUST BE PRETTY SWEET BEING WOLVERINE, HUH? A SHOWER, A CHANGE OF CLOTHES AND THEN BACK ON THE ROAD IN SEARCH OF THOSE WEAPON X LOSERS.
YOU DON'T SEE THE PROFESSOR MAKING HIM TAKE ANY EXAMS.
TO TELL YOU THE TRUTH, I'M NOT SURE I COULD SEE HIM FILLING OUT ANY APPLICATIONS FOR JOBS EITHER, BOBBY.
AT LEAST PROFESSOR XAVIER THINKS THERE IS STILL A CHANCE YOU AND I CAN BE REINTEGRATED INTO SOCIETY.
IT'S THE WAY HE COMES AND GOES WITHOUT ANYBODY EVEN SEEING HIM. MAN, THAT'S JUST SO COOL.
WHAT ELSE DO YOU THINK THEY TEACH YOU IN BLACK OPS, COLOSSUS?
THE RECKLESSNESS OF BUGGING FIVE HUNDRED POUND RUSSIANS WHEN THEY'RE BENCH-PRESSING, PERHAPS. HOW DID THINGS GO WITH YOUR OLD GIRLFRIEND, INCIDENTALLY?

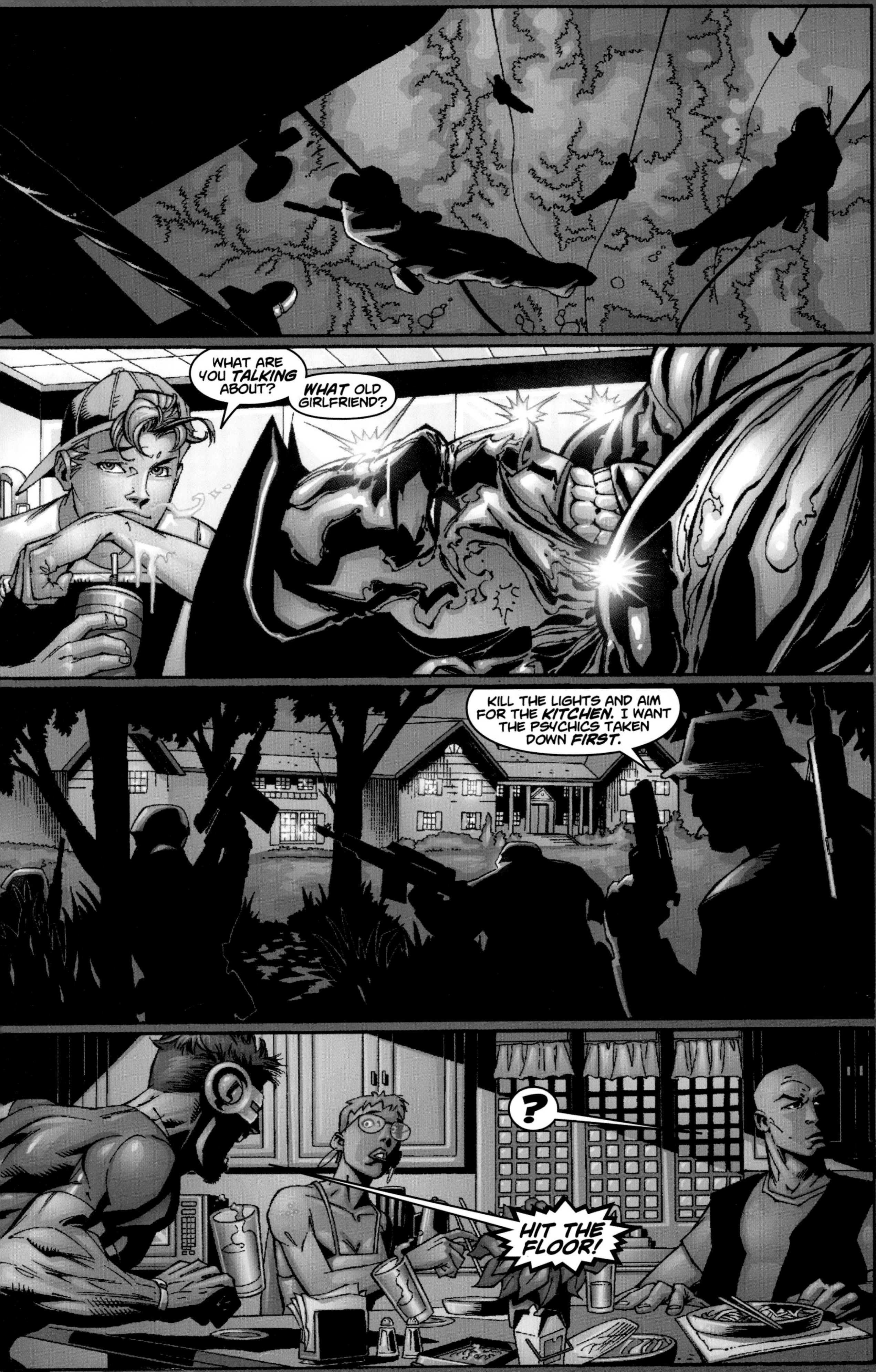
WHAT ARE YOU TALKING ABOUT?
WHAT OLD GIRLFRIEND?
KILL THE LIGHTS AND AIM FOR THE KITCHEN. I WANT THE PSYCHICS TAKEN DOWN FIRST.
?
HIT THE FLOOR!

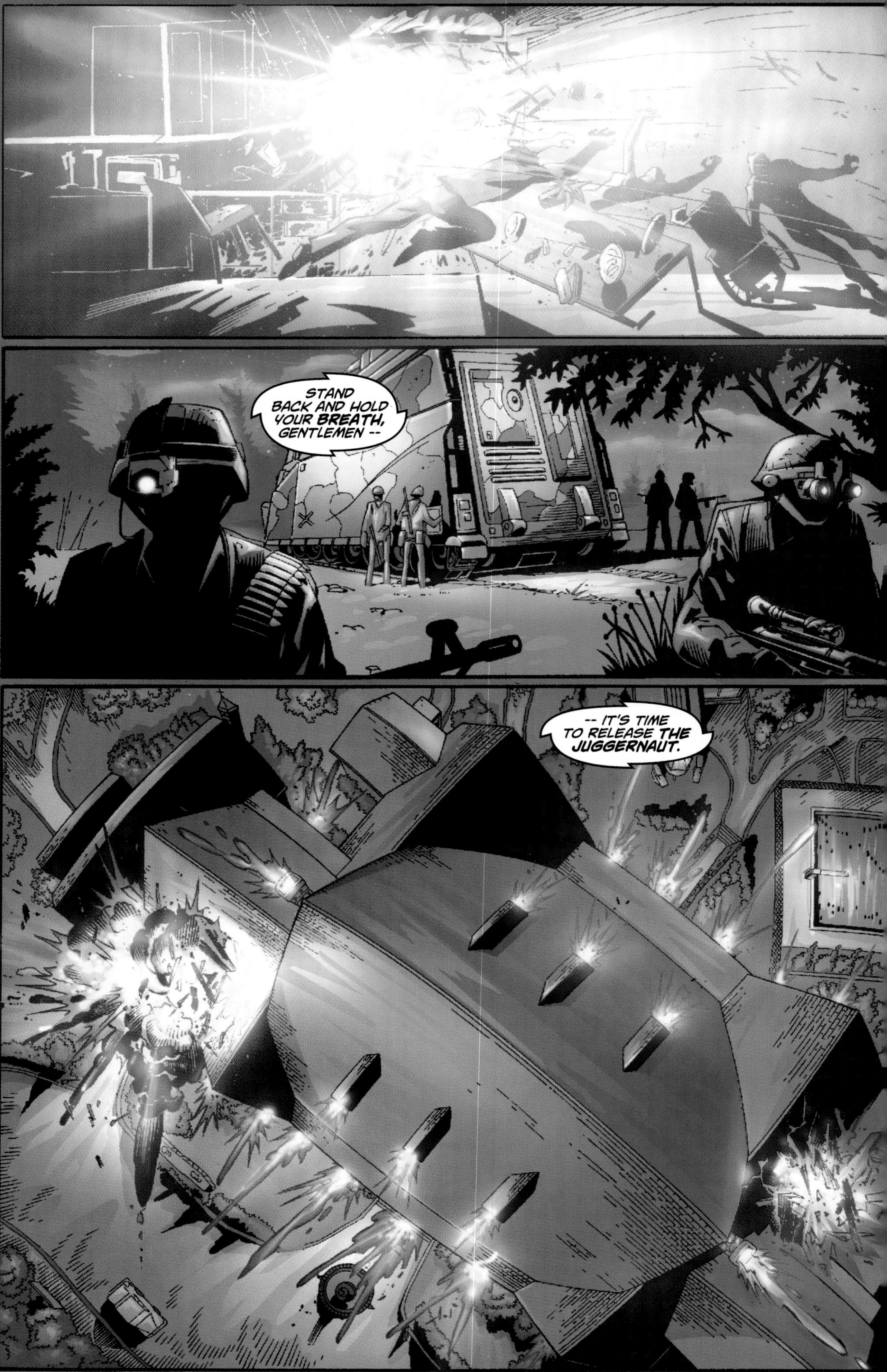
STAND BACK AND HOLD YOUR BREATH, GENTLEMEN --
-- IT'S TIME TO RELEASE THE JUGGERNAUT.

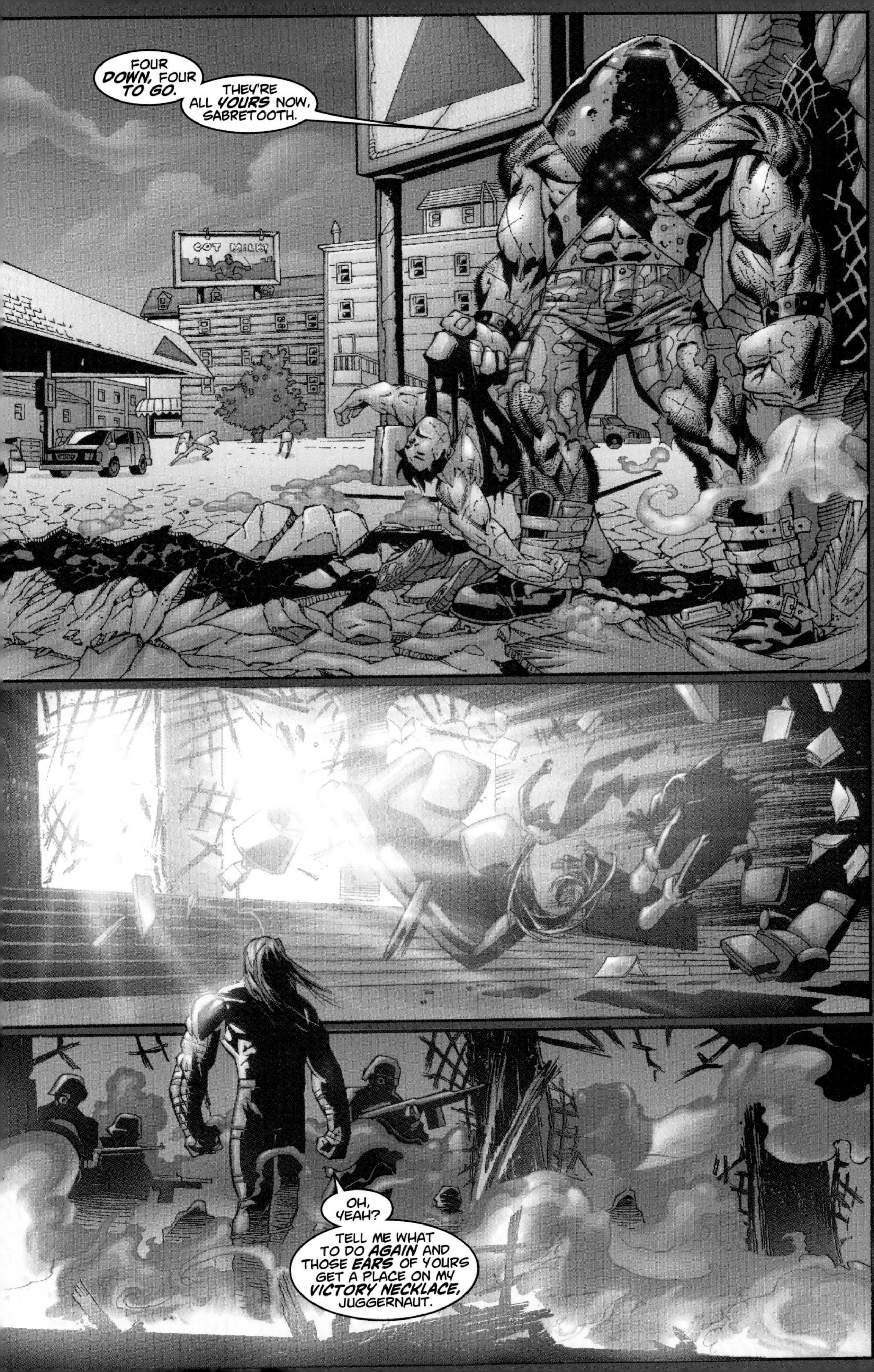
FOUR DOWN, FOUR TO GO.
THEY'RE ALL YOURS NOW, SABRETOOTH.
GOT MILK?
OH, YEAH?
TELL ME WHAT TO DO AGAIN AND THOSE EARS OF YOURS GET A PLACE ON MY VICTORY NECKLACE, JUGGERNAUT.

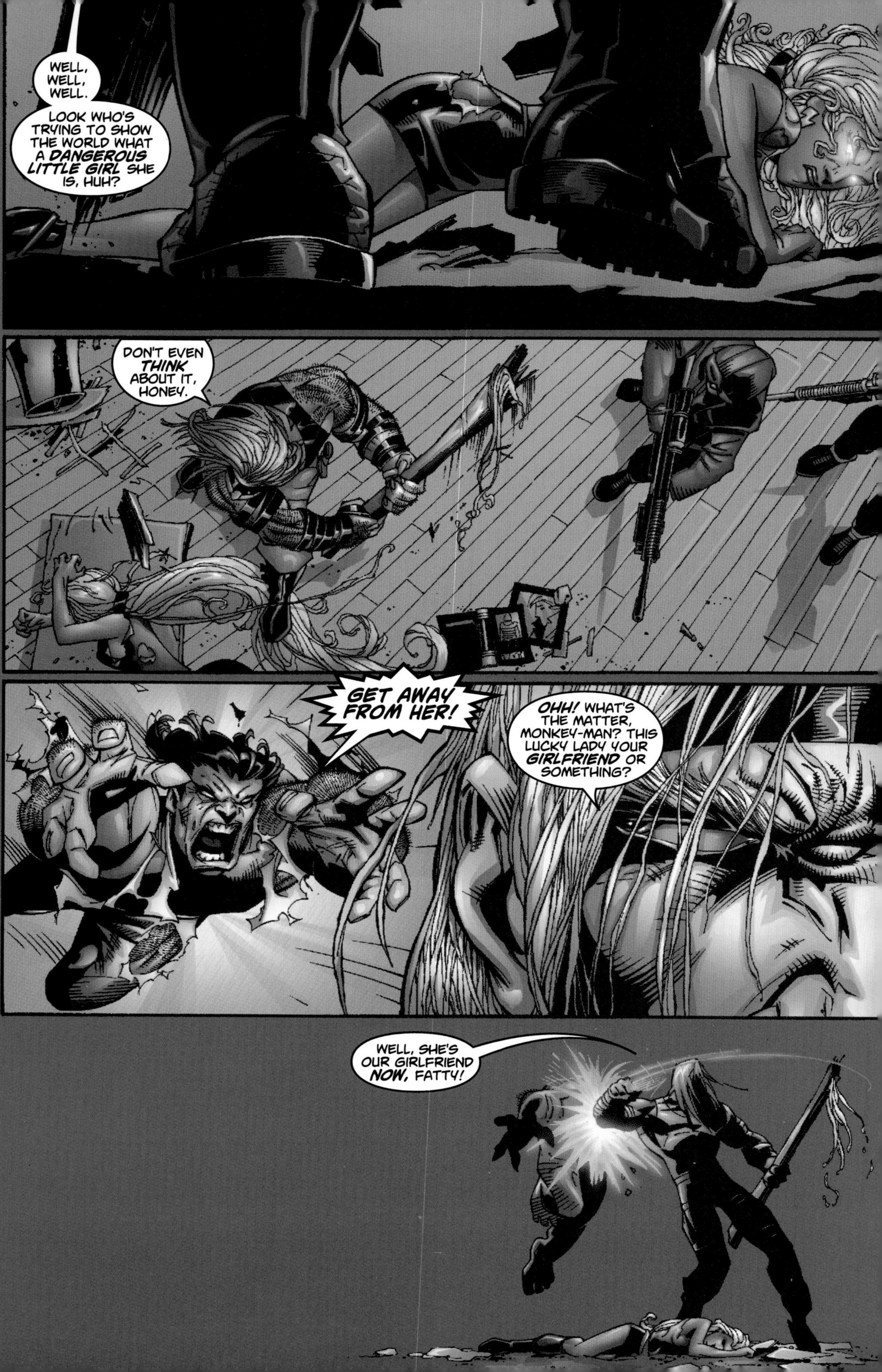
WELL, WELL, WELL.
LOOK WHO'S TRYING TO SHOW THE WORLD WHAT A DANGEROUS LITTLE GIRL SHE IS, HUH?
DON'T EVEN THINK ABOUT IT, HONEY.
GET AWAY FROM HER!
OHH! WHAT'S THE MATTER, MONKEY-MAN? THIS LUCKY LADY YOUR GIRLFRIEND OR SOMETHING?
WELL, SHE'S OUR GIRLFRIEND NOW, FATTY!

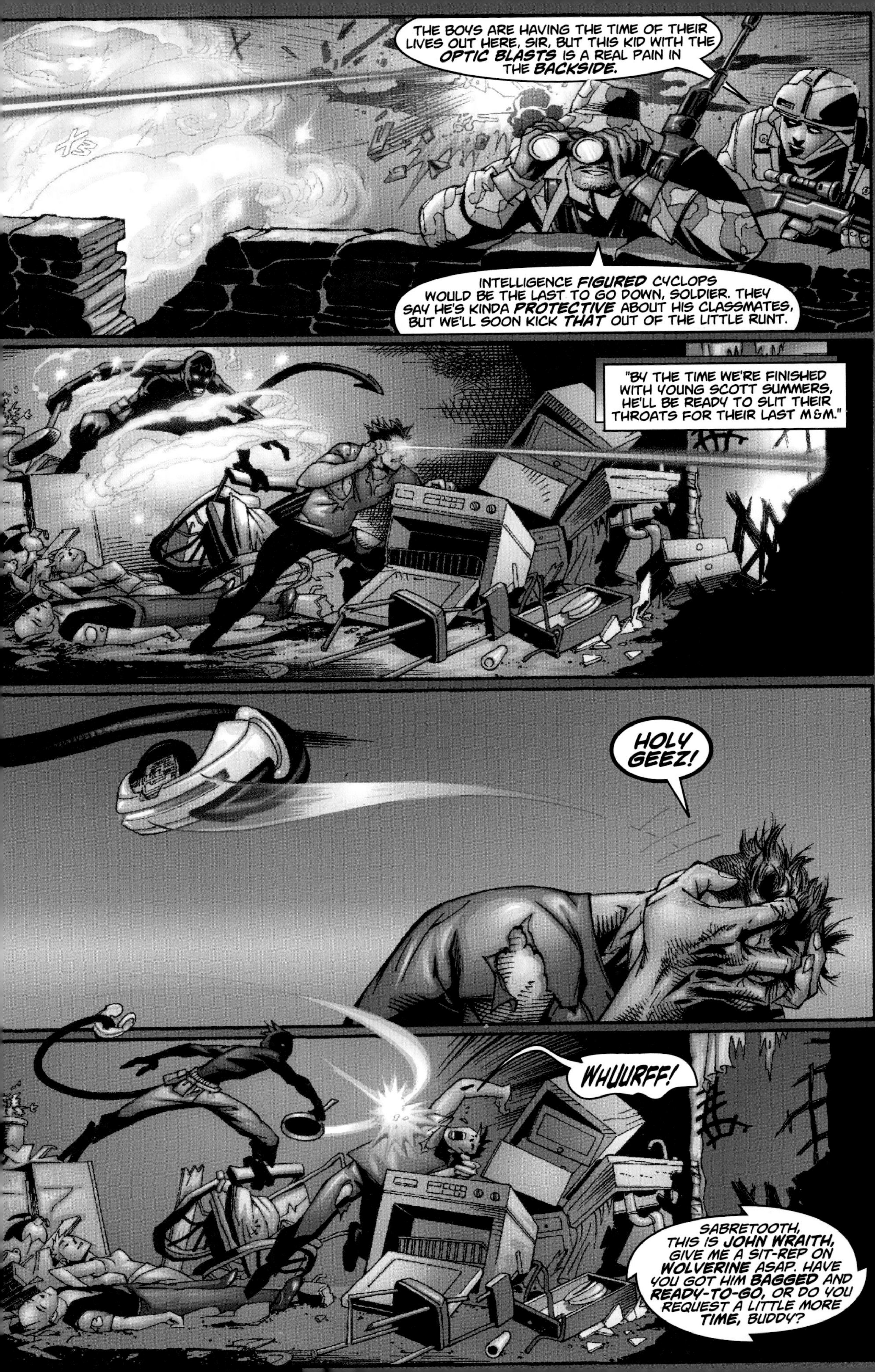
THE BOYS ARE HAVING THE TIME OF THEIR LIVES OUT HERE, SIR, BUT THIS KID WITH THE OPTIC BLASTS IS A REAL PAIN IN THE BACKSIDE.
INTELLIGENCE FIGURED CYCLOPS WOULD BE THE LAST TO GO DOWN, SOLDIER. THEY SAY HE'S KINDA PROTECTIVE ABOUT HIS CLASSMATES, BUT WE'LL SOON KICK THAT OUT OF THE LITTLE RUNT.
"BY THE TIME WE'RE FINISHED WITH YOUNG SCOTT SUMMERS, HE'LL BE READY TO SLIT THEIR THROATS FOR THEIR LAST M&M."
HOLY GEEZ!
WHUURFF!
SABRETOOTH, THIS IS JOHN WRAITH, GIVE ME A SIT-REP ON WOLVERINE ASAP. HAVE YOU GOT HIM BAGGED AND READY-TO-GO, OR DO YOU REQUEST A LITTLE MORE TIME, BUDDY?

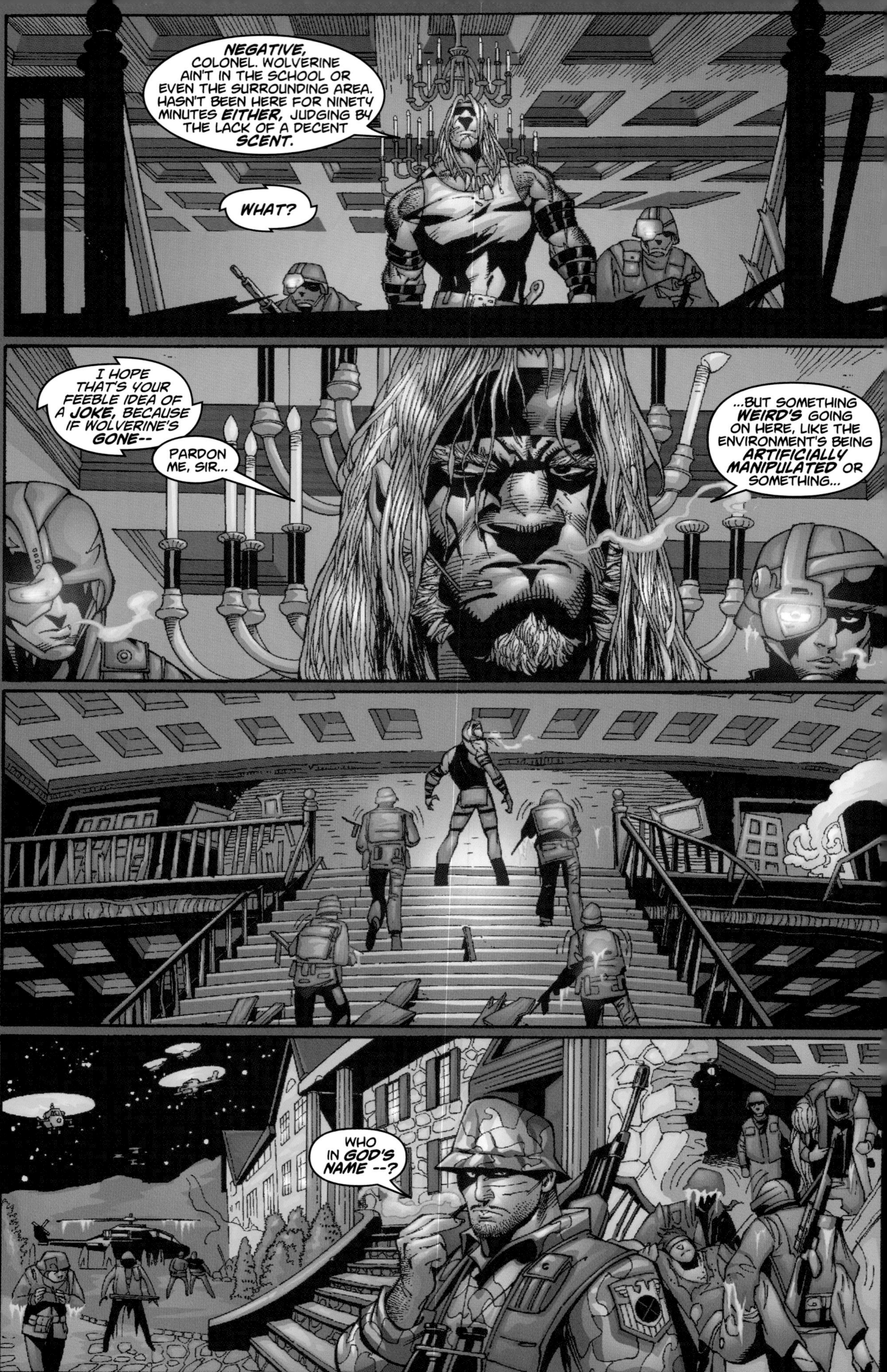
NEGATIVE, COLONEL. WOLVERINE AIN'T IN THE SCHOOL OR EVEN THE SURROUNDING AREA. HASN'T BEEN HERE FOR NINETY MINUTES EITHER, JUDGING BY THE LACK OF A DECENT SCENT.
WHAT?
I HOPE THAT'S YOUR FEEBLE IDEA OF A JOKE, BECAUSE IF WOLVERINE'S GONE--
PARDON ME, SIR...
...BUT SOMETHING WEIRD'S GOING ON HERE, LIKE THE ENVIRONMENT'S BEING ARTIFICIALLY MANIPULATED OR SOMETHING...
WHO IN GOD'S NAME --?

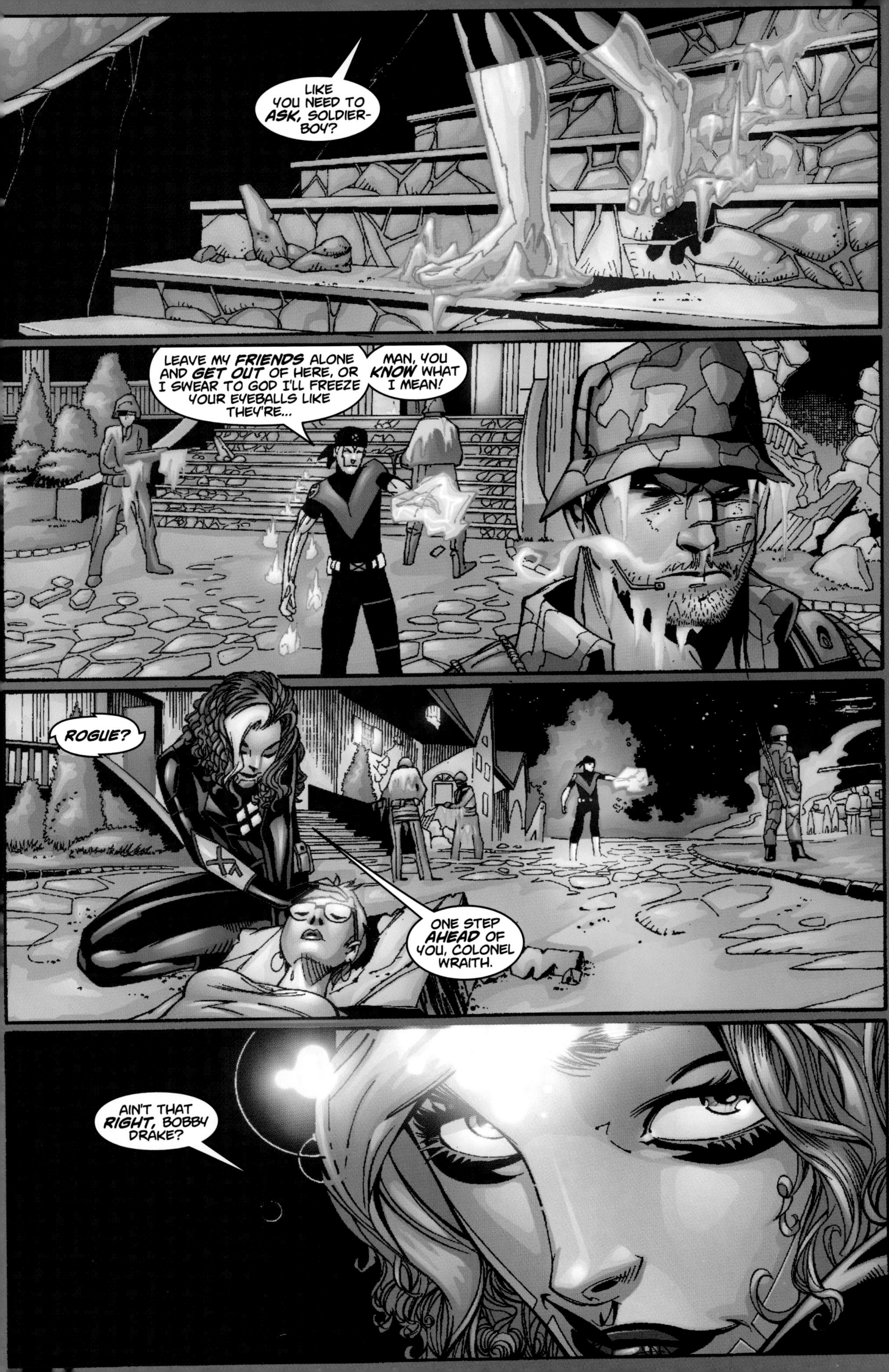
LIKE YOU NEED TO ASK, SOLDIER-BOY?
LEAVE MY FRIENDS ALONE AND GET OUT OF HERE, OR I SWEAR TO GOD I'LL FREEZE YOUR EYEBALLS LIKE THEY'RE...
MAN, YOU KNOW WHAT I MEAN!
ROGUE?
ONE STEP AHEAD OF YOU, COLONEL WRAITH.
AIN'T THAT RIGHT, BOBBY DRAKE?

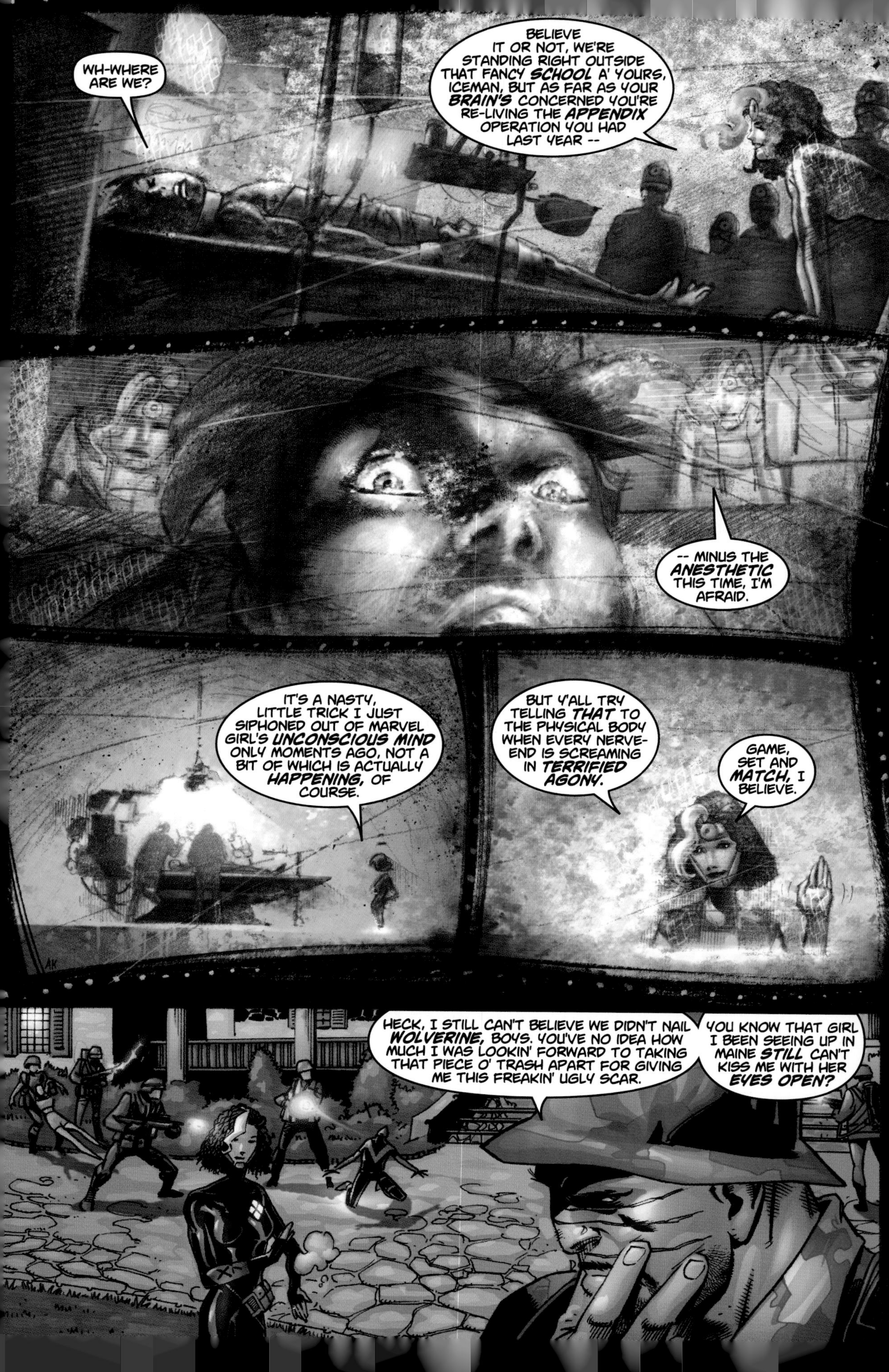
WH-WHERE ARE WE?
BELIEVE IT OR NOT, WE'RE STANDING RIGHT OUTSIDE THAT FANCY SCHOOL A' YOURS, ICEMAN, BUT AS FAR AS YOUR BRAIN'S CONCERNED YOU'RE RE-LIVING THE APPENDIX OPERATION YOU HAD LAST YEAR --
-- MINUS THE ANESTHETIC THIS TIME, I'M AFRAID.
IT'S A NASTY, LITTLE TRICK I JUST SIPHONED OUT OF MARVEL GIRL'S UNCONSCIOUS MIND ONLY MOMENTS AGO, NOT A BIT OF WHICH IS ACTUALLY HAPPENING, OF COURSE.
BUT Y'ALL TRY TELLING THAT TO THE PHYSICAL BODY WHEN EVERY NERVE-END IS SCREAMING IN TERRIFIED AGONY.
GAME, SET AND MATCH, I BELIEVE.
HECK, I STILL CAN'T BELIEVE WE DIDN'T NAIL WOLVERINE, BOYS. YOU'VE NO IDEA HOW MUCH I WAS LOOKIN' FORWARD TO TAKING THAT PIECE O' TRASH APART FOR GIVING ME THIS FREAKIN' UGLY SCAR.
YOU KNOW THAT GIRL I BEEN SEEING UP IN MAINE STILL CAN'T KISS ME WITH HER EYES OPEN?

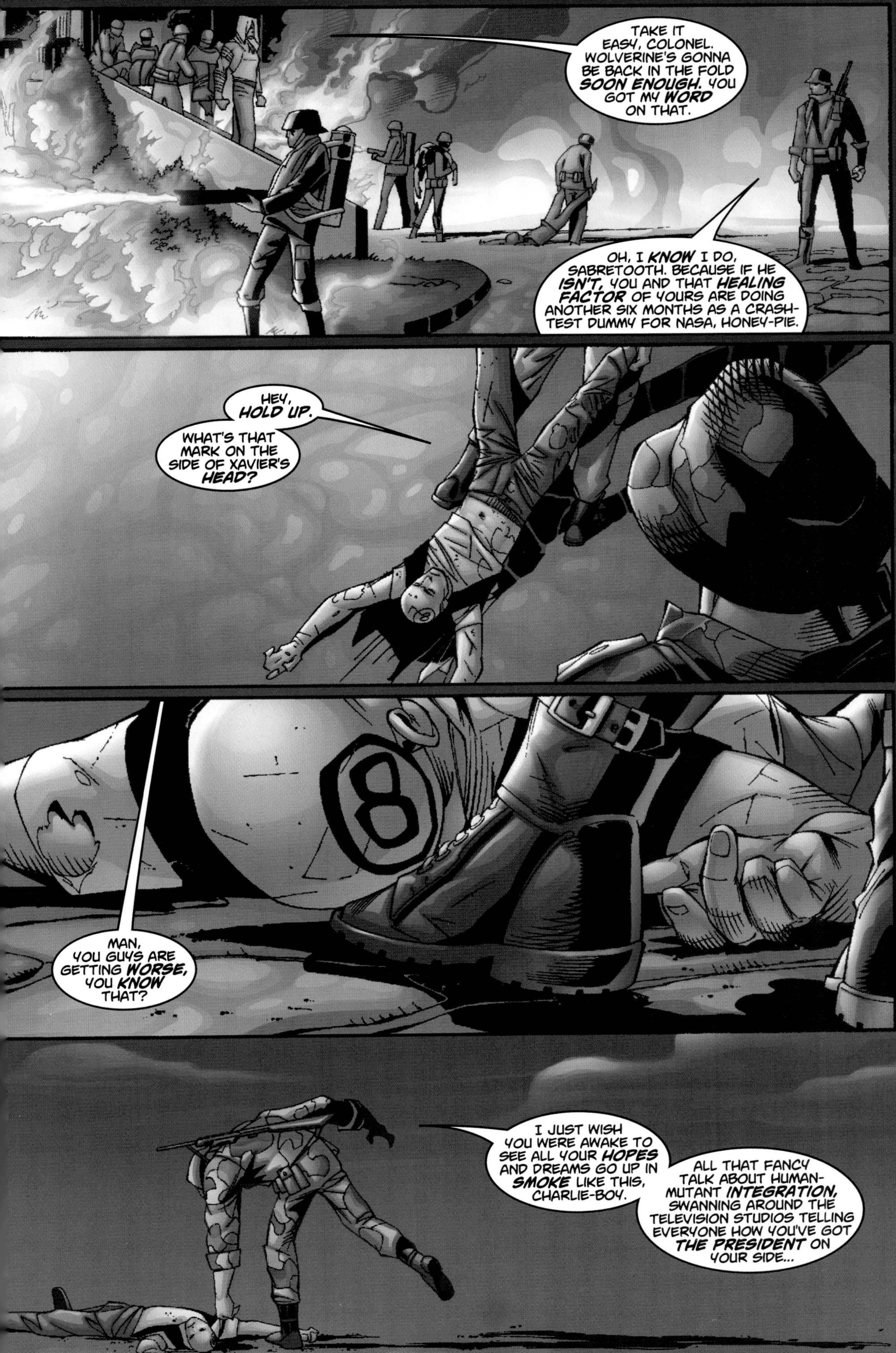
TAKE IT EASY, COLONEL. WOLVERINE'S GONNA BE BACK IN THE FOLD SOON ENOUGH. YOU GOT MY WORD ON THAT.
OH, I KNOW I DO, SABRETOOTH. BECAUSE IF HE ISN'T, YOU AND THAT HEALING FACTOR OF YOURS ARE DOING ANOTHER SIX MONTHS AS A CRASH-TEST DUMMY FOR NASA, HONEY-PIE.
HEY, HOLD UP.
WHAT'S THAT MARK ON THE SIDE OF XAVIER'S HEAD?
MAN, YOU GUYS ARE GETTING WORSE, YOU KNOW THAT?
I JUST WISH YOU WERE AWAKE TO SEE ALL YOUR HOPES AND DREAMS GO UP IN SMOKE LIKE THIS, CHARLIE-BOY.
ALL THAT FANCY TALK ABOUT HUMAN-MUTANT INTEGRATION, SWANNING AROUND THE TELEVISION STUDIOS TELLING EVERYONE HOW YOU'VE GOT THE PRESIDENT ON YOUR SIDE...

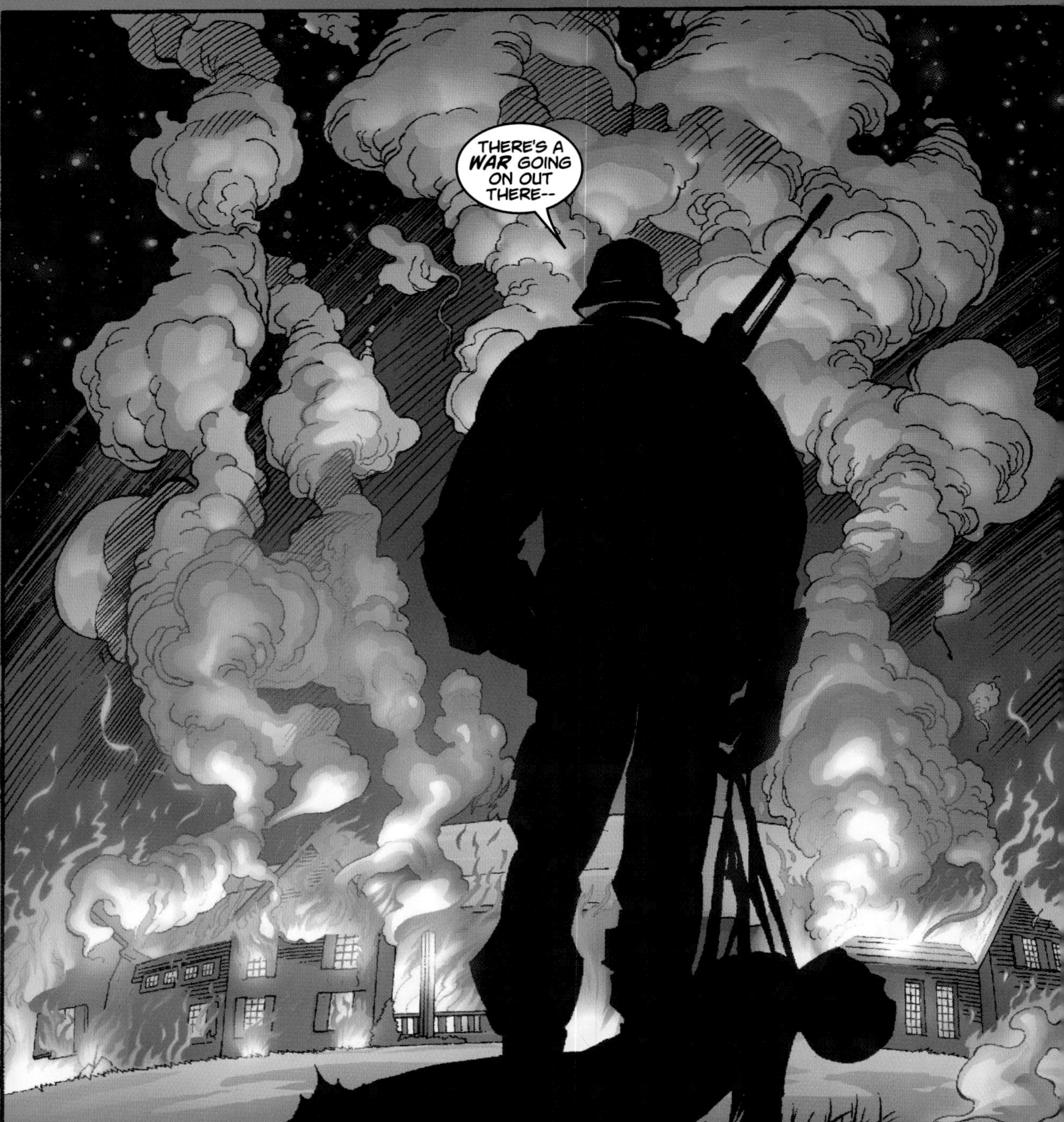
THERE'S A WAR GOING ON OUT THERE--

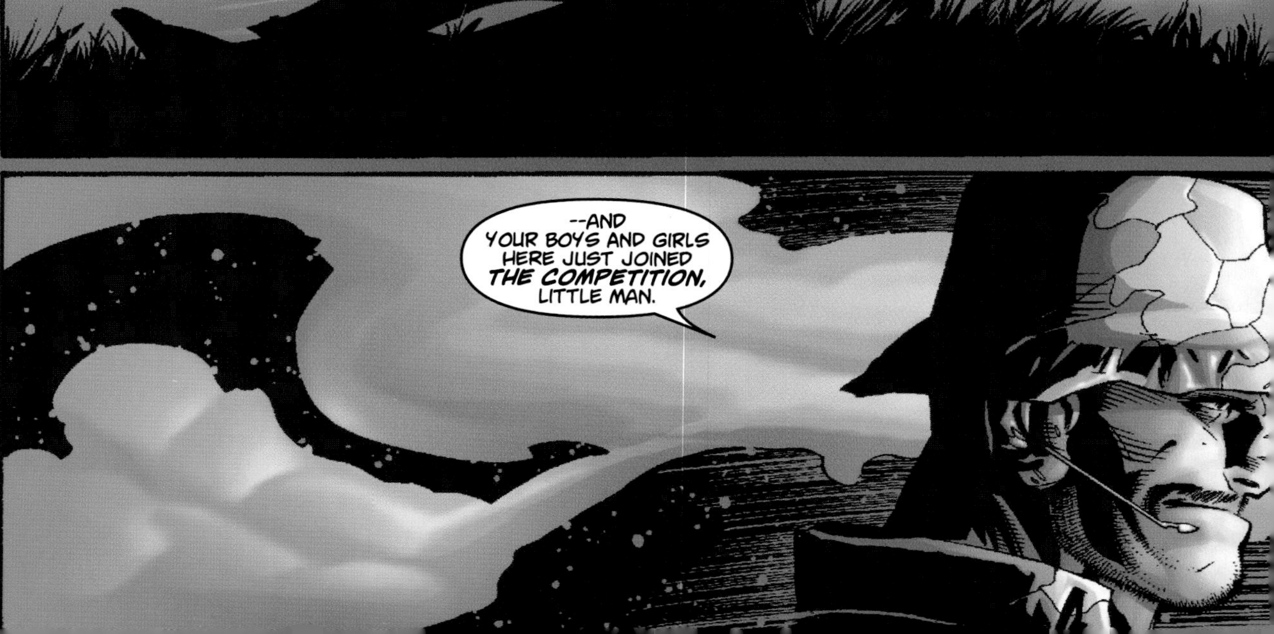
--AND YOUR BOYS AND GIRLS HERE JUST JOINED THE COMPETITION, LITTLE MAN.

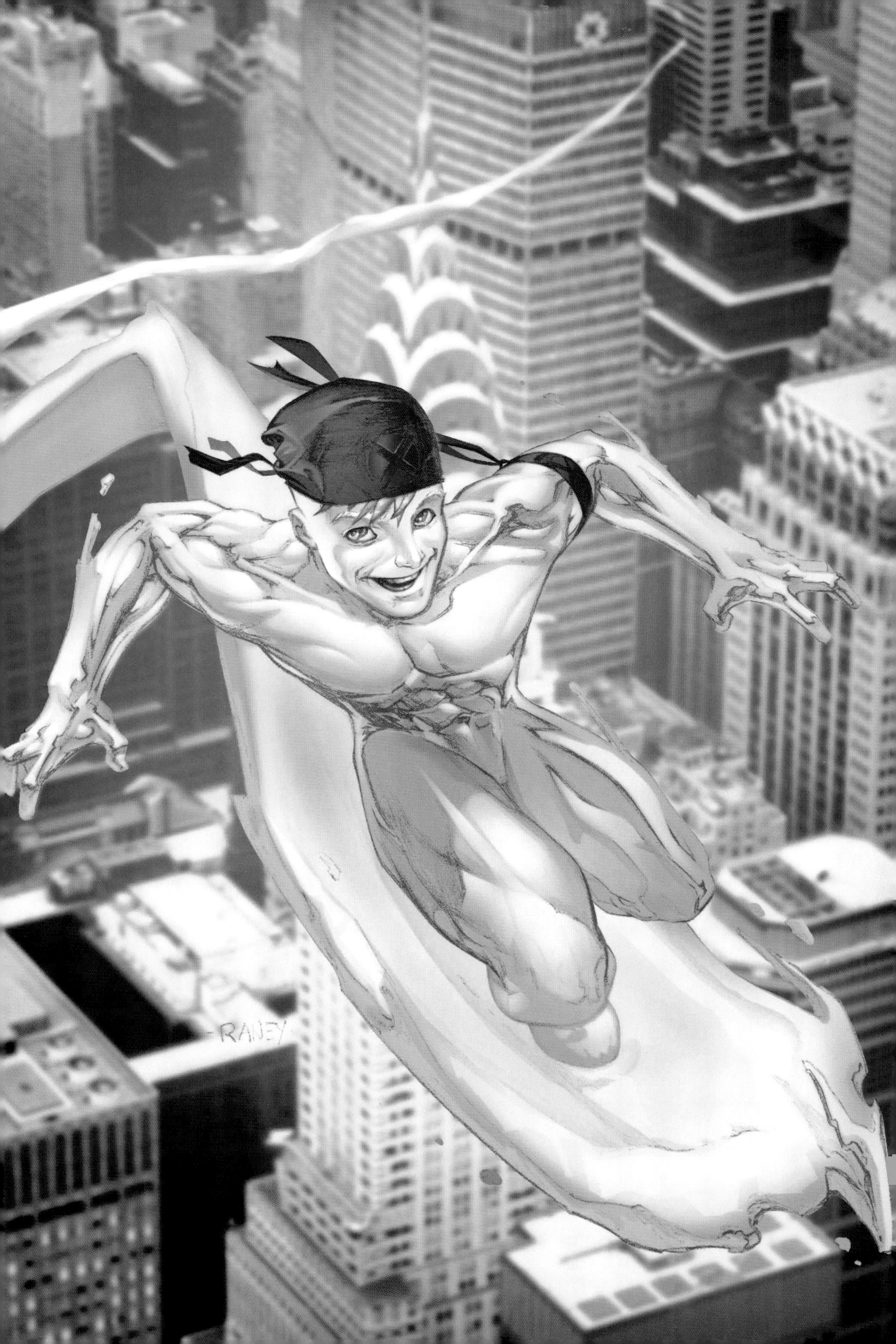
RANEY

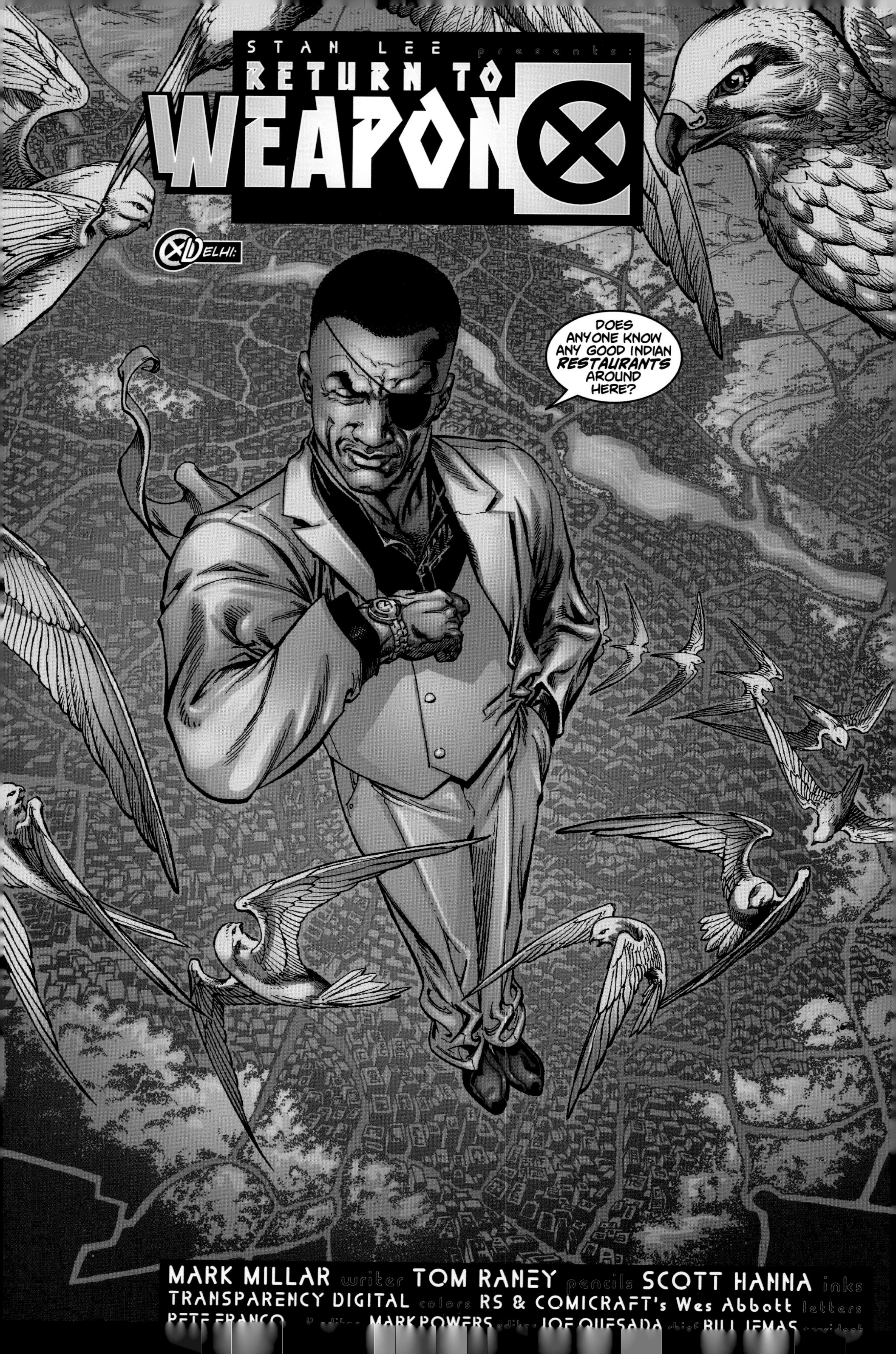
STAN LEE presents:
RETURN TO WEAPON X
DELHI:
DOES ANYONE KNOW ANY GOOD INDIAN RESTAURANTS AROUND HERE?
MARK MILLAR writer TOM RANEY pencils SCOTT HANNA inks
TRANSPARENCY DIGITAL colors RS & COMICRAFT's Wes Abbott letters
PETE FRANCO MARK POWERS JOE QUESADA BILL JEMAS

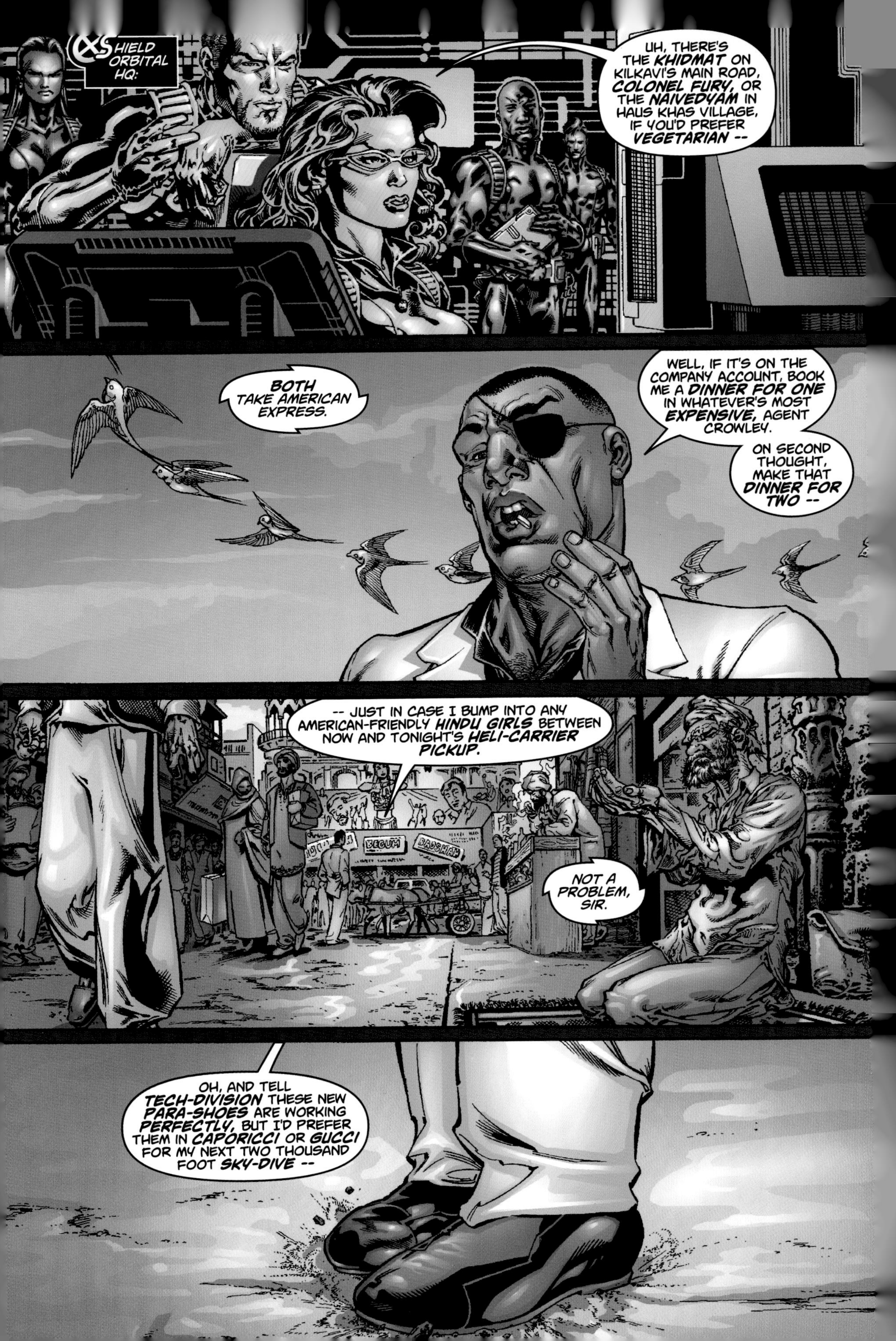
SHIELD ORBITAL HQ:
UH, THERE'S THE KHIDMAT ON KILKAVI'S MAIN ROAD, COLONEL FURY, OR THE NAIVEDYAM IN HAUS KHAS VILLAGE, IF YOU'D PREFER VEGETARIAN --
BOTH TAKE AMERICAN EXPRESS.
WELL, IF IT'S ON THE COMPANY ACCOUNT, BOOK ME A DINNER FOR ONE IN WHATEVER'S MOST EXPENSIVE, AGENT CROWLEY.
ON SECOND THOUGHT, MAKE THAT DINNER FOR TWO --
-- JUST IN CASE I BUMP INTO ANY AMERICAN-FRIENDLY HINDU GIRLS BETWEEN NOW AND TONIGHT'S HELI-CARRIER PICKUP.
BEGUM
BADSHAH
NOT A PROBLEM, SIR.
OH, AND TELL TECH-DIVISION THESE NEW PARA-SHOES ARE WORKING PERFECTLY, BUT I'D PREFER THEM IN CAPORICCI OR GUCCI FOR MY NEXT TWO THOUSAND FOOT SKY-DIVE --

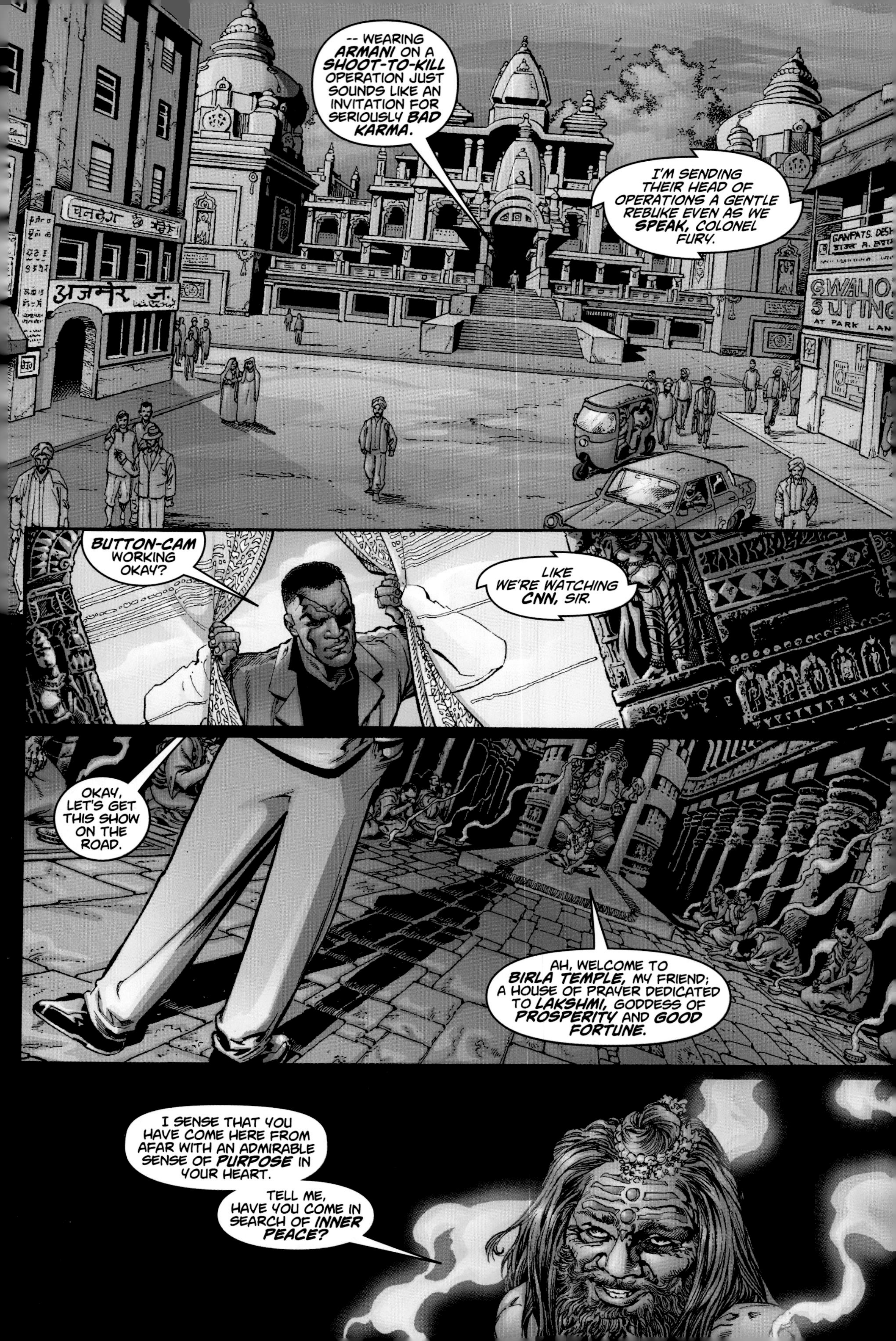
-- WEARING ARMANI ON A SHOOT-TO-KILL OPERATION JUST SOUNDS LIKE AN INVITATION FOR SERIOUSLY BAD KARMA.
I'M SENDING THEIR HEAD OF OPERATIONS A GENTLE REBUKE EVEN AS WE SPEAK, COLONEL FURY.
BUTTON-CAM WORKING OKAY?
LIKE WE'RE WATCHING CNN, SIR.
OKAY, LET'S GET THIS SHOW ON THE ROAD.
AH, WELCOME TO BIRLA TEMPLE, MY FRIEND; A HOUSE OF PRAYER DEDICATED TO LAKSHMI, GODDESS OF PROSPERITY AND GOOD FORTUNE.
I SENSE THAT YOU HAVE COME HERE FROM AFAR WITH AN ADMIRABLE SENSE OF PURPOSE IN YOUR HEART.
TELL ME, HAVE YOU COME IN SEARCH OF INNER PEACE?

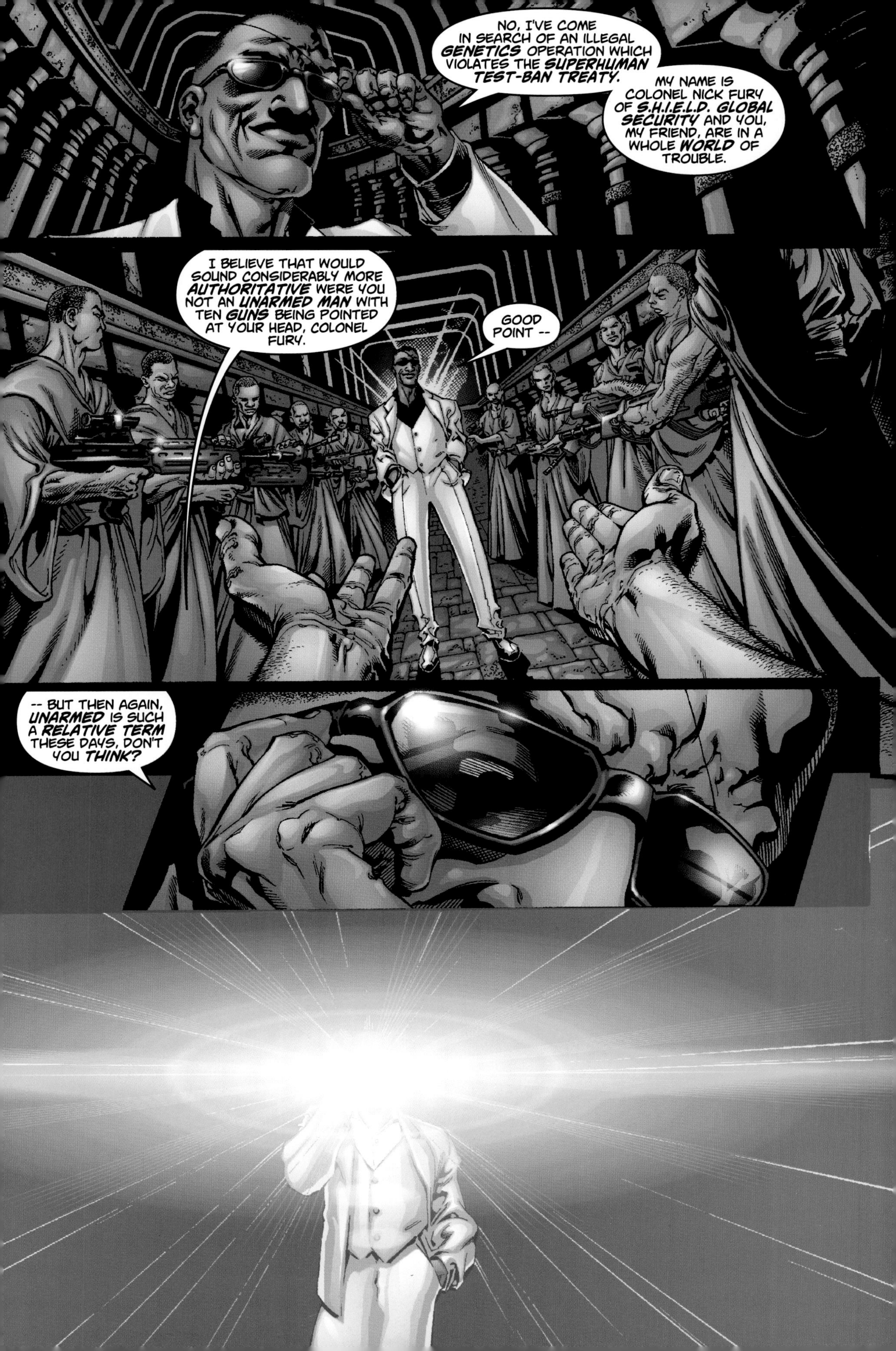
NO, I'VE COME IN SEARCH OF AN ILLEGAL GENETICS OPERATION WHICH VIOLATES THE SUPERHUMAN TEST-BAN TREATY.
MY NAME IS COLONEL NICK FURY OF S.H.I.E.L.D. GLOBAL SECURITY AND YOU, MY FRIEND, ARE IN A WHOLE WORLD OF TROUBLE.
I BELIEVE THAT WOULD SOUND CONSIDERABLY MORE AUTHORITATIVE WERE YOU NOT AN UNARMED MAN WITH TEN GUNS BEING POINTED AT YOUR HEAD, COLONEL FURY.
GOOD POINT --
-- BUT THEN AGAIN, UNARMED IS SUCH A RELATIVE TERM THESE DAYS, DON'T YOU THINK?

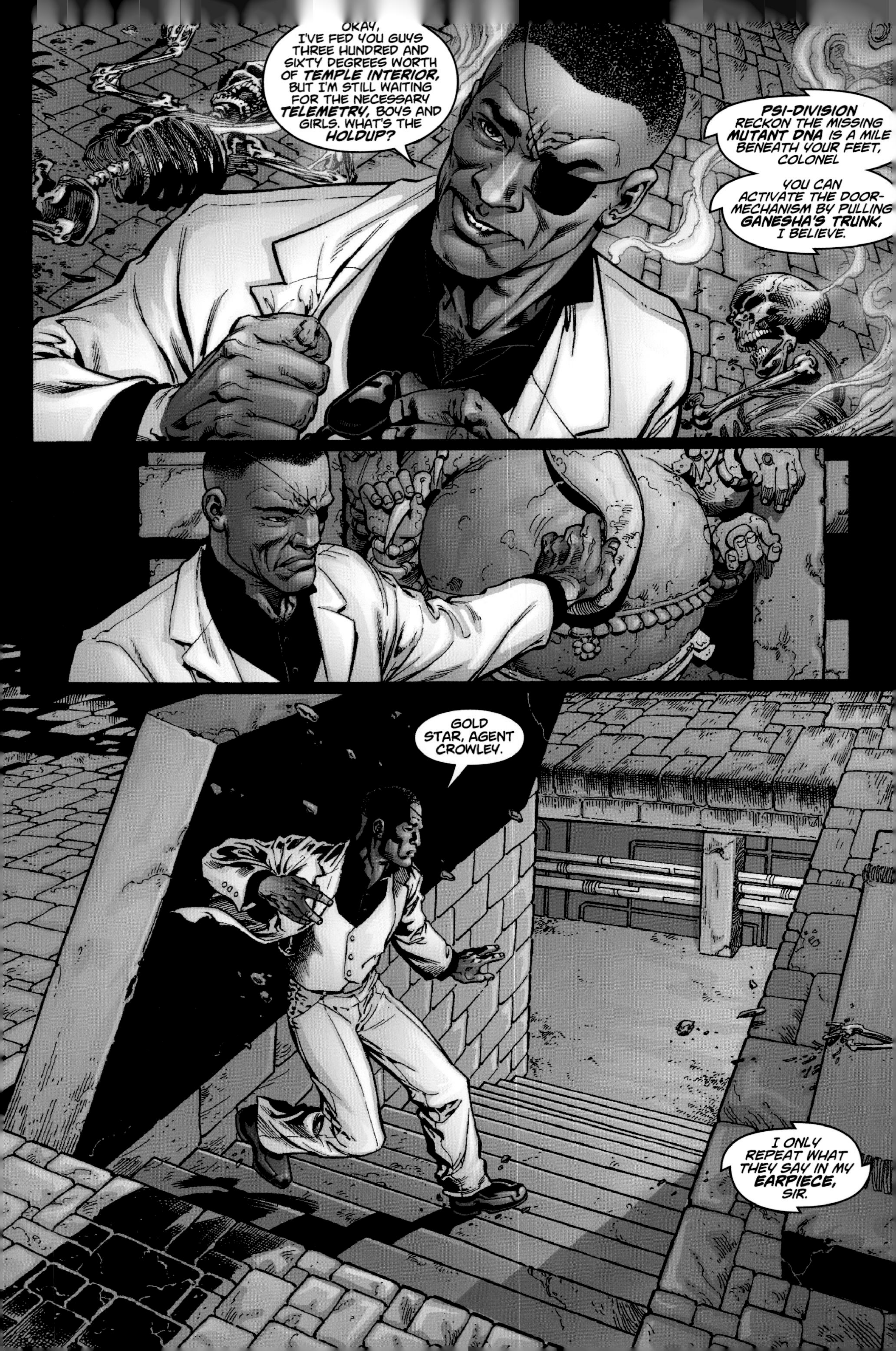
OKAY, I'VE FED YOU GUYS THREE HUNDRED AND SIXTY DEGREES WORTH OF TEMPLE INTERIOR, BUT I'M STILL WAITING FOR THE NECESSARY TELEMETRY, BOYS AND GIRLS. WHAT'S THE HOLDUP?
PSI-DIVISION RECKON THE MISSING MUTANT DNA IS A MILE BENEATH YOUR FEET, COLONEL
YOU CAN ACTIVATE THE DOOR-MECHANISM BY PULLING GANESHA'S TRUNK, I BELIEVE.
GOLD STAR, AGENT CROWLEY.
I ONLY REPEAT WHAT THEY SAY IN MY EARPIECE, SIR.

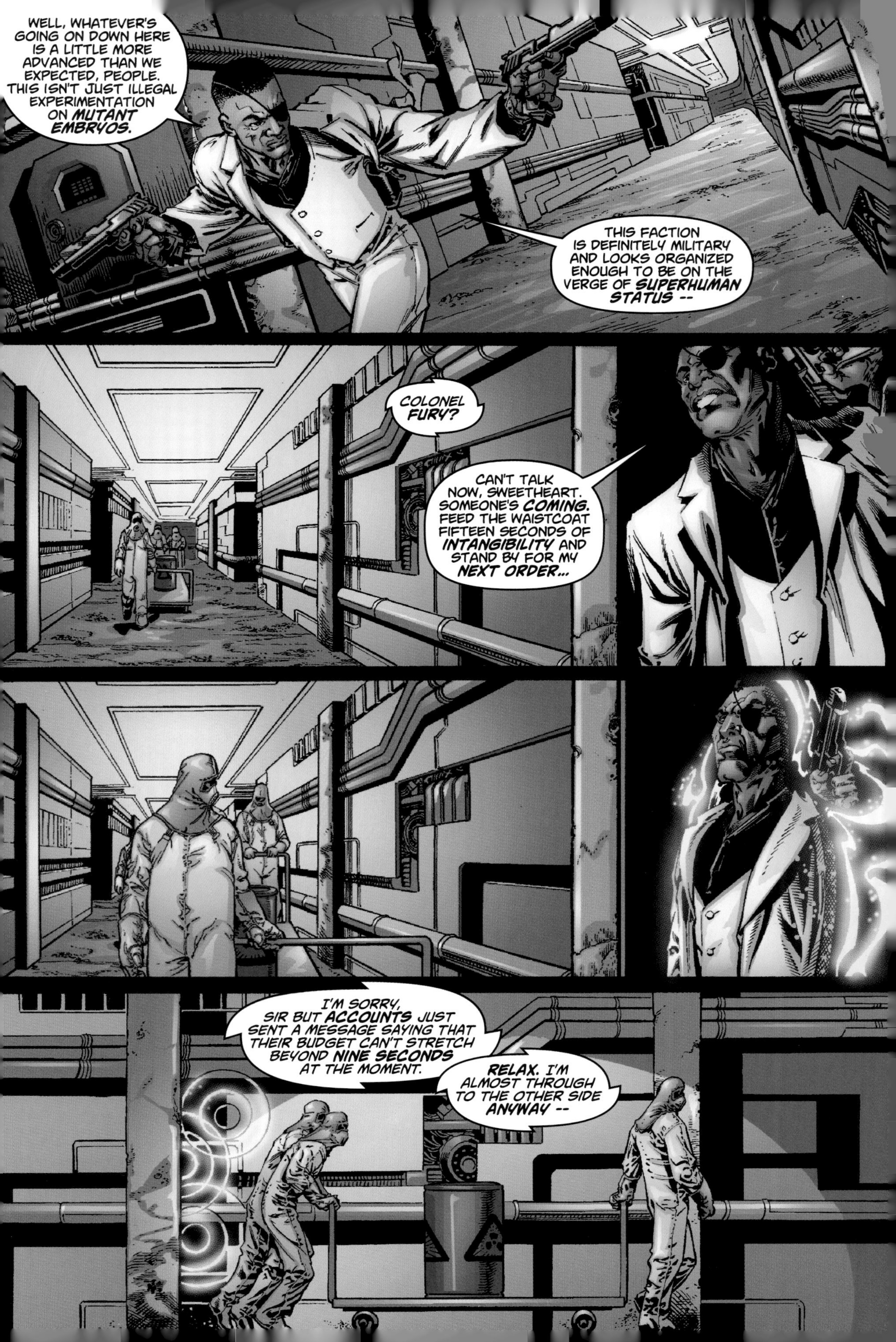
WELL, WHATEVER'S GOING ON DOWN HERE IS A LITTLE MORE ADVANCED THAN WE EXPECTED, PEOPLE. THIS ISN'T JUST ILLEGAL EXPERIMENTATION ON MUTANT EMBRYOS.
THIS FACTION IS DEFINITELY MILITARY AND LOOKS ORGANIZED ENOUGH TO BE ON THE VERGE OF SUPERHUMAN STATUS --
COLONEL FURY?
CAN'T TALK NOW, SWEETHEART. SOMEONE'S COMING. FEED THE WAISTCOAT FIFTEEN SECONDS OF INTANGIBILITY AND STAND BY FOR MY NEXT ORDER...
I'M SORRY, SIR BUT ACCOUNTS JUST SENT A MESSAGE SAYING THAT THEIR BUDGET CAN'T STRETCH BEYOND NINE SECONDS AT THE MOMENT.
RELAX. I'M ALMOST THROUGH TO THE OTHER SIDE ANYWAY --

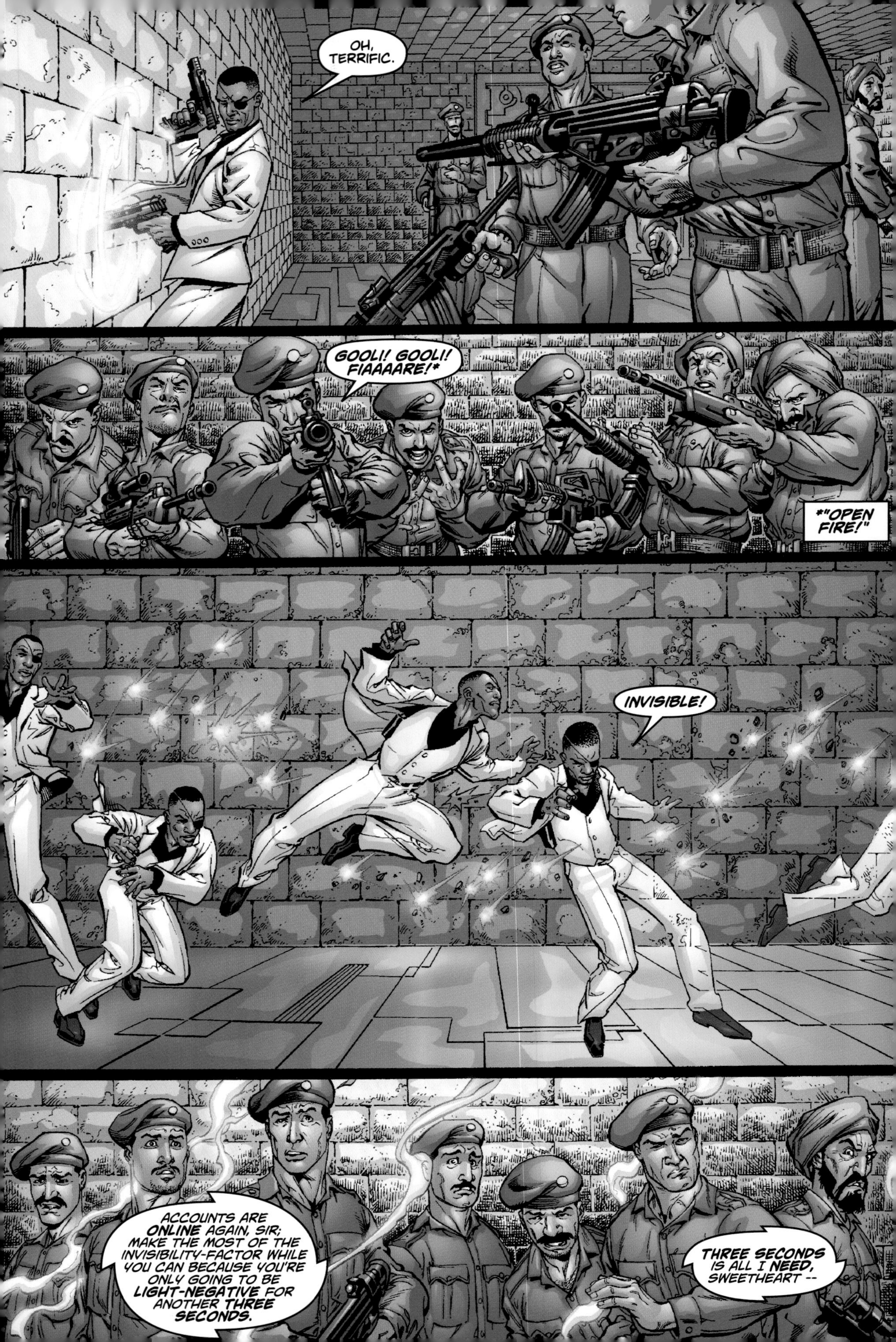

OH, TERRIFIC.
GOOLI! GOOLI! FIAAAARE!*
*"OPEN FIRE!"
INVISIBLE!
ACCOUNTS ARE ONLINE AGAIN, SIR; MAKE THE MOST OF THE INVISIBILITY-FACTOR WHILE YOU CAN BECAUSE YOU'RE ONLY GOING TO BE LIGHT-NEGATIVE FOR ANOTHER THREE SECONDS.
THREE SECONDS IS ALL I NEED, SWEETHEART --

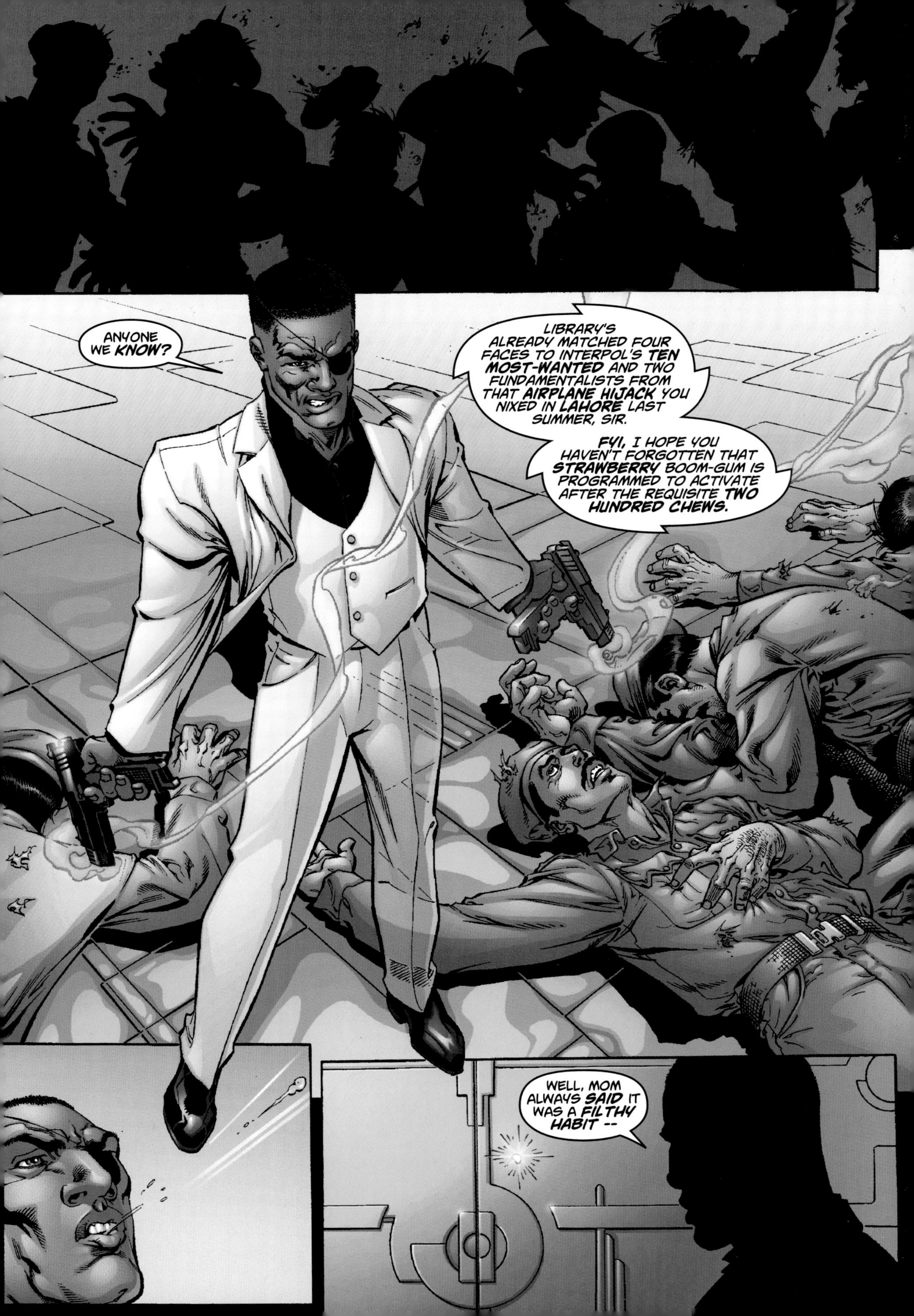
ANYONE WE KNOW?
LIBRARY'S ALREADY MATCHED FOUR FACES TO INTERPOL'S TEN MOST-WANTED AND TWO FUNDAMENTALISTS FROM THAT AIRPLANE HIJACK YOU NIXED IN LAHORE LAST SUMMER, SIR.
FYI, I HOPE YOU HAVEN'T FORGOTTEN THAT STRAWBERRY BOOM-GUM IS PROGRAMMED TO ACTIVATE AFTER THE REQUISITE TWO HUNDRED CHEWS.
WELL, MOM ALWAYS SAID IT WAS A FILTHY HABIT --

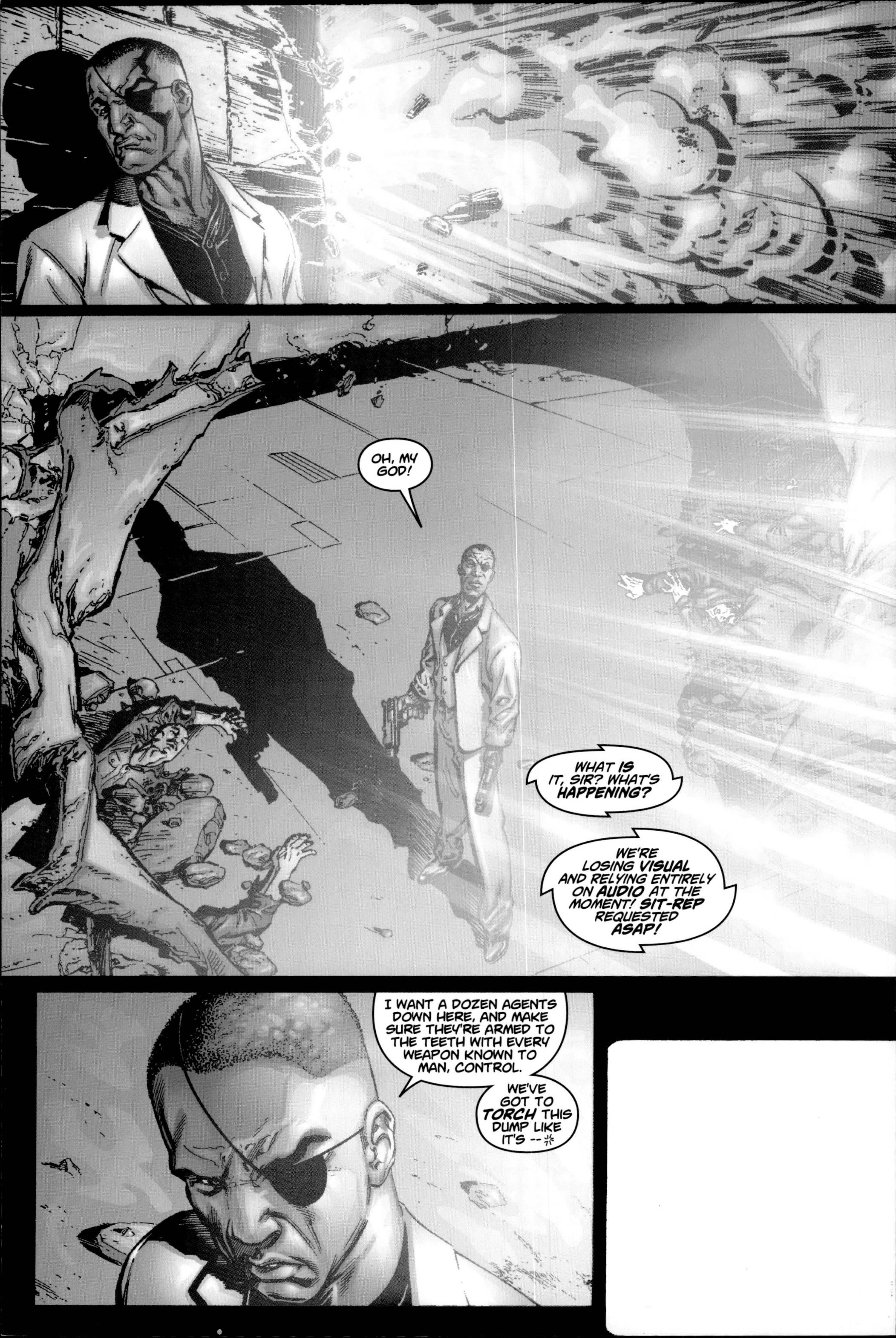
OH, MY GOD!
WHAT IS IT, SIR? WHAT'S HAPPENING?
WE'RE LOSING VISUAL AND RELYING ENTIRELY ON AUDIO AT THE MOMENT! SIT-REP REQUESTED ASAP!
I WANT A DOZEN AGENTS DOWN HERE, AND MAKE SURE THEY'RE ARMED TO THE TEETH WITH EVERY WEAPON KNOWN TO MAN, CONTROL.
WE'VE GOT TO TORCH THIS DUMP LIKE IT'S --

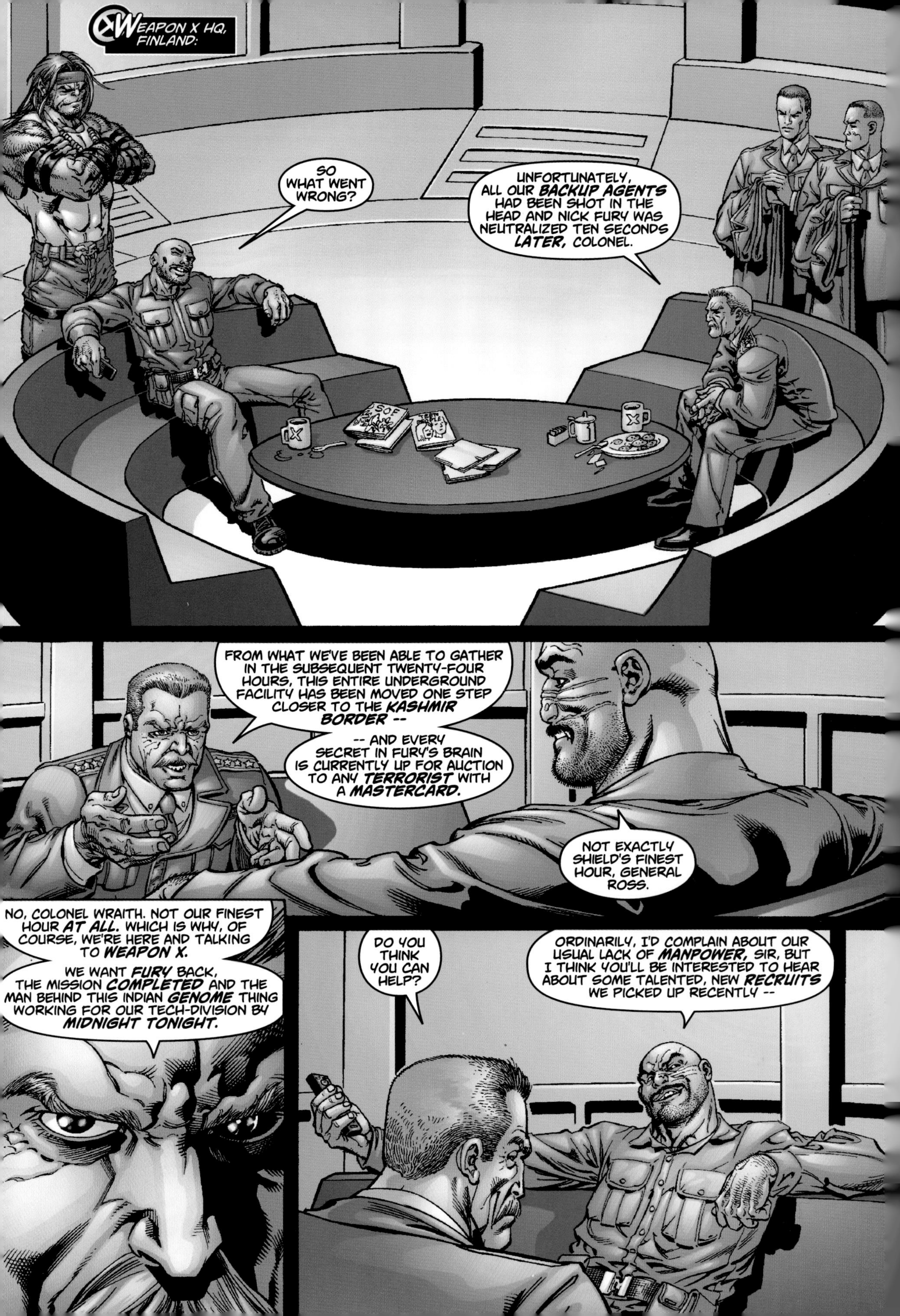
WEAPON X HQ, FINLAND:
SO WHAT WENT WRONG?
UNFORTUNATELY, ALL OUR BACKUP AGENTS HAD BEEN SHOT IN THE HEAD AND NICK FURY WAS NEUTRALIZED TEN SECONDS LATER, COLONEL.
FROM WHAT WE'VE BEEN ABLE TO GATHER IN THE SUBSEQUENT TWENTY-FOUR HOURS, THIS ENTIRE UNDERGROUND FACILITY HAS BEEN MOVED ONE STEP CLOSER TO THE KASHMIR BORDER --
-- AND EVERY SECRET IN FURY'S BRAIN IS CURRENTLY UP FOR AUCTION TO ANY TERRORIST WITH A MASTERCARD.
NOT EXACTLY SHIELD'S FINEST HOUR, GENERAL ROSS.
NO, COLONEL WRAITH. NOT OUR FINEST HOUR AT ALL. WHICH IS WHY, OF COURSE, WE'RE HERE AND TALKING TO WEAPON X.
WE WANT FURY BACK, THE MISSION COMPLETED AND THE MAN BEHIND THIS INDIAN GENOME THING WORKING FOR OUR TECH-DIVISION BY MIDNIGHT TONIGHT.
DO YOU THINK YOU CAN HELP?
ORDINARILY, I'D COMPLAIN ABOUT OUR USUAL LACK OF MANPOWER, SIR, BUT I THINK YOU'LL BE INTERESTED TO HEAR ABOUT SOME TALENTED, NEW RECRUITS WE PICKED UP RECENTLY --

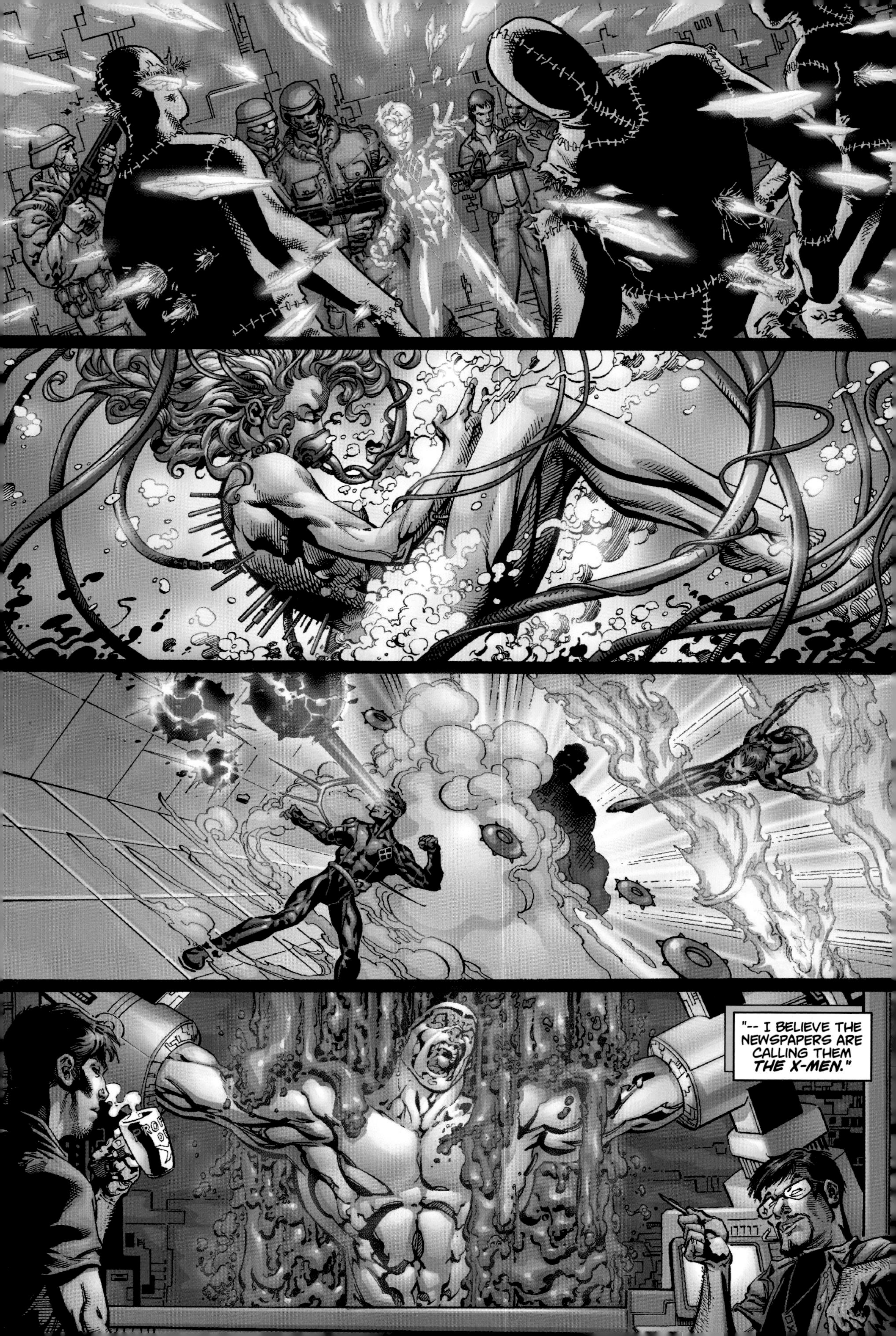
"-- I BELIEVE THE NEWSPAPERS ARE CALLING THEM THE X-MEN."

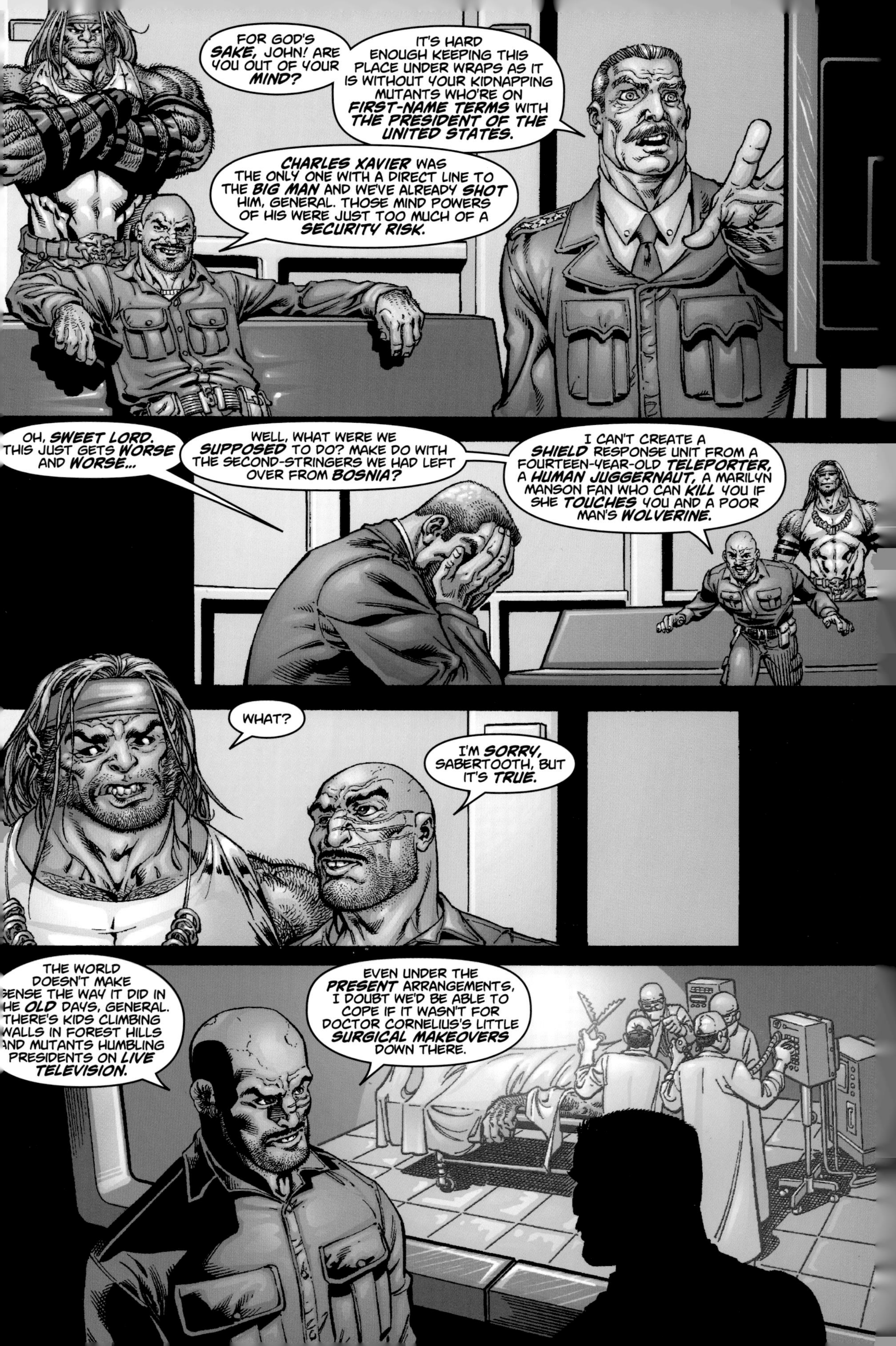
FOR GOD'S SAKE, JOHN! ARE YOU OUT OF YOUR MIND?
IT'S HARD ENOUGH KEEPING THIS PLACE UNDER WRAPS AS IT IS WITHOUT YOUR KIDNAPPING MUTANTS WHO'RE ON FIRST-NAME TERMS WITH THE PRESIDENT OF THE UNITED STATES.
CHARLES XAVIER WAS THE ONLY ONE WITH A DIRECT LINE TO THE BIG MAN AND WE'VE ALREADY SHOT HIM, GENERAL. THOSE MIND POWERS OF HIS WERE JUST TOO MUCH OF A SECURITY RISK.
OH, SWEET LORD. THIS JUST GETS WORSE AND WORSE...
WELL, WHAT WERE WE SUPPOSED TO DO? MAKE DO WITH THE SECOND-STRINGERS WE HAD LEFT OVER FROM BOSNIA?
I CAN'T CREATE A SHIELD RESPONSE UNIT FROM A FOURTEEN-YEAR-OLD TELEPORTER, A HUMAN JUGGERNAUT, A MARILYN MANSON FAN WHO CAN KILL YOU IF SHE TOUCHES YOU AND A POOR MAN'S WOLVERINE.
WHAT?
I'M SORRY, SABERTOOTH, BUT IT'S TRUE.
THE WORLD DOESN'T MAKE SENSE THE WAY IT DID IN THE OLD DAYS, GENERAL. THERE'S KIDS CLIMBING WALLS IN FOREST HILLS AND MUTANTS HUMBLING PRESIDENTS ON LIVE TELEVISION.
EVEN UNDER THE PRESENT ARRANGEMENTS, I DOUBT WE'D BE ABLE TO COPE IF IT WASN'T FOR DOCTOR CORNELIUS'S LITTLE SURGICAL MAKEOVERS DOWN THERE.

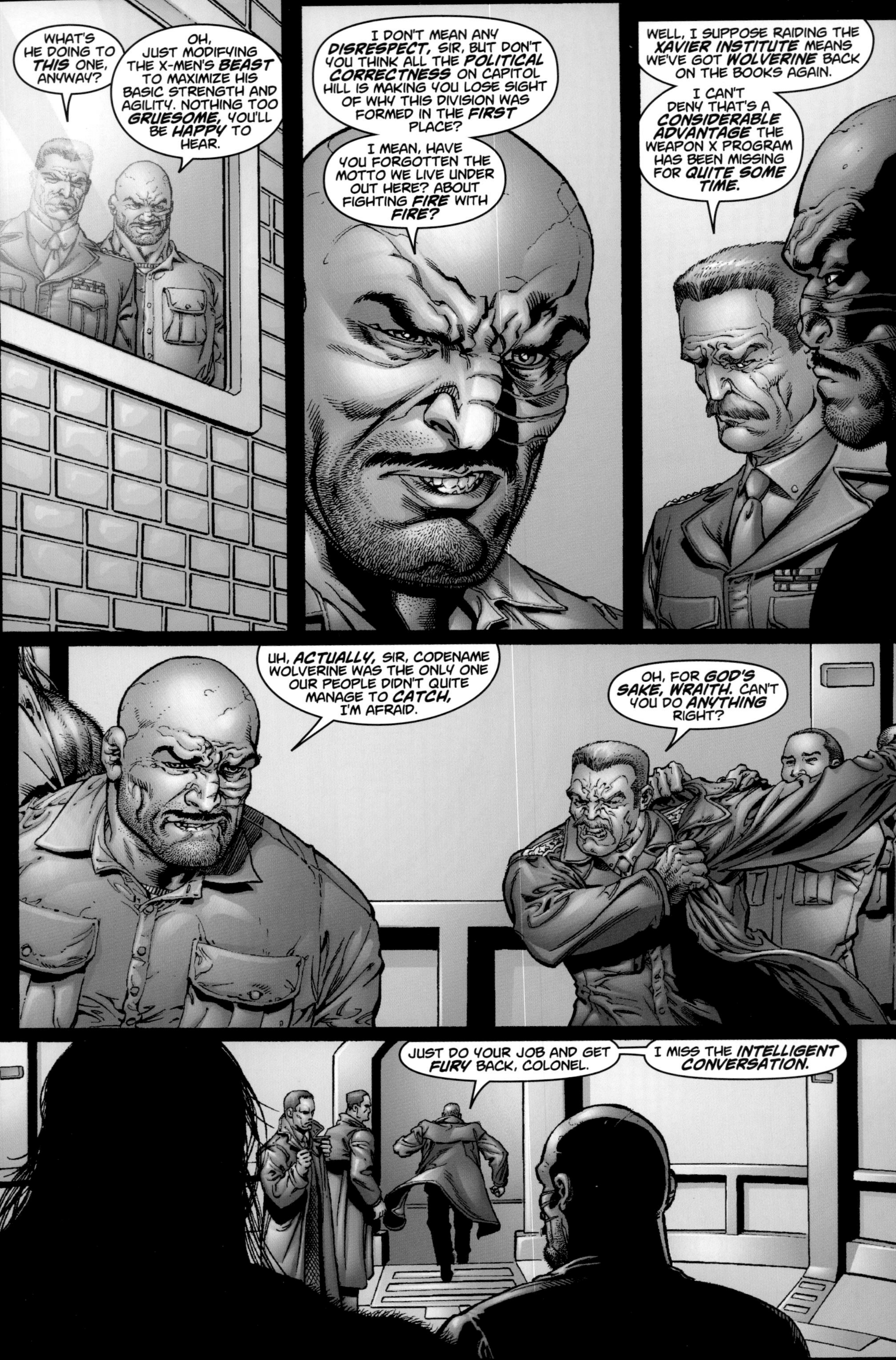
WHAT'S HE DOING TO THIS ONE, ANYWAY?
OH, JUST MODIFYING THE X-MEN'S BEAST TO MAXIMIZE HIS BASIC STRENGTH AND AGILITY. NOTHING TOO GRUESOME, YOU'LL BE HAPPY TO HEAR.
I DON'T MEAN ANY DISRESPECT, SIR, BUT DON'T YOU THINK ALL THE POLITICAL CORRECTNESS ON CAPITOL HILL IS MAKING YOU LOSE SIGHT OF WHY THIS DIVISION WAS FORMED IN THE FIRST PLACE?
I MEAN, HAVE YOU FORGOTTEN THE MOTTO WE LIVE UNDER OUT HERE? ABOUT FIGHTING FIRE WITH FIRE?
WELL, I SUPPOSE RAIDING THE XAVIER INSTITUTE MEANS WE'VE GOT WOLVERINE BACK ON THE BOOKS AGAIN.
I CAN'T DENY THAT'S A CONSIDERABLE ADVANTAGE THE WEAPON X PROGRAM HAS BEEN MISSING FOR QUITE SOME TIME.
UH, ACTUALLY, SIR, CODENAME WOLVERINE WAS THE ONLY ONE OUR PEOPLE DIDN'T QUITE MANAGE TO CATCH, I'M AFRAID.
OH, FOR GOD'S SAKE, WRAITH. CAN'T YOU DO ANYTHING RIGHT?
JUST DO YOUR JOB AND GET FURY BACK, COLONEL.
I MISS THE INTELLIGENT CONVERSATION.

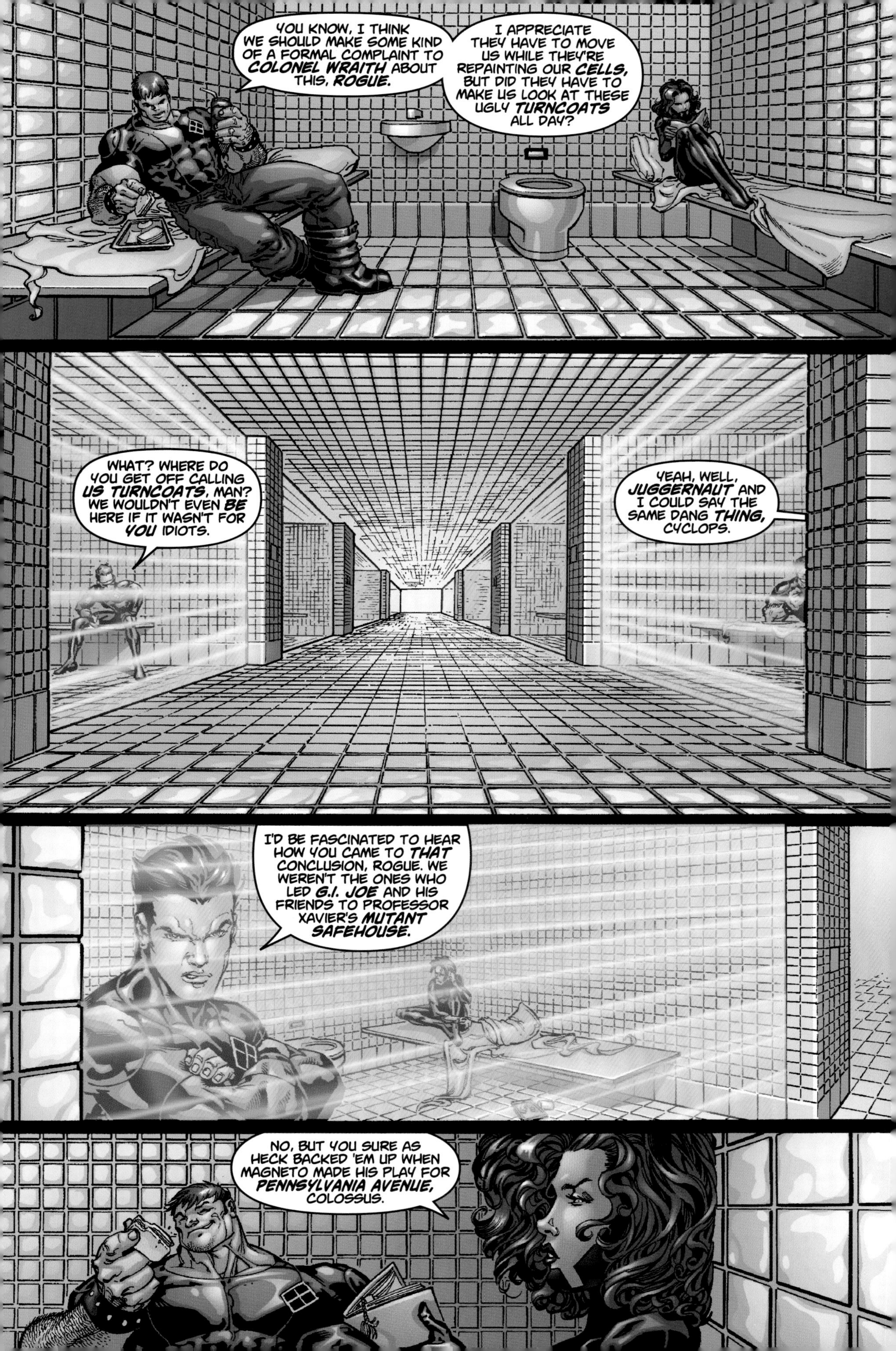
YOU KNOW, I THINK WE SHOULD MAKE SOME KIND OF A FORMAL COMPLAINT TO COLONEL WRAITH ABOUT THIS, ROGUE.
I APPRECIATE THEY HAVE TO MOVE US WHILE THEY'RE REPAINTING OUR CELLS, BUT DID THEY HAVE TO MAKE US LOOK AT THESE UGLY TURNCOATS ALL DAY?
WHAT? WHERE DO YOU GET OFF CALLING US TURNCOATS, MAN? WE WOULDN'T EVEN BE HERE IF IT WASN'T FOR YOU IDIOTS.
YEAH, WELL, JUGGERNAUT AND I COULD SAY THE SAME DANG THING, CYCLOPS.
I'D BE FASCINATED TO HEAR HOW YOU CAME TO THAT CONCLUSION, ROGUE. WE WEREN'T THE ONES WHO LED G.I. JOE AND HIS FRIENDS TO PROFESSOR XAVIER'S MUTANT SAFEHOUSE.
NO, BUT YOU SURE AS HECK BACKED 'EM UP WHEN MAGNETO MADE HIS PLAY FOR PENNSYLVANIA AVENUE, COLOSSUS.

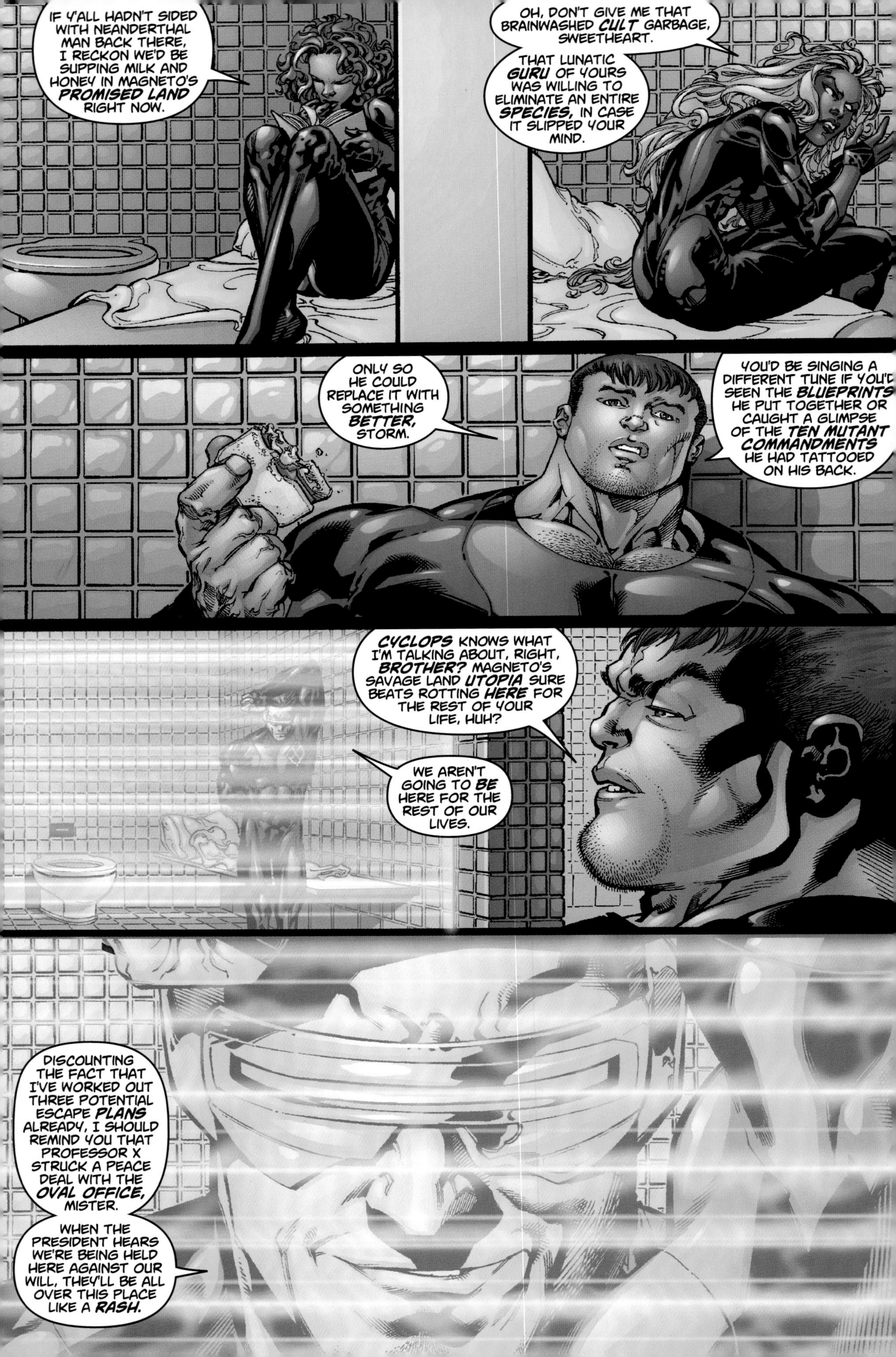
IF Y'ALL HADN'T SIDED WITH NEANDERTHAL MAN BACK THERE, I RECKON WE'D BE SUPPING MILK AND HONEY IN MAGNETO'S PROMISED LAND RIGHT NOW.
OH, DON'T GIVE ME THAT BRAINWASHED CULT GARBAGE, SWEETHEART.
THAT LUNATIC GURU OF YOURS WAS WILLING TO ELIMINATE AN ENTIRE SPECIES, IN CASE IT SLIPPED YOUR MIND.
ONLY SO HE COULD REPLACE IT WITH SOMETHING BETTER, STORM.
YOU'D BE SINGING A DIFFERENT TUNE IF YOU'D SEEN THE BLUEPRINTS HE PUT TOGETHER OR CAUGHT A GLIMPSE OF THE TEN MUTANT COMMANDMENTS HE HAD TATTOOED ON HIS BACK.
CYCLOPS KNOWS WHAT I'M TALKING ABOUT, RIGHT, BROTHER? MAGNETO'S SAVAGE LAND UTOPIA SURE BEATS ROTTING HERE FOR THE REST OF YOUR LIFE, HUH?
WE AREN'T GOING TO BE HERE FOR THE REST OF OUR LIVES.
DISCOUNTING THE FACT THAT I'VE WORKED OUT THREE POTENTIAL ESCAPE PLANS ALREADY, I SHOULD REMIND YOU THAT PROFESSOR X STRUCK A PEACE DEAL WITH THE OVAL OFFICE, MISTER.
WHEN THE PRESIDENT HEARS WE'RE BEING HELD HERE AGAINST OUR WILL, THEY'LL BE ALL OVER THIS PLACE LIKE A RASH.

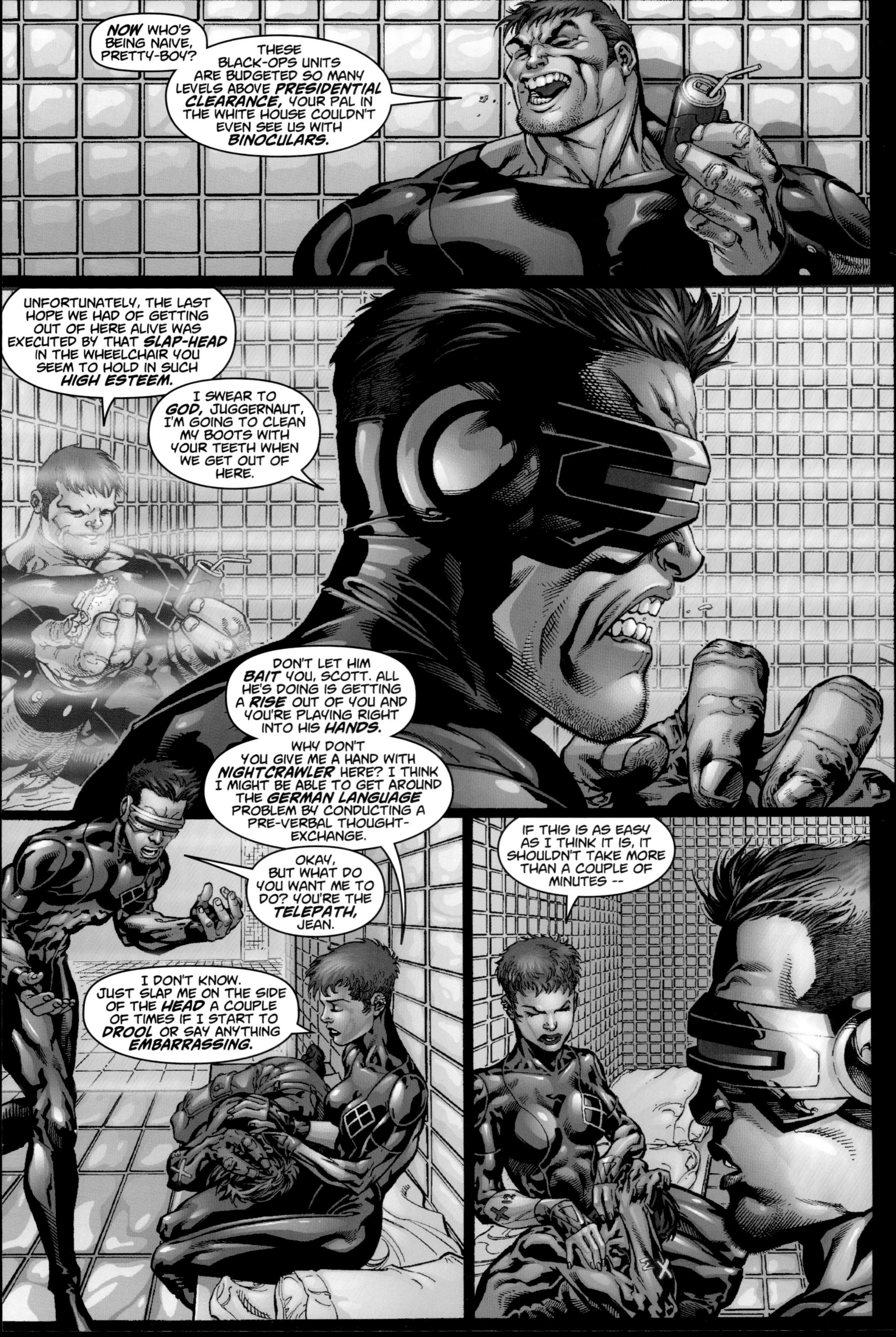
NOW WHO'S BEING NAIVE, PRETTY-BOY?
THESE BLACK-OPS UNITS ARE BUDGETED SO MANY LEVELS ABOVE PRESIDENTIAL CLEARANCE, YOUR PAL IN THE WHITE HOUSE COULDN'T EVEN SEE US WITH BINOCULARS.
UNFORTUNATELY, THE LAST HOPE WE HAD OF GETTING OUT OF HERE ALIVE WAS EXECUTED BY THAT SLAP-HEAD IN THE WHEELCHAIR YOU SEEM TO HOLD IN SUCH HIGH ESTEEM.
I SWEAR TO GOD, JUGGERNAUT, I'M GOING TO CLEAN MY BOOTS WITH YOUR TEETH WHEN WE GET OUT OF HERE.
DON'T LET HIM BAIT YOU, SCOTT. ALL HE'S DOING IS GETTING A RISE OUT OF YOU AND YOU'RE PLAYING RIGHT INTO HIS HANDS.
WHY DON'T YOU GIVE ME A HAND WITH NIGHTCRAWLER HERE? I THINK I MIGHT BE ABLE TO GET AROUND THE GERMAN LANGUAGE PROBLEM BY CONDUCTING A PRE-VERBAL THOUGHT-EXCHANGE.
OKAY, BUT WHAT DO YOU WANT ME TO DO? YOU'RE THE TELEPATH, JEAN.
I DON'T KNOW. JUST SLAP ME ON THE SIDE OF THE HEAD A COUPLE OF TIMES IF I START TO DROOL OR SAY ANYTHING EMBARRASSING.
IF THIS IS AS EASY AS I THINK IT IS, IT SHOULDN'T TAKE MORE THAN A COUPLE OF MINUTES --

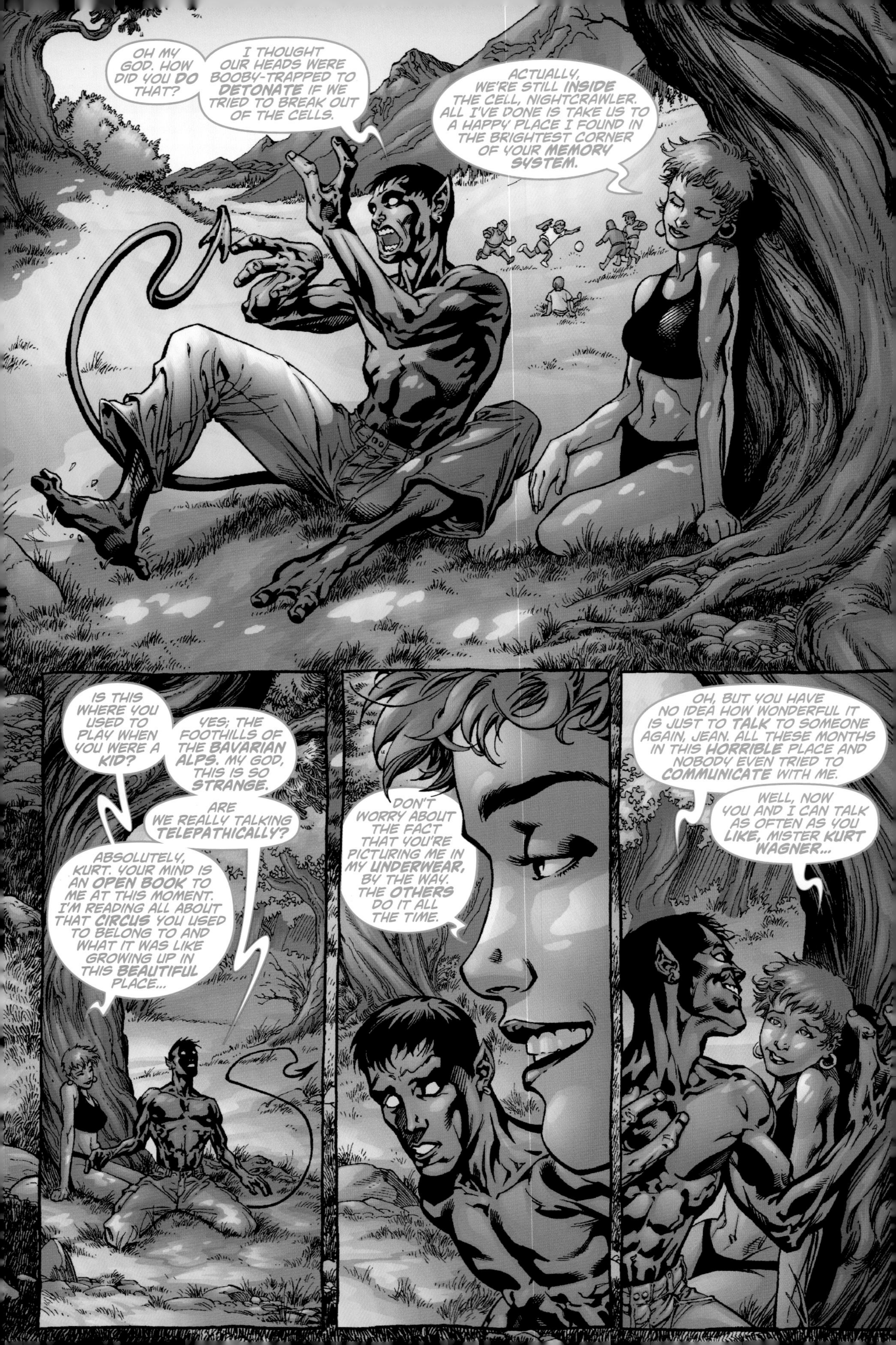
OH MY GOD. HOW DID YOU DO THAT?
I THOUGHT OUR HEADS WERE BOOBY-TRAPPED TO DETONATE IF WE TRIED TO BREAK OUT OF THE CELLS.
ACTUALLY, WE'RE STILL INSIDE THE CELL, NIGHTCRAWLER. ALL I'VE DONE IS TAKE US TO A HAPPY PLACE I FOUND IN THE BRIGHTEST CORNER OF YOUR MEMORY SYSTEM.
IS THIS WHERE YOU USED TO PLAY WHEN YOU WERE A KID?
YES; THE FOOTHILLS OF THE BAVARIAN ALPS. MY GOD, THIS IS SO STRANGE.
ARE WE REALLY TALKING TELEPATHICALLY?
ABSOLUTELY, KURT. YOUR MIND IS AN OPEN BOOK TO ME AT THIS MOMENT. I'M READING ALL ABOUT THAT CIRCUS YOU USED TO BELONG TO AND WHAT IT WAS LIKE GROWING UP IN THIS BEAUTIFUL PLACE...
DON'T WORRY ABOUT THE FACT THAT YOU'RE PICTURING ME IN MY UNDERWEAR, BY THE WAY. THE OTHERS DO IT ALL THE TIME.
OH, BUT YOU HAVE NO IDEA HOW WONDERFUL IT IS JUST TO TALK TO SOMEONE AGAIN, JEAN. ALL THESE MONTHS IN THIS HORRIBLE PLACE AND NOBODY EVEN TRIED TO COMMUNICATE WITH ME.
WELL, NOW YOU AND I CAN TALK AS OFTEN AS YOU LIKE, MISTER KURT WAGNER...

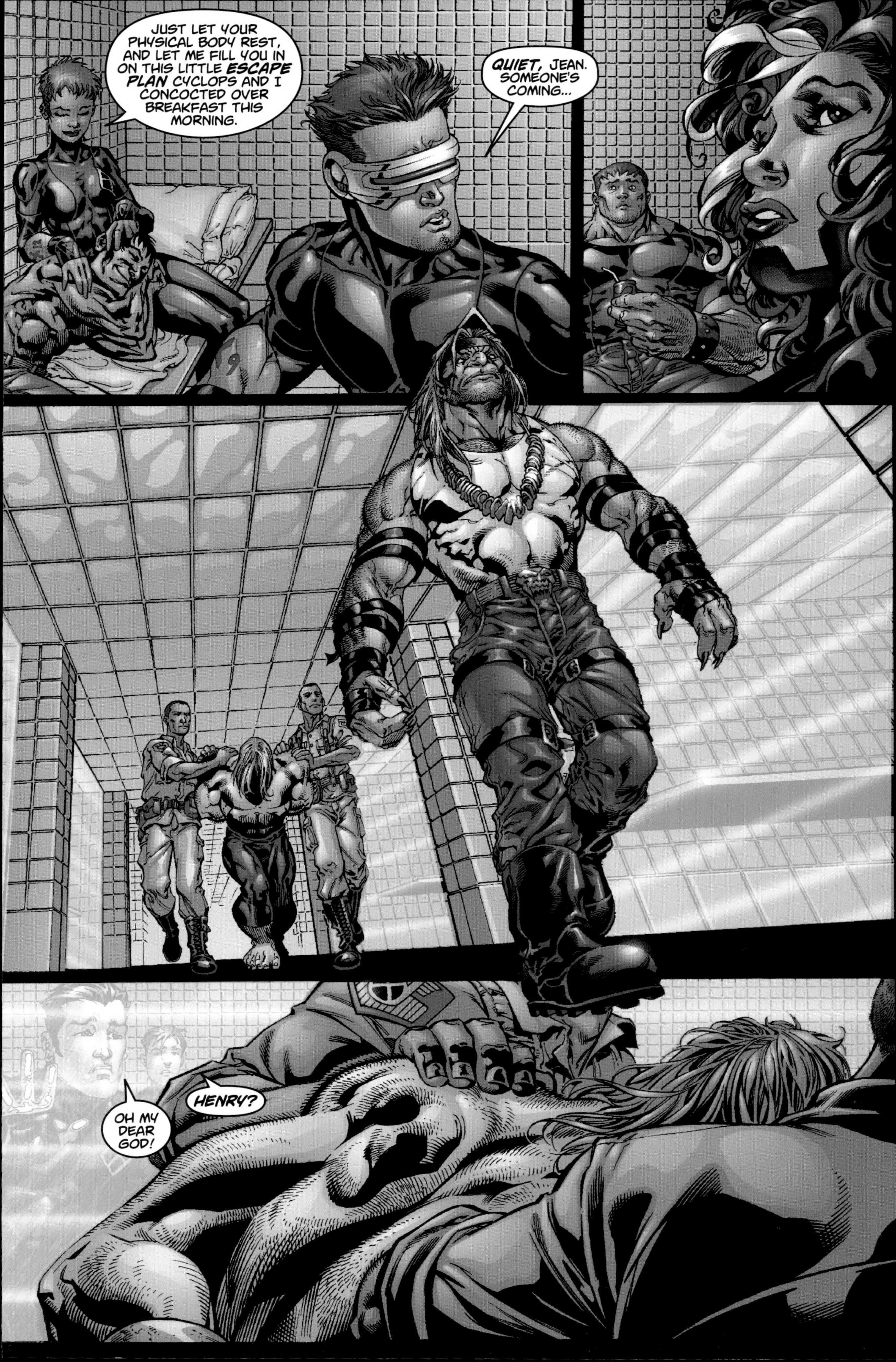
JUST LET YOUR PHYSICAL BODY REST, AND LET ME FILL YOU IN ON THIS LITTLE **ESCAPE PLAN** CYCLOPS AND I CONCOCTED OVER BREAKFAST THIS MORNING.
QUIET, JEAN. SOMEONE'S COMING...
HENRY?
OH MY DEAR GOD!

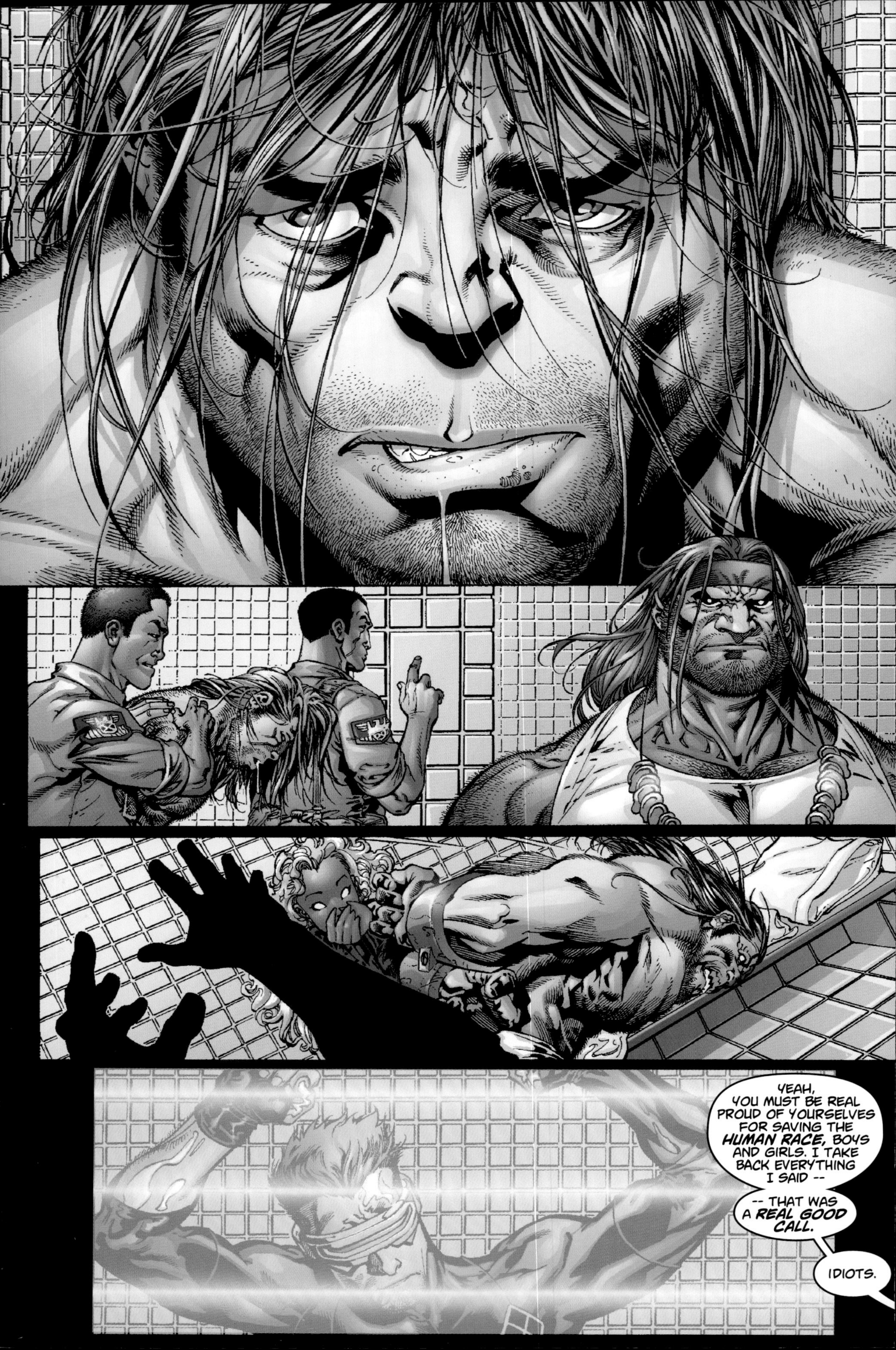
YEAH, YOU MUST BE REAL PROUD OF YOURSELVES FOR SAVING THE **HUMAN RACE,** BOYS AND GIRLS. I TAKE BACK EVERYTHING I SAID --
-- THAT WAS A **REAL GOOD CALL.**
IDIOTS.

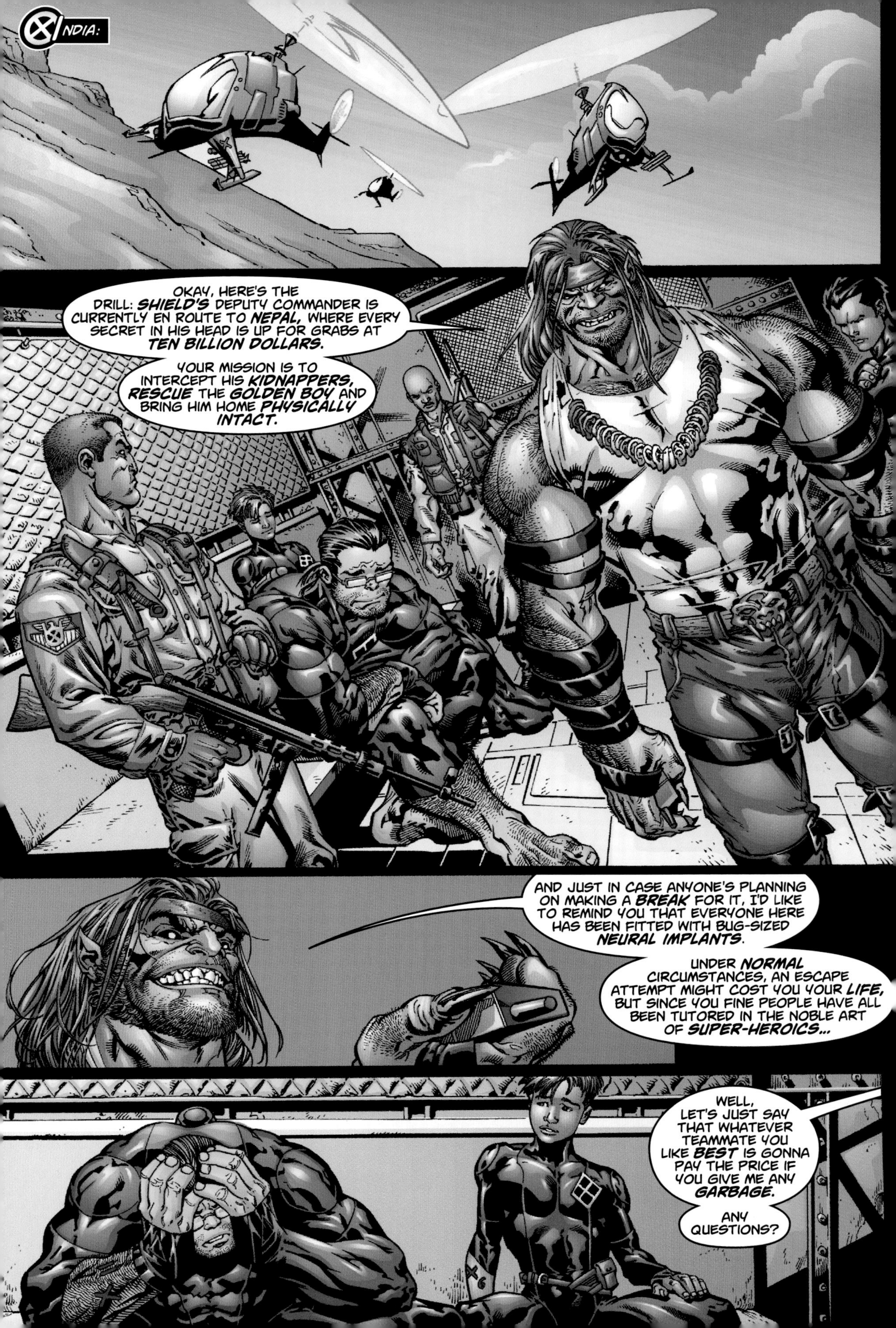
X INDIA:
OKAY, HERE'S THE DRILL: SHIELD'S DEPUTY COMMANDER IS CURRENTLY EN ROUTE TO NEPAL, WHERE EVERY SECRET IN HIS HEAD IS UP FOR GRABS AT TEN BILLION DOLLARS.
YOUR MISSION IS TO INTERCEPT HIS KIDNAPPERS, RESCUE THE GOLDEN BOY AND BRING HIM HOME PHYSICALLY INTACT.
AND JUST IN CASE ANYONE'S PLANNING ON MAKING A BREAK FOR IT, I'D LIKE TO REMIND YOU THAT EVERYONE HERE HAS BEEN FITTED WITH BUG-SIZED NEURAL IMPLANTS.
UNDER NORMAL CIRCUMSTANCES, AN ESCAPE ATTEMPT MIGHT COST YOU YOUR LIFE, BUT SINCE YOU FINE PEOPLE HAVE ALL BEEN TUTORED IN THE NOBLE ART OF SUPER-HEROICS...
WELL, LET'S JUST SAY THAT WHATEVER TEAMMATE YOU LIKE BEST IS GONNA PAY THE PRICE IF YOU GIVE ME ANY GARBAGE.
ANY QUESTIONS?

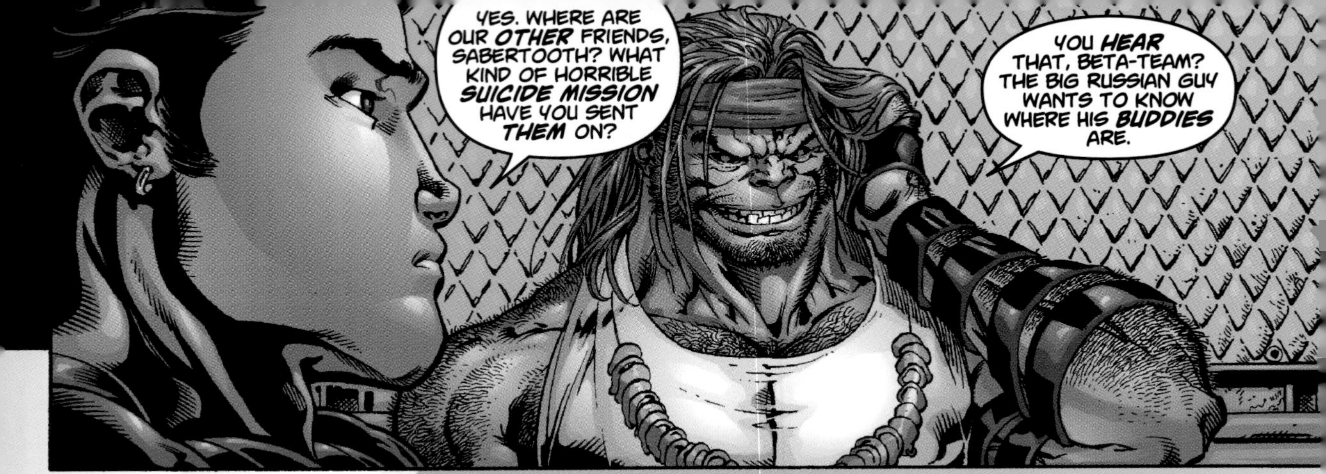
YES. WHERE ARE OUR OTHER FRIENDS, SABERTOOTH? WHAT KIND OF HORRIBLE SUICIDE MISSION HAVE YOU SENT THEM ON?
YOU HEAR THAT, BETA-TEAM? THE BIG RUSSIAN GUY WANTS TO KNOW WHERE HIS BUDDIES ARE.

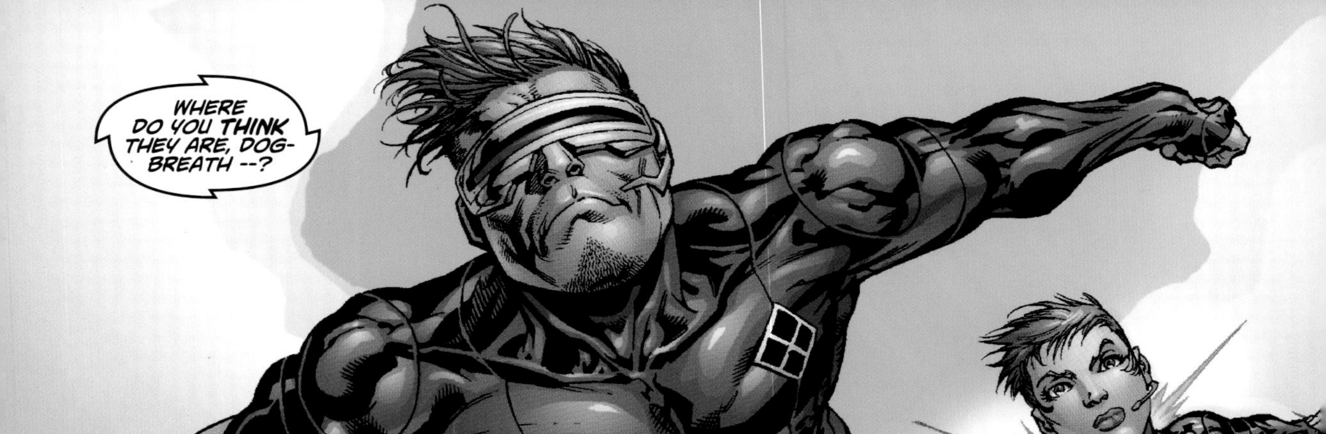
WHERE DO YOU THINK THEY ARE, DOG-BREATH --?

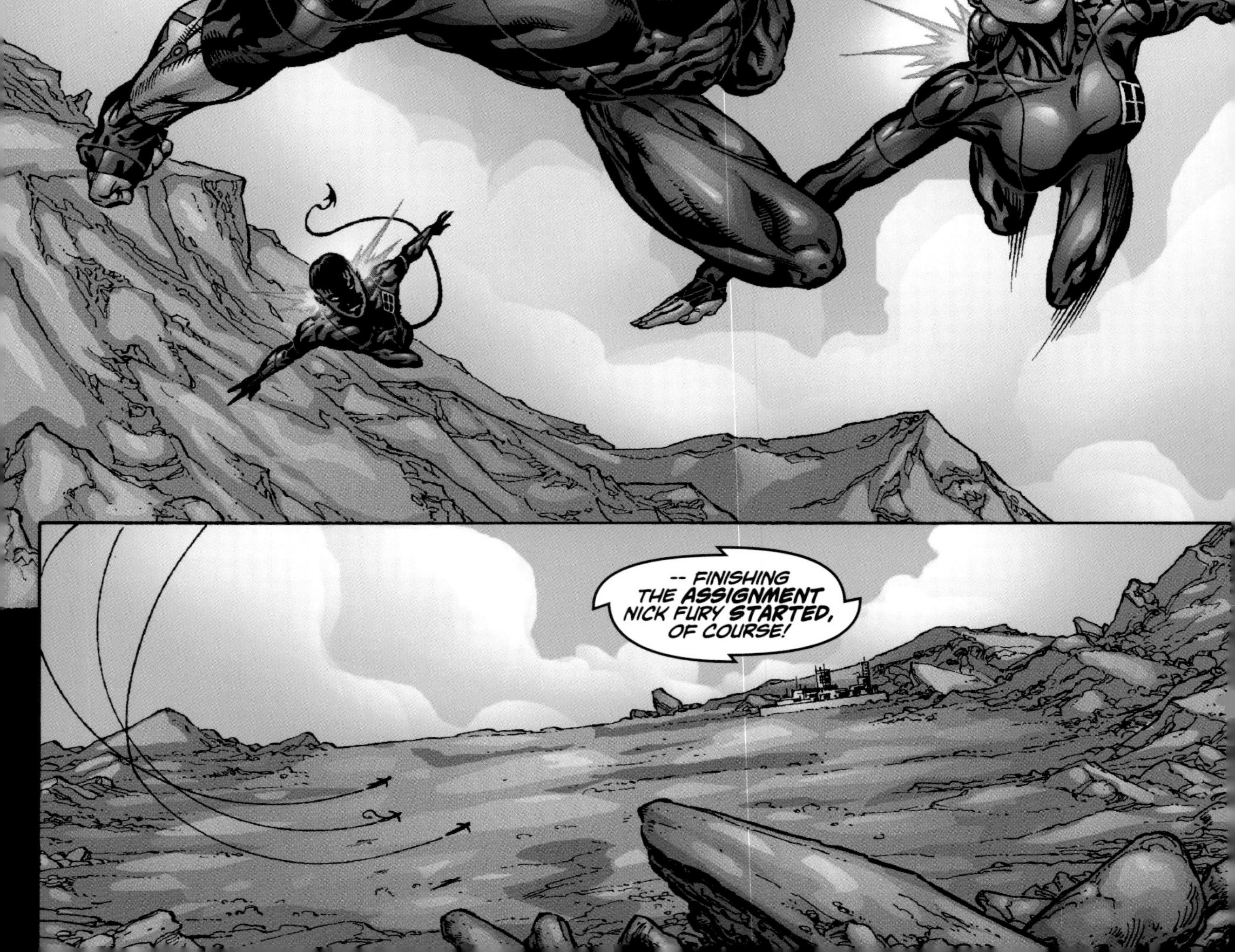
-- FINISHING THE ASSIGNMENT NICK FURY STARTED, OF COURSE!

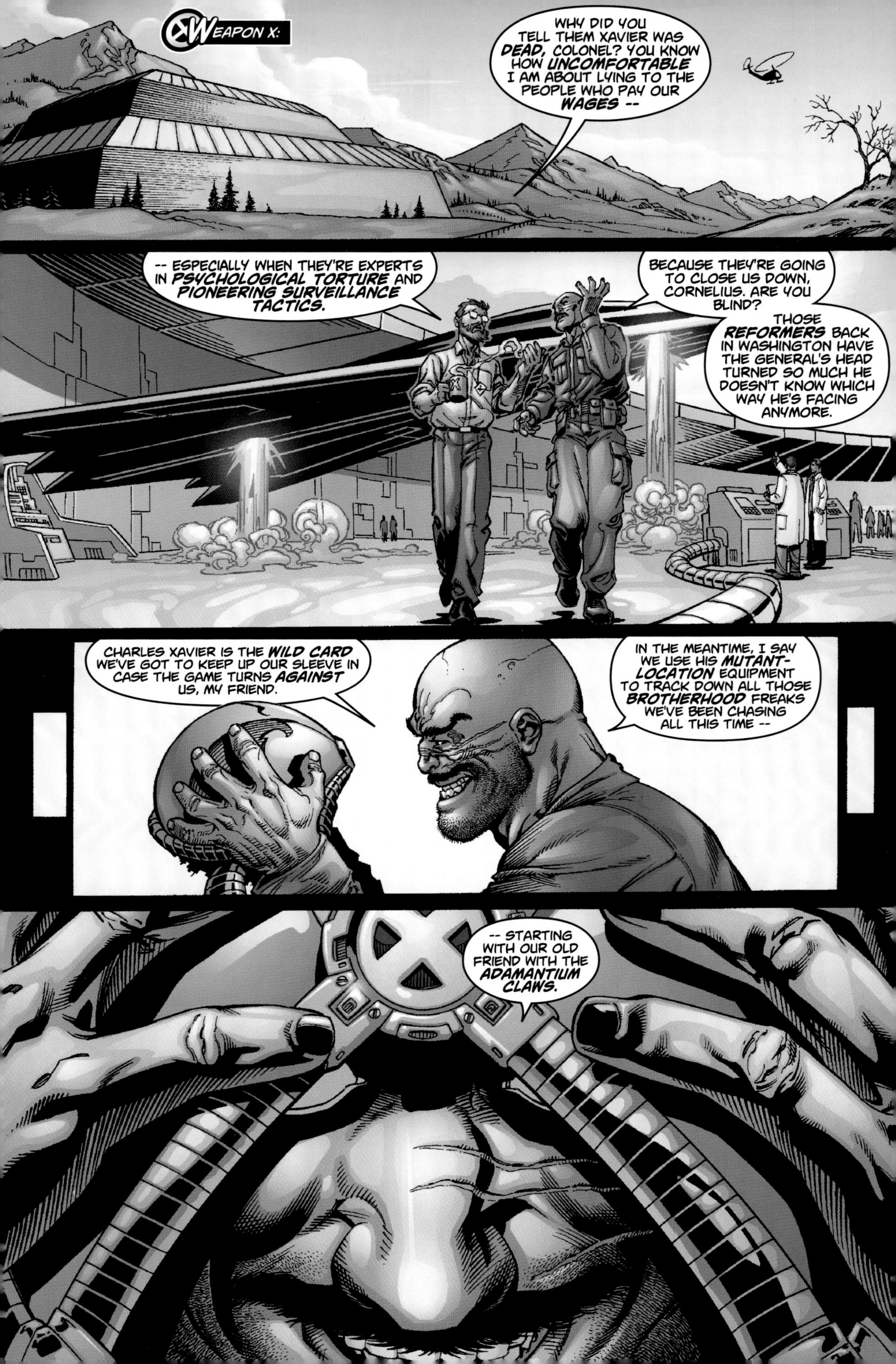
WEAPON X:
WHY DID YOU TELL THEM XAVIER WAS DEAD, COLONEL? YOU KNOW HOW UNCOMFORTABLE I AM ABOUT LYING TO THE PEOPLE WHO PAY OUR WAGES --
-- ESPECIALLY WHEN THEY'RE EXPERTS IN PSYCHOLOGICAL TORTURE AND PIONEERING SURVEILLANCE TACTICS.
BECAUSE THEY'RE GOING TO CLOSE US DOWN, CORNELIUS. ARE YOU BLIND?
THOSE REFORMERS BACK IN WASHINGTON HAVE THE GENERAL'S HEAD TURNED SO MUCH HE DOESN'T KNOW WHICH WAY HE'S FACING ANYMORE.
CHARLES XAVIER IS THE WILD CARD WE'VE GOT TO KEEP UP OUR SLEEVE IN CASE THE GAME TURNS AGAINST US, MY FRIEND.
IN THE MEANTIME, I SAY WE USE HIS MUTANT-LOCATION EQUIPMENT TO TRACK DOWN ALL THOSE BROTHERHOOD FREAKS WE'VE BEEN CHASING ALL THIS TIME --
-- STARTING WITH OUR OLD FRIEND WITH THE ADAMANTIUM CLAWS.

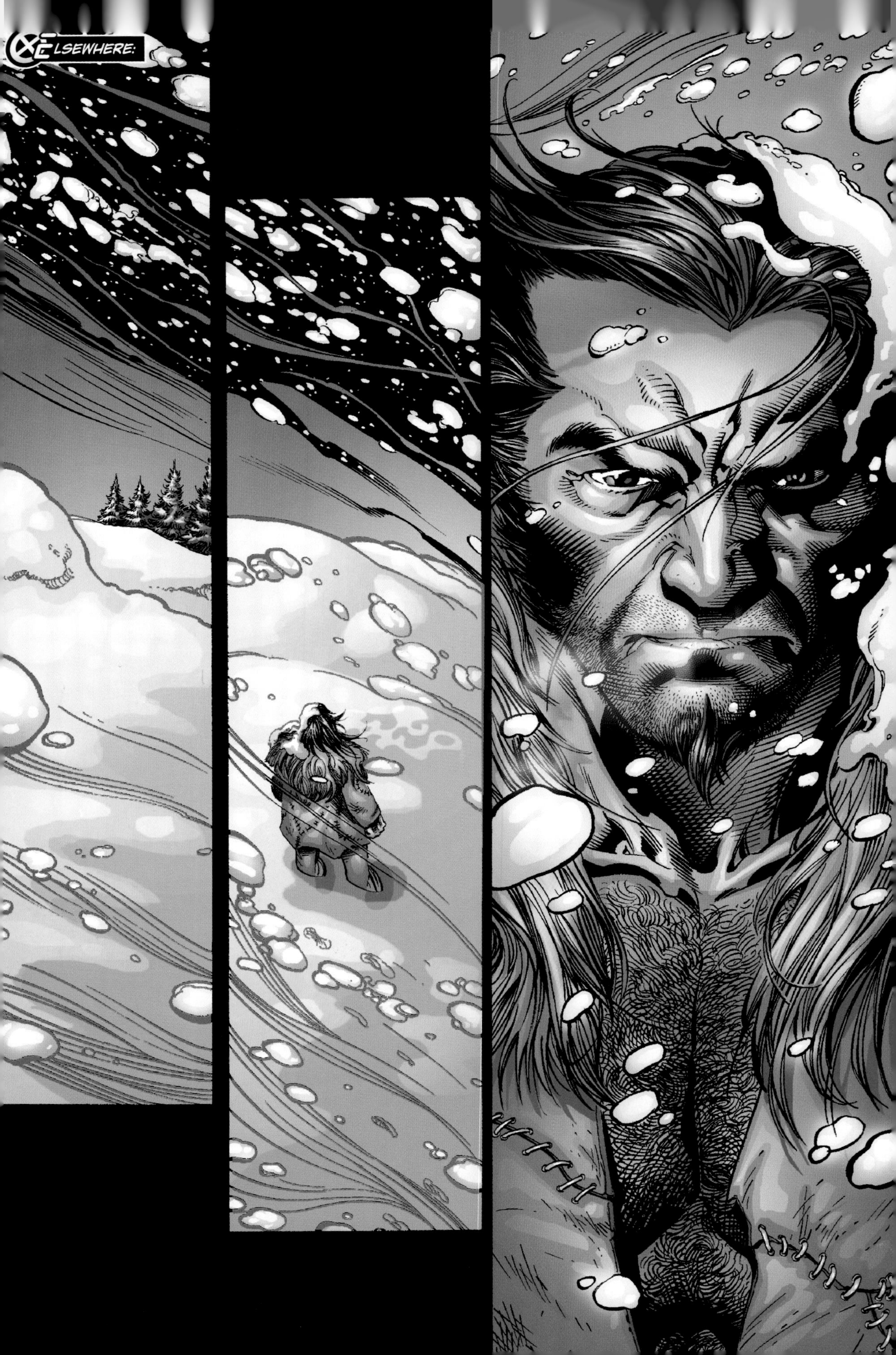
ELSEWHERE:

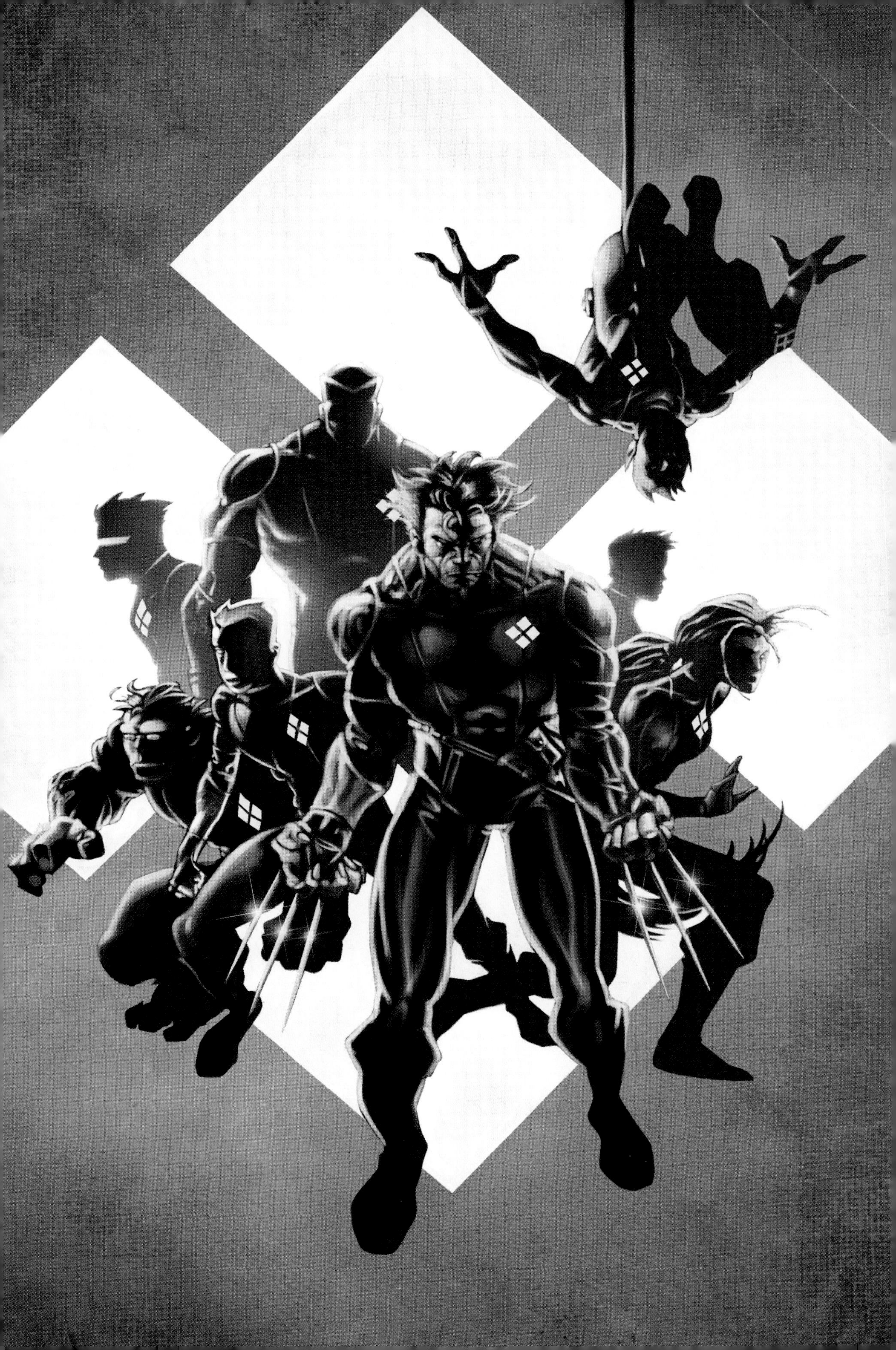

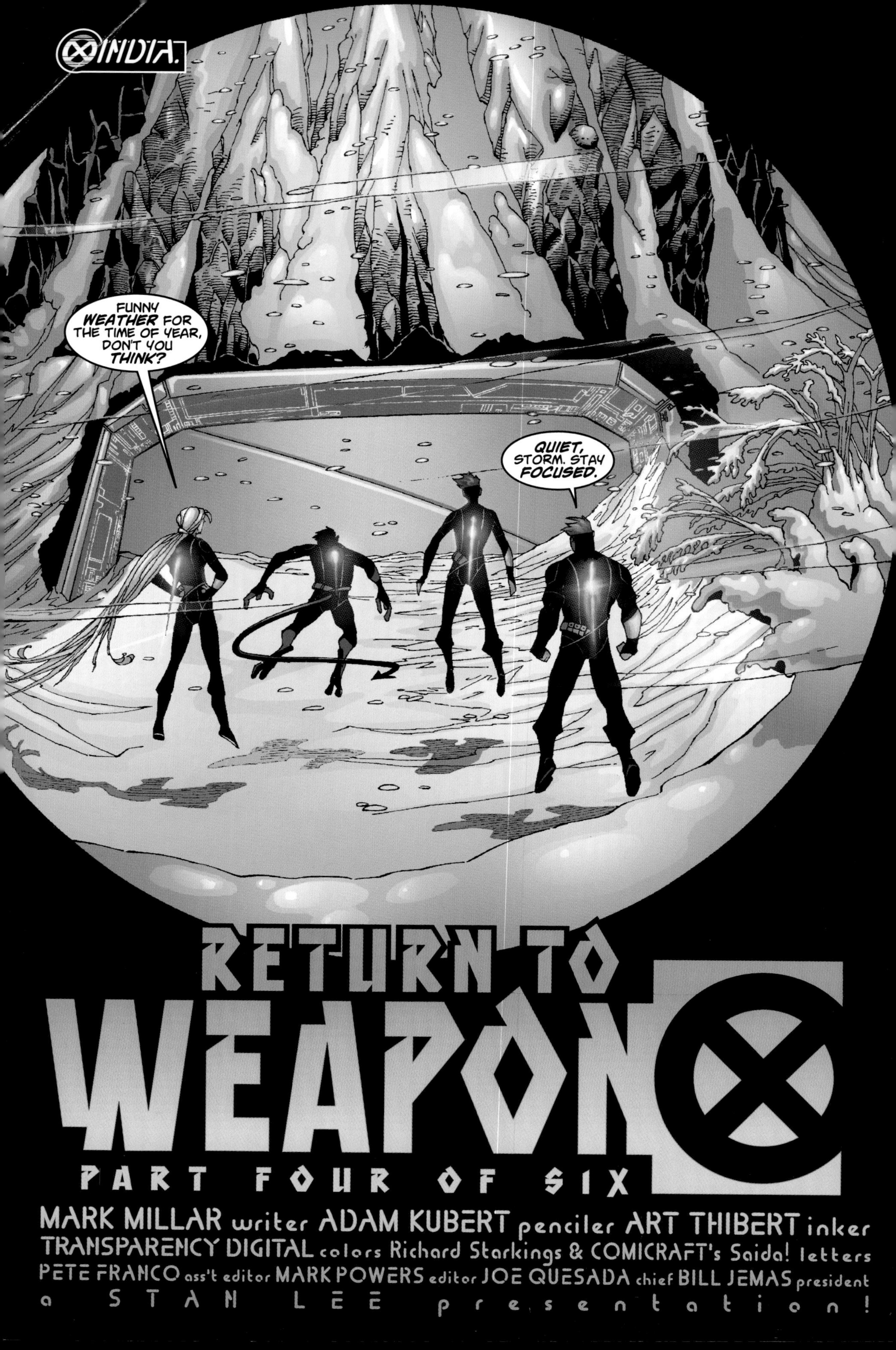
FUNNY WEATHER FOR THE TIME OF YEAR, DON'T YOU THINK?
QUIET, STORM. STAY FOCUSED.

RETURN TO WEAPON X

PART FOUR OF SIX

MARK MILLAR writer ADAM KUBERT penciler ART THIBERT inker
TRANSPARENCY DIGITAL colors Richard Starkings & COMICRAFT's Saida! letters
PETE FRANCO ass't editor MARK POWERS editor JOE QUESADA chief BILL JEMAS president
a STAN LEE presentation!

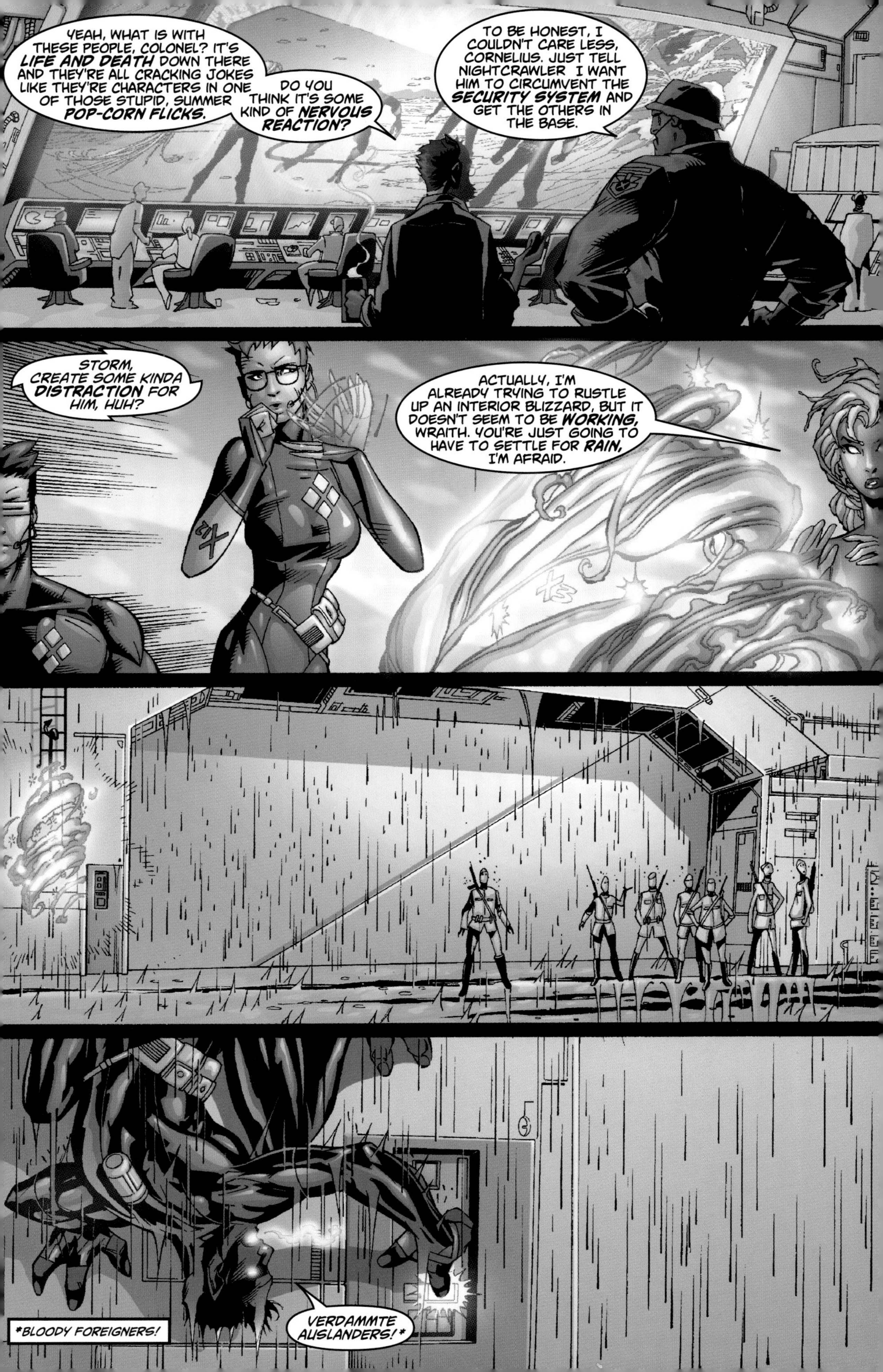
YEAH, WHAT IS WITH THESE PEOPLE, COLONEL? IT'S LIFE AND DEATH DOWN THERE AND THEY'RE ALL CRACKING JOKES LIKE THEY'RE CHARACTERS IN ONE OF THOSE STUPID, SUMMER POP-CORN FLICKS.
DO YOU THINK IT'S SOME KIND OF NERVOUS REACTION?
TO BE HONEST, I COULDN'T CARE LESS, CORNELIUS. JUST TELL NIGHTCRAWLER I WANT HIM TO CIRCUMVENT THE SECURITY SYSTEM AND GET THE OTHERS IN THE BASE.
STORM, CREATE SOME KINDA DISTRACTION FOR HIM, HUH?
ACTUALLY, I'M ALREADY TRYING TO RUSTLE UP AN INTERIOR BLIZZARD, BUT IT DOESN'T SEEM TO BE WORKING, WRAITH. YOU'RE JUST GOING TO HAVE TO SETTLE FOR RAIN, I'M AFRAID.
VERDAMMTE AUSLANDERS!*
*BLOODY FOREIGNERS!

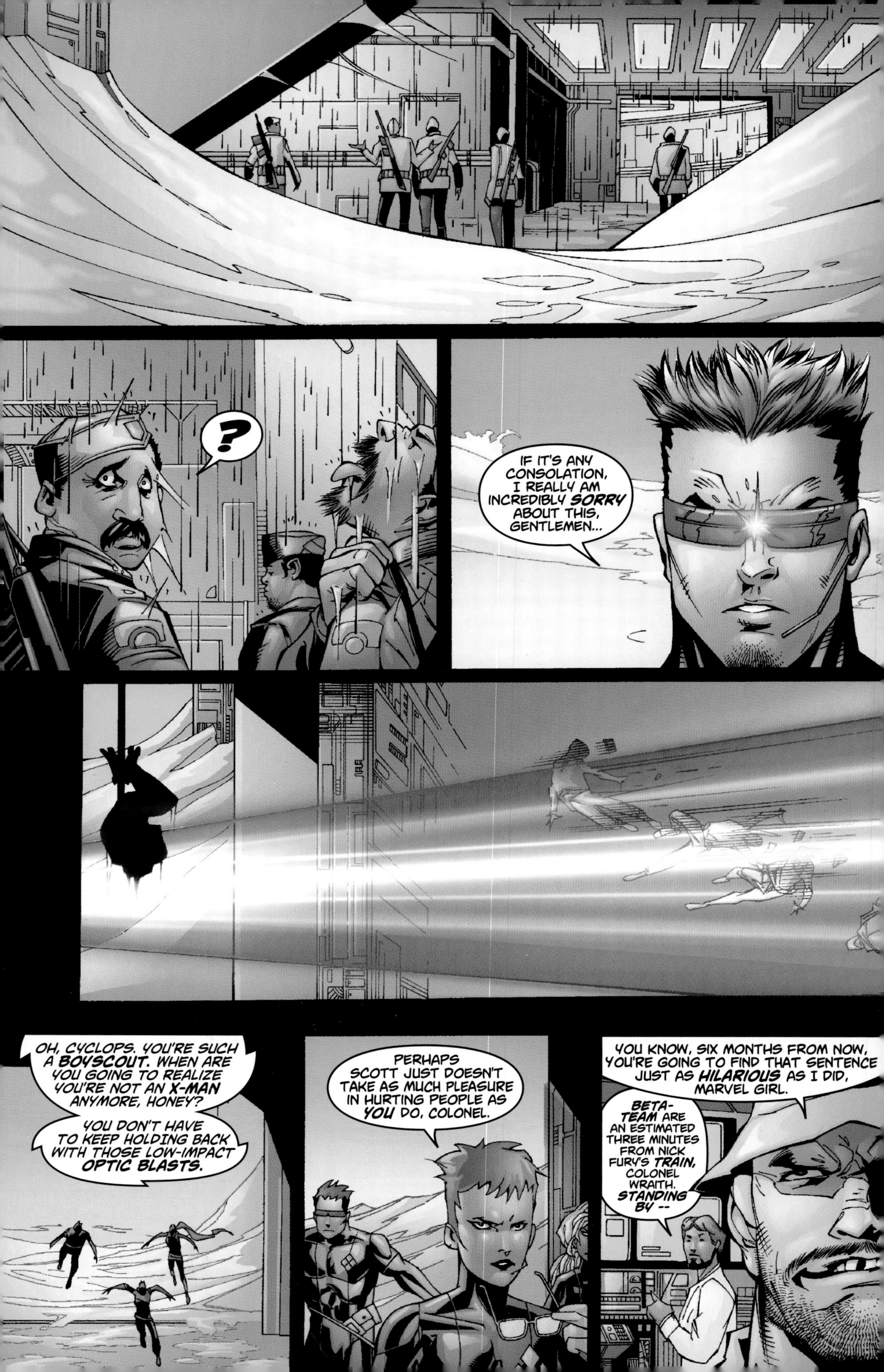
?
IF IT'S ANY CONSOLATION, I REALLY AM INCREDIBLY SORRY ABOUT THIS, GENTLEMEN...
OH, CYCLOPS. YOU'RE SUCH A BOYSCOUT. WHEN ARE YOU GOING TO REALIZE YOU'RE NOT AN X-MAN ANYMORE, HONEY?
YOU DON'T HAVE TO KEEP HOLDING BACK WITH THOSE LOW-IMPACT OPTIC BLASTS.
PERHAPS SCOTT JUST DOESN'T TAKE AS MUCH PLEASURE IN HURTING PEOPLE AS YOU DO, COLONEL.
YOU KNOW, SIX MONTHS FROM NOW, YOU'RE GOING TO FIND THAT SENTENCE JUST AS HILARIOUS AS I DID, MARVEL GIRL.
BETA-TEAM ARE AN ESTIMATED THREE MINUTES FROM NICK FURY'S TRAIN, COLONEL WRAITH. STANDING BY --

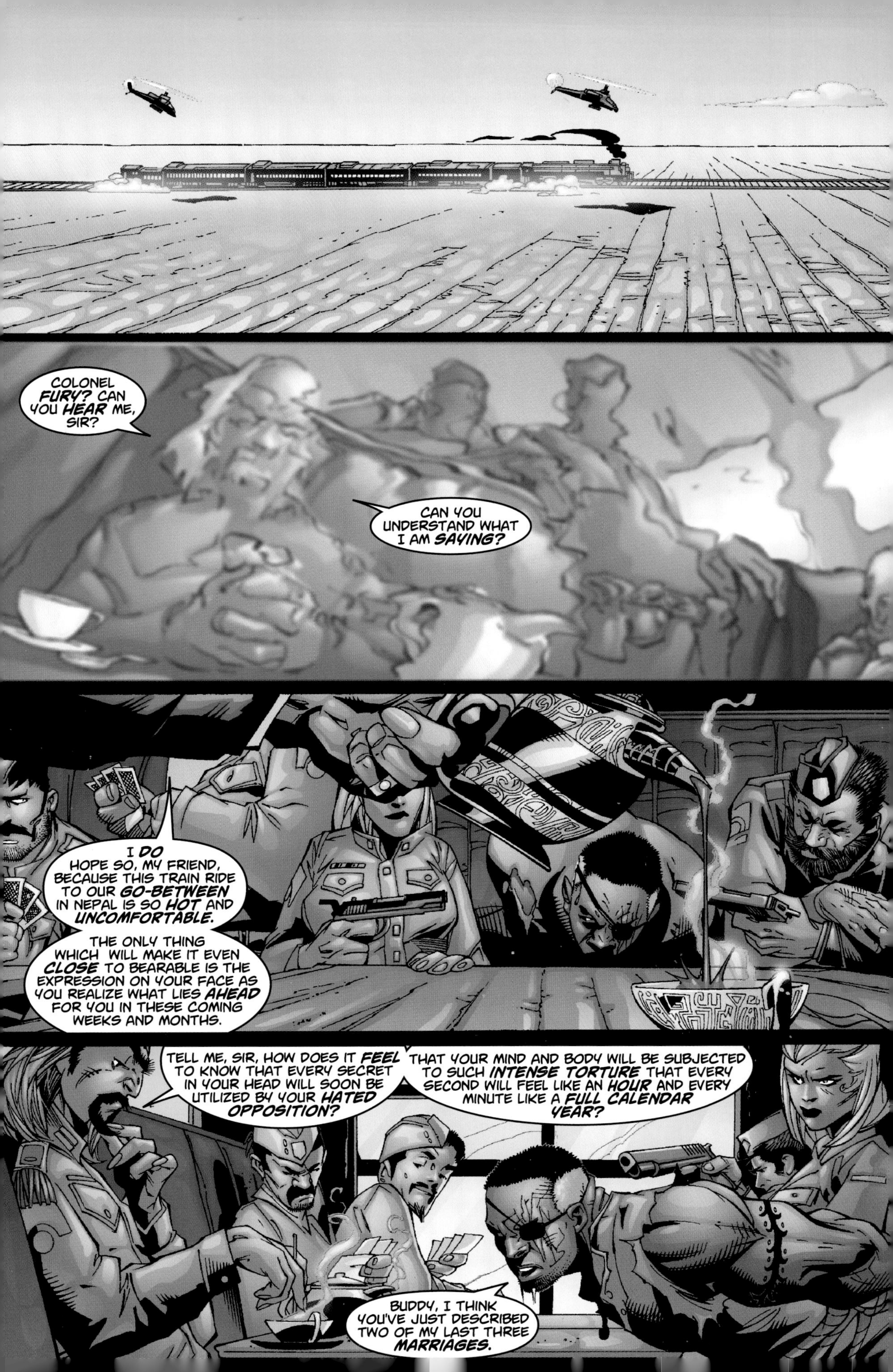
COLONEL FURY? CAN YOU HEAR ME, SIR?
CAN YOU UNDERSTAND WHAT I AM SAYING?
I DO HOPE SO, MY FRIEND, BECAUSE THIS TRAIN RIDE TO OUR GO-BETWEEN IN NEPAL IS SO HOT AND UNCOMFORTABLE.
THE ONLY THING WHICH WILL MAKE IT EVEN CLOSE TO BEARABLE IS THE EXPRESSION ON YOUR FACE AS YOU REALIZE WHAT LIES AHEAD FOR YOU IN THESE COMING WEEKS AND MONTHS.
TELL ME, SIR, HOW DOES IT FEEL TO KNOW THAT EVERY SECRET IN YOUR HEAD WILL SOON BE UTILIZED BY YOUR HATED OPPOSITION?
THAT YOUR MIND AND BODY WILL BE SUBJECTED TO SUCH INTENSE TORTURE THAT EVERY SECOND WILL FEEL LIKE AN HOUR AND EVERY MINUTE LIKE A FULL CALENDAR YEAR?
BUDDY, I THINK YOU'VE JUST DESCRIBED TWO OF MY LAST THREE MARRIAGES.

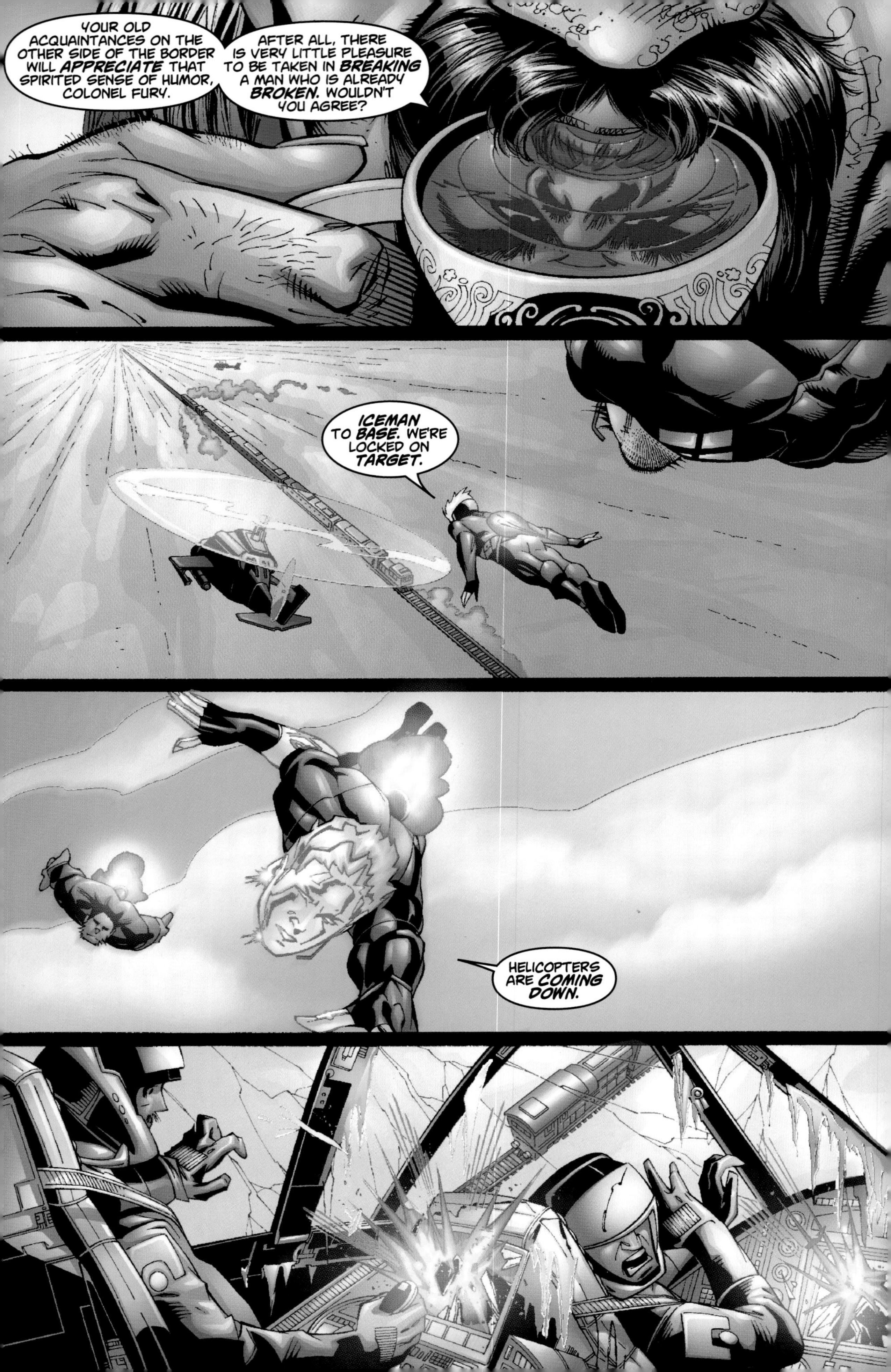
YOUR OLD ACQUAINTANCES ON THE OTHER SIDE OF THE BORDER WILL APPRECIATE THAT SPIRITED SENSE OF HUMOR, COLONEL FURY.
AFTER ALL, THERE IS VERY LITTLE PLEASURE TO BE TAKEN IN BREAKING A MAN WHO IS ALREADY BROKEN. WOULDN'T YOU AGREE?
ICEMAN TO BASE. WE'RE LOCKED ON TARGET.
HELICOPTERS ARE COMING DOWN.

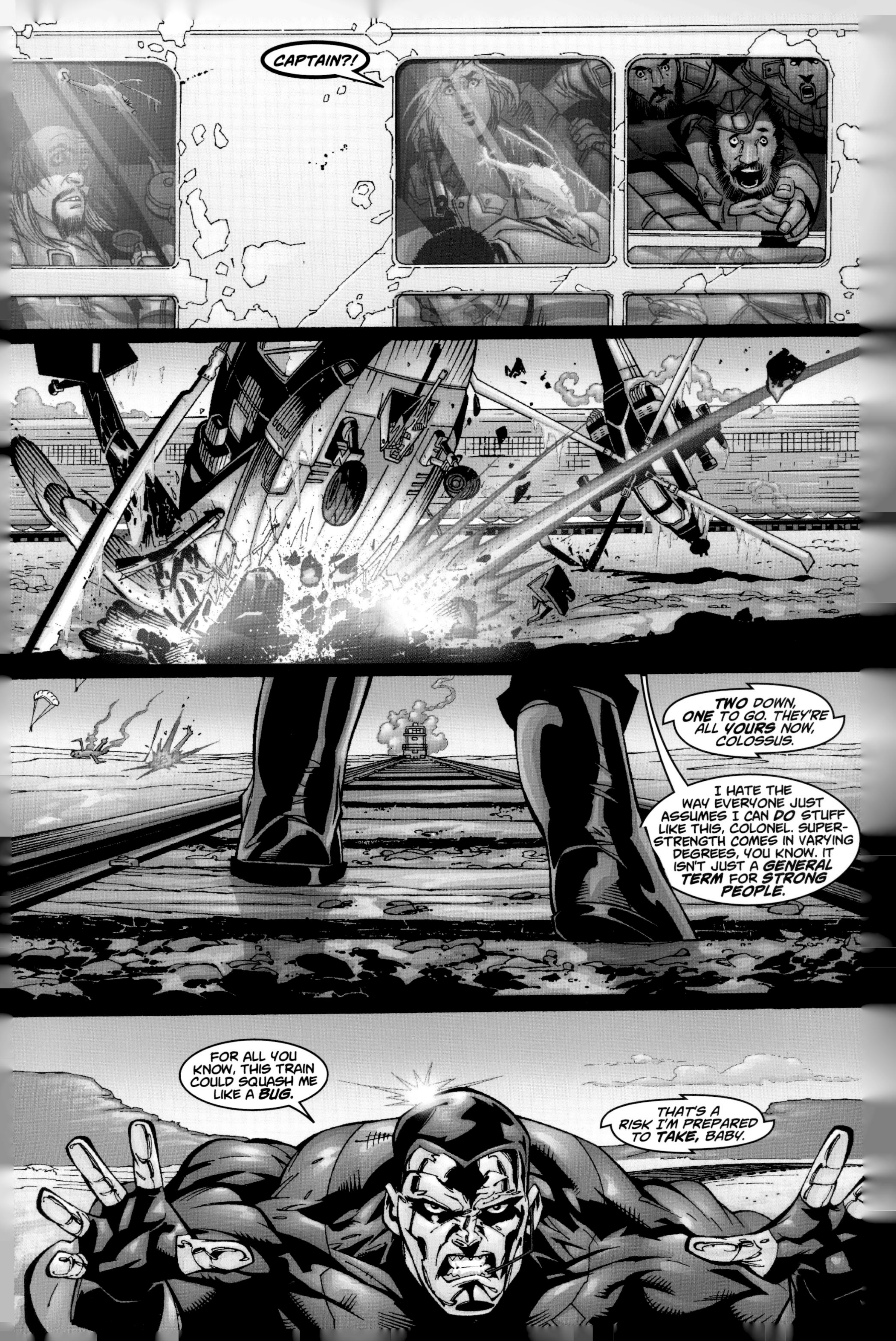
CAPTAIN?!
TWO DOWN, ONE TO GO. THEY'RE ALL YOURS NOW, COLOSSUS.
I HATE THE WAY EVERYONE JUST ASSUMES I CAN DO STUFF LIKE THIS, COLONEL. SUPER-STRENGTH COMES IN VARYING DEGREES, YOU KNOW. IT ISN'T JUST A GENERAL TERM FOR STRONG PEOPLE.
FOR ALL YOU KNOW, THIS TRAIN COULD SQUASH ME LIKE A BUG.
THAT'S A RISK I'M PREPARED TO TAKE, BABY.

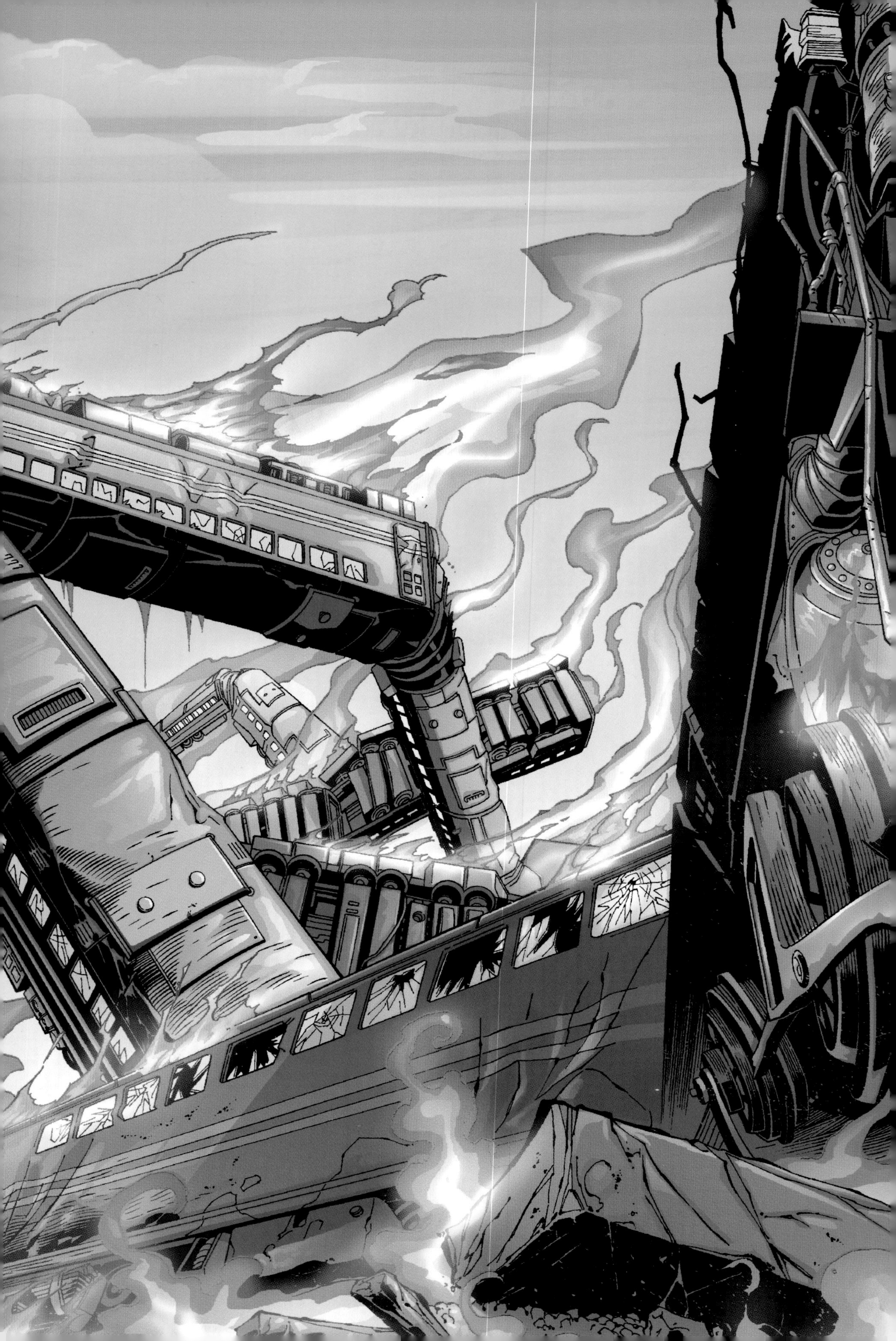

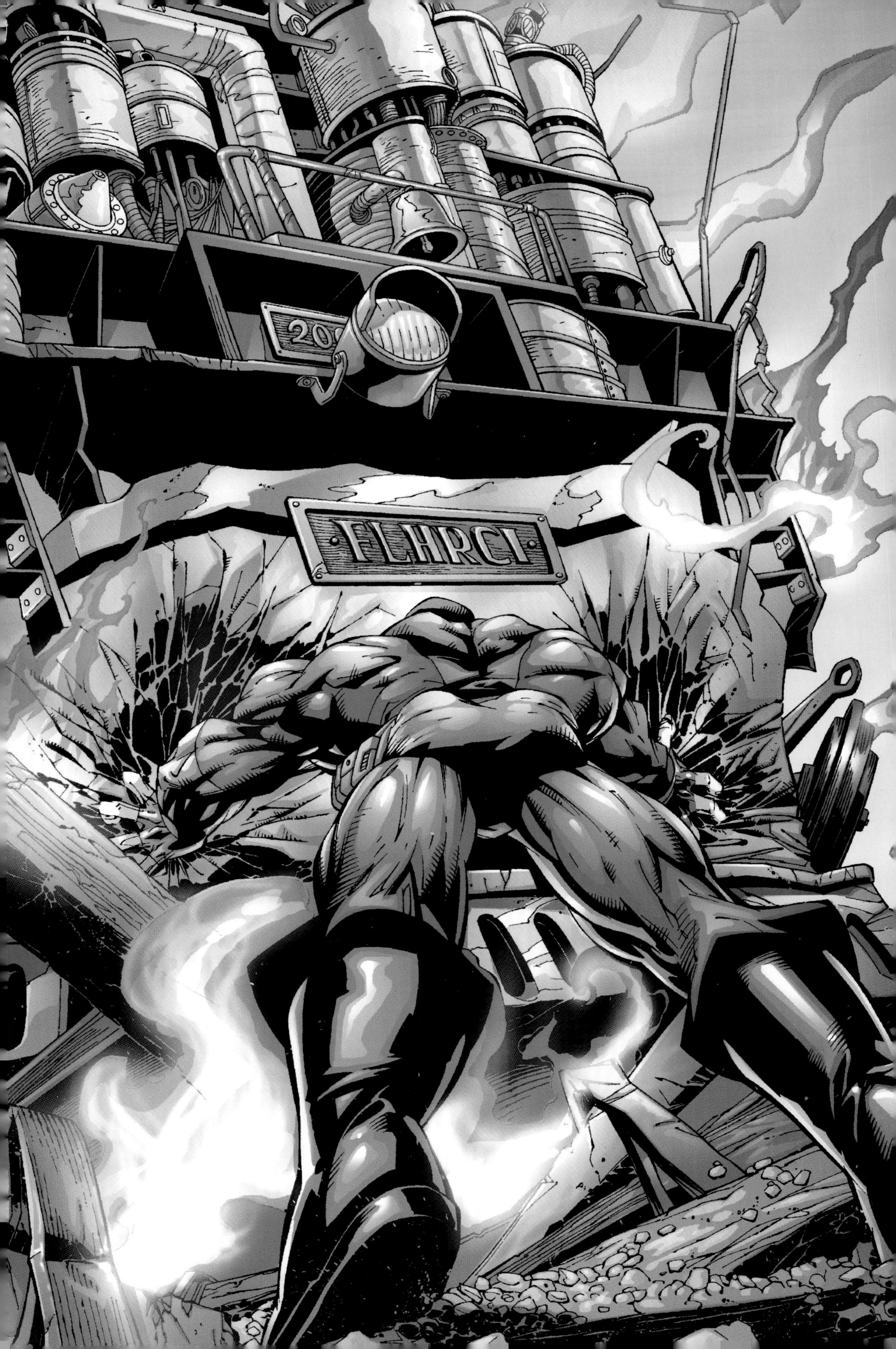
FLHRCI

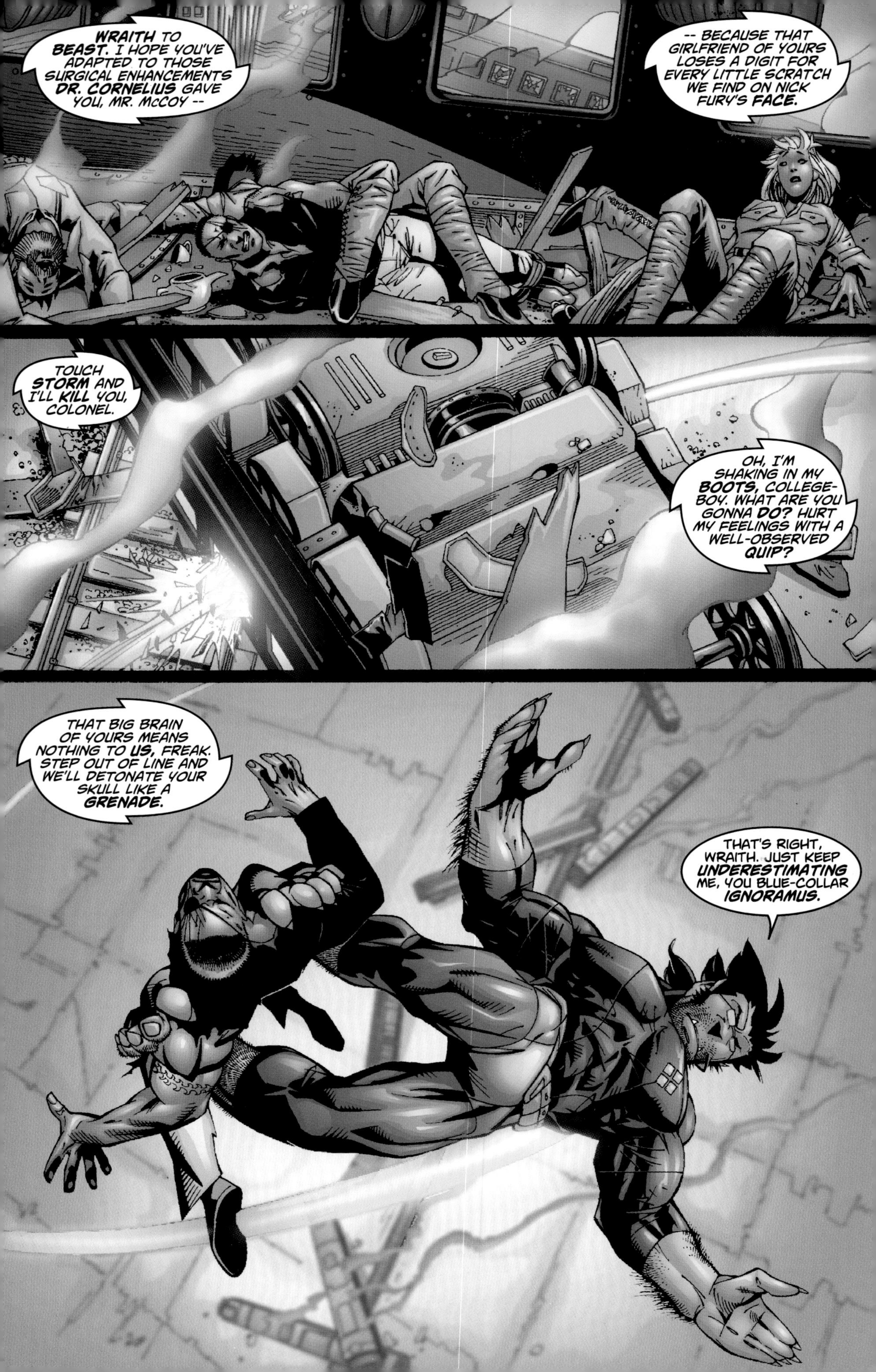
WRAITH TO BEAST. I HOPE YOU'VE ADAPTED TO THOSE SURGICAL ENHANCEMENTS DR. CORNELIUS GAVE YOU, MR. McCOY --
-- BECAUSE THAT GIRLFRIEND OF YOURS LOSES A DIGIT FOR EVERY LITTLE SCRATCH WE FIND ON NICK FURY'S FACE.
TOUCH STORM AND I'LL KILL YOU, COLONEL.
OH, I'M SHAKING IN MY BOOTS, COLLEGE-BOY. WHAT ARE YOU GONNA DO? HURT MY FEELINGS WITH A WELL-OBSERVED QUIP?
THAT BIG BRAIN OF YOURS MEANS NOTHING TO US, FREAK. STEP OUT OF LINE AND WE'LL DETONATE YOUR SKULL LIKE A GRENADE.
THAT'S RIGHT, WRAITH. JUST KEEP UNDERESTIMATING ME, YOU BLUE-COLLAR IGNORAMUS.

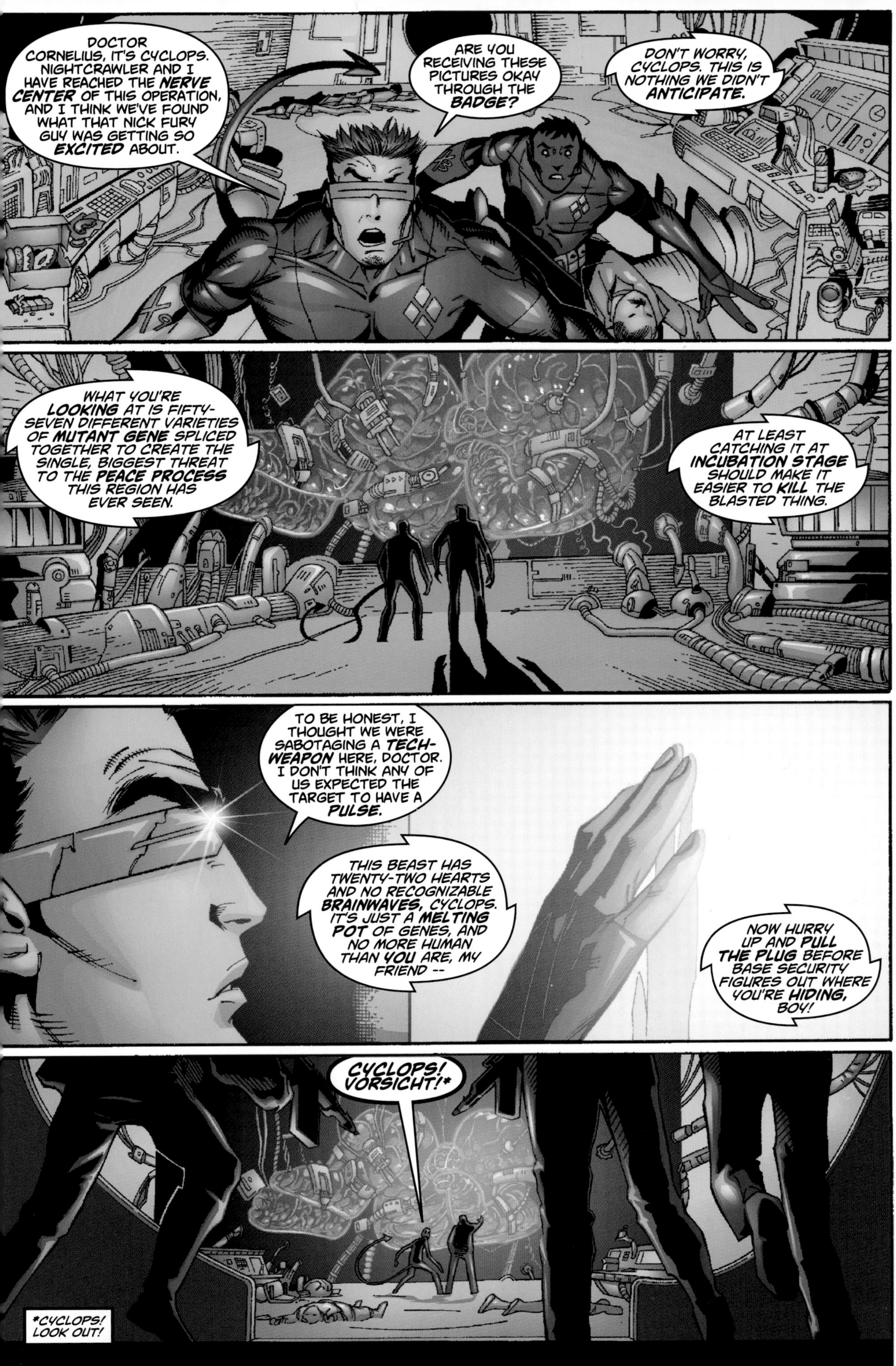
DOCTOR CORNELIUS, IT'S CYCLOPS. NIGHTCRAWLER AND I HAVE REACHED THE NERVE CENTER OF THIS OPERATION, AND I THINK WE'VE FOUND WHAT THAT NICK FURY GUY WAS GETTING SO EXCITED ABOUT.
ARE YOU RECEIVING THESE PICTURES OKAY THROUGH THE BADGE?
DON'T WORRY, CYCLOPS. THIS IS NOTHING WE DIDN'T ANTICIPATE.
WHAT YOU'RE LOOKING AT IS FIFTY-SEVEN DIFFERENT VARIETIES OF MUTANT GENE SPLICED TOGETHER TO CREATE THE SINGLE, BIGGEST THREAT TO THE PEACE PROCESS THIS REGION HAS EVER SEEN.
AT LEAST CATCHING IT AT INCUBATION STAGE SHOULD MAKE IT EASIER TO KILL THE BLASTED THING.
TO BE HONEST, I THOUGHT WE WERE SABOTAGING A TECH-WEAPON HERE, DOCTOR. I DON'T THINK ANY OF US EXPECTED THE TARGET TO HAVE A PULSE.
THIS BEAST HAS TWENTY-TWO HEARTS AND NO RECOGNIZABLE BRAINWAVES, CYCLOPS. IT'S JUST A MELTING POT OF GENES, AND NO MORE HUMAN THAN YOU ARE, MY FRIEND --
NOW HURRY UP AND PULL THE PLUG BEFORE BASE SECURITY FIGURES OUT WHERE YOU'RE HIDING, BOY!
CYCLOPS! VORSICHT!*
*CYCLOPS! LOOK OUT!

WHAT?

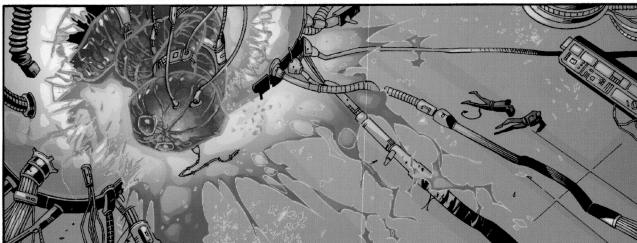

OH MY GOD!

WHAT ARE YOU WAITING FOR, NIGHTCRAWLER? GET US OUT OF HERE, MAN!

*HIT THE DETONATOR, YOU IDIOT! HIT IT!

DRUEK AUF DEN ASLOESER! DRUEK ES!*

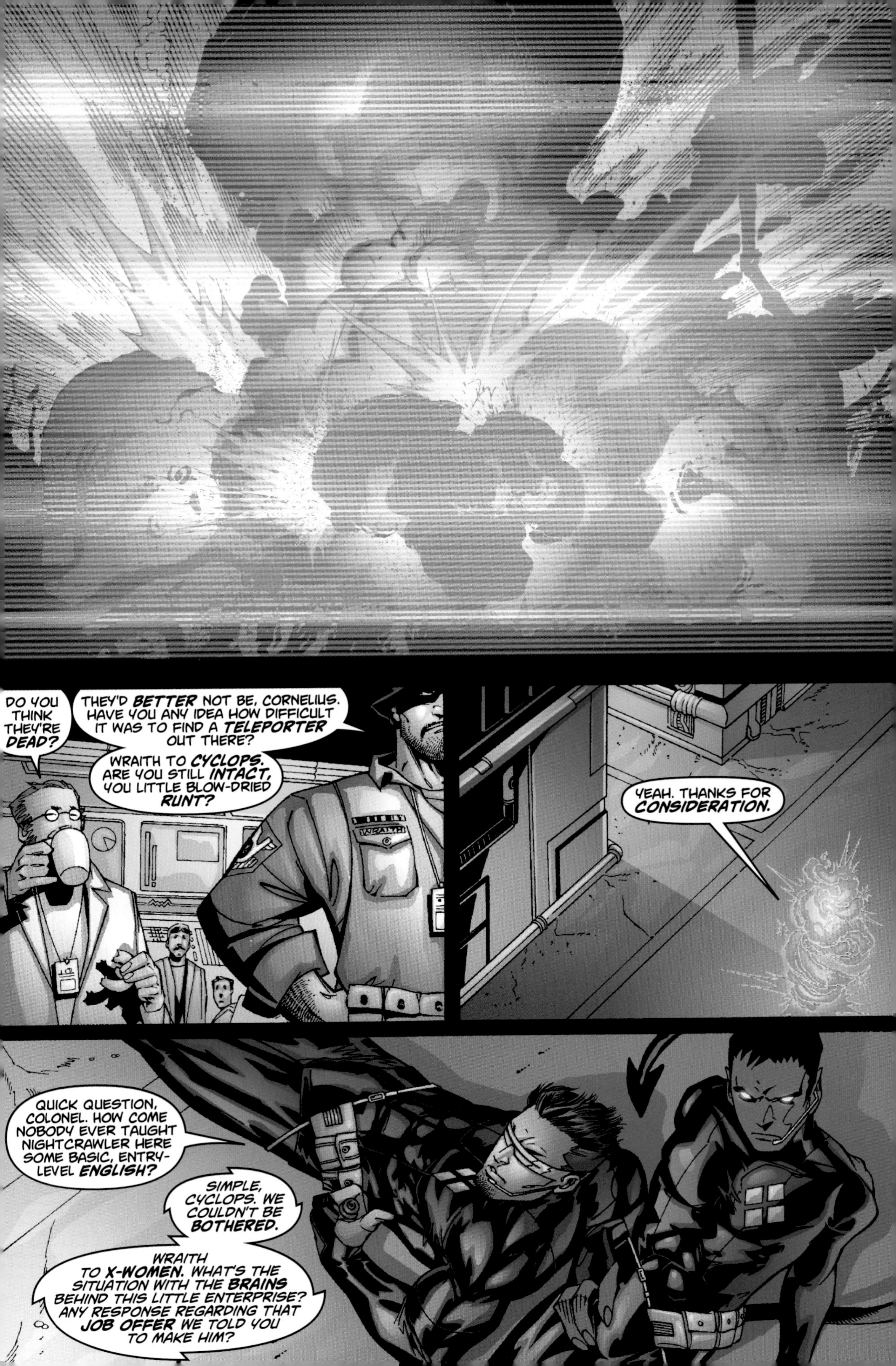
DO YOU THINK THEY'RE DEAD?
THEY'D BETTER NOT BE, CORNELIUS. HAVE YOU ANY IDEA HOW DIFFICULT IT WAS TO FIND A TELEPORTER OUT THERE?
WRAITH TO CYCLOPS. ARE YOU STILL INTACT, YOU LITTLE BLOW-DRIED RUNT?
WRAITH
YEAH. THANKS FOR CONSIDERATION.
QUICK QUESTION, COLONEL. HOW COME NOBODY EVER TAUGHT NIGHTCRAWLER HERE SOME BASIC, ENTRY-LEVEL ENGLISH?
SIMPLE, CYCLOPS. WE COULDN'T BE BOTHERED.
WRAITH TO X-WOMEN. WHAT'S THE SITUATION WITH THE BRAINS BEHIND THIS LITTLE ENTERPRISE? ANY RESPONSE REGARDING THAT JOB OFFER WE TOLD YOU TO MAKE HIM?

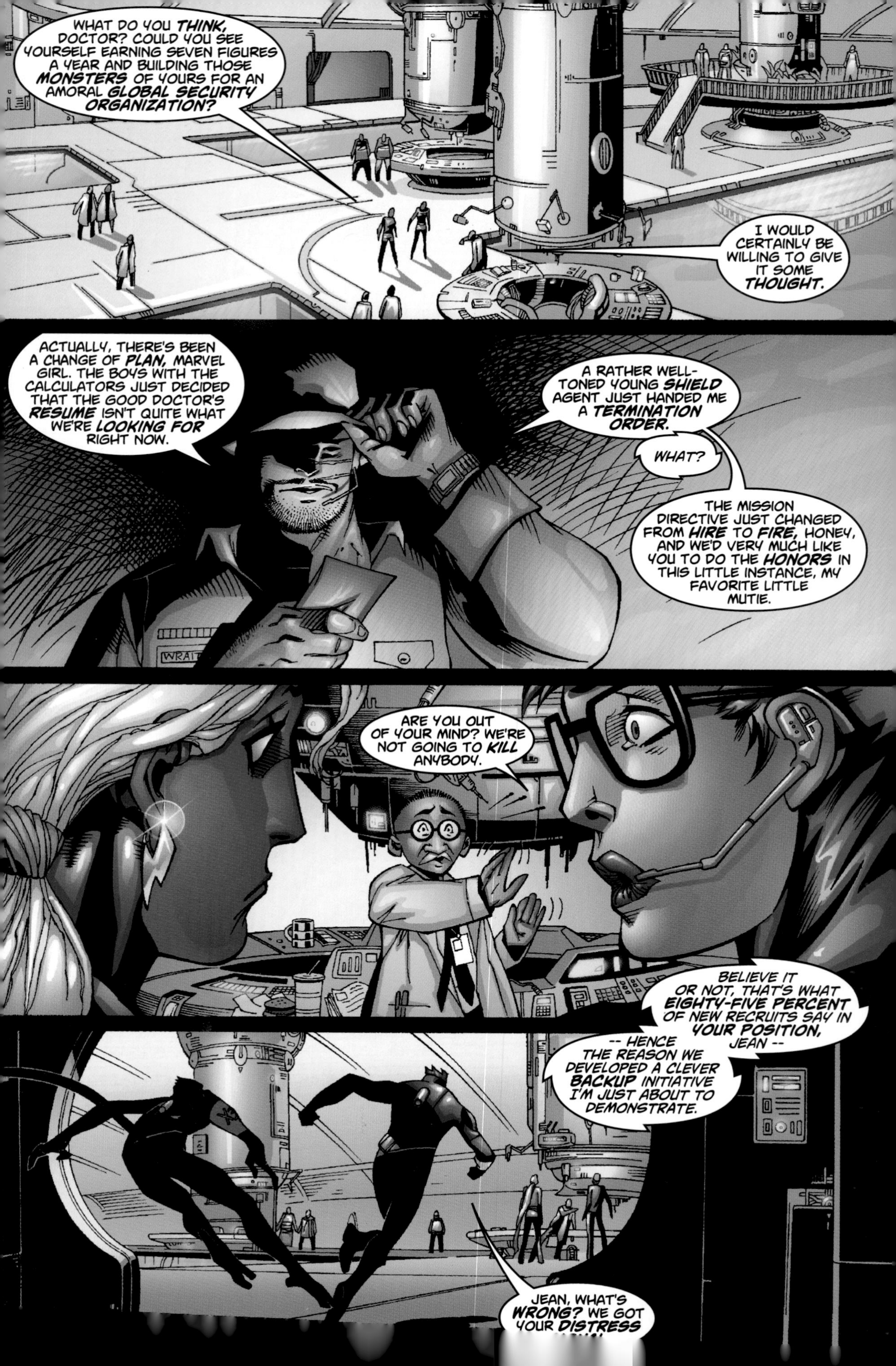
WHAT DO YOU THINK, DOCTOR? COULD YOU SEE YOURSELF EARNING SEVEN FIGURES A YEAR AND BUILDING THOSE MONSTERS OF YOURS FOR AN AMORAL GLOBAL SECURITY ORGANIZATION?
I WOULD CERTAINLY BE WILLING TO GIVE IT SOME THOUGHT.
ACTUALLY, THERE'S BEEN A CHANGE OF PLAN, MARVEL GIRL. THE BOYS WITH THE CALCULATORS JUST DECIDED THAT THE GOOD DOCTOR'S RESUME ISN'T QUITE WHAT WE'RE LOOKING FOR RIGHT NOW.
A RATHER WELL-TONED YOUNG SHIELD AGENT JUST HANDED ME A TERMINATION ORDER.
WHAT?
THE MISSION DIRECTIVE JUST CHANGED FROM HIRE TO FIRE, HONEY, AND WE'D VERY MUCH LIKE YOU TO DO THE HONORS IN THIS LITTLE INSTANCE, MY FAVORITE LITTLE MUTIE.
ARE YOU OUT OF YOUR MIND? WE'RE NOT GOING TO KILL ANYBODY.
BELIEVE IT OR NOT, THAT'S WHAT EIGHTY-FIVE PERCENT OF NEW RECRUITS SAY IN YOUR POSITION, JEAN --
-- HENCE THE REASON WE DEVELOPED A CLEVER BACKUP INITIATIVE I'M JUST ABOUT TO DEMONSTRATE.
JEAN, WHAT'S WRONG? WE GOT YOUR DISTRESS

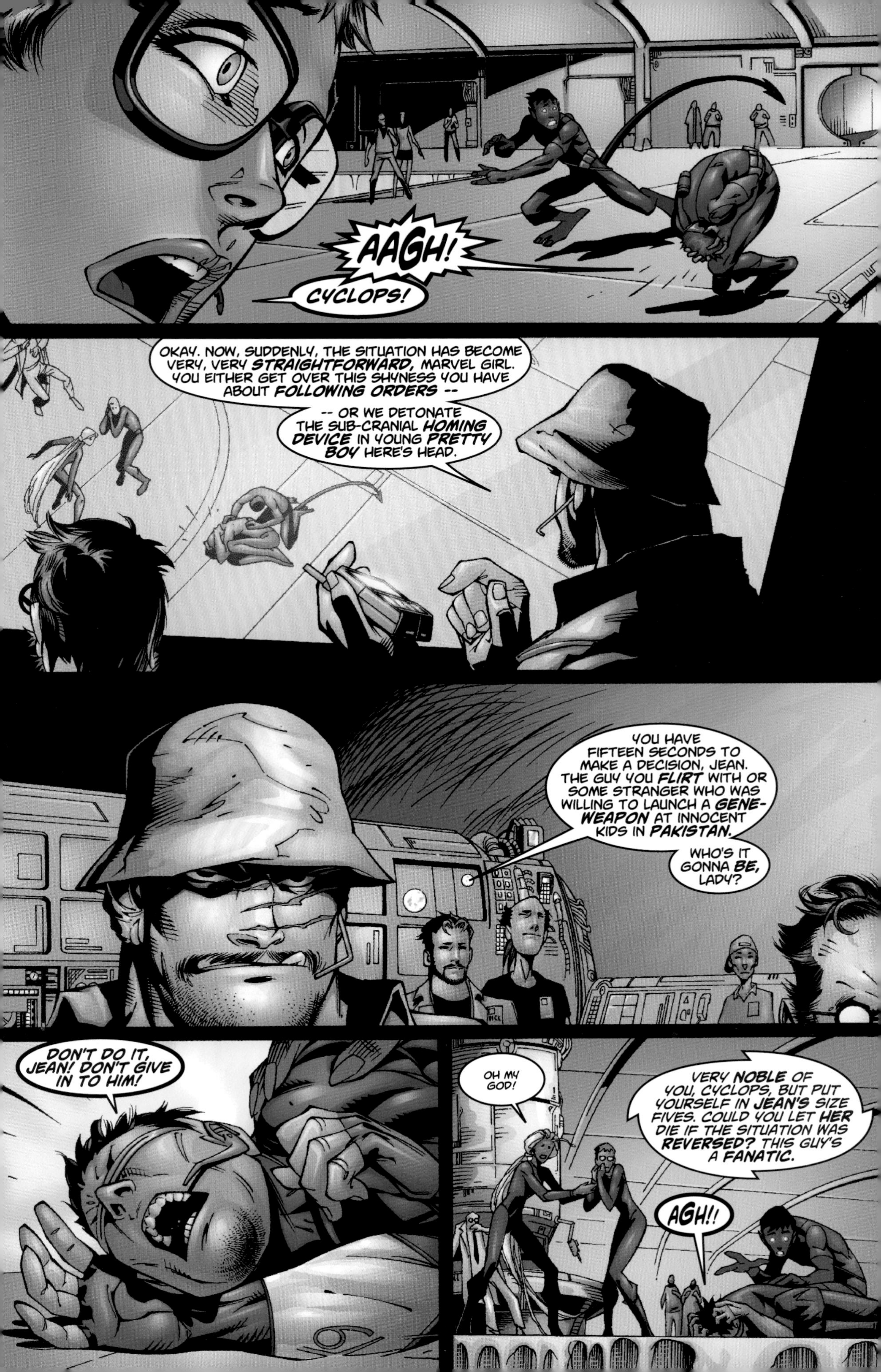
AAGH!
CYCLOPS!
OKAY. NOW, SUDDENLY, THE SITUATION HAS BECOME VERY, VERY STRAIGHTFORWARD, MARVEL GIRL. YOU EITHER GET OVER THIS SHYNESS YOU HAVE ABOUT FOLLOWING ORDERS --
-- OR WE DETONATE THE SUB-CRANIAL HOMING DEVICE IN YOUNG PRETTY BOY HERE'S HEAD.
YOU HAVE FIFTEEN SECONDS TO MAKE A DECISION, JEAN. THE GUY YOU FLIRT WITH OR SOME STRANGER WHO WAS WILLING TO LAUNCH A GENE-WEAPON AT INNOCENT KIDS IN PAKISTAN.
WHO'S IT GONNA BE, LADY?
DON'T DO IT, JEAN! DON'T GIVE IN TO HIM!
OH MY GOD!
VERY NOBLE OF YOU, CYCLOPS, BUT PUT YOURSELF IN JEAN'S SIZE FIVES. COULD YOU LET HER DIE IF THE SITUATION WAS REVERSED? THIS GUY'S A FANATIC.
AGH!!

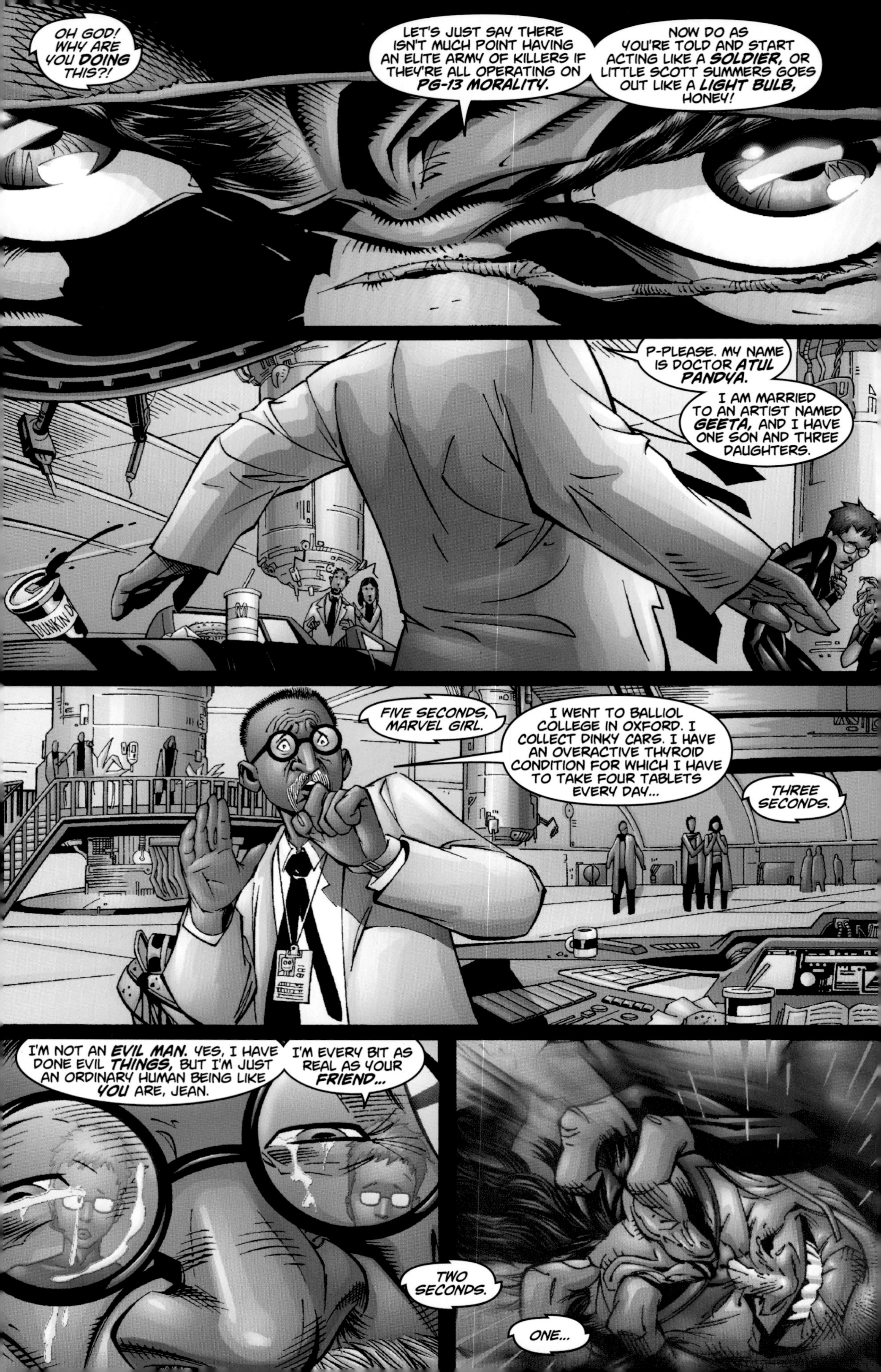
OH GOD! WHY ARE YOU DOING THIS?!
LET'S JUST SAY THERE ISN'T MUCH POINT HAVING AN ELITE ARMY OF KILLERS IF THEY'RE ALL OPERATING ON PG-13 MORALITY.
NOW DO AS YOU'RE TOLD AND START ACTING LIKE A SOLDIER, OR LITTLE SCOTT SUMMERS GOES OUT LIKE A LIGHT BULB, HONEY!
P-PLEASE. MY NAME IS DOCTOR ATUL PANDYA.
I AM MARRIED TO AN ARTIST NAMED GEETA, AND I HAVE ONE SON AND THREE DAUGHTERS.
FIVE SECONDS, MARVEL GIRL.
I WENT TO BALLIOL COLLEGE IN OXFORD. I COLLECT DINKY CARS. I HAVE AN OVERACTIVE THYROID CONDITION FOR WHICH I HAVE TO TAKE FOUR TABLETS EVERY DAY...
THREE SECONDS.
I'M NOT AN EVIL MAN. YES, I HAVE DONE EVIL THINGS, BUT I'M JUST AN ORDINARY HUMAN BEING LIKE YOU ARE, JEAN.
I'M EVERY BIT AS REAL AS YOUR FRIEND...
TWO SECONDS.
ONE...

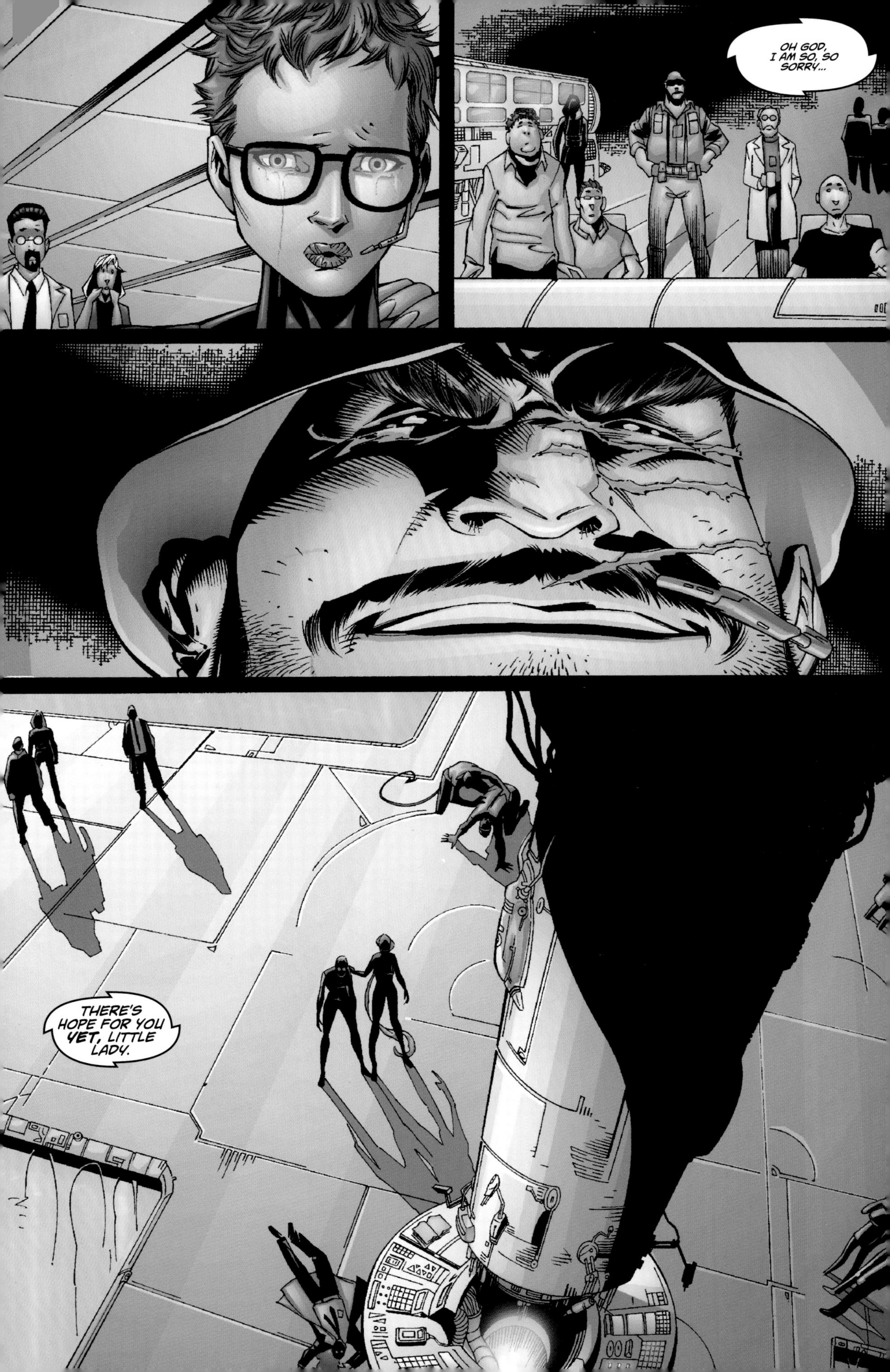
OH GOD, I AM SO, SO SORRY...
THERE'S HOPE FOR YOU YET, LITTLE LADY.

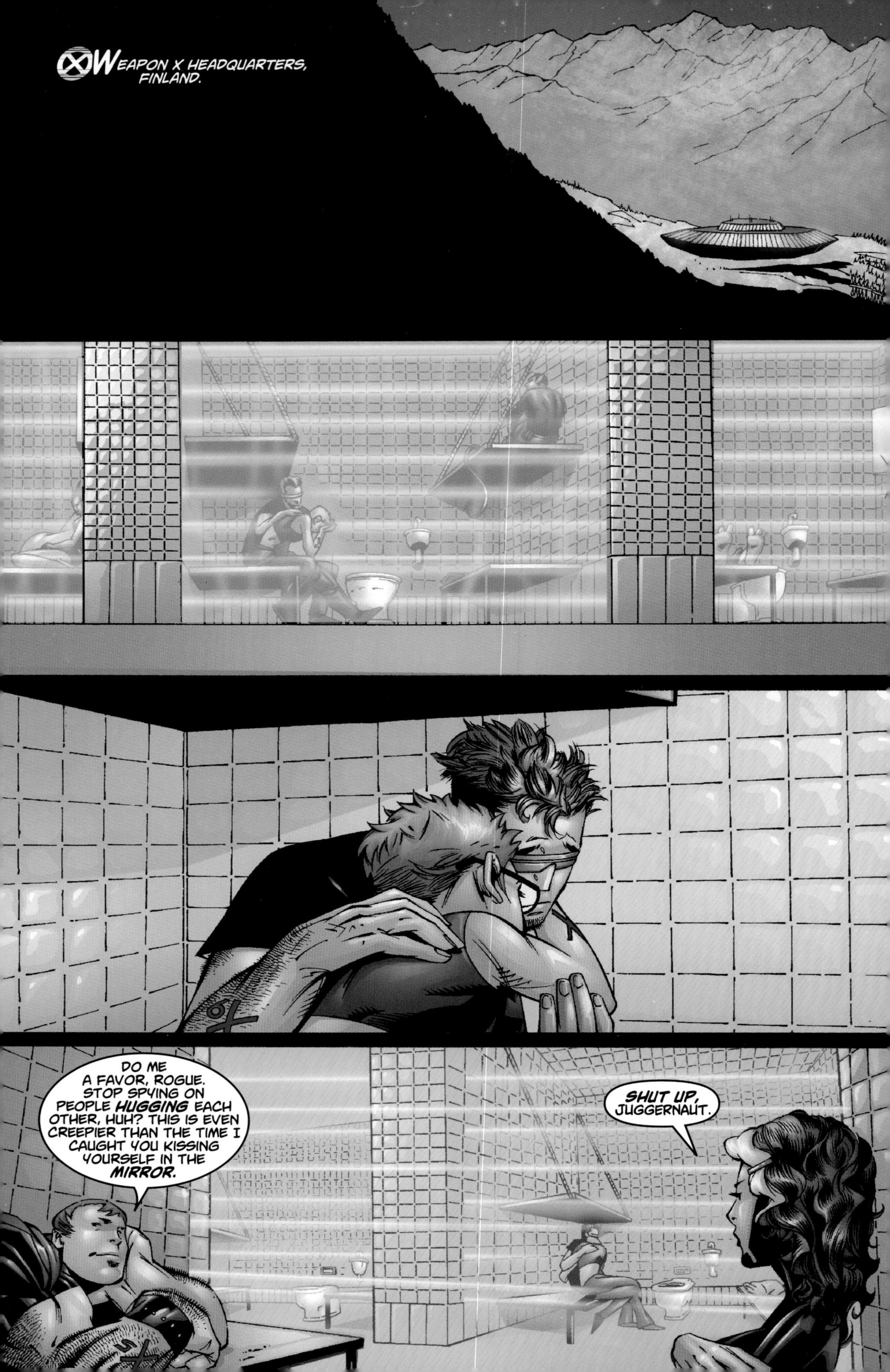
WEAPON X HEADQUARTERS, FINLAND.
DO ME A FAVOR, ROGUE. STOP SPYING ON PEOPLE HUGGING EACH OTHER, HUH? THIS IS EVEN CREEPIER THAN THE TIME I CAUGHT YOU KISSING YOURSELF IN THE MIRROR.
SHUT UP, JUGGERNAUT.

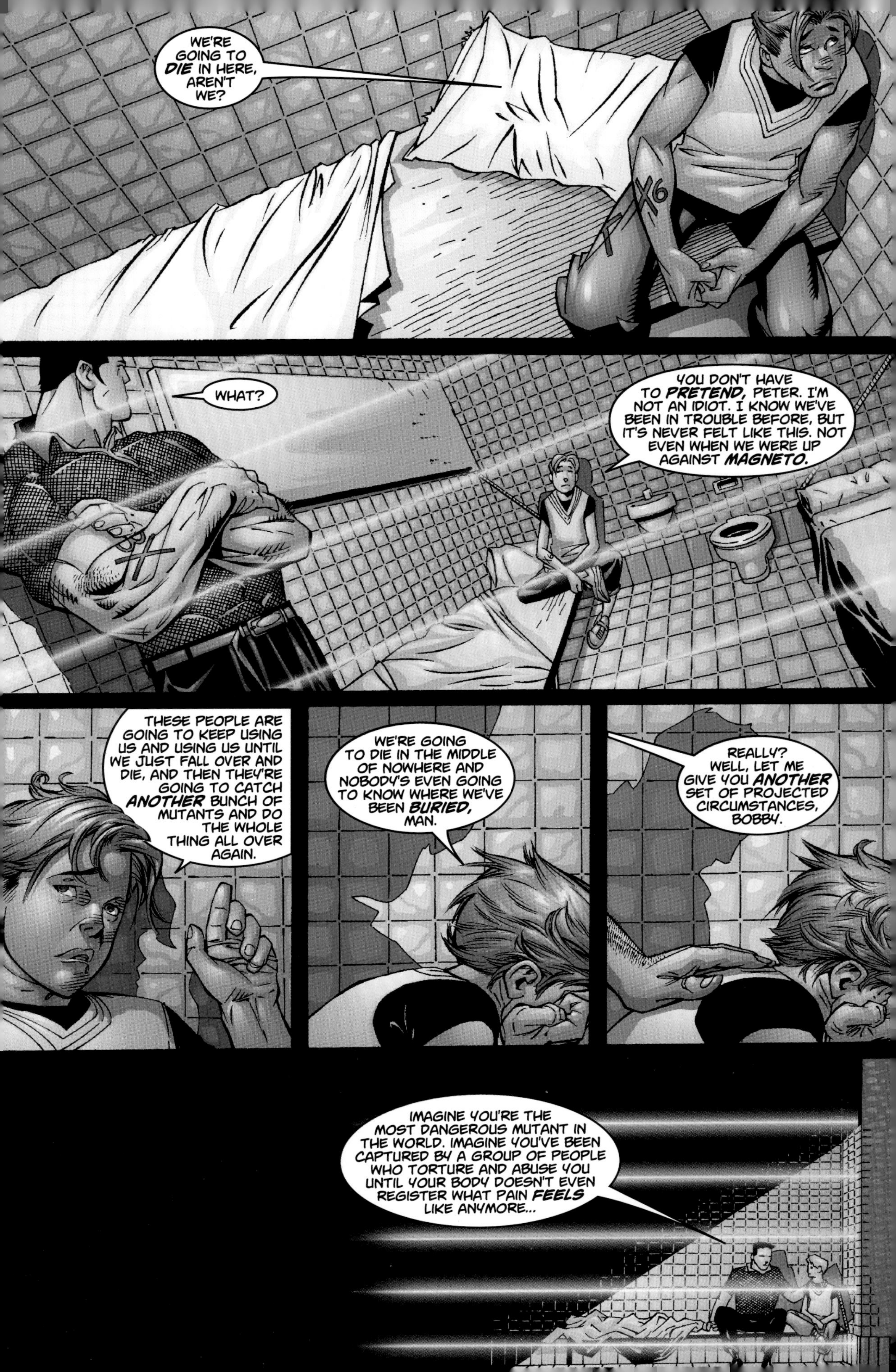

WE'RE GOING TO DIE IN HERE, AREN'T WE?
WHAT?
YOU DON'T HAVE TO PRETEND, PETER. I'M NOT AN IDIOT. I KNOW WE'VE BEEN IN TROUBLE BEFORE, BUT IT'S NEVER FELT LIKE THIS. NOT EVEN WHEN WE WERE UP AGAINST MAGNETO.
THESE PEOPLE ARE GOING TO KEEP USING US AND USING US UNTIL WE JUST FALL OVER AND DIE, AND THEN THEY'RE GOING TO CATCH ANOTHER BUNCH OF MUTANTS AND DO THE WHOLE THING ALL OVER AGAIN.
WE'RE GOING TO DIE IN THE MIDDLE OF NOWHERE AND NOBODY'S EVEN GOING TO KNOW WHERE WE'VE BEEN BURIED, MAN.
REALLY? WELL, LET ME GIVE YOU ANOTHER SET OF PROJECTED CIRCUMSTANCES, BOBBY.
IMAGINE YOU'RE THE MOST DANGEROUS MUTANT IN THE WORLD. IMAGINE YOU'VE BEEN CAPTURED BY A GROUP OF PEOPLE WHO TORTURE AND ABUSE YOU UNTIL YOUR BODY DOESN'T EVEN REGISTER WHAT PAIN FEELS LIKE ANYMORE...

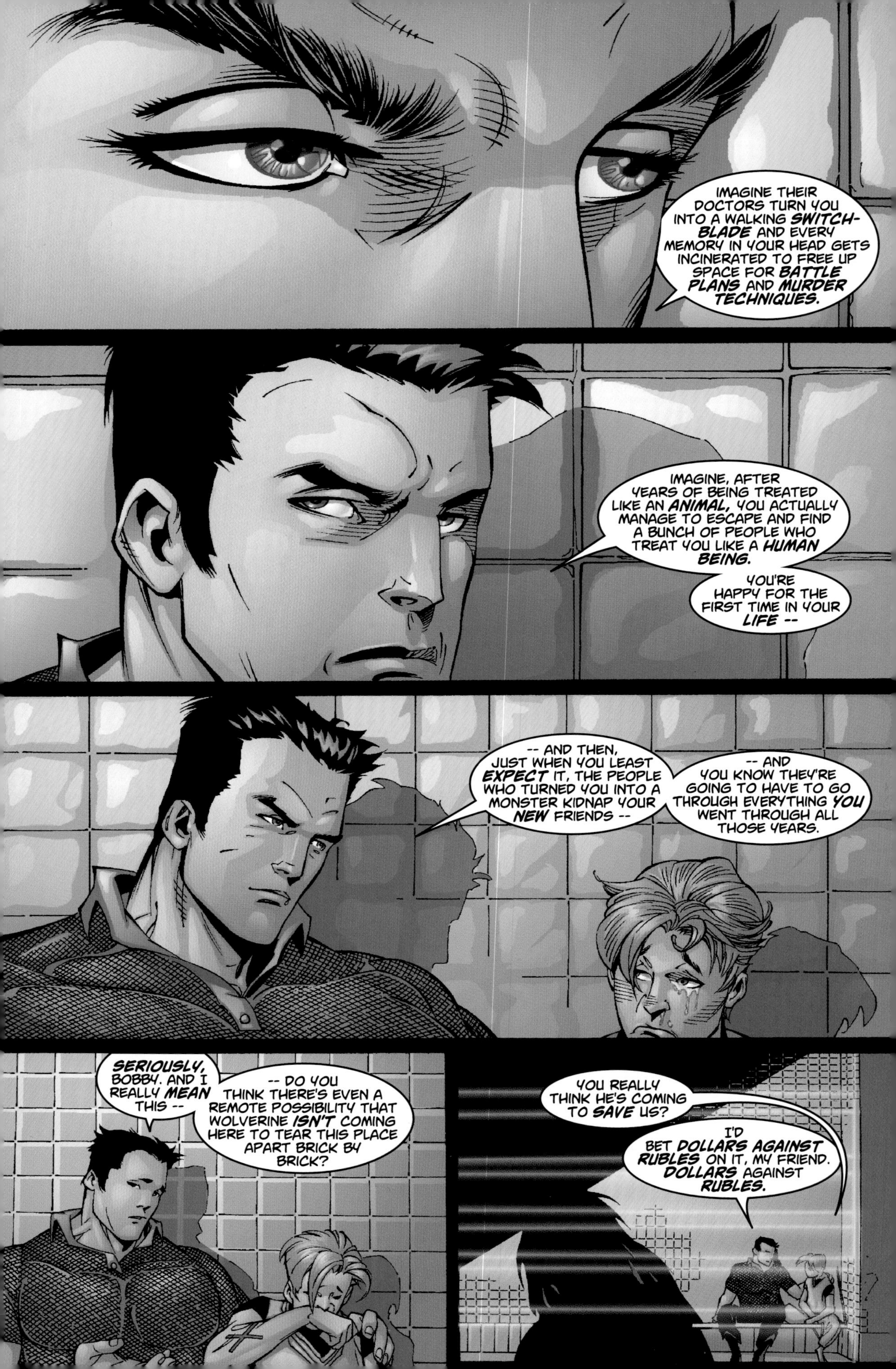
IMAGINE THEIR DOCTORS TURN YOU INTO A WALKING SWITCH-BLADE AND EVERY MEMORY IN YOUR HEAD GETS INCINERATED TO FREE UP SPACE FOR BATTLE PLANS AND MURDER TECHNIQUES.
IMAGINE, AFTER YEARS OF BEING TREATED LIKE AN ANIMAL, YOU ACTUALLY MANAGE TO ESCAPE AND FIND A BUNCH OF PEOPLE WHO TREAT YOU LIKE A HUMAN BEING.
YOU'RE HAPPY FOR THE FIRST TIME IN YOUR LIFE --
-- AND THEN, JUST WHEN YOU LEAST EXPECT IT, THE PEOPLE WHO TURNED YOU INTO A MONSTER KIDNAP YOUR NEW FRIENDS --
-- AND YOU KNOW THEY'RE GOING TO HAVE TO GO THROUGH EVERYTHING YOU WENT THROUGH ALL THOSE YEARS.
SERIOUSLY, BOBBY. AND I REALLY MEAN THIS --
-- DO YOU THINK THERE'S EVEN A REMOTE POSSIBILITY THAT WOLVERINE ISN'T COMING HERE TO TEAR THIS PLACE APART BRICK BY BRICK?
YOU REALLY THINK HE'S COMING TO SAVE US?
I'D BET DOLLARS AGAINST RUBLES ON IT, MY FRIEND. DOLLARS AGAINST RUBLES.

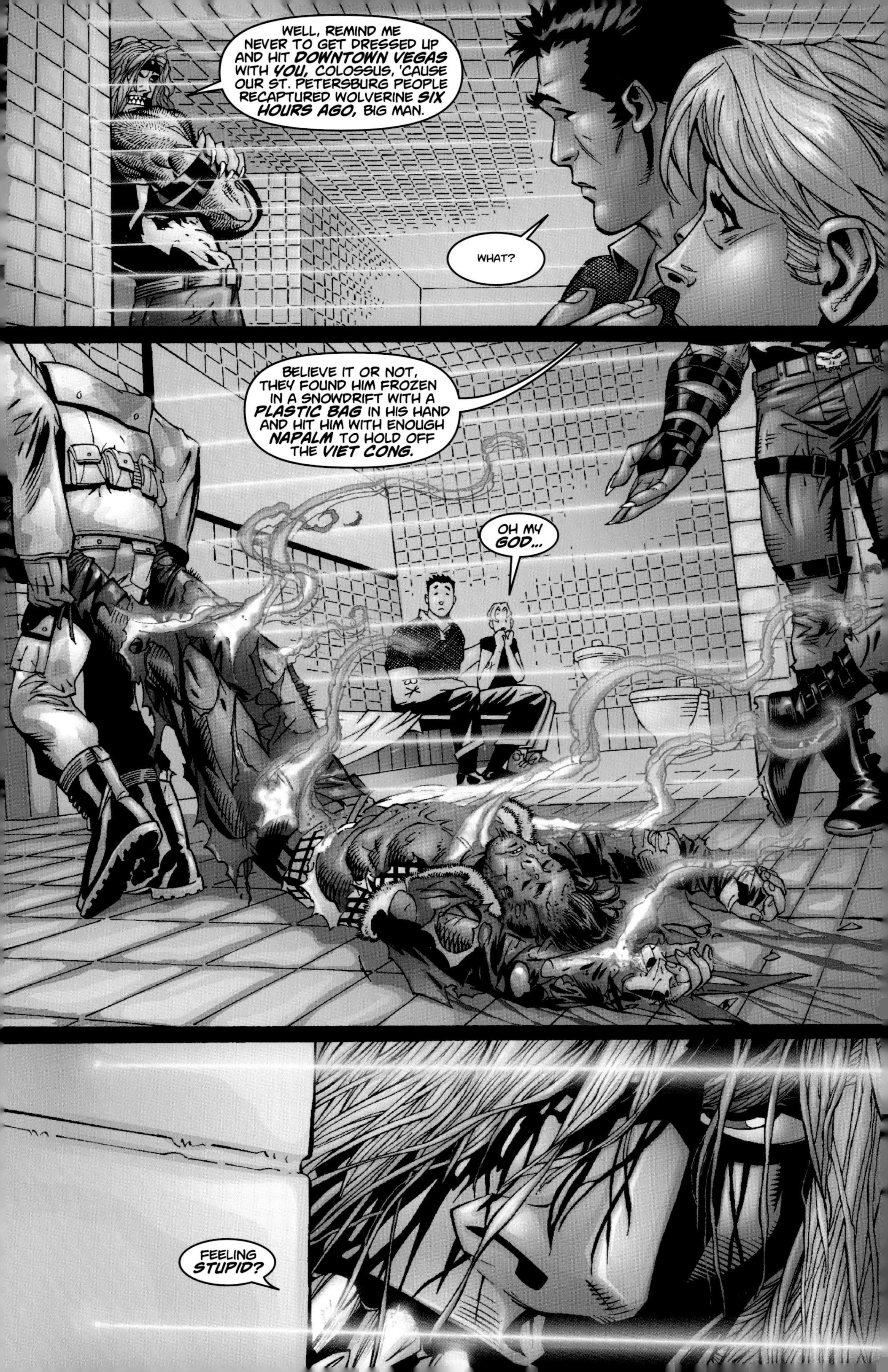
WELL, REMIND ME NEVER TO GET DRESSED UP AND HIT DOWNTOWN VEGAS WITH YOU, COLOSSUS, 'CAUSE OUR ST. PETERSBURG PEOPLE RECAPTURED WOLVERINE SIX HOURS AGO, BIG MAN.
WHAT?
BELIEVE IT OR NOT, THEY FOUND HIM FROZEN IN A SNOWDRIFT WITH A PLASTIC BAG IN HIS HAND AND HIT HIM WITH ENOUGH NAPALM TO HOLD OFF THE VIET CONG.
OH MY GOD...
FEELING STUPID?

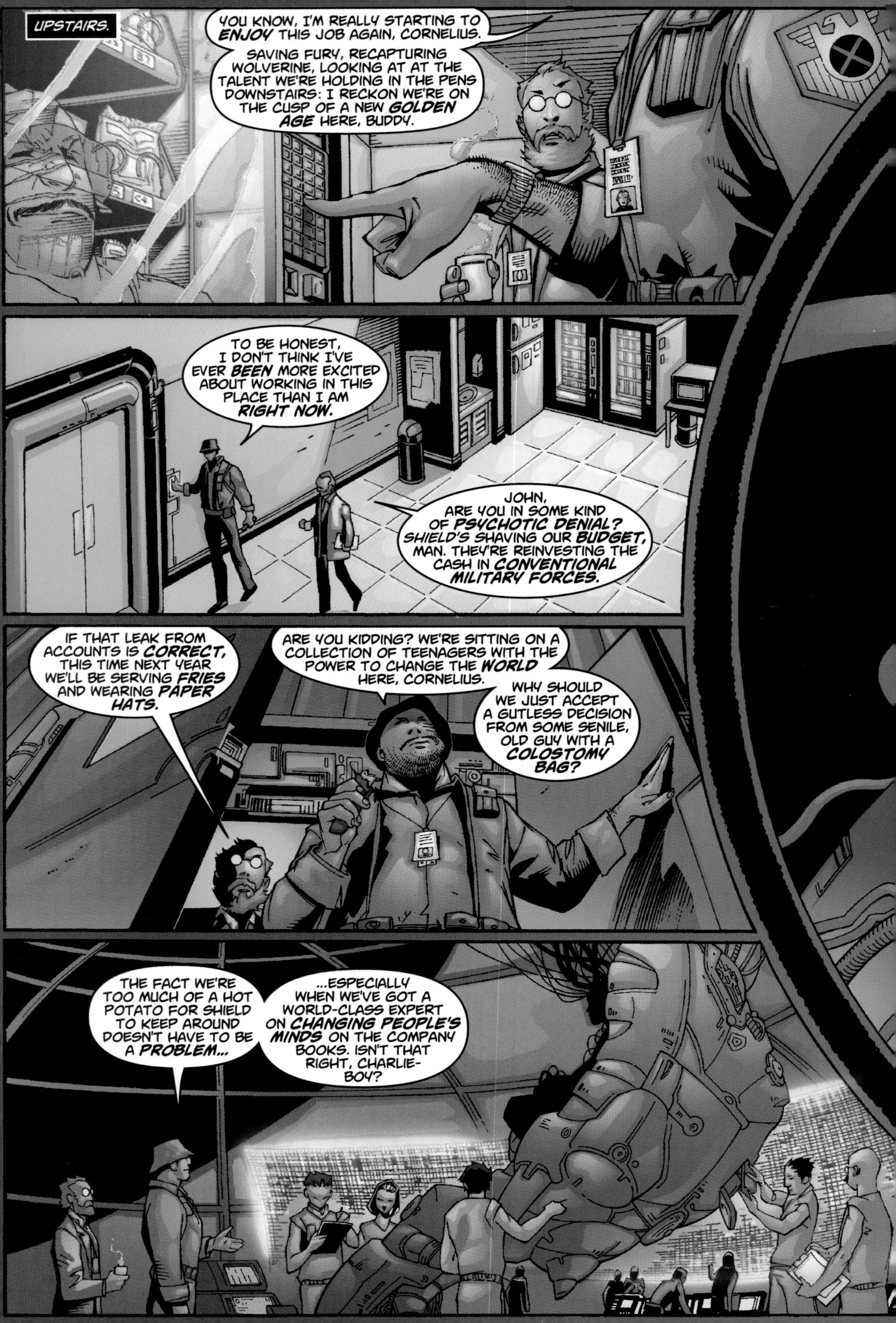
UPSTAIRS.
YOU KNOW, I'M REALLY STARTING TO ENJOY THIS JOB AGAIN, CORNELIUS.
SAVING FURY, RECAPTURING WOLVERINE, LOOKING AT AT THE TALENT WE'RE HOLDING IN THE PENS DOWNSTAIRS: I RECKON WE'RE ON THE CUSP OF A NEW GOLDEN AGE HERE, BUDDY.
TO BE HONEST, I DON'T THINK I'VE EVER BEEN MORE EXCITED ABOUT WORKING IN THIS PLACE THAN I AM RIGHT NOW.
JOHN, ARE YOU IN SOME KIND OF PSYCHOTIC DENIAL? SHIELD'S SHAVING OUR BUDGET, MAN. THEY'RE REINVESTING THE CASH IN CONVENTIONAL MILITARY FORCES.
IF THAT LEAK FROM ACCOUNTS IS CORRECT, THIS TIME NEXT YEAR WE'LL BE SERVING FRIES AND WEARING PAPER HATS.
ARE YOU KIDDING? WE'RE SITTING ON A COLLECTION OF TEENAGERS WITH THE POWER TO CHANGE THE WORLD HERE, CORNELIUS.
WHY SHOULD WE JUST ACCEPT A GUTLESS DECISION FROM SOME SENILE, OLD GUY WITH A COLOSTOMY BAG?
THE FACT WE'RE TOO MUCH OF A HOT POTATO FOR SHIELD TO KEEP AROUND DOESN'T HAVE TO BE A PROBLEM...
...ESPECIALLY WHEN WE'VE GOT A WORLD-CLASS EXPERT ON CHANGING PEOPLE'S MINDS ON THE COMPANY BOOKS. ISN'T THAT RIGHT, CHARLIE-BOY?

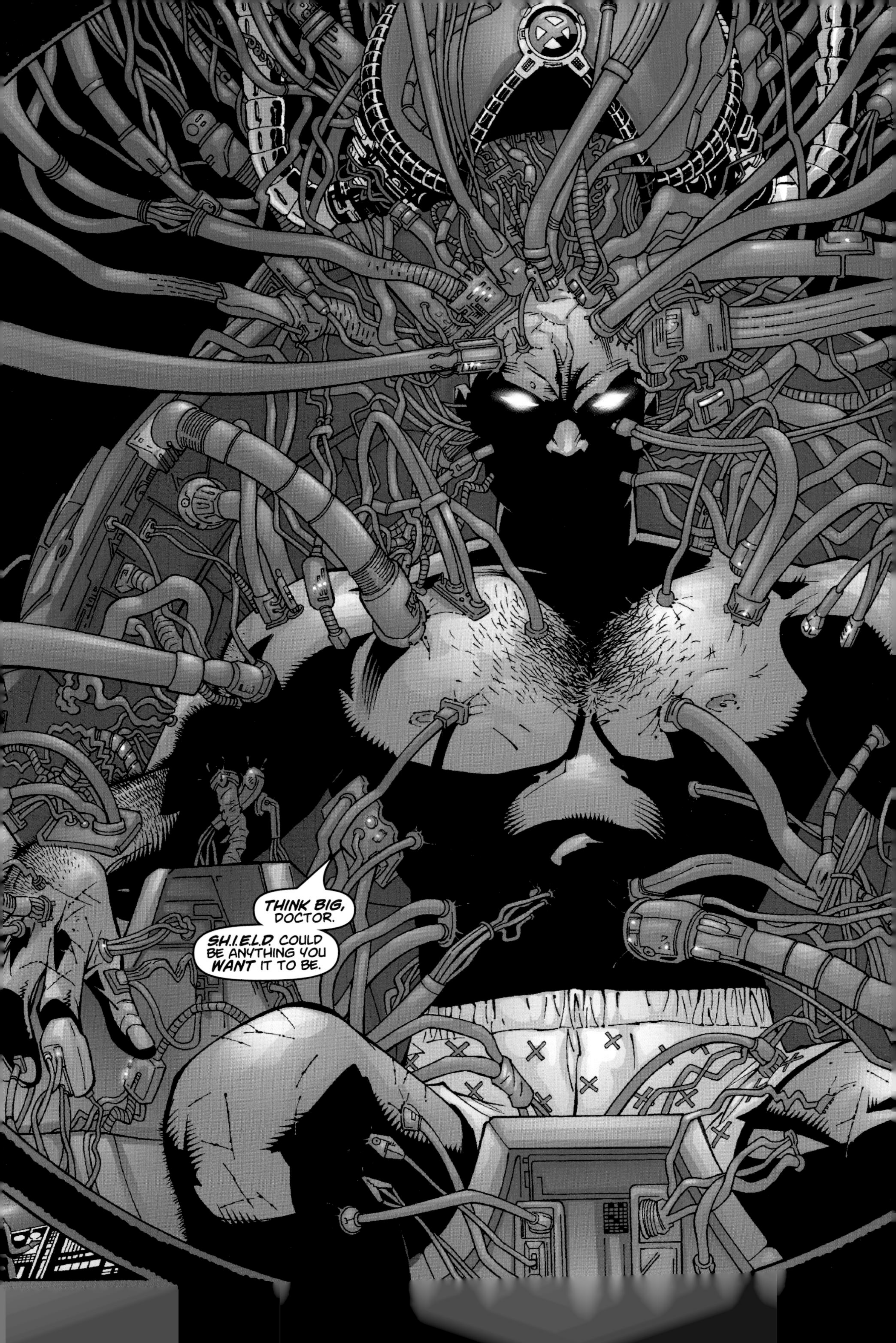
THINK BIG, DOCTOR.
S.H.I.E.L.D COULD BE ANYTHING YOU WANT IT TO BE.

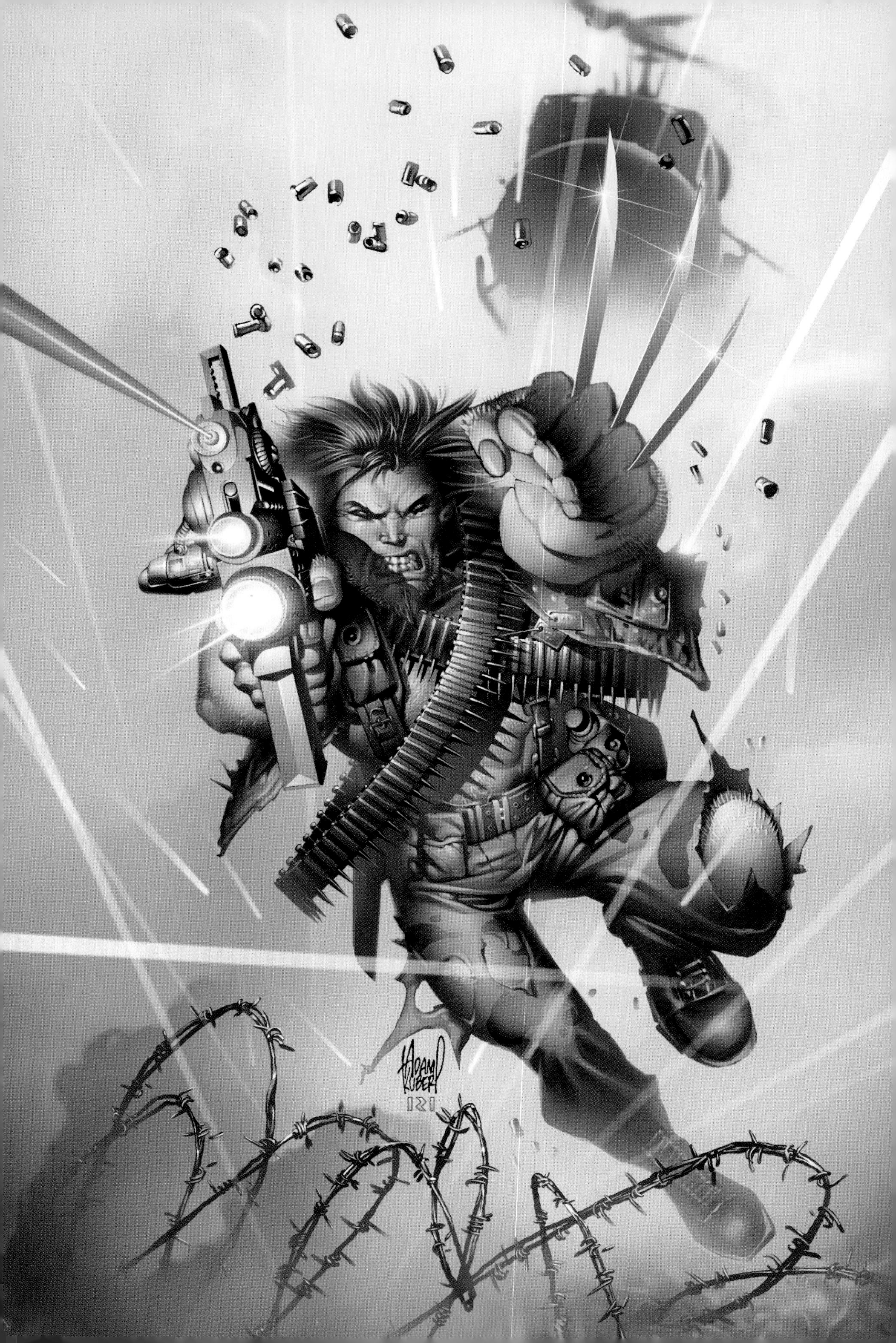

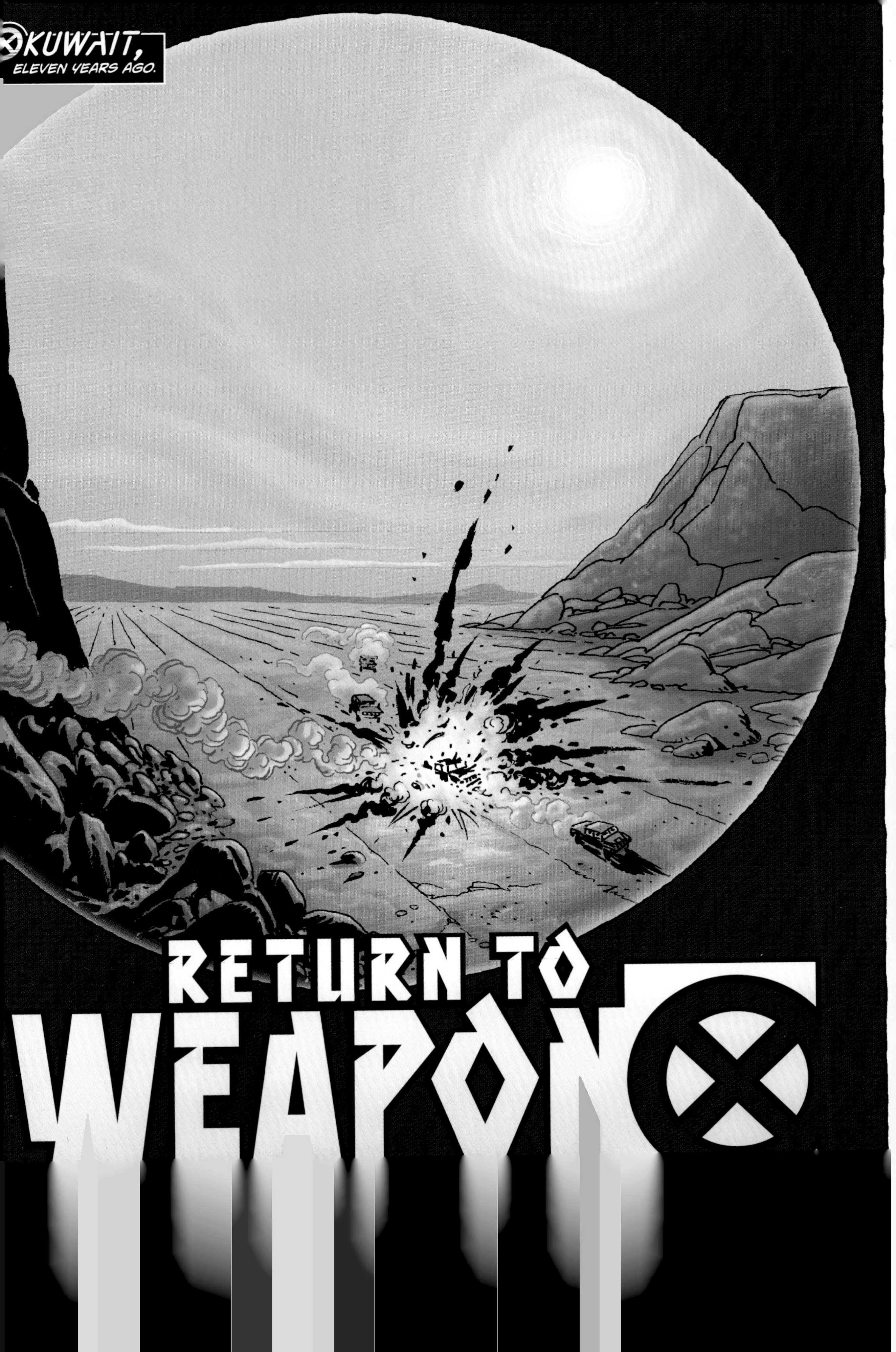
KUWAIT,
ELEVEN YEARS AGO.
RETURN TO
WEAPON X

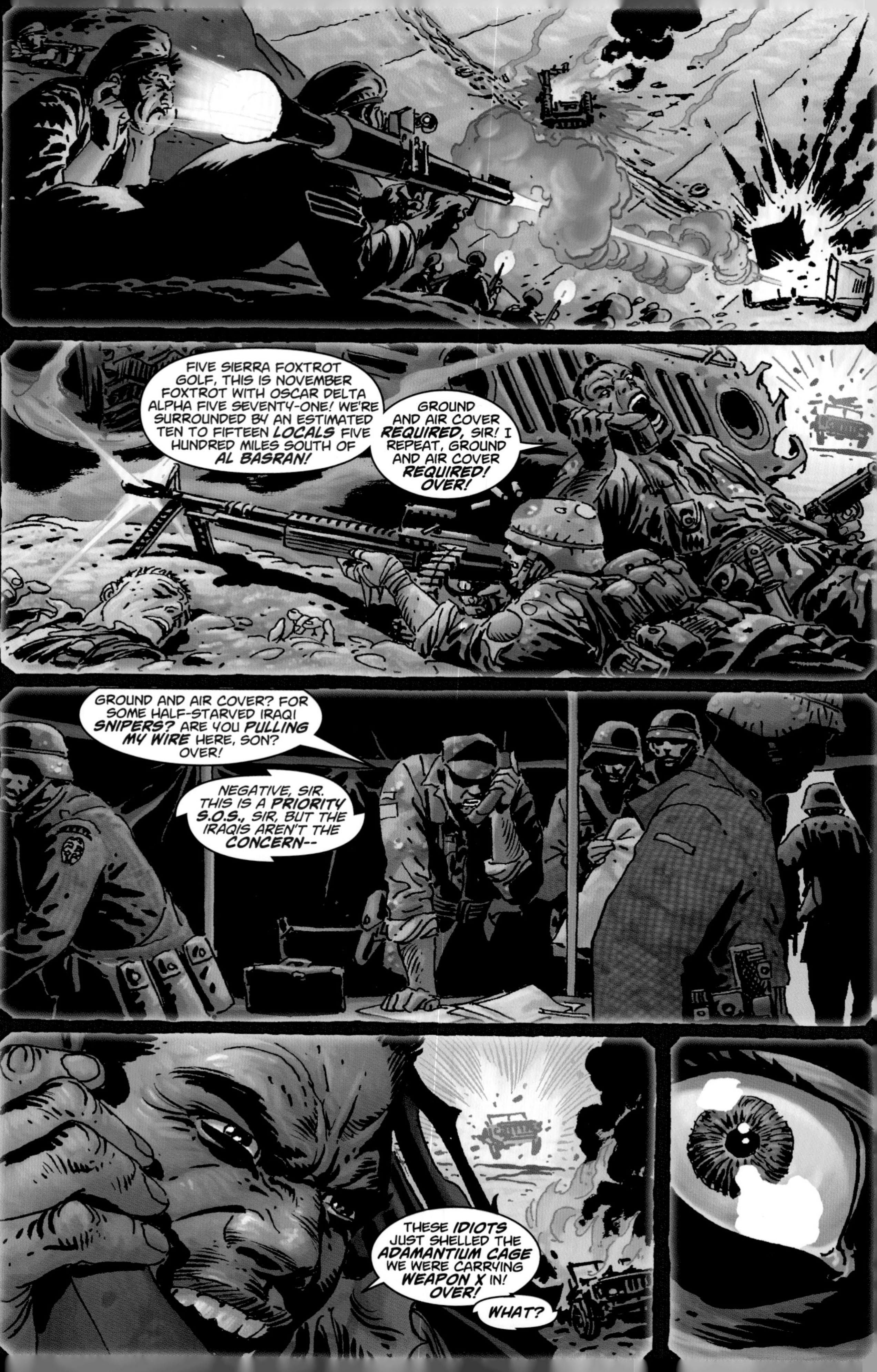
FIVE SIERRA FOXTROT GOLF, THIS IS NOVEMBER FOXTROT WITH OSCAR DELTA ALPHA FIVE SEVENTY-ONE! WE'RE SURROUNDED BY AN ESTIMATED TEN TO FIFTEEN LOCALS FIVE HUNDRED MILES SOUTH OF AL BASRAN!
GROUND AND AIR COVER REQUIRED, SIR! I REPEAT, GROUND AND AIR COVER REQUIRED! OVER!
GROUND AND AIR COVER? FOR SOME HALF-STARVED IRAQI SNIPERS? ARE YOU PULLING MY WIRE HERE, SON? OVER!
NEGATIVE, SIR. THIS IS A PRIORITY S.O.S., SIR, BUT THE IRAQIS AREN'T THE CONCERN--
THESE IDIOTS JUST SHELLED THE ADAMANTIUM CAGE WE WERE CARRYING WEAPON X IN! OVER!
WHAT?

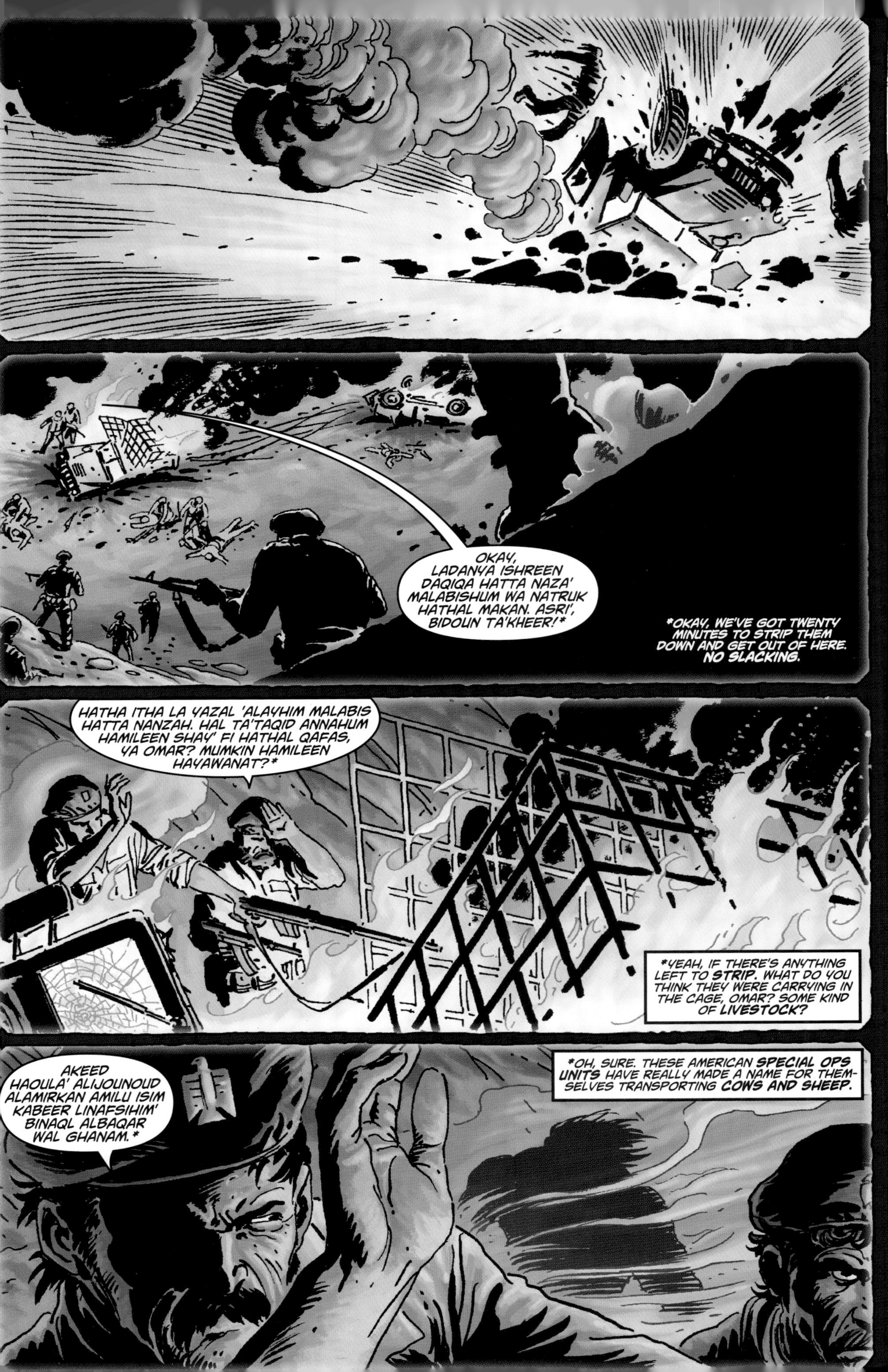
OKAY, LADANYA ISHREEN DAQIQA HATTA NAZA' MALABISHUM WA NATRUK HATHAL MAKAN. ASRI', BIDOUN TA'KHEER!*
*OKAY, WE'VE GOT TWENTY MINUTES TO STRIP THEM DOWN AND GET OUT OF HERE. NO SLACKING.
HATHA ITHA LA YAZAL 'ALAYHIM MALABIS HATTA NANZAH. HAL TA'TAQID ANNAHUM HAMILEEN SHAY' FI HATHAL QAFAS, YA OMAR? MUMKIN HAMILEEN HAYAWANAT?*
*YEAH, IF THERE'S ANYTHING LEFT TO STRIP. WHAT DO YOU THINK THEY WERE CARRYING IN THE CAGE, OMAR? SOME KIND OF LIVESTOCK?
AKEED HAOULA' ALIJOUNOUD ALAMIRKAN AMILU ISIM KABEER LINAFSIHIM' BINAQL ALBAQAR WAL GHANAM.*
*OH, SURE. THESE AMERICAN SPECIAL OPS UNITS HAVE REALLY MADE A NAME FOR THEMSELVES TRANSPORTING COWS AND SHEEP.

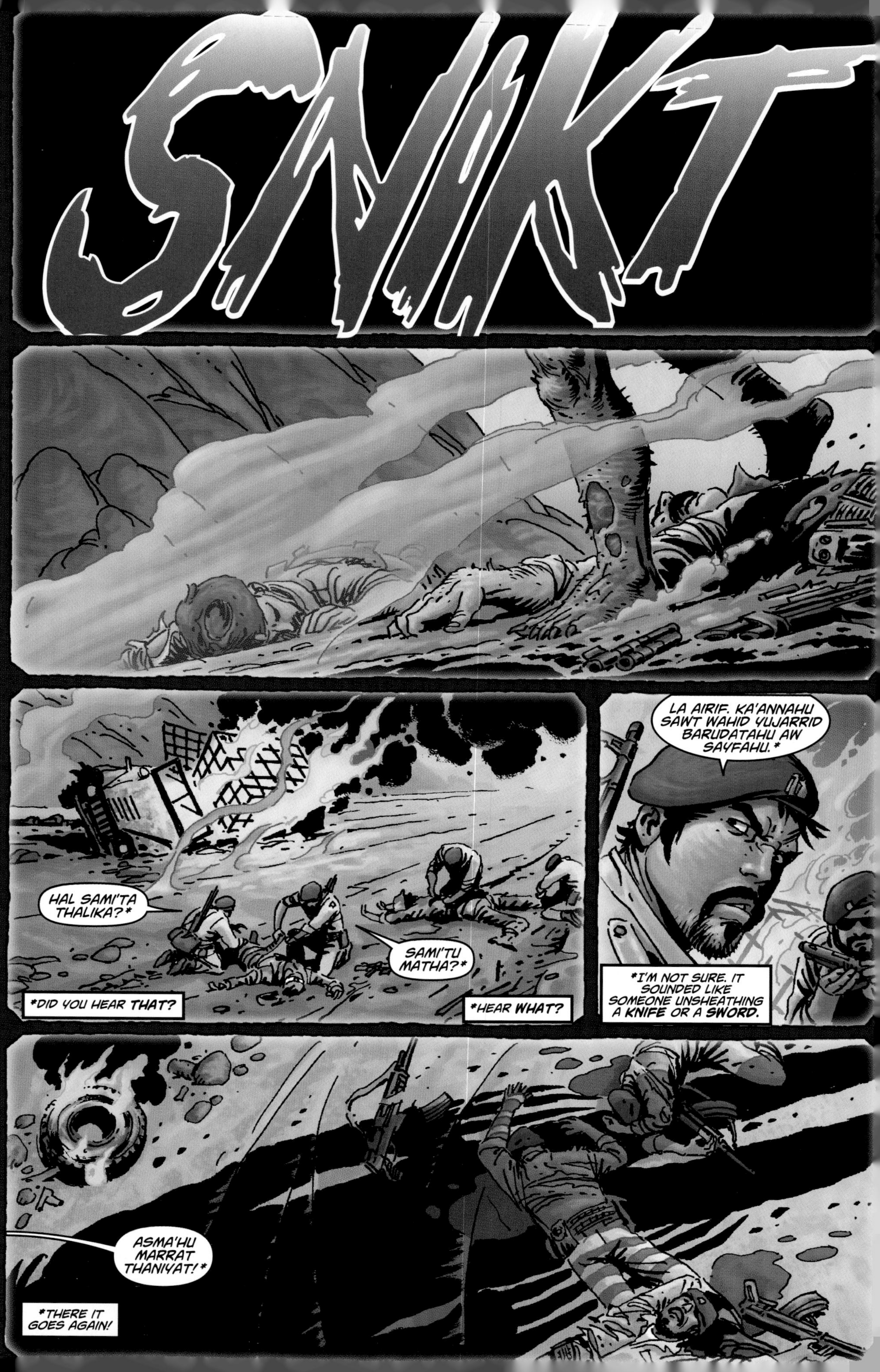
SNIKT
HAL SAMI'TA THALIKA?*
SAMI'TU MATHA?*
*DID YOU HEAR THAT?
*HEAR WHAT?
LA AIRIF. KA'ANNAHU SAWT WAHID YUJARRID BARUDATAHU AW SAYFAHU.*
*I'M NOT SURE. IT SOUNDED LIKE SOMEONE UNSHEATHING A KNIFE OR A SWORD.
ASMA'HU MARRAT THANIYAT!*
*THERE IT GOES AGAIN!

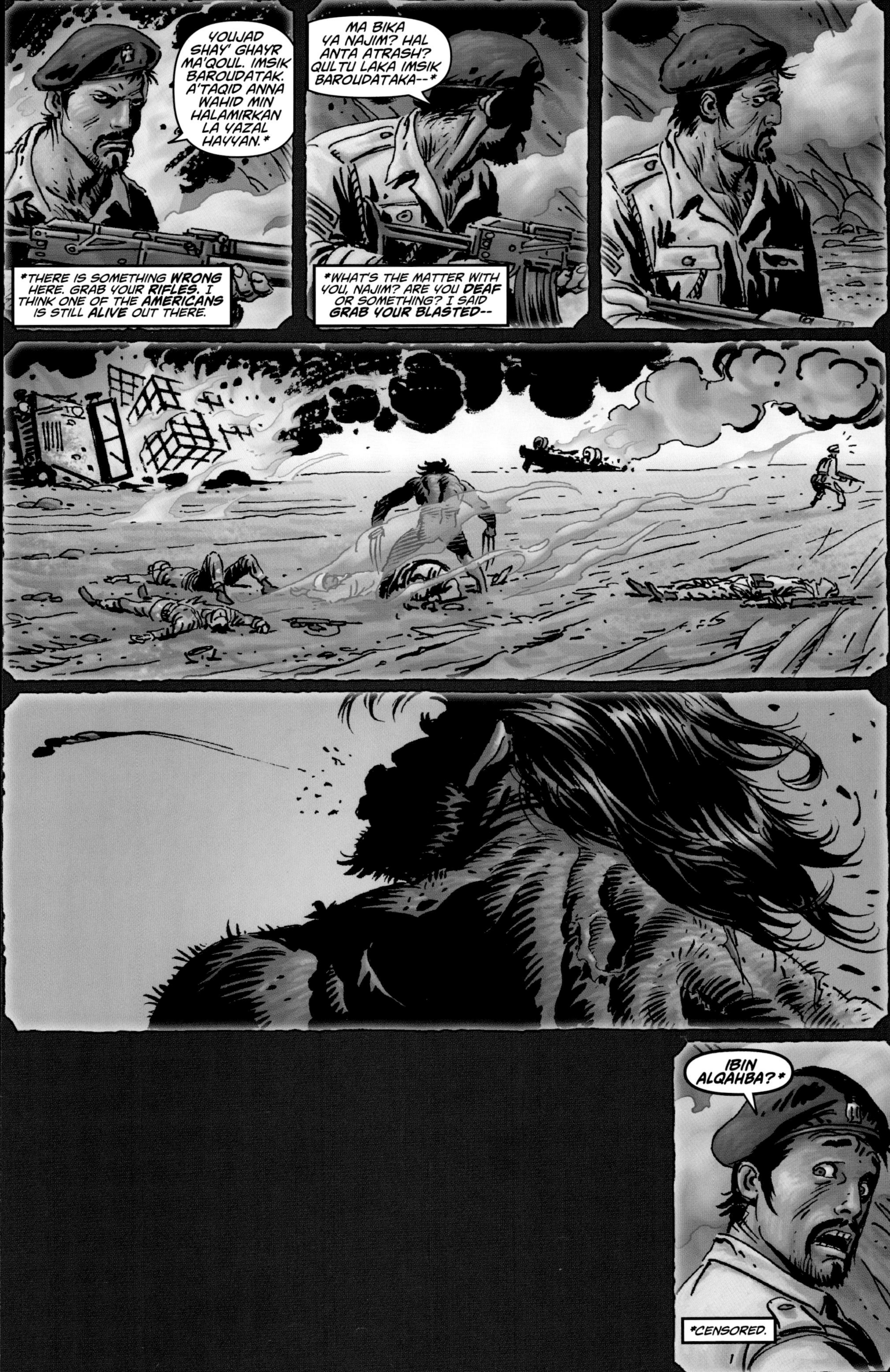
YOUJAD SHAY' GHAYR MA'QOUL. IMSIK BAROUDATAK. A'TAQID ANNA WAHID MIN HALAMIRKAN LA YAZAL HAYYAN.*
*THERE IS SOMETHING WRONG HERE. GRAB YOUR RIFLES. I THINK ONE OF THE AMERICANS IS STILL ALIVE OUT THERE.
MA BIKA YA NAJIM? HAL ANTA ATRASH? QULTU LAKA IMSIK BAROUDATAKA--*
*WHAT'S THE MATTER WITH YOU, NAJIM? ARE YOU DEAF OR SOMETHING? I SAID GRAB YOUR BLASTED--
IBIN ALQAHBA?*
*CENSORED.

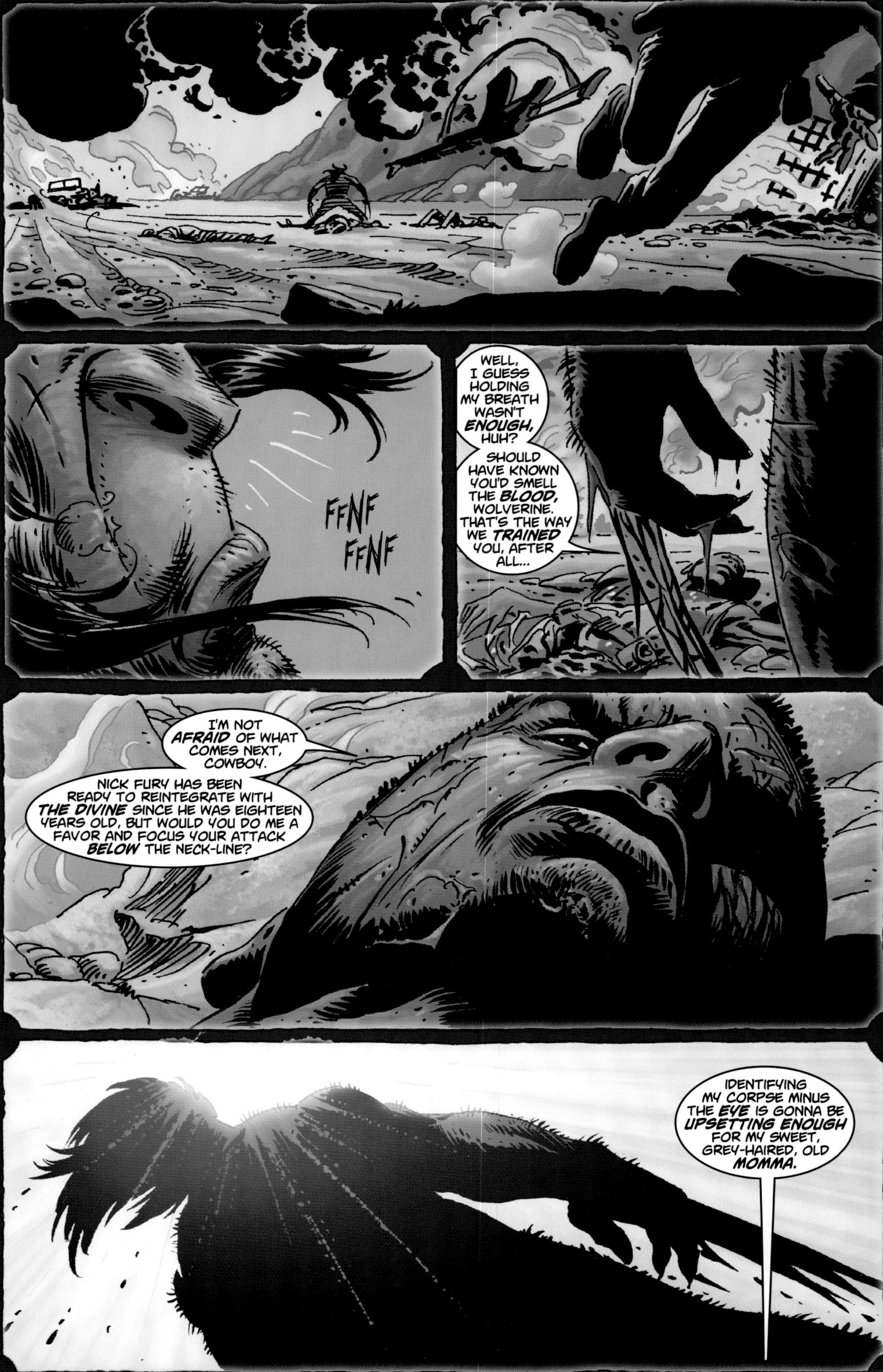
FFNF FFNF
WELL, I GUESS HOLDING MY BREATH WASN'T ENOUGH, HUH?
SHOULD HAVE KNOWN YOU'D SMELL THE BLOOD, WOLVERINE. THAT'S THE WAY WE TRAINED YOU, AFTER ALL...
I'M NOT AFRAID OF WHAT COMES NEXT, COWBOY.
NICK FURY HAS BEEN READY TO REINTEGRATE WITH THE DIVINE SINCE HE WAS EIGHTEEN YEARS OLD, BUT WOULD YOU DO ME A FAVOR AND FOCUS YOUR ATTACK BELOW THE NECK-LINE?
IDENTIFYING MY CORPSE MINUS THE EYE IS GONNA BE UPSETTING ENOUGH FOR MY SWEET, GREY-HAIRED, OLD MOMMA.

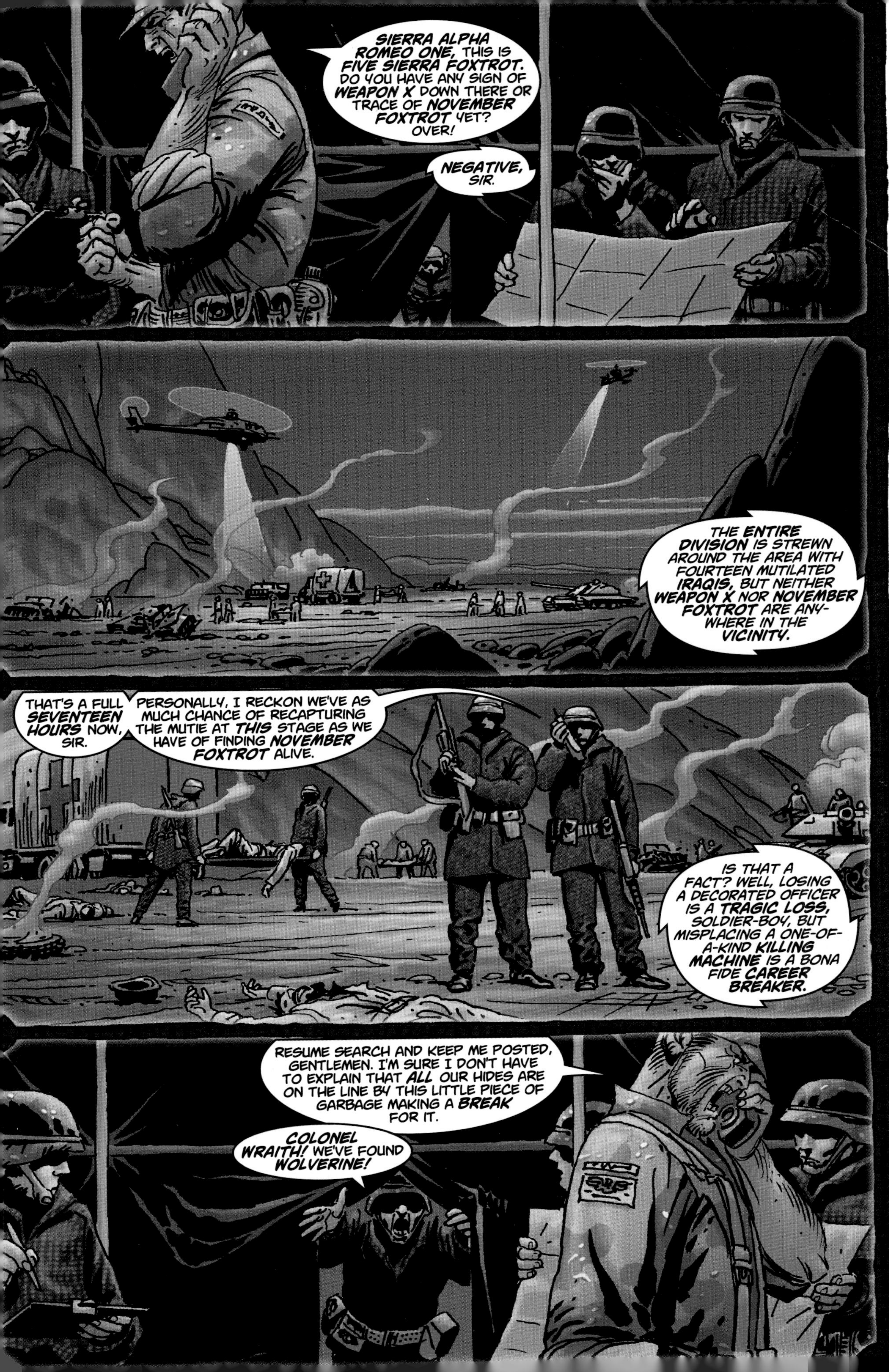
SIERRA ALPHA ROMEO ONE, THIS IS FIVE SIERRA FOXTROT. DO YOU HAVE ANY SIGN OF WEAPON X DOWN THERE OR TRACE OF NOVEMBER FOXTROT YET? OVER!
NEGATIVE, SIR.
THE ENTIRE DIVISION IS STREWN AROUND THE AREA WITH FOURTEEN MUTILATED IRAQIS, BUT NEITHER WEAPON X NOR NOVEMBER FOXTROT ARE ANYWHERE IN THE VICINITY.
THAT'S A FULL SEVENTEEN HOURS NOW, SIR.
PERSONALLY, I RECKON WE'VE AS MUCH CHANCE OF RECAPTURING THE MUTIE AT THIS STAGE AS WE HAVE OF FINDING NOVEMBER FOXTROT ALIVE.
IS THAT A FACT? WELL, LOSING A DECORATED OFFICER IS A TRAGIC LOSS, SOLDIER-BOY, BUT MISPLACING A ONE-OF-A-KIND KILLING MACHINE IS A BONA FIDE CAREER BREAKER.
RESUME SEARCH AND KEEP ME POSTED, GENTLEMEN. I'M SURE I DON'T HAVE TO EXPLAIN THAT ALL OUR HIDES ARE ON THE LINE BY THIS LITTLE PIECE OF GARBAGE MAKING A BREAK FOR IT.
COLONEL WRAITH! WE'VE FOUND WOLVERINE!

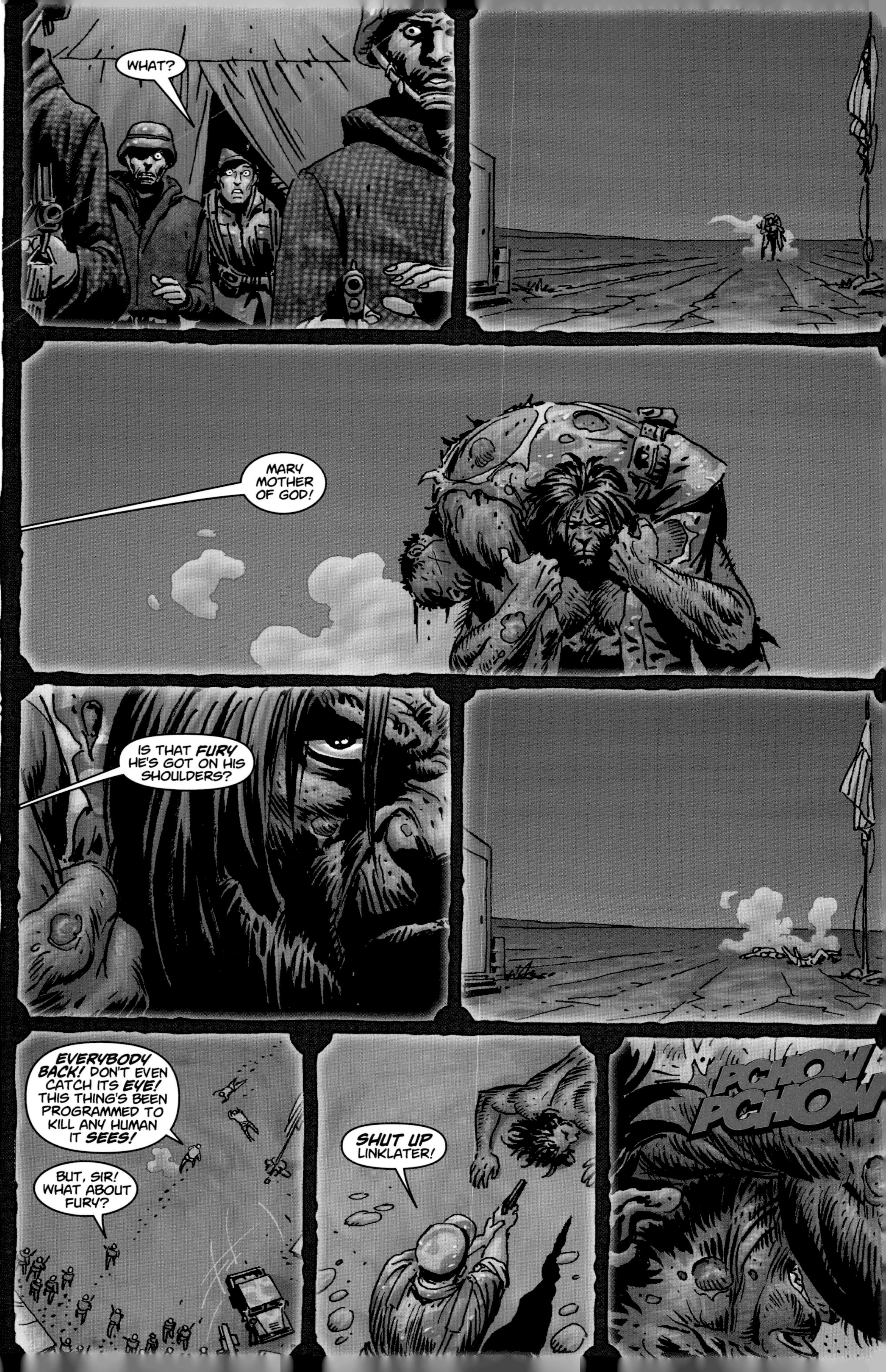
WHAT?
MARY MOTHER OF GOD!
IS THAT FURY HE'S GOT ON HIS SHOULDERS?
EVERYBODY BACK! DON'T EVEN CATCH ITS EYE! THIS THING'S BEEN PROGRAMMED TO KILL ANY HUMAN IT SEES!
BUT, SIR! WHAT ABOUT FURY?
SHUT UP LINKLATER!
PCHOW PCHOW

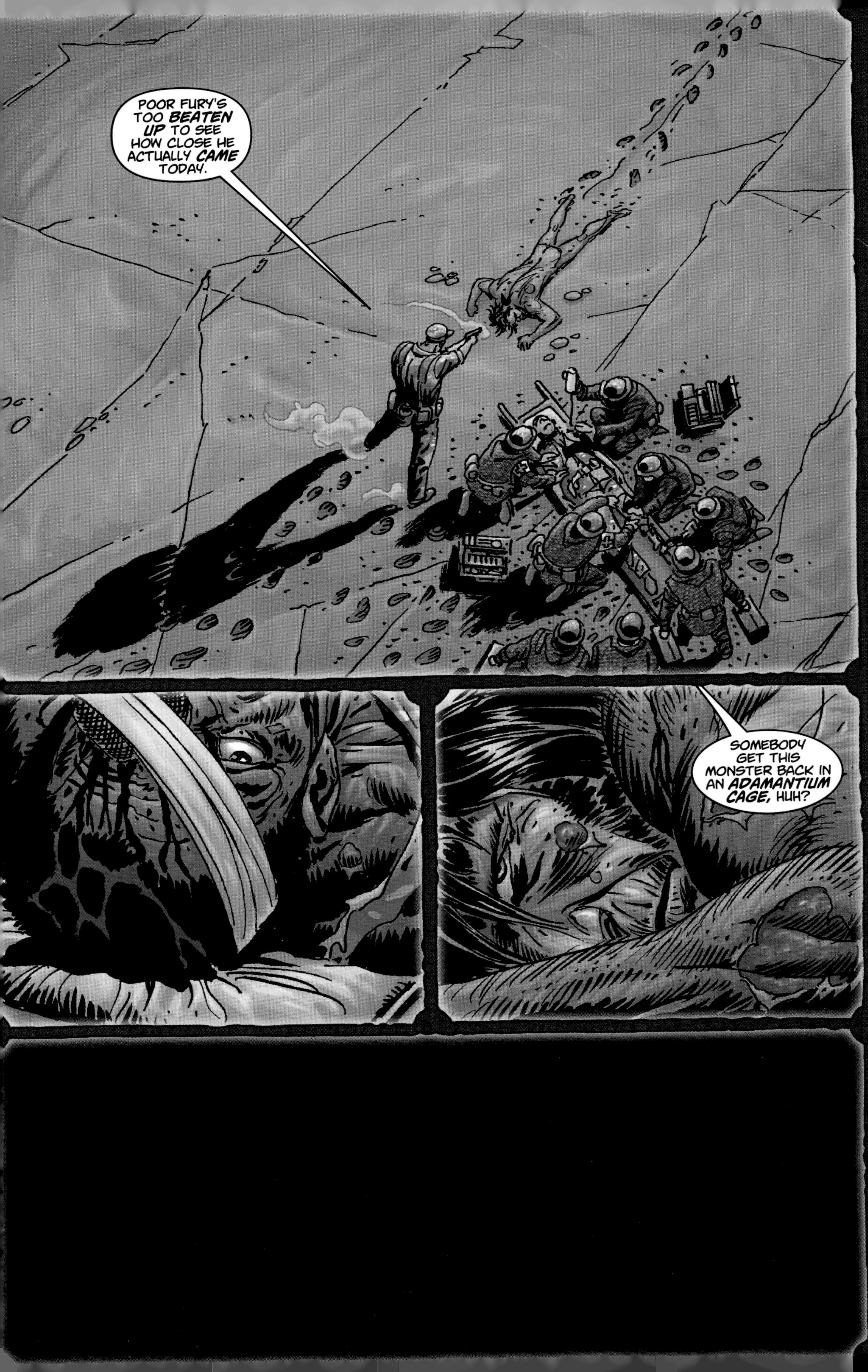
POOR FURY'S TOO **BEATEN UP** TO SEE HOW CLOSE HE ACTUALLY **CAME** TODAY.
SOMEBODY GET THIS MONSTER BACK IN AN **ADAMANTIUM CAGE,** HUH?

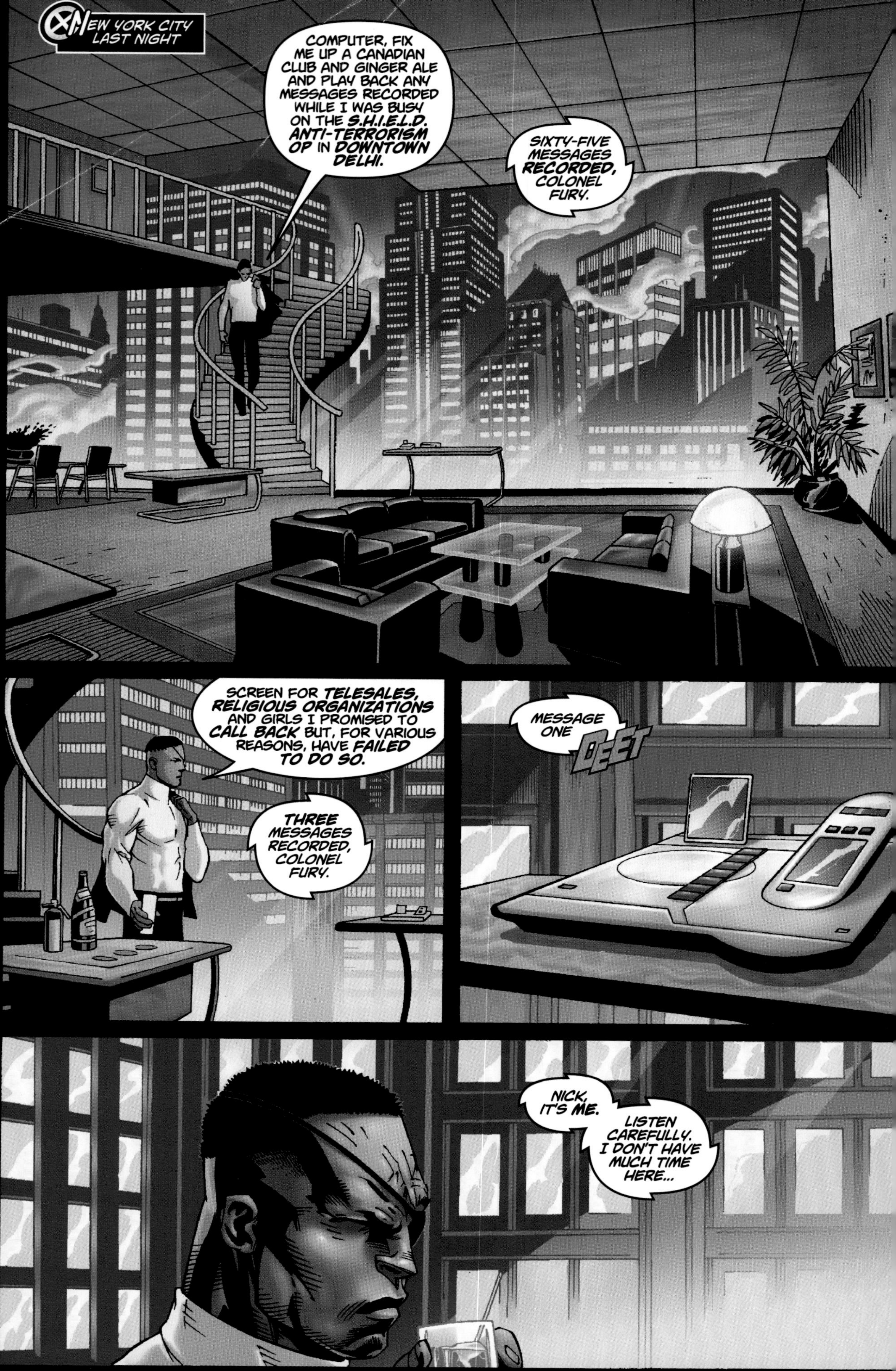
NEW YORK CITY
LAST NIGHT
COMPUTER, FIX ME UP A CANADIAN CLUB AND GINGER ALE AND PLAY BACK ANY MESSAGES RECORDED WHILE I WAS BUSY ON THE S.H.I.E.L.D. ANTI-TERRORISM OP IN DOWNTOWN DELHI.
SIXTY-FIVE MESSAGES RECORDED, COLONEL FURY.
SCREEN FOR TELESALES, RELIGIOUS ORGANIZATIONS AND GIRLS I PROMISED TO CALL BACK BUT, FOR VARIOUS REASONS, HAVE FAILED TO DO SO.
THREE MESSAGES RECORDED, COLONEL FURY.
MESSAGE ONE
DEET
NICK, IT'S ME.
LISTEN CAREFULLY. I DON'T HAVE MUCH TIME HERE...

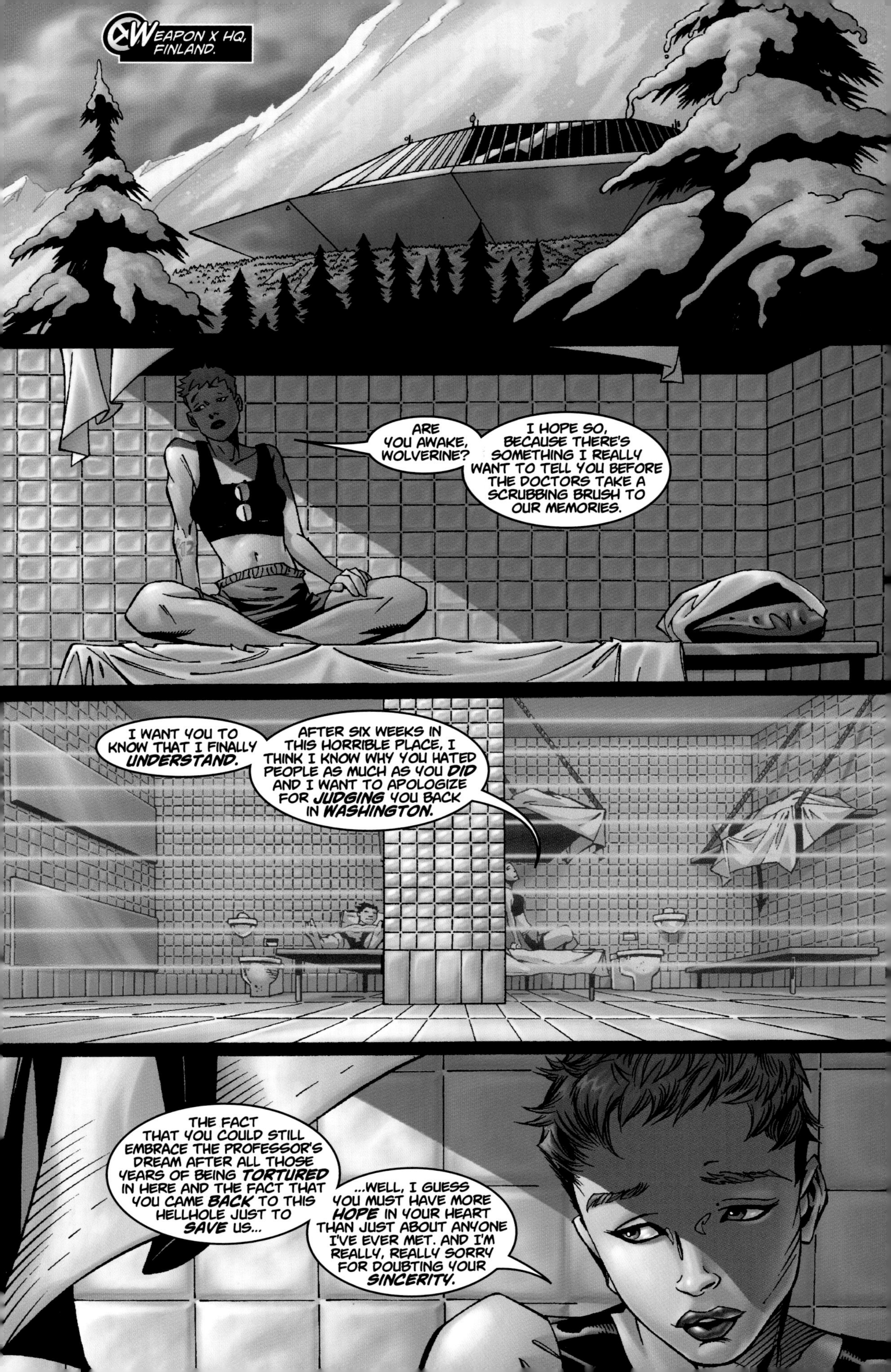
WEAPON X HQ, FINLAND.
ARE YOU AWAKE, WOLVERINE?
I HOPE SO, BECAUSE THERE'S SOMETHING I REALLY WANT TO TELL YOU BEFORE THE DOCTORS TAKE A SCRUBBING BRUSH TO OUR MEMORIES.
I WANT YOU TO KNOW THAT I FINALLY UNDERSTAND.
AFTER SIX WEEKS IN THIS HORRIBLE PLACE, I THINK I KNOW WHY YOU HATED PEOPLE AS MUCH AS YOU DID AND I WANT TO APOLOGIZE FOR JUDGING YOU BACK IN WASHINGTON.
THE FACT THAT YOU COULD STILL EMBRACE THE PROFESSOR'S DREAM AFTER ALL THOSE YEARS OF BEING TORTURED IN HERE AND THE FACT THAT YOU CAME BACK TO THIS HELLHOLE JUST TO SAVE US...
...WELL, I GUESS YOU MUST HAVE MORE HOPE IN YOUR HEART THAN JUST ABOUT ANYONE I'VE EVER MET. AND I'M REALLY, REALLY SORRY FOR DOUBTING YOUR SINCERITY.

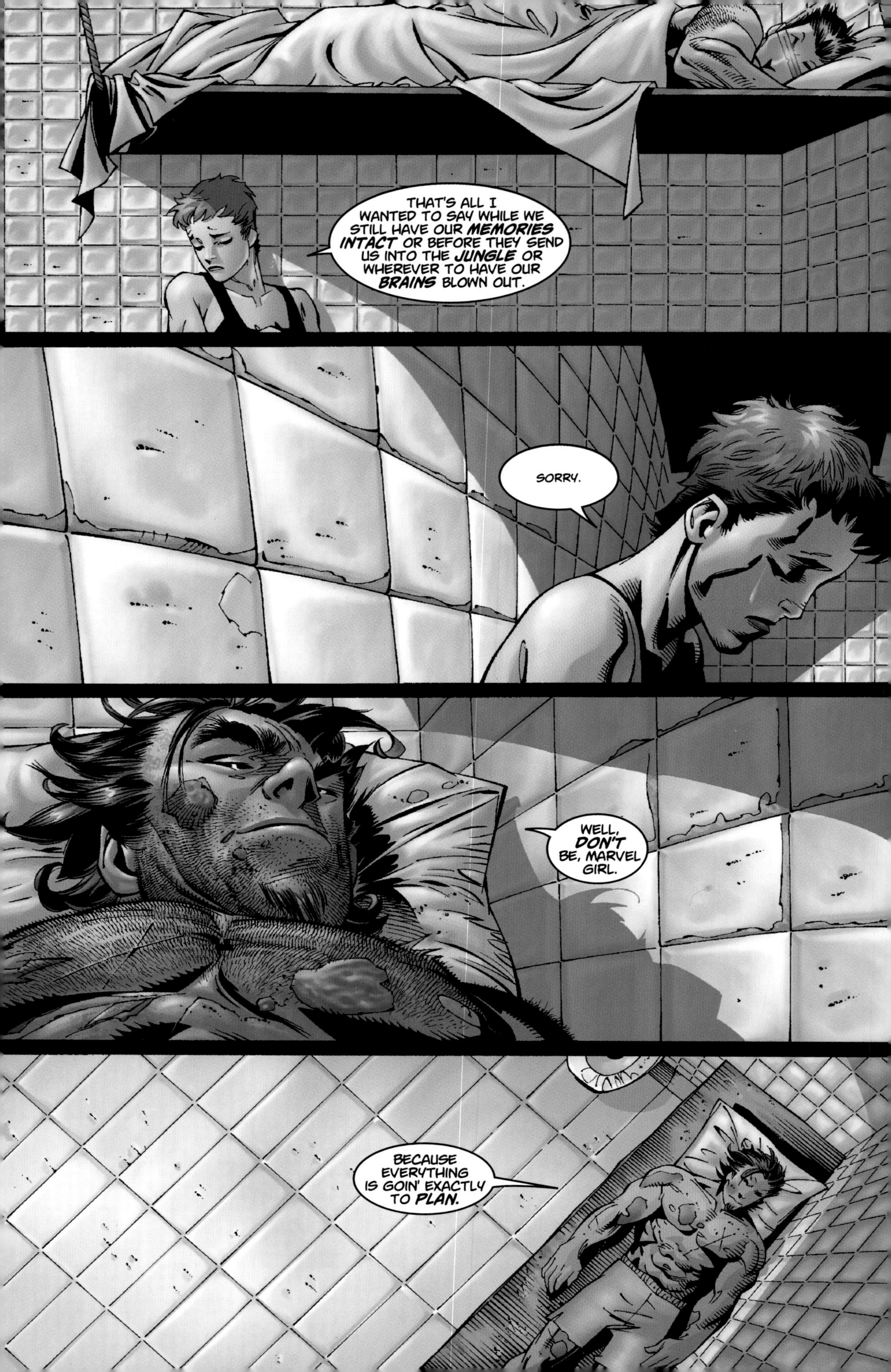
THAT'S ALL I WANTED TO SAY WHILE WE STILL HAVE OUR MEMORIES INTACT OR BEFORE THEY SEND US INTO THE JUNGLE OR WHEREVER TO HAVE OUR BRAINS BLOWN OUT.
SORRY.
WELL, DON'T BE, MARVEL GIRL.
BECAUSE EVERYTHING IS GOIN' EXACTLY TO PLAN.

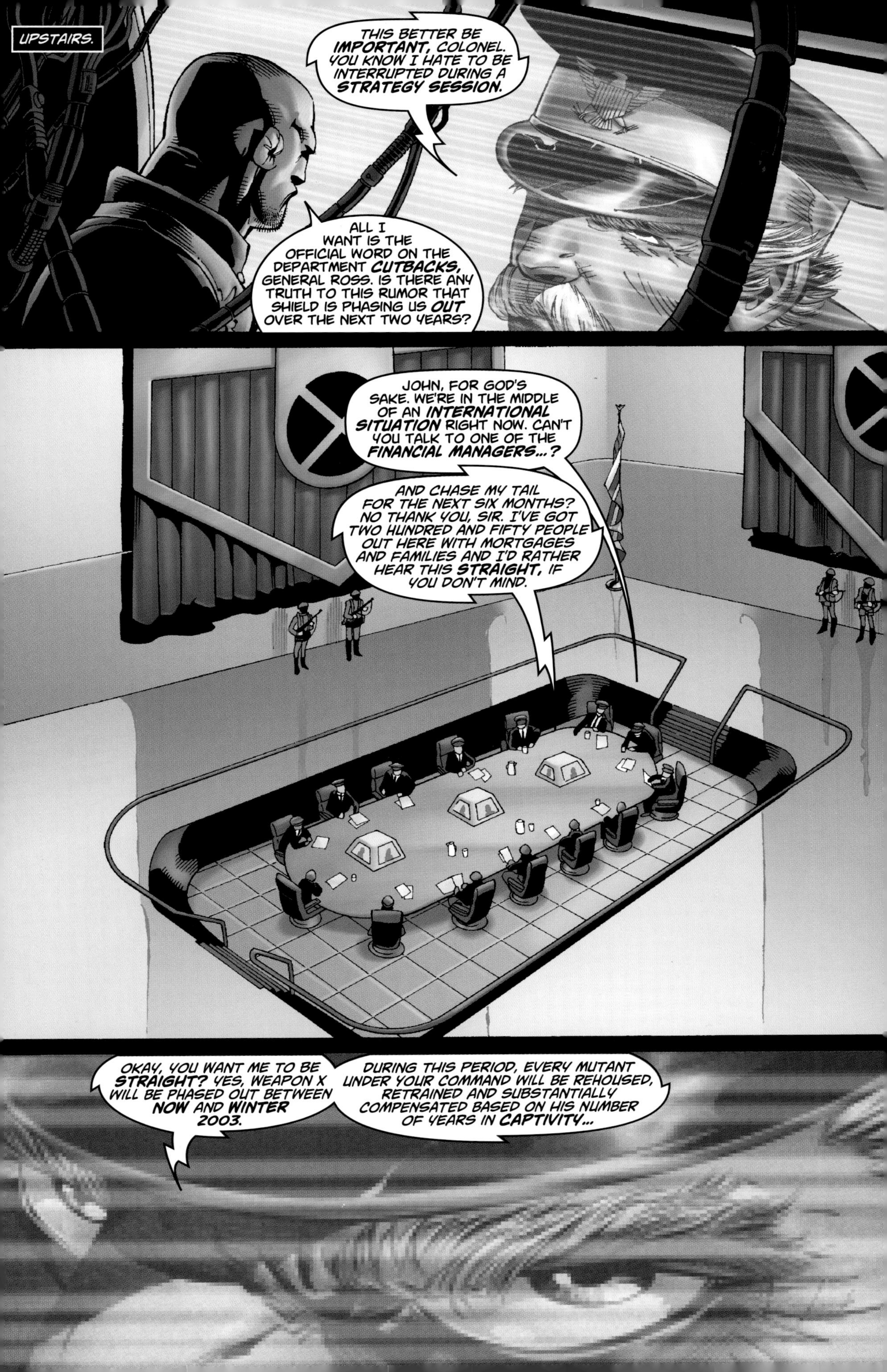
UPSTAIRS.
THIS BETTER BE IMPORTANT, COLONEL. YOU KNOW I HATE TO BE INTERRUPTED DURING A STRATEGY SESSION.
ALL I WANT IS THE OFFICIAL WORD ON THE DEPARTMENT CUTBACKS, GENERAL ROSS. IS THERE ANY TRUTH TO THIS RUMOR THAT SHIELD IS PHASING US OUT OVER THE NEXT TWO YEARS?
JOHN, FOR GOD'S SAKE. WE'RE IN THE MIDDLE OF AN INTERNATIONAL SITUATION RIGHT NOW. CAN'T YOU TALK TO ONE OF THE FINANCIAL MANAGERS...?
AND CHASE MY TAIL FOR THE NEXT SIX MONTHS? NO THANK YOU, SIR. I'VE GOT TWO HUNDRED AND FIFTY PEOPLE OUT HERE WITH MORTGAGES AND FAMILIES AND I'D RATHER HEAR THIS STRAIGHT, IF YOU DON'T MIND.
OKAY, YOU WANT ME TO BE STRAIGHT? YES, WEAPON X WILL BE PHASED OUT BETWEEN NOW AND WINTER 2003.
DURING THIS PERIOD, EVERY MUTANT UNDER YOUR COMMAND WILL BE REHOUSED, RETRAINED AND SUBSTANTIALLY COMPENSATED BASED ON HIS NUMBER OF YEARS IN CAPTIVITY...

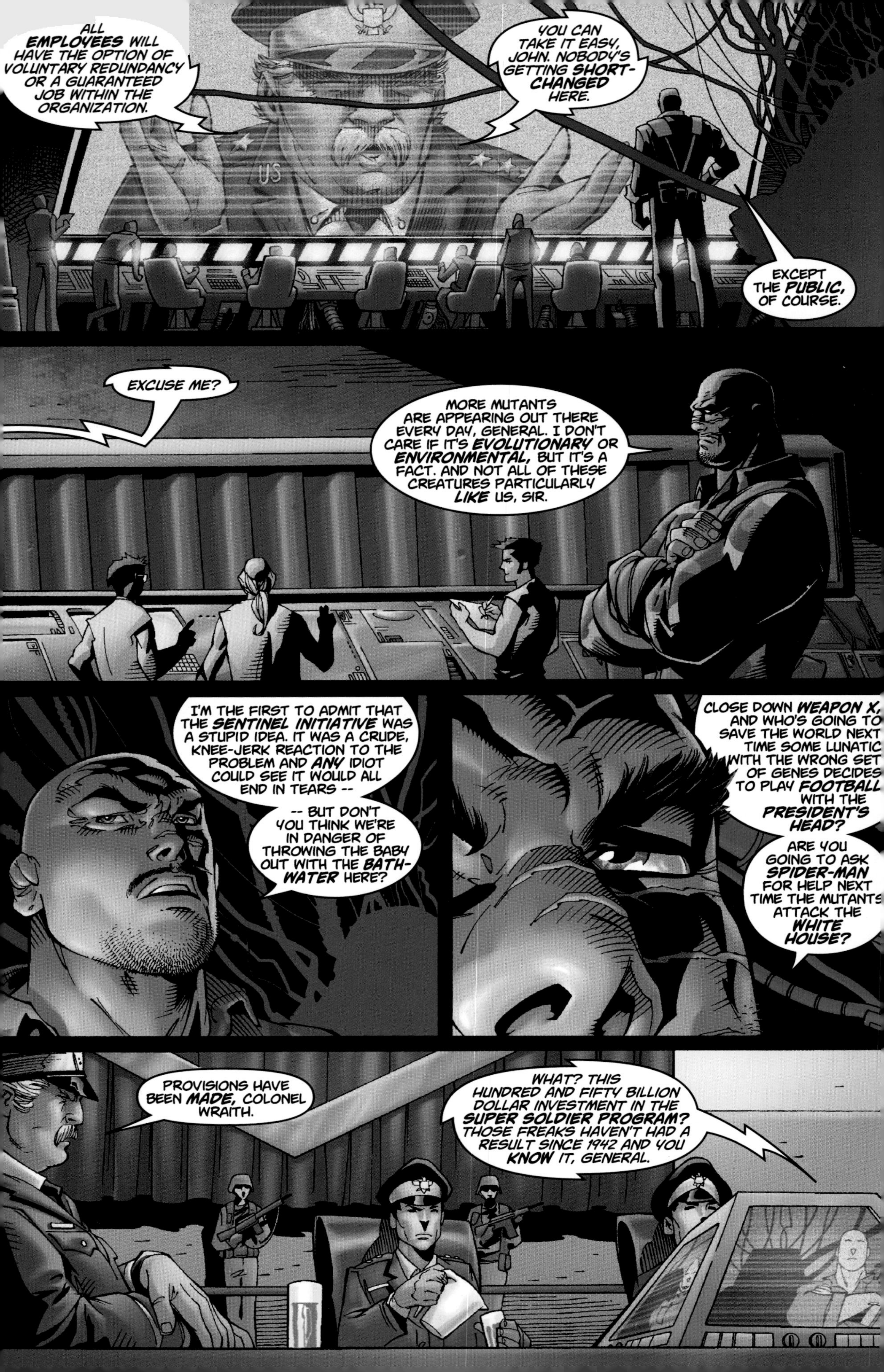
ALL EMPLOYEES WILL HAVE THE OPTION OF VOLUNTARY REDUNDANCY OR A GUARANTEED JOB WITHIN THE ORGANIZATION.
YOU CAN TAKE IT EASY, JOHN. NOBODY'S GETTING SHORT-CHANGED HERE.
EXCEPT THE PUBLIC, OF COURSE.
EXCUSE ME?
MORE MUTANTS ARE APPEARING OUT THERE EVERY DAY, GENERAL. I DON'T CARE IF IT'S EVOLUTIONARY OR ENVIRONMENTAL, BUT IT'S A FACT. AND NOT ALL OF THESE CREATURES PARTICULARLY LIKE US, SIR.
I'M THE FIRST TO ADMIT THAT THE SENTINEL INITIATIVE WAS A STUPID IDEA. IT WAS A CRUDE, KNEE-JERK REACTION TO THE PROBLEM AND ANY IDIOT COULD SEE IT WOULD ALL END IN TEARS --
-- BUT DON'T YOU THINK WE'RE IN DANGER OF THROWING THE BABY OUT WITH THE BATH-WATER HERE?
CLOSE DOWN WEAPON X, AND WHO'S GOING TO SAVE THE WORLD NEXT TIME SOME LUNATIC WITH THE WRONG SET OF GENES DECIDES TO PLAY FOOTBALL WITH THE PRESIDENT'S HEAD?
ARE YOU GOING TO ASK SPIDER-MAN FOR HELP NEXT TIME THE MUTANTS ATTACK THE WHITE HOUSE?
PROVISIONS HAVE BEEN MADE, COLONEL WRAITH.
WHAT? THIS HUNDRED AND FIFTY BILLION DOLLAR INVESTMENT IN THE SUPER SOLDIER PROGRAM? THOSE FREAKS HAVEN'T HAD A RESULT SINCE 1942 AND YOU KNOW IT, GENERAL.

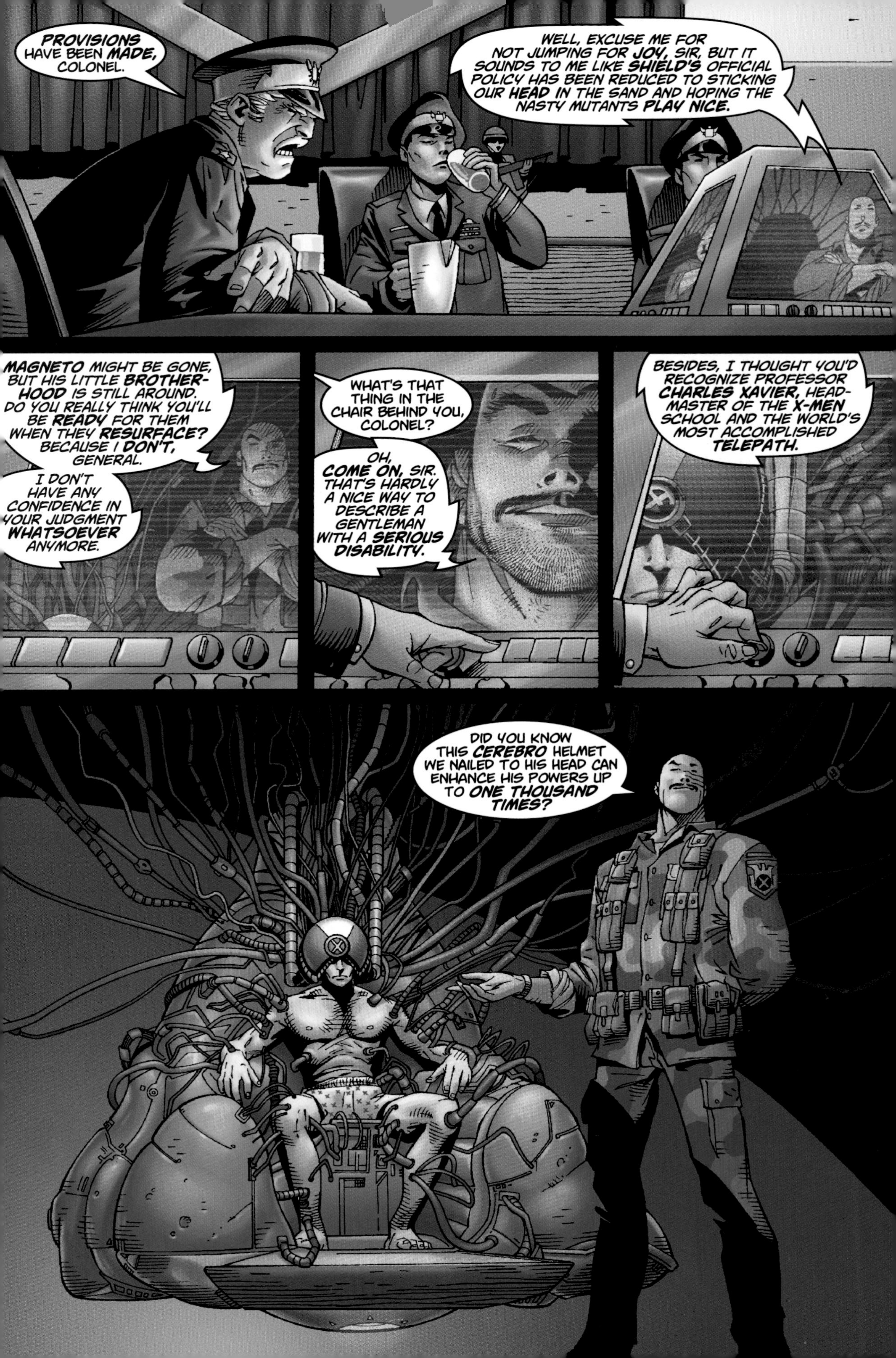
PROVISIONS HAVE BEEN MADE, COLONEL.
WELL, EXCUSE ME FOR NOT JUMPING FOR JOY, SIR, BUT IT SOUNDS TO ME LIKE SHIELD'S OFFICIAL POLICY HAS BEEN REDUCED TO STICKING OUR HEAD IN THE SAND AND HOPING THE NASTY MUTANTS PLAY NICE.
MAGNETO MIGHT BE GONE, BUT HIS LITTLE BROTHER-HOOD IS STILL AROUND. DO YOU REALLY THINK YOU'LL BE READY FOR THEM WHEN THEY RESURFACE? BECAUSE I DON'T, GENERAL.
I DON'T HAVE ANY CONFIDENCE IN YOUR JUDGMENT WHATSOEVER ANYMORE.
WHAT'S THAT THING IN THE CHAIR BEHIND YOU, COLONEL?
OH, COME ON, SIR. THAT'S HARDLY A NICE WAY TO DESCRIBE A GENTLEMAN WITH A SERIOUS DISABILITY.
BESIDES, I THOUGHT YOU'D RECOGNIZE PROFESSOR CHARLES XAVIER, HEAD-MASTER OF THE X-MEN SCHOOL AND THE WORLD'S MOST ACCOMPLISHED TELEPATH.
DID YOU KNOW THIS CEREBRO HELMET WE NAILED TO HIS HEAD CAN ENHANCE HIS POWERS UP TO ONE THOUSAND TIMES?

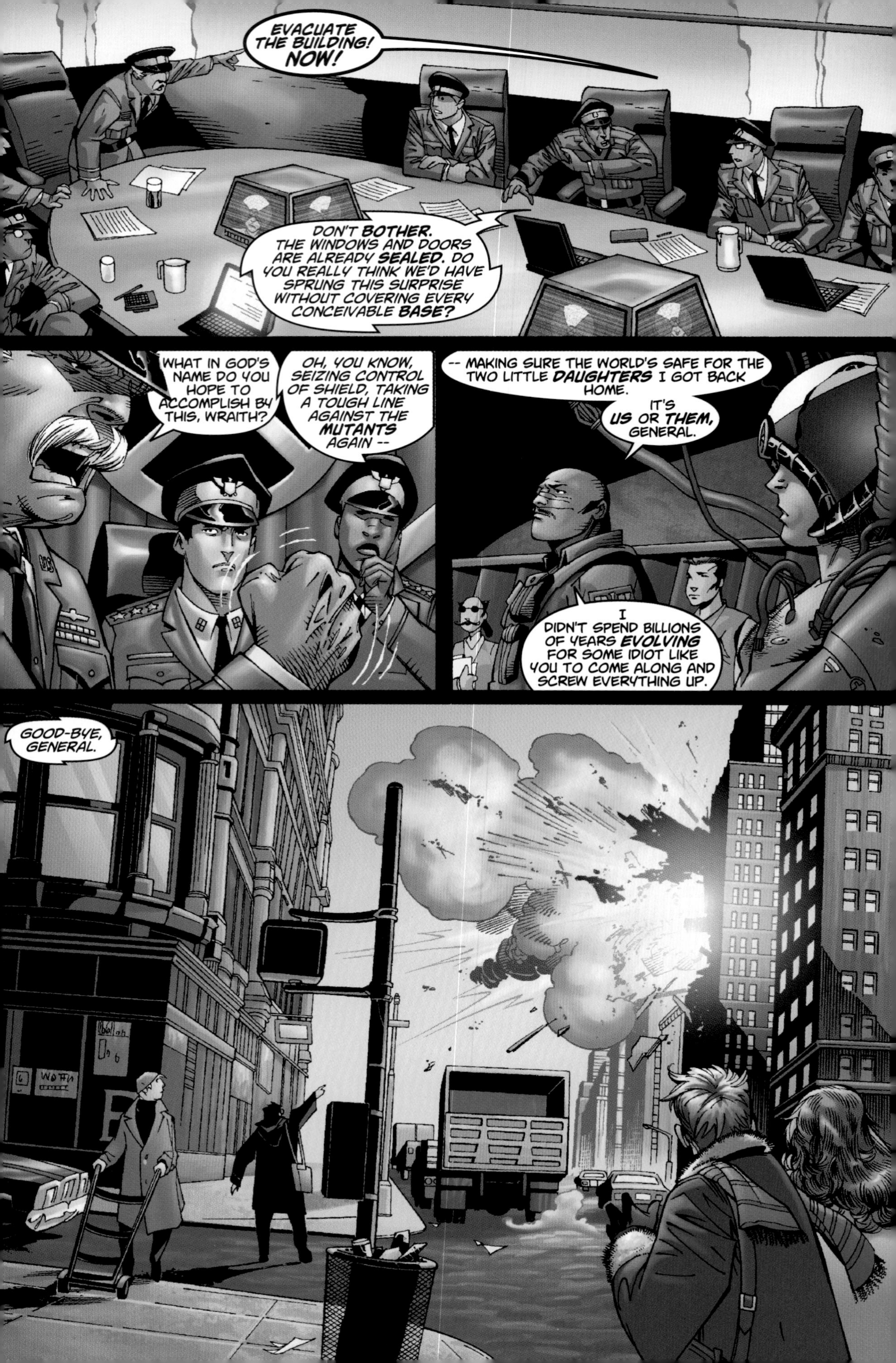

EVACUATE THE BUILDING! NOW!
DON'T BOTHER. THE WINDOWS AND DOORS ARE ALREADY SEALED. DO YOU REALLY THINK WE'D HAVE SPRUNG THIS SURPRISE WITHOUT COVERING EVERY CONCEIVABLE BASE?
WHAT IN GOD'S NAME DO YOU HOPE TO ACCOMPLISH BY THIS, WRAITH?
OH, YOU KNOW, SEIZING CONTROL OF SHIELD, TAKING A TOUGH LINE AGAINST THE MUTANTS AGAIN --
-- MAKING SURE THE WORLD'S SAFE FOR THE TWO LITTLE DAUGHTERS I GOT BACK HOME.
IT'S US OR THEM, GENERAL.
I DIDN'T SPEND BILLIONS OF YEARS EVOLVING FOR SOME IDIOT LIKE YOU TO COME ALONG AND SCREW EVERYTHING UP.
GOOD-BYE, GENERAL.

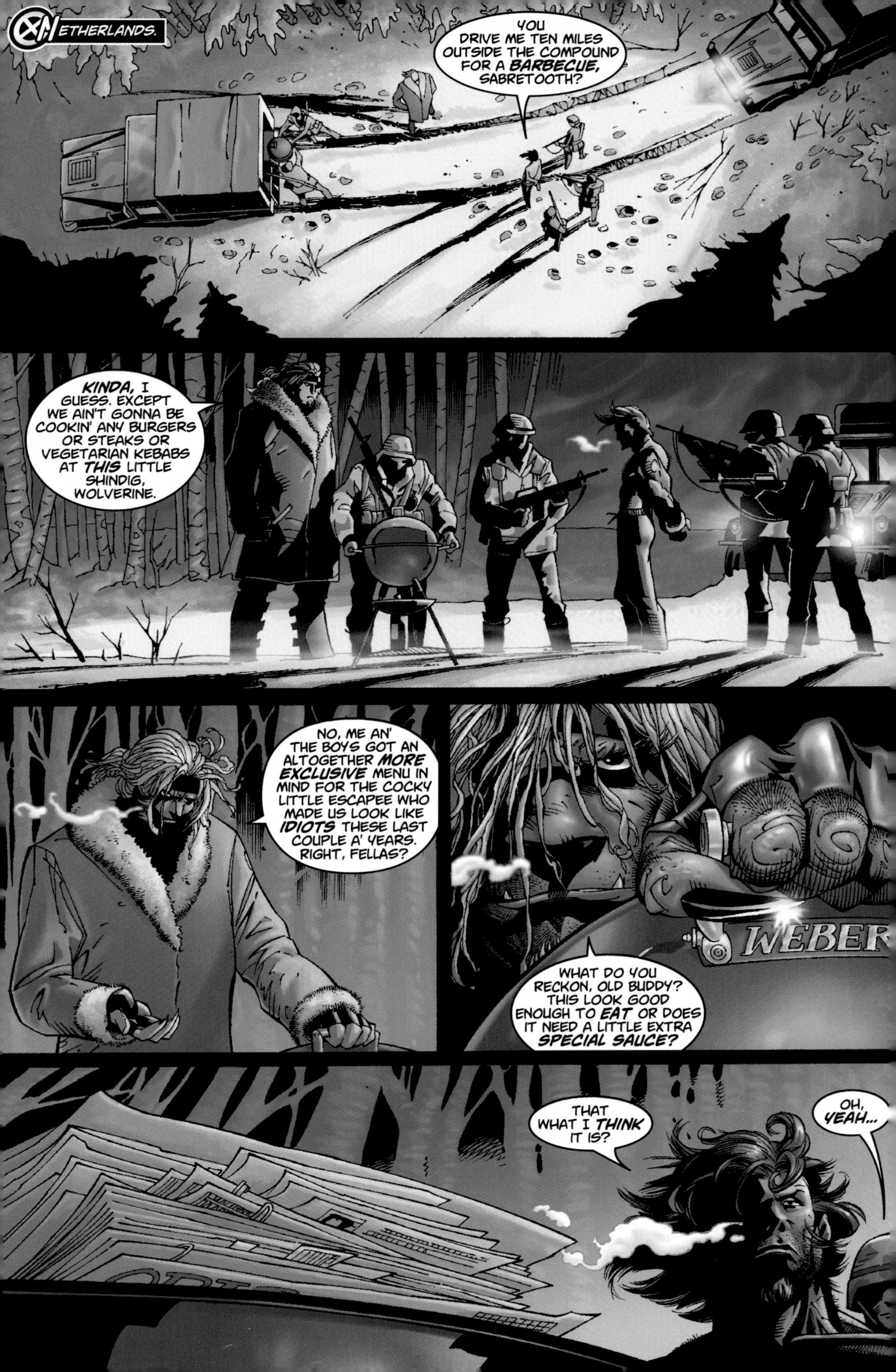
NETHERLANDS.
YOU DRIVE ME TEN MILES OUTSIDE THE COMPOUND FOR A BARBECUE, SABRETOOTH?
KINDA, I GUESS. EXCEPT WE AIN'T GONNA BE COOKIN' ANY BURGERS OR STEAKS OR VEGETARIAN KEBABS AT THIS LITTLE SHINDIG, WOLVERINE.
NO, ME AN' THE BOYS GOT AN ALTOGETHER MORE EXCLUSIVE MENU IN MIND FOR THE COCKY LITTLE ESCAPEE WHO MADE US LOOK LIKE IDIOTS THESE LAST COUPLE A' YEARS. RIGHT, FELLAS?
WEBER
WHAT DO YOU RECKON, OLD BUDDY? THIS LOOK GOOD ENOUGH TO EAT OR DOES IT NEED A LITTLE EXTRA SPECIAL SAUCE?
THAT WHAT I THINK IT IS?
OH, YEAH...

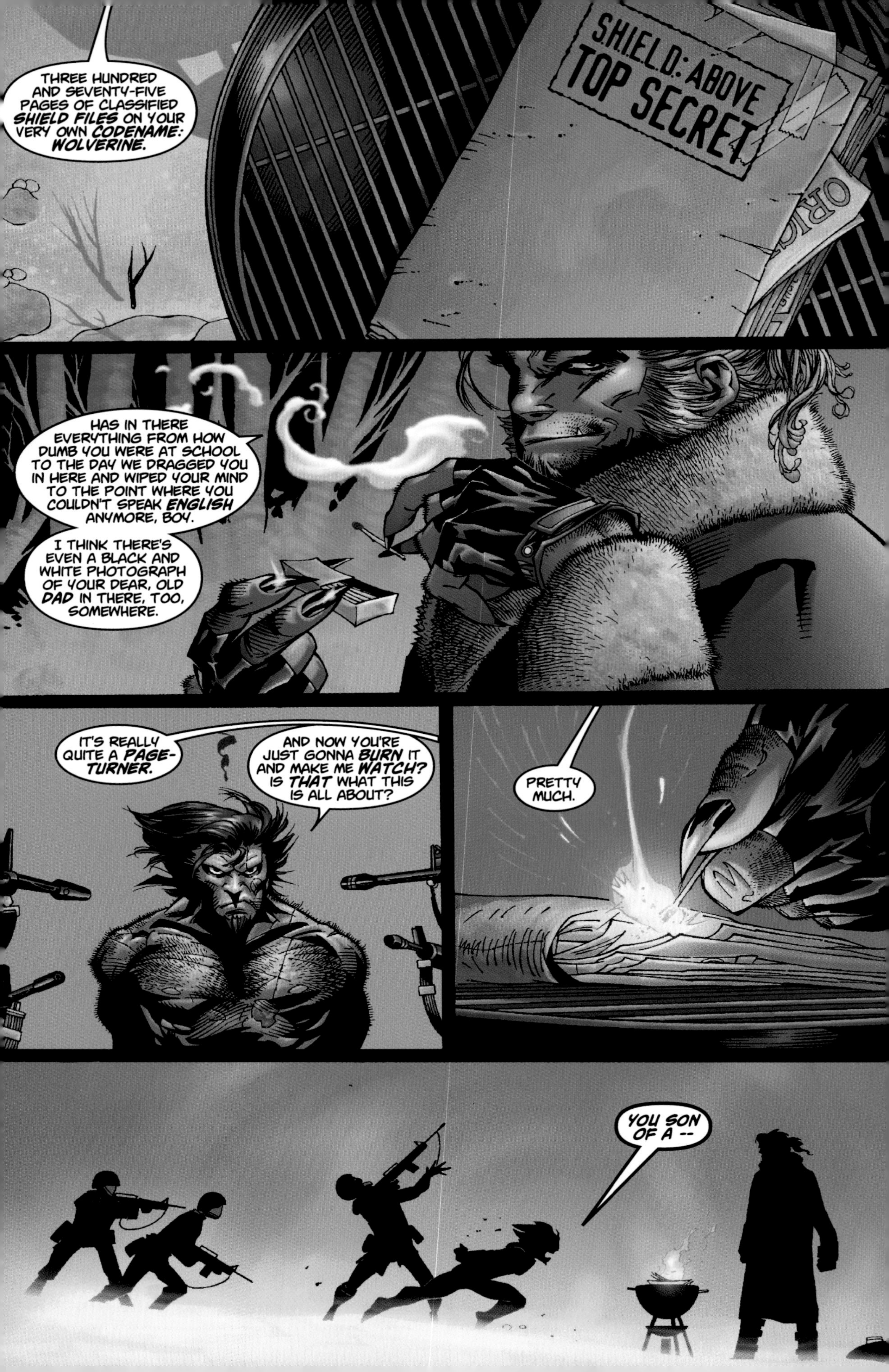
THREE HUNDRED AND SEVENTY-FIVE PAGES OF CLASSIFIED SHIELD FILES ON YOUR VERY OWN CODENAME: WOLVERINE.
S.H.I.E.L.D.: ABOVE TOP SECRET
HAS IN THERE EVERYTHING FROM HOW DUMB YOU WERE AT SCHOOL TO THE DAY WE DRAGGED YOU IN HERE AND WIPED YOUR MIND TO THE POINT WHERE YOU COULDN'T SPEAK ENGLISH ANYMORE, BOY.
I THINK THERE'S EVEN A BLACK AND WHITE PHOTOGRAPH OF YOUR DEAR, OLD DAD IN THERE, TOO, SOMEWHERE.
IT'S REALLY QUITE A PAGE-TURNER.
AND NOW YOU'RE JUST GONNA BURN IT AND MAKE ME WATCH? IS THAT WHAT THIS IS ALL ABOUT?
PRETTY MUCH.
YOU SON OF A --

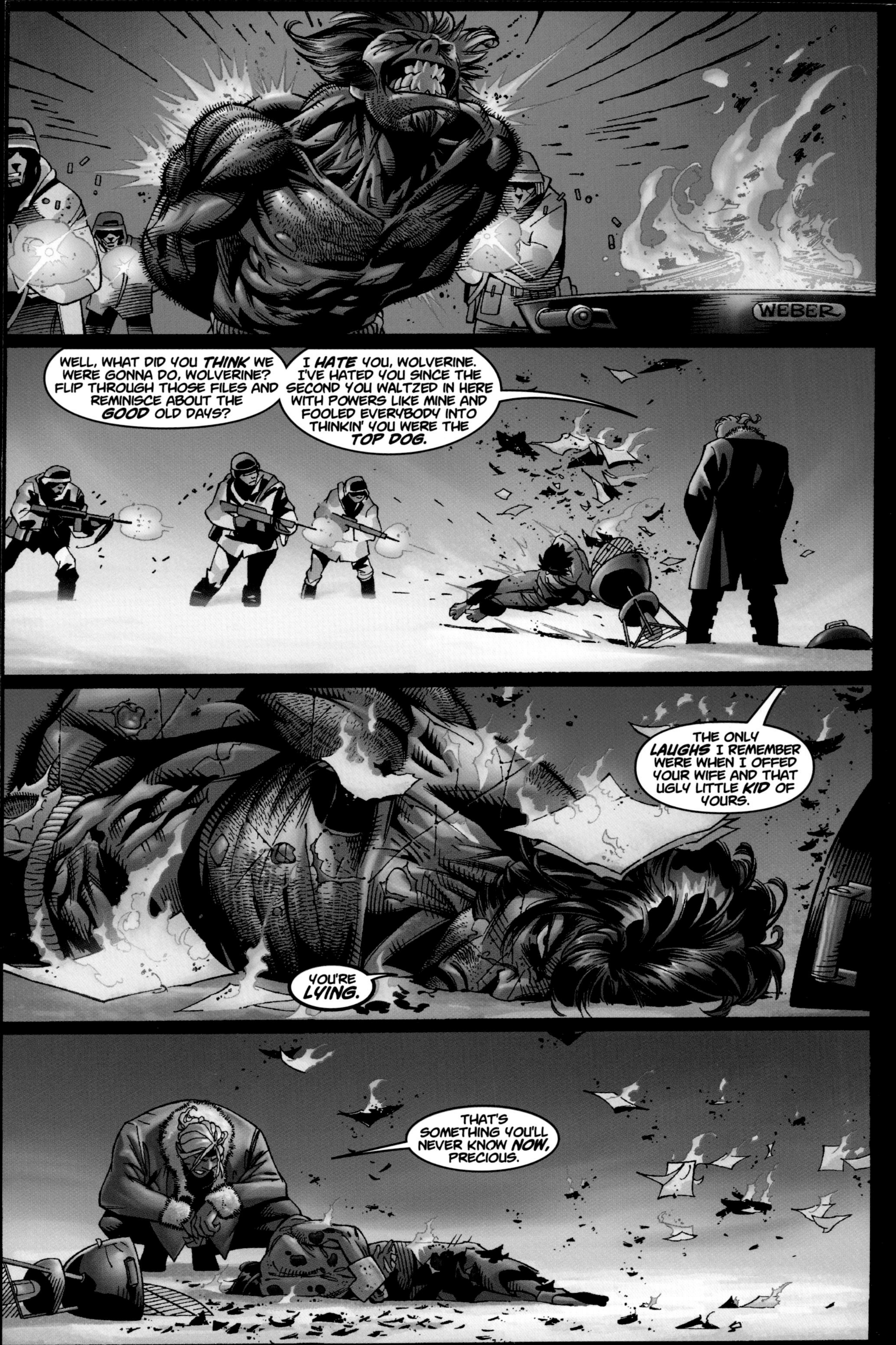
WEBER
WELL, WHAT DID YOU THINK WE WERE GONNA DO, WOLVERINE? FLIP THROUGH THOSE FILES AND REMINISCE ABOUT THE GOOD OLD DAYS?
I HATE YOU, WOLVERINE. I'VE HATED YOU SINCE THE SECOND YOU WALTZED IN HERE WITH POWERS LIKE MINE AND FOOLED EVERYBODY INTO THINKIN' YOU WERE THE TOP DOG.
THE ONLY LAUGHS I REMEMBER WERE WHEN I OFFED YOUR WIFE AND THAT UGLY LITTLE KID OF YOURS.
YOU'RE LYING.
THAT'S SOMETHING YOU'LL NEVER KNOW NOW, PRECIOUS.

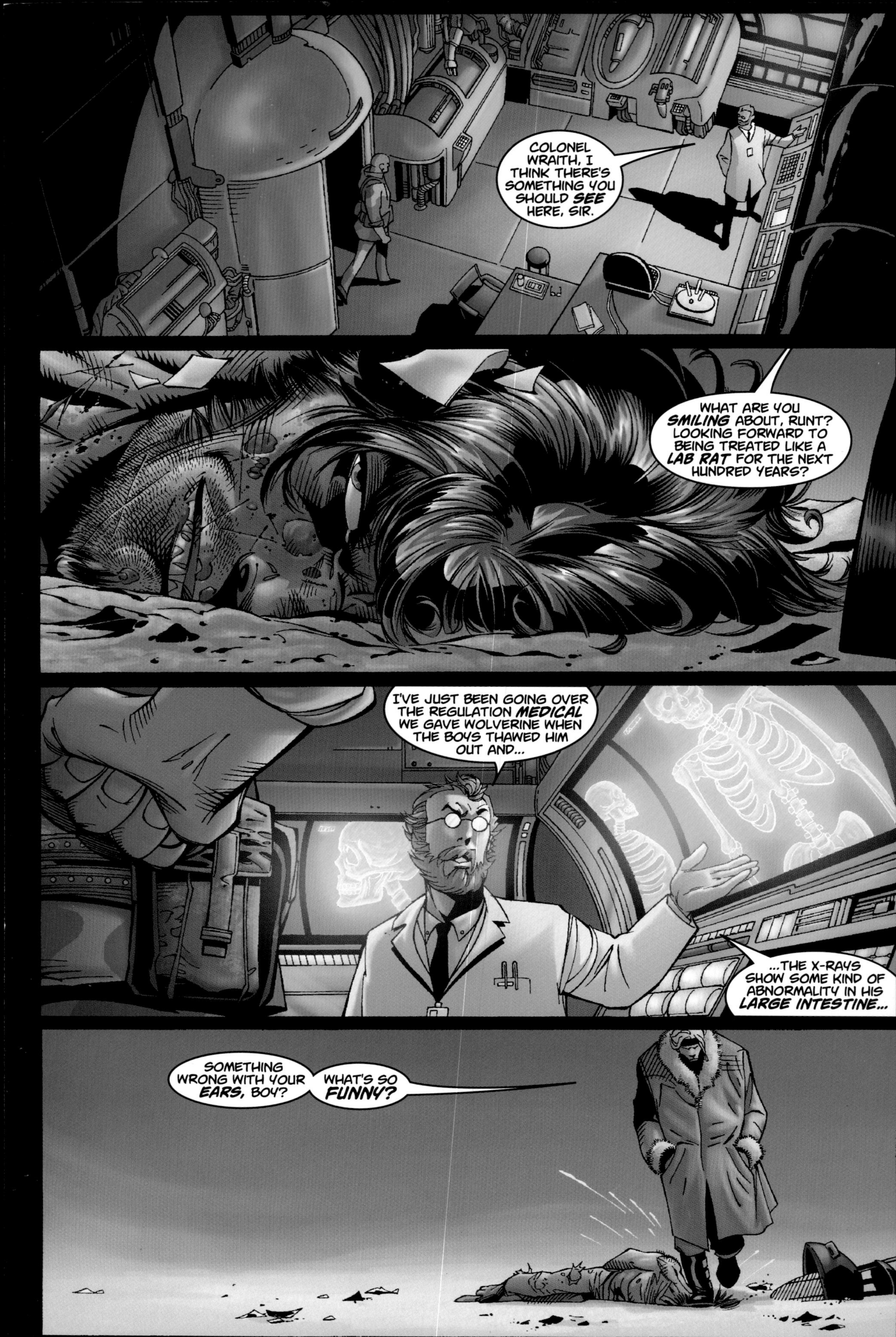
COLONEL WRAITH, I THINK THERE'S SOMETHING YOU SHOULD SEE HERE, SIR.
WHAT ARE YOU SMILING ABOUT, RUNT? LOOKING FORWARD TO BEING TREATED LIKE A LAB RAT FOR THE NEXT HUNDRED YEARS?
I'VE JUST BEEN GOING OVER THE REGULATION MEDICAL WE GAVE WOLVERINE WHEN THE BOYS THAWED HIM OUT AND...
...THE X-RAYS SHOW SOME KIND OF ABNORMALITY IN HIS LARGE INTESTINE...
SOMETHING WRONG WITH YOUR EARS, BOY?
WHAT'S SO FUNNY?

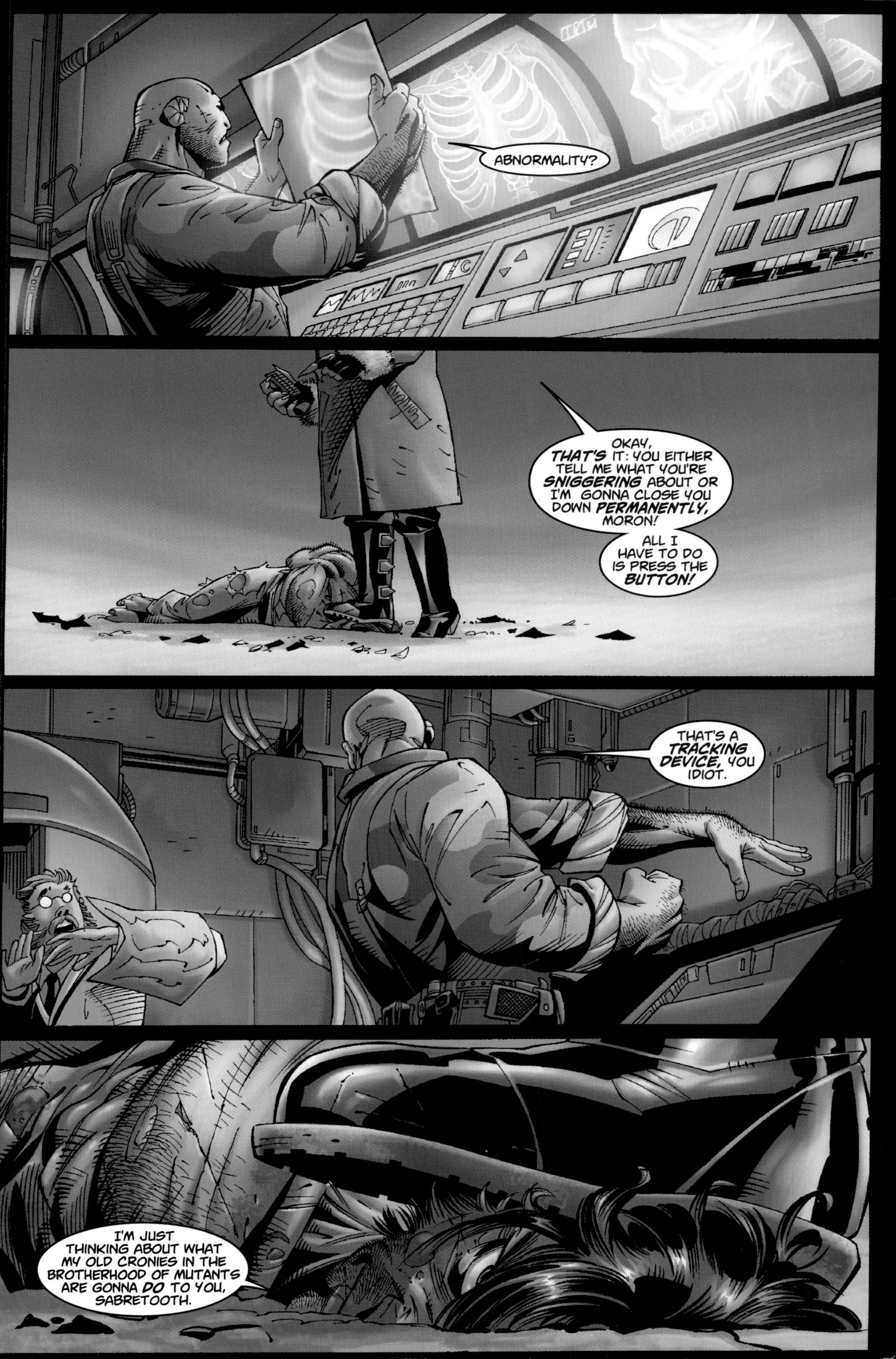

ABNORMALITY?
OKAY, THAT'S IT: YOU EITHER TELL ME WHAT YOU'RE SNIGGERING ABOUT OR I'M GONNA CLOSE YOU DOWN PERMANENTLY, MORON!
ALL I HAVE TO DO IS PRESS THE BUTTON!
THAT'S A TRACKING DEVICE, YOU IDIOT.
I'M JUST THINKING ABOUT WHAT MY OLD CRONIES IN THE BROTHERHOOD OF MUTANTS ARE GONNA DO TO YOU, SABRETOOTH.

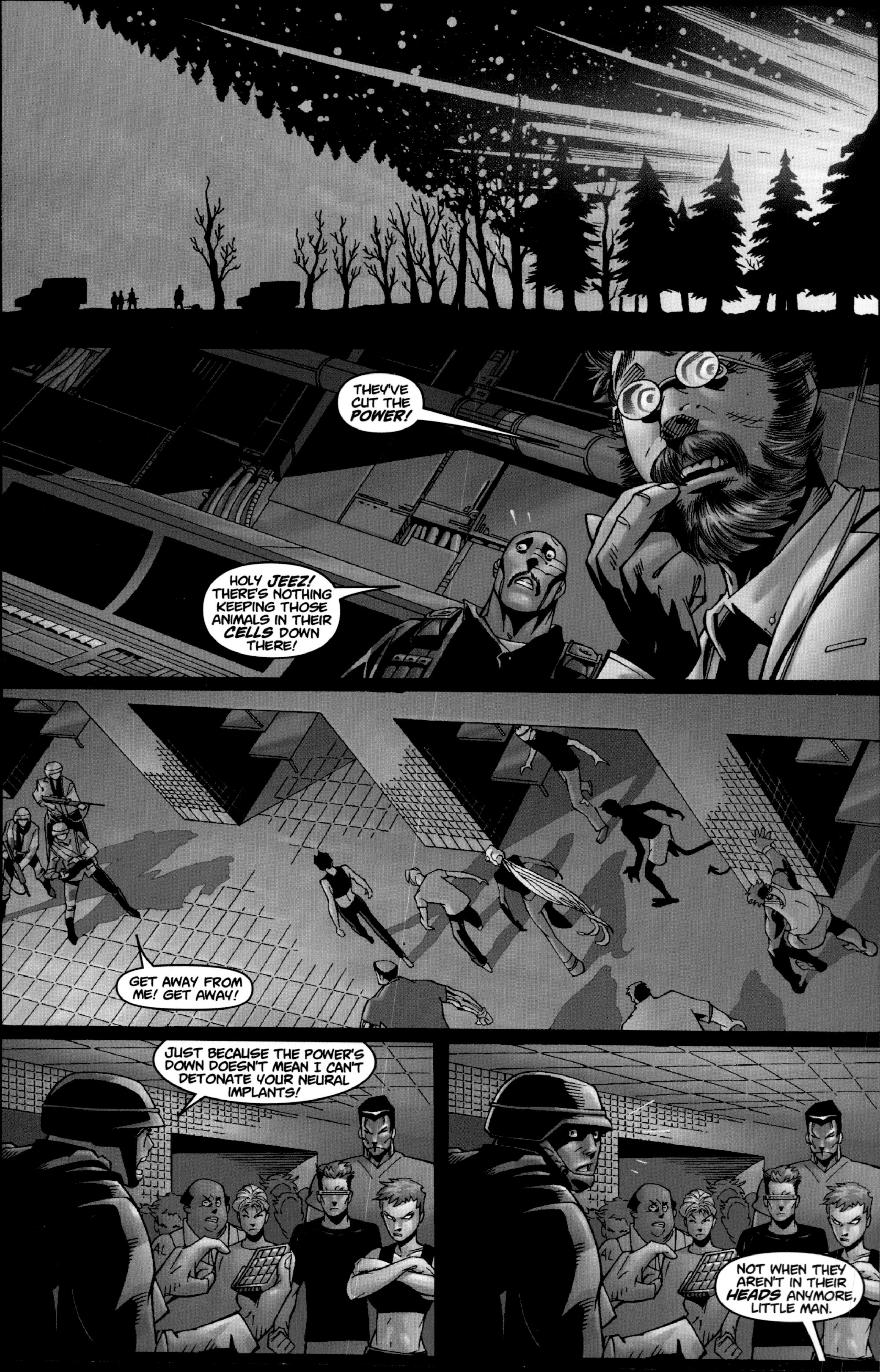
THEY'VE CUT THE POWER!
HOLY JEEZ! THERE'S NOTHING KEEPING THOSE ANIMALS IN THEIR CELLS DOWN THERE!
GET AWAY FROM ME! GET AWAY!
JUST BECAUSE THE POWER'S DOWN DOESN'T MEAN I CAN'T DETONATE YOUR NEURAL IMPLANTS!
NOT WHEN THEY AREN'T IN THEIR HEADS ANYMORE, LITTLE MAN.

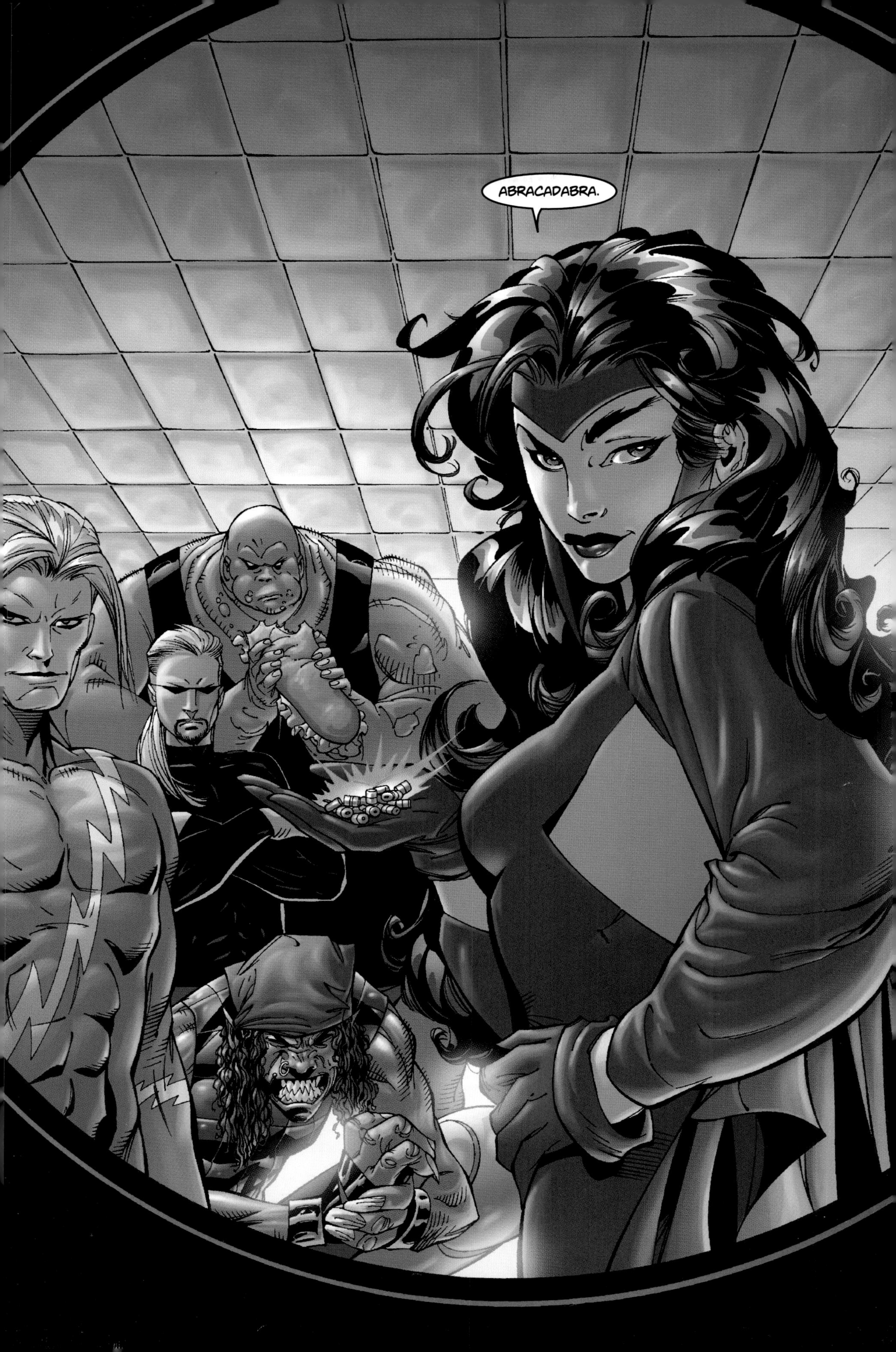
ABRACADABRA.

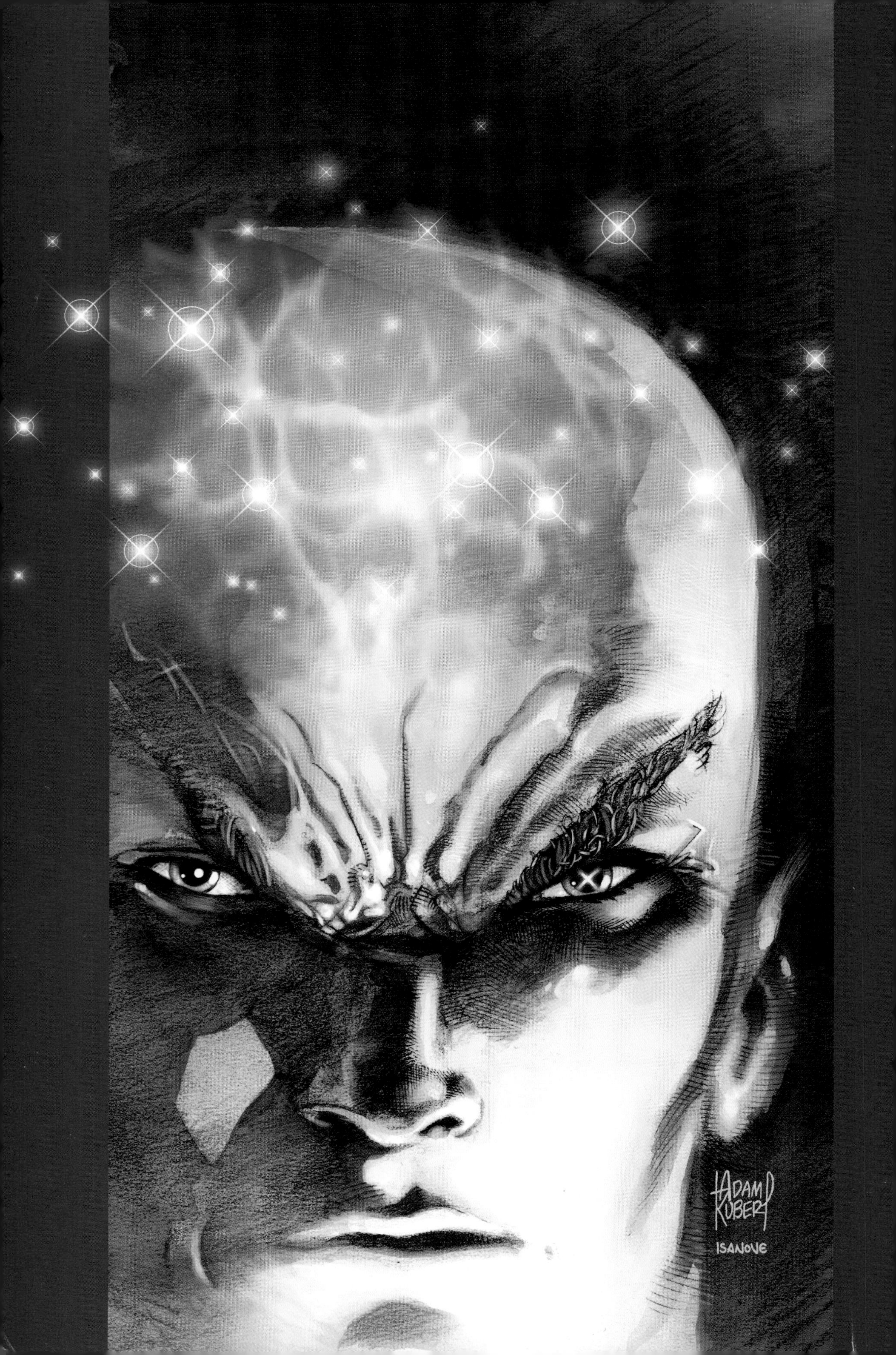
ADAM KUBERT
ISANOVE

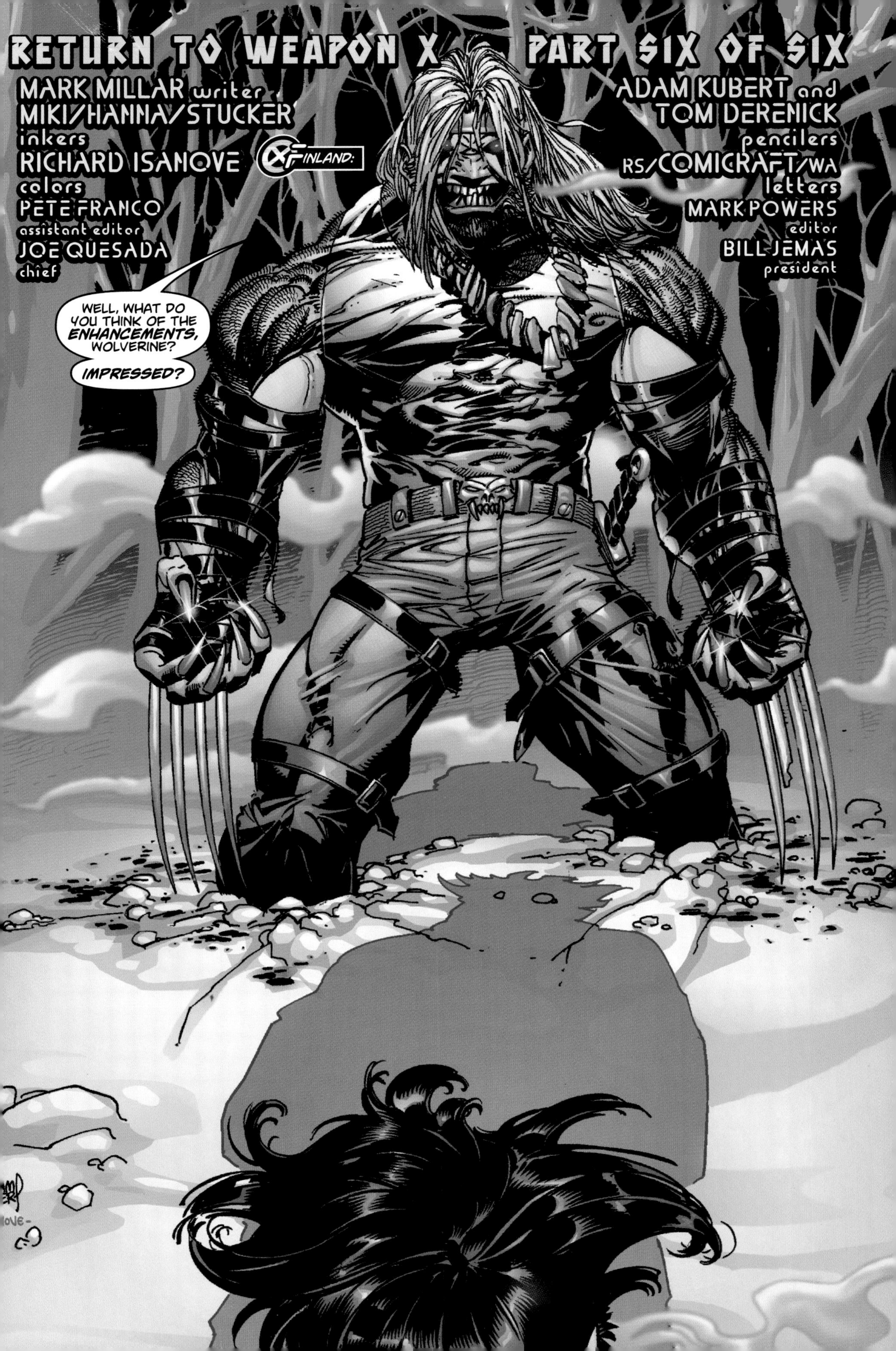

RETURN TO WEAPON X PART SIX OF SIX
MARK MILLAR writer
MIKI/HANNA/STUCKER inkers
RICHARD ISANOVE colors
PETE FRANCO assistant editor
JOE QUESADA chief
X FINLAND:
ADAM KUBERT and TOM DERENICK pencilers
RS/COMICRAFT/WA letters
MARK POWERS editor
BILL JEMAS president
WELL, WHAT DO YOU THINK OF THE ENHANCEMENTS, WOLVERINE?
IMPRESSED?

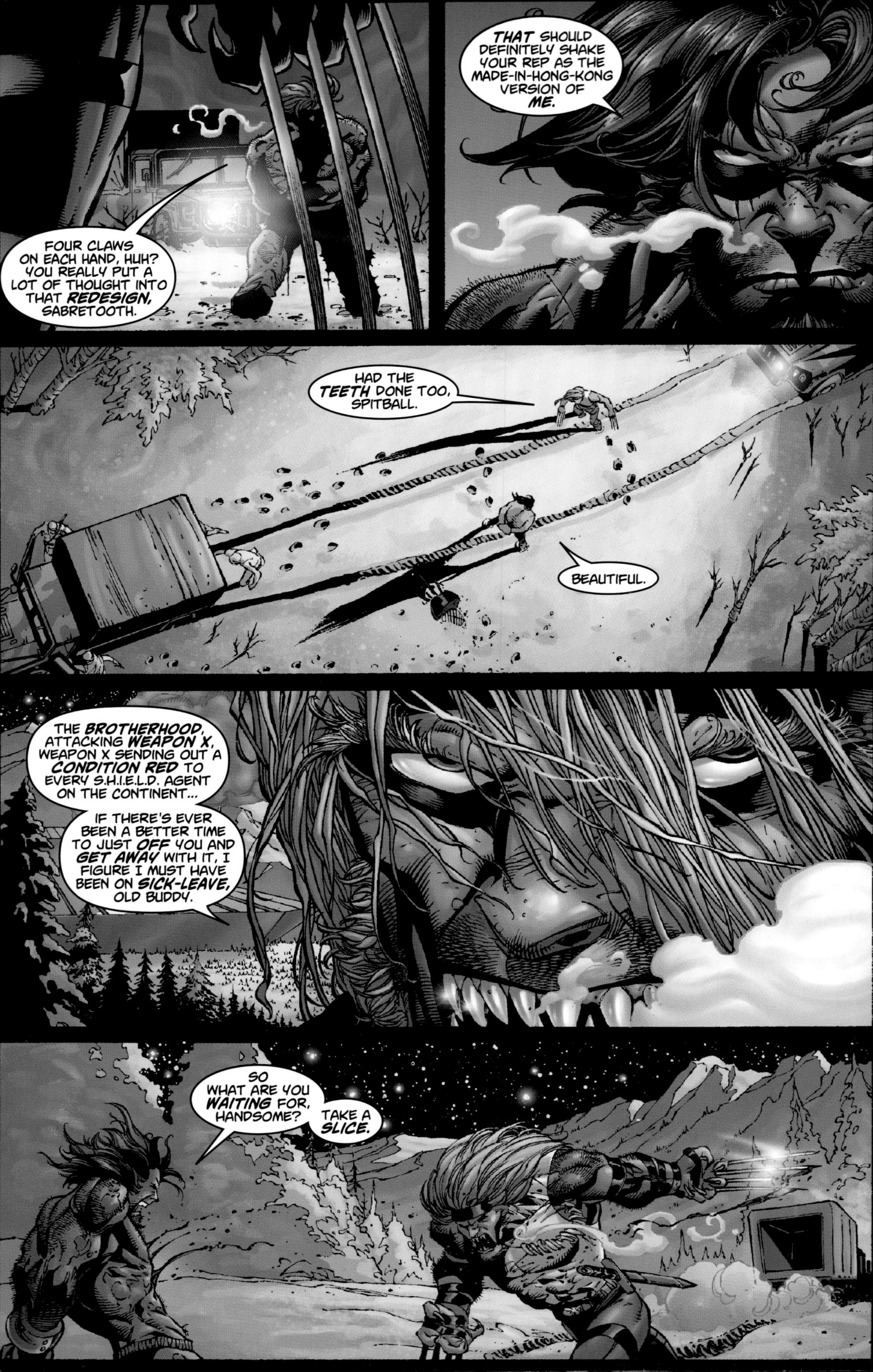
FOUR CLAWS ON EACH HAND, HUH? YOU REALLY PUT A LOT OF THOUGHT INTO THAT REDESIGN, SABRETOOTH.
THAT SHOULD DEFINITELY SHAKE YOUR REP AS THE MADE-IN-HONG-KONG VERSION OF ME.
HAD THE TEETH DONE TOO, SPITBALL.
BEAUTIFUL.
THE BROTHERHOOD, ATTACKING WEAPON X, WEAPON X SENDING OUT A CONDITION RED TO EVERY S.H.I.E.L.D. AGENT ON THE CONTINENT...
IF THERE'S EVER BEEN A BETTER TIME TO JUST OFF YOU AND GET AWAY WITH IT, I FIGURE I MUST HAVE BEEN ON SICK-LEAVE, OLD BUDDY.
SO WHAT ARE YOU WAITING FOR, HANDSOME?
TAKE A SLICE.

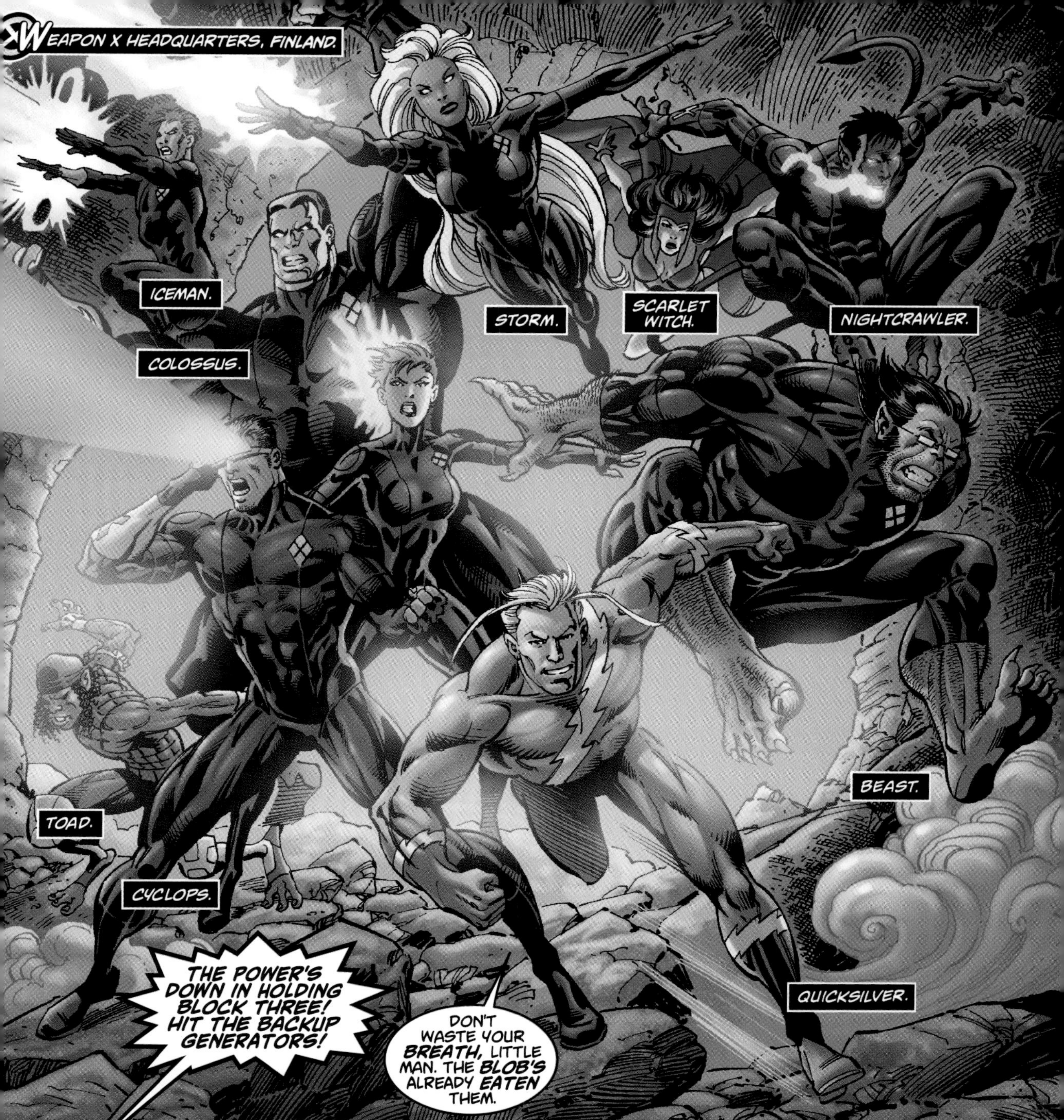
WEAPON X HEADQUARTERS, FINLAND.
ICEMAN.
COLOSSUS.
STORM.
SCARLET WITCH.
NIGHTCRAWLER.
TOAD.
CYCLOPS.
BEAST.
QUICKSILVER.
THE POWER'S DOWN IN HOLDING BLOCK THREE! HIT THE BACKUP GENERATORS!
DON'T WASTE YOUR BREATH, LITTLE MAN. THE BLOB'S ALREADY EATEN THEM.

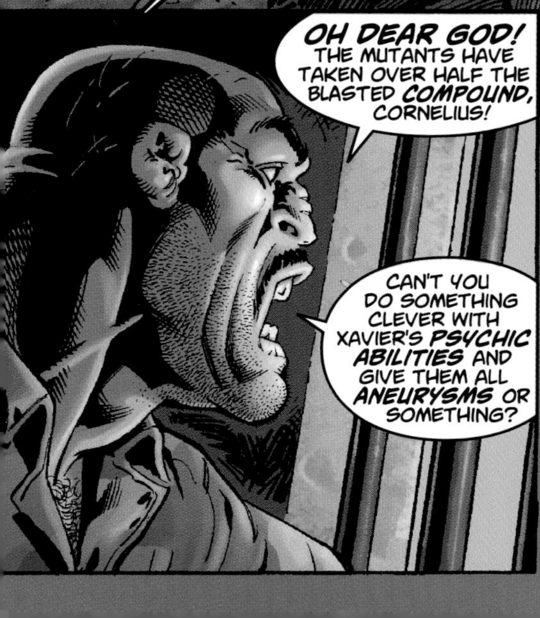
OH DEAR GOD! THE MUTANTS HAVE TAKEN OVER HALF THE BLASTED COMPOUND, CORNELIUS!
CAN'T YOU DO SOMETHING CLEVER WITH XAVIER'S PSYCHIC ABILITIES AND GIVE THEM ALL ANEURYSMS OR SOMETHING?

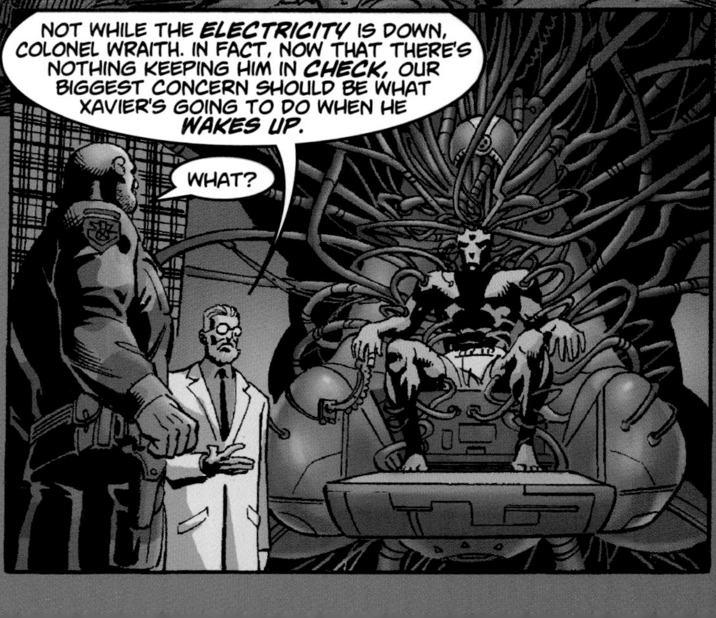
NOT WHILE THE ELECTRICITY IS DOWN, COLONEL WRAITH. IN FACT, NOW THAT THERE'S NOTHING KEEPING HIM IN CHECK, OUR BIGGEST CONCERN SHOULD BE WHAT XAVIER'S GOING TO DO WHEN HE WAKES UP.
WHAT?

FREEZE, YOU *FREAKS!*

YOU KNOW, YOU REALLY *SHOULDN'T* GIVE ICEMAN *OPENINGS* LIKE THAT, MISTER.

WHAT MAKES YOU THINK HE'S GONNA WAKE UP?

WELL, WHY *SHOULDN'T* HE? THE ONLY THING THAT WAS LETTING US *CONTROL* HIM WERE THE *NEURAL CLAMPS,* AND NOW THAT THE *MACHINE* ISN'T WORKING...

...WELL, MY GUESS IS WE'VE GOT APPROXIMATELY FIVE TO TEN MINUTES TO GET *OUT* OF HERE.

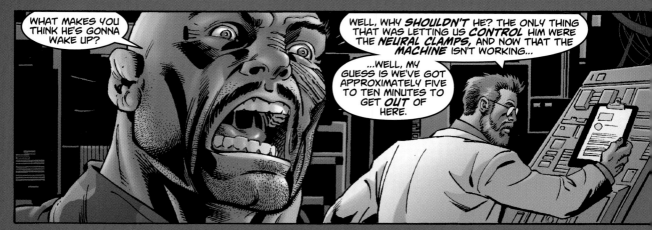

UNACCEPTABLE, CORNELIUS. ABSOLUTELY *OFF-THE-SCALE* UNACCEPTABLE...

WRAITH! WHAT ON EARTH ARE YOU *DOING?*

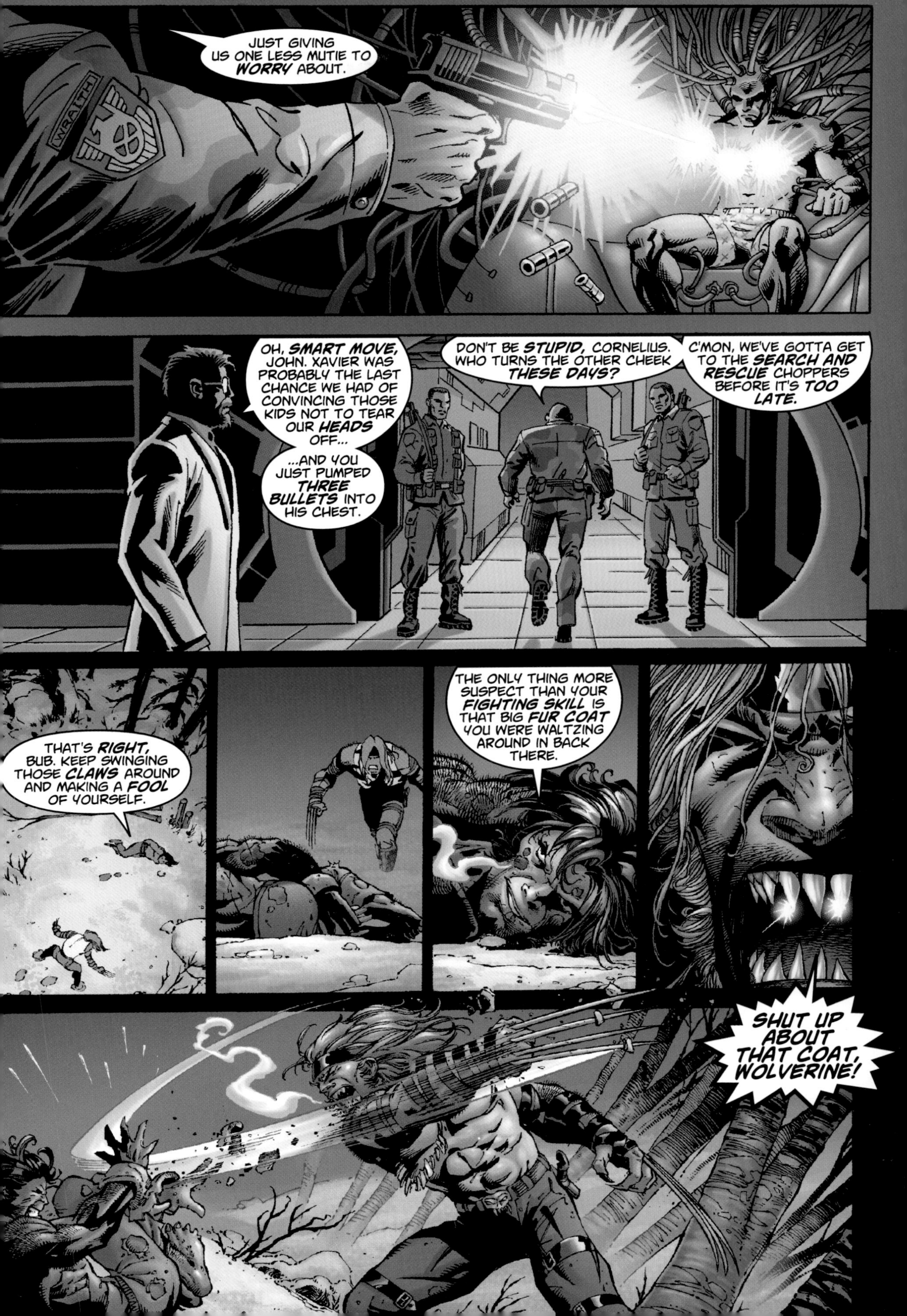

JUST GIVING US ONE LESS MUTIE TO WORRY ABOUT.
WRAITH
OH, SMART MOVE, JOHN. XAVIER WAS PROBABLY THE LAST CHANCE WE HAD OF CONVINCING THOSE KIDS NOT TO TEAR OUR HEADS OFF...
...AND YOU JUST PUMPED THREE BULLETS INTO HIS CHEST.
DON'T BE STUPID, CORNELIUS. WHO TURNS THE OTHER CHEEK THESE DAYS?
C'MON, WE'VE GOTTA GET TO THE SEARCH AND RESCUE CHOPPERS BEFORE IT'S TOO LATE.
THAT'S RIGHT, BUB. KEEP SWINGING THOSE CLAWS AROUND AND MAKING A FOOL OF YOURSELF.
THE ONLY THING MORE SUSPECT THAN YOUR FIGHTING SKILL IS THAT BIG FUR COAT YOU WERE WALTZING AROUND IN BACK THERE.
SHUT UP ABOUT THAT COAT, WOLVERINE!

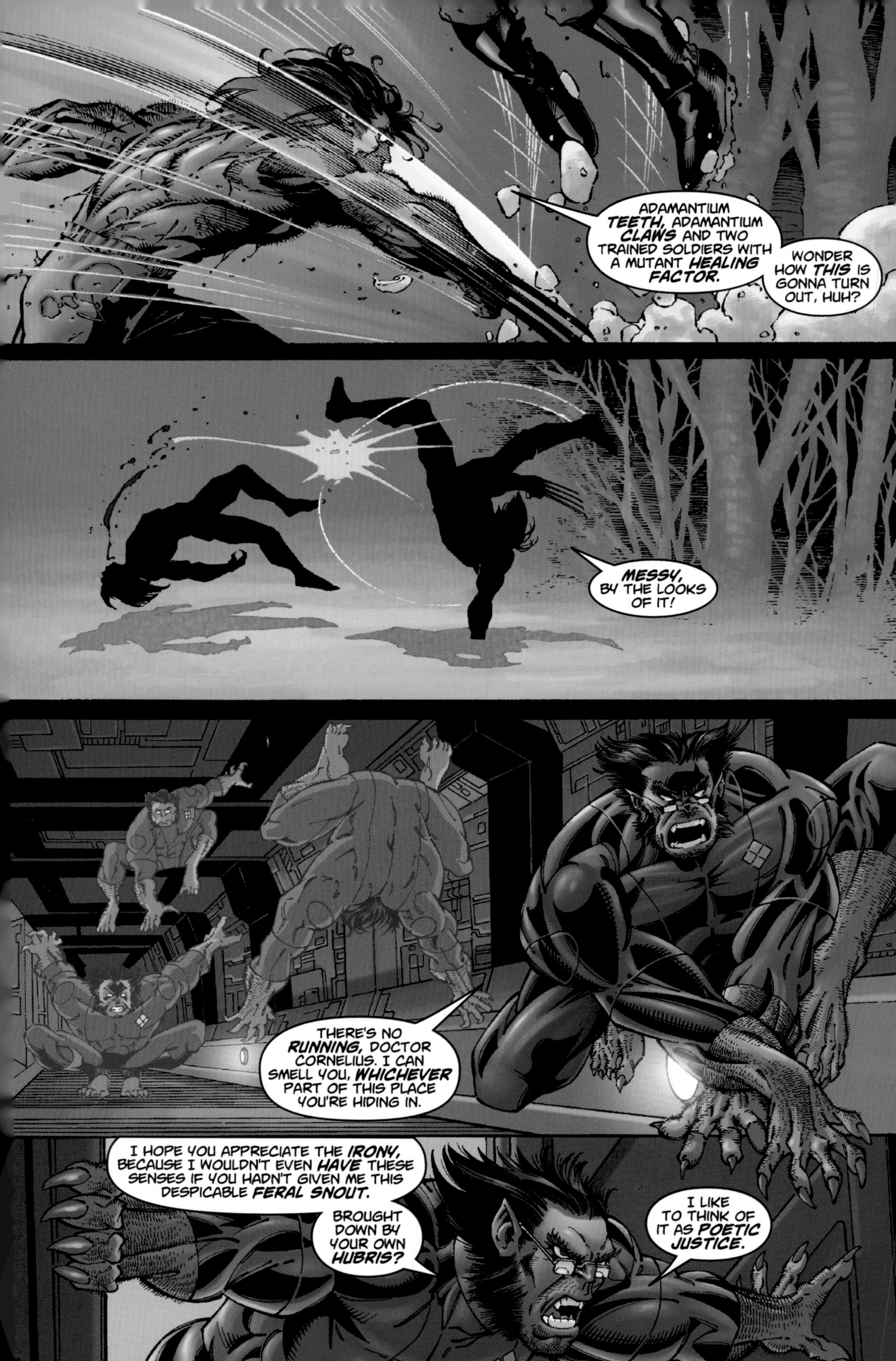
ADAMANTIUM TEETH, ADAMANTIUM CLAWS AND TWO TRAINED SOLDIERS WITH A MUTANT HEALING FACTOR.
WONDER HOW THIS IS GONNA TURN OUT, HUH?
MESSY, BY THE LOOKS OF IT!
THERE'S NO RUNNING, DOCTOR CORNELIUS. I CAN SMELL YOU, WHICHEVER PART OF THIS PLACE YOU'RE HIDING IN.
I HOPE YOU APPRECIATE THE IRONY, BECAUSE I WOULDN'T EVEN HAVE THESE SENSES IF YOU HADN'T GIVEN ME THIS DESPICABLE FERAL SNOUT.
BROUGHT DOWN BY YOUR OWN HUBRIS?
I LIKE TO THINK OF IT AS POETIC JUSTICE.

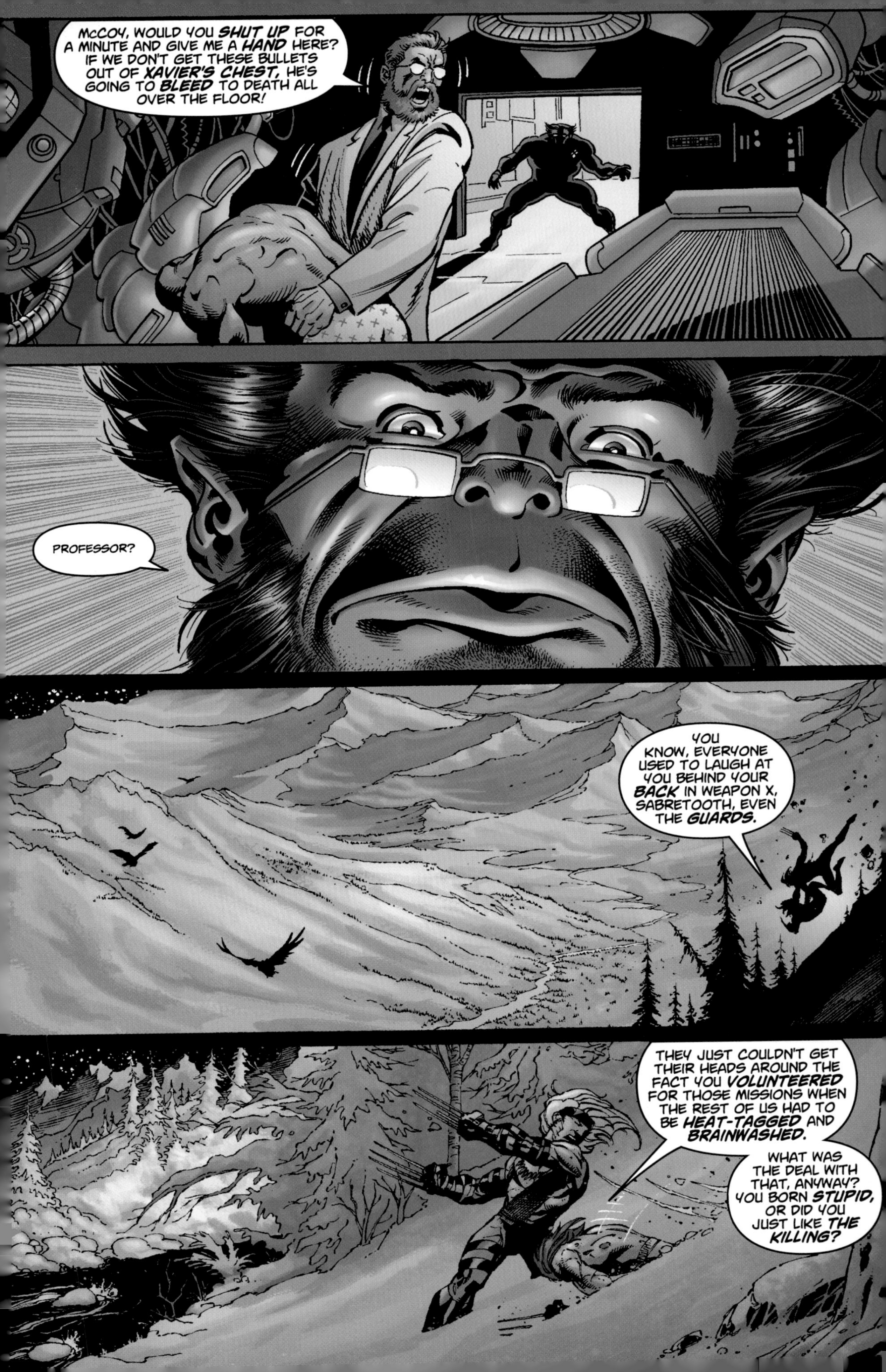
McCOY, WOULD YOU SHUT UP FOR A MINUTE AND GIVE ME A HAND HERE? IF WE DON'T GET THESE BULLETS OUT OF XAVIER'S CHEST, HE'S GOING TO BLEED TO DEATH ALL OVER THE FLOOR!
PROFESSOR?
YOU KNOW, EVERYONE USED TO LAUGH AT YOU BEHIND YOUR BACK IN WEAPON X, SABRETOOTH, EVEN THE GUARDS.
THEY JUST COULDN'T GET THEIR HEADS AROUND THE FACT YOU VOLUNTEERED FOR THOSE MISSIONS WHEN THE REST OF US HAD TO BE HEAT-TAGGED AND BRAINWASHED.
WHAT WAS THE DEAL WITH THAT, ANYWAY? YOU BORN STUPID, OR DID YOU JUST LIKE THE KILLING?

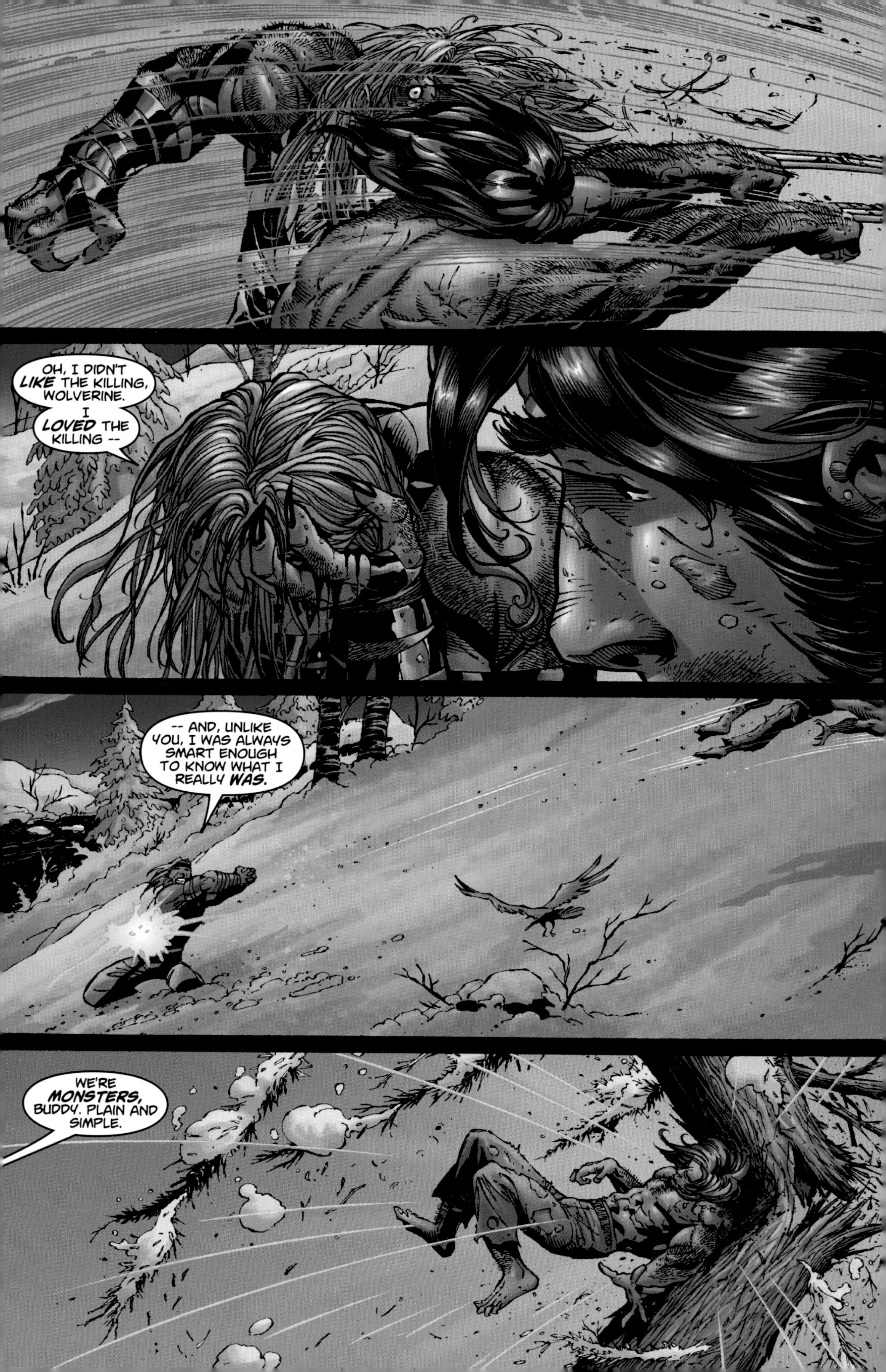

OH, I DIDN'T **LIKE** THE KILLING, WOLVERINE. I **LOVED** THE KILLING --
-- AND, UNLIKE YOU, I WAS ALWAYS SMART ENOUGH TO KNOW WHAT I REALLY **WAS**.
WE'RE **MONSTERS**, BUDDY. PLAIN AND SIMPLE.

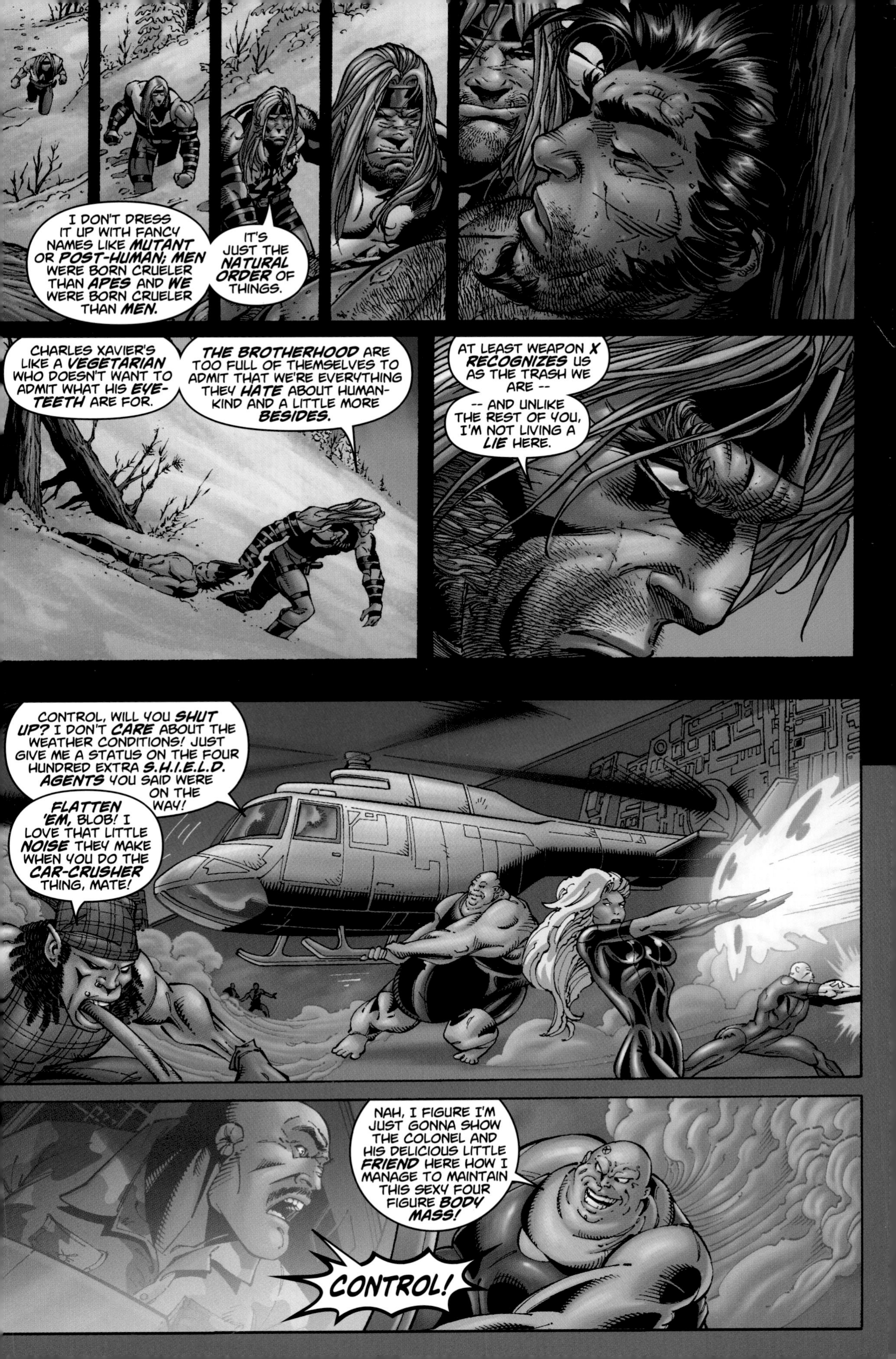

I DON'T DRESS IT UP WITH FANCY NAMES LIKE MUTANT OR POST-HUMAN; MEN WERE BORN CRUELER THAN APES AND WE WERE BORN CRUELER THAN MEN.
IT'S JUST THE NATURAL ORDER OF THINGS.
CHARLES XAVIER'S LIKE A VEGETARIAN WHO DOESN'T WANT TO ADMIT WHAT HIS EYE-TEETH ARE FOR.
THE BROTHERHOOD ARE TOO FULL OF THEMSELVES TO ADMIT THAT WE'RE EVERYTHING THEY HATE ABOUT HUMAN-KIND AND A LITTLE MORE BESIDES.
AT LEAST WEAPON X RECOGNIZES US AS THE TRASH WE ARE --
-- AND UNLIKE THE REST OF YOU, I'M NOT LIVING A LIE HERE.
CONTROL, WILL YOU SHUT UP? I DON'T CARE ABOUT THE WEATHER CONDITIONS! JUST GIVE ME A STATUS ON THE FOUR HUNDRED EXTRA S.H.I.E.L.D. AGENTS YOU SAID WERE ON THE WAY!
FLATTEN 'EM, BLOB! I LOVE THAT LITTLE NOISE THEY MAKE WHEN YOU DO THE CAR-CRUSHER THING, MATE!
NAH, I FIGURE I'M JUST GONNA SHOW THE COLONEL AND HIS DELICIOUS LITTLE FRIEND HERE HOW I MANAGE TO MAINTAIN THIS SEXY FOUR FIGURE BODY MASS!
CONTROL!

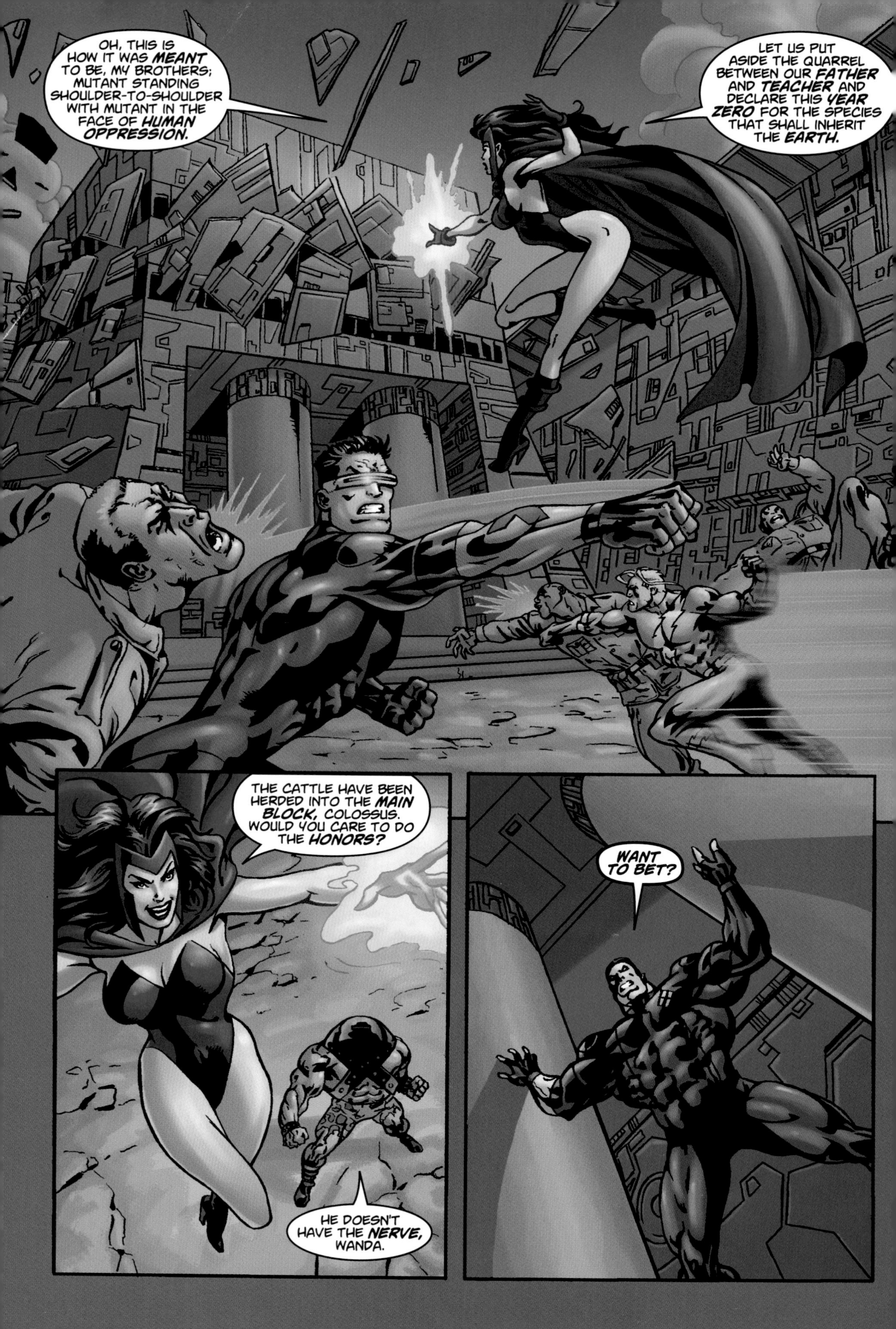
OH, THIS IS HOW IT WAS MEANT TO BE, MY BROTHERS; MUTANT STANDING SHOULDER-TO-SHOULDER WITH MUTANT IN THE FACE OF HUMAN OPPRESSION.
LET US PUT ASIDE THE QUARREL BETWEEN OUR FATHER AND TEACHER AND DECLARE THIS YEAR ZERO FOR THE SPECIES THAT SHALL INHERIT THE EARTH.
THE CATTLE HAVE BEEN HERDED INTO THE MAIN BLOCK, COLOSSUS. WOULD YOU CARE TO DO THE HONORS?
HE DOESN'T HAVE THE NERVE, WANDA.
WANT TO BET?

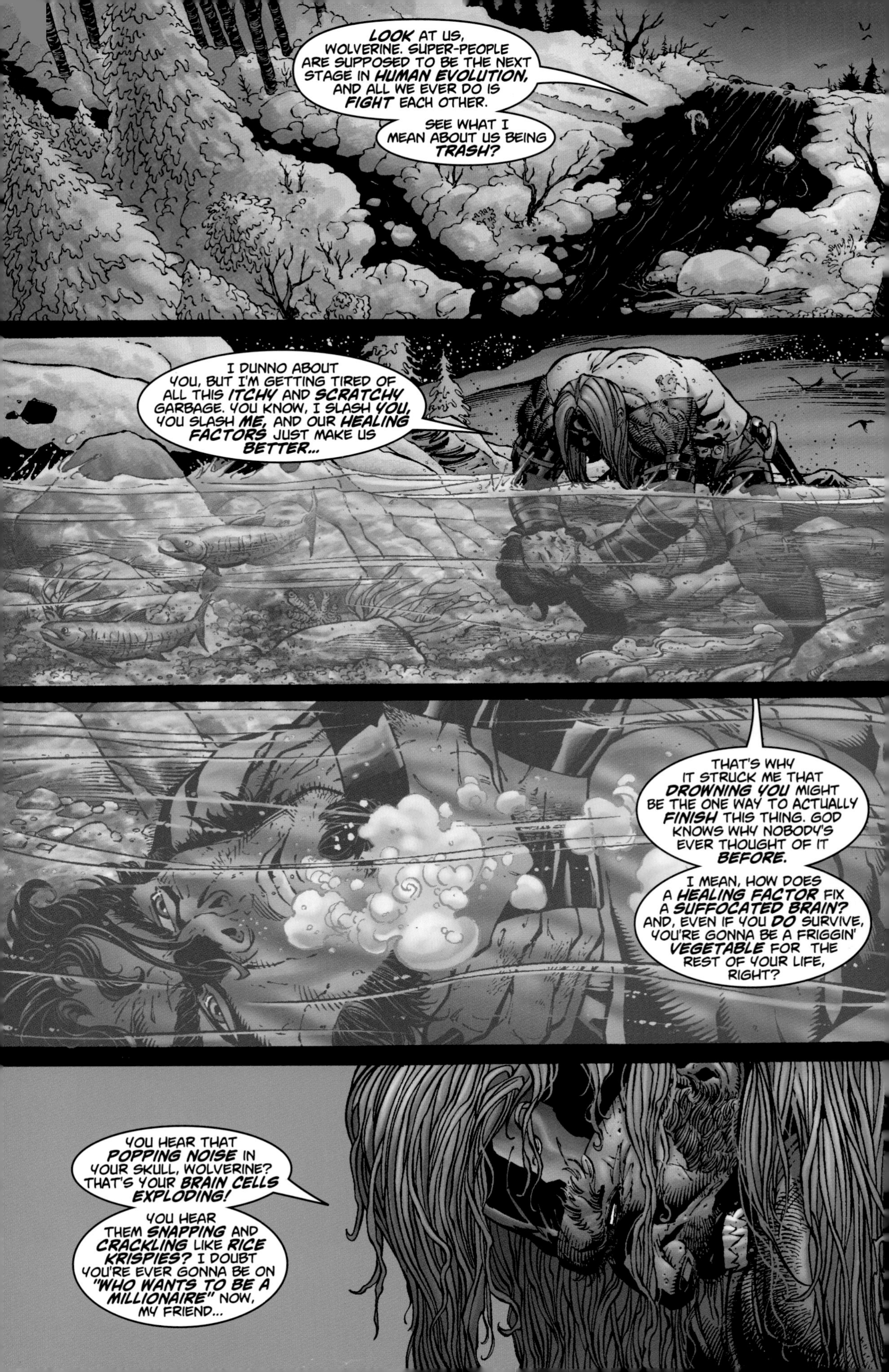
LOOK AT US, WOLVERINE. SUPER-PEOPLE ARE SUPPOSED TO BE THE NEXT STAGE IN HUMAN EVOLUTION, AND ALL WE EVER DO IS FIGHT EACH OTHER.
SEE WHAT I MEAN ABOUT US BEING TRASH?
I DUNNO ABOUT YOU, BUT I'M GETTING TIRED OF ALL THIS ITCHY AND SCRATCHY GARBAGE. YOU KNOW, I SLASH YOU, YOU SLASH ME, AND OUR HEALING FACTORS JUST MAKE US BETTER...
THAT'S WHY IT STRUCK ME THAT DROWNING YOU MIGHT BE THE ONE WAY TO ACTUALLY FINISH THIS THING. GOD KNOWS WHY NOBODY'S EVER THOUGHT OF IT BEFORE.
I MEAN, HOW DOES A HEALING FACTOR FIX A SUFFOCATED BRAIN? AND, EVEN IF YOU DO SURVIVE, YOU'RE GONNA BE A FRIGGIN' VEGETABLE FOR THE REST OF YOUR LIFE, RIGHT?
YOU HEAR THAT POPPING NOISE IN YOUR SKULL, WOLVERINE? THAT'S YOUR BRAIN CELLS EXPLODING!
YOU HEAR THEM SNAPPING AND CRACKLING LIKE RICE KRISPIES? I DOUBT YOU'RE EVER GONNA BE ON "WHO WANTS TO BE A MILLIONAIRE" NOW, MY FRIEND...

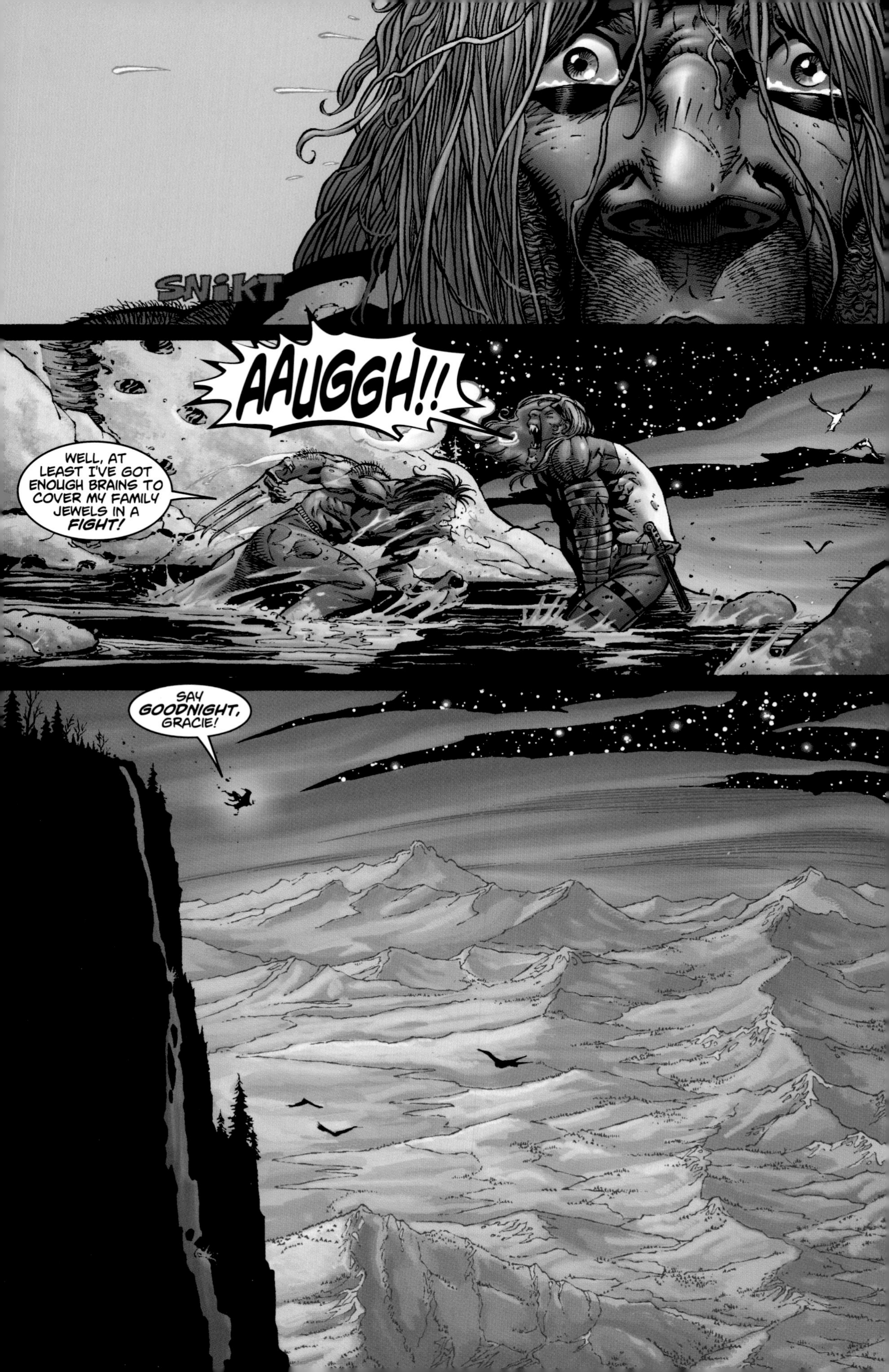
SNIKT
AAUGGH!!
WELL, AT LEAST I'VE GOT ENOUGH BRAINS TO COVER MY FAMILY JEWELS IN A FIGHT!
SAY GOODNIGHT, GRACIE!

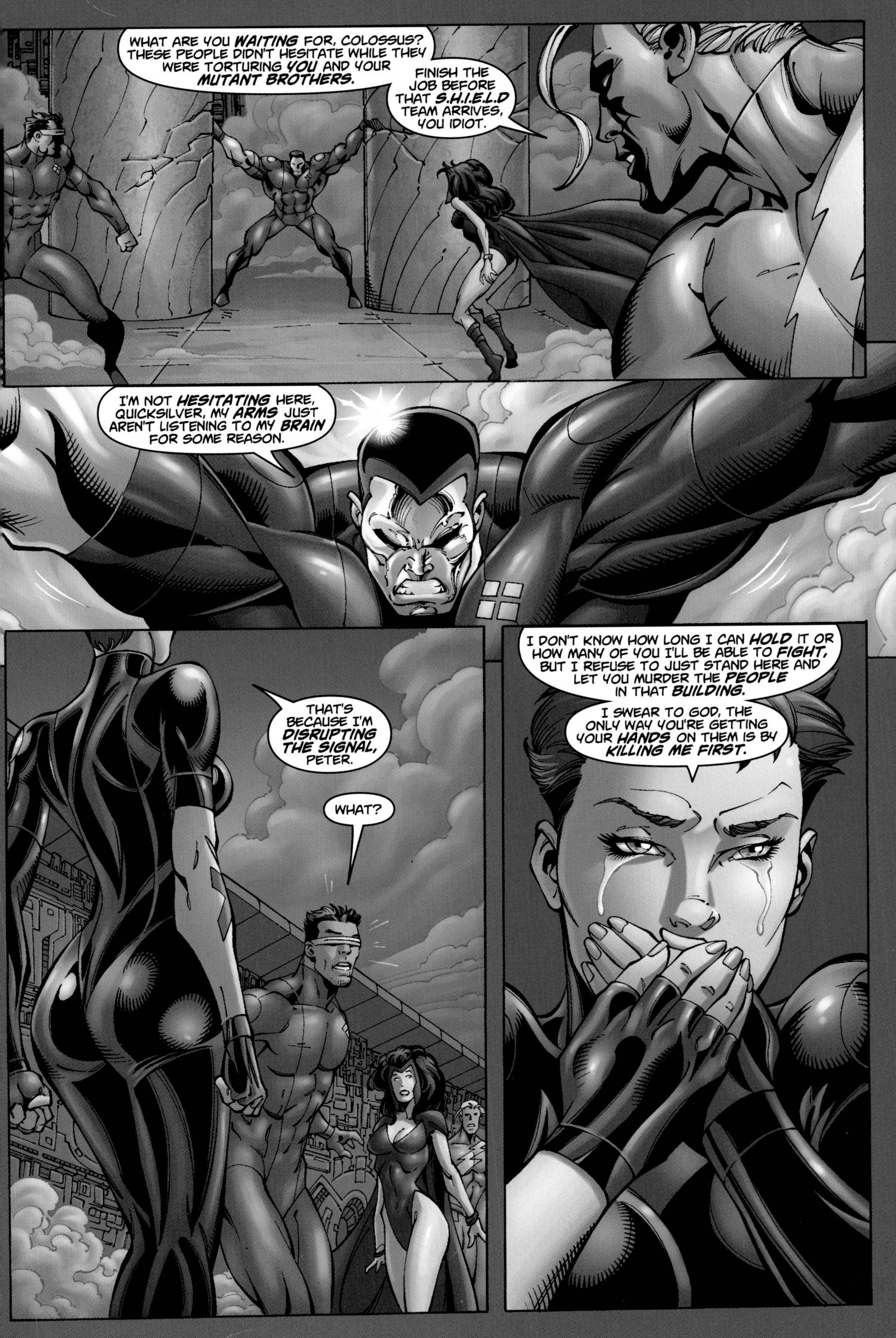
WHAT ARE YOU WAITING FOR, COLOSSUS? THESE PEOPLE DIDN'T HESITATE WHILE THEY WERE TORTURING YOU AND YOUR MUTANT BROTHERS.
FINISH THE JOB BEFORE THAT S.H.I.E.L.D TEAM ARRIVES, YOU IDIOT.
I'M NOT HESITATING HERE, QUICKSILVER, MY ARMS JUST AREN'T LISTENING TO MY BRAIN FOR SOME REASON.
THAT'S BECAUSE I'M DISRUPTING THE SIGNAL, PETER.
WHAT?
I DON'T KNOW HOW LONG I CAN HOLD IT OR HOW MANY OF YOU I'LL BE ABLE TO FIGHT, BUT I REFUSE TO JUST STAND HERE AND LET YOU MURDER THE PEOPLE IN THAT BUILDING.
I SWEAR TO GOD, THE ONLY WAY YOU'RE GETTING YOUR HANDS ON THEM IS BY KILLING ME FIRST.

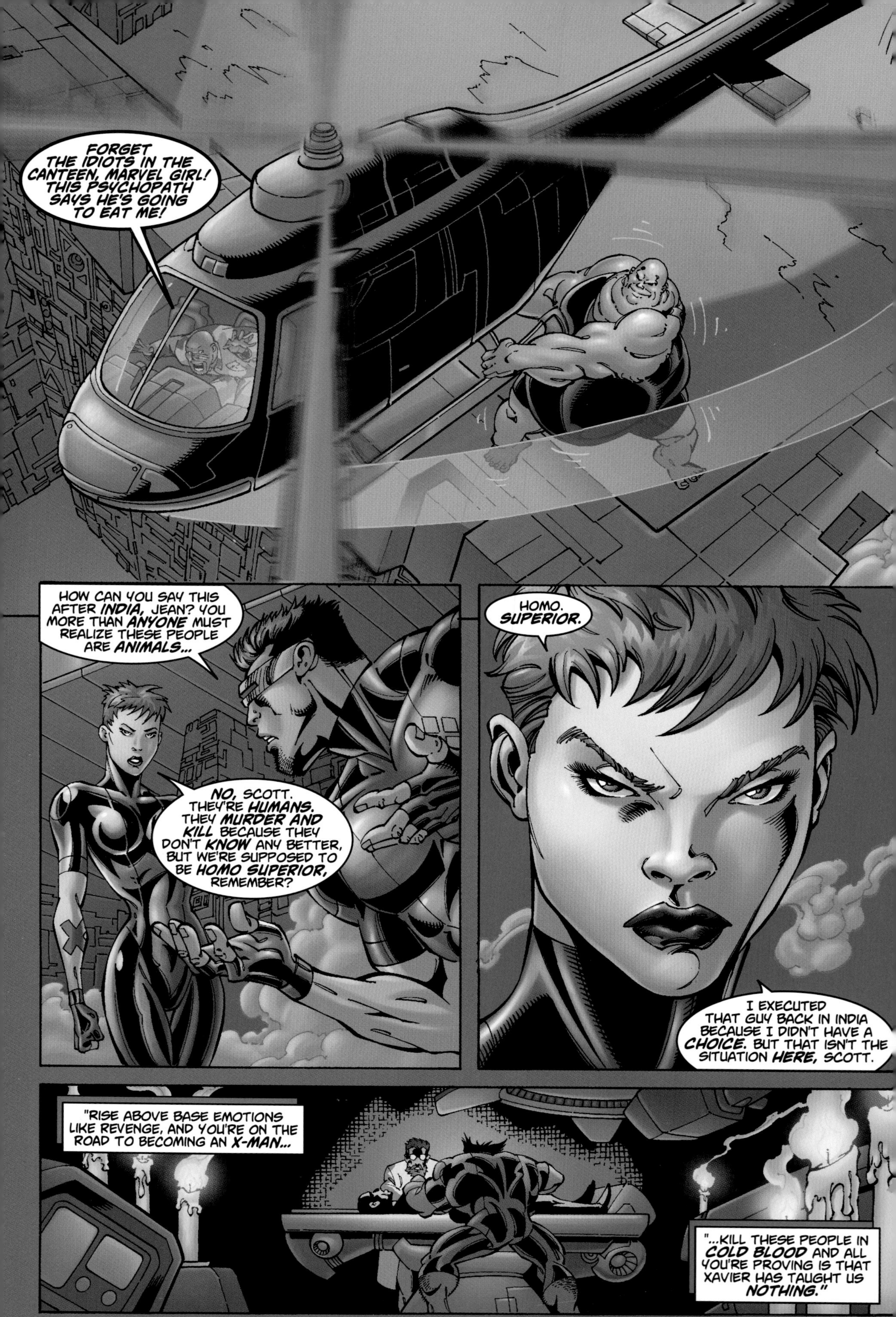

FORGET THE IDIOTS IN THE CANTEEN, MARVEL GIRL! THIS PSYCHOPATH SAYS HE'S GOING TO EAT ME!
HOW CAN YOU SAY THIS AFTER INDIA, JEAN? YOU MORE THAN ANYONE MUST REALIZE THESE PEOPLE ARE ANIMALS...
NO, SCOTT. THEY'RE HUMANS. THEY MURDER AND KILL BECAUSE THEY DON'T KNOW ANY BETTER, BUT WE'RE SUPPOSED TO BE HOMO SUPERIOR, REMEMBER?
HOMO. SUPERIOR.
I EXECUTED THAT GUY BACK IN INDIA BECAUSE I DIDN'T HAVE A CHOICE. BUT THAT ISN'T THE SITUATION HERE, SCOTT.
"RISE ABOVE BASE EMOTIONS LIKE REVENGE, AND YOU'RE ON THE ROAD TO BECOMING AN X-MAN...
"...KILL THESE PEOPLE IN COLD BLOOD AND ALL YOU'RE PROVING IS THAT XAVIER HAS TAUGHT US NOTHING."

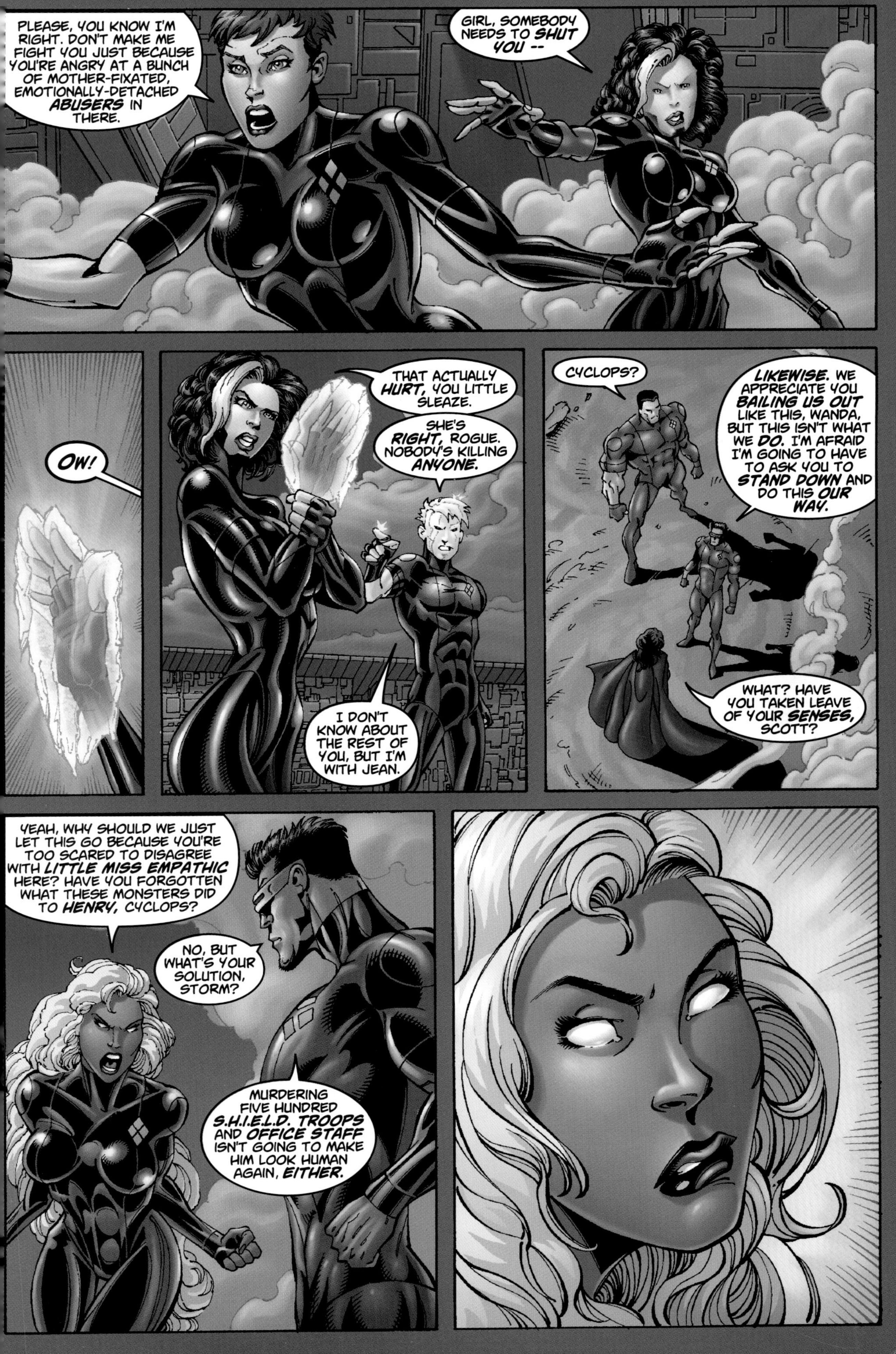
PLEASE, YOU KNOW I'M RIGHT. DON'T MAKE ME FIGHT YOU JUST BECAUSE YOU'RE ANGRY AT A BUNCH OF MOTHER-FIXATED, EMOTIONALLY-DETACHED ABUSERS IN THERE.
GIRL, SOMEBODY NEEDS TO SHUT YOU --
OW!
THAT ACTUALLY HURT, YOU LITTLE SLEAZE.
SHE'S RIGHT, ROGUE. NOBODY'S KILLING ANYONE.
I DON'T KNOW ABOUT THE REST OF YOU, BUT I'M WITH JEAN.
CYCLOPS?
LIKEWISE. WE APPRECIATE YOU BAILING US OUT LIKE THIS, WANDA, BUT THIS ISN'T WHAT WE DO. I'M AFRAID I'M GOING TO HAVE TO ASK YOU TO STAND DOWN AND DO THIS OUR WAY.
WHAT? HAVE YOU TAKEN LEAVE OF YOUR SENSES, SCOTT?
YEAH, WHY SHOULD WE JUST LET THIS GO BECAUSE YOU'RE TOO SCARED TO DISAGREE WITH LITTLE MISS EMPATHIC HERE? HAVE YOU FORGOTTEN WHAT THESE MONSTERS DID TO HENRY, CYCLOPS?
NO, BUT WHAT'S YOUR SOLUTION, STORM?
MURDERING FIVE HUNDRED S.H.I.E.L.D. TROOPS AND OFFICE STAFF ISN'T GOING TO MAKE HIM LOOK HUMAN AGAIN, EITHER.

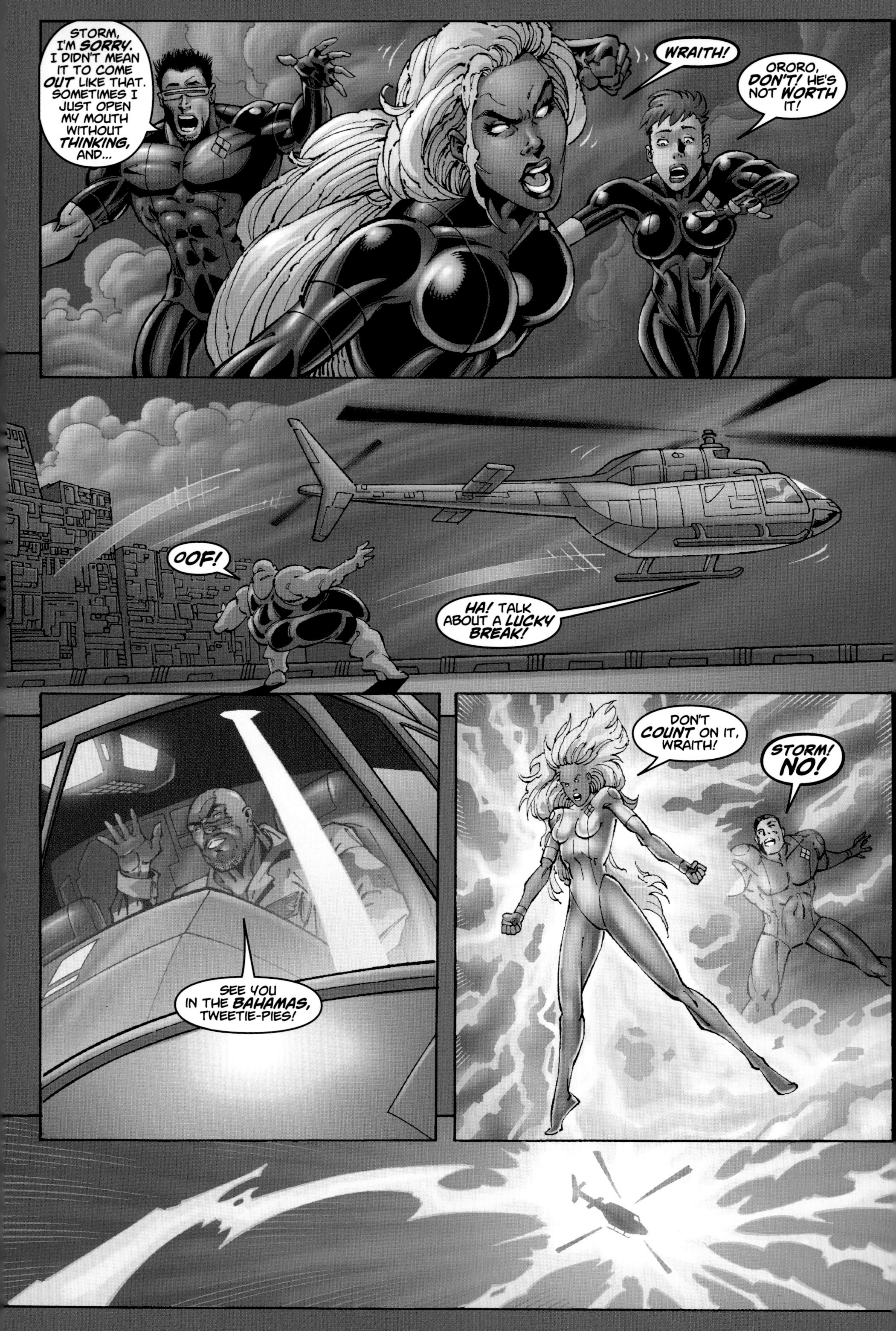
STORM, I'M SORRY. I DIDN'T MEAN IT TO COME OUT LIKE THAT. SOMETIMES I JUST OPEN MY MOUTH WITHOUT THINKING, AND...
WRAITH!
ORORO, DON'T! HE'S NOT WORTH IT!
OOF!
HA! TALK ABOUT A LUCKY BREAK!
SEE YOU IN THE BAHAMAS, TWEETIE-PIES!
DON'T COUNT ON IT, WRAITH!
STORM! NO!

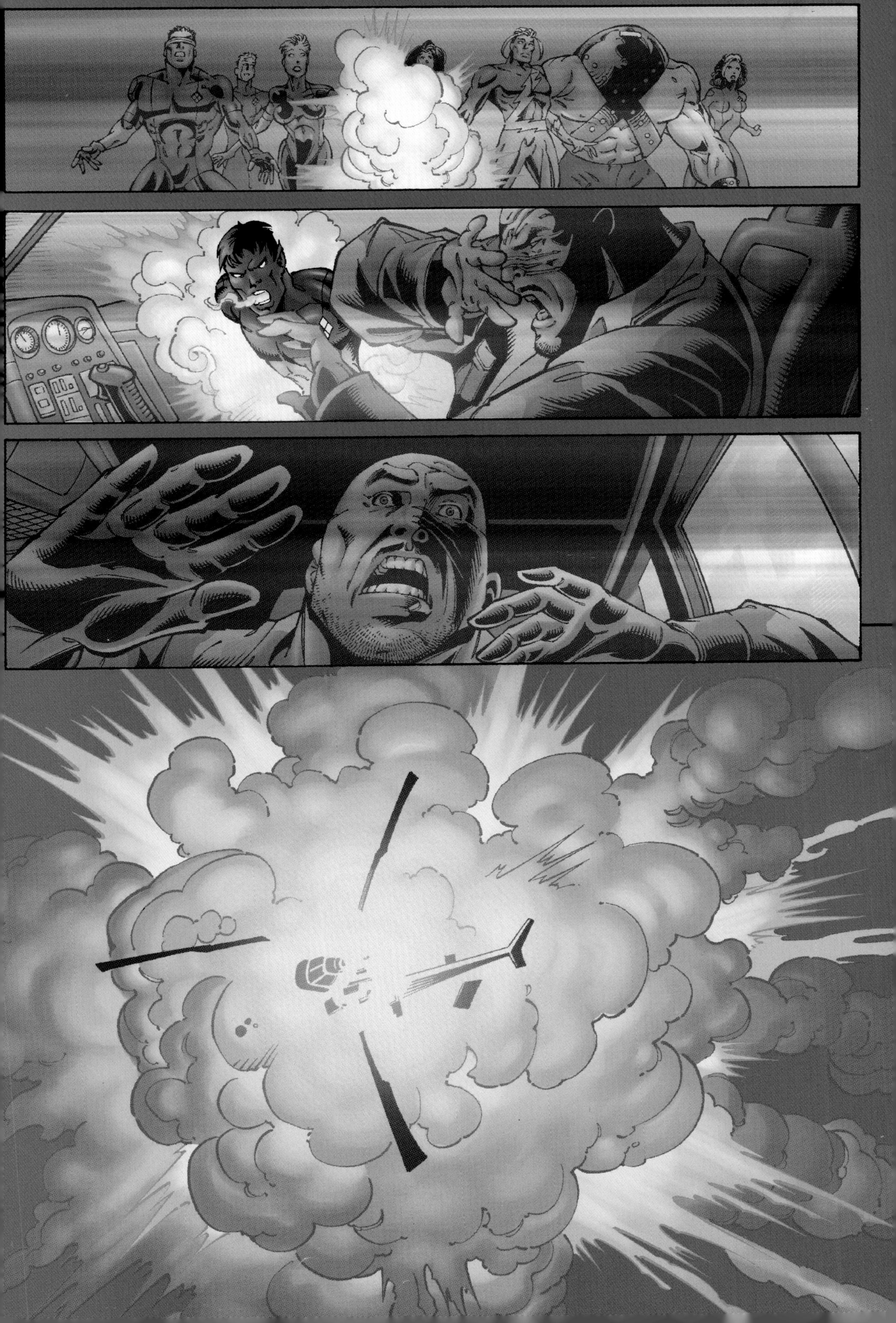

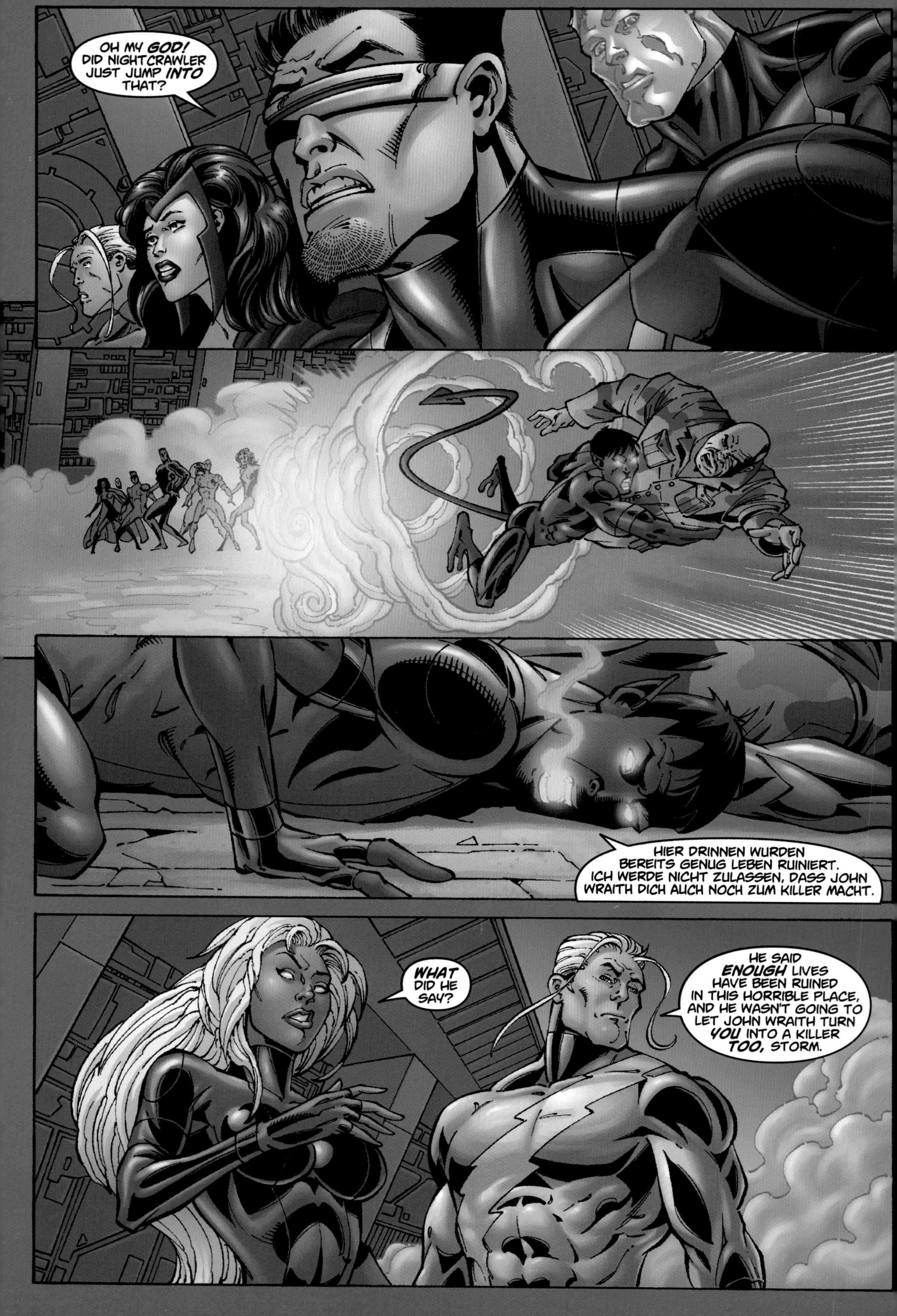
OH MY GOD! DID NIGHTCRAWLER JUST JUMP INTO THAT?
HIER DRINNEN WURDEN BEREITS GENUG LEBEN RUINIERT. ICH WERDE NICHT ZULASSEN, DASS JOHN WRAITH DICH AUCH NOCH ZUM KILLER MACHT.
WHAT DID HE SAY?
HE SAID ENOUGH LIVES HAVE BEEN RUINED IN THIS HORRIBLE PLACE, AND HE WASN'T GOING TO LET JOHN WRAITH TURN YOU INTO A KILLER TOO, STORM.

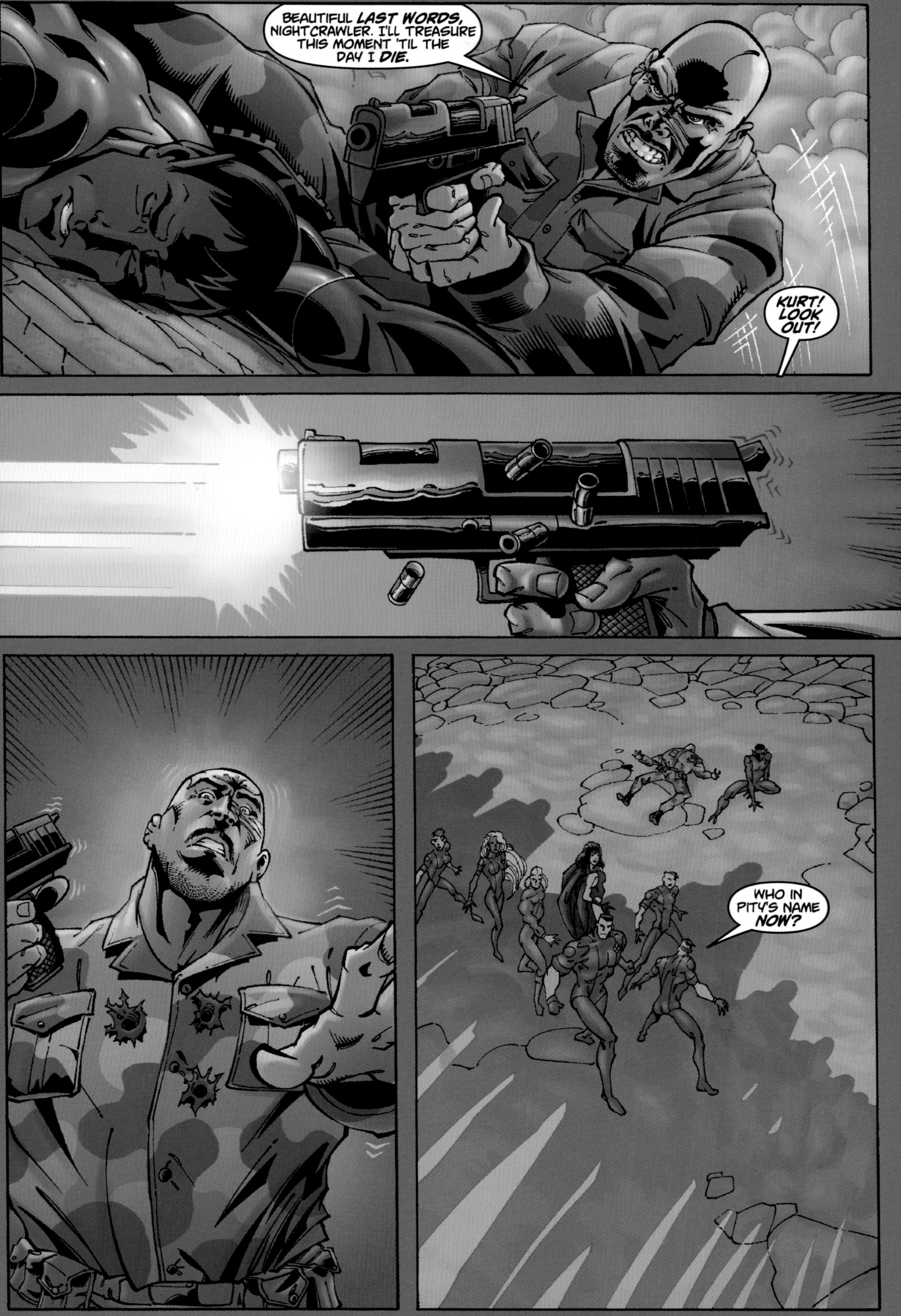
BEAUTIFUL LAST WORDS, NIGHTCRAWLER. I'LL TREASURE THIS MOMENT 'TIL THE DAY I DIE.
KURT! LOOK OUT!
WHO IN PITY'S NAME NOW?

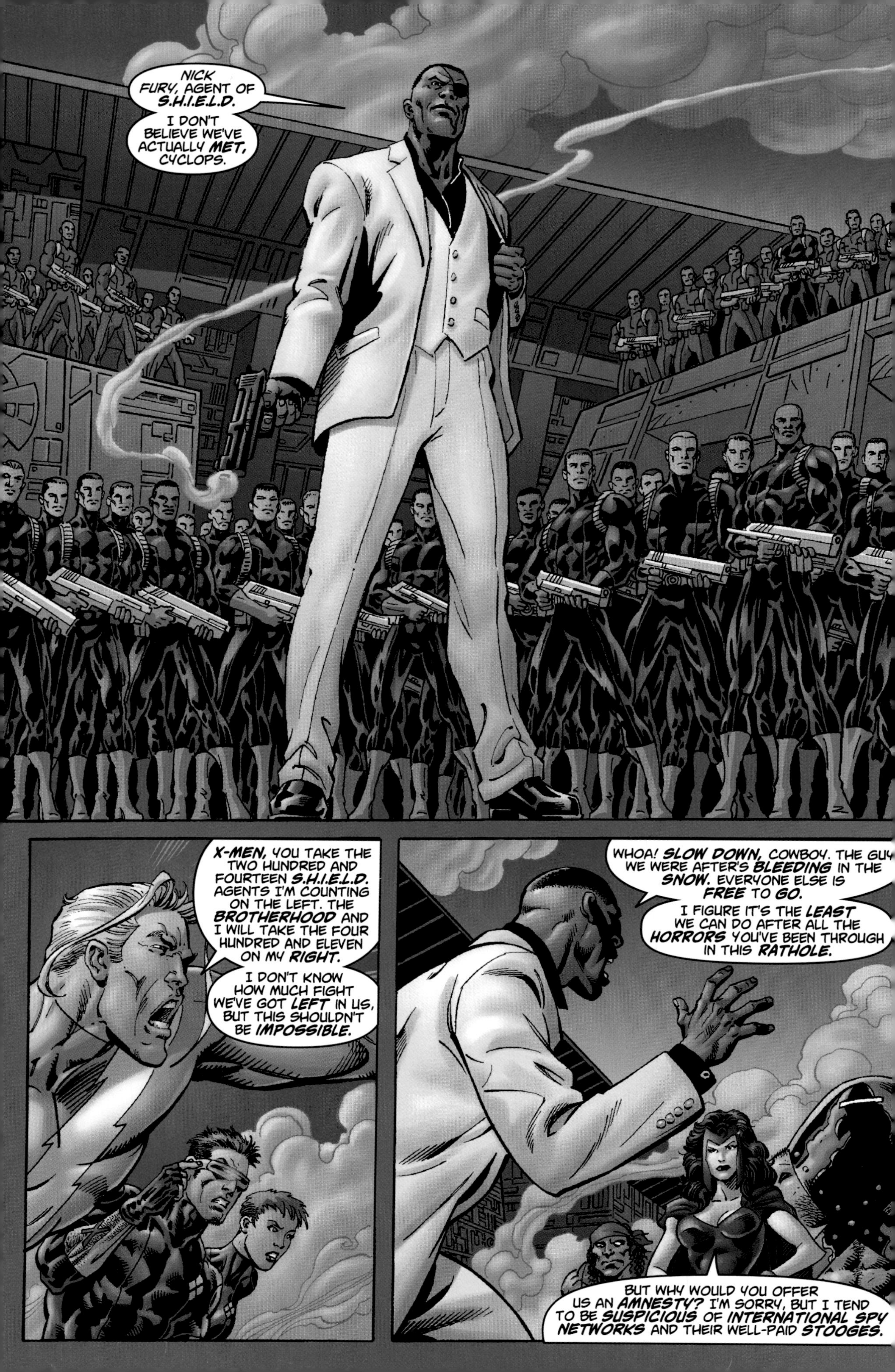
NICK FURY, AGENT OF S.H.I.E.L.D.
I DON'T BELIEVE WE'VE ACTUALLY MET, CYCLOPS.
X-MEN, YOU TAKE THE TWO HUNDRED AND FOURTEEN S.H.I.E.L.D. AGENTS I'M COUNTING ON THE LEFT. THE BROTHERHOOD AND I WILL TAKE THE FOUR HUNDRED AND ELEVEN ON MY RIGHT.
I DON'T KNOW HOW MUCH FIGHT WE'VE GOT LEFT IN US, BUT THIS SHOULDN'T BE IMPOSSIBLE.
WHOA! SLOW DOWN, COWBOY. THE GUY WE WERE AFTER'S BLEEDING IN THE SNOW. EVERYONE ELSE IS FREE TO GO.
I FIGURE IT'S THE LEAST WE CAN DO AFTER ALL THE HORRORS YOU'VE BEEN THROUGH IN THIS RATHOLE.
BUT WHY WOULD YOU OFFER US AN AMNESTY? I'M SORRY, BUT I TEND TO BE SUSPICIOUS OF INTERNATIONAL SPY NETWORKS AND THEIR WELL-PAID STOOGES.

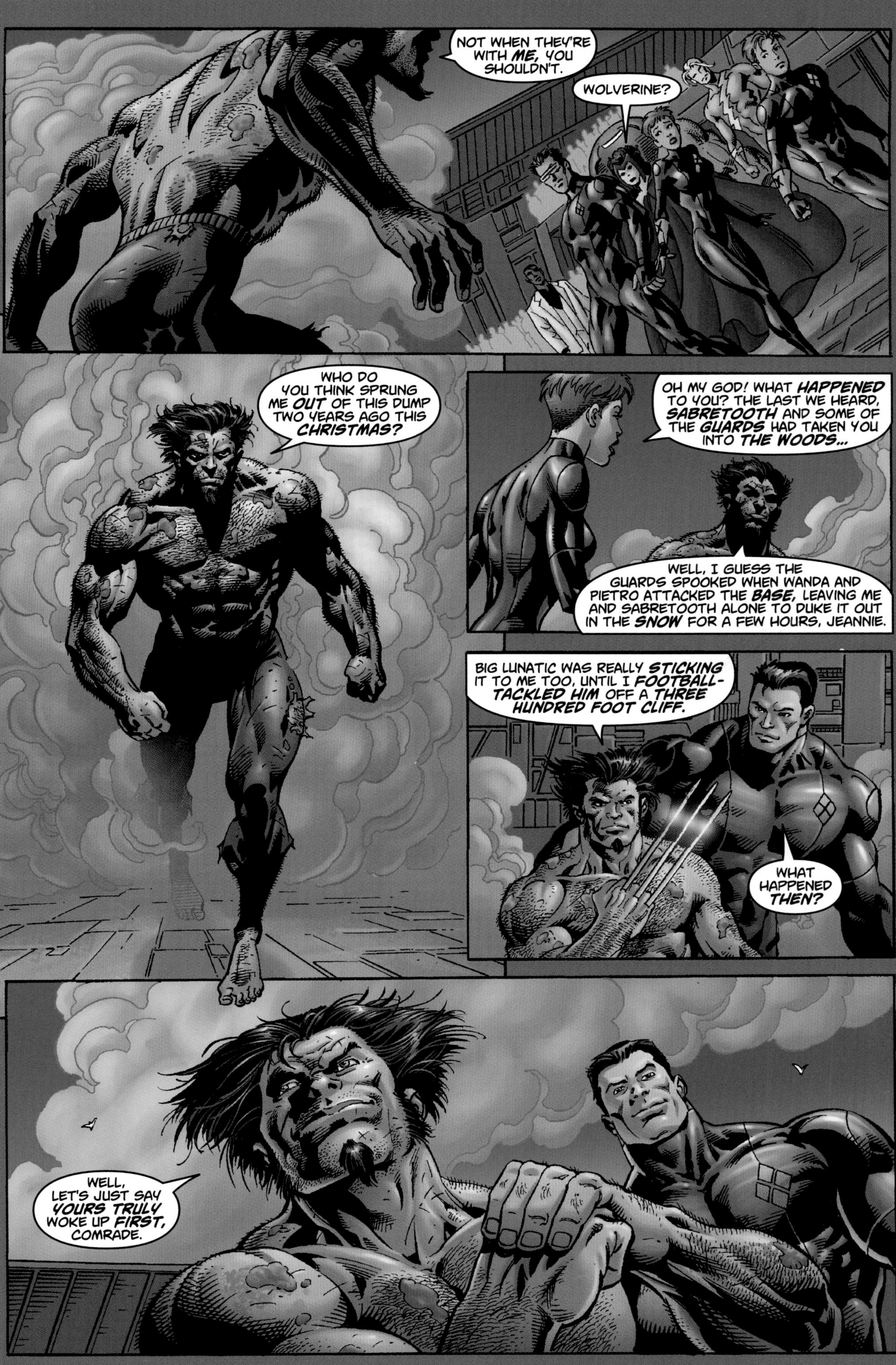

NOT WHEN THEY'RE WITH ME, YOU SHOULDN'T.
WOLVERINE?
WHO DO YOU THINK SPRUNG ME OUT OF THIS DUMP TWO YEARS AGO THIS CHRISTMAS?
OH MY GOD! WHAT HAPPENED TO YOU? THE LAST WE HEARD, SABRETOOTH AND SOME OF THE GUARDS HAD TAKEN YOU INTO THE WOODS...
WELL, I GUESS THE GUARDS SPOOKED WHEN WANDA AND PIETRO ATTACKED THE BASE, LEAVING ME AND SABRETOOTH ALONE TO DUKE IT OUT IN THE SNOW FOR A FEW HOURS, JEANNIE.
BIG LUNATIC WAS REALLY STICKING IT TO ME TOO, UNTIL I FOOTBALL-TACKLED HIM OFF A THREE HUNDRED FOOT CLIFF.
WHAT HAPPENED THEN?
WELL, LET'S JUST SAY YOURS TRULY WOKE UP FIRST, COMRADE.

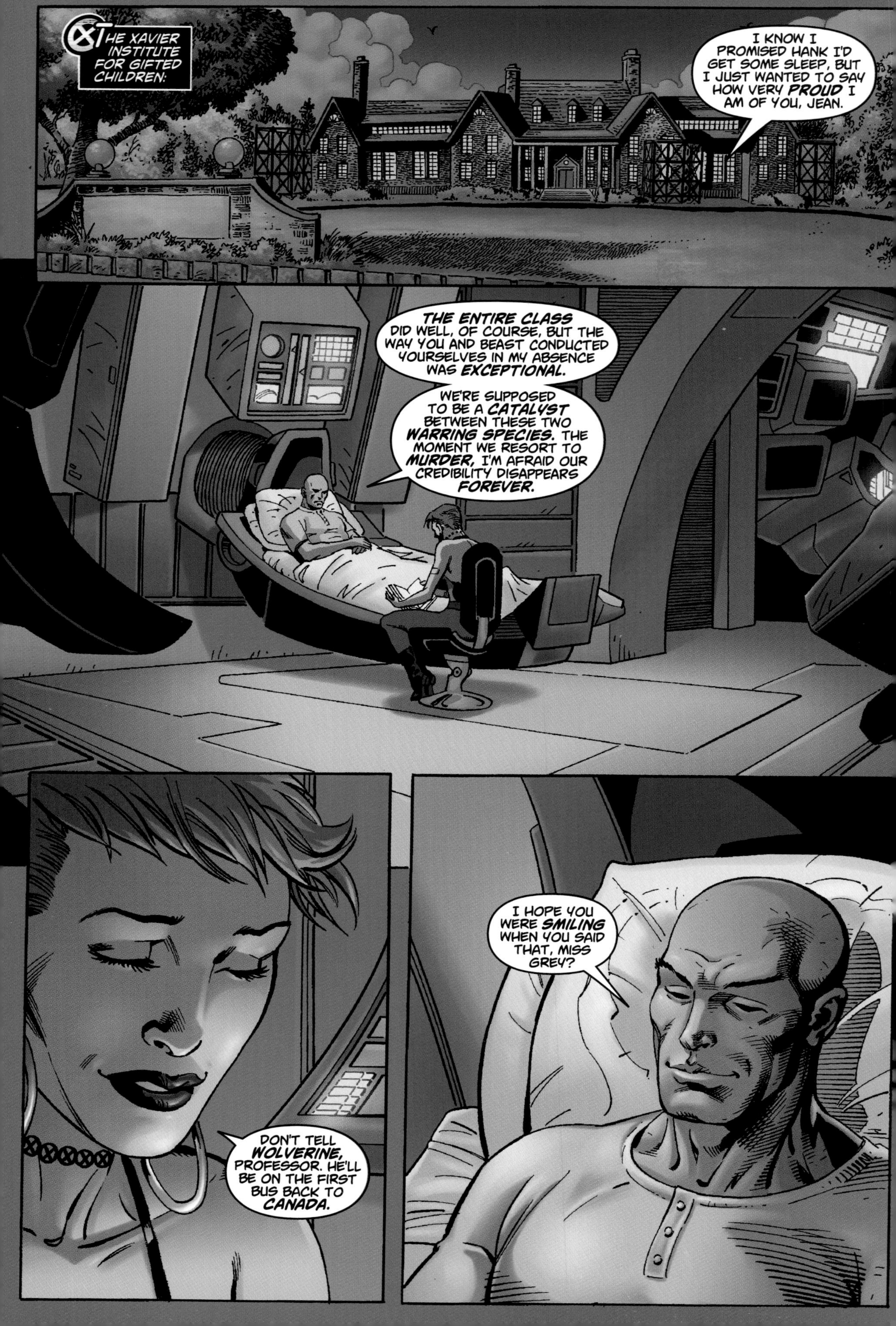
THE XAVIER INSTITUTE FOR GIFTED CHILDREN:
I KNOW I PROMISED HANK I'D GET SOME SLEEP, BUT I JUST WANTED TO SAY HOW VERY PROUD I AM OF YOU, JEAN.
THE ENTIRE CLASS DID WELL, OF COURSE, BUT THE WAY YOU AND BEAST CONDUCTED YOURSELVES IN MY ABSENCE WAS EXCEPTIONAL.
WE'RE SUPPOSED TO BE A CATALYST BETWEEN THESE TWO WARRING SPECIES. THE MOMENT WE RESORT TO MURDER, I'M AFRAID OUR CREDIBILITY DISAPPEARS FOREVER.
DON'T TELL WOLVERINE, PROFESSOR. HE'LL BE ON THE FIRST BUS BACK TO CANADA.
I HOPE YOU WERE SMILING WHEN YOU SAID THAT, MISS GREY?

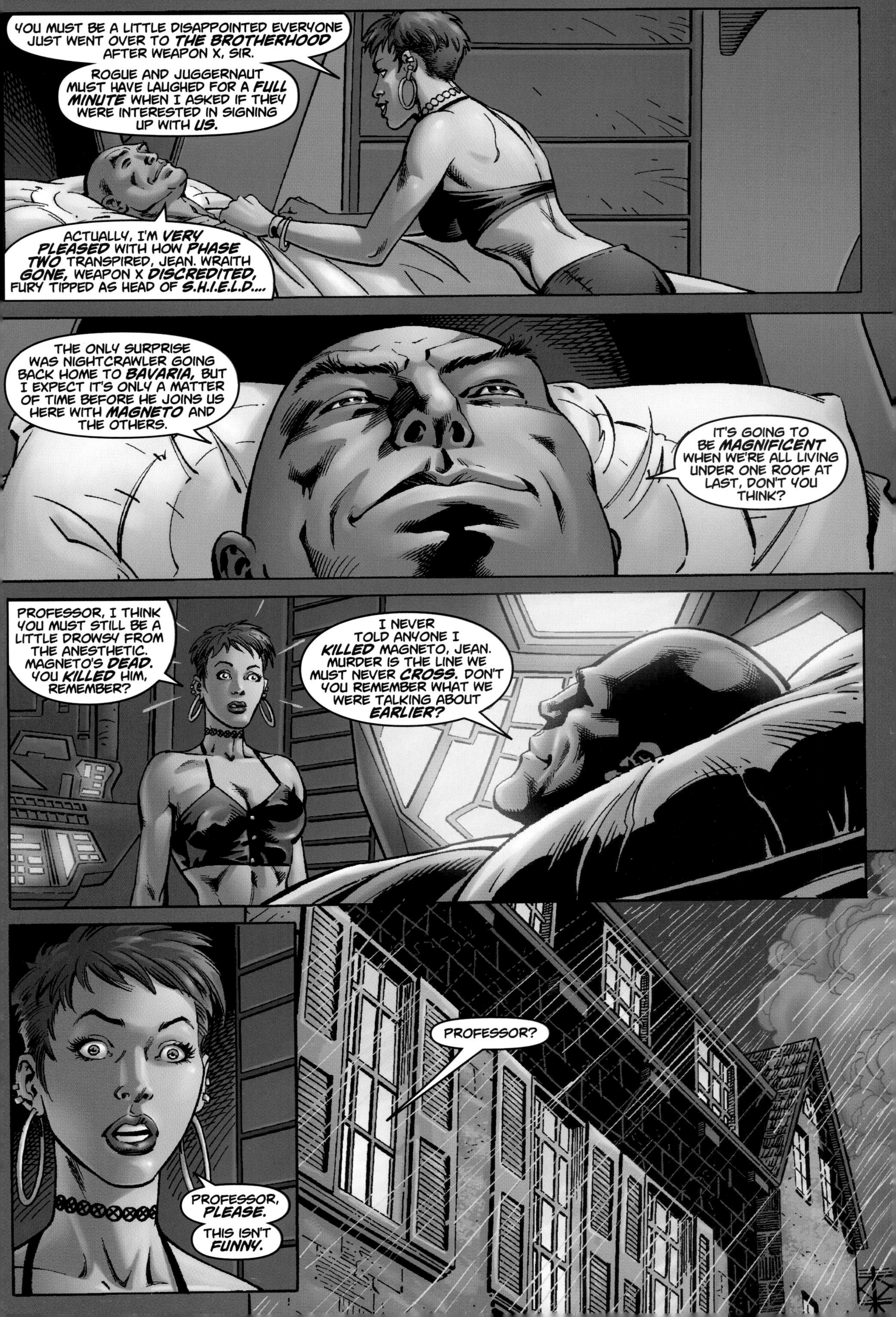
YOU MUST BE A LITTLE DISAPPOINTED EVERYONE JUST WENT OVER TO THE BROTHERHOOD AFTER WEAPON X, SIR.
ROGUE AND JUGGERNAUT MUST HAVE LAUGHED FOR A FULL MINUTE WHEN I ASKED IF THEY WERE INTERESTED IN SIGNING UP WITH US.
ACTUALLY, I'M VERY PLEASED WITH HOW PHASE TWO TRANSPIRED, JEAN. WRAITH GONE, WEAPON X DISCREDITED, FURY TIPPED AS HEAD OF S.H.I.E.L.D....
THE ONLY SURPRISE WAS NIGHTCRAWLER GOING BACK HOME TO BAVARIA, BUT I EXPECT IT'S ONLY A MATTER OF TIME BEFORE HE JOINS US HERE WITH MAGNETO AND THE OTHERS.
IT'S GOING TO BE MAGNIFICENT WHEN WE'RE ALL LIVING UNDER ONE ROOF AT LAST, DON'T YOU THINK?
PROFESSOR, I THINK YOU MUST STILL BE A LITTLE DROWSY FROM THE ANESTHETIC. MAGNETO'S DEAD. YOU KILLED HIM, REMEMBER?
I NEVER TOLD ANYONE I KILLED MAGNETO, JEAN. MURDER IS THE LINE WE MUST NEVER CROSS. DON'T YOU REMEMBER WHAT WE WERE TALKING ABOUT EARLIER?
PROFESSOR?
PROFESSOR, PLEASE.
THIS ISN'T FUNNY.

MARK MILLAR

Before it was decided that the Ultimate X-Men should more closely resemble their movie counterparts, writer Mark Millar penned the following plot outline for the series' first six issues ...

Ultimate X-Men 6-Issue Plot Outline

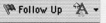

Reply | Reply All | Forward | Follow Up

From: Mark Millar
To: X-Office
Cc: Bill Jemas, Joe Quesada
Sent: Friday, June 23, 2000 2:39 PM
Subject: Ultimate X-Men 6-Issue Plot Outline

INTRODUCTION:

Okay, you already know the basics of this so I'll try to keep this as brief as possible. The actual characters to be used have still to be finalized, but I'm working on the assumption that we're going with Professor X, Cyclops, Wolverine, Jean Grey, The Beast, Mystique and Storm. I'd also like to introduce a new character into what, when the book opens, is an already-established team. This gives the readers an identification figure who can meet the characters and status quo around the same time they do.

Ideally, I'd like to have broken the issues down and given you a scene by scene description of what happens in each, but time restrictions means I'll just have to be much broader at the moment.

PLOTS (1-6)

The first issue opens with a covert operation being carried out by a disguised group of teenage X-Men on behalf of the Pentagon. Wolverine, Jean Grey, The Beast, Mystique and Storm are all involved in this Mission Impossible-style opening, wearing sun-glasses, talking into wrist-watches and busting an international operation being carried out by a terrorist cell from the Brotherhood of Evil Mutants. I'd like to play down costumes here and play up leathers, designer clothes and exotic locations to give this a much more spy-movie feel than the X-Men comic and establish the tone immediately. The nature of the terrorist operation is still to be decided, but the basic idea is that the Brotherhood of Evil Mutants are out to destroy the kind of things which you capitalists would call The American Way of Life. The Brotherhood, under the command of the unseen Magneto, target nuclear power stations, corporations which exploit the Third World, arms manufacturers and so on. All worthy targets, of course, but they obviously don't care how many ordinary human lives are exterminated in the process.

Opening scene should be high-octane action which allows us to see each of the characters use their powers at least once and radio home to base to say that the anti-terrorist mission has been successful. Cut from here to campaigners outside the White House picketing against the President's rumoured sanction of mutants in the military. Mutants claim they're mankind's replacement and our natural enemy. How can the President trust them with national security. It's a convincing

MORE

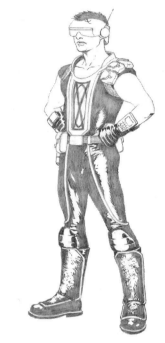

attachment: cyke.jpg
art by: J.H. Williams III

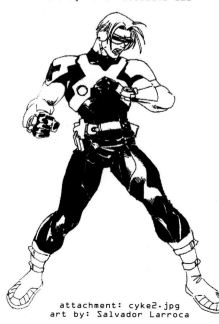

attachment: cyke2.jpg
art by: Salvador Larroca

Ultimate X-Men 6-Issue Plot Outline

Reply Reply All Forward Follow Up

From: Mark Millar
To: X-Office
Cc: Bill Jemas, Joe Quesada
Sent: Friday, June 23, 2000 2:39 PM
Subject: Ultimate X-Men 6-Issue Plot Outline

argument and one which Senator Kelly is trying to get out of the President. There's an official 'no comment' from the White House on the issue at the moment, but Kelly is pressing hard for an answer.

The whole X-Men initiative was the brain-child of Charles Xavier; a bald, intense George Stephanopolous-style genius in the White House who has advised the President on domestic, economic and foreign policy initiatives since he was eighteen years old. He's openly a mutant within the corridors of power and has convinced Clinton that the best way of dealing with the growing threat of mutant terrorism is to incorporate mutants into the establishment. Working together can benefit both sides and, if more people's mutant genes are activating every day, isn't it better to swim with the tide than against it? Senator Kelly is completely opposed to what he sees as mutant appeasement and wants to blow this whole thing wide open. The President is dithering on the matter, but plans to stick with the program for now because the X-Men have been a huge success since their initiative began a few months ago.

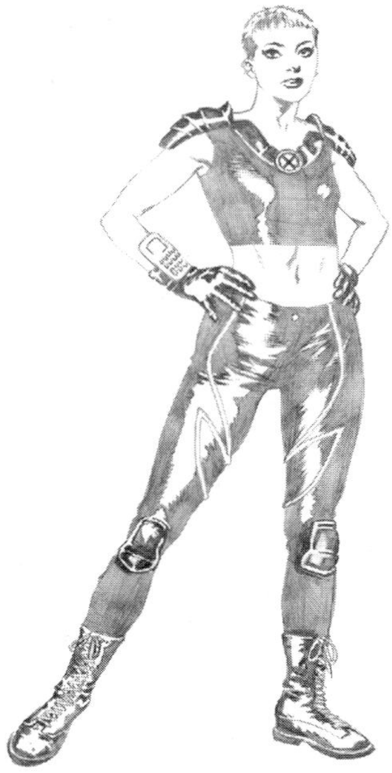

attachment: jean.jpg
art by: J.H. Williams III

Cut from here to the military base where the X-Men hang out. These kids are all misfits and outcasts from society, disowned by their own parents in many cases, whom Charles Xavier gathered together and has mobilized as a fighting unit. They're suspicious of him to various degrees and don't like the covert nature of the operations, annoyed that the other soldiers refuse to talk to them and that their missions are never allowed to reach the newspapers. However, it's a lot better than the lives they led prior to their recruitment and the X-Men at least gives them some direction where they can be around other kids who don't want to hang them from the nearest tree. They've grown pretty tight as a group, but treat Charles a little like the way a bunch of teenage friends treat an older brother when he walks into a room. They respect him, but they're not particularly at ease around him.

Using the perfected Cerebro system developed by the super-genius Beast, the X-Men are able to locate mutant genes in unsuspecting humans which are on the verge of activation. This means that sometimes the X-Men know someone is a mutant before they even realize it themselves. The new recruit is a kid called Bobby Drake and his capture is organized with almost militaristic precision as the kids go undercover in his school and find this poor kid who turned blue and went

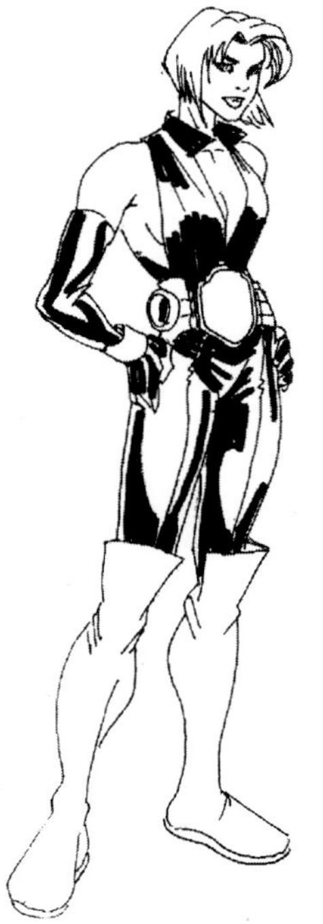

attachment: jean2.jpg
art by: Salvador Larroca

MORE

Ultimate X-Men 6-Issue Plot Outline

Reply | Reply All | Forward | Follow Up

From: Mark Millar
To: X-Office
Cc: Bill Jemas, Joe Quesada
Sent: Friday, June 23, 2000 2:39 PM
Subject: Ultimate X-Men 6-Issue Plot Outline

missing several weeks ago. I think the younger readers in particular would get off on the idea of the X-Men posing as school pupils (with perhaps the 20 year old Wolverine posing as a student teacher) in order to capture the kid who turns out to be Iceman. Bobby's broken into the team, has the entire status quo explained to him, receives his new code-name and gets trained to be an X-Man.

This would be a good opportunity to update concepts like the Danger Room and give it more of a virtual reality, Matrix-style training camp feel where literally anything in time and space can be used against the mutants as they hone their skills. Cyclops and The Beast should be the guys behind training, Professor X taking a more background role throughout and observing their progress from a distance. It's also where we hammer home the fact that people all over the world are turning into mutants every day.

Professor X's initiative is that we'd rather have them in the tent out than outside the tent in and he wants these kids tracked down and embraced by the establishment as soon as possible. This is the only way mutants are going to be accepted. The unseen Magneto, we discover, has a different ideology. His Brotherhood of Evil Mutants are collecting an army of their own in some unknown location and a Gene War is promised as soon as his numbers are big enough. For the moment, he's just striking mankind where it hurts, his acolytes crippling sources of power and government through acts of mutant terrorism. The mutants are the future, he maintains. Why try to put the brakes on evolution?

The third issue is Iceman's baptism of fire as all the training is put to the test in a field operation. Again, this should be an international act of mutant terrorism (although completely different from the first one) where the team can really cut loose. It should also be a really topical set-up and situation and a threat the team demolish with genuine style. Iceman, of course, should save the day and the buzz should be really upbeat until a final sequence where The Beast is trapped, unable to save himself after saving countless lives. Cyclops is telling the military back-up that they have to go back for him, but the slight risks involved mean they're unwilling to chance losing human lives for the sake of a mutant. This hammers it home to the X-Men, and Cyclops in particular, how lowly they're regarded by the people they're willing to die for and

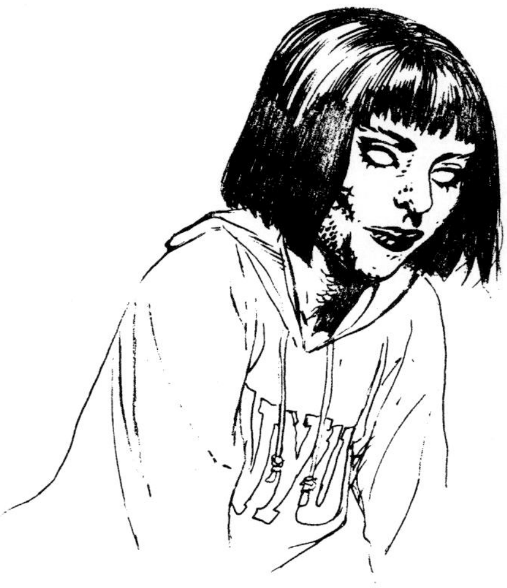

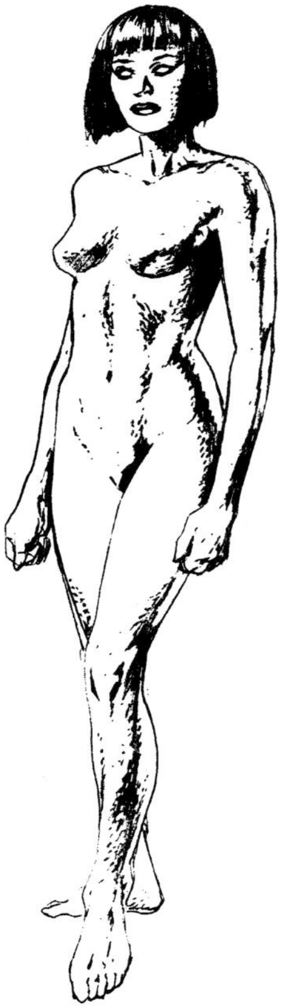

attachment: mystique.jpg
art by: J.H. Williams III

MORE

Ultimate X-Men 6-Issue Plot Outline

Reply Reply All Forward Follow Up

From: Mark Millar
To: X-Office
Cc: Bill Jemas, Joe Quesada
Sent: Friday, June 23, 2000 2:39 PM
Subject: Ultimate X-Men 6-Issue Plot Outline

we should have a really emotive moment as The Beast very clearly and very definitely is left behind to perish.

Xavier is horrified by this turn of events, but the soldiers responsible aren't even punished. The Beast's sacrifice, despite the fact that he saved thousands of people, isn't even reported in the newspapers. Cyclops has had it with the X-Men. There's a huge confrontation where he lashes out at Xavier and quits. Wolverine, Storm and Mystique leave with him and issue three ends as they leave their old life behind and go in search of something new. Only Jean Grey and the recently recruited Iceman stay behind with a genuinely rattled Professor X.

I'd like to introduce a sub-plot where Cyclops was being tempted by someone in the opposite camp during the earlier issues and his eventual resignation from the X-Men leads this little renegade band straight to Magneto and his hidden sanctuary. Hidden from the outside world, he's created a mutant paradise in a place regular Marvel fans would recognize as The Savage Land. He and his Evil Brotherhood have tamed the human population using mind-control implants and created a utopian city within the dense jungle which acts as a microcosm of his eventual plans for the outside world. Magneto, as I don't need to point out, is Half-Manson/Half-Christ and his charismatic argument that humans are destroying the Earth homo-superior was supposed to inherit spellbinds Cyclops, Wolvie and the others.

It's a logical evolutionary argument that the mutants are the masters of the humans and it's also very natural that the humans should resent and fear their replacements as the dominant species on planet Earth. Charles Xavier is too rooted in humanity to realize that sharing the planet is as impossible as the President sharing the Oval Office with an ape. However, humanity far outnumbers the mutant species, but their numbers are growing every day. By hacking into the Cerebro system, they can locate and kidnap X-active mutants and introduce them into Magneto's cult. Better this than being lap-dogs of the status quo and acting as weapons for the same establishment who allow half their own species to starve.

What follows, much to everyone's surprise, is four of the original X-Men joining the Brotherhood and taking part in the terrorist activity against everything unfair in the capi-

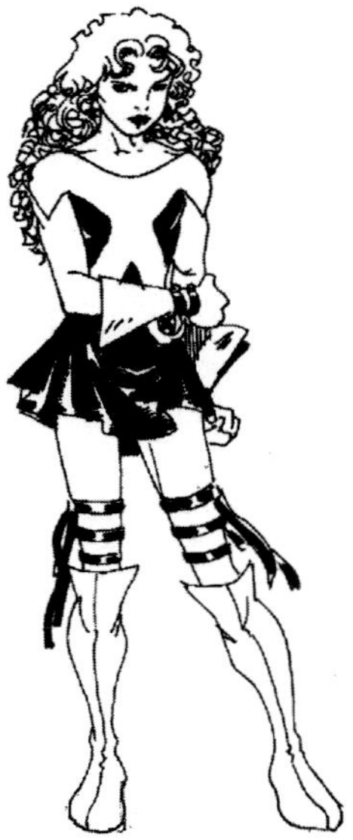

attachment: kitty.jpg
art by: Salvador Larroca

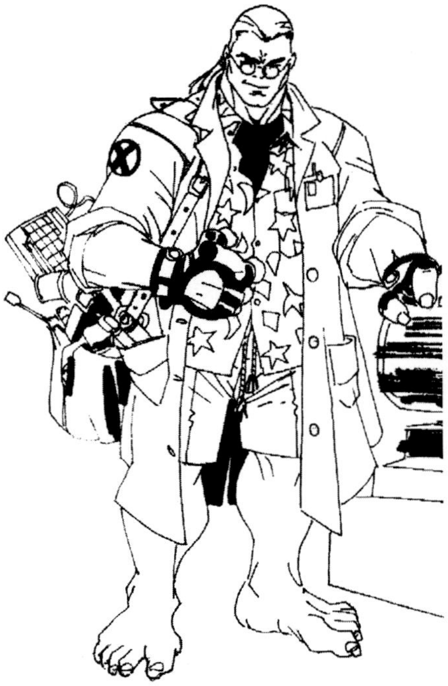

attachment: hank.jpg
art by: Salvador Larroca

MORE

Ultimate X-Men 6-Issue Plot Outline

Reply Reply All Forward Follow Up

From: Mark Millar

To: X-Office

Cc: Bill Jemas, Joe Quesada

Sent: Friday, June 23, 2000 2:39 PM

Subject: Ultimate X-Men 6-Issue Plot Outline

talist world. Of course, this brings them up against Jean, Iceman and Professor X, but it also plays directly into the hands of Senator Kelly and his anti-mutant sympathizers in the military establishment. The story that the President (under the guidance of Charles Xavier) used muties in the military who have since broken cover and joined Magneto's Brotherhood of Evil Mutants is leaked to the media and all Hell breaks loose. The terrorist strikes are reaching the very heart of the American, European and Asian financial communities and something has to be done. Xavier is horrified to discover that the X-Men project is temporarily suspended and a back-up plan, which he knew nothing about, is initiated. Imagine the image of the ground shaking in a military testing camp as enormous silo-covers are pulled back and we turn the page for a huge, double-page image of dozens of eighty foot Sentinels firing off into the sky and dwarfing the people down below. Mutant gene-locating killers (using Cerebro technology) are sent after the rogue X-Men and their instructions are to destroy them and Magneto's secret Savage Land paradise.

Issue five features the most awesome destruction imaginable as this beautiful place built by Magneto is obliterated by the squadron of airborne Sentinels and all the mutants who sought sanctuary here meet a grisly, but exciting end. Cyclops and the renegade X-Men do their best to chop the numbers of these creatures, but they're overwhelmed until Magneto steps out and goes into action for the first time. The Sentinels literally stop dead in the air and cease functioning. Slowly, they form a circle around Magneto and bow their heads. He floats between them and magnetically opens up their shells, raises their CPUs into the air and reprograms the machines in a matter of minutes. Now, instead of hunting and killing anyone with a mutant gene, they've been redesigned to do precisely the opposite. He looks around at the utter devastation wrought by the world's establishment and all these dead mutants who followed him and he promises he'll do much, much worse as he fires the Sentinels back towards the United States. Magneto and the renegade X-Men follow, the Gene War promised between human and mutant looking set to happen at last.

The big fight therefore takes place between the conventional military and the remaining X-Men and the Sentinels over Washington as Magneto heads for the White House. I like the idea of him marching past all the guards, stopping bullets in

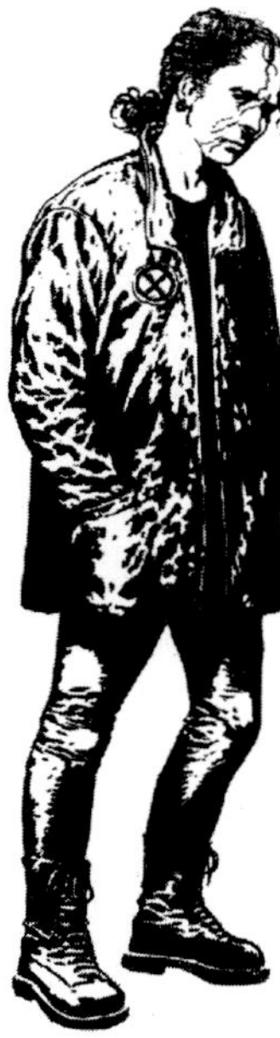

attachment: gambit.jpg
art by: J.H. Williams III

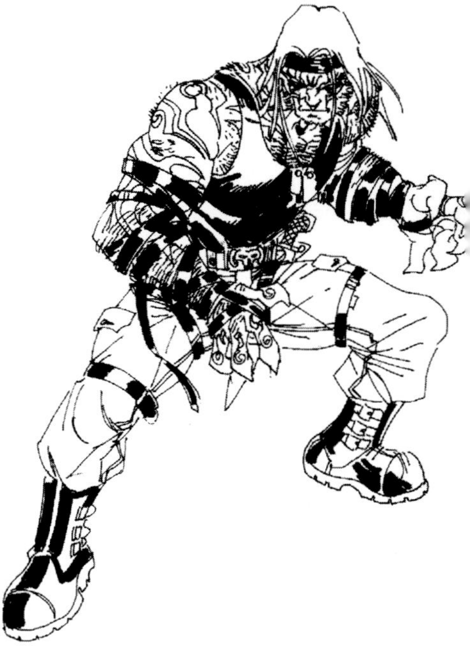

attachment: sabretooth.jpg
art by: Salvador Larroca

MORE

Ultimate X-Men 6-Issue Plot Outline

Reply   Reply All   Forward   Follow Up

From: Mark Millar

To: X-Office
Cc: Bill Jemas, Joe Quesada
Sent: Friday, June 23, 2000 2:39 PM
Subject: Ultimate X-Men 6-Issue Plot Outline

the air and firing them back towards the troops, wiping out all the security people, crunching people up inside cars, etc, until he finally reaches the President and a single, middle-aged security man with a gun in his shaking hand. A bald, overweight security officer with a PACE-MAKER fitted to his heart? How interesting, he says as he raises a hand and we subtly watch the pace-maker float from off-panel and into his grip. The President is alone and terrified and Magneto drags him outside and talks to the cameras, saying he's going to keep the most powerful human being in the world alive so he can see what Magneto plans to do to the human race.

The wild cards in all this, of course, are the renegade X-Men. They hate the establishment who shunned them, killed their friends, are destroying the world and tried to kill them, but they can't shake that final part of humanity which tells them that Magneto is as bad as the other side. Charles Xavier is the embodiment of both sides working together and he urges the X-Men to help them defeat Magneto and the Sentinels, but it's Jean Grey who saves the day by pulling Cyclops back to the side of the angels and fighting back.

The actual details of this big, final fight and Magneto's defeat and disappearance (supposed death) can be worked out if and when we get to the script, but the end result should be the warring X-Men coming together as a family again at the end and Charles Xavier conceding that he was as wrong as Magneto. Siding with one group of ideologues is just as bad as siding with another. Why should they be puppets of the establishment when they can fight the good fight in an underground capacity and be accountable to no-one? The Blackbird jet which should have been featured in earlier missions, the virtual Danger Room and all their cool gadgets bought and paid for by military technicians are stolen and the sixth issue ends with this underground gang established and ready for new adventures, existing somewhere between humanity and the shadow world of the mutants. The actual set-up by this point is much closer to the established X-Men scenario, except their origins are different, they're on the run from both sides and the kids are more autonomous than they are under the direct leadership of Professor X. He's really more of an organizer and advisor here. However, they're still hated and very, very misunderstood and that's the main thing, right?

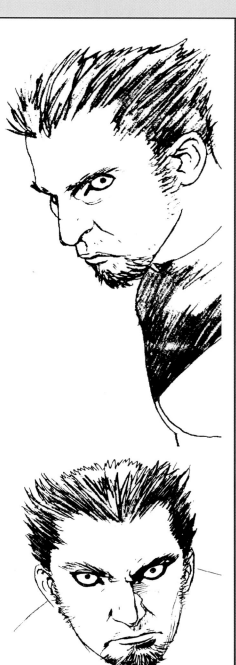

END

attachment: wolverine.jpg
art by: J.H. Williams III

MUTANT GENESIS
BRIAN MICHAEL BENDIS

Although he later turned down the gig, Ultimate Spider-Man scribe Brian Michael Bendis offered up his own take on the Ultimate X-Men during the Project's early stages. The following are selections from his script for issue #1 ...

X-Men/ Ground Zero Project Script/ Issue One/ by Brian Michael Bendis

Page 4-

1- Tight on the face of CHARLES XAVIER. Bald, handsome. Late thirties. His gaze is focused. He is addressing a room. It was his voice in the voice-over.

XAVIER
A good example of this, if you think about it, is the Kennedy Presidency.

Many believe it would never have survived the media saturated political landscape that we have now.

The plague of scandal would have driven him from office, if it had even let him get there in the first place.

2- Wide of college classroom. PROFESSOR CHARLES XAVIER SITS IN HIS WHEELCHAIR and addresses his modest sized classroom of students. The rooms design is sparse but lived in. Not a lot of clutter. Just desks and students. They are mostly writing in their notebooks because they are being given an assignment. Taking notes. a young girl stares at Charles intently. A young man is close to falling asleep.

XAVIER (CONT'D)
This is a lesson of modern political science-

-and this is what you are going to tell me about in your papers.

3- Charles is looking over at one student in particular. The dozing teen.

XAVIER (CONT'D)
Today, if the media chooses to focus on you- on anyone- there is no sin that cannot be uncovered-

4- Tight on the dozing teen.

XAVIER (CONT'D)
And there is no statute of limitations on a mistake of youth.

5- The dozing teen jolts awake. Something woke him. He is looking at Xavier dumbfounded. (Xavier woke him with a little psychic jolt?)

XAVIER (CONT'D)
The media microscope sees far into the past and under every rock.

6- Same as 3. Charles smirks to himself as he continues on. Behind him at the window at the door we can see a man in a suit standing.

XAVIER (CONT'D)
So, when you write your papers- for your final grade-

I want you to contemplate what kind of a person would want to put themselves and their family into the world of politics.

7- Same as six. Xavier looks away from his students to the man at the door.

XAVIER (CONT'D)
-into a situation so intrusive.

8- Charles is looking at the man behind the glass window of the door in awe but still talking to his students.

XAVIER (CONT'D)
What kind of a person would sacrifice everything for the power to lead others?

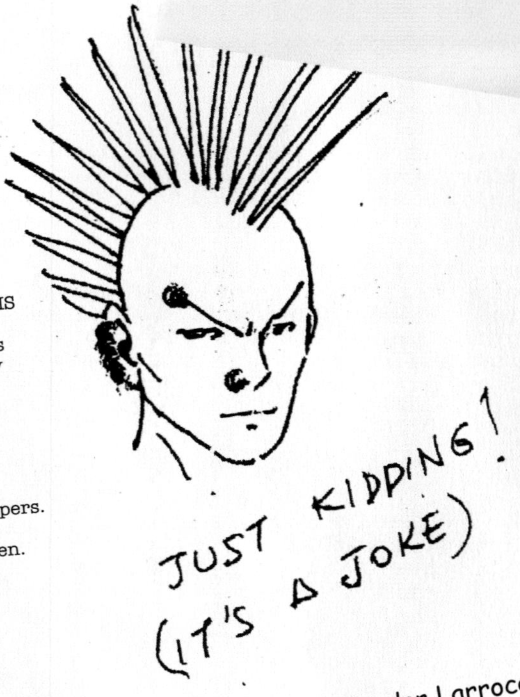
JUST KIDDING!
(IT'S A JOKE)

Professor X by Salvador Larroca

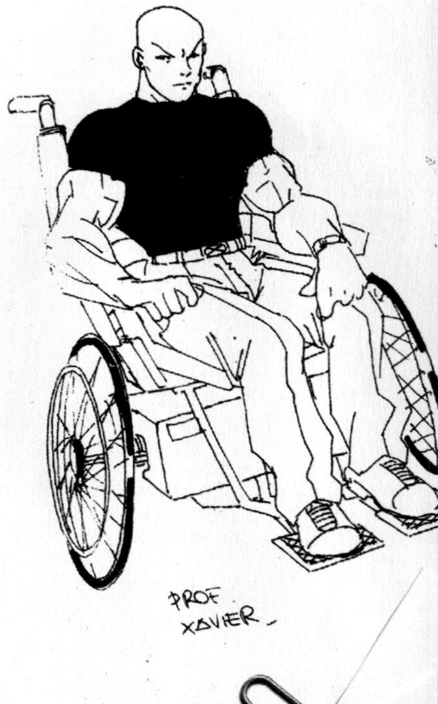
PROF XAVIER

- Wide shot of park. Ororo has just performed her poem for a smattering of ıer peers and a couple of walk bys. A smattering of applause to her beautiful poem. She accepts it gracefully.
It is a beautiful day in a small city park in Chicago.

LYNDSAY
YAY!
ORORO
Thank you guys. Thanks.

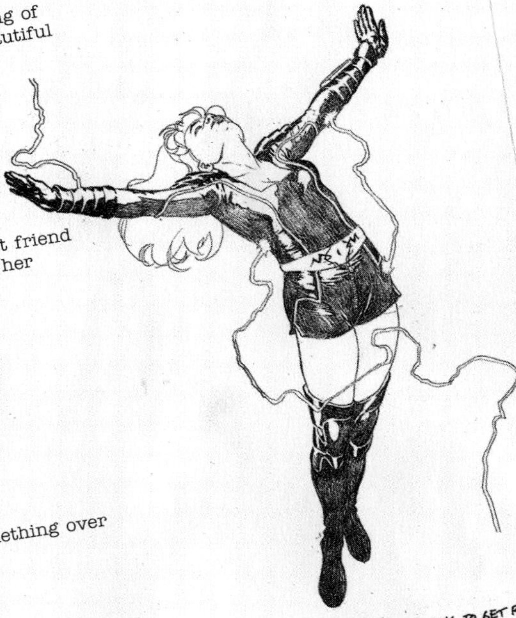

Page 25-
1- Over Ororo's shoulder, from the small crowd, Lindsey, Ororo's best friend (think Brandi), leaps up from the crowd in approval and support of her friend's performance.
Most of the rest of the crowd is talking amongst themselves.
Maybe a skateboarding guy is staring at Ororo in the background.
Awestruck by her beauty.

LYNDSAY
Ororo, that was amazing!! You did it!
ORORO
It was OK.
LYNDSAY
Girl! You are so the performer!

2- Same, but Lyndsay's face has dropped. She is looking at something over Ororo's shoulder. Something she is sad to see.

LYNDSAY (CONT'D)
That was really fun to-

STORM-ORORO: I THOUGHT IT MORE INTERESTING TO GET RID OF THE CAPE. IT SEEMS TO GIVE HER MORE ATTITUDE WITHOUT IT. SHE HAS A MORE VOLUPTUOUS BODY COMPARED TO JEAN GREY. NOTE THE TRIBAL TATTOOS.

3- Same angle, Ororo turns her head around to see what her friend Lindsay is looking at so miserably.

LYNDSAY (CONT'D)
That dog-

4- Over both Lindsay and Ororo's shoulder, they have both turned their bodies to face...
A handsome young BLACK MAN who is hanging all over a fly girl.
The couple are oblivious to the fact that they are being watched by the two young girls. There is a small smattering of people walking around the open park.

5- Tighter on the young couple slobbering on each other

6- Lyndsay and Ororo frowning at the sight. Ororo looks really hurt. This is obviously her boyfriend or a boy she liked.
The SKY BEHIND THEM IS TURNING DARKER with a twinge of orange from an electrical orange. The wind is picking up.

LYNDSAY (CONT'D)
He's a dog, O.

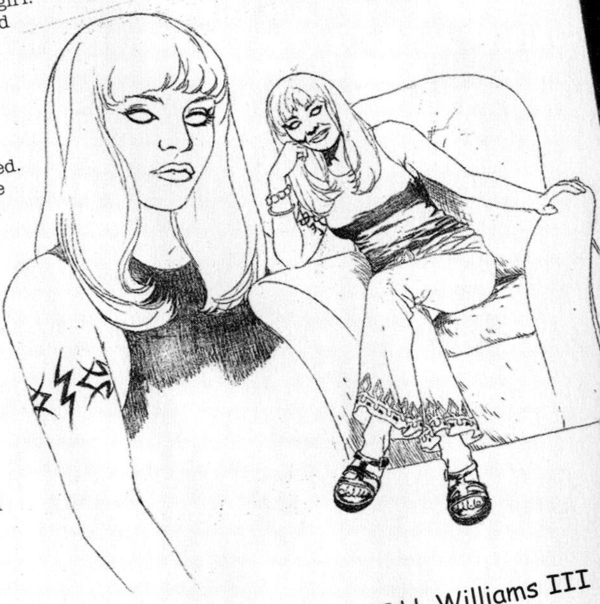

Page 26-
1- Tight on Ororo. She is really mad and hurt. We can see that Ororo is no wallflower. She is emotional and tempestuous-

2- Mid shot of the two girls. Lyndsay yells out toward the couple. Ororo still stares ahead in quiet rage.
The WIND has really picked up. Leaves are blowing.
The people in the park are starting to run.
A STORM IS COMING. Behind them the sky has turned into A DARK STORMY WEATHER COLOR.
The fury of the Earth is brewing.

LYNDSAY (CONT'D)
YOU DOG!!!

Storm by J.H. Williams III

3- The couple breaks their revelry. The girl looks to the sky noticing the crazy weather all of a sudden.
The boy looks right at Ororo.

4- Ororo looks right at him. a single tear falls down one of her angry eyes.
Way behind her A HUGE LIGHTNING BOLT TOUCHES DOWN.
A lone raindrop hits her forehead.

Page 33-
1- The lawyer props his expensive suitcase on the patio table.

> LAWYER
> Doctor, my clients love their boy very much.
>
> That is why this position was so intriguing to them.
> The next solution was going to be surgery, but that is
> a risky venture at best.

2- Xavier uncomfortable in the direction this is going.

> XAVIER
> Can I meet the boy?

3- The lawyer looks to Travis.

> TRAVIS
> He will be here momentarily. He is out for his
> morning...stroll.
> LAWYER
> So, how much are you looking for Xavier?

4- Same as 2.

> XAVIER
> I'm sorry?

5- Same as 3.

> LAWYER
> How much will it take for you to take him off their hands?

6- Xavier winces at this statement.

> XAVIER
> I don't think you understand the nature of-

7- Same as 2.

> LAWYER
> We absolutely understand.
>
> Mr. Worthington wants to be clear that his obligations to the
> boy financially are unbounding.

8- Xavier totally perplexed by this tone.

> XAVIER
> This isn't a financial transaction. This is about the boy.

9- The lawyer pulls out the document.

> LAWYER
> Then you understand that you will, in essence, be his legal
> guardian absolving the Worthington's of any obligations.

10- Xavier practically growls at the slimy lawyer.

> TRAVIS
> Sirs, Master Warren is approaching...

Page 34-
1- Wide shot of the patio.
In the foreground, we can see the figure of what seems like a
HUGE BIRD approaching. It is backlit to the sun.
2- Same but the figure swoops down from the sky. The same
arcing trajectory of a bird coming in for a landing.
They all watch.
3- Big, big panel. But it isn't a bird.
It is the beautiful WINGED FIGURE OF WARREN
WORTHINGTON 3... A beautiful blond boy of 17.
(think Kurt Cobain) He has a six foot WHITE WINGSPAN
spread wide as he has stopped and hovers just above ground
level in front of the meeting. His face is humble almost
embarrassed. He doesn't look anyone in the eye. His left wing gleams
off the sun... He truly looks like AN ANGEL.

<39>

shakes
too similar
to Cyclops?

No Goggles
Yes early
costume

ANGEL: THE RICH YUPPY KID. THE TOTAL OPPOSITE OF GAMBIT BUT
STILL HAS THE TYPICAL 15 YEAROLD ATTITUDE. HE IS A LOT
MORE MAN NAIVE THAN GAMBIT ABOUT THE WORLD AROUND
HIM.

Angel by J.H. Williams III

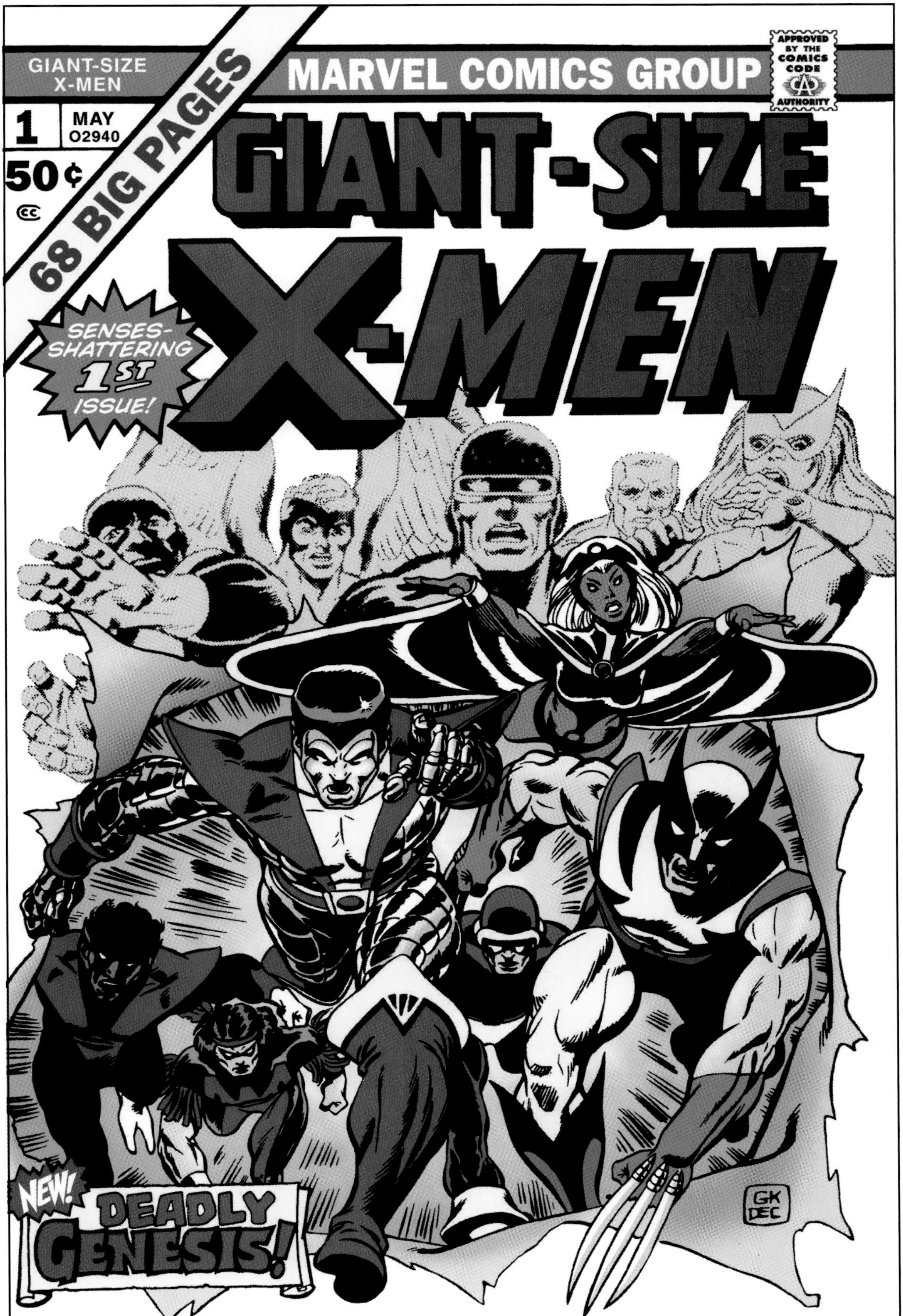
GIANT-SIZE
X-MEN
1
MAY
02940
50¢
68 BIG PAGES
MARVEL COMICS GROUP
APPROVED
BY THE
COMICS
CODE
AUTHORITY
GIANT-SIZE
X-MEN
SENSES-
SHATTERING
1ST
ISSUE!
NEW!
DEADLY
GENESIS!
GK
DEC

Marvel's mutant heroes were reborn once before, in the pages of 1975's *Giant-Size X-Men #1*. Now, experience the origin of the "all-new, all-different" Children of the Atom ...

Stan Lee PRESENTS: THE UNCANNY X-MEN!™

LEN WEIN WRITER EDITOR & DAVE COCKRUM ILLUSTRATOR / GLYNIS WEIN colorist / JOHN COSTANZA letterer
- CO-CREATORS -

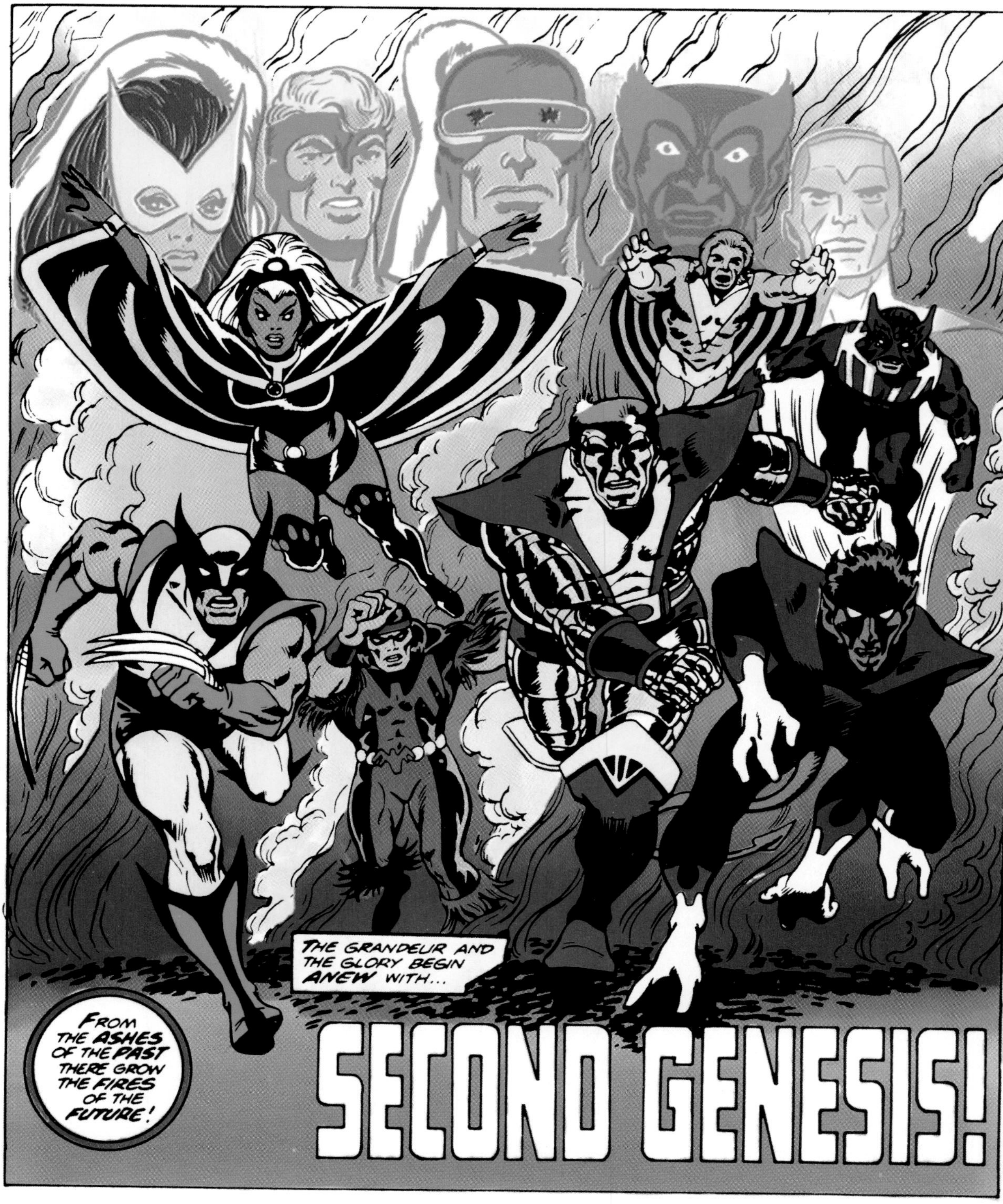
THE GRANDEUR AND THE GLORY BEGIN ANEW WITH...
FROM THE ASHES OF THE PAST THERE GROW THE FIRES OF THE FUTURE!
SECOND GENESIS!

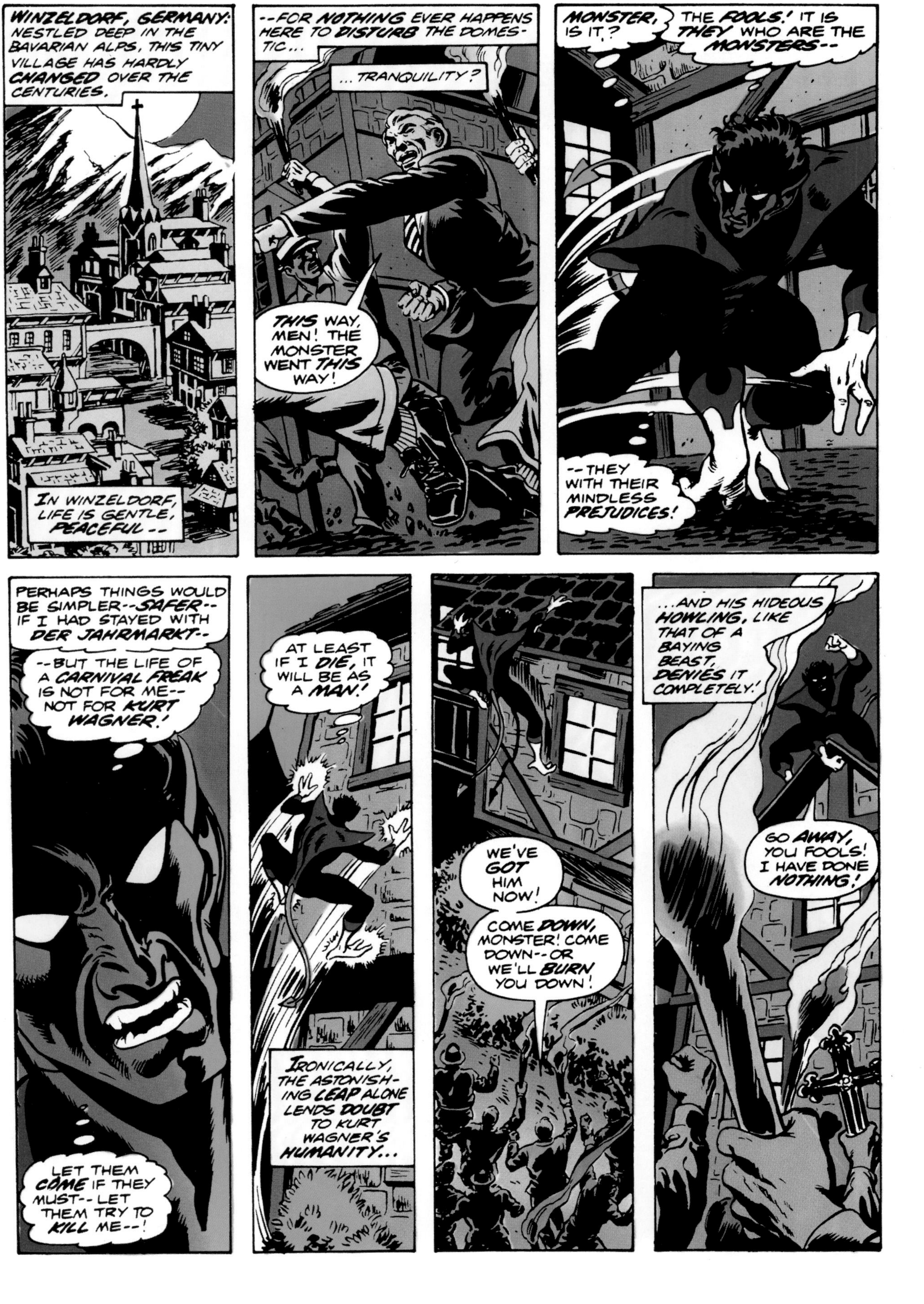
WINZELDORF, GERMANY: NESTLED DEEP IN THE BAVARIAN ALPS, THIS TINY VILLAGE HAS HARDLY CHANGED OVER THE CENTURIES.
IN WINZELDORF, LIFE IS GENTLE, PEACEFUL --
--FOR NOTHING EVER HAPPENS HERE TO DISTURB THE DOMESTIC...
...TRANQUILITY?
THIS WAY, MEN! THE MONSTER WENT THIS WAY!
MONSTER, IS IT?
THE FOOLS! IT IS THEY WHO ARE THE MONSTERS--
--THEY WITH THEIR MINDLESS PREJUDICES!
PERHAPS THINGS WOULD BE SIMPLER--SAFER--IF I HAD STAYED WITH DER JAHRMARKT--
--BUT THE LIFE OF A CARNIVAL FREAK IS NOT FOR ME--NOT FOR KURT WAGNER!
LET THEM COME IF THEY MUST--LET THEM TRY TO KILL ME--!
AT LEAST IF I DIE, IT WILL BE AS A MAN!
IRONICALLY, THE ASTONISHING LEAP ALONE LENDS DOUBT TO KURT WAGNER'S HUMANITY...
WE'VE GOT HIM NOW!
COME DOWN, MONSTER! COME DOWN--OR WE'LL BURN YOU DOWN!
...AND HIS HIDEOUS HOWLING, LIKE THAT OF A BAYING BEAST, DENIES IT COMPLETELY!
GO AWAY, YOU FOOLS! I HAVE DONE NOTHING!

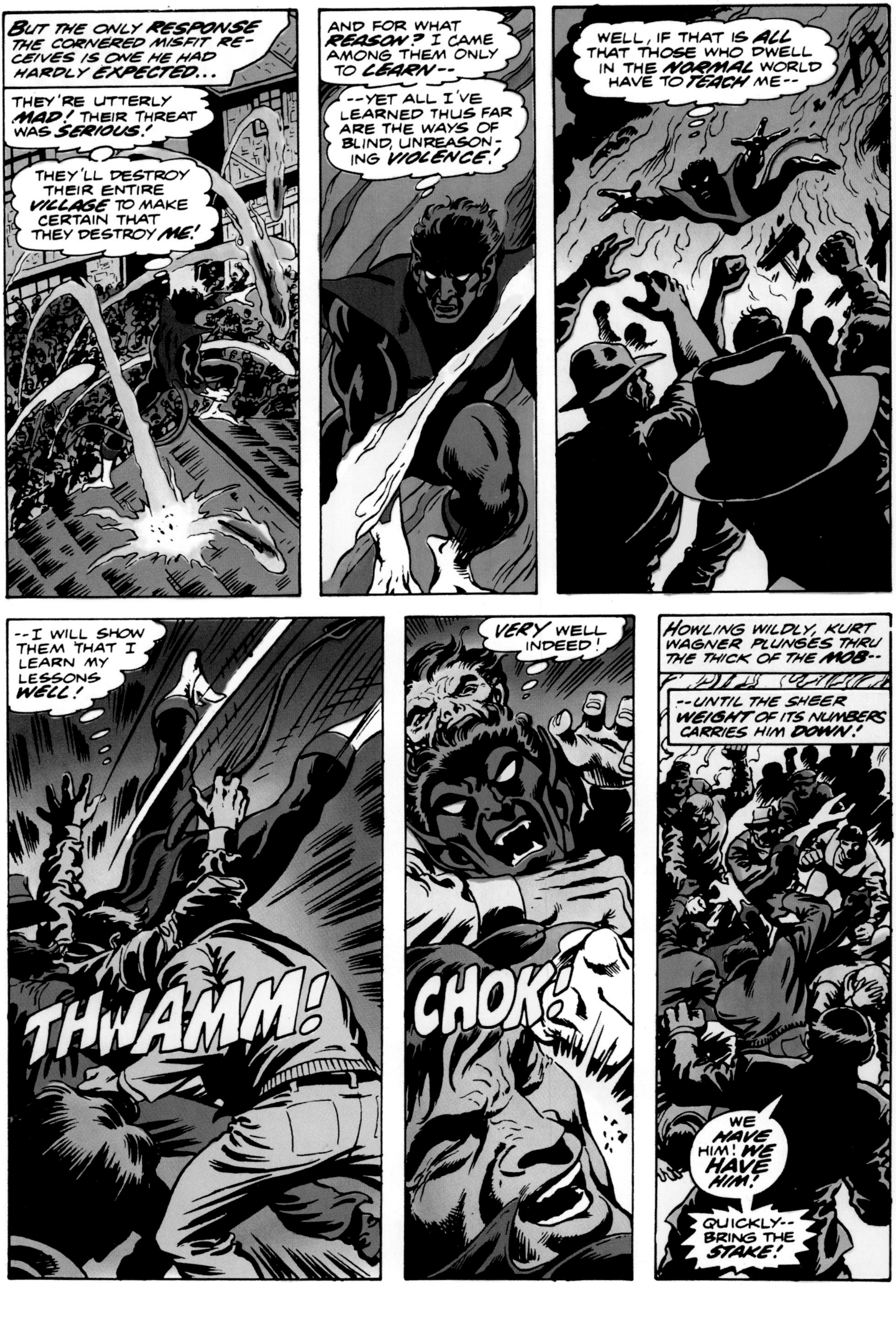
BUT THE ONLY RESPONSE THE CORNERED MISFIT RECEIVES IS ONE HE HAD HARDLY EXPECTED...
THEY'RE UTTERLY MAD! THEIR THREAT WAS SERIOUS!
THEY'LL DESTROY THEIR ENTIRE VILLAGE TO MAKE CERTAIN THAT THEY DESTROY ME!
AND FOR WHAT REASON? I CAME AMONG THEM ONLY TO LEARN--
--YET ALL I'VE LEARNED THUS FAR ARE THE WAYS OF BLIND, UNREASONING VIOLENCE!
WELL, IF THAT IS ALL THAT THOSE WHO DWELL IN THE NORMAL WORLD HAVE TO TEACH ME--
--I WILL SHOW THEM THAT I LEARN MY LESSONS WELL!
THWAMM!
VERY WELL INDEED!
CHOK!
HOWLING WILDLY, KURT WAGNER PLUNGES THRU THE THICK OF THE MOB--
--UNTIL THE SHEER WEIGHT OF ITS NUMBERS CARRIES HIM DOWN!
WE HAVE HIM! WE HAVE HIM!
QUICKLY-- BRING THE STAKE!

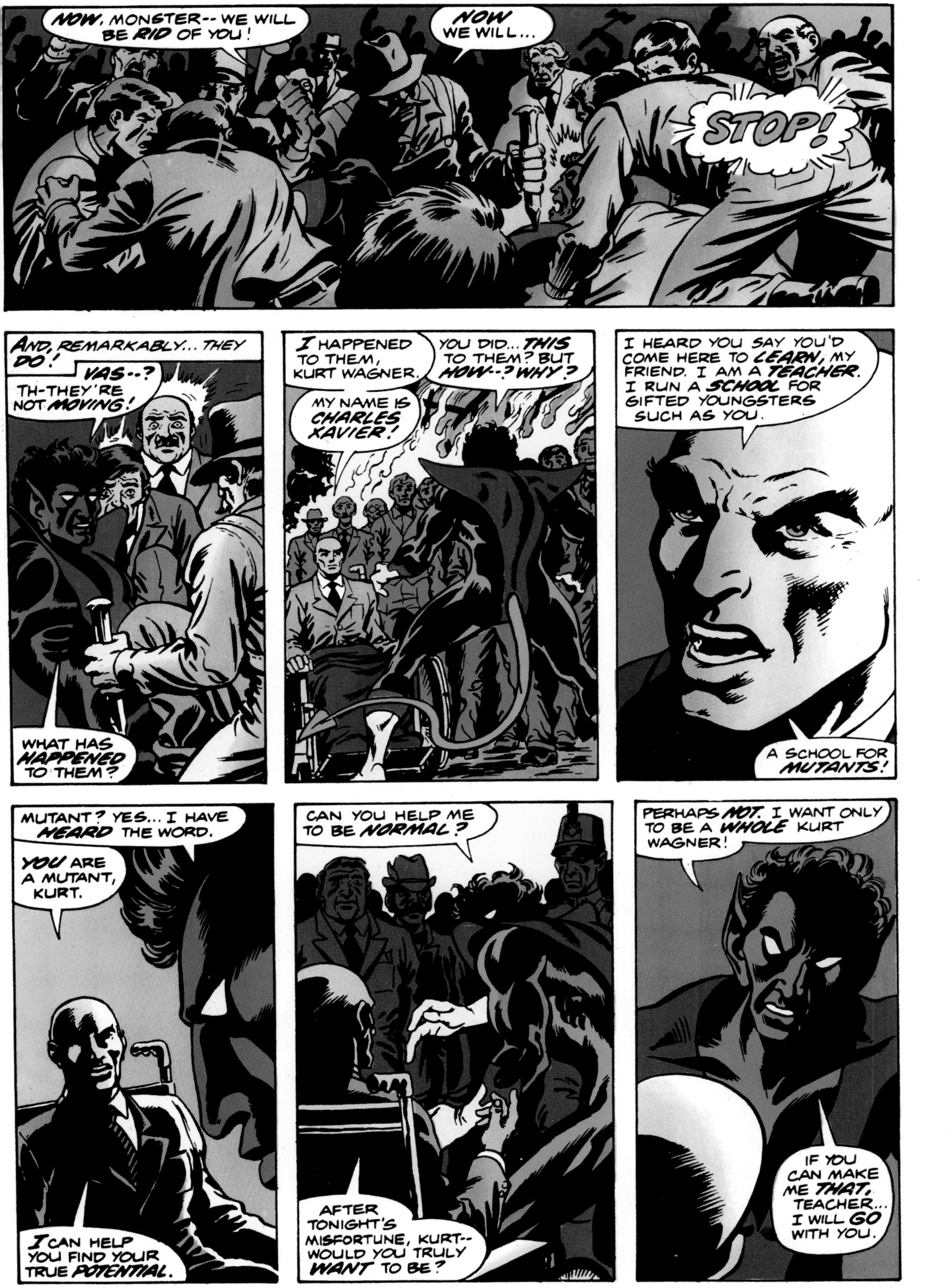
NOW, MONSTER-- WE WILL BE RID OF YOU!
NOW WE WILL...
STOP!
AND, REMARKABLY... THEY DO!
VAS--?
TH-THEY'RE NOT MOVING!
WHAT HAS HAPPENED TO THEM?
I HAPPENED TO THEM, KURT WAGNER.
YOU DID... THIS TO THEM? BUT HOW--? WHY?
MY NAME IS CHARLES XAVIER!
I HEARD YOU SAY YOU'D COME HERE TO LEARN, MY FRIEND. I AM A TEACHER. I RUN A SCHOOL FOR GIFTED YOUNGSTERS SUCH AS YOU.
A SCHOOL FOR MUTANTS!
MUTANT? YES... I HAVE HEARD THE WORD.
YOU ARE A MUTANT, KURT.
I CAN HELP YOU FIND YOUR TRUE POTENTIAL.
CAN YOU HELP ME TO BE NORMAL?
AFTER TONIGHT'S MISFORTUNE, KURT-- WOULD YOU TRULY WANT TO BE?
PERHAPS NOT. I WANT ONLY TO BE A WHOLE KURT WAGNER!
IF YOU CAN MAKE ME THAT, TEACHER... I WILL GO WITH YOU.

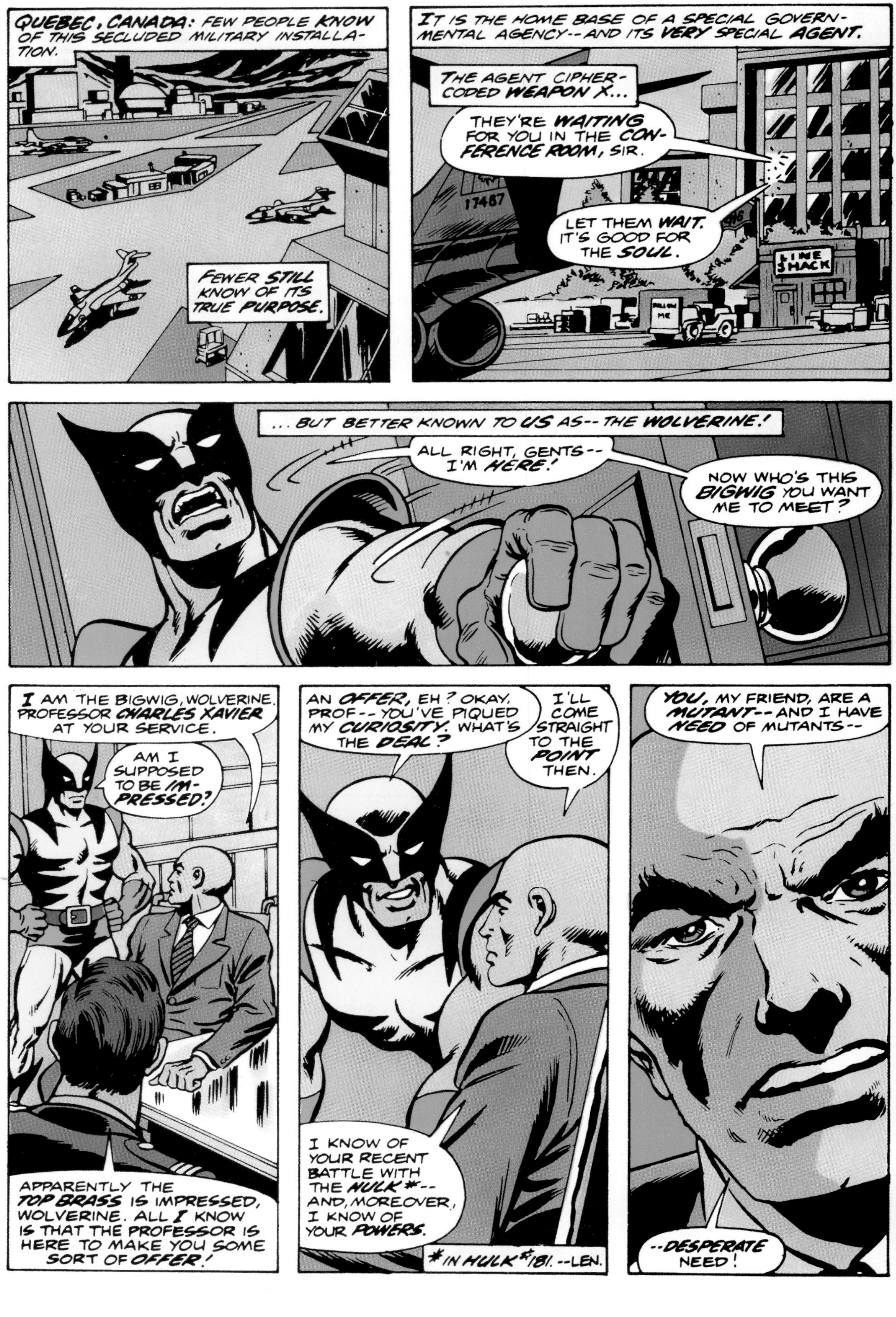
QUEBEC, CANADA: FEW PEOPLE KNOW OF THIS SECLUDED MILITARY INSTALLATION.
FEWER STILL KNOW OF ITS TRUE PURPOSE.
IT IS THE HOME BASE OF A SPECIAL GOVERNMENTAL AGENCY--AND ITS VERY SPECIAL AGENT.
THE AGENT CIPHER-CODED WEAPON X...
THEY'RE WAITING FOR YOU IN THE CONFERENCE ROOM, SIR.
LET THEM WAIT. IT'S GOOD FOR THE SOUL.
LINE SHACK
17487
...BUT BETTER KNOWN TO US AS--THE WOLVERINE!
ALL RIGHT, GENTS--I'M HERE!
NOW WHO'S THIS BIGWIG YOU WANT ME TO MEET?
I AM THE BIGWIG, WOLVERINE. PROFESSOR CHARLES XAVIER AT YOUR SERVICE.
AM I SUPPOSED TO BE IMPRESSED?
APPARENTLY THE TOP BRASS IS IMPRESSED, WOLVERINE. ALL I KNOW IS THAT THE PROFESSOR IS HERE TO MAKE YOU SOME SORT OF OFFER!
AN OFFER, EH? OKAY, PROF--YOU'VE PIQUED MY CURIOSITY. WHAT'S THE DEAL?
I'LL COME STRAIGHT TO THE POINT THEN.
I KNOW OF YOUR RECENT BATTLE WITH THE HULK*--AND, MOREOVER, I KNOW OF YOUR POWERS.
*IN HULK #181. --LEN.
YOU, MY FRIEND, ARE A MUTANT--AND I HAVE NEED OF MUTANTS--
--DESPERATE NEED!

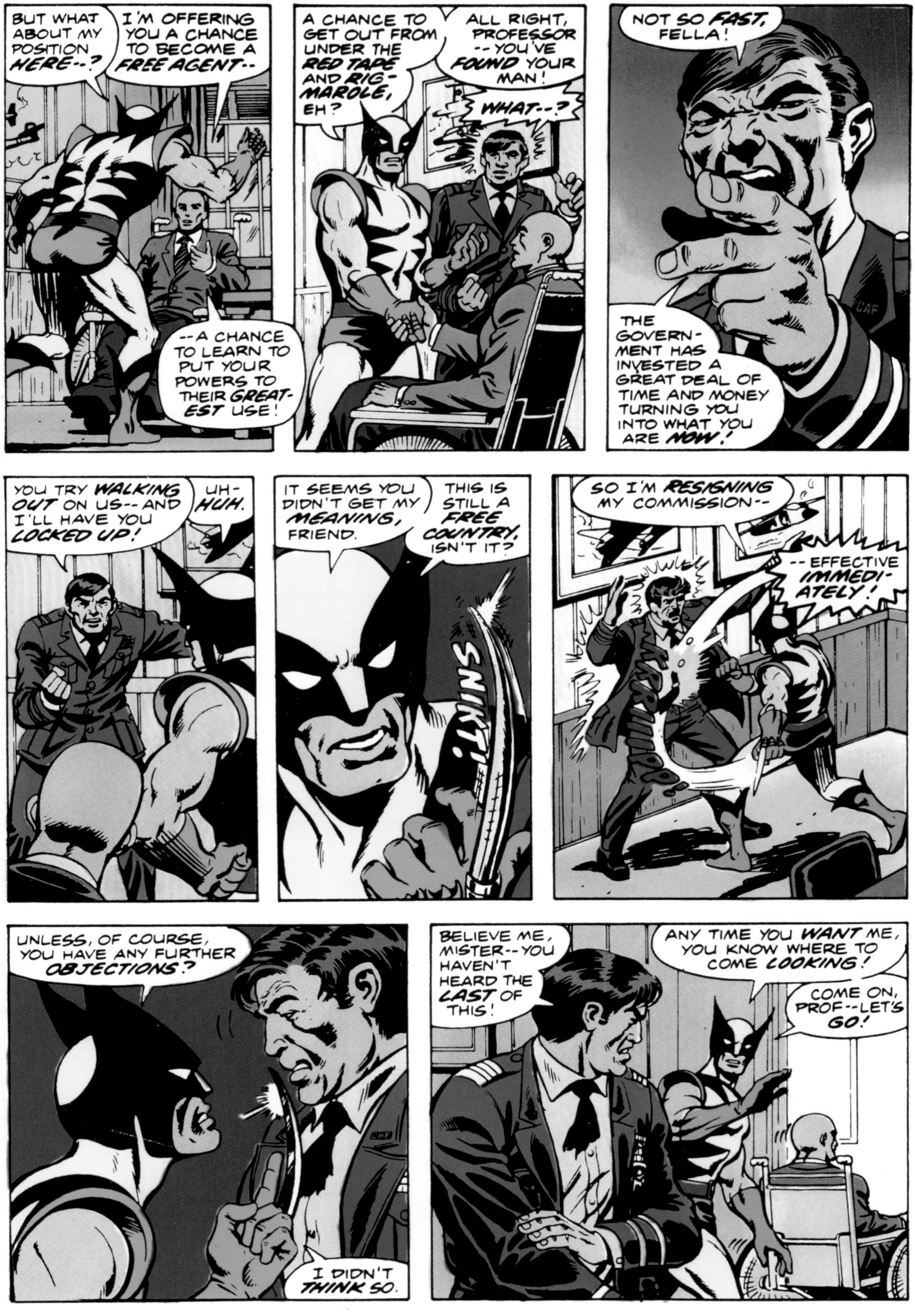
BUT WHAT ABOUT MY POSITION HERE--?
I'M OFFERING YOU A CHANCE TO BECOME A FREE AGENT--
--A CHANCE TO LEARN TO PUT YOUR POWERS TO THEIR GREATEST USE!
A CHANCE TO GET OUT FROM UNDER THE RED TAPE AND RIGMAROLE, EH?
ALL RIGHT, PROFESSOR --YOU'VE FOUND YOUR MAN!
WHAT--?
NOT SO FAST, FELLA!
THE GOVERNMENT HAS INVESTED A GREAT DEAL OF TIME AND MONEY TURNING YOU INTO WHAT YOU ARE NOW!
YOU TRY WALKING OUT ON US--AND I'LL HAVE YOU LOCKED UP!
UH-HUH.
IT SEEMS YOU DIDN'T GET MY MEANING, FRIEND.
THIS IS STILL A FREE COUNTRY, ISN'T IT?
SNIKT!
SO I'M RESIGNING MY COMMISSION--
--EFFECTIVE IMMEDIATELY!
UNLESS, OF COURSE, YOU HAVE ANY FURTHER OBJECTIONS?
I DIDN'T THINK SO.
BELIEVE ME, MISTER--YOU HAVEN'T HEARD THE LAST OF THIS!
ANY TIME YOU WANT ME, YOU KNOW WHERE TO COME LOOKING!
COME ON, PROF--LET'S GO!

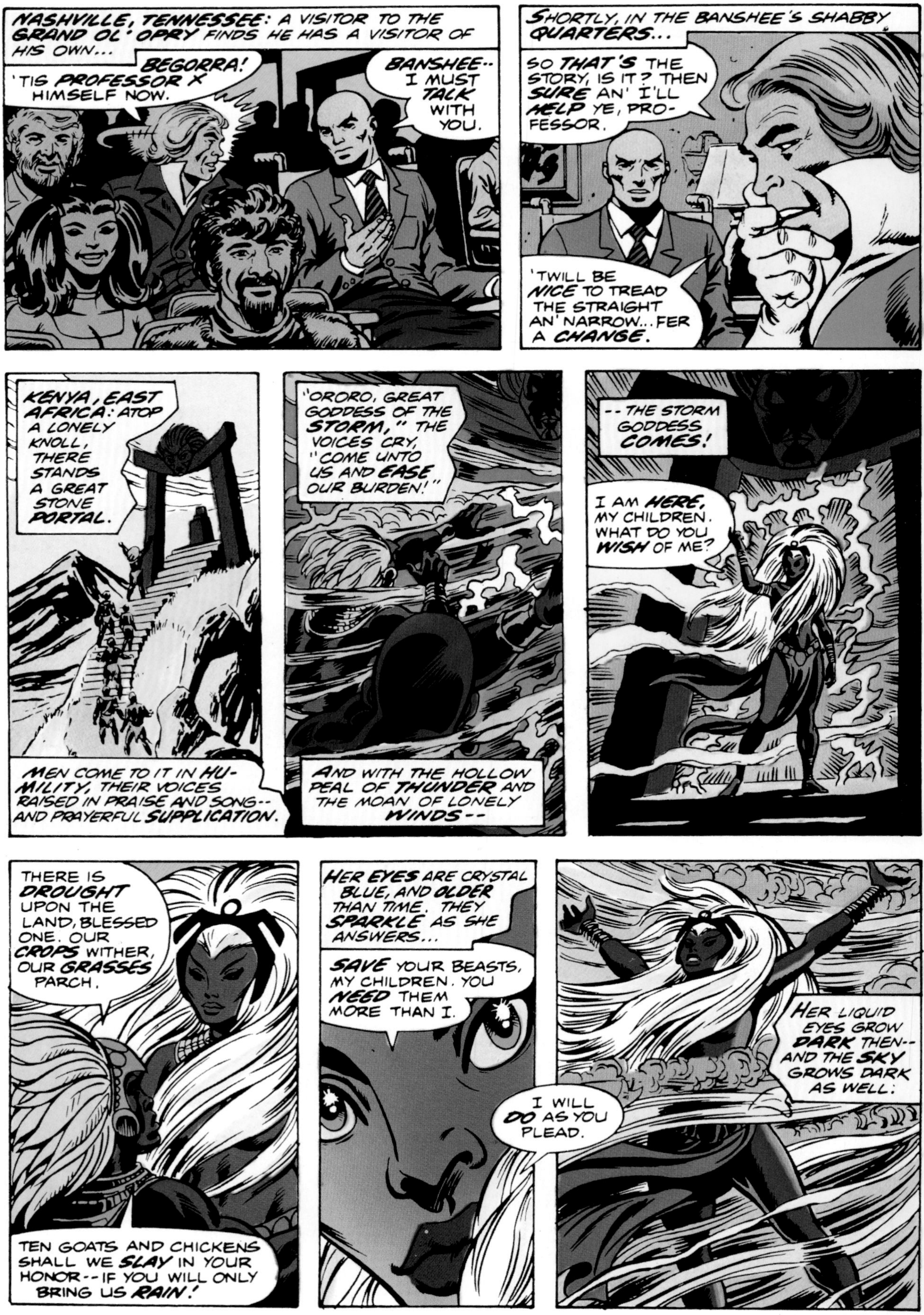
NASHVILLE, TENNESSEE: A VISITOR TO THE GRAND OL' OPRY FINDS HE HAS A VISITOR OF HIS OWN...
BEGORRA! 'TIS PROFESSOR X HIMSELF NOW.
BANSHEE.. I MUST TALK WITH YOU.
SHORTLY, IN THE BANSHEE'S SHABBY QUARTERS...
SO THAT'S THE STORY, IS IT? THEN SURE AN' I'LL HELP YE, PROFESSOR.
'TWILL BE NICE TO TREAD THE STRAIGHT AN' NARROW... FER A CHANGE.
KENYA, EAST AFRICA: ATOP A LONELY KNOLL, THERE STANDS A GREAT STONE PORTAL.
MEN COME TO IT IN HUMILITY, THEIR VOICES RAISED IN PRAISE AND SONG-- AND PRAYERFUL SUPPLICATION.
"ORORO, GREAT GODDESS OF THE STORM," THE VOICES CRY, "COME UNTO US AND EASE OUR BURDEN!"
AND WITH THE HOLLOW PEAL OF THUNDER AND THE MOAN OF LONELY WINDS--
--THE STORM GODDESS COMES!
I AM HERE, MY CHILDREN. WHAT DO YOU WISH OF ME?
THERE IS DROUGHT UPON THE LAND, BLESSED ONE. OUR CROPS WITHER, OUR GRASSES PARCH.
TEN GOATS AND CHICKENS SHALL WE SLAY IN YOUR HONOR-- IF YOU WILL ONLY BRING US RAIN!
HER EYES ARE CRYSTAL BLUE, AND OLDER THAN TIME. THEY SPARKLE AS SHE ANSWERS...
SAVE YOUR BEASTS, MY CHILDREN. YOU NEED THEM MORE THAN I.
HER LIQUID EYES GROW DARK THEN-- AND THE SKY GROWS DARK AS WELL:
I WILL DO AS YOU PLEAD.

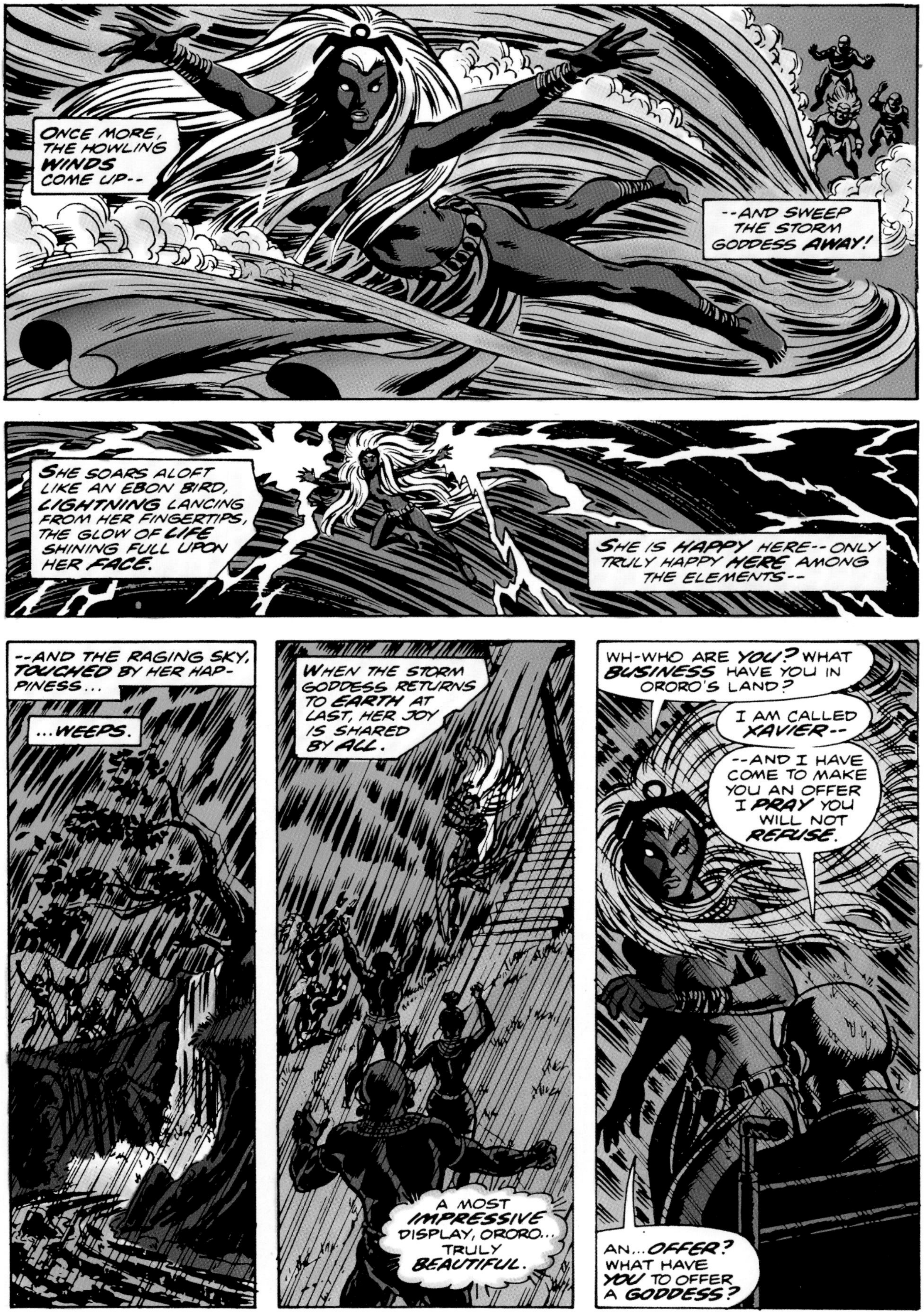
ONCE MORE, THE HOWLING WINDS COME UP--
--AND SWEEP THE STORM GODDESS AWAY!
SHE SOARS ALOFT LIKE AN EBON BIRD, LIGHTNING LANCING FROM HER FINGERTIPS, THE GLOW OF LIFE SHINING FULL UPON HER FACE.
SHE IS HAPPY HERE--ONLY TRULY HAPPY HERE AMONG THE ELEMENTS--
--AND THE RAGING SKY, TOUCHED BY HER HAPPINESS...
...WEEPS.
WHEN THE STORM GODDESS RETURNS TO EARTH AT LAST, HER JOY IS SHARED BY ALL.
A MOST IMPRESSIVE DISPLAY, ORORO... TRULY BEAUTIFUL.
WH-WHO ARE YOU? WHAT BUSINESS HAVE YOU IN ORORO'S LAND?
I AM CALLED XAVIER--
--AND I HAVE COME TO MAKE YOU AN OFFER I PRAY YOU WILL NOT REFUSE.
AN...OFFER? WHAT HAVE YOU TO OFFER A GODDESS?

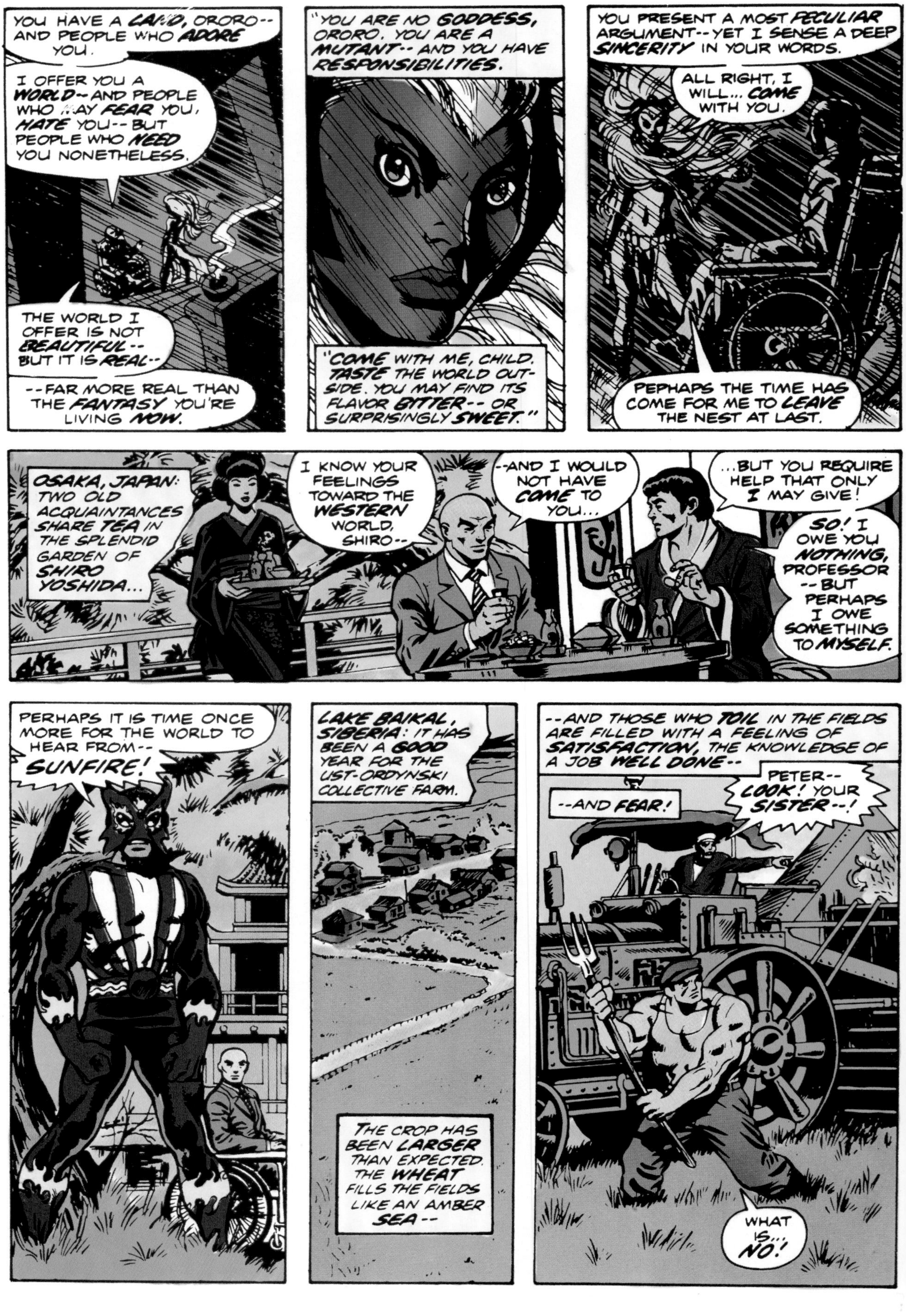
YOU HAVE A LAND, ORORO-- AND PEOPLE WHO ADORE YOU.
I OFFER YOU A WORLD-- AND PEOPLE WHO MAY FEAR YOU, HATE YOU-- BUT PEOPLE WHO NEED YOU NONETHELESS.
THE WORLD I OFFER IS NOT BEAUTIFUL-- BUT IT IS REAL--
--FAR MORE REAL THAN THE FANTASY YOU'RE LIVING NOW.
"YOU ARE NO GODDESS, ORORO. YOU ARE A MUTANT-- AND YOU HAVE RESPONSIBILITIES.
"COME WITH ME, CHILD. TASTE THE WORLD OUTSIDE. YOU MAY FIND ITS FLAVOR BITTER-- OR SURPRISINGLY SWEET."
YOU PRESENT A MOST PECULIAR ARGUMENT--YET I SENSE A DEEP SINCERITY IN YOUR WORDS.
ALL RIGHT, I WILL... COME WITH YOU.
PEPHAPS THE TIME HAS COME FOR ME TO LEAVE THE NEST AT LAST.
OSAKA, JAPAN: TWO OLD ACQUAINTANCES SHARE TEA IN THE SPLENDID GARDEN OF SHIRO YOSHIDA...
I KNOW YOUR FEELINGS TOWARD THE WESTERN WORLD, SHIRO--
--AND I WOULD NOT HAVE COME TO YOU...
...BUT YOU REQUIRE HELP THAT ONLY I MAY GIVE!
SO! I OWE YOU NOTHING, PROFESSOR --BUT PERHAPS I OWE SOMETHING TO MYSELF.
PERHAPS IT IS TIME ONCE MORE FOR THE WORLD TO HEAR FROM-- SUNFIRE!
LAKE BAIKAL, SIBERIA: IT HAS BEEN A GOOD YEAR FOR THE UST-ORDYNSKI COLLECTIVE FARM.
THE CROP HAS BEEN LARGER THAN EXPECTED. THE WHEAT FILLS THE FIELDS LIKE AN AMBER SEA--
--AND THOSE WHO TOIL IN THE FIELDS ARE FILLED WITH A FEELING OF SATISFACTION, THE KNOWLEDGE OF A JOB WELL DONE--
--AND FEAR!
PETER-- LOOK! YOUR SISTER--!
WHAT IS... NO!

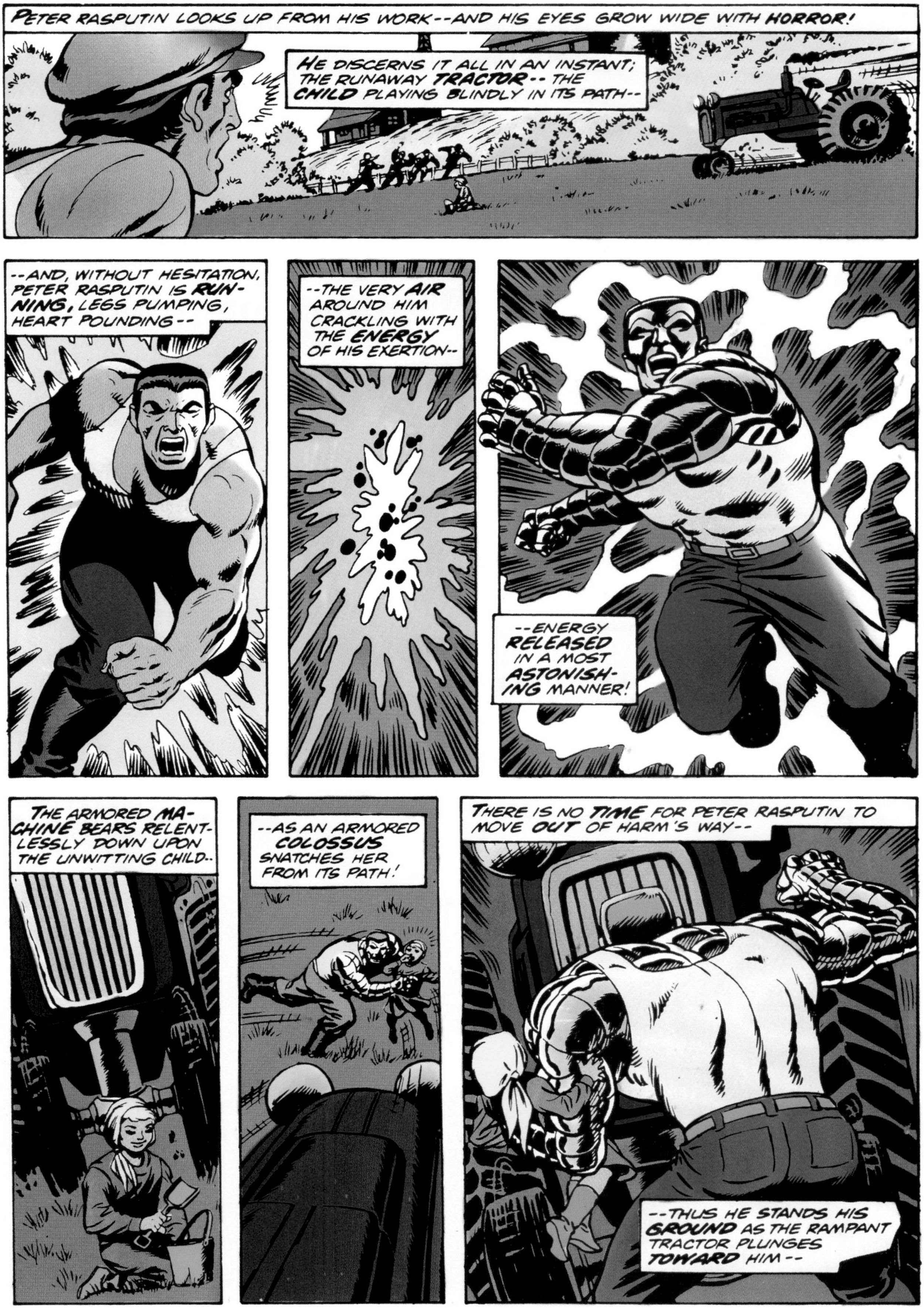

PETER RASPUTIN LOOKS UP FROM HIS WORK--AND HIS EYES GROW WIDE WITH HORROR!
HE DISCERNS IT ALL IN AN INSTANT; THE RUNAWAY TRACTOR-- THE CHILD PLAYING BLINDLY IN ITS PATH--
--AND, WITHOUT HESITATION, PETER RASPUTIN IS RUNNING, LEGS PUMPING, HEART POUNDING--
--THE VERY AIR AROUND HIM CRACKLING WITH THE ENERGY OF HIS EXERTION--
--ENERGY RELEASED IN A MOST ASTONISHING MANNER!
THE ARMORED MACHINE BEARS RELENTLESSLY DOWN UPON THE UNWITTING CHILD..
--AS AN ARMORED COLOSSUS SNATCHES HER FROM ITS PATH!
THERE IS NO TIME FOR PETER RASPUTIN TO MOVE OUT OF HARM'S WAY--
--THUS HE STANDS HIS GROUND AS THE RAMPANT TRACTOR PLUNGES TOWARD HIM--

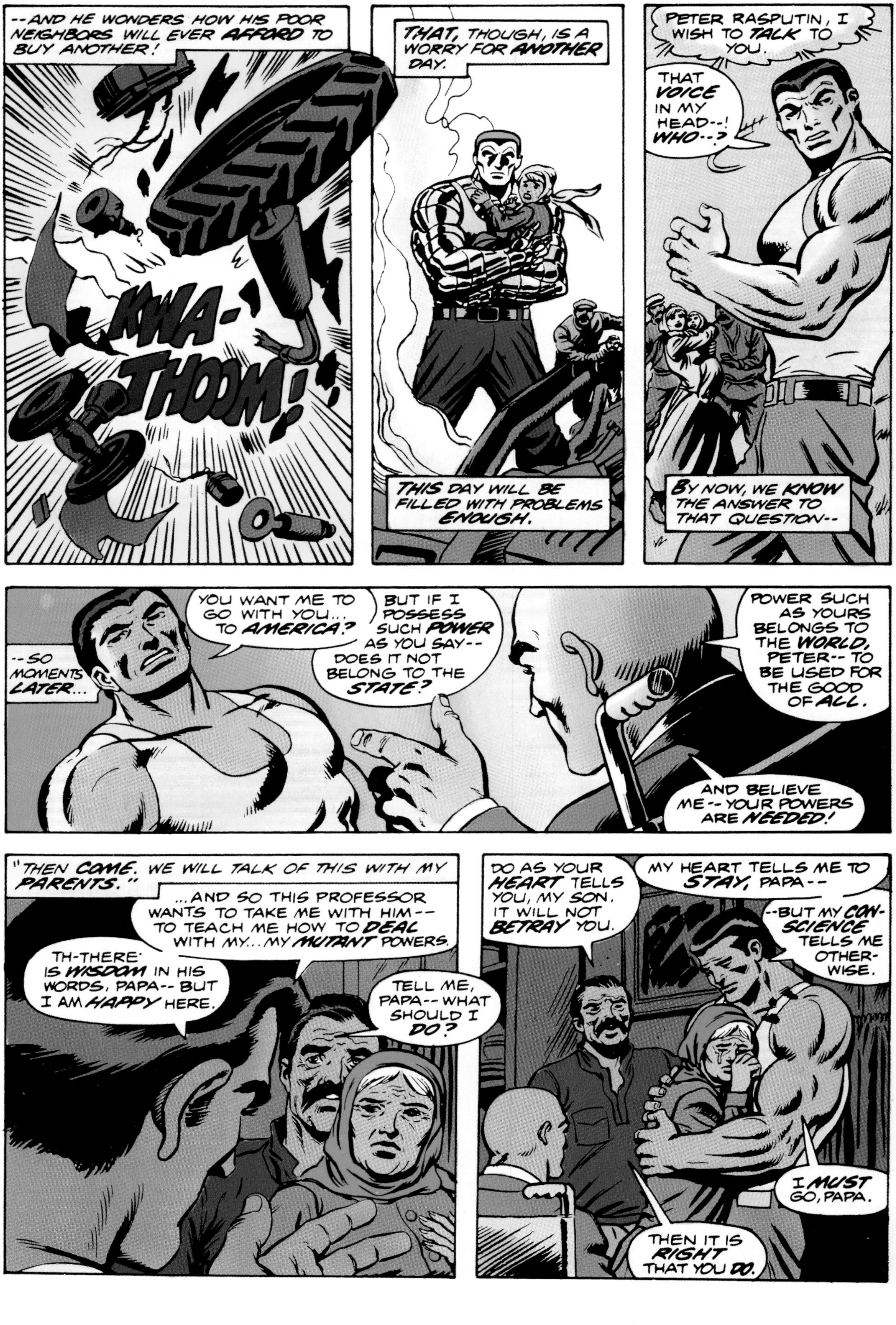

--AND HE WONDERS HOW HIS POOR NEIGHBORS WILL EVER AFFORD TO BUY ANOTHER!
KWA-THOOM!
THAT, THOUGH, IS A WORRY FOR ANOTHER DAY.
THIS DAY WILL BE FILLED WITH PROBLEMS ENOUGH.
PETER RASPUTIN, I WISH TO TALK TO YOU.
THAT VOICE IN MY HEAD--! WHO--?
BY NOW, WE KNOW THE ANSWER TO THAT QUESTION--
--SO MOMENTS LATER...
YOU WANT ME TO GO WITH YOU... TO AMERICA?
BUT IF I POSSESS SUCH POWER AS YOU SAY-- DOES IT NOT BELONG TO THE STATE?
POWER SUCH AS YOURS BELONGS TO THE WORLD, PETER-- TO BE USED FOR THE GOOD OF ALL.
AND BELIEVE ME-- YOUR POWERS ARE NEEDED!
"THEN COME. WE WILL TALK OF THIS WITH MY PARENTS."
...AND SO THIS PROFESSOR WANTS TO TAKE ME WITH HIM-- TO TEACH ME HOW TO DEAL WITH MY... MY MUTANT POWERS.
TH-THERE IS WISDOM IN HIS WORDS, PAPA-- BUT I AM HAPPY HERE.
TELL ME, PAPA-- WHAT SHOULD I DO?
DO AS YOUR HEART TELLS YOU, MY SON. IT WILL NOT BETRAY YOU.
MY HEART TELLS ME TO STAY, PAPA--
--BUT MY CON-SCIENCE TELLS ME OTHER-WISE.
I MUST GO, PAPA.
THEN IT IS RIGHT THAT YOU DO.

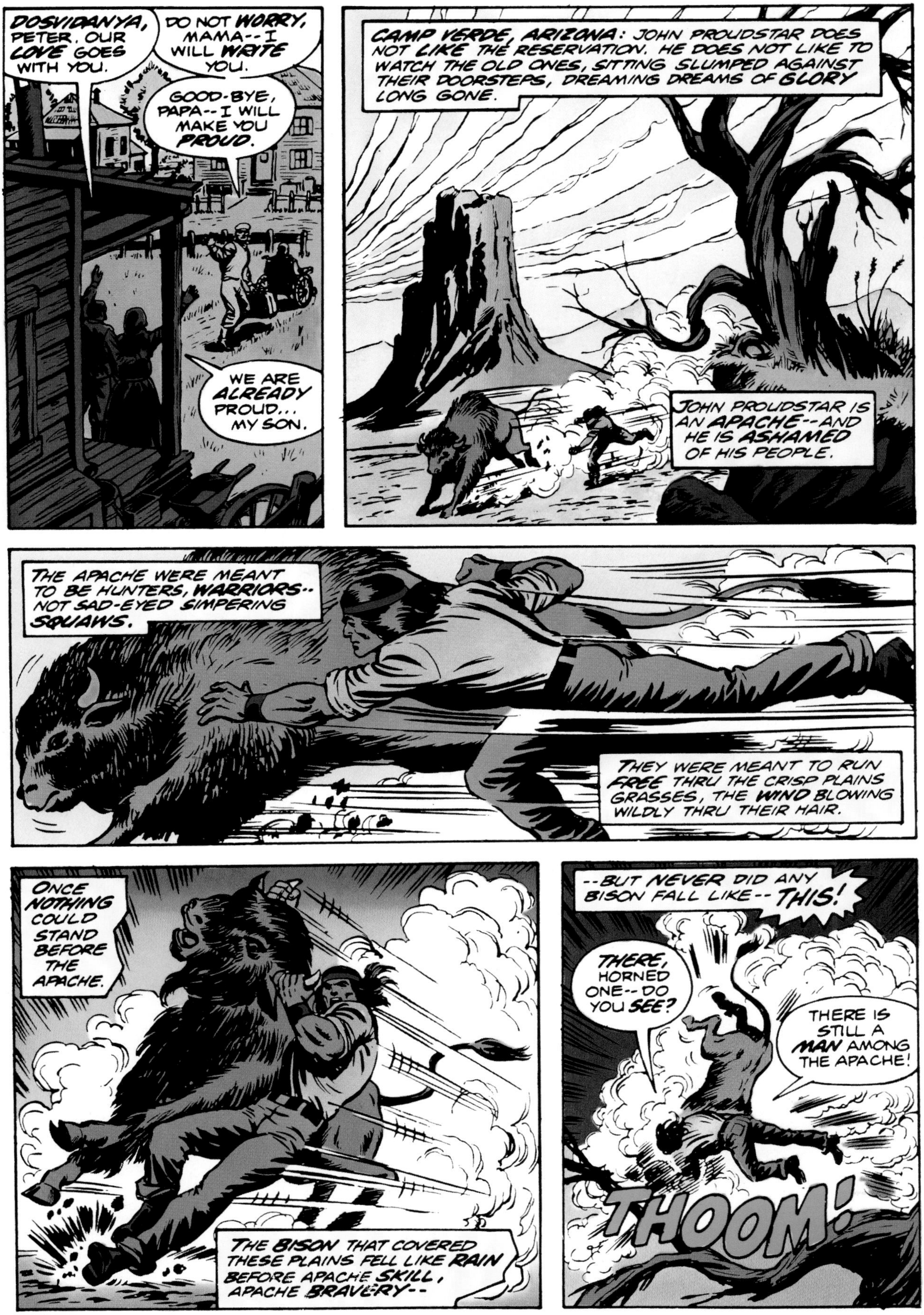
DOSVIDANYA, PETER. OUR LOVE GOES WITH YOU.
DO NOT WORRY, MAMA--I WILL WRITE YOU.
GOOD-BYE, PAPA--I WILL MAKE YOU PROUD.
WE ARE ALREADY PROUD... MY SON.
CAMP VERDE, ARIZONA: JOHN PROUDSTAR DOES NOT LIKE THE RESERVATION. HE DOES NOT LIKE TO WATCH THE OLD ONES, SITTING SLUMPED AGAINST THEIR DOORSTEPS, DREAMING DREAMS OF GLORY LONG GONE.
JOHN PROUDSTAR IS AN APACHE--AND HE IS ASHAMED OF HIS PEOPLE.
THE APACHE WERE MEANT TO BE HUNTERS, WARRIORS.. NOT SAD-EYED SIMPERING SQUAWS.
THEY WERE MEANT TO RUN FREE THRU THE CRISP PLAINS GRASSES, THE WIND BLOWING WILDLY THRU THEIR HAIR.
ONCE NOTHING COULD STAND BEFORE THE APACHE.
THE BISON THAT COVERED THESE PLAINS FELL LIKE RAIN BEFORE APACHE SKILL, APACHE BRAVERY--
--BUT NEVER DID ANY BISON FALL LIKE--THIS!
THERE, HORNED ONE--DO YOU SEE?
THERE IS STILL A MAN AMONG THE APACHE!
THOOM!

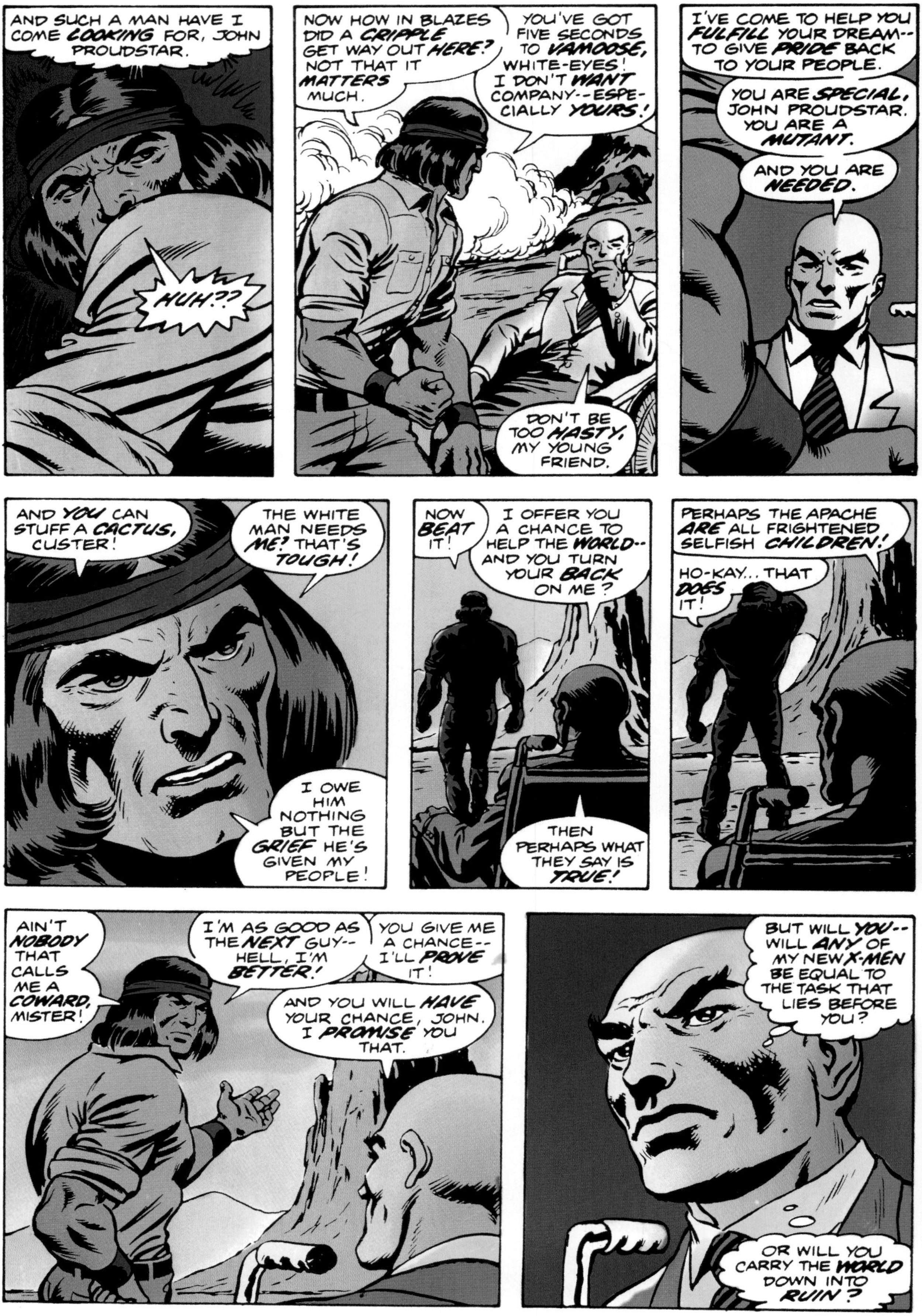

AND SUCH A MAN HAVE I COME LOOKING FOR, JOHN PROUDSTAR.
HUH??
NOW HOW IN BLAZES DID A CRIPPLE GET WAY OUT HERE? NOT THAT IT MATTERS MUCH.
YOU'VE GOT FIVE SECONDS TO VAMOOSE, WHITE-EYES! I DON'T WANT COMPANY--ESPECIALLY YOURS!
DON'T BE TOO HASTY, MY YOUNG FRIEND.
I'VE COME TO HELP YOU FULFILL YOUR DREAM--TO GIVE PRIDE BACK TO YOUR PEOPLE.
YOU ARE SPECIAL, JOHN PROUDSTAR. YOU ARE A MUTANT.
AND YOU ARE NEEDED.
AND YOU CAN STUFF A CACTUS, CUSTER!
THE WHITE MAN NEEDS ME? THAT'S TOUGH!
I OWE HIM NOTHING BUT THE GRIEF HE'S GIVEN MY PEOPLE!
NOW BEAT IT!
I OFFER YOU A CHANCE TO HELP THE WORLD--AND YOU TURN YOUR BACK ON ME?
THEN PERHAPS WHAT THEY SAY IS TRUE!
PERHAPS THE APACHE ARE ALL FRIGHTENED SELFISH CHILDREN!
HO-KAY... THAT DOES IT!
AIN'T NOBODY THAT CALLS ME A COWARD, MISTER!
I'M AS GOOD AS THE NEXT GUY--HELL, I'M BETTER!
YOU GIVE ME A CHANCE--I'LL PROVE IT!
AND YOU WILL HAVE YOUR CHANCE, JOHN. I PROMISE YOU THAT.
BUT WILL YOU--WILL ANY OF MY NEW X-MEN BE EQUAL TO THE TASK THAT LIES BEFORE YOU?
OR WILL YOU CARRY THE WORLD DOWN INTO RUIN?

CHAPTER II "...AND WHEN THERE WAS ONE!"

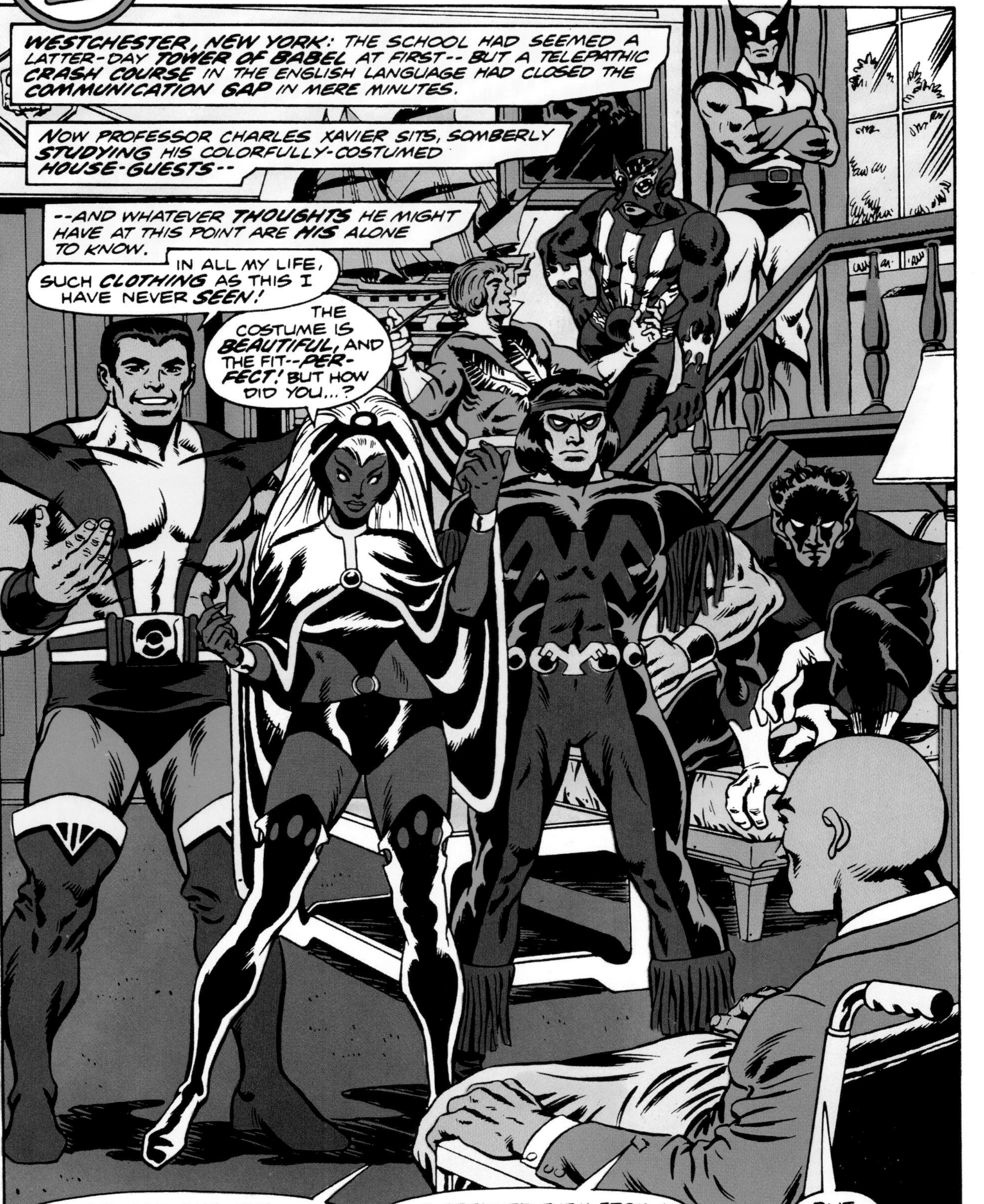

WESTCHESTER, NEW YORK: THE SCHOOL HAD SEEMED A LATTER-DAY TOWER OF BABEL AT FIRST-- BUT A TELEPATHIC CRASH COURSE IN THE ENGLISH LANGUAGE HAD CLOSED THE COMMUNICATION GAP IN MERE MINUTES.
NOW PROFESSOR CHARLES XAVIER SITS, SOMBERLY STUDYING HIS COLORFULLY-COSTUMED HOUSE-GUESTS--
--AND WHATEVER THOUGHTS HE MIGHT HAVE AT THIS POINT ARE HIS ALONE TO KNOW.
IN ALL MY LIFE, SUCH CLOTHING AS THIS I HAVE NEVER SEEN!
THE COSTUME IS BEAUTIFUL, AND THE FIT--PERFECT! BUT HOW DID YOU...?
THE UNIFORMS ARE CONSTRUCTED FROM UNSTABLE MOLECULES, WHICH ADJUST THEMSELVES WHERE NECESSARY.
I OBTAINED THEM FROM A MAN NAMED REED RICHARDS, AND I'M CERTAIN YOU'LL LEARN MORE OF HIM AND HIS FRIENDS LATER.
BUT RIGHT NOW...

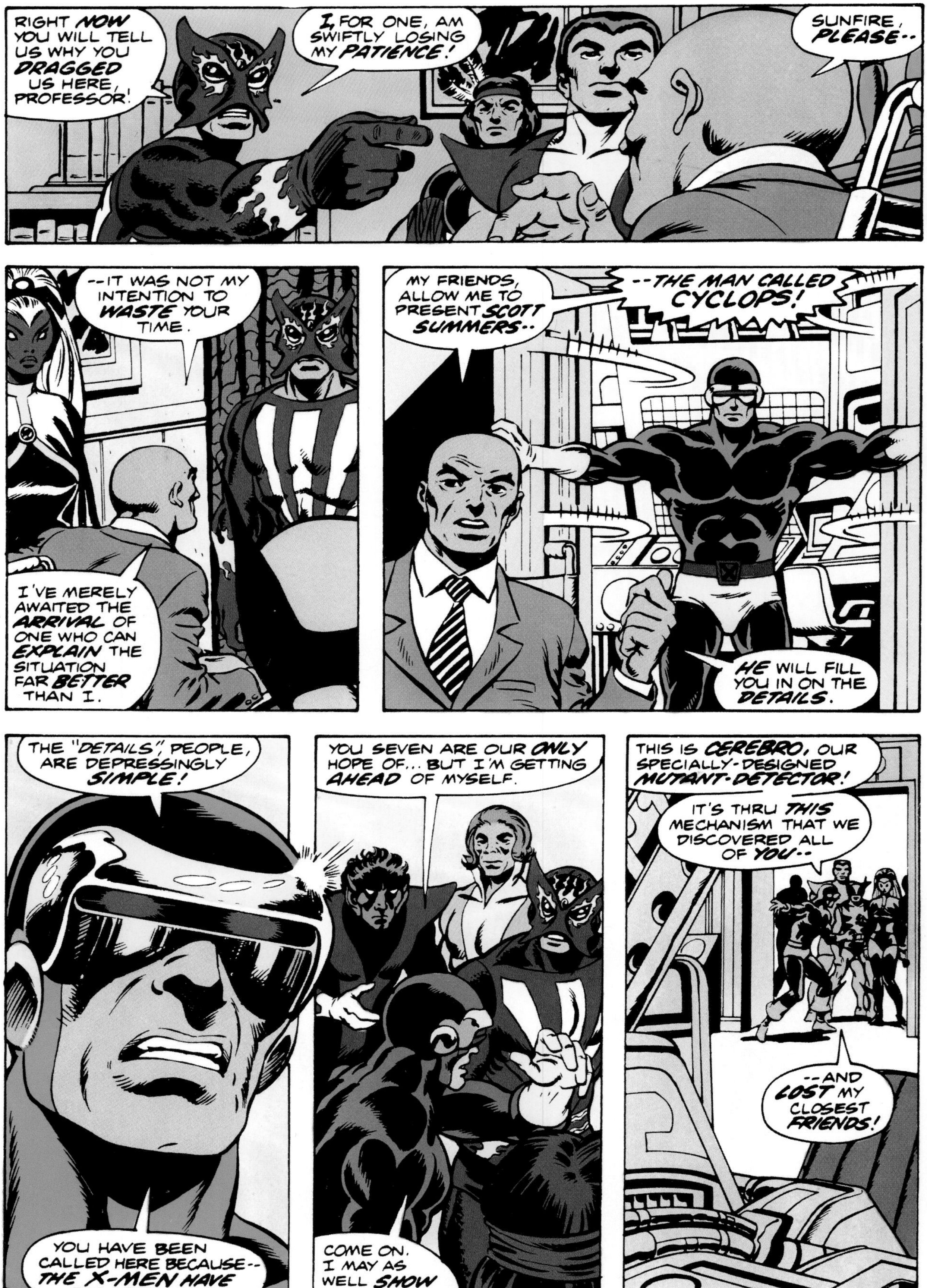
RIGHT NOW YOU WILL TELL US WHY YOU DRAGGED US HERE, PROFESSOR!
I, FOR ONE, AM SWIFTLY LOSING MY PATIENCE!
SUNFIRE, PLEASE--
--IT WAS NOT MY INTENTION TO WASTE YOUR TIME.
I'VE MERELY AWAITED THE ARRIVAL OF ONE WHO CAN EXPLAIN THE SITUATION FAR BETTER THAN I.
MY FRIENDS, ALLOW ME TO PRESENT SCOTT SUMMERS--
--THE MAN CALLED CYCLOPS!
HE WILL FILL YOU IN ON THE DETAILS.
THE "DETAILS," PEOPLE, ARE DEPRESSINGLY SIMPLE!
YOU HAVE BEEN CALLED HERE BECAUSE-- THE X-MEN HAVE DISAPPEARED!
YOU SEVEN ARE OUR ONLY HOPE OF... BUT I'M GETTING AHEAD OF MYSELF.
COME ON. I MAY AS WELL SHOW YOU WHERE IT ALL BEGAN!
THIS IS CEREBRO, OUR SPECIALLY-DESIGNED MUTANT-DETECTOR!
IT'S THRU THIS MECHANISM THAT WE DISCOVERED ALL OF YOU--
--AND LOST MY CLOSEST FRIENDS!

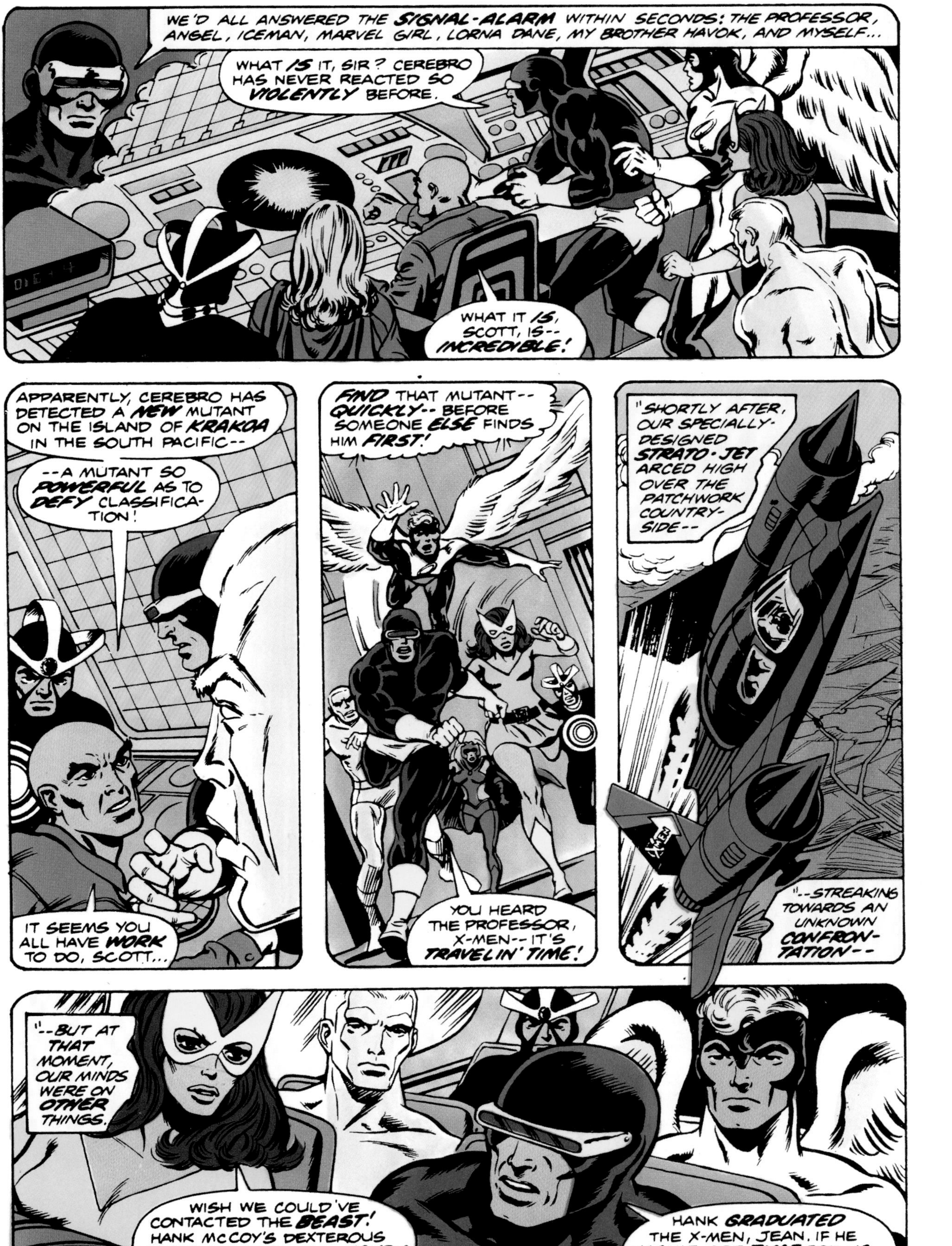
WE'D ALL ANSWERED THE SIGNAL-ALARM WITHIN SECONDS: THE PROFESSOR, ANGEL, ICEMAN, MARVEL GIRL, LORNA DANE, MY BROTHER HAVOK, AND MYSELF...
WHAT IS IT, SIR? CEREBRO HAS NEVER REACTED SO VIOLENTLY BEFORE.
WHAT IT IS, SCOTT, IS--INCREDIBLE!
APPARENTLY, CEREBRO HAS DETECTED A NEW MUTANT ON THE ISLAND OF KRAKOA IN THE SOUTH PACIFIC--
--A MUTANT SO POWERFUL AS TO DEFY CLASSIFICATION!
IT SEEMS YOU ALL HAVE WORK TO DO, SCOTT...
FIND THAT MUTANT--QUICKLY--BEFORE SOMEONE ELSE FINDS HIM FIRST!
YOU HEARD THE PROFESSOR, X-MEN--IT'S TRAVELIN' TIME!
"SHORTLY AFTER, OUR SPECIALLY-DESIGNED STRATO-JET ARCED HIGH OVER THE PATCHWORK COUNTRYSIDE--
"--STREAKING TOWARDS AN UNKNOWN CONFRONTATION--
"--BUT AT THAT MOMENT, OUR MINDS WERE ON OTHER THINGS.
WISH WE COULD'VE CONTACTED THE BEAST! HANK McCOY'S DEXTEROUS DIGITS MIGHT BE--EH--HANDY ON A JOB LIKE THIS.
HANK GRADUATED THE X-MEN, JEAN. IF HE HASN'T GOT TIME FOR US NOW, THAT'S HIS BUSINESS.

RIGHT NOW WE'VE GOT BUSINESS OF OUR *OWN* TO WORRY ABOUT.

THAT'S *KRAKOA* DEAD AHEAD!

YEECH--YOU'D NEED A SUPER-POWER JUST TO *SURVIVE* ON THAT DESOLATE MUD-BAR.

ENOUGH *BANTER!* STRAP IN FOR *LANDING!*

"WE TOUCHED DOWN MOMENTS LATER, OUR *VTOL* ✱ JETS LOWERING US TO EARTH AS GENTLY AS AN INFANT IS LOWERED INTO ITS CRADLE--

✱*VERTICAL TAKE-OFF AND LANDING. --ENCYCLOPEDIC LEN.*

"--BUT WE WERE *NOT* INFANTS--AND THIS WAS DEFINITELY NO *CHILD'S GAME!*

I THINK WE TOOK THE *WRONG* BUS, GANG. THIS PLACE SURE DOESN'T LOOK LIKE *CLEVELAND.*

ALL THE *INSECTS* IN THE AIR-- THE OVERGROWN *JUNGLE--!*

ON SECOND THOUGHT, MAYBE THIS *IS* CLEVELAND.

I TOLD YOU *BEFORE,* ICEMAN--*SHELVE* THE SNAPPY PATTER!

WE HAVE A *DIFFICULT* JOB AHEAD OF US, FINDING THAT NEW *MUTANT--!*

MAYBE AN *IMPOSSIBLE* ONE, CYKE--WHEN YOU CONSIDER WE HAVE *NO* IDEA WHAT WE'RE *LOOKING* FOR!

POINT *TAKEN,* ANGEL. LET'S *FAN OUT* AND SEE IF...

BEHIND US-- L-LOOK! IT'S...IT'S...

QUICK, EVERYBODY-- *SCATTER!*

GET *MOVING* BEFORE WE...

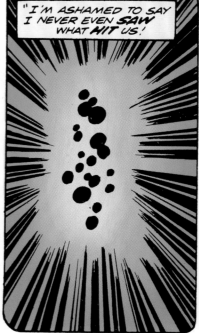

"I'M ASHAMED TO SAY I NEVER EVEN *SAW* WHAT *HIT* US!"

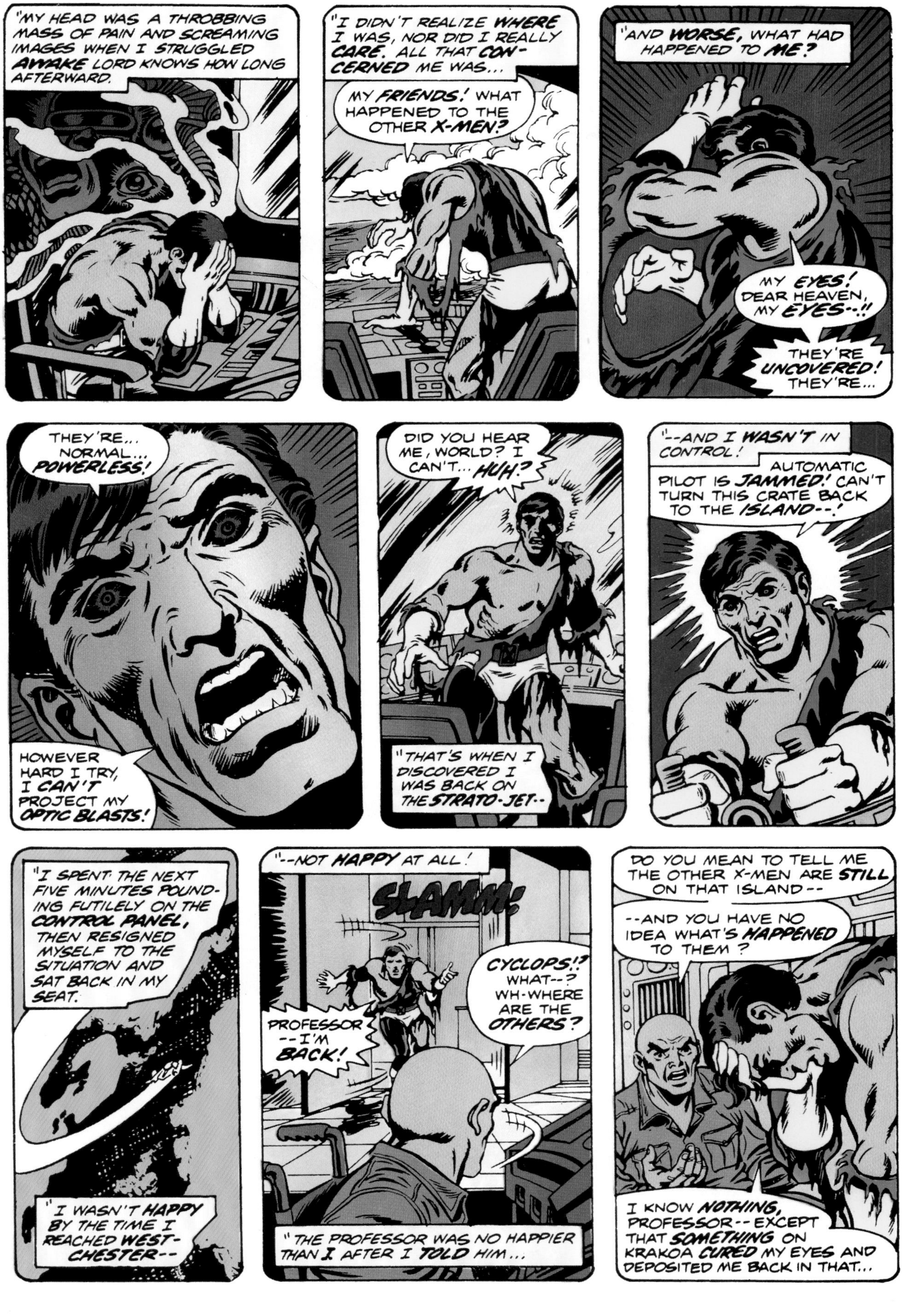
"MY HEAD WAS A THROBBING MASS OF PAIN AND SCREAMING IMAGES WHEN I STRUGGLED AWAKE LORD KNOWS HOW LONG AFTERWARD.
"I DIDN'T REALIZE WHERE I WAS, NOR DID I REALLY CARE. ALL THAT CONCERNED ME WAS...
MY FRIENDS! WHAT HAPPENED TO THE OTHER X-MEN?
"AND WORSE, WHAT HAD HAPPENED TO ME?
MY EYES! DEAR HEAVEN, MY EYES--!!
THEY'RE UNCOVERED! THEY'RE...
THEY'RE... NORMAL... POWERLESS!
HOWEVER HARD I TRY, I CAN'T PROJECT MY OPTIC BLASTS!
DID YOU HEAR ME, WORLD? I CAN'T... HUH?
"THAT'S WHEN I DISCOVERED I WAS BACK ON THE STRATO-JET--
"--AND I WASN'T IN CONTROL!
AUTOMATIC PILOT IS JAMMED! CAN'T TURN THIS CRATE BACK TO THE ISLAND--!
"I SPENT THE NEXT FIVE MINUTES POUNDING FUTILELY ON THE CONTROL PANEL, THEN RESIGNED MYSELF TO THE SITUATION AND SAT BACK IN MY SEAT.
"I WASN'T HAPPY BY THE TIME I REACHED WESTCHESTER--
"--NOT HAPPY AT ALL!
SLAMM!
PROFESSOR --I'M BACK!
CYCLOPS!? WHAT--? WH-WHERE ARE THE OTHERS?
"THE PROFESSOR WAS NO HAPPIER THAN I AFTER I TOLD HIM...
DO YOU MEAN TO TELL ME THE OTHER X-MEN ARE STILL ON THAT ISLAND--
--AND YOU HAVE NO IDEA WHAT'S HAPPENED TO THEM ?
I KNOW NOTHING, PROFESSOR-- EXCEPT THAT SOMETHING ON KRAKOA CURED MY EYES AND DEPOSITED ME BACK IN THAT...

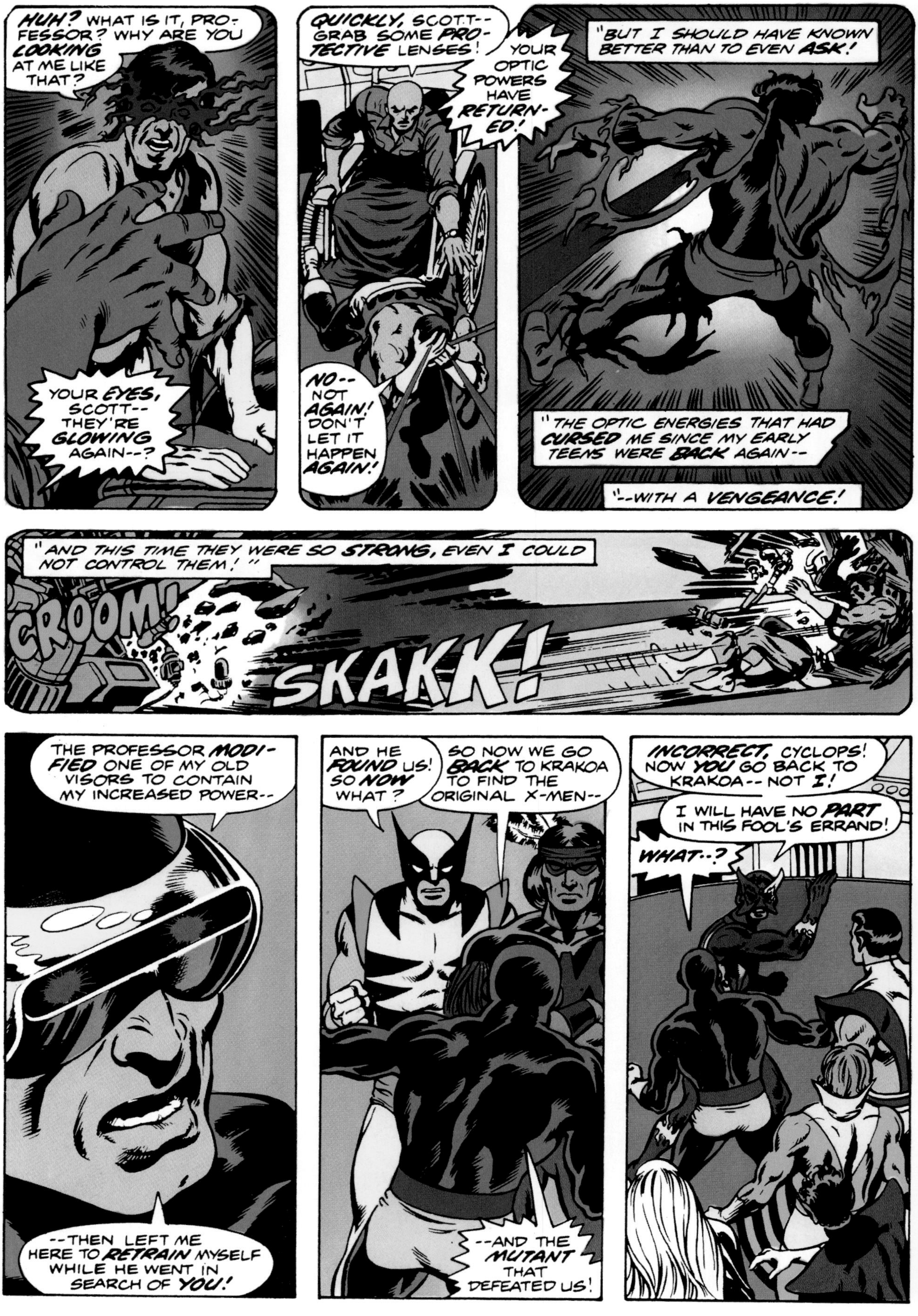
HUH? WHAT IS IT, PROFESSOR? WHY ARE YOU LOOKING AT ME LIKE THAT?
YOUR EYES, SCOTT-- THEY'RE GLOWING AGAIN--?
QUICKLY, SCOTT-- GRAB SOME PROTECTIVE LENSES!
YOUR OPTIC POWERS HAVE RETURNED!
NO-- NOT AGAIN! DON'T LET IT HAPPEN AGAIN!
"BUT I SHOULD HAVE KNOWN BETTER THAN TO EVEN ASK!
"THE OPTIC ENERGIES THAT HAD CURSED ME SINCE MY EARLY TEENS WERE BACK AGAIN--
"--WITH A VENGEANCE!
"AND THIS TIME THEY WERE SO STRONG, EVEN I COULD NOT CONTROL THEM!"
CROOM!
SKAKK!
THE PROFESSOR MODIFIED ONE OF MY OLD VISORS TO CONTAIN MY INCREASED POWER--
--THEN LEFT ME HERE TO RETRAIN MYSELF WHILE HE WENT IN SEARCH OF YOU!
AND HE FOUND US! SO NOW WHAT?
SO NOW WE GO BACK TO KRAKOA TO FIND THE ORIGINAL X-MEN--
--AND THE MUTANT THAT DEFEATED US!
INCORRECT, CYCLOPS! NOW YOU GO BACK TO KRAKOA-- NOT I!
I WILL HAVE NO PART IN THIS FOOL'S ERRAND!
WHAT--?

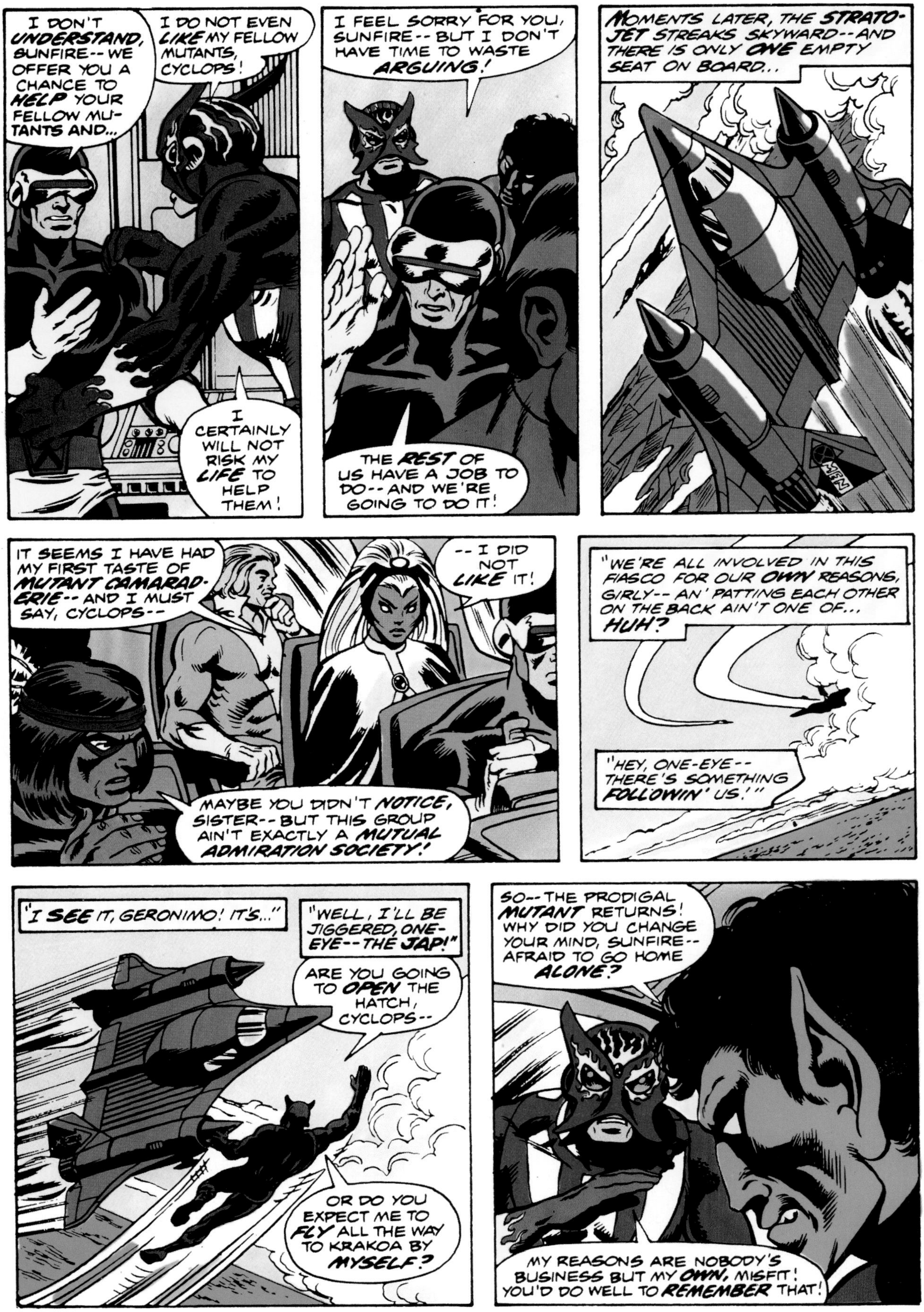

I DON'T UNDERSTAND, SUNFIRE-- WE OFFER YOU A CHANCE TO HELP YOUR FELLOW MUTANTS AND...
I DO NOT EVEN LIKE MY FELLOW MUTANTS, CYCLOPS!
I CERTAINLY WILL NOT RISK MY LIFE TO HELP THEM!
I FEEL SORRY FOR YOU, SUNFIRE-- BUT I DON'T HAVE TIME TO WASTE ARGUING!
THE REST OF US HAVE A JOB TO DO-- AND WE'RE GOING TO DO IT!
MOMENTS LATER, THE STRATO-JET STREAKS SKYWARD-- AND THERE IS ONLY ONE EMPTY SEAT ON BOARD...
IT SEEMS I HAVE HAD MY FIRST TASTE OF MUTANT CAMARADERIE-- AND I MUST SAY, CYCLOPS--
-- I DID NOT LIKE IT!
MAYBE YOU DIDN'T NOTICE, SISTER-- BUT THIS GROUP AIN'T EXACTLY A MUTUAL ADMIRATION SOCIETY!
"WE'RE ALL INVOLVED IN THIS FIASCO FOR OUR OWN REASONS, GIRLY-- AN' PATTING EACH OTHER ON THE BACK AIN'T ONE OF... HUH?
"HEY, ONE-EYE-- THERE'S SOMETHING FOLLOWIN' US!"
"I SEE IT, GERONIMO! IT'S..."
"WELL, I'LL BE JIGGERED, ONE-EYE-- THE JAP!"
ARE YOU GOING TO OPEN THE HATCH, CYCLOPS--
OR DO YOU EXPECT ME TO FLY ALL THE WAY TO KRAKOA BY MYSELF?
SO-- THE PRODIGAL MUTANT RETURNS! WHY DID YOU CHANGE YOUR MIND, SUNFIRE-- AFRAID TO GO HOME ALONE?
MY REASONS ARE NOBODY'S BUSINESS BUT MY OWN, MISFIT! YOU'D DO WELL TO REMEMBER THAT!

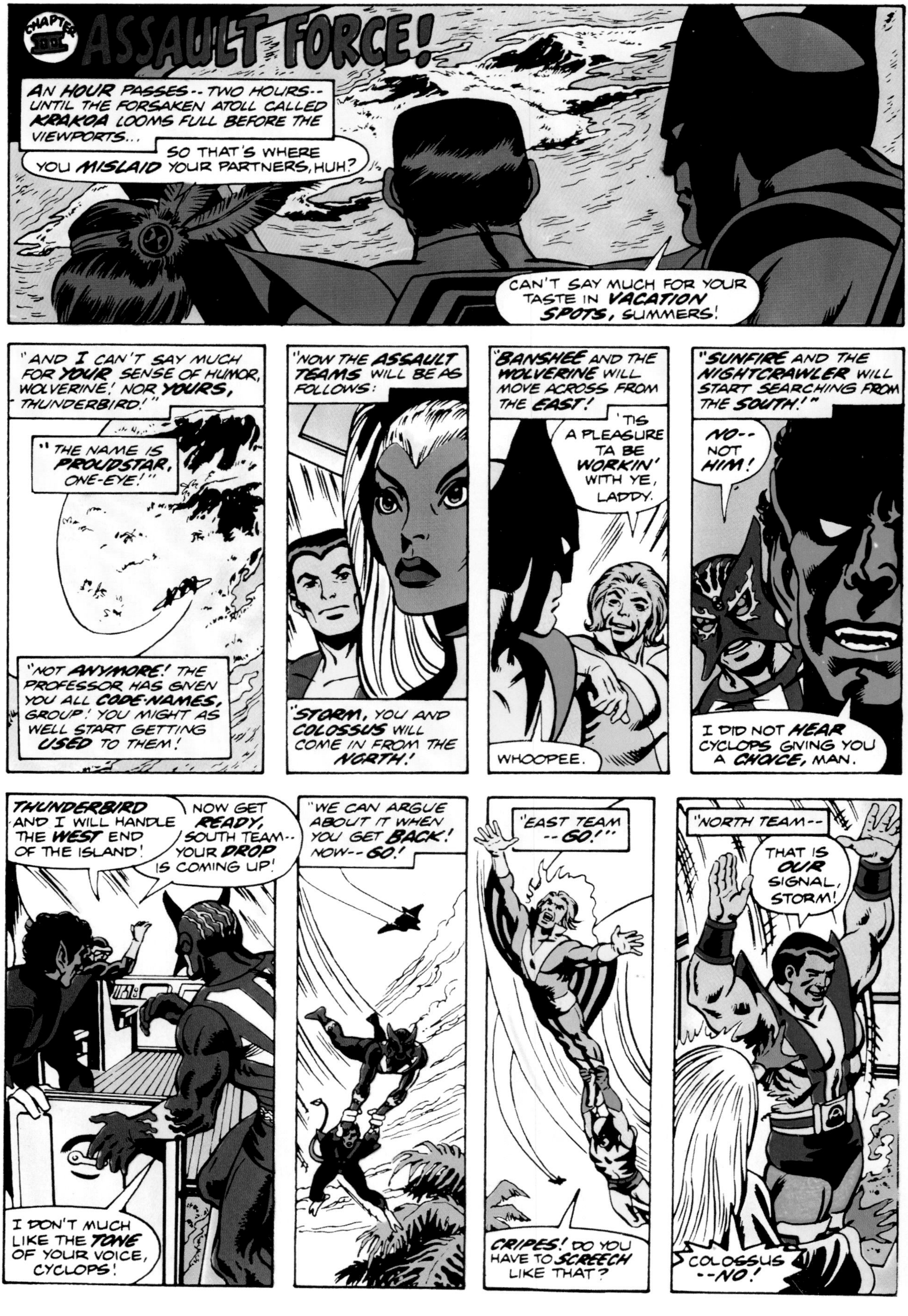

CHAPTER III
ASSAULT FORCE!
AN HOUR PASSES--TWO HOURS--UNTIL THE FORSAKEN ATOLL CALLED KRAKOA LOOMS FULL BEFORE THE VIEWPORTS...
SO THAT'S WHERE YOU MISLAID YOUR PARTNERS, HUH?
CAN'T SAY MUCH FOR YOUR TASTE IN VACATION SPOTS, SUMMERS!
"AND I CAN'T SAY MUCH FOR YOUR SENSE OF HUMOR, WOLVERINE! NOR YOURS, THUNDERBIRD!"
"THE NAME IS PROUDSTAR, ONE-EYE!"
"NOT ANYMORE! THE PROFESSOR HAS GIVEN YOU ALL CODE-NAMES, GROUP! YOU MIGHT AS WELL START GETTING USED TO THEM!
"NOW THE ASSAULT TEAMS WILL BE AS FOLLOWS:
"STORM, YOU AND COLOSSUS WILL COME IN FROM THE NORTH!
"BANSHEE AND THE WOLVERINE WILL MOVE ACROSS FROM THE EAST!
'TIS A PLEASURE TA BE WORKIN' WITH YE, LADDY.
WHOOPEE.
"SUNFIRE AND THE NIGHTCRAWLER WILL START SEARCHING FROM THE SOUTH!"
NO--NOT HIM!
I DID NOT HEAR CYCLOPS GIVING YOU A CHOICE, MAN.
THUNDERBIRD AND I WILL HANDLE THE WEST END OF THE ISLAND!
NOW GET READY, SOUTH TEAM--YOUR DROP IS COMING UP!
I DON'T MUCH LIKE THE TONE OF YOUR VOICE, CYCLOPS!
"WE CAN ARGUE ABOUT IT WHEN YOU GET BACK! NOW--GO!
"EAST TEAM --GO!"
CRIPES! DO YOU HAVE TO SCREECH LIKE THAT?
"NORTH TEAM--
THAT IS OUR SIGNAL, STORM!
COLOSSUS --NO!

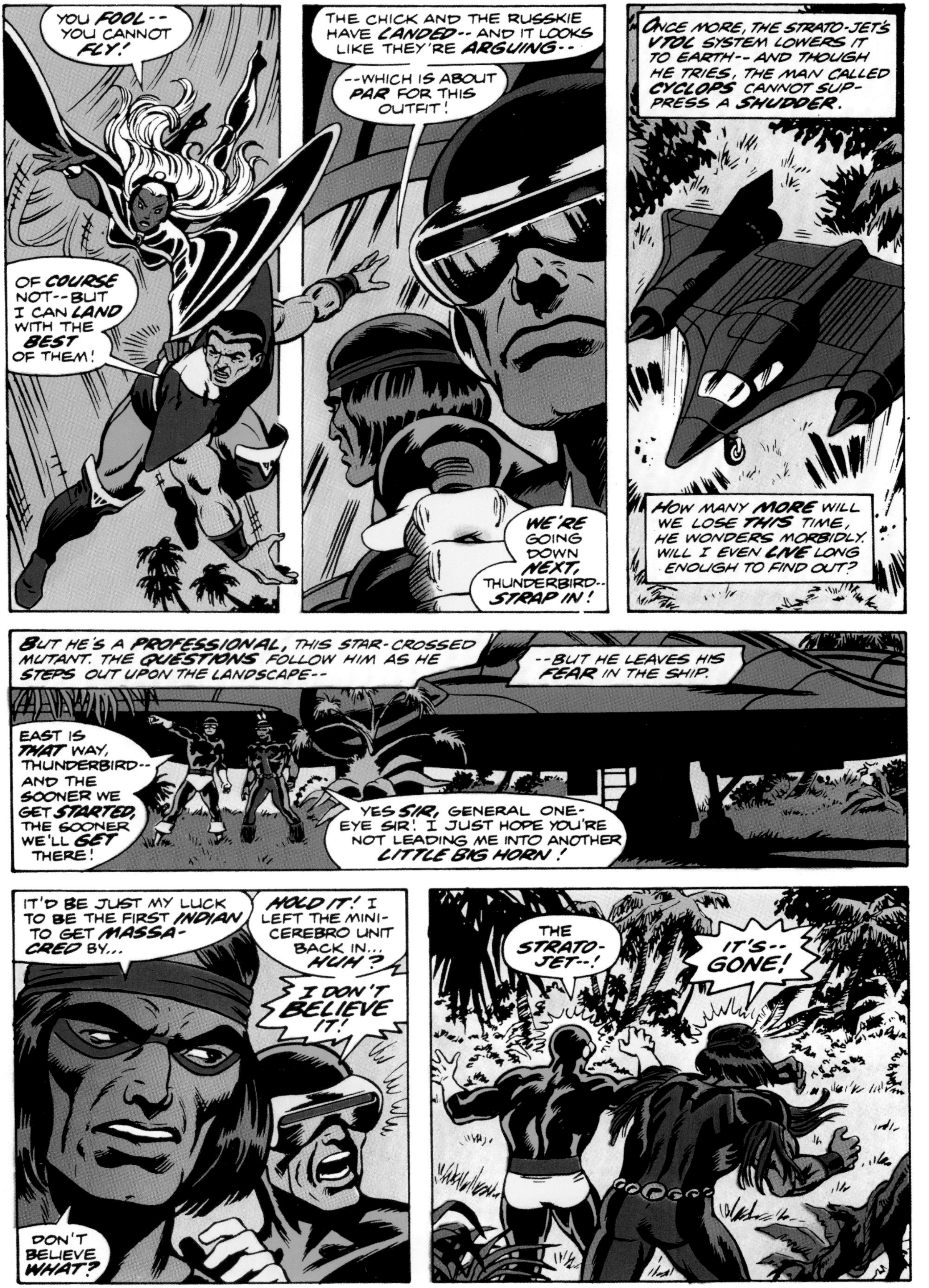

YOU FOOL-- YOU CANNOT FLY!
OF COURSE NOT--BUT I CAN LAND WITH THE BEST OF THEM!
THE CHICK AND THE RUSSKIE HAVE LANDED-- AND IT LOOKS LIKE THEY'RE ARGUING--
--WHICH IS ABOUT PAR FOR THIS OUTFIT!
WE'RE GOING DOWN NEXT, THUNDERBIRD-- STRAP IN!
ONCE MORE, THE STRATO-JET'S VTOL SYSTEM LOWERS IT TO EARTH-- AND THOUGH HE TRIES, THE MAN CALLED CYCLOPS CANNOT SUPPRESS A SHUDDER.
HOW MANY MORE WILL WE LOSE THIS TIME, HE WONDERS MORBIDLY. WILL I EVEN LIVE LONG ENOUGH TO FIND OUT?
BUT HE'S A PROFESSIONAL, THIS STAR-CROSSED MUTANT. THE QUESTIONS FOLLOW HIM AS HE STEPS OUT UPON THE LANDSCAPE--
--BUT HE LEAVES HIS FEAR IN THE SHIP.
EAST IS THAT WAY, THUNDERBIRD-- AND THE SOONER WE GET STARTED, THE SOONER WE'LL GET THERE!
YES SIR, GENERAL ONE-EYE SIR! I JUST HOPE YOU'RE NOT LEADING ME INTO ANOTHER LITTLE BIG HORN!
IT'D BE JUST MY LUCK TO BE THE FIRST INDIAN TO GET MASSACRED BY...
HOLD IT! I LEFT THE MINI-CEREBRO UNIT BACK IN... HUH?
I DON'T BELIEVE IT!
DON'T BELIEVE WHAT?
THE STRATO-JET--!
IT'S-- GONE!

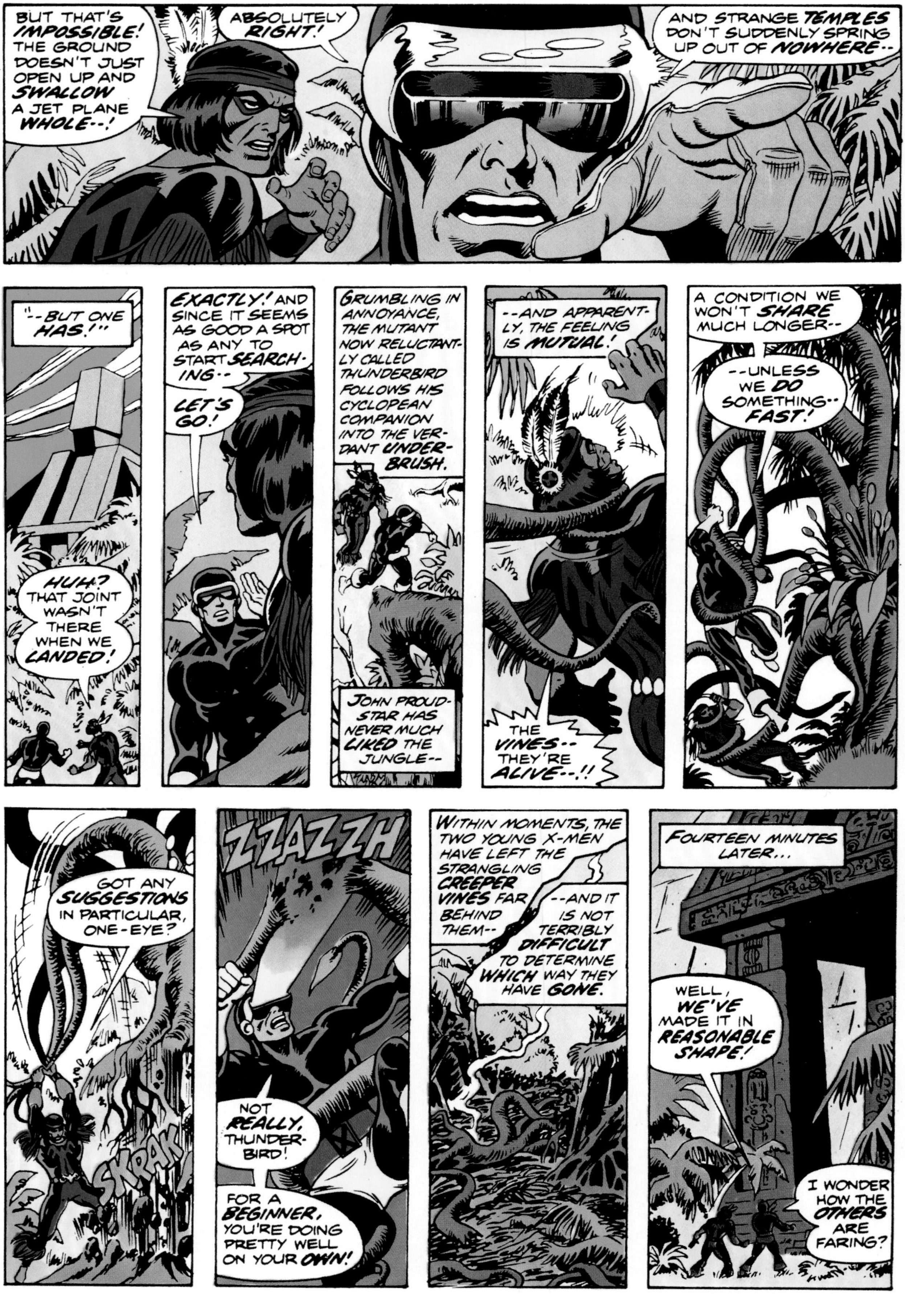

BUT THAT'S IMPOSSIBLE! THE GROUND DOESN'T JUST OPEN UP AND SWALLOW A JET PLANE WHOLE--!
ABSOLUTELY RIGHT!
AND STRANGE TEMPLES DON'T SUDDENLY SPRING UP OUT OF NOWHERE--
"--BUT ONE HAS!"
HUH? THAT JOINT WASN'T THERE WHEN WE LANDED!
EXACTLY! AND SINCE IT SEEMS AS GOOD A SPOT AS ANY TO START SEARCHING--
LET'S GO!
GRUMBLING IN ANNOYANCE, THE MUTANT NOW RELUCTANTLY CALLED THUNDERBIRD FOLLOWS HIS CYCLOPEAN COMPANION INTO THE VERDANT UNDERBRUSH.
JOHN PROUDSTAR HAS NEVER MUCH LIKED THE JUNGLE--
--AND APPARENTLY, THE FEELING IS MUTUAL!
THE VINES--THEY'RE ALIVE--!!
A CONDITION WE WON'T SHARE MUCH LONGER--
--UNLESS WE DO SOMETHING--FAST!
GOT ANY SUGGESTIONS IN PARTICULAR, ONE-EYE?
SKRAK
ZZAZZH
NOT REALLY, THUNDERBIRD!
FOR A BEGINNER, YOU'RE DOING PRETTY WELL ON YOUR OWN!
WITHIN MOMENTS, THE TWO YOUNG X-MEN HAVE LEFT THE STRANGLING CREEPER VINES FAR BEHIND THEM--
--AND IT IS NOT TERRIBLY DIFFICULT TO DETERMINE WHICH WAY THEY HAVE GONE.
FOURTEEN MINUTES LATER...
WELL, WE'VE MADE IT IN REASONABLE SHAPE!
I WONDER HOW THE OTHERS ARE FARING?

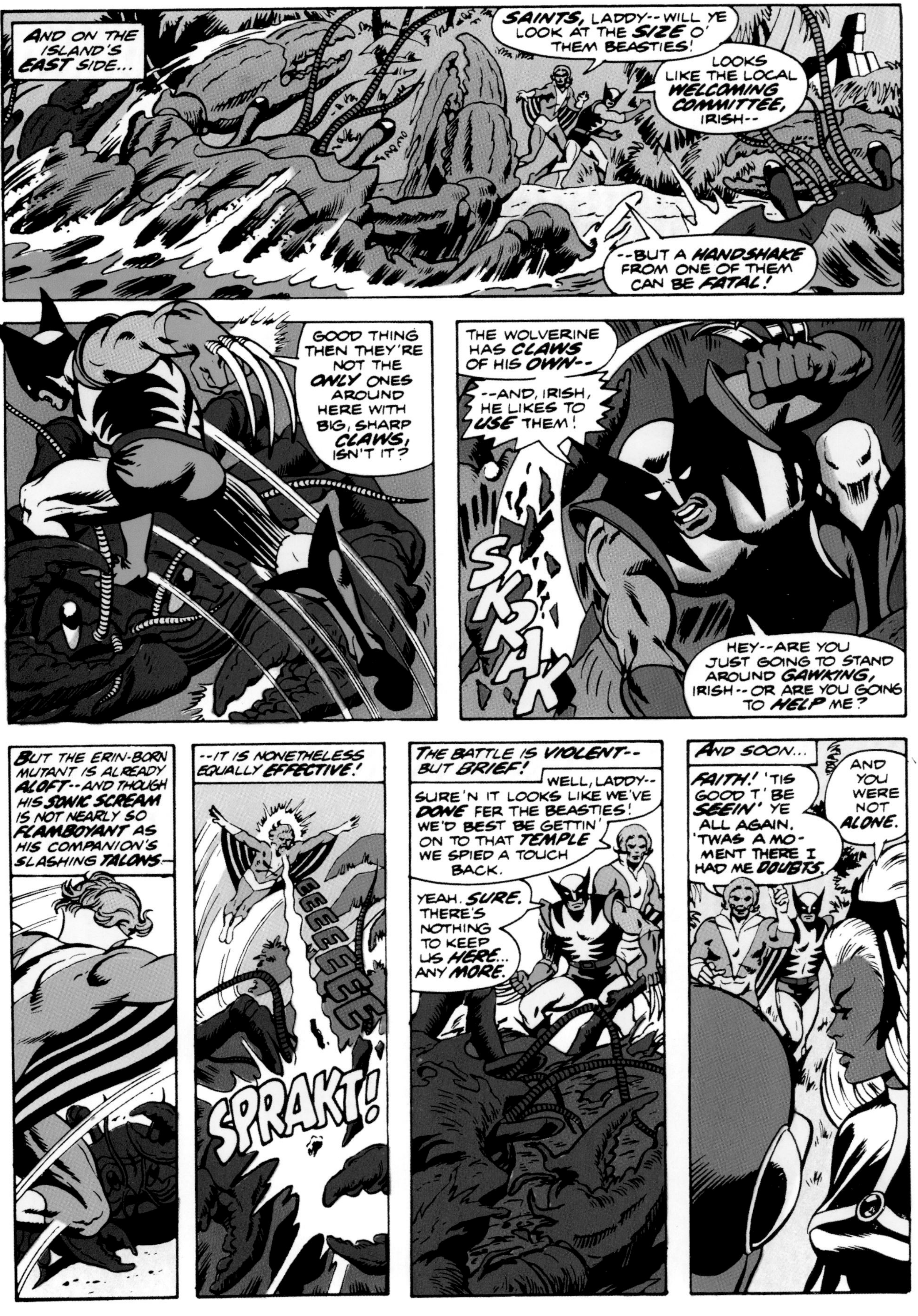
AND ON THE ISLAND'S EAST SIDE...
SAINTS, LADDY--WILL YE LOOK AT THE SIZE O' THEM BEASTIES!
LOOKS LIKE THE LOCAL WELCOMING COMMITTEE, IRISH--
--BUT A HANDSHAKE FROM ONE OF THEM CAN BE FATAL!
GOOD THING THEN THEY'RE NOT THE ONLY ONES AROUND HERE WITH BIG, SHARP CLAWS, ISN'T IT?
THE WOLVERINE HAS CLAWS OF HIS OWN--
--AND, IRISH, HE LIKES TO USE THEM!
SKRAK
HEY--ARE YOU JUST GOING TO STAND AROUND GAWKING, IRISH--OR ARE YOU GOING TO HELP ME?
BUT THE ERIN-BORN MUTANT IS ALREADY ALOFT--AND THOUGH HIS SONIC SCREAM IS NOT NEARLY SO FLAMBOYANT AS HIS COMPANION'S SLASHING TALONS--
--IT IS NONETHELESS EQUALLY EFFECTIVE!
EEEEEEE
SPRAKT!
THE BATTLE IS VIOLENT--BUT BRIEF!
WELL, LADDY--SURE'N IT LOOKS LIKE WE'VE DONE FER THE BEASTIES! WE'D BEST BE GETTIN' ON TO THAT TEMPLE WE SPIED A TOUCH BACK.
YEAH. SURE. THERE'S NOTHING TO KEEP US HERE... ANY MORE.
AND SOON...
FAITH! 'TIS GOOD T' BE SEEIN' YE ALL AGAIN. 'TWAS A MO-MENT THERE I HAD ME DOUBTS.
AND YOU WERE NOT ALONE.

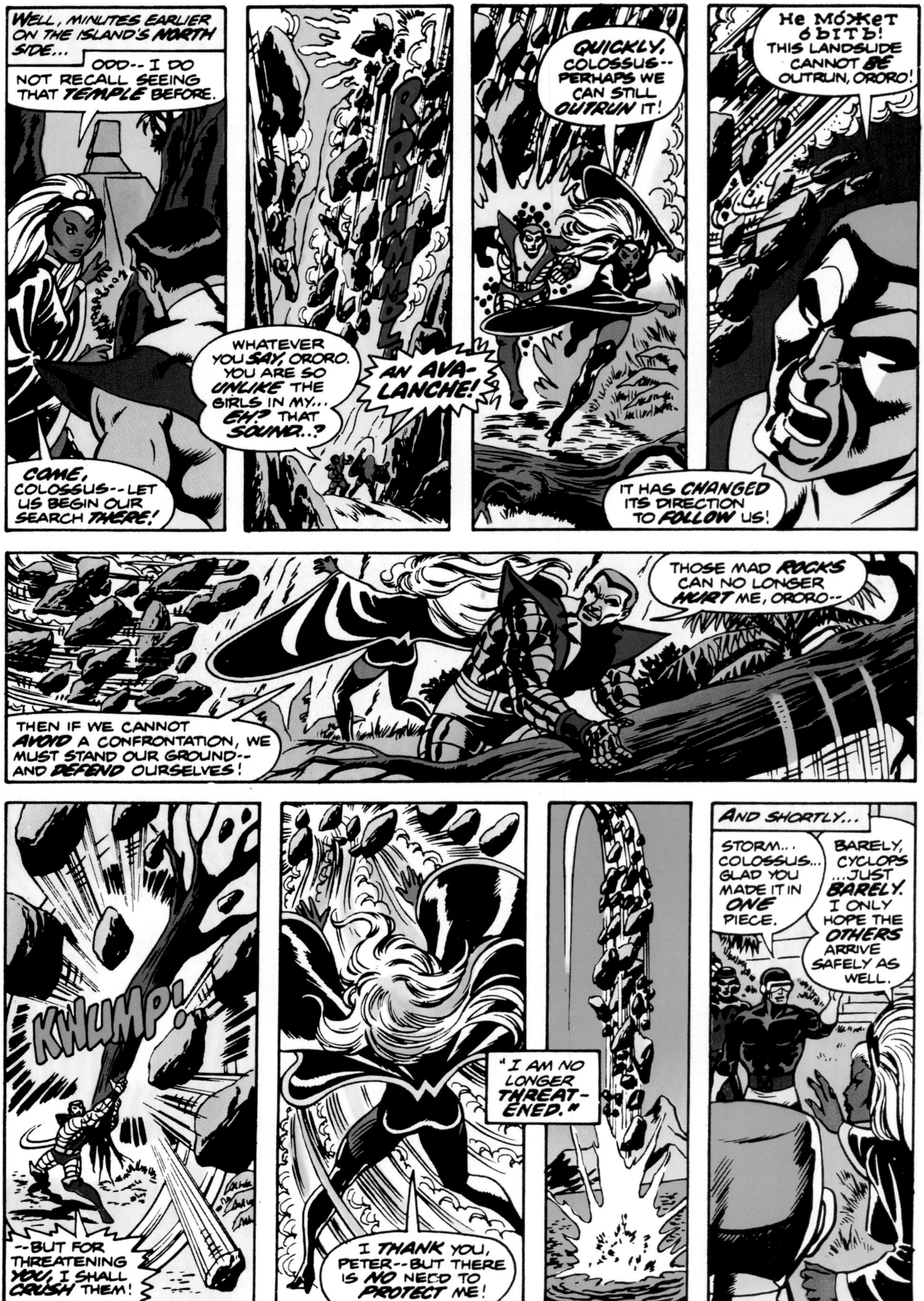
WELL, MINUTES EARLIER ON THE ISLAND'S NORTH SIDE...
ODD-- I DO NOT RECALL SEEING THAT TEMPLE BEFORE.
COME, COLOSSUS--LET US BEGIN OUR SEARCH THERE!
WHATEVER YOU SAY, ORORO. YOU ARE SO UNLIKE THE GIRLS IN MY... EH? THAT SOUND...?
RRUMMBL
AN AVA-LANCHE!
QUICKLY, COLOSSUS-- PERHAPS WE CAN STILL OUTRUN IT!
Не Мо́жет быть! THIS LANDSLIDE CANNOT BE OUTRUN, ORORO!
IT HAS CHANGED ITS DIRECTION TO FOLLOW US!
THOSE MAD ROCKS CAN NO LONGER HURT ME, ORORO--
THEN IF WE CANNOT AVOID A CONFRONTATION, WE MUST STAND OUR GROUND-- AND DEFEND OURSELVES!
KWUMP!
--BUT FOR THREATENING YOU, I SHALL CRUSH THEM!
I THANK YOU, PETER--BUT THERE IS NO NEED TO PROTECT ME!
"I AM NO LONGER THREAT-ENED."
AND SHORTLY...
STORM... COLOSSUS... GLAD YOU MADE IT IN ONE PIECE.
BARELY, CYCLOPS ...JUST BARELY. I ONLY HOPE THE OTHERS ARRIVE SAFELY AS WELL.

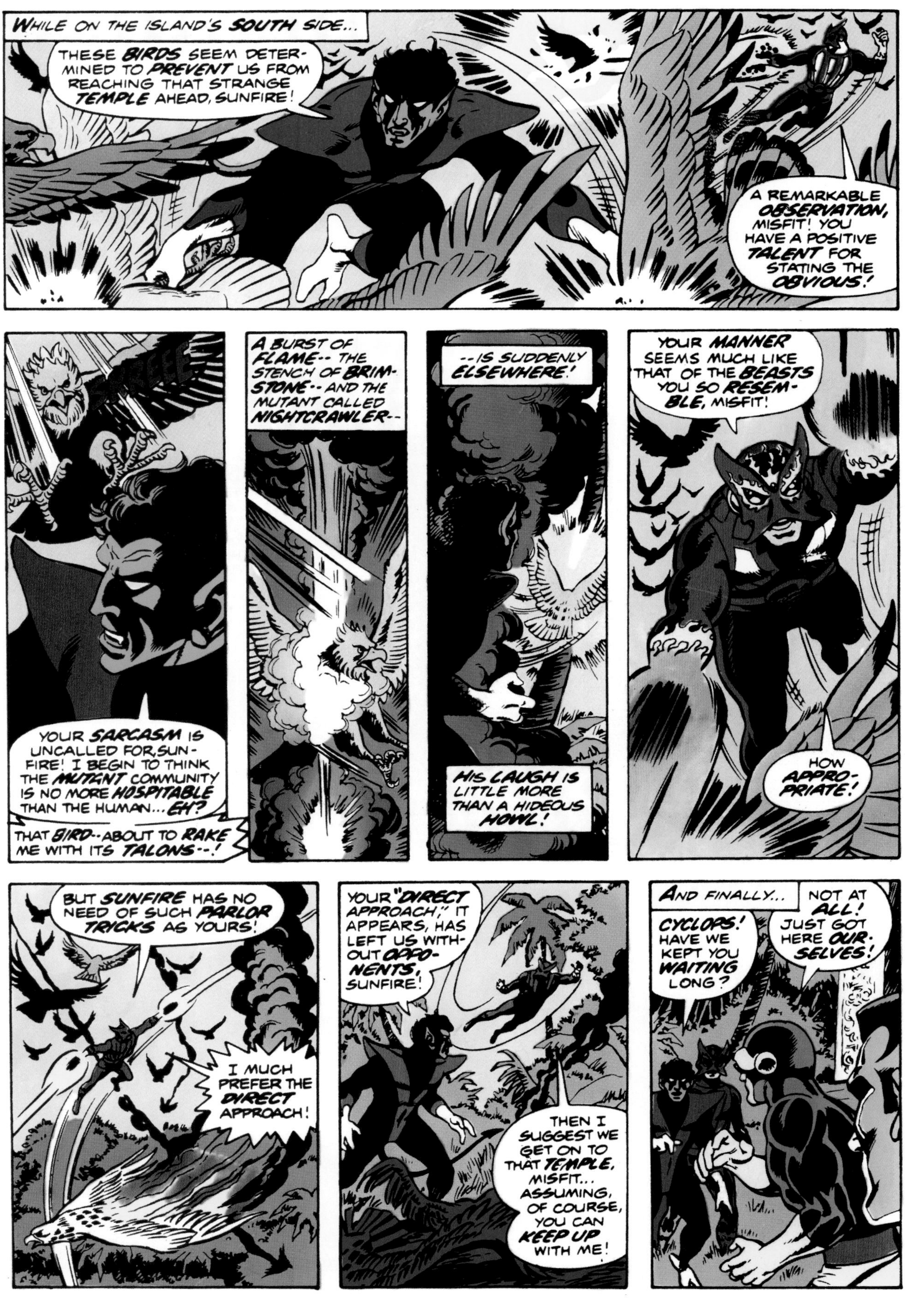
WHILE ON THE ISLAND'S SOUTH SIDE...
THESE BIRDS SEEM DETERMINED TO PREVENT US FROM REACHING THAT STRANGE TEMPLE AHEAD, SUNFIRE!
A REMARKABLE OBSERVATION, MISFIT! YOU HAVE A POSITIVE TALENT FOR STATING THE OBVIOUS!
SKREEEE
YOUR SARCASM IS UNCALLED FOR, SUN-FIRE! I BEGIN TO THINK THE MUTANT COMMUNITY IS NO MORE HOSPITABLE THAN THE HUMAN... EH?
THAT BIRD--ABOUT TO RAKE ME WITH ITS TALONS--!
A BURST OF FLAME-- THE STENCH OF BRIMSTONE--AND THE MUTANT CALLED NIGHTCRAWLER--
--IS SUDDENLY ELSEWHERE!
HIS LAUGH IS LITTLE MORE THAN A HIDEOUS HOWL!
YOUR MANNER SEEMS MUCH LIKE THAT OF THE BEASTS YOU SO RESEMBLE, MISFIT!
HOW APPROPRIATE!
BUT SUNFIRE HAS NO NEED OF SUCH PARLOR TRICKS AS YOURS!
I MUCH PREFER THE DIRECT APPROACH!
YOUR "DIRECT APPROACH," IT APPEARS, HAS LEFT US WITHOUT OPPONENTS, SUNFIRE!
THEN I SUGGEST WE GET ON TO THAT TEMPLE, MISFIT... ASSUMING, OF COURSE, YOU CAN KEEP UP WITH ME!
AND FINALLY...
CYCLOPS! HAVE WE KEPT YOU WAITING LONG?
NOT AT ALL! JUST GOT HERE OURSELVES!

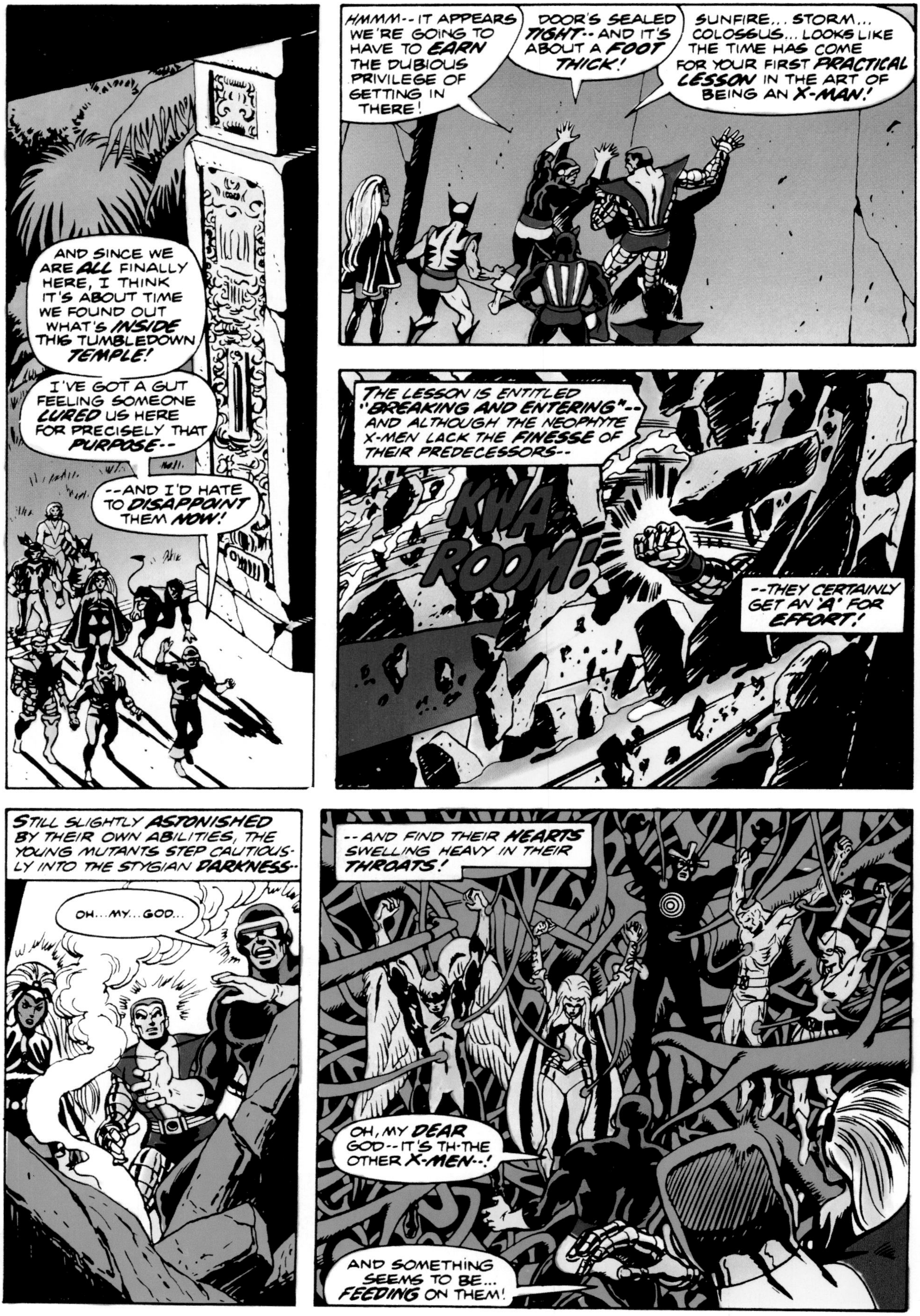
AND SINCE WE ARE ALL FINALLY HERE, I THINK IT'S ABOUT TIME WE FOUND OUT WHAT'S INSIDE THIS TUMBLEDOWN TEMPLE!
I'VE GOT A GUT FEELING SOMEONE LURED US HERE FOR PRECISELY THAT PURPOSE--
--AND I'D HATE TO DISAPPOINT THEM NOW!
HMMM--IT APPEARS WE'RE GOING TO HAVE TO EARN THE DUBIOUS PRIVILEGE OF GETTING IN THERE!
DOOR'S SEALED TIGHT--AND IT'S ABOUT A FOOT THICK!
SUNFIRE... STORM... COLOSSUS... LOOKS LIKE THE TIME HAS COME FOR YOUR FIRST PRACTICAL LESSON IN THE ART OF BEING AN X-MAN!
THE LESSON IS ENTITLED "BREAKING AND ENTERING"--AND ALTHOUGH THE NEOPHYTE X-MEN LACK THE FINESSE OF THEIR PREDECESSORS--
KWA-ROOM!
--THEY CERTAINLY GET AN 'A' FOR EFFORT!
STILL SLIGHTLY ASTONISHED BY THEIR OWN ABILITIES, THE YOUNG MUTANTS STEP CAUTIOUSLY INTO THE STYGIAN DARKNESS--
OH...MY...GOD...
--AND FIND THEIR HEARTS SWELLING HEAVY IN THEIR THROATS!
OH, MY DEAR GOD--IT'S TH-THE OTHER X-MEN--!
AND SOMETHING SEEMS TO BE... FEEDING ON THEM!

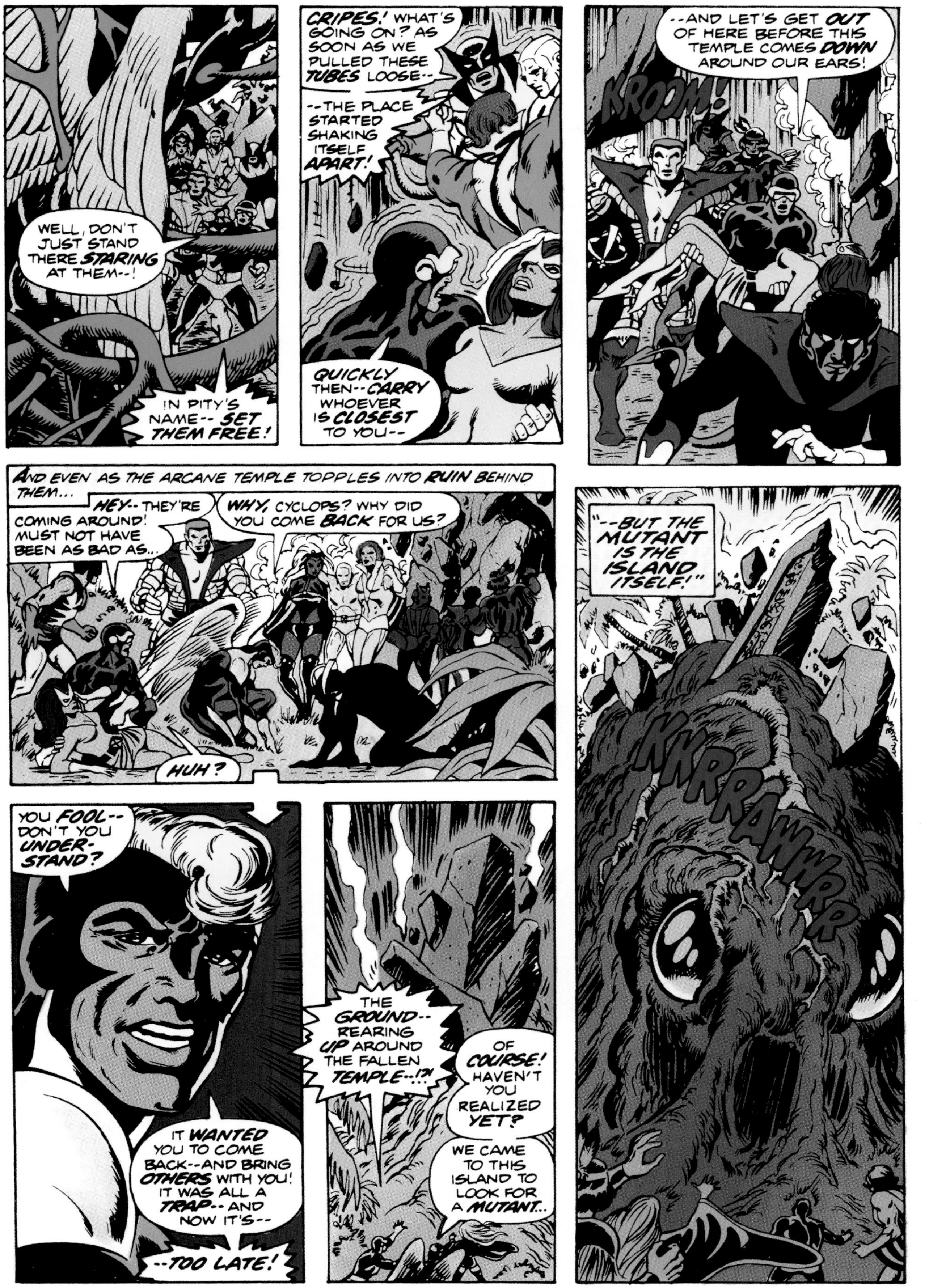

WELL, DON'T JUST STAND THERE STARING AT THEM--!
IN PITY'S NAME-- SET THEM FREE!
CRIPES! WHAT'S GOING ON? AS SOON AS WE PULLED THESE TUBES LOOSE--
--THE PLACE STARTED SHAKING ITSELF APART!
QUICKLY THEN--CARRY WHOEVER IS CLOSEST TO YOU--
--AND LET'S GET OUT OF HERE BEFORE THIS TEMPLE COMES DOWN AROUND OUR EARS!
KROOM!
AND EVEN AS THE ARCANE TEMPLE TOPPLES INTO RUIN BEHIND THEM...
HEY-- THEY'RE COMING AROUND! MUST NOT HAVE BEEN AS BAD AS...
WHY, CYCLOPS? WHY DID YOU COME BACK FOR US?
HUH?
YOU FOOL-- DON'T YOU UNDER-STAND?
IT WANTED YOU TO COME BACK--AND BRING OTHERS WITH YOU! IT WAS ALL A TRAP-- AND NOW IT'S--
--TOO LATE!
THE GROUND-- REARING UP AROUND THE FALLEN TEMPLE--!?!
OF COURSE! HAVEN'T YOU REALIZED YET?
WE CAME TO THIS ISLAND TO LOOK FOR A MUTANT...
"--BUT THE MUTANT IS THE ISLAND ITSELF!"
KNRRAWHRR

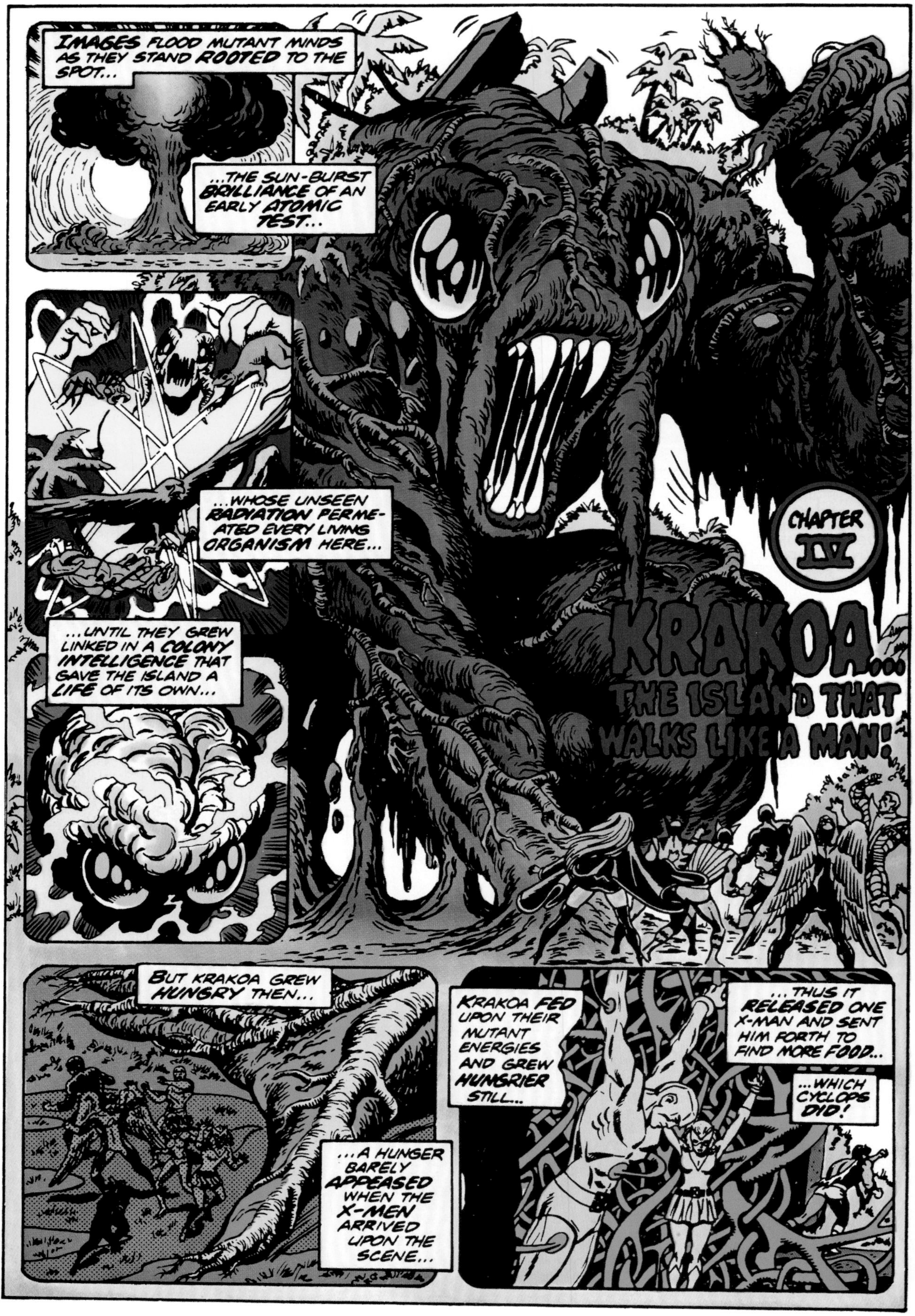
IMAGES FLOOD MUTANT MINDS AS THEY STAND ROOTED TO THE SPOT...
...THE SUN-BURST BRILLIANCE OF AN EARLY ATOMIC TEST...
...WHOSE UNSEEN RADIATION PERMEATED EVERY LIVING ORGANISM HERE...
...UNTIL THEY GREW LINKED IN A COLONY INTELLIGENCE THAT GAVE THE ISLAND A LIFE OF ITS OWN...
CHAPTER IV
KRAKOA... THE ISLAND THAT WALKS LIKE A MAN!
BUT KRAKOA GREW HUNGRY THEN...
...A HUNGER BARELY APPEASED WHEN THE X-MEN ARRIVED UPON THE SCENE...
KRAKOA FED UPON THEIR MUTANT ENERGIES AND GREW HUNGRIER STILL...
...THUS IT RELEASED ONE X-MAN AND SENT HIM FORTH TO FIND MORE FOOD...
...WHICH CYCLOPS DID!

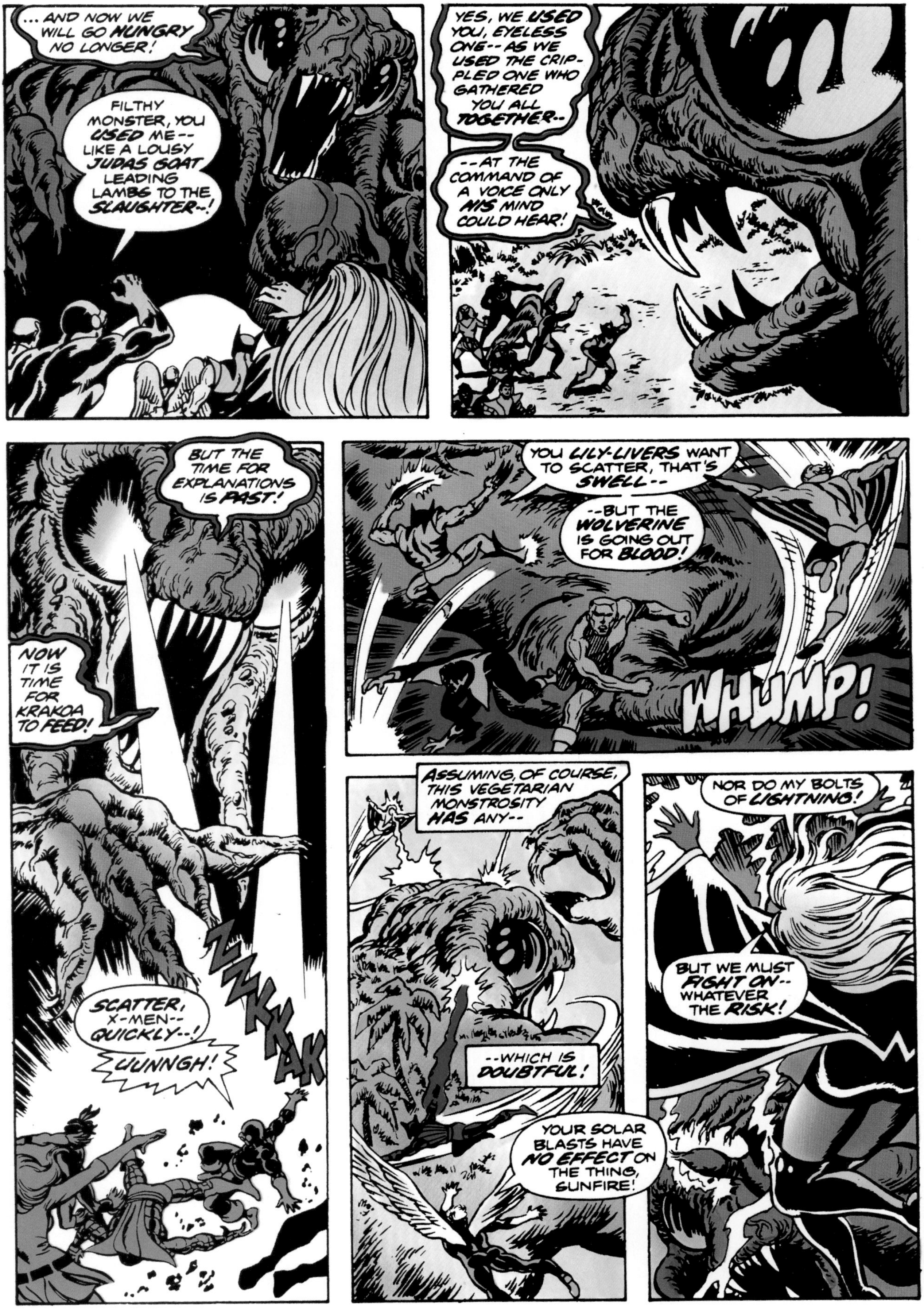

... AND NOW WE WILL GO HUNGRY NO LONGER!
FILTHY MONSTER, YOU USED ME -- LIKE A LOUSY JUDAS GOAT LEADING LAMBS TO THE SLAUGHTER--!
YES, WE USED YOU, EYELESS ONE -- AS WE USED THE CRIPPLED ONE WHO GATHERED YOU ALL TOGETHER--
--AT THE COMMAND OF A VOICE ONLY HIS MIND COULD HEAR!
BUT THE TIME FOR EXPLANATIONS IS PAST!
NOW IT IS TIME FOR KRAKOA TO FEED!
ZNKKAK
SCATTER, X-MEN -- QUICKLY--!
UUNNGH!
YOU LILY-LIVERS WANT TO SCATTER, THAT'S SWELL--
--BUT THE WOLVERINE IS GOING OUT FOR BLOOD!
WHUMP!
ASSUMING, OF COURSE, THIS VEGETARIAN MONSTROSITY HAS ANY--
--WHICH IS DOUBTFUL!
YOUR SOLAR BLASTS HAVE NO EFFECT ON THE THING, SUNFIRE!
NOR DO MY BOLTS OF LIGHTNING!
BUT WE MUST FIGHT ON -- WHATEVER THE RISK!

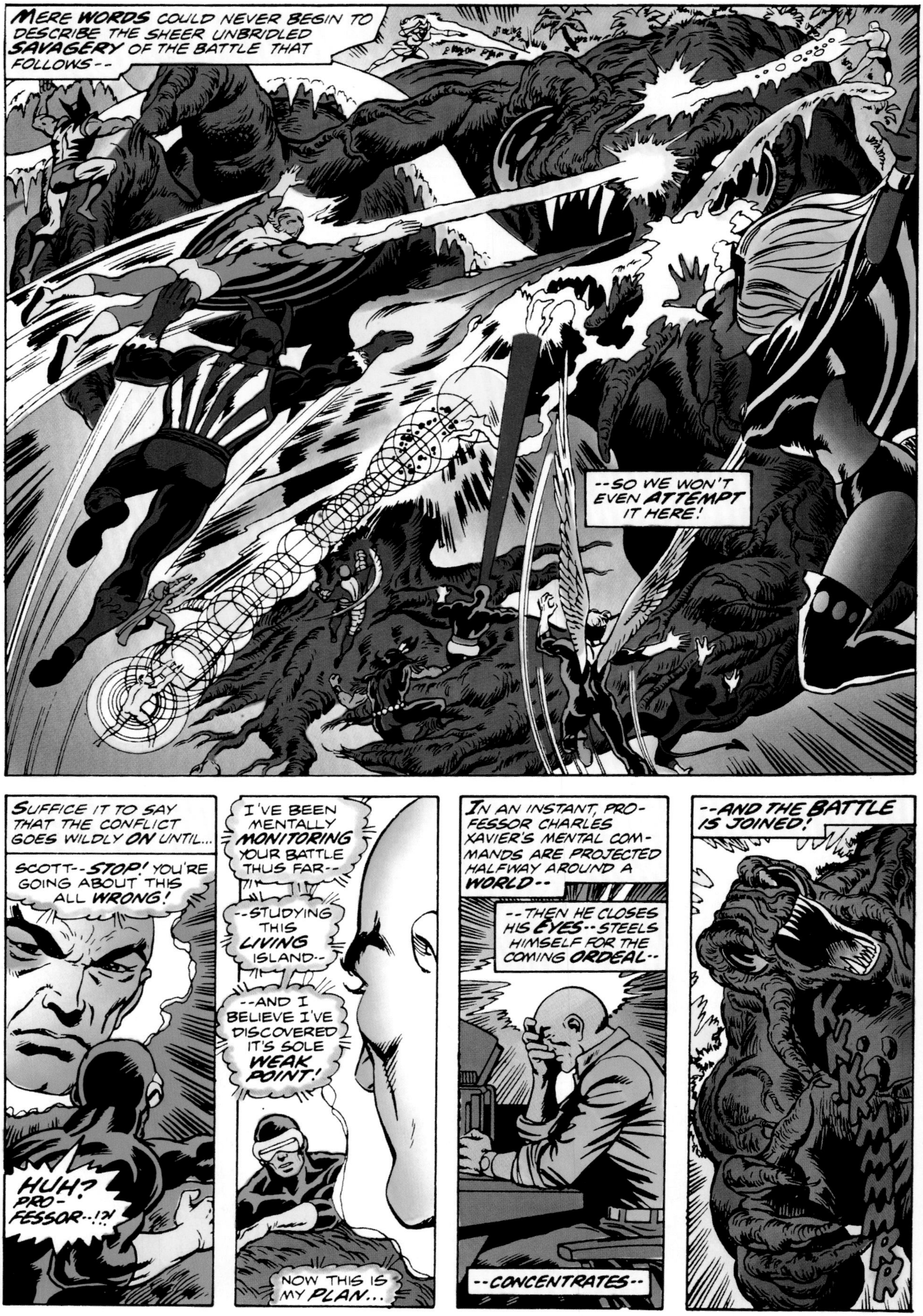
MERE WORDS COULD NEVER BEGIN TO DESCRIBE THE SHEER UNBRIDLED SAVAGERY OF THE BATTLE THAT FOLLOWS--
--SO WE WON'T EVEN ATTEMPT IT HERE!
SUFFICE IT TO SAY THAT THE CONFLICT GOES WILDLY ON UNTIL...
SCOTT--STOP! YOU'RE GOING ABOUT THIS ALL WRONG!
HUH? PRO-FESSOR--!?!
I'VE BEEN MENTALLY MONITORING YOUR BATTLE THUS FAR--
--STUDYING THIS LIVING ISLAND--
--AND I BELIEVE I'VE DISCOVERED IT'S SOLE WEAK POINT!
NOW THIS IS MY PLAN...
IN AN INSTANT, PRO-FESSOR CHARLES XAVIER'S MENTAL COM-MANDS ARE PROJECTED HALFWAY AROUND A WORLD--
--THEN HE CLOSES HIS EYES--STEELS HIMSELF FOR THE COMING ORDEAL--
--CONCENTRATES--
--AND THE BATTLE IS JOINED!

IT IS A WAR FOUGHT ON *TWO* FRONTS-- AS PROFESSOR X WAGES DEADLY MENTAL COMBAT WITH A CRAZED *COMMUNITY INTELLECT*-- WHILE HIS STUDENTS RACE TO CARRY OUT HIS *PLAN*...

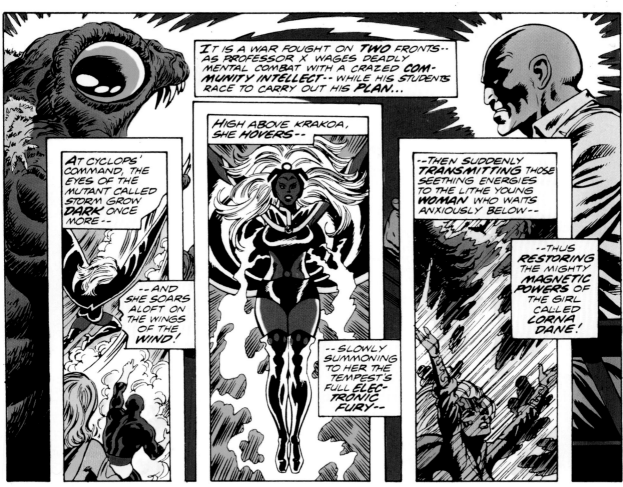

HIGH ABOVE KRAKOA, SHE *HOVERS*--

AT CYCLOPS' COMMAND, THE EYES OF THE MUTANT CALLED STORM GROW *DARK* ONCE MORE--

--AND SHE SOARS ALOFT ON THE WINGS OF THE *WIND!*

--SLOWLY SUMMONING TO HER THE TEMPEST'S FULL *ELECTRONIC FURY*--

--THEN SUDDENLY *TRANSMITTING* THOSE SEETHING ENERGIES TO THE LITHE YOUNG *WOMAN* WHO WAITS ANXIOUSLY BELOW--

--THUS *RESTORING* THE MIGHTY *MAGNETIC POWERS* OF THE GIRL CALLED *LORNA DANE!*

--AND LORNA DANE *SCREAMS* IN ANGUISH AS HER PHYSICAL LIMITS ARE *REACHED*--

--AND *EXCEEDED!*

WITHIN MOMENTS, THE CIRCUIT IS *COMPLETED*--

DON'T *STOP!* LORD, WHATEVER YOU DO-- *DON'T STOP!*

YOU'VE GOT TO *CALL IT OFF,* SCOTT! LORNA CAN'T *TAKE* THAT KIND OF PUNISHMENT!

SHE'LL BE *KILLED!*

ALEX-- I *CAN'T!*

I CAN'T SACRIFICE A *WORLD* TO SAVE ONE *WOMAN,* ALEX--

--EVEN IF SHE *IS* THE WOMAN YOU *LOVE!*

I SWEAR TO YOU-- *BROTHER* OR *NO* BROTHER, IF SHE *DIES*...

THE REMAINDER OF HAVOK'S ANGRY OUTBURST IS *SLAIN* BY THE CRACKLING ROAR OF THE THUNDROUS *DOWN-POUR*--

--EVEN AS THE TORRENTIAL WATERS LEND *LIFE* TO SOMETHING *ELSE!*

BEGORRAH! THE BLINKIN' BEASTIE'S GETTIN' *STRONGER* NOW!

BUT *HOW*--?

CYCLOPS, THE ISLAND'S MIND HAS SUDDENLY GROWN MORE *FORCEFUL!*

I--I CAN'T MAINTAIN MY *ASSAULT* ANY LONGER--!

FORGIVE ME, SCOTT...

...BUT I FEAR... YOU'RE... ON... YOUR... OWN...

FOOLS! YOU BROUGHT *RAIN* FROM THE SKY TO *DESTROY* US--

--BUT IT SERVES ONLY TO *RE-PLENISH* US--

--AND GIVE US *STRENGTH* TO DESTROY *YOU!*

BUT AS BEFORE, THE X-MEN *ARGUE* THAT POINT--

--QUITE *STRONGLY!*

WE CAN'T HOLD THAT THING OFF *FOREVER,* SCOTT! IF THE PROFESSOR'S PLAN DOESN'T *WORK...*

WE'LL *KNOW* IF IT WORKS SOON ENOUGH, JEAN! GET EVERY-BODY *BACK!*

WE'RE READY TO *BEGIN!*

WITH THAT, A SOLEMN SCOTT SUMMERS *TURNS*--TO FIND THAT THE FIGURE OF LORNA DANE HAS BECOME *LOST* WITHIN A *CORUSCATING INCAN-DESCENT* TOWER OF SHEER *MAGNETIC* FORCE.

HIS MUTANT EYES *NARROW*-- AND A SINGLE *WORD* FORMS UPON HIS LIPS:

NOW!

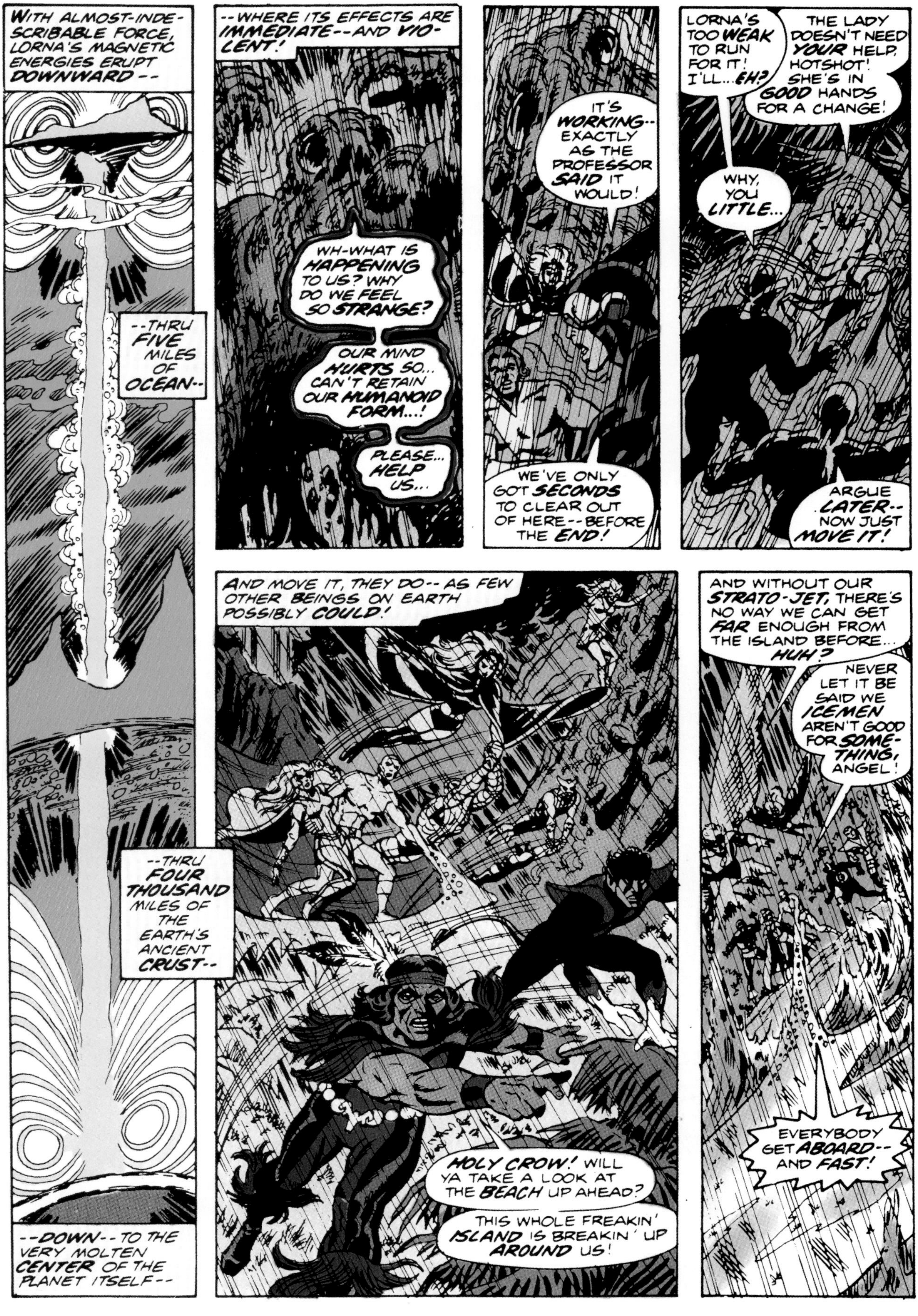
WITH ALMOST-INDESCRIBABLE FORCE, LORNA'S MAGNETIC ENERGIES ERUPT DOWNWARD--
--THRU FIVE MILES OF OCEAN--
--THRU FOUR THOUSAND MILES OF THE EARTH'S ANCIENT CRUST--
--DOWN--TO THE VERY MOLTEN CENTER OF THE PLANET ITSELF--
--WHERE ITS EFFECTS ARE IMMEDIATE--AND VIOLENT!
WH-WHAT IS HAPPENING TO US? WHY DO WE FEEL SO STRANGE?
OUR MIND HURTS SO... CAN'T RETAIN OUR HUMANOID FORM...!
PLEASE... HELP US...
IT'S WORKING-- EXACTLY AS THE PROFESSOR SAID IT WOULD!
WE'VE ONLY GOT SECONDS TO CLEAR OUT OF HERE--BEFORE THE END!
LORNA'S TOO WEAK TO RUN FOR IT! I'LL... EH?
THE LADY DOESN'T NEED YOUR HELP, HOTSHOT! SHE'S IN GOOD HANDS FOR A CHANGE!
WHY, YOU LITTLE...
ARGUE LATER-- NOW JUST MOVE IT!
AND MOVE IT, THEY DO--AS FEW OTHER BEINGS ON EARTH POSSIBLY COULD!
HOLY CROW! WILL YA TAKE A LOOK AT THE BEACH UP AHEAD?
THIS WHOLE FREAKIN' ISLAND IS BREAKIN' UP AROUND US!
AND WITHOUT OUR STRATO-JET, THERE'S NO WAY WE CAN GET FAR ENOUGH FROM THE ISLAND BEFORE... HUH?
NEVER LET IT BE SAID WE ICEMEN AREN'T GOOD FOR SOMETHING, ANGEL!
EVERYBODY GET ABOARD-- AND FAST!

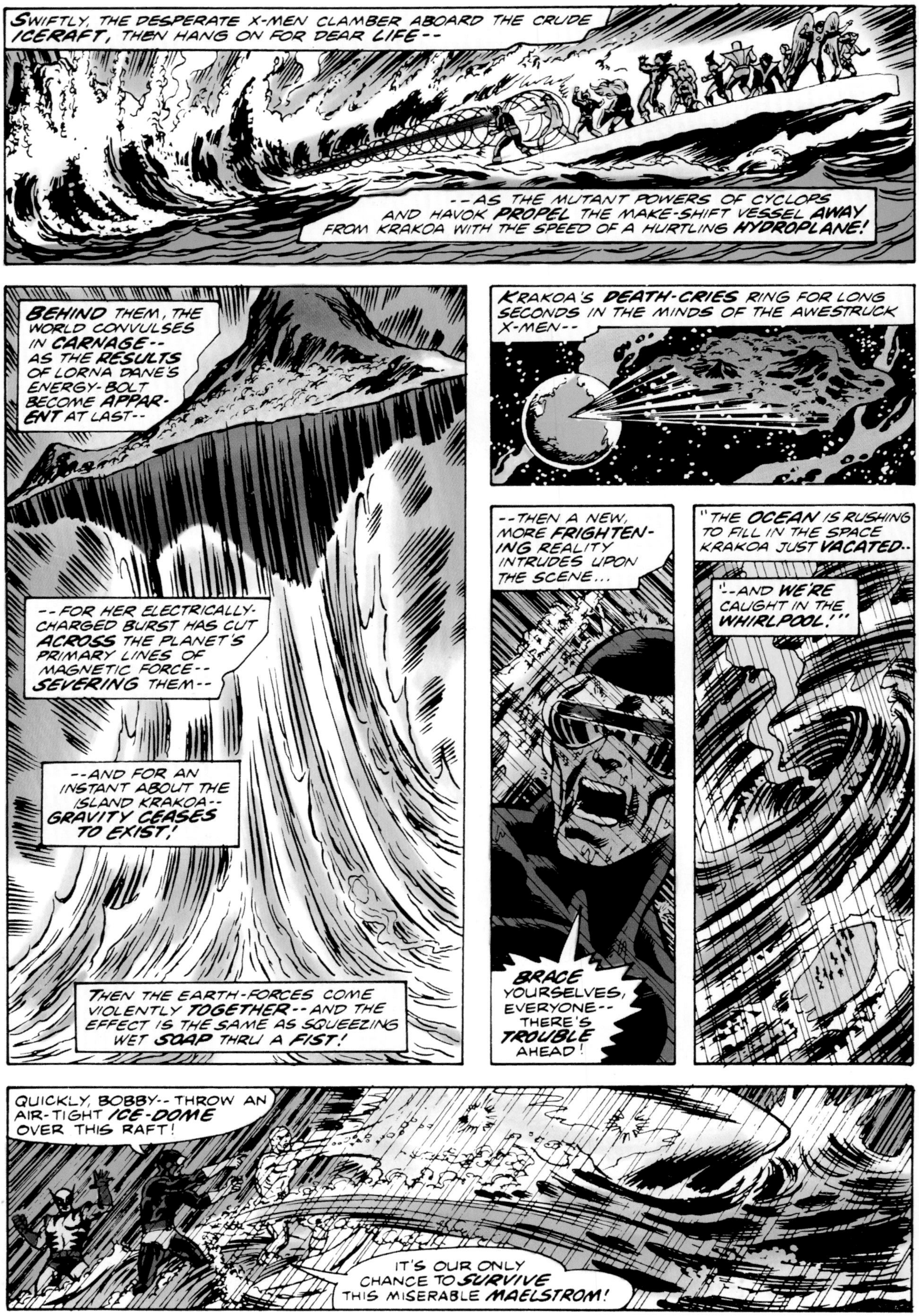
SWIFTLY, THE DESPERATE X-MEN CLAMBER ABOARD THE CRUDE ICERAFT, THEN HANG ON FOR DEAR LIFE--
--AS THE MUTANT POWERS OF CYCLOPS AND HAVOK PROPEL THE MAKE-SHIFT VESSEL AWAY FROM KRAKOA WITH THE SPEED OF A HURTLING HYDROPLANE!
BEHIND THEM, THE WORLD CONVULSES IN CARNAGE-- AS THE RESULTS OF LORNA DANE'S ENERGY-BOLT BECOME APPARENT AT LAST--
--FOR HER ELECTRICALLY-CHARGED BURST HAS CUT ACROSS THE PLANET'S PRIMARY LINES OF MAGNETIC FORCE-- SEVERING THEM--
--AND FOR AN INSTANT ABOUT THE ISLAND KRAKOA-- GRAVITY CEASES TO EXIST!
THEN THE EARTH-FORCES COME VIOLENTLY TOGETHER--AND THE EFFECT IS THE SAME AS SQUEEZING WET SOAP THRU A FIST!
KRAKOA'S DEATH-CRIES RING FOR LONG SECONDS IN THE MINDS OF THE AWESTRUCK X-MEN--
--THEN A NEW, MORE FRIGHTENING REALITY INTRUDES UPON THE SCENE...
BRACE YOURSELVES, EVERYONE-- THERE'S TROUBLE AHEAD!
"THE OCEAN IS RUSHING TO FILL IN THE SPACE KRAKOA JUST VACATED..
"--AND WE'RE CAUGHT IN THE WHIRLPOOL!"
QUICKLY, BOBBY--THROW AN AIR-TIGHT ICE-DOME OVER THIS RAFT!
IT'S OUR ONLY CHANCE TO SURVIVE THIS MISERABLE MAELSTROM!

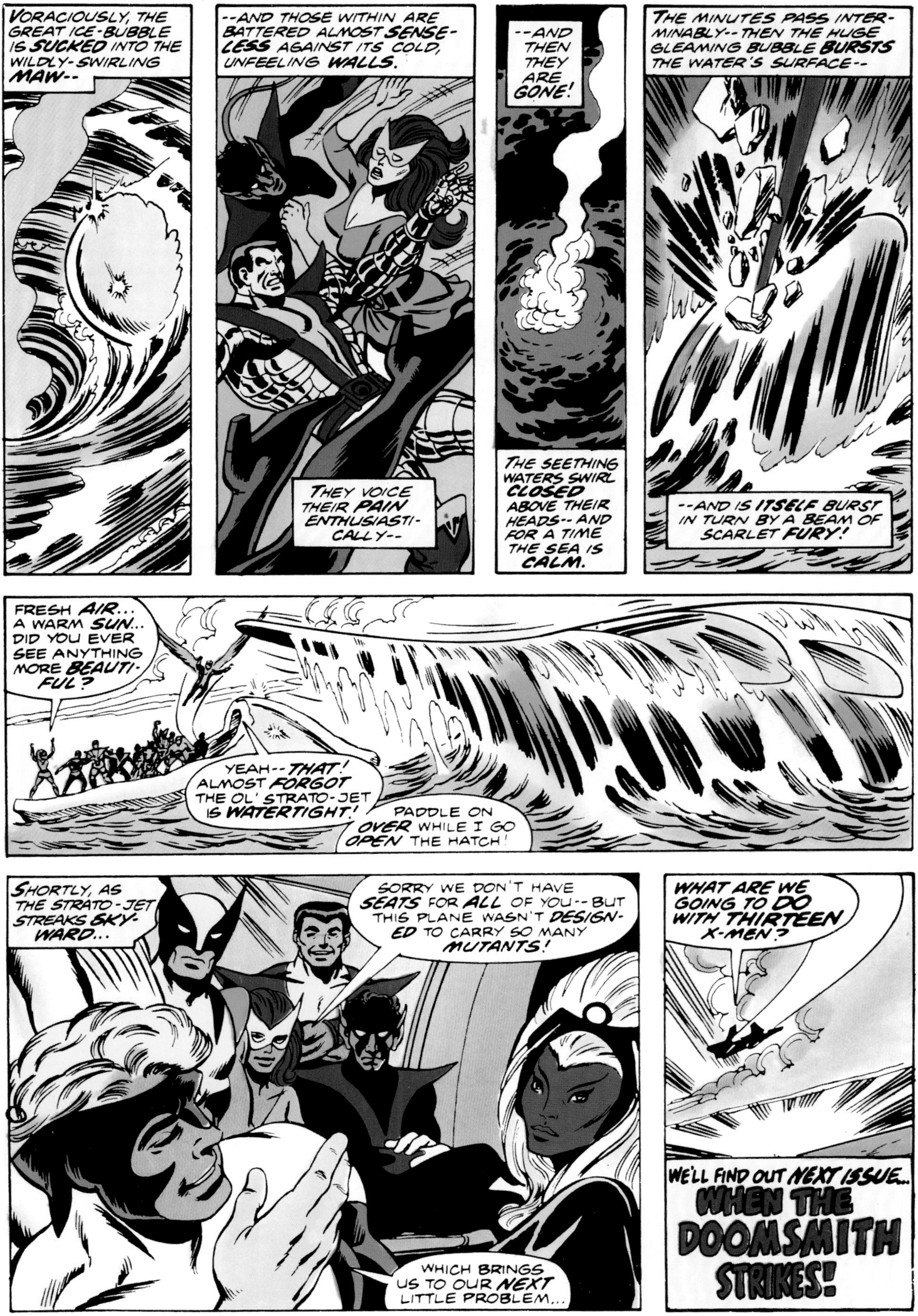
VORACIOUSLY, THE GREAT ICE-BUBBLE IS SUCKED INTO THE WILDLY-SWIRLING MAW--
--AND THOSE WITHIN ARE BATTERED ALMOST SENSELESS AGAINST ITS COLD, UNFEELING WALLS.
THEY VOICE THEIR PAIN ENTHUSIASTICALLY--
--AND THEN THEY ARE GONE!
THE SEETHING WATERS SWIRL CLOSED ABOVE THEIR HEADS-- AND FOR A TIME THE SEA IS CALM.
THE MINUTES PASS INTERMINABLY-- THEN THE HUGE GLEAMING BUBBLE BURSTS THE WATER'S SURFACE--
--AND IS ITSELF BURST IN TURN BY A BEAM OF SCARLET FURY!
FRESH AIR... A WARM SUN... DID YOU EVER SEE ANYTHING MORE BEAUTIFUL?
YEAH--THAT! ALMOST FORGOT THE OL' STRATO-JET IS WATERTIGHT!
PADDLE ON OVER WHILE I GO OPEN THE HATCH!
SHORTLY, AS THE STRATO-JET STREAKS SKYWARD...
SORRY WE DON'T HAVE SEATS FOR ALL OF YOU-- BUT THIS PLANE WASN'T DESIGNED TO CARRY SO MANY MUTANTS!
WHICH BRINGS US TO OUR NEXT LITTLE PROBLEM...
WHAT ARE WE GOING TO DO WITH THIRTEEN X-MEN?
WE'LL FIND OUT NEXT ISSUE...
WHEN THE DOOMSMITH STRIKES!

AFTERWORD

THE MARVEL UNIVERSE MAY BE THE LONGEST-RUNNING CONTINUOUS STORY IN MODERN HISTORY.

STAN LEE AND HIS CREATIVE TEAM LAID A STRONG BASE OF CHARACTERS AND THEMES. THEN, EVERY YEAR, FOR THE LAST FOUR DECADES, EACH MARVEL COMIC HAS BEEN PLACED CAREFULLY UPON THAT FOUNDATION. WELL OVER 20,000 BOOKS -- PRODUCED BY THOUSANDS OF WRITERS, ARTISTS, AND EDITORS -- FORM THE UNIVERSAL STORY STRUCTURE WE CALL "CONTINUITY." THE STRENGTH OF MARVEL COMICS IS THAT OUR LOYAL FANS, OUR "TRUE BELIEVERS," FULLY EMBRACE OUR COMPLEX AND RICH CONTINUITY.

BUT, ULTIMATE X-MEN HAS NEARLY NOTHING TO DO WITH ANY OF THAT.

JOE QUESADA AND I STARTED THE ULTIMATE BOOKS BECAUSE WE WANTED MARVEL TO GET BACK IN TOUCH WITH KIDS. WE WANTED MARVEL'S GREAT TEEN HEROES -- SPIDEY AND THE X-MEN -- TO STAR IN COMICS FOR 2001 KIDS. EVERYBODY KNOWS KIDS AND TEENS LIKE READING ABOUT KIDS AND TEENS, BUT MARVEL'S TEEN STARS WENT AND GOT OLD. IN OUR MAINLINE BOOKS, OUR FORMER TEEN STARS ARE PUSHING 30 YEARS OLD, MANY ARE MARRIED, AND SOME HAVE KIDS OF THEIR OWN. MOREOVER, THE "CONTINUITY" STOOD AS A HUGE BARRIER TO ENTRY FOR READERS OF ANY AGE. WITH EVERY COMIC CRAFTED TO FIT IN WITH 20,000 OTHERS, NO ONE BOOK WAS EASY FOR A NEW READER TO PICK UP AND READ.

IN THE PAST, MARVEL EDITORS RARELY MESSED AROUND WITH THE CONTINUITY, FOR FEAR OF "BETRAYING" THE VOCAL MEMBERS OF OUR LOYAL ADULT FAN BASE WHO COMPLAIN ABOUT EVERYTHING THAT CONTRADICTS THE STORIES THEY HAVE BEEN READING FOR 10, 20 OR 30 YEARS. FRANKLY, THE SHEER FEAR OF ADULT-FAN BACKLASH FORCED MARVEL EDITORS INTO DOZENS OF LAME TEEN-PUBLISHING PROGRAMS. THESE FELL INTO FOUR BASIC CATEGORIES:

1. "UNTOLD STORIES": TURN BACK THE CLOCK TO 1962 AND TELL STORIES THAT HAD NOT YET BEEN "REVEALED." IN OTHER WORDS, WE FORCED CYCLOPS AND PHOENIX INTO SKINNY TIES AND BOBBY SOCKS, AND MADE THEM FIGHT GIANT ANTS CREATED BY ATOMIC-BOMB TESTING.

2. "ADVENTURES": PUBLISH COMICS BASED ON MARVEL KIDS' CARTOONS. IN OTHER WORDS, WE FORCED COMIC CREATORS TO USE THE SIMPLISTIC ARTISTIC AND STORY-TELLING STYLES THAT COULDN'T POSSIBLY WORK ANYWHERE ELSE BUT IN ACTION ANIMATION.

3. "WHAT IF": GIVE THE WRITERS AND ARTISTS CREATIVE FREEDOM TO WRITE AND DRAW THE CHARACTERS THEY LOVE IN MODERN, REAL WORLD, SETTINGS. BUT, PUT SOME NIM "ALTERNATE UNIVERSE" LABEL ON THE COVERS SO FANS KNOW THE BOOKS REALLY "DON'T COUNT."

4. "PACKS": CREATE ALL NEW KIDS' TEAMS -- I.E., MARVEL'S OWN XFL.

AND THEN, MARVEL MANAGEMENT HAD THE REAL CHALLENGE OF TRYING TO LOOK SURPRISED WHEN ALL THOSE PUBLISHING PROGRAMS FLAT OUT FAILED.

BUT NOW, HERE IS ULTIMATE X-MEN -- NO BACKSTORY, NO TURNING BACK THE CLOCK, NO HANDS TIED BEHIND THE CREATORS' BACKS, NO APOLOGY, AND NO FEAR -- JUST THE REAL X-MEN PORTRAYED AS TEENAGERS IN THE REAL WORLD. THIS SIX-ISSUE STORY ARC HIT THE COMIC INDUSTRY LIKE SIX TONS OF BRICKS, LAUNCHING AS THE NO. 1 BOOK IN THE BUSINESS AND GROWING IN READERSHIP WITH EACH NEW RELEASE.

AND HERE IS THE WONDERFUL SURPRISE FOR THIS MARVEL MANAGEMENT TEAM: SUCCESS. NOT JUST AMONG NEW READERS, BUT AMONG MARVEL'S LOYAL ADULT FOLLOWING. IT TURNS OUT TRUE MARVEL FANS ARE NOT JUST "TRUE BELIEVERS" IN THE OLD STORIES. THEY GLADLY EMBRACE GREAT WORK, EVEN IF IT IS NOT TIED TO THE OLD STORY LINES.

MARK MILLAR CAPTURED LIGHTNING IN A BOTTLE: THE SPIRIT AND ESSENCE OF THE X-MEN AS TEENAGERS. THEN, HE UNPOPPED THE CORK ON THIS INCREDIBLE MORAL AND MILITARY STRUGGLE FOR GLOBAL DOMINATION. MARVEL'S MOST POPULAR PENCILERS, ADAM AND ANDY KUBERT, HAVE RAISED THEIR CRAFT TO AN ALL-TIME HIGH -- SPLASHING THE STORY ACROSS PAGE AFTER PAGE IN THEIR UNIQUELY BOLD AND CLEAR GRAPHIC STYLE. INKERS, ART THIBERT AND DANNY MIKI, ALONG WITH COLORISTS, RICHARD ISANOVE AND BRIAN HABERLIN, MADE OUTSTANDING CONTRIBUTIONS TO THE LOOK OF THIS BOOK. MARK POWERS AND PETER FRANCO HAVE KEPT ALL OF THE MOVING PARTS TOGETHER, AND MANAGED TO TRANSLATE MY COMPLAINTS INTO CREATIVE INPUT FOR MILLAR AND THE KUBERTS. COMBINED WITH BRIAN BENDIS AND MARK BAGLEY ON SPIDER-MAN, ULTIMATE MARVEL HAS BEEN AN UNQUALIFIED HIT.

AND NOW, I WOULD LIKE TO MAKE AN UNUSUAL DEDICATION FOR MARVEL'S HOTTEST TEEN BOOK. ULTIMATE X-MEN IS DEDICATED TO OUR ADULT FANS, WHO HAVE OPENED THEIR HEARTS AND MINDS TO OUR NEW MARVEL UNIVERSE.

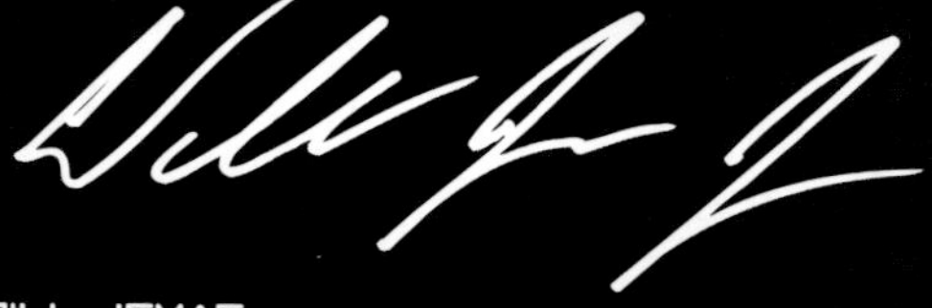

BILL JEMAS
PRESIDENT, MARVEL ENTERPRISES